TRANSLITERATED DICTIONARY
OF THE
RUSSIAN
LANGUAGE

*An abridged dictionary consisting
of Russian-to-English and
English-to-Russian sections.*

EUGENE GARFIELD
Editor

iSi
PRESS™
Philadelphia
1979

Published by

a division of the

Institute for Scientific Information®
3501 Market St.
University City Science Center
Philadelphia, Pennsylvania 19104

Library of Congress Cataloging in Publication Data
Main entry under title:

Transliterated Dictionary of the Russian Language.

1. Russian language—Dictionaries—English.
2. English language—Dictionaries—Russian.
I. Garfield, Eugene.
PG2640. T7   491.7′3′21   79-14068
ISBN 0-89495-003-7 (Hardcover Edition)
ISBN 0-89495-011-8 (Softcover Edition)

Printed in the United States of America

Contents

Introduction
and Acknowledgments

This unconventional dictionary is designed to help scholars and educated lay persons of all types to deal with a variety of Cyrillic texts. For the librarian, this may mean bibliographic citations. For the scientist it may be a journal article. For the tourist it may be a poster, a sign, or a spoken word.

Whatever its application, the dictionary results from my long-term interest in the transliteration of non-Roman alphabets.[1, 2] Transliteration is the spelling of words from one language with characters from the alphabet of another. Ideally, it is a one-for-one character-by-character replacement. For example, *LONDON* is the Roman transliteration of the Russian word ЛОНДОН. Publication of this dictionary reflects my conviction that transliteration can help improve communications between countries that use non-Roman alphabets and those that do not.

This conviction stems from first-hand knowledge that the Cyrillic alphabet (introduced in the ninth century by St. Cyril, who combined letters from the Greek and Roman alphabets) presents an obstacle in using the Russian language that is vastly underestimated. I can well remember the difficulty of using standard Russian-English dictionaries in my recent travels in the Soviet Union. However, the original inspiration for this dictionary was my frustration in examining Russian scientific texts printed in Cyrillic. Since I was never able to "keep up" with my Russian, the letters of the Cyrillic alphabet were not indelibly fixed in my mind.

But even when I recognized the letters, I faced the frustrating task of dealing with an entirely foreign alphabetic ordering scheme. We learn the order of our alphabet as children through endless repetitions until we know it by rote. As adults, everyday use of alphabetically arranged material reinforces our skill. But this learning approach is not feasible for most people who must deal with Russian. As a result, I know people who can converse in Russian but still stumble over the order of the letters in the Cyrillic alphabet.

This dictionary presents solutions to both the problems of letter recognition and letter order. It contains a dual conversion table that makes it possible to quickly determine the Roman equivalent for any cyrillic letter. In this way, Russian text can be transliterated with minimum effort. In fact, this purely mechanical procedure can even be performed by a machine. The transliterated word may then be found in the Russian-English section of the dictionary, where the Russian words are organized in *Roman* alphabetical order.

While this dictionary is designed primarily for reading Russian texts, there is also an English-to-Russian section. When you need the Russian equivalent of an English word, just look up the word in the English-to-Russian section. This provides the Russian word in transliterated form. You can then use the dual conversion table to reconstruct the transliterated word into its Cyrillic form.

The 27th edition of the Akhmanova-Wilson *Russian English Dictionary,* published by the Russian Language Press, Moscow, 1975 is the main source for the terms included in this first edition. This approach to word selection is significant because the Akhmanova-Wilson dictionary covers the words most frequently encountered in Russian texts. Nearly one thousand words of a more technical nature were selected by the ISI staff to supplement the basic Akhmanova-Wilson list. I also considered the inclusion of other sources of technical terms such as glossaries and thesauri. However, to serve the widest possible audience, decided to reduce the dictionary's size and publish it at a lower cost.

If this dictionary is successful, I hope to supplement this first edition with a volume including additional technical terms, especially those whose meanings are not obvious in transliteration. The remarkable fact is that the number of such words is relatively small. That is why transliteration "works." Once you have transliterated the truly Slavic terms in a text, you have little or no difficulty comprehending the rest. A large percentage of Russian technical words are cognate terms used in English, French, or German.

I believe this transliterated Russian-English dictionary will be of use to a variety of people who wish to read or translate Russian. Librarians involved in cataloging Russian materials will find it a great time saver as should anyone who must index or abstract Russian material. Instructors teaching introductory courses in Russian should find this dictionary a handy study aid for their students. It will help overcome an initial resistance for the reasons cited before. Finally, the traveler to the Soviet Union will find this dictionary a welcome companion.

Serious scholars who make continuous use of Russian may regard this dictionary as an unnecessary crutch. If such people can recite the Russian alphabet as rapidly as their own then I would have to agree. But most scientists and scholars cannot; nor can they afford the luxury of keeping up with their Russian. This dictionary is designed to save them a lot of time and energy.

As much as I have been personally involved with the conception and creation of this dictionary, it simply would not have been possible to complete it without the assistance of my close colleague and friend, the late Robert Hayne.[3] As the Chief Editor of the Institute for Scientific Information, he assisted me in clarifying the objectives and design of the dictionary. He also launched the data gathering effort and worked out the details of the composition system. After his death the project waned but was given new life with the establishment of ISI Press.

I also wish to recognize the technical assistance of Yuri Meerovich in the transliteration work itself. Mr. Meerovich is currently teaching in the "English for Speakers of Other Languages" program of the Philadelphia Board of Education. Until 1974 he was an instructor at the Institute of Foreign Languages and a teacher in the Moscow public schools. Excellent advice was also received from Dr. Michael Zarechnak, of the Department of Languages and Linguistics at Georgetown University.

Eugene Garfield
President
Institute for Scientific Information® (ISI®)
Philadelphia, PA, USA

References

1. Garfield E. Transliteration ≠ Transcription ≠ Translation. *Current Contents* (16):5-7, 21 April 1975.*
2. ————. Why not stop worrying about Cyrillic and read Russian! *Current Contents* (21):5-10, 26 May 1975.*
3. Garfield E. To remember my brother, Robert L. Hayne. *Current Contents* (34):5-6, 22 August 1977.

* Reprinted in: Garfield E. *Essays of an information scientist.* Philadelphia: ISI Press, 1977. 2 vols.

User's Guide

Content of Major Sections

This dictionary consists of two major sections. The Russian-to-English section lists nearly 17,000 Russian words that have been transliterated from the Cyrillic to the Roman alphabet. These words are listed according to the order of the Roman alphabet. In addition to the transliterated form, brief definitions and designations of parts of speech are provided for each Russian word. In the English-to-Russian section, English words are listed in Roman alphabetic order with each word followed by its transliterated Russian equivalent and a part of speech designation for the Russian word.

The English-Russian section of this dictionary is unusual in many respects. It was compiled by *re-sorting* the Russian-English section. Since the Akhmanova-Wilson dictionary includes the most frequently used Russian words, one might conclude that the re-sorted version would include all of the most commonly used English words. This is not the case. A number of the most familiar English words did not appear in the Akhmanova-Wilson translations of Russian words. The result is that the omitted words do not appear as entries in the English-Russian section.

The English-Russian section does, however, illustrate the richness of the Russian language in providing many subtle shades of meanings. This is shown by the array of Russian terms required to translate some of the English words that were used by Akhmanova-Wilson. For example, five different Russian words are provided as translations for the English word "departure." Also, in English a "deviation" may be a departure from the norm. In Russian the term closest to this is "otklonenie." However, several other Russian words convey different shades of meanings: "deviatsiya" means "deviation," as in a compass; while "uklon" means "deviation or deflection," in a political sense.

Transliteration System

Conversion tables in this guide and at the endleaves allow the user to convert Cyrillic letters into their Roman equivalents and vice versa. The words contained in this dictionary were transliterated by the staff of the Institute for Scientific Information following the system of the British Standards Institute (BSI). This system was used because it seemed to combine the best features of two other leading systems, the Library of Congress and Board of Geographic Names. The British Standards Institute system's lack of ambiguity and absence of ligatures make it a useful system for personnel untrained in linguistics. In addition, it is a system that has been used by several English-language publishers of Russian materials and by many agencies of the United States government, such as the National Science Foundation and the Department of Agriculture. Since the Library of Congress system agrees with the BSI system in all but a few instances, it is a simple matter to convert one system to the other. There may be, however, some effect on the *ordering* of words when one system or the other is used.

There are few transliteration systems that can be applied in practical situations exactly as conceived. In this dictionary it was necessary to modify the BSI system slightly by ignoring the diacritical marks over the Cyrillic Ё and Й. Thus, the Cyrillic Ё is transliterated as a Roman e, and Й is transliterated as a Roman i. All other transliterations are in strict conformity to the BSI system. (Individuals interested in learning more about transliteration systems will find a wealth of useful information in H. H. Wellisch: *The Conversion of Scripts*, John Wiley & Sons, 1978.)

Conversion Tables

The following tables show the characters of the Cyrillic alphabet and their Roman equivalents as used in this dictionary. The Cyrillic-to-Roman table is arranged in order of the Cyrillic alphabet. The Roman-to-Cyrillic table is arranged in the order of the Roman alphabet. Since the Cyrillic alphabet contains more letters than the Roman, combinations of Roman

Cyrillic	Roman	Roman	Cyrillic
А	a	a	А
Б(б)	b	b	Б(б)
В	v	ch	Ч
Г	g	d	Д
Д	d	e	Е,Ё
Е,Ё	e	é	Э
Ж	zh	f	Ф
З	z	g	Г
И,Й	i	i	И,Й
К	k	k	К
Л	l	kh	Х
М	m	l	Л
Н	n	m	М
О	o	n	Н
П	p	o	О
Р	r	p	П
С	s	r	Р
Т	t	s	С
У	u	sh	Ш
Ф	f	shch	Щ
Х	kh	t	Т
Ц	ts	ts	Ц
Ч	ch	u	У
Ш	sh	v	В
Щ	shch	y	Ы
Ъ	"	ya	Я
Ы	y	yu	Ю
Ь	'	z	З
Э	é	zh	Ж
Ю	yu	'	Ь
Я	ya	"	Ъ

letters and two special symbols are used to represent those Cyrillic letters for which there are no corresponding characters in the Roman alphabet. The latter include the so-called "soft" (ь) and "hard" (ъ) signs, also known as the "silent letters," for which the single prime (ʹ) and double prime (ʺ) symbols are used.

The reader should note carefully that unambiguous, one-to-one reversibility of *Roman* characters to their Cyrillic equivalents is difficult. This is because some Roman letters, such as "h," "j," "q," "w," and "x," represent sounds that are hard to reproduce in an unambiguous way with Cyrillic letters. The Russians approximate these sounds as follows:

Roman letter	Cyrillic approximation	
h	Г	(g)
j	ДЖ	(dzh)
q	КВ	(kv)
w	В	(v)
x	КС	(ks)

Thus, the name *Hilbert* is cited as *Gilbert,* *Woodward* as *Voodvard.* While this precludes complete letter-for-letter reversibility, the method typically used by the Russians to transliterate English words serves the needs of the Russian reader, just as the system used to transliterate the Russian words in this dictionary serves the needs of the English-speaking reader.

Typical Entry (*Russian-English Section*)

The following is a typical entry in the transliterated Russian-to-English section as it would appear for the Russian word АЛЬМАНАХ:.

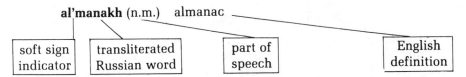

The boldface entry is the transliterated Russian word. The abbreviation next to each transliterated word indicates the part of speech in accordance with the following scheme:

abbr.	abbreviation	n. n.	noun neuter
adj.	adjective	n. pl.	noun plural
adv.	adverb	num.	numeral
col.	colloquialism	p.	pronoun
conj.	conjunction	part.	particle
interj.	interjection	pred.	predicate use
intro.	introductory word	prep.	preposition
n. collect.	collective noun	v. impf.	verb in the imperfective aspect
n. f.	noun feminine		
n. m.	noun masculine	v. impf. & pf.	verb; can be either perfective or imperfective
n. m. & f.	noun; could be either masculine or feminine	v. pf.	verb in the perfective aspect

Following the part of speech is a simple (usually one-word) English definition. Occasionally, secondary definitions or shades of meanings are provided. Definitions taken from the Akhmanova-Wilson dictionary that were archaic or oriented to British usage have been modified to conform as much as possible to modern American usage. Information related to etymology, idiomatic use, and syntactic or semantic requirements is omitted.

Some additional conventions followed in this dictionary are as follows:

—the hard and soft signs are ignored in the alphabetization of transliterated Russian words in which they appear, as is the accent mark over the é.

—the reflexive ending *sya* appears in parenthesis following certain verbs. When this occurs, it indicates that the English definition is the same for the verb stem when it is combined with the *sya* ending as it is for the stem alone.

—pronouns, days of the week, months, and most proper adjectives are not capitalized in Russian. Geographic designations are capitalized when they apply to formal political institutions or units.

—a few Russian words have English definitions that would seem to require additional clarification. In such instances, a modifying word has been added, parenthetically. Example:

kumys (n.m.)   koumiss (a type of beverage)

Typical Entry (*English-Russian Section*)

All conventions followed in the English-to-transliterated-Russian section have been described previously. The following is a typical entry in this section:

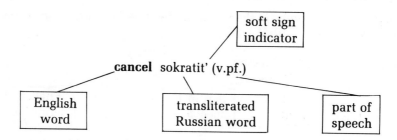

Grammar

Each entry contains only a single form of the transliterated Russian word rather than the usual range of grammatical and lexical variations found in most traditional dictionaries. In view of this, the following general discussion of Russian grammar may be helpful to the user who wishes to go beyond the primary purpose of the dictionary.

Grammatical categories in Russian consist of the following features: voice, person, number, gender, case, mood, tense, and some others. By combining these features into a bundle, a particular part of speech is formed. Thus, noun endings combined with the stem form the categories of case, number, gender, and animateness. Verbs are formed by combining the categories of tense, person, number, voice, and mood. Adjectives are characterized by case, number, and gender. Parts of speech such as those mentioned above are called inflected. If no grammatical categories are added to the stem of the lexical meaning, as is the case with the adverbs, prepositions, conjunctions, and particles, these words are called uninflected. In most specific terms, inflected words are subdivided into those which are subject to declension (nominal inflection) and those which are subject to conjugation (verbal inflection).

The inflected forms are represented only by a specific form from the set of related inflected forms. Thus, the nouns are represented by the nominative case, gender, singular number; verbs by their infinitive form; adjectives by singular number, nominative case, and masculine gender. Pronouns, due to their small number and high frequency, are entered in all their forms. Therefore, the pronoun *ya* (I), is included as well as the declined forms *menya, mne, mnoi*. So are the other pronouns. The dictionary entries as defined above are referred to as canonical forms.

Canonical forms are the basis for the lookup. The user should match the word from the text, say, *podpiskami*, letter by letter from left to right until either the whole word or part of it is matched against the dictionary entry. If there are two matching forms of varying length, the longer form should be chosen. The remaining portion of the word should not consist of more than three letters (or four, in the case of the ending *-yami* which indicates the instrumental plural for palatalized noun stems). In our case, we will find two entries: *podpis'* and podpiska. We choose *podpiska* because it is the longest match, leaving the portion *-mi*. Combining the entry with the stem *-mi* we get *podpiskami*, where the ending *-ami* shows instrumental plural for nonpalatalized nouns.

RUSSIAN-ENGLISH SECTION

A (A)

abazhur (n.m.) lamp shade
abbat (n.m.) abbot
aberratsiya (n.f.) aberration
abkhazets (n.m.) Abkhazian
abonement (n.m.) subscription
aborigen (n.m.) aboriginal
abort (n.m.) abortion
abrikos (n.m.) apricot
absolyutnyi (adj.) absolute
absorbtsiya (n.f.) absorption
abstraktnyi (adj.) abstract
abstraktsionizm (n.m.) abstractionism
abstsissa (n.f.) abscissa
absurd (n.m.) absurdity
abzats (n.m.) paragraph
ad (n.m.) hell
administrator (n.m.) administrator
administrativnyi (adj.) administrative
admiral (n.m.) admiral
adres (n.m.) address
adskii (adj.) hellish
advokat (n.m.) lawyer
ad"yutant (n.m.) aide
adzharets (n.m.) Adzhar
aérodrom (n.m.) airport
aéroklub (n.m.) amateur flying club
aéronavigatsiya (n.f.) airnavigation
aéroplan (n.m.) airplane
afera (n.f.) shady transaction
afganets (n.m.) Afghan
afisha (n.f.) bill
aforizm (n.m.) aphorism
agent (n.m.) agent
agitator (n.m.) propagandist
agitbrigada (n.f.) propaganda team
agitirovat' (v.impf.) agitate
agitpunkt (n.m.) propaganda station
agoniya (n.f.) agony
agrarnyi (adj.) agrarian
agregat (n.m.) unit
agressiya (n.f.) aggression
agressivnyi (adj.) aggressive
agrobiologiya (n.f.) agricultural biology
agronom (n.m.) agronomist
agrotekhnika (n.f.) agrotechnics

aist (n.m.) stork
akademik (n.m.) academician
akademiya (n.f.) academy
akatsiya (n.f.) acacia
akh (interj.) ah
akhnut' (v.pf.) gasp
akklimatizirovat'sya (v.impf.) acclimatize
    oneself
akkompanirovat' (v.impf.) accompany
akkord (n.m.) chord
akkordeon (n.m.) accordion
akkreditiv (n.m.) letter of credit
akkumulyator (n.m.) accumulator
akkuratnyi (adj.) punctual, neat
akrobat (n.m.) acrobat
aksioma (n.f.) axiom
akt (n.m.) act
akter (n.m.) actor
aktiv (n.m.) most active members
aktiv (n.m.) assets
aktivizirovat' (v.impf.&pf.) activate
aktivnost' (n.f.) activity
aktivnyi (adj.) active
aktrisa (n.f.) actress
aktsent (n.m.) accent
aktsioner (n.m.) shareholder
aktsiya (n.f.) share
aktsiya (n.f.) action
aktual'nyi (adj.) present-day
akula (n.f.) shark
akusherka (n.f.) midwife
akustika (n.f.) acoustics
akvarel' (n.f.) watercolor
akvarium (n.m.) aquarium
albanets (n.m.) Albanian
al'bom (n.m.) album
alchnost' (n.f.) greediness
alet' (v.impf.) redden
alfavit (n.m.) alphabet
algebra (n.f.) algebra
algoritm (n.m.) algorithm
alimenty (n.pl.) alimony
alkogolizm (n.m.) alcoholism
allegoriya (n.f.) allegory
alleya (n.f.) avenue

1

allo (interj.) hello!
al'manakh (n.m.) almanac
almaz (n.m.) diamond
al'piiskii (adj.) alpine
al'pinizm (n.m.) mountaineering
alyi (adj.) scarlet
alyuminii (n.m.) aluminum
ambrazura (n.f.) embrasure
ambulatoriya (n.f.) dispensary
amerikanets (n.m.) American
amfiteatr (n.m.) amphitheater
aminokislota (n.f.) amino acid
ammiak (n.m.) ammonia
amnistiya (n.f.) amnesty
amoral'nyi (adj.) amoral
amortizatsiya (n.f.) depreciation
amper (n.m.) ampere
amplituda (n.f.) amplitude
amplua (n.n.) line
amputatsiya (n.f.) amputation
amunitsiya (n.f.) military equipment
anakhronizm (n.m.) anachronism
analiticheskii (adj.) analytic
analiz (n.m.) analysis
analog (n.m.) analog
analogiya (n.f.) analogy
ananas (n.m.) pineapple
anarkhiya (n.f.) anarchy
anarkhizm (n.m.) anarchism
anatom (n.m.) anatomist
anatomirovat' (v.impf.) dissect
anatomiya (n.f.) anatomy
anekdot (n.m.) joke
angar (n.m.) hangar
angel (n.m.) angel
angina (n.f.) quinsy
anglichanin (n.m.) Englishman
angliiskii (adj.) English
anglosaksonskii (adj.) Anglo-Saxon
anketa (n.f.) form
annotatsiya (n.f.) abstract
annulirovat' (v.impf.&pf.) annul
anod (n.m.) anode
anomaliya (n.f.) anomaly
anonimnyi (adj.) anonymous
anons (n.m.) announcement
ansambl' (n.m.) ensemble
anshlag (n.m.) full house

antagonizm (n.m.) antagonism
antenna (n.f.) aerial
antibiotik (n.m.) antibiotic
antichnyi (adj.) antique
antifashist (n.m.) anti-fascist
antiimperialisticheskii (adj.) anti-imperialist
antikvar (n.m.) antiquary
antimilitaristicheskii (adj.) anti-military
antinarodnyi (adj.) anti-national
antiobshchestvennyi (adj.) antisocial
antipatiya (n.f.) antipathy
antireligioznyi (adj.) anti-religious
antisanitarnyi (adj.) insanitary
antisemitizm (n.m.) anti-Semitism
antisovetskii (adj.) anti-Soviet
antivoennyi (adj.) anti-war
antonim (n.m.) antonym
antrakt (n.m.) intermission
antratsit (n.m.) anthracite
antreprener (n.m.) manager
apatichnyi (adj.) apathetic
apatiya (n.f.) apathy
apellirovat' (v.pf.) appeal
apel'sin (n.m.) orange
aplodirovat' (v.impf.) applaud
aplomb (n.m.) assurance
apofeoz (n.m.) apotheosis
apogei (n.m.) apogee
apolitichnyi (adj.) apolitical
apostrof (n.m.) apostrophe
apparat (n.m.) device
appenditsit (n.m.) appendicitis
appetit (n.m.) appetite
aprel' (n.m.) April
apteka (n.f.) drug store
arab (n.m.) Arab
arbitr (n.m.) arbiter
arbuz (n.m.) watermelon
arena (n.f.) arena
arenda (n.f.) lease
ar'ergard (n.m.) rear-guard
arest (n.m.) arrest
arfa (n.f.) harp
argentinets (n.m.) Argentinian
argument (n.m.) argument
arifmetika (n.f.) arithmetic
aristokrat (n.m.) aristocrat
ariya (n.f.) aria

arka (n.f.) arch
arkhaizm (n.m.) archaism
arkheolog (n.m.) archaeologist
arkheologiya (n.f.) archaeology
arkhipelag (n.m.) archipelago
arkhitektor (n.m.) architect
arkhiv (n.m.) archives
arkticheskii (adj.) arctic
armeiskii (adj.) army
armiya (n.f.) army
armyanin (n.m.) Armenian
armyanskii (adj.) Armenian
aromat (n.m.) aroma
arsenal (n.m.) arsenal
artel' (n.f.) artel
arteriya (n.f.) artery
artezianskii (adj.) artesian
artilleriiskii (adj.) artillery
artillerist (n.m.) artilleryman
artilleriya (n.f.) artillery
artist (n.m.) artist
aryk (n.m.) irrigation ditch
asfal't (n.m.) asphalt
asimmetriya (n.f.) asymmetry
asket (n.m.) ascetic
aspirant (n.m.) postgraduate
assambleya (n.f.) assembly
assignovanie (n.n.) appropriation
assimilirovat'sya (v.impf.&pf.) assimilate
assistent (n.m.) assistant
assortiment (n.m.) assortment
assotsiatsiya (n.f.) association
asteroid (n.m.) asteroid
astma (n.f.) asthma
astra (n.f.) aster
astrofizik (n.m.) astrophysicist
astronavt (n.m.) astronaut
astronom (n.m.) astronomer
ataka (n.f.) attack
atavizm (n.m.) atavism
ateizm (n.m.) atheism
atel'e (n.n.) studio
atlas (n.m.) atlas
atlas (n.m.) satin
atlet (n.m.) athlete
atmosfera (n.f.) atmosphere
atom (n.m.) atom
atomnyi (adj.) atomic

atribut (n.m.) attribute
atrofirovat'sya (v.impf.&pf.) atrophy
attashe (n.m.) attache
attestat (n.m.) certificate
auditoriya (n.f.) lecture hall
auktsion (n.m.) auction
avangard (n.m.) vanguard
avans (n.m.) prepayment
avanstsena (n.f.) proscenium
avantyura (n.f.) adventure
avariinyi (adj.) emergency
avariya (n.f.) accident
avgust (n.m.) August
aviabaza (n.f.) airbase
aviatsionnyi (adj.) aircraft
aviatsiya (n.f.) aviation
avitaminoz (n.m.) avitaminosis
avos' (adv.) perhaps
avral (n.m.) all hands on deck
avstraliets (n.m.) Australian
avstriets (n.m.) Austrian
avtobaza (n.f.) garage
avtobiografiya (n.f.) autobiography
avtoblokirovka (n.f.) automatic block system
avtobus (n.m.) bus
avtogennyi (adj.) autogenous
avtograf (n.m.) autograph
avtomat (n.m.) automatic machine
avtomatchik (n.m.) submachine gunner
avtomaticheskii (adj.) automatic
avtomatizatsiya (n.f.) automation
avtomobil' (n.m.) automobile
avtonomiya (n.f.) autonomy
avtoportret (n.m.) self-portrait
avtor (n.m.) author
avtoritet (n.m.) authority
avtoruchka (n.f.) fountain pen
avtostrada (n.f.) highway
avtotraktornyi (adj.) motor and tractor
avtotransport (n.m.) motor transport
avtozavod (n.m.) automobile works
azart (n.m.) excitement
azbuka (n.f.) alphabet
azerbaidzhanets (n.m.) Azerbaijanian
aziatskii (adj.) Asian
azot (n.m.) nitrogen

B (Б)

baba (n.f.) woman
babochka (n.f.) butterfly
babushka (n.f.) grandmother
bad'ya (n.f.) bucket
bagazh (n.m.) luggage
bagrovyi (adj.) purple
baidarka (n.f.) canoe
bak (n.m.) cistern
bakaleinyi (adj.) grocery
bakaleya (n.f.) grocery
bakhroma (n.f.) fringe
bakhval'stvo (n.n.) bragging
bakteriolog (n.m.) bacteriologist
bakteriologiya (n.f.) bacteriology
bakteriya (n.f.) bacterium
bal (n.m.) ball
balagan (n.m.) show booth
balalaika (n.f.) balalaika
balans (n.m.) balance
balerina (n.f.) ballet dancer
balet (n.m.) ballet
balka (n.f.) beam
balkanskii (adj.) Balkan
balkon (n.m.) balcony
ball (n.m.) point
ballada (n.f.) ballad
ballast (n.m.) ballast
ballistika (n.f.) ballistics
ballon (n.m.) cylinder
ballotirovat'sya (v.impf.) be a candidate
balovat' (v.impf.) spoil
baloven' (n.m.) favorite
baltiiskii (adj.) Baltic
bal'zamirovat' (v.impf.) embalm
bambuk (n.m.) bamboo
banal'nyi (adj.) commonplace
banan (n.m.) banana
banda (n.f.) gang
bandazh (n.m.) truss
banderol' (n.f.) printed matter
bandit (n.m.) bandit
bank (n.m.) bank
banka (n.f.) can
banket (n.m.) banquet
bankir (n.m.) banker

bankrot (n.m.) bankrupt
bant (n.m.) bow
banya (n.f.) bathhouse
baraban (n.m.) drum
barak (n.m.) barrack
baran (n.m.) ram
barashek (n.m.) lamb
barel'ef (n.m.) bas-relief
bar'er (n.m.) barrier
barii (n.m.) barium
barin (n.m.) gentleman
bariton (n.m.) baritone
barkhat (n.m.) velvet
barokamera (n.f.) pressure chamber
barometr (n.m.) barometer
barrikada (n.f.) barricade
barskii (adj.) lordly
barsuk (n.m.) badger
barynya (n.f.) lady
barysh (n.m.) profit
baryshnya (n.f.) young lady
barzha (n.f.) barge
bas (n.m.) bass
bashenka (n.f.) turret
bashkir (n.m.) Bashkir
bashmak (n.m.) shoe
bashnya (n.f.) tower
basketbol (n.m.) basketball
basnoslovnyi (adj.) fabulous
basnya (n.f.) fable
bassein (n.m.) pool
bastovat' (v.impf.) be on strike
batal'on (n.m.) battalion
batareya (n.f.) battery
batisfera (n.f.) bathysphere
batist (n.m.) cambric
baton (n.m.) long loaf
batrak (n.m.) farmhand
batsilla (n.f.) bacillus
bayan (n.m.) bayan accordion
baza (n.f.) base
baza (n.f.) storehouse
bazar (n.m.) market
bazirovat'sya (v.impf.) be based on
bazis (n.m.) basis

bditel'nost' (n.f.) vigilance
bechevka (n.f.) string
beda (n.f.) misfortune
bednet' (v.impf.) grow poor
bednost' (n.f.) poverty
bedovyi (adj.) foolhardy
bedro (n.n.) thigh
bedstvovat' (v.impf.) live in poverty
beg (n.m.) running
begat' (v.impf.) run
begemot (n.m.) hippopotamus
beglets (n.m.) fugitive
beglo (adv.) fluently
begom (adv.) running
begotnya (n.f.) bustle
begovoi (adj.) race
begstvo (n.n.) flight
begun (n.m.) runner
bel'e (n.n.) linen
belet' (v.impf.) become white
bel'etazh (n.m.) first floor
bel'giets (n.m.) Belgian
belichii (adj.) squirrel
belila (n.pl.) zinc white
belit' (v.impf.) bleach
belizna (n.f.) whiteness
belka (n.f.) squirrel
belkovyi (adj.) albuminous
belletristika (n.f.) fiction
bel'mo (n.n.) walleye
belogvardeets (n.m.) White Guard
belok (n.m.) white, albumen
belokuryi (adj.) blond
belorus (n.m.) Byelorussian
beloshveika (n.f.) seamstress
belosnezhnyi (adj.) snow-white
beluga (n.f.) beluga sturgeon
belyi (adj.) white
bemol' (n.m.) flat
benzin (n.m.) benzine
benzokolonka (n.f.) filling-station
berech' (v.impf.) take care
bereg (n.m.) shore
beregis' (v.impf.) look out!
beregovoi (adj.) coast
beremennaya (adj.) pregnant
beret (n.m.) beret
bereza (n.f.) birch

berezhlivyi (adj.) thrifty
berezhnyi (adj.) careful
berillii (n.m.) beryllium
berloga (n.f.) den
bes (n.m.) demon
beschelovechnyi (adj.) inhuman
beschestnyi (adj.) dishonorable
beschinstvo (n.n.) excess
beschislennyi (adj.) countless
beschuvstvennyi (adj.) insensible
beseda (n.f.) conversation
besedka (n.f.) summerhouse
besedovat' (v.impf.) talk
besformennyi (adj.) formless
beshenstvo (n.n.) rage
besit' (v.impf.) madden
beskharakternyi (adj.) weak willed
beskhitrostnyi (adj.) artless
beskhozyaistvennost' (n.f.) mismanagement
besklassovyi (adj.) classless
beskonechnost' (n.f.) infinity
beskonechnyi (adj.) endless
beskontrol'nyi (adj.) uncontrolled
beskorystnyi (adj.) disinterested
besnovat'sya (v.impf.) rave
bespamyatstvo (n.n.) unconsciousness
bespartiinyi (adj.) nonparty
bespechnyi (adj.) careless
bespereboinyi (adj.) uninterrupted
besperesadochnyi (adj.) direct
besplanovyi (adj.) unplanned
besplatnyi (adj.) free of charge
besplodnyi (adj.) sterile
bespochvennyi (adj.) groundless
bespodobnyi (adj.) incomparable
bespokoinyi (adj.) restless
bespokoit' (v.impf.) disturb
bespoleznyi (adj.) useless
bespomoshchnyi (adj.) helpless
besporyadok (n.m.) disorder
besposadochnyi (adj.) nonstop
besposhchadnyi (adj.) ruthless
besposhlinnyi (adj.) duty-free
bespovorotnyi (adj.) irrevocable
bespozvonochnye (n.pl.) invertebrates
bespravnyi (adj.) deprived of rights
bespredel'nyi (adj.) unlimited
besprekoslovnyi (adj.) unquestioning

besprepyatstvennyi (adj.) unimpeded
bespreryvnyi (adj.) continuous
bespretsedentnyi (adj.) unprecedented
besprichinnyi (adj.) groundless
besprimernyi (adj.) unprecedented
besprintsipnyi (adj.) unscrupulous
bespristrastnyi (adj.) impartial
besprizornyi (adj.) uncared for
besprobudnyi (adj.) deep
besproigryshnyi (adj.) safe
besprosvetnyi (adj.) pitch-dark
besprotsentnyi (adj.) interest free
besprovolochnyi (adj.) wireless
besputnyi (adj.) dissolute
besserdechnyi (adj.) heartless
besshumnyi (adj.) noiseless
bessil'nyi (adj.) weak
bessistemnyi (adj.) unsystematic
besslavnyi (adj.) ignominious
besslednyi (adj.) traceless
besslovesnyi (adj.) dumb
bessmennyi (adj.) permanent
bessmertnyi (adj.) immortal
bessmyslennyi (adj.) senseless
bessoderzhatel'nyi (adj.) empty
bessonnyi (adj.) sleepless
bessovestnyi (adj.) unscrupulous
bessoznatel'nyi (adj.) unconscious
b.spornyi (adj.) indisputable
bessrochnyi (adj.) indefinite
besstrashnyi (adj.) fearless
besstrastnyi (adj.) impassive
besstydnyi (adj.) shameless
bessvyaznyi (adj.) incoherent
bestaktnyi (adj.) tactless
bestolkovyi (adj.) stupid
bestsel'nyi (adj.) aimless
bestsennyi (adj.) priceless
bestsenok (n.m.) very cheaply
bestseremonnyi (adj.) unceremonious
bestsvetnyi (adj.) colorless
beta luchi (n.pl.) beta rays
beton (n.m.) concrete
betonomeshalka (n.f.) concrete mixer
bez (prep.) without
bezalabernyi (adj.) disorganized
bezapellyatsionnyi (adj.) peremptory
bezbelkovyi (adj.) protein-free

bezboleznennyi (adj.) painless
bezbozhnik (n.m.) atheist
bezbrezhnyi (adj.) boundless
bezdarnyi (adj.) untalented
bezdeistvie (n.n.) inaction
bezdel'e (n.n.) idleness
bezdelitsa (n.f.) trifle
bezdelushka (n.f.) trinket
bezdenezh'e (n.n.) lack of money
bezdetnyi (adj.) childless
bezdna (n.f.) abyss
bezdomnyi (adj.) homeless
bezdonnyi (adj.) bottomless
bezdorozh'e (n.n.) lack of roads
bezdushnyi (adj.) heartless
bezdykhannyi (adj.) lifeless
bezgolosyi (adj.) voiceless
bezgolovyi (adj.) brainless
bezgramotnyi (adj.) illiterate
bezgranichnyi (adj.) boundless
bezhat' (v.impf.) run
bezhenets (n.m.) refugee
bezlichnyi (adj.) impersonal
bezlyudnyi (adj.) lonely
bezmernyi (adj.) immeasurable
bezmolvnyi (adj.) silent
bezmozglyi (adj.) brainless
bezmyatezhnyi (adj.) serene
beznadezhnyi (adj.) hopeless
beznakazannyi (adj.) unpunished
beznogii (adj.) legless
beznravstvennyi (adj.) immoral
bezobidnyi (adj.) harmless
bezoblachnyi (adj.) cloudless
bezobraznyi (adj.) ugly
bezogovorochnyi (adj.) unconditional
bezopasnyi (adj.) safe
bezoruzhnyi (adj.) unarmed
bezoshibochnyi (adj.) faultless
bezostanovochnyi (adj.) unceasing
bezotchetnyi (adj.) instinctive
bezotradnyi (adj.) cheerless
bezotvetstvennyi (adj.) irresponsible
bezrabotnyi (adj.) unemployed
bezrassudnyi (adj.) reckless
bezrazlichnyi (adj.) indifferent
bezrezul'tatnyi (adj.) futile
bezropotnyi (adj.) uncomplaining

bezrukii (adj.) armless
bezuchastnyi (adj.) listless
bezudarnyi (adj.) unstressed
bezuderzhnyi (adj.) unrestrained
bezukoriznennyi (adj.) irreproachable
bezumnyi (adj.) insane
bez umolku (adv.) incessantly
bezumstvo (n.n.) madness
bezuprechnyi (adj.) irreproachable
bezuslovno (adv.) undoubtedly
bezuspeshnyi (adj.) unsuccessful
bezuteshnyi (adj.) inconsolable
bezvestnyi (adj.) unknown
bezvkusnyi (adj.) tasteless
bezvlastie (n.n.) anarchy
bezvodnyi (adj.) arid
bezvolie (n.n.) weak will
bezvozdushnyi (adj.) airless
bezvozmezdnyi (adj.) gratuitous
bezvozvratnyi (adj.) irretrievable
bezvrednyi (adj.) harmless
bezvykhodnyi (adj.) hopeless
bezydeinyi (adj.) unprincipled
bezymyannyi (adj.) anonymous
bezyskhodnyi (adj.) endless
bezzabotnyi (adj.) carefree
bezzakonnyi (adj.) lawless
bezzashchitnyi (adj.) defenseless
bezzastenchivyi (adj.) shameless
bezzavetnyi (adj.) wholehearted
bezzemel'nyi (adj.) landless
bezzhalostnyi (adj.) ruthless
bezzlobnyi (adj.) good-natured
bezzubyi (adj.) toothless
bezzvuchnyi (adj.) soundless
bibliografiya (n.f.) bibliography
biblioteka (n.f.) library
bibliya (n.f.) bible
bich (n.m.) lash
bidon (n.m.) can
bienie (n.n.) throbbing
bilet (n.m.) ticket
bil'yard (n.m.) billiards
binokl' (n.m.) field glasses
binom (n.m.) binominal
bint (n.m.) bandage
biofizika (n.f.) biophysics
biografiya (n.f.) biography

biokhimiya (n.f.) biochemistry
biologiya (n.f.) biology
bionika (n.f.) bionics
biopsiya (n.f.) biopsy
birmanets (n.m.) Burmese
birzha (n.f.) exchange
bis (interj.) encore
biser (n.m.) beads
biskvit (n.m.) sponge cake
bissektrisa (n.f.) bisector
bit' (v.impf.) beat
bitkom (adv.) packed
bit'sya (v.impf.) fight
bitva (n.f.) battle
bityi (adj.) beaten
blago (n.n.) welfare
blagodarit' (v.impf.) thank
blagodarnyi (adj.) grateful
blagodarya (prep.) thanks to
blagodetel' (n.m.) benefactor
blagodeyanie (n.n.) good deed
blagodushie (n.n.) placidity
blagonadezhnyi (adj.) reliable
blagopoluchnyi (adj.) happy
blagopriyatnyi (adj.) favorable
blagorazumnyi (adj.) reasonable
blagorodnyi (adj.) noble
blagosklonnyi (adj.) benevolent
blagoslovit' (v.pf.) bless
blagosostoyanie (n.n.) well-being
blagotvoritel'nost' (n.f.) charity
blagotvornyi (adj.) beneficial
blagoukhanie (n.n.) fragrance
blagoustroennyi (adj.) comfortable
blagovidnyi (adj.) specious
blagovospitannyi (adj.) well-bred
blagozhelatel'nyi (adj.) well-disposed
blagozvuchnyi (adj.) harmonious
blank (n.m.) form
blazhenstvo (n.n.) bliss
blednet' (v.impf.) turn pale
blednost' (n.f.) pallor
bleklyi (adj.) faded
blesk (n.m.) luster
blesna (n.f.) fish lure
blesnut' (v.pf.) flash
blestet' (v.impf.) shine
blestyashchii (adj.) shining

blik (n.m.) light
blin (n.m.) pancake
blindazh (n.m.) dugout
blistat' (v.impf.) shine
bliz (prep.) near
blizhaishii (adj.) nearest
blizhnie (n.pl.) fellow creatures
blizhnii (adj.) neighboring, near
blizit'sya (v.impf.) approach
blizkie (n.pl.) family
blizkii (adj.) near
bliznets (n.m.) twin
blizorukii (adj.) myopic
blizost' (n.f.) proximity
blok (n.m.) bloc
blok (n.m.) block, pulley
blokada (n.f.) blockade
blokha (n.f.) flea
blokirovka (n.f.) block signalling
bloknot (n.m.) writing pad
blondin (n.m.) fair-haired man
bluza (n.f.) blouse
bluzhdat' (v.impf.) roam
blyudechko (n.n.) saucer
blyudo (n.n.) dish
blyudtse (n.n.) saucer
blyusti (v.impf.) guard
bob (n.m.) bean
bober (n.m.) beaver
bobrik (n.m.) castor
bobrovyi (adj.) beaver
bochka (n.f.) barrel
bochonok (n.m.) keg
bodat' (v.impf.) butt
bodrit' (v.impf.) invigorate
bodrost' (n.f.) cheerfulness
bodryashchii (adj.) bracing
boepripasy (n.pl.) ammunition
boesposobnost' (n.f.) fighting efficiency
boets (n.m.) private
boevoi (adj.) fighting
bog (n.m.) God
bogatet' (v.impf.) grow rich
bogatstvo (n.n.) riches
bogatyi (adj.) rich
boi (n.m.) battle
boikii (adj.) smart, sharp, glib
boikot (n.m.) boycott

boinitsa (n.f.) loophole
boinya (n.f.) slaughterhouse
bok (n.m.) side
bokal (n.m.) goblet
bokom (adv.) sideways
bokovoi (adj.) lateral
boks (n.m.) boxing
bol' (n.f.) pain
bolee (adv.) more
bolel'shchik (n.m.) fan
bolen (adj.) sick
bolet' (v.impf.) be ill
boleutolyayushchee (n.n.) sedative
bolezn' (n.f.) illness
boleznennyi (adj.) sickly
bolgarin (n.m.) Bulgarian
bol'nichnyi (adj.) hospital
bol'nitsa (n.f.) hospital
bol'no (adv.) it hurts
bol'no (adv.) badly
bol'noi (adj.) sick
bolotistyi (adj.) swampy
bolotnyi (adj.) swampy
boloto (n.n.) swamp
bol'she (adj.) more
bol'shevik (n.m.) Bolshevik
bol'shinstvo (n.n.) majority
bol'shoi (adj.) big, large, great
bolt (n.m.) bolt
boltat' (v.impf.) stir
boltat' (v.impf.) chatter
boltat'sya (v.impf.) dangle
boltlivyi (adj.) talkative
boltun (n.m.) chatterbox
bolvan (n.m.) blockhead
bolyachka (n.f.) sore
bomba (n.f.) bomb
bombardirovat' (v.impf.) bombard
bombardirovshchik (n.m.) bomber
bomboubezhishche (n.n.) bomb shelter
bor (n.m.) pine forest
bor'ba (n.f.) fight, struggle
borets (n.m.) fighter
bormotat' (v.impf.) mutter
bornyi (adj.) boric
boroda (n.f.) beard
borodatyi (adj.) bearded
borodavka (n.f.) wart

borona (n.f.)   harrow
borot'sya (v.impf.)   fight, struggle
borozda (n.f.)   furrow
bort (n.m.)   side
bosikom (adv.)   barefoot
botanika (n.f.)   botany
botiki (n.pl.)   high overshoes
botinok (n.m.)   shoe
boyat'sya (v.impf.)   be afraid
boyazlivyi (adj.)   timid
boyazn' (n.f.)   fear
brachnyi (adj.)   conjugal
brak (n.m.)   marriage
brak (n.m.)   defect
bran' (n.f.)   swearing
branit' (v.impf.)   scold
brannyi (adj.)   abusive
braslet (n.m.)   bracelet
brat (n.m.)   brother
brat' (v.impf.)   take
bratskii (adj.)   brotherly
brazilets (n.m.)   Brazilian
bred (n.m.)   delirium
bremya (n.n.)   burden
bresh' (n.f.)   breach
bresti (v.impf.)   shuffle along
brevenchatyi (adj.)   timbered
brevno (n.n.)   log
breyushchii (adj.)   low-level
brezent (n.m.)   tarpaulin
brezgat' (v.impf.)   be squeamish
brezglivyi (adj.)   squeamish
brigada (n.f.)   brigade
bril'yant (n.m.)   diamond
brit' (v.impf.)   shave
britanskii (adj.)   British
britva (n.f.)   razor
brod (n.m.)   ford
brodit' (v.impf.)   wander
brodit' (v.impf.)   ferment
brom (n.m.)   bromine
broneboinyi (adj.)   armor-piercing
bronenosets (n.m.)   battleship
bronepoezd (n.m.)   armored train
bronevik (n.m.)   armored car
bronirovannyi (adj.)   armored
bronirovat' (v.impf.)   armor
bronirovat' (v.impf.)   reserve

bronkh (n.m.)   bronchus
bronkhit (n.m.)   bronchitis
bronya (n.f.)   reserved place
bronya (n.f.)   armor
bronza (n.f.)   bronze
brosat' (v.impf.)   throw
broshennyi (adj.)   abandoned
broshka, brosh' (n.f.)   brooch
broshyura (n.f.)   booklet
brosit' (v.pf.)   throw
brov' (n.f.)   eyebrow
brozhenie (n.n.)   fermentation
brus (n.m.)   beam
brusnika (n.f.)   red bilberry
brusok (n.m.)   bar
bryatsat' (v.impf.)   clank
brykat'sya (v. impf.)   kick
bryuki (n.pl.)   trousers
bryukva (n.f.)   turnip
bryunet (n.m.)   dark-haired man
bryushnoi (adj.)   abdominal
bryuzga (n.m.&f.)   grumbler
bryuzzhat' (v.impf.)   grumble
bryzgat' (v.impf.)   splash
bryznut' (v.pf.)   splash
bubny (n.pl.)   diamonds
budet (pred.)   that'll do
budil'nik (n.m.)   alarm clock
budit' (v.impf.)   wake
budka (n.f.)   box
budni (n.pl.)   weekdays
budorazhit' (v.impf.)   disturb
budto (conj.)   as if
budushchee (n.n.)   future
budushchii (adj.)   future
bufer (n.m.)   buffer
bufet (n.m.)   sideboard
bugor (n.m.)   hillock
buinyi (adj.)   violent
buistvo (n.n.)   tumult
buivol (n.m.)   buffalo
buk (n.m.)   beech
bukashka (n.f.)   insect
buket (n.m.)   bouquet
bukhgalter (n.m.)   bookkeeper
bukhta (n.f.)   bay
bukinist (n.m.)   secondhand bookseller
buksir (n.m.)   tugboat

bukva (n.f.) letter
bukval'no (adv.) literally
bukvar' (n.m.) ABC-book
bulavka (n.f.) pin
bul'dog (n.m.) bulldog
bul'dozer (n.m.) bulldozer
bulka (n.f.) roll
bulochnaya (n.f.) baker's shop
bul'on (n.m.) broth
bul'var (n.m.) boulevard
bulyzhnik (n.m.) cobblestone
bumaga (n.f.) paper
bumazhnik (n.m.) wallet
bumazhnyi (adj.) paper
bumazhnyi (adj.) cotton
bunt (n.m.) riot
buran (n.m.) snowstorm
burav (n.m.) gimlet
burda (n.f.) dishwater
burenie (n.n.) drilling
burevestnik (n.m.) storm petrel
burit' (v.impf.) bore
burka (n.f.) felt cloak
burki (n.pl.) felt boots
burlit' (v.impf.) seethe
burnyi (adj.) stormy
burovoi (adj.) boring
burya (n.f.) storm
buryi (adj.) grayish-brown
burzhua (n.m.) bourgeois
burzhuaznyi (adj.) bourgeois

bushevat' (v.impf.) storm, rage
busy (n.pl.) beads
butaforiya (n.f.) properties
buterbrod (n.m.) sandwich
buton (n.m.) bud
butsy (n.pl.) football shoes
butylka (n.f.) bottle
buyan (n.m.) rowdy
byaz' (n.f.) unbleached calico
byk (n.m.) bull
byk (n.m.) pier
byl' (n.f.) true story
byloe (n.n.) past
bystro (adv.) quickly
bystrodeistvuyushchii (adj.) fast
bystrota (n.f.) speed
bystryi (adj.) quick
byt (n.m.) mode of life
byt' (v.impf.) be
bytie (n.n.) existence
bytovoi (adj.) social
byudzhet (n.m.) budget
byulleten' (n.m.) bulletin
byuro (n.n.) bureau
byurokrat (n.m.) bureaucrat
byust (n.m.) bust
byustgal'ter (n.m.) brassiere
byvalyi (adj.) worldly-wise
byvat' (v.impf.) be, happen
byvshii (adj.) former

C (Ч)

chaban (n.m.) shepherd
chad (n.m.) fumes
chai (n.m.) tea
chaika (n.f.) seagull
chainik (n.m.) teapot
chakhlyi (adj.) wilted
chakhotka (n.f.) consumption
chalma (n.f.) turban
chan (n.m.) vat
charuyushchii (adj.) fascinating

chas (n.m.) hour
chasha (n.f.) scale
chashcha (n.f.) thicket
chashche (adj.) more often
chashka (n.f.) cup
chasovnya (n.f.) chapel
chasovoi (adj.) hour, hour's
chasovoi (n.m.) sentry
chasovshchik (n.m.) watchmaker
chast' (n.f.) part

chastitsa (n.f.) particle
chastnoe (n.n.) quotient
chastnost' (n.f.) particular
chasto (adv.) often
chastota (n.f.) frequency
chastotno-modulirovannyi (adj.) frequency-
  modulated
chastushki (n.pl.) sung couplets
chastyi (adj.) frequent
chasy (n.pl.) watch
chayanie (n.n.) hope
ch'e (p.) whose
chechevitsa (n.f.) lentil
chego (p.) what
chei (p.) whose
chek (n.m.) receipt, check
chekanit' (v.impf.) mint
chekh (n.m.) Czech
chekharda (n.f.) leapfrog
chekhol (n.m.) cover
cheln (n.m.) canoe
chelnok (n.m.) canoe
chelnok (n.m.) shuttle
chelovechestvo (n.n.) humanity
chelovechnyi (adj.) humane
chelovek (n.m.) human being
chelovekolyubie (n.n.) human kindness
chelyust' (n.f.) jaw
chem (conj.) than
chemodan (n.m.) suitcase
chempion (n.m.) champion
chempionat (n.m.) championship
chepchik (n.m.) nightcap
chepukha (n.f.) nonsense
cherchenie (n.n.) drawing
cherdak (n.m.) attic
chered (n.m.) turn
cheredovanie (n.n.) alternation
cheremukha (n.f.) bird cherry tree
cherep (n.m.) skull
cherepakha (n.f.) tortoise
cherepitsa (n.f.) tile
chereschur (adv.) too
chereshnya (n.f.) cherry
cherez (prep.) across, over, through
cherknut' (v.pf.) drop a line
chernet' (v.impf.) turn black
chernika (n.f.) bilberry

chernila (n.pl.) ink
chernit' (v.impf.) blacken
cherno-buryi (adj.) silver fox
chernokozhii (adj.) black-skinned
chernomorskii (adj.) Black Sea
chernorabochii (adj.) manual worker
chernosliv (n.m.) prunes
chernovik (n.m.) rough copy
chernozem (n.m.) black earth
chernyi (adj.) black
cherpat' (v.impf.) scoop
cherstvet' (v.impf.) grow stale
cherstvyi (adj.) stale
chert (n.m.) devil
cherta (n.f.) line
chertezh (n.m.) draught
chertit' (v.impf.) draw
cherv' (n.m.) worm
chervivyi (adj.) wormeaten
chervonnyi (adj.) pure gold
chervy (n.pl.) hearts
chesat' (v.impf.) comb, scratch
chesat'sya (v.impf.) scratch, itch
cheshskii (adj.) Czech
cheshuya (n.f.) scales
chesnok (n.m.) garlic
chesotka (n.f.) itch
chest' (n.f.) honor
chestnost' (n.f.) honesty
chestolyubie (n.n.) ambition
chestolyubivyi (adj.) ambitious
chestvovat' (v.impf.) celebrate
cheta (n.f.) couple
chetkii (adj.) clear, legible
chetnost' (n.f.) parity
chetnyi (adj.) even
chetveren'ki (n.pl.) all four
chetverka (n.f.) four
chetvero (num.) four
chetveronogii (n.m.) four-footed
chetvert' (n.f.) quarter
chetvertyi (adj.) fourth
chetyre (num.) four
chetyrekhétazhnyi (adj.) four-storied
chetyrekhletnii (adj.) four-year
chetyrekhmestnyi (adj.) four-seater
chetyrekhugol'nyi (adj.) quadrangular
chetyrnadtsat' (num.) fourteen

chikhat' (v.impf.) sneeze
chiliets (n.m.) Chilean
chiliiskii (adj.) Chilean
chin (n.m.) rank
chinit' (v.impf.) repair
chinit' (v.impf.) sharpen
chinit' (v.impf.) put obstacles
chinovnik (n.m.) official
chirikat' (v.impf.) chirp
chirkat' (v.impf.) strike
chislennost' (n.f.) quantity
chislitel' (n.m.) numerator
chislitel'noe (n.n.) numeral
chislit'sya (v.impf.) be on the list
chislo (n.n.) number
chislovoi (adj.) numerical
chistit' (v.impf.) clean
chistil'shchik (n.m.) bootblack
chisto (adv.) cleanly
chistokrovnyi (adj.) thoroughbred
chistopisanie (n.n.) calligraphy
chistoplotnyi (adj.) clean
chistoserdechnyi (adj.) sincere
chistota (n.f.) cleanliness
chistyi (adj.) clean
chital'nya (n.f.) reading-room
chitat' (v.impf.) read
chitatel' (n.m.) reader
chitka (n.f.) reading
chizh (n.m.) siskin
chlen (n.m.) member
chlen (n.m.) article
chlen-korrespondent (n.m.) corresponding
    member
chlenorazdel'nyi (adj.) articulate
chlenskii (adj.) membership
chokat'sya (v.impf.) clink glasses
chopornyi (adj.) stiff
chrevatyi (adj.) pregnant, fraught
chrezmernyi (adj.) excessive
chrezvychainyi (ajd.) extraordinary

chtenie (n.n.) reading
chtets (n.m.) reciter
chtit' (v.impf.) honor
chto (p.) what
chto (conj.) that
chto (p.) why
chtoby (conj.) in order to
chto-libo (p.) something, anything
chto-to (p.) something, somehow
chuchelo (n.n.) stuffed animal, scarecrow
chudak (n.m.) crank
chudesnyi (adj.) wonderful
chudit'sya (v.impf.) seem
chudno (adv.) wonderfully
chudnoi (adj.) odd
chudnyi (adj.) wonderful
chudo (n.n.) miracle
chudodeistvennyi (adj.) miraculous
chudovishche (n.n.) monster
chugun (n.m.) cast-iron
chulan (n.m.) storeroom
chulok (n.m.) stocking
chuma (n.f.) plague
churban (n.m.) block
chush' (n.f.) nonsense
chut' (adv.) slightly
chut'-chut' (adv.) just a little
chut'e (n.n.) scent
chutkii (adj.) sensitive
chuvash (n.m.) Chuvash
chuvstvennost' (n.f.) sensuality
chuvstvitel'nost' (n.f.) sensitiveness
chuvstvo (n.n.) sense
chuyat' (v.impf.) smell, scent
chuzhbina (n.f.) alien land
chuzhdat'sya (v.impf.) avoid
chuzhdyi (adj.) alien
chuzhezemnyi (adj.) foreign
chuzhoi (adj.) alien
chvanstvo (n.n.) swaggering

D (Д)

da (part.) yes
dacha (n.f.) summer cottage
dal' (n.f.) distance
dalee (adv.) further
dalekii (adj.) far
daleko (adv.) far off
dal'neishii (adj.) further
dal'nii (adj.) distant
dal'noboinyi (adj.) long-range
dal'nost' (n.f.) distance
dal'novidnyi (adj.) farsighted
dal'nozorkii (adj.) farsighted
dal'she (adj.) further
dal'tonizm (n.m.) color-blindness
dama (n.f.) lady
damba (n.f.) dam
damka (n.f.) king
damskii (adj.) lady's
dan' (n.f.) tribute, levy
dannye (n.pl.) data
dannyi (adj.) given
dar (n.m.) gift
darit' (v.impf.) make a present
darom (adv.) gratis
darovanie (n.n.) gift, talent
darovoi (adj.) free
darvinizm (n.m.) Darwinism
dat' (v.pf.) give
data (n.f.) date
datchik (n.m.) sensor, transducer
datel'nyi (adj.) dative
datirovat' (v.impf.) date
datskii (adj.) Danish
davat' (v.impf.) give
davit' (v.impf.) press
davit'sya (v.impf.) choke
davka (n.f.) crush
davlenie (n.n.) pressure
davnii (adj.) old
davno (adv.) long ago
davnost' (n.f.) remoteness
dazhe (part.) even
debaty (n.pl.) debate
debet (n.m.) debit
debri (n.pl.) thickets

debyut (n.m.) debut
defekt (n.m.) defect
defitsit (n.m.) deficit
degazatsiya (n.f.) decontamination
degidrirovanie (n.n.) dehydrogenation
deistvitel'no (adv.) actually
deistvovat' (v.impf.) act
deistvuyushchii (adj.) acting
deiterii (n.m.) deuterium
dekabr' (n.m.) December
dekada (n.f.) ten-day period
dekan (n.m.) dean
deklamirovat' (v.impf.) recite
deklaratsiya (n.f.) declaration
dekoratsiya (n.f.) scenery
dekret (n.m.) decree
delannyi (adj.) feigned
delat' (v.impf.) do, make
delat'sya (v.impf.) become, grow
delegatsiya (n.f.) delegation
delenie (n.n.) division
delets (n.m.) businessman
delezh (n.m.) sharing
del'fin (n.m.) dolphin
delimoe (n.n.) dividend
delikatnost' (n.f.) tact
delit' (v.impf.) divide
delitel' (n.m.) divisor
del'nyi (adj.) efficient
delo (n.n.) affair, business
delovoi (adj.) businesslike
demagog (n.m.) demagogue
demarkatsionnyi (adj.) demarcation
demilitarizatsiya (n.f.) demilitarization
demobilizatsiya (n.f.) demobilization
demokrat (n.m.) democrat
demokratiya (n.f.) democracy
demonstrativnyi (adj.) deliberate,
    demonstrative
demonstratsiya (n.f.) demonstration
demoralizatsiya (n.f.) demoralization
den' (n.m.) day
denezhnyi (adj.) money, monetary,
    pecuniary
den'gi (n.pl.) money

depo (n.n.) depot
depressiya (n.f.) depression
deputat (n.m.) deputy
derevenskii (adj.) rural
derevnya (n.f.) village
derevo (n.n.) tree
derevyannyi (adj.) wooden
dergat' (v.impf.) pull
dermatologiya (n.f.) dermatology
dern (n.m.) turf
dernut'(sya) (v.pf.) twitch
derzat' (v.impf.) dare
derzhat' (v.impf.) hold
derzhat'sya (v.impf.) hold on to
derzhava (n.f.) state
derzkii (adj.) impertinent
derznovennyi (adj.) daring
derznut' (v.pf.) dare
derzost' (n.f.) impertinence
desant (n.m.) landing
desert (n.m.) dessert
deshevet' (v.impf.) fall in price
deshevo (adv.) cheaply
deshevyi (adj.) cheap
desna (n.f.) gum
despot (n.m.) despot
desyat' (num.) ten
desyatichnyi (adj.) decimal
desyatidnevnyi (adj.) ten-day
desyatikratnyi (adj.) tenfold
desyatiletie (n.n.) decade
desyatiletnii (adj.) ten-year
desyatka (n.f.) ten-ruble bill
desyatnik (n.m.) foreman
desyatok (n.m.) ten
det' (v.pf.) do with, put
detal' (n.f.) detail, part
detenysh (n.m.) baby animal
deti (n.pl.) children
detvora (n.pl.) children
deval'vatsiya (n.f.) devaluation
devat'(sya) (v.impf.) disappear
deviatsiya (n.f.) deviation
devitsa (n.f.) girl
deviz (n.m.) motto
devochka (n.f.) girl
devstvennyi (adj.) virgin
devushka (n.f.) girl
devyanosto (num.) ninety

devyat' (num.) nine
devyatka (n.f.) nine
devyatnadtsat' (num.) nineteen
devyat'sot (num.) nine hundred
devyatyi (adj.) ninth
deyatel' (n.m.) statesman
dezaktivatsiya (n.f.) decontamination
dezinfektsiya (n.f.) disinfection
diabet (n.m.) diabetes
diafragma (n.f.) diaphragm
diagnoz (n.m.) diagnosis
diagonal' (n.f.) diagonal
diagramma (n.f.) diagram, chart
dialekt (n.m.) dialect
dialektika (n.f.) dialectics
dialog (n.m.) dialogue
diametr (n.m.) diameter
diapazon (n.m.) range
dich' (n.f.) game
dich' (n.f.) nonsense
dichit'sya (v.impf.) be unsociable
dieta (n.f.) diet
diez (n.m.) sharp
differentsial (n.m.) differential
differentsirovat' (v.impf.) differentiate
diffuziya (n.f.) diffusion
difterit (n.m.) diphtheria
diftong (n.m.) diphthong
dikar' (n.m.) savage
dikii (adj.) wild
dikost' (n.f.) savagery
diktant (n.m.) dictation
diktator (n.m.) dictator
diktatura (n.f.) dictatorship
diktor (n.m.) announcer
diktovat' (v.impf.) dictate
diktsiya (n.f.) articulation
diletant (n.m.) amateur
dinamicheskii (adj.) dynamic
dinamika (n.f.) dynamics
dinamit (n.m.) dynamite
dinamo-mashina (n.f.) dynamo
dinastiya (n.f.) dynasty
diod (n.m.) diode
diplom (n.m.) diploma
diplomat (n.m.) diplomat
diplomnyi (adj.) graduation
direktiva (n.f.) instructions

direktor (n.m.) director
dirizhabl' (n.m.) dirigible
dirizher (n.m.) conductor
disk (n.m.) disk
diskreditirovat' (v.impf.&pf.) discredit
diskriminatsiya (n.f.) discrimination
diskussiya (n.f.) discussion
dispanser (n.m.) dispensary
dispepsiya (n.f.) dyspepsia
dispersiya (n.f.) dispersion, variance
dispetcher (n.m.) controller
disput (n.m.) disputation
dissertatsiya (n.f.) thesis
dissonans (n.m.) dissonance
distantsiya (n.f.) distance
distillirovannyi (adj.) distilled
distsiplina (n.f.) discipline
ditya (n.n.) child
divan (n.m.) sofa
diversant (n.m.) saboteur
diversiya (n.f.) sabotage
diviziya (n.f.) division
divnyi (adj.) marvellous
dizel' (n.m.) diesel
dizenteriya (n.f.) dysentery
dlina (n.f.) length
dlinnyi (adj.) long
dlitel'nyi (adj.) long
dlit'sya (v.impf.) continue
dlya (prep.) for
dnem (adv.) in the daytime
dnevnik (n.m.) diary
dnevnoi (adj.) day, daily
dno (n.n.) bottom
dobavit' (v.pf.) add
dobegat' (v.impf.) run up to
dobela (adv.) white hot
dobirat'sya (v.impf.) reach
dobit' (v.pf.) finish off
dobit'sya (v.pf.) obtain
dobivat' (v.impf.) finish off
dobivat'sya (v.impf.) strive
doblest' (n.f.) valor
doblestnyi (adj.) valiant
dobrat'sya (v.pf.) reach
dobro (n.n.) good
dobro pozhalovat' (col.) welcome
dobrodetel' (n.f.) virtue

dobrodushnyi (adj.) good-natured
dobrokachestvennyi (adj.) of good quality
dobrosovestnyi (adj.) conscientious
dobrota (n.f.) kindness
dobrovol'nyi (adj.) voluntary
dobrozhelatel'nyi (adj.) benevolent
dobryi (adj.) kind
dobycha (n.f.) mining
dobyt' (v.pf.) obtain
dobyvat' (v.impf.) mine
dochista (adv.) completely
dochitat' (v.pf.) finish
dochka (n.f.) daughter
dodelat' (v.pf.) complete
dodumat'sya (v.pf.) arrive at
doedat' (v.pf.) finish eating
doekhat' (v.pf.) reach, get to
doest' (v.pf.) finish eating
doezzhat' (v.pf.) reach, get to
dog (n.m.) mastiff
dogadat'sya (v.pf.) guess
dogadka (n.f.) guess
dogma (n.f.) dogma
dognat' (v.pf.) catch up
dogonyat' (v.impf.) catch up
dogorat' (v.impf.) burn out
dogovarivat' (v.impf) finish talking
dogovarivat'sya (v.impf.) reach agreement
dogovor (n.m.) agreement
dogovorit' (v.pf.) finish talking
dogovorit'sya (v.pf.) reach agreement
doigrat' (v.pf.) finish playing
doigryvat' (v.impf.) finish playing
doinyi (adj.) milking
doiskat'sya (v.pf.) find out
doiskivat'sya (v.impf.) search for
doistoricheskii (adj.) prehistoric
doit' (v.impf.) milk
doiti (v.pf.) reach
dok (n.m.) dock
dokanchivat' (v.impf.) finish
dokazat' (v.pf.) prove
dokazatel'stvo (n.n.) proof
doker (n.m.) docker
dokhlyi (adj.) dead
dokhod (n.m.) income
dokhodit' (v.impf.) reach
dokhodnyi (adj.) profitable

doklad (n.m.) report
dokonat' (v.pf.) ruin
dokonchit' (v.pf.) finish
dokrasna (adv.) red-hot
doktor (n.m.) doctor
doktrina (n.f.) doctrine
dokument (n.m.) document
dolbit' (v.impf.) hollow
dolee (adv.) longer
dolg (n.m.) debt
dolgii (adj.) long
dolgoigrayushchii (adj.) long-playing
dolgoletnii (adj.) of many years
dolgosrochnyi (adj.) long-term
dolgota (n.f.) longitude
dolgovechnyi (adj.) lasting
dolgovremennyi (adj.) of long duration
dolgozhdannyi (adj.) long-awaited
dolina (n.f.) valley
dol'ka (n.f.) lobule
dollar (n.m.) dollar
doloi (adv.) away, down with
doloto (n.n.) chisel
dolozhit' (v.pf.) make a report
dol'she (adv.) longer
dolya (n.f.) part
dolya (n.f.) fate
dolzhen (adj.) must
dolzhnik (n.m.) debtor
dolzhnost' (n.f.) position
dolzhnyi (adj.) due, proper
dom (n.m.) house
domashnii (adj.) domestic
domennyi (adj.) blast furnace
dominanta (n.f.) dominant
dominion (n.m.) dominion
domkrat (n.m.) jack
domna (n.f.) blast furnace
domogat'sya (v.impf.) solicit
domoi (adv.) home
domoupravlenie (n.n.) apartment
    management
domovladelets (n.m.) landlord
domovyi (adj.) house, household
donesenie (n.n.) report
donesti (v.pf.) carry to
donesti (v.pf.) inform
donestis' (v.pf.) reach one's ears

donizu (adv.) to the bottom
donor (n.m.) donor
donos (n.m.) denunciation
donoschik (n.m.) informer
donosit'sya (v.impf.) reach
dopisat' (v.pf.) finish writing
dopit' (v.pf.) drink up
dopivat' (v.impf.) drink up
doplachivat' (v.impf.) pay in addition
doplata (n.f.) additional payment
doplyvat' (v.impf.) swim
dopolnenie (n.n.) addition
dopolnit' (v.pf.) supplement
dopolnitel'nyi (adj.) additional
doprashivat' (v.impf.) interrogate
doprizyvnik (n.m.) youth of premilitary age
dopros (n.m.) interrogation
dopushchenie (n.n.) assumption
dopusk (n.m.) pass, tolerance
dopuskat' (v.impf.) admit
dopustimyi (adj.) permissible
dopustit' (v.pf.) admit
dopytyvat'sya (v.impf.) try to find out
dorevolyutsionnyi (adj.) prerevolutionary
dorodnyi (adj.) corpulent
doroga (n.f.) road
dorogoi (adj.) expensive
dorozhat' (v.impf.) rise in price
dorozhit' (v.impf.) value
dorozhka (n.f.) path
dorozhnyi (adj.) road
dorvat'sya (v.pf.) seize upon
dosada (n.f.) annoyance
dosazhdat' (v.impf.) annoy
doshchatyi (adj.) of planks
doshkol'nyi (adj.) preschool
doska (n.f.) board
doslovno (adv.) literally
dosrochno (adv.) ahead of schedule
dostat' (v.pf.) reach
dostatochnyi (adj.) sufficient
dostavat'sya (v.impf.) fall to someone's lot
dostavit' (v.pf.) deliver
dostavlyat' (v.impf.) deliver
dostich' (v.pf.) reach
dostizhenie (n.n.) achievement
dostoinstvo (n.n.) dignity
dostoinyi (adj.) worthy

dostoprimechatel'nyi (adj.) remarkable
dostovernost' (n.f.) authenticity
dostovernyi (adj.) reliable
dostoyanie (n.n.) property
dostup (n.m.) access
dostupnyi (adj.) accessible
dosug (n.m.) leisure
dosukha (adv.) dry
dotatsiya (n.f.) grant
dotla (adv.) utterly
dotragivat'sya (v.impf.) touch
dotsent (n.m.) senior lecturer
doverennost' (n.f.) power of attorney
doverie (n.n.) trust
dovershenie (n.n.) completion
doveryat' (v.impf.) trust
dovesti (v.pf.) accompany
dovezti (v.pf.) take (to, as far as)
dovod (n.m.) argument
dovodit' (v.impf.) accompany
dovoennyi (adj.) prewar
dovol'no (adv.) rather
dovol'nyi (adj.) content
dovol'stvo (n.n.) satisfaction
dovol'stvovat'sya (v.impf.) be content
dovozit' (v.impf.) lead
doyarka (n.f.) milkmaid
doza (n.f.) dose
dozhd' (n.m.) rain
dozhdat'sya (v.pf.) wait
dozhdevoi (adj.) rain
dozhdlivyi (adj.) rainy
dozhidat'sya (v.impf.) wait
dozhit' (v.pf.) live
dozhivat' (v.impf.) live
dozor (n.m.) patrol
dozrevat' (v.impf.) ripen
dozvolyat' (v.impf.) permit
dozvonit'sya (v.pf.) call
dozvukovoi (adj.) subsonic
dragotsennyi (adj.) precious
draka (n.f.) fight
drakon (n.m.) dragon
drama (n.f.) drama
drap (n.m.) thick cloth
drat' (v.impf.) tear
drat'sya (v.impf.) fight
draznit' (v.impf.) tease

drebezzhat' (v.impf.) rattle
dreif (n.m.) drift
dremat' (v.impf.) doze
dremota (n.f.) drowsiness
dremuchii (adj.) dense
drenazh (n.m.) drainage
dressirovat' (v.impf.) train
drevesina (n.f.) wood
drevesnyi (adj.) wood
drevko (n.n.) flagpole
drevnii (adj.) ancient
drezina (n.f.) trolley
drob' (n.f.) shot
drob' (n.f.) fraction
drobit' (v.impf.) crush
drognut' (v.pf.) shake
drognut' (v.pf.) shiver
drova (n.pl.) firewood
drovosek (n.m.) woodcutter
drozd (n.m.) thrush
drozh' (n.f.) trembling
drozhat' (v.impf.) tremble
drozhzhi (n.pl.) yeast
drug (n.m.) friend
drugie (n.pl.) others
drugoi (adj.) other
druzhba (n.f.) friendship
druzhit' (v.impf.) be friends
druzhnyi (adj.) friendly
dryakhlyi (adj.) decrepit
dryan' (n.f.) trash
dub (n.m.) oak
dubina (n.f.) cudgel
dublikat (n.m.) duplicate
dublirovanie (n.n.) standby system
dublirovat' (v.impf.) duplicate
dubovyi (adj.) oaken
dudka (n.f.) pipe
duél' (n.f.) duel
duét (n.m.) duet
duga (n.f.) arc
dukh (n.m.) spirit
dukhi (n.pl.) perfume
dukhota (n.f.) closeness
dukhovenstvo (n.n.) clergy
dukhovka (n.f.) oven
dukhovnyi (adj.) spiritual
dukhovoi (adj.) wind

dulo (n.n.) muzzle
duma (n.f.) thought
duma (n.f.) duma
dumat' (v.impf.) think
dunovenie (n.n.) breath
dunut' (v.pf.) blow
duplo (n.n.) hollow
dur' (n.f.) folly
dura (n.f.) fool
durman (n.m.) narcotic
durnet' (v.impf.) grow ugly
durno (adv.) badly
durnota (n.f.) giddiness
dush (n.m.) shower
dusha (n.f.) soul
dushegubka (n.f.) gas chamber
dushevnobol'noi (adj.) lunatic
dushevnyi (adj.) sincere
dushistyi (adj.) fragrant
dushit' (v.impf.) strangle
dushit'sya (v.impf.) to perfume
dushno (adj.) stuffy
dut' (v.impf.) blow
dut'sya (v.impf.) be sulky
dutyi (adj.) exaggerated
dva (num.) two
dvadtsat' (num.) twenty
dvadtsatiletie (n.n.) twentieth anniversary
dvadtsatyi (adj.) twentieth
dvazhdy (adv.) twice
dvenadtsat' (num.) twelve
dver' (n.f.) door
dvesti (num.) two hundred
dvigatel' (n.m.) motor
dvinut' (v.impf.) move
dvizhenie (n.n.) movement
dvizhushchii (adj.) driving
dvoe (num.) two
dvoetochie (n.n.) colon
dvoichnyi (adj.) binary
dvoika (n.f.) two
dvoinik (n.m.) double

dvoinoi (adj.) double
dvoinya (n.f.) twins
dvoistvennyi (adj.) ambivalent
dvor (n.m.) court
dvorets (n.m.) palace
dvornik (n.m.) janitor
dvornyazhka (n.f.) mongrel
dvortsovyi (adj.) court
dvoryanin (n.m.) nobleman
dvoyakii (adj.) double
dvoyurodnyi (adj.) cousin
dvubortnyi (adj.) double-breasted
dvuchlen (n.m.) binominal
dvukhétazhnyi (adj.) two-storied
dvukhgodichnyi (adj.) two-year
dvukhletnii (adj.) of two years
dvukhmestnyi (adj.) two-seater
dvukhmesyachnyi (adj.) two-month
dvukhnedel'nyi (adj.) for two weeks
dvukratnyi (adj.) twofold
dvulichnyi (adj.) double-faced
dvupolyi (adj.) bisexual
dvupolyusnyi (adj.) bipolar
dvurushnik (n.m.) double-dealer
dvusmyslennyi (adj.) ambiguous
dvuspal'nyi (adj.) double-bed
dvustoronnii (adj.) bilateral
dyadya (n.m.) uncle
dyatel (n.m.) woodpecker
d'yavol (n.m.) devil
dykhanie (n.n.) breathing
dym (n.m.) smoke
dymokhod (n.m.) flue
dynya (n.f.) melon
dyra (n.f.) hole
dyryavyi (adj.) full of holes
dyshat' (v.impf.) breathe
dyuna (n.f.) dune
dyuzhina (n.f.) dozen
dzhemper (n.m.) jumper
dzhungli (n.pl.) jungle

E (E, Ë, Э)

eda (n.f.) food

edinenie (n.n.) unity

edinitsa (n.f.) unit

edinodushie (n.n.) unanimity

edinoglasnyi (adj.) unanimous

edinolichnyi (adj.) individual

edinomyshlennik (n.m.) adherent

edinonachalie (n.n.) one-man management

edinoobrazie (n.n.) uniformity

edinovremennyi (adj.) one time grant

edinstvennyi (adj.) the only

edinstvo (n.n.) unity

edinyi (adj.) united

edkii (adj.) caustic

edok (n.m.) eater

edva (adv.) hardly

éfes (n.m.) sword-hilt

éffekt (n.m.) effect

éffektivnyi (adj.) effective

éffektnyi (adj.) spectacular

éfir (n.m.) ether

efreitor (n.m.) lance corporal

egipetskii (adj.) Egyptian

égoizm (n.m.) selfishness

ekhat' (v.impf.) drive

ekhidnyi (adj.) malicious

ékho (n.n.) echo

ékipazh (n.m.) carriage

ékipazh (n.m.) crew

ékipirovat' (v.impf.&pf.) equip

ékonomika (n.f.) economics

ékonomicheskii (adj.) economic

ékonomit' (v.impf.) economize

ékonomiya (n.f.) economy

ékran (n.m.) screen

ékskavator (n.m.) excavator

ékskursiya (n.f.) excursion

ékspeditsiya (n.f.) expedition

éksperiment (n.m.) experiment

ékspert (n.m.) expert

ékspluatirovat' (v.impf.) exploit

éksponat (n.m.) exhibit

éksport (n.m.) export

ékspozitsiya (n.f.) exposition

ékspromt (n.m.) impromptu

ékspropriirovat' (v.impf.&pf.) expropriate

ékstaz (n.m.) ecstasy

éksterritorial'nyi (adj.) exterritorial

ékstravagantnyi (adj.) extravagant

ékstrennyi (adj.) special

ékstsentrichnyi (adj.) eccentric

ékstsess (n.m.) excess

ékvator (n.m.) equator

ékvivalent (n.m.) equivalent

ékzamen (n.m.) examination

ékzamenator (n.m.) examiner

ékzamenovat' (v.impf.) examine

ékzemplyar (n.m.) specimen

el' (n.f.) fir

élastichnyi (adj.) elastic

ele (adv.) hardly

élegantnyi (adj.) elegant

élektricheskii (adj.) electric

élektrifitsirovat' (v.impf.&pf.) electrify

élektrod (n.m.) electrode

elektrodvigatel' (n.m.) electric motor

élektroenergiya (n.f.) electrical energy

élektromonter (n.m.) electrician

élektron (n.m.) electron

élektronika (n.f.) electronics

élektronno-vychislitel' naya mashina (n.f.) electronic computer

élektropoloter (n.m.) electric floor polisher

élektroprovodnost' (n.f.) electrical conductivity

élektrostantsiya (n.f.) electric power station

élektrotekhnik (n.m.) electrical engineer

élektrovoz (n.m.) electric locomotive

élement (n.m.) element

élementarnyi (adj.) elementary

élevator (n.m.) elevator

elka (n.f.) fir tree

elovyi (adj.) fir

émal' (n.f.) enamel

émalirovannyi (adj.) enamelled

émansipatsiya (n.f.) emancipation

émblema (n.f.) emblem

émigrant (n.m.) emigrant

emkii (adj.) capacious

émotsional'nyi (adj.) emotional

émotsiya (n.f.) emotion
émpiriokrititsizm (n.m.) empiriocriticism
emu (p.) him
énergetika (n.f.) power engineering
énergichnyi (adj.) energetic
énergiya (n.f.) energy
enot (n.m.) raccoon
éntsiklopediya (n.f.) encyclopedia
éntuziazm (n.m.) enthusiasm
épicheskii (adj.) epic
épidemiologiya (n.f.) epidemiology
épidemiya (n.f.) epidemic
épigraf (n.m.) epigraph
épigramma (n.f.) epigram
épilog (n.m.) epilogue
episkop (n.m.) bishop
épitafiya (n.f.) epitaph
épitet (n.m.) epithet
épizod (n.m.) episode
épokha (n.f.) epoch
épopeya (n.f.) epic
épos (n.m.) epos
éra (n.f.) era
eres' (n.f.) heresy
eretik (n.m.) heretic
éroticheskii (adj.) erotic
éruditsiya (n.f.) erudition
erunda (n.f.) nonsense
érzat' (v.impf.) fidget
éshafot (n.m.) scaffold
eshche (adv.) still, more, yet
éshelon (n.m.) echelon
éskadra (n.f.) squadron
éskadril'ya (n.f.) squadron
éskalator (n.m.) escalator
éskimo (n.n.) chocolate ice
éskimos (n.m.) Eskimo
éskiz (n.m.) sketch
éskort (n.m.) escort
esli (conj.) if

ésminets (n.m.) destroyer
éssentsiya (n.f.) essence
est' (v.impf.) eat
éstafeta (n.f.) relay race
estestvennyi (adj.) natural
estestvoznanie (n.n.) natural history
éstetika (n.f.) aesthetics
éstonets (n.m.) Estonian
éstrada (n.f.) stage
éta (p.) this
étazh (n.m.) floor
étazherka (n.f.) bookcase
éti (p.) these
étichnyi (adj.) ethical
étika (n.f.) ethics
étiket (n.m.) etiquette
étiketka (n.f.) label
étimologiya (n.f.) etymology
étnografiya (n.f.) ethnography
éto (p.) this
étot (p.) this
étyud (n.m.) study
évakuatsiya (n.f.) evacuation
evangelie (n.m.) gospel
evgenika (n.f.) eugenics
évolyutsionnyi (adj.) evolutionary
evrei (n.m.) Jew
évristicheskii (adj.) heuristic
Evropa (n.f.) Europe
eyu (p.) her
ezda (n.f.) drive
ezdit' (v.impf.) drive
ezh (n.m.) hedgehog
ezhechasno (adv.) hourly
ezhednevno (adv.) daily
ezhegodnyi (adj.) annual
ezhemesyachnyi (adj.) monthly
ezheminutno (adv.) every minute
ezhenedel'nyi (adj.) weekly
ezhevika (n.f.) blackberry

F (Ф)

fabrichnyi (adj.) factory
fabrika (n.f.) factory
fabula (n.f.) plot
fagotsit (n.m.) phagocyte
fakel (n.m.) torch
fakir (n.m.) fakir
fakt (n.m.) fact
faktor (n.m.) factor
fakul'tativnyi (adj.) optional
fakul'tet (n.m.) department
fal'sh' (n.f.) falsity
fal'shivyi (adj.) false
fal'sifitsirovat' (v.impf.) falsify
familiya (n.f.) surname
famil'yarnyi (adj.) unceremonious
fanatik (n.m.) fanatic
fanatizm (n.m.) fanaticism
fanera (n.f.) veneer
fantasticheskii (adj.) fantastic
fantazer (n.m.) dreamer
fantaziya (n.f.) fantasy
fara (n.f.) headlight
farfor (n.m.) china
faringit (n.m.) pharyngitis
farmakologiya (n.f.) pharmacology
farmakopeya (n.f.) pharmacopoeia
farmatsevt (n.m.) pharmacist
fars (n.m.) farce
farsh (n.m.) stuffing
fartuk (n.m.) apron
farvater (n.m.) fairway
fasad (n.m.) facade
fashizm (n.m.) fascism
fasol' (n.f.) haricot bean
fason (n.m.) fashion
fatalizm (n.m.) fatalism
fatal'nyi (adj.) fatal
fauna (n.f.) fauna
fayans (n.m.) glazed earthenware
faza (n.f.) phase
fazan (n.m.) pheasant
federal'nyi (adj.) federal
federativnyi (adj.) federative
federatsiya (n.f.) federation
feericheskii (adj.) magic

feierverk (n.m.) fireworks
fekhtovanie (n.n.) fencing
fel'dmarshal (n.m.) field marshal
fel'dsher (n.m.) medical assistant
fel'eton (n.m.) satirical article
fenil (n.m.) phenyl
fenomen (n.m.) phenomenon
feodal (n.m.) feudal lord
feodal'nyi (adj.) feudal
ferma (n.f.) farm
ferma (n.f.) girder
ferment (n.m.) enzyme
fermentatsiya (n.f.) fermentation
fermer (n.m.) farmer
ferz' (n.m.) queen
feshenebel'nyi (adj.) fashionable
festival' (n.m.) festival
fetish (n.m.) fetish
fetr (n.m.) felt
fevral' (n.m.) February
feya (n.f.) fairy
fialka (n.f.) violet
fiasko (n.n.) fiasco
figlyar (n.m.) mountebank
figura (n.f.) figure
figural'nyi (adj.) figurative
figurirovat' (v.impf.) appear as
figurist (n.m.) figure skater
figurnyi (adj.) figured
fiksirovat' (v.impf.) fix
fiktivnyi (adj.) fictitious
fiktsiya (n.f.) fiction
filantrop (n.m.) philanthropist
filarmoniya (n.f.) philharmonic society
filial (n.m.) branch office
filin (n.m.) eagle-owl
fil'm (n.m.) film
filolog (n.m.) philologist
filosof (n.m.) philosopher
fil'tr (n.m.) filter
finn (n.m.) Finn
final (n.m.) end
finansirovat' (v.impf.) finance
finansovyi (adj.) financial
finik (n.m.) date

finish (n.m.)   finish
fioletovyi (adj.)   violet
firma (n.f.)   firm
fisgarmoniya (n.f.)   harmonium
fitil' (n.m.)   wick
fitopatologiya (n.f.)   phytopathology
fizicheskii (adj.)   physical
fizik (n.m.)   physicist
fizika (n.f.)   physics
fiziolog (n.m.)   physiologist
fiziologiya (n.f.)   physiology
fizionomiya (n.f.)   physiognomy
fizioterapiya (n.f.)   physiotherapy
fizkul'tura (n.f.)   physical culture
flag (n.m.)   flag
flakon (n.m.)   bottle
flanel' (n.f.)   flannel
flang (n.m.)   flank
flegmatichnyi (adj.)   phlegmatic
fleita (n.f.)   flute
fleksiya (n.f.)   inflection
fligel' (n.m.)   wing
flirt (n.m.)   flirtation
flora (n.f.)   flora
flot (n.m.)   fleet
flotatsiya (n.f.)   flotation
fluorestsentsiya (n.f.)   fluorescence
flyaga (n.f.)   flask
flyuger (n.m.)   weathercock
flyus (n.m.)   gumboil
flyus (n.m.)   flux
foie (n.n.)   foyer
fokstrot (n.m.)   foxtrot
fokus (n.m.)   focus
fokus (n.m.)   trick
fol'ga (n.f.)   foil
foliant (n.m.)   folio
fol'klor (n.m.)   folklore
fon (n.m.)   background
fonar' (n.m.)   lantern
fond (n.m.)   fund
fonetika (n.f.)   phonetics
fontan (n.m.)   fountain
forel' (n.f.)   trout
forma (n.f.)   form
formalizm (n.m.)   formalism
formal'nost' (n.f.)   formality
format (n.m.)   size

formatsiya (n.f.)   formation
formennyi (adj.)   uniform
formirovat' (v.impf.)   form
formovat' (v.impf.)   mold
formovshchik (n.m.)   molder
formula (n.f.)   formula
forpost (n.m.)   outpost
forsirovat' (v.impf.)   force
fort (n.m.)   fort
fortepiano (n.n.)   piano
fortochka (n.f.)   ventilation window
fosfat (n.m.)   phosphate
fosfor (n.m.)   phosphorus
fotoapparat (n.m.)   camera
fotoélement (n.m.)   photoelectric cell
fotograf (n.m.)   photographer
fotografiya (n.f.)   photograph
fotokhimiya (n.f.)   photochemistry
fotosintez (n.m.)   photosynthesis
fragment (n.m.)   fragment
frak (n.m.)   tailcoat
frakht (n.m.)   freight
fraktsionnyi (adj.)   factional
fraktsiya (n.f.)   faction
frant (n.m.)   dandy
frantsuz (n.m.)   Frenchman
frantsuzskii (adj.)   French
frantsuzy (n.pl.)   French
fraza (n.f.)   phrase
frazeologiya (n.f.)   phraseology
frazer (n.m.)   phrasemonger
french (n.m.)   service jacket
freska (n.f.)   fresco
freza (n.f.)   milling cutter
frivol'nyi (adj.)   frivolous
front (n.m.)   front
frontovik (n.m.)   front-line soldier
frukt (n.m.)   fruit
ftor (n.m.)   fluorine
ftorirovanie (n.n.)   fluorination
fufaika (n.f.)   jersey
fugasnyi (adj.)   high explosive
fundament (n.m.)   foundation
fungitsid (n.m.)   fungicide
funikuler (n.m.)   funicular
funktsionirovat' (v.impf.)   function
funktsiya (n.f.)   function
funt (n.m.)   pound

furazh (n.m.)   fodder
furazhka (n.f.)   peaked cap
furgon (n.m.)   van
furor (n.m.)   furore
furunkul (n.m.)   boil

futbol (n.m.)   football
futlyar (n.m.)   cover
fyrkat' (v.impf.)   snort
fyuzelyazh (n.m.)   fuselage

G (Г)

ga (n.m.)   hectare
gad (n.m.)   reptile
gadalka (n.f.)   fortune-teller
gadit' (v.impf.)   foul
gadkii (adj.)   nasty
gadyuka (n.f.)   adder
gagachii (adj.)   eider duck
gaika (n.f.)   nut
galantereya (n.f.)   haberdashery
galereya (n.f.)   gallery
galerka (n.f.)   gallery
galka (n.f.)   jackdaw bird
gal'ka (n.f.)   pebbles
gallii (n.m.)   gallium
gallyutsinatsiya (n.f.)   hallucination
galogen (n.m.)   halogen
galop (n.m.)   gallop
galoshi (n.pl.)   galoshes
galstuk (n.m.)   tie
gal'vanicheskii (adj.)   galvanic
gal'vanizatsiya (n.f.)   galvanizing
gam (n.m.)   uproar
gamak (n.m.)   hammock
gamma (n.f.)   scale
gamma-izluchenie (n.n.)   gama-radiation
gangrena (n.f.)   gangrene
ganteli (n.pl.)   dumbbells
gar' (n.f.)   burning
garantirovat' (v.impf.&pf.)   guarantee
garantiya (n.f.)   guarantee
garazh (n.m.)   garage
garderob (n.m.)   cloakroom
gardina (n.f.)   window curtain
garmonichnyi (adj.)   harmonious
garmonika (n.f.)   accordion
garmonirovat' (v.impf.)   harmonize

garmonist (n.m.)   accordion player
garmoniya (n.f.)   harmony
garnir (n.m.)   garnish
garnitur (n.m.)   set
garnizon (n.m.)   garrison
gartsevat' (v.impf.)   prance
gasit' (v.impf.)   extinguish
gasnut' (v.impf.)   go out
gastrit (n.m.)   gastritis
gastrolirovat' (v.impf.)   tour
gastronomicheskii (adj.)   grocery
gauptvakhta (n.f.)   guardhouse
gavan' (n.f.)   harbor
gaz (n.m.)   gas
gazeta (n.f.)   newspaper
gazirovannyi (adj.)   aerated
gazogenerator (n.m.)   gas generator
gazon (n.m.)   lawn
gazoobraznyi (adj.)   gaseous
gazoprovod (n.m.)   gas main
gazoubezhishche (n.n.)   gas shelter
gazovyi (adj.)   gas
gde (adv.)   where
gde-libo (adv.)   somewhere
gegemoniya (n.f.)   hegemony
gektar (n.m.)   hectare
gelii (n.m.)   helium
gelioénergetika (n.f.)   solar power
   engineering
gemoglobin (n.m.)   hemoglobin
gemoliz (n.m.)   hemolysis
genealogiya (n.f.)   genealogy
general (n.m.)   general
generalissimus (n.m.)   generalissimo
general-leitenant (n.m.)   lieutenant general
general'nyi (adj.)   general

generator (n.m.) generator
genetika (n.f.) genetics
genezis (n.m.) genesis
genial'nyi (adj.) brilliant
genii (n.m.) genius
geodeziya (n.f.) land surveying
geofizicheskii (adj.) geophysical
geograf (n.m.) geographer
geokhimiya (n.f.) geochemistry
geolog (n.m.) geologist
geologorazvedka (n.f.) geological survey
geomagnetizm (n.m.) geomagnetism
geometriya (n.f.) geometry
georgin (n.m.) dahlia
geran' (n.f.) geranium
gerb (n.m.) coat of arms
gerbarii (n.m.) herbarium
gerbovyi (adj.) heraldic
germanskii (adj.) German
germeticheskii (adj.) hermetically sealed
germetizirovat' (v.impf.) pressurize
geroi (n.m.) hero
geroizm (n.m.) heroism
geterotsiklicheskii (adj.) heterocyclic
getry (n.pl.) gaiters
giatsint (n.m.) hyacinth
gibel' (n.f.) ruin
gibkii (adj.) flexible
giblyi (adj.) bad
gibnut' (v.impf.) perish
gibrid (n.m.) hybrid
gid (n.m.) guide
gidravlika (n.f.) hydraulics
gidrobiologiya (n.f.) hydrobiology
gidrodinamika (n.f.) hydrodynamics
gidroliz (n.m.) hydrolysis
gidroplan (n.m.) hydroplane
gidrostantsiya (n.f.) hydroelectric power
  station
gidrotekhnika (n.f.) hydraulic engineering
giena (n.f.) hyena
gigant (n.m.) giant
gigiena (n.f.) hygiene
gigroskopicheskii (adj.) hygroscopic
gil'za (n.f.) cartridge case
gimn (n.m.) hymn
gimnast (n.m.) gymnast
ginekolog (n.m.) gynecologist

ginekologiya (n.f.) gynecology
giperbola (n.f.) hyperbole
gipertoniya (n.f.) hypertension
gipertrofiya (n.f.) hypertrophy
gipnoz (n.m.) hypnosis
gipotenuza (n.f.) hypotenuse
gipoteza (n.f.) hypothesis
gips (n.m.) gypsum
girlyanda (n.f.) garland
girya (n.f.) weight
gistologiya (n.f.) histology
gitara (n.f.) guitar
glad' (n.f.) smooth surface
glad' (n.f.) satin stitch
gladit' (v.impf.) stroke
gladkii (adj.) smooth
glagol (n.m.) verb
glagol-svyazka (n.f.) linking-verb
glanda (n.f.) tonsil
glasnost' (n.f.) publicity
glasnyi (adj.) public
glasnyi (adj.) vowel
glava (n.f.) head
glava (n.f.) chapter
glavar' (n.m.) ringleader
glavenstvo (n.n.) supremacy
glavnokomanduyushchii (n.m.) commander
  in chief
glavnyi (adj.) chief
glaz (n.m.) eye
glazet' (v.impf.) stare
glazhen'e (n.n.) ironing
glaznoi (adj.) eye
glazok (n.m.) peephole
glazun'ya (n.f.) fried eggs
glazur' (n.f.) icing
gletcher (n.m.) glacier
glina (n.f.) clay
glinyanyi (adj.) clay
glisser (n.m.) speedboat
glist (n.m.) intestinal worm
glitserin (n.m.) glycerine
globus (n.m.) globe
glodat' (v.impf.) gnaw
glokhnut' (v.impf.) grow deaf
glotat' (v.impf.) swallow
glotka (n.f.) throat
glotok (n.m.) sip

glub' (n.f.) depth
glubina (n.f.) depth
glubokii (adj.) deep
gluboko (adv.) deeply
glubokomyslennyi (adj.) thoughtful
glukhie (n.collect.) the deaf
glukhonemoi (adj.) deaf-mute
glukhota (n.f.) deafness
glumit'sya (v.impf.) sneer
glupet' (v.impf.) grow stupid
glupo (adv.) stupidly
glush' (n.f.) backwoods
glushitel' (n.m.) muffler
glyadet' (v.impf.) stare
glyanets (n.m.) luster
glyatsiologiya (n.f.) glaciology
glyba (n.f.) block
glyukoza (n.f.) glucose
gnat' (v.impf.) drive
gnedoi (adj.) bay
gnet (n.m.) oppression
gnetushchii (adj.) depressing
gnev (n.m.) anger
gnezdit'sya (v.impf.) nest
gnezdo (n.n.) nest
gnienie (n.n.) rotting
gniloi (adj.) rotten
gnit' (v.impf.) rot
gnoi (n.m.) pus
gnoinik (n.m.) abscess
gnoit'sya (v.impf.) fester
gnusavit' (v.impf.) speak with a nasal twang
gnushat'sya (v.impf.) shun
gnusnyi (adj.) infamous
gnut' (v.impf.) bend
god (n.m.) year
godichnyi (adj.) annual
godit'sya (v.impf.) be suitable
godnyi (adj.) fit
godovalyi (adj.) one year old
godovshchina (n.f.) anniversary
gofrirovannyi (adj.) corrugated
gogotat' (v.impf.) roar with laughter
gol (n.m.) goal
golenishche (n.n.) top of a boot
gollandets (n.m.) Dutch
golod (n.m.) hunger
golodnyi (n.m.) hungry

golodovka (n.f.) hunger strike
gololeditsa (n.f.) icy condition of roads
golos (n.m.) voice
goloslovno (adv.) without proof
golosovanie (n.n.) voting
golosovoi (adj.) vocal
golova (n.f.) head
golovastik (n.m.) tadpole
goloveshka (n.f.) firebrand
golovka (n.f.) head
golovokruzhenie (n.n.) dizziness
golovolomka (n.f.) puzzle
golovomoika (n.f.) severe scolding
golovorez (n.m.) cutthroat
golovotyap (n.m.) bungler
golub' (n.m.) pigeon
goluboi (adj.) blue
golyi (adj.) naked
gomeopatiya (n.f.) homeopathy
gomogennyi (adj.) homogeneous
gomolog (n.m.) homologue
gonchar (n.m.) potter
gonchaya (n.f.) hound
gondola (n.f.) gondola
gonenie (n.n.) persecution
gonets (n.m.) messenger
gonka (n.f.) haste, race
gonki (n.pl.) races
gonochnyi (adj.) racing
gonor (n.m.) arrogance
gonorar (n.m.) fee
gonyat' (v.impf.) drive
gore (n.n.) grief
gora (n.f.) mountain
gorazdo (adv.) much
gorb (n.m.) hump
gorbit'sya (v.impf.) stoop
gorbushka (n.f.) crust
gorchichnik (n.m.) mustard plaster
gorchit' (v.impf.) taste bitter
gorchitsa (n.f.) mustard
gordelivyi (adj.) proud
gordit'sya (v.impf.) be proud
gordost' (n.f.) pride
gorech' (n.f.) bitter taste
gorelka (n.f.) burner
gorelyi (adj.) burnt
gorenie (n.n.) burning

gorestnyi (adj.) sad
goret' (v.impf.) burn
gorets (n.m.) highlander
goristyi (adj.) mountainous
gorizont (n.m.) horizon
gorka (n.f.) hill
gor'kii (adj.) bitter
gorlo (n.n.) throat
gorlyshko (n.n.) neck
gormon (n.m.) hormone
gorn (n.m.) furnace
gorn (n.m.) bugle
gornorabochii (n.m.) miner
gornostai (n.m.) ermine
gornozavodskii (adj.) mining and
   metallurgical
gornyi (adj.) mountainous
gorod (n.m.) town
gorokh (n.m.) peas
goroshek (n.m.) peas
gorozhanin (n.m.) townsman
gorshok (n.m.) pot
gorst' (n.f.) handfull
gortan' (n.f.) larynx
goryachii (adj.) hot
goryacho (adv.) hot
goryuchee (n.n.) fuel
gosbank (n.m.) state bank
gospital' (n.m.) hospital
gosplan (n.m.) state planning commission
gospodin (n.m.) gentleman
gospodstvo (n.n.) domination
gospozha (n.f.) lady
gosstrakh (n.m.) state insurance
gost' (n.m.) guest
gostepriimnyi (adj.) hospitable
gostinaya (n.f.) living room
gostinitsa (n.f.) hotel
gostit' (v.impf.) stay with
gosudarstvennyi (adj.) state
gosudarstvo (n.n.) state
goticheskii (adj.) Gothic
gotoval'nya (n.f.) case of drawing
   instruments
gotovit' (v.impf.) prepare
gotovnost' (n.f.) readiness
gotovyi (adj.) ready
govor (n.m.) murmur

govorit' (v.impf.) speak
govorlivyi (adj.) talkative
govyadina (n.f.) beef
grabezh (n.m.) robbery
grabit' (v.impf.) rob
grabli (n.pl.) rake
grach (n.m.) rook
grad (n.m.) hail
gradom (adv.) thick and fast
gradus (n.m.) degree
graf (n.m.) count
grafa (n.f.) column
graficheskii (adj.) graphic
grafik (n.m.) timetable
grafika (n.f.) graphic arts
grafin (n.m.) carafe
grafinya (n.f.) countess
grafit (n.m.) graphite
gramm (n.m.) gram
grammatika (n.f.) grammar
gramota (n.f.) reading and writing
gramotnyi (adj.) literate
gramzapis' (n.f.) recording
gran' (n.f.) side
granat (n.m.) pomegranate
granat (n.m.) garnet
granata (n.f.) grenade
grandioznyi (adj.) grandiose
granenyi (adj.) faceted
granit (n.m.) granite
granitsa (n.f.) border
granka (n.f.) galley-proof
granulema (n.f.) granuloma
gratsioznyi (adj.) graceful
gratsiya (n.f.) grace
graver (n.m.) engraver
gravii (n.m.) gravel
gravirovat' (v.impf.) engrave
gravitatsiya (n.f.) gravitation
gravyura (n.f.) engraving
grazhdanin (n.m.) citizen
grazhdanskii (adj.) civil
grazhdanstvo (n.n.) citizenship
greben' (n.m.) comb
grebenka (n.f.) comb
grebets (n.m.) oarsman
greblya (n.f.) rowing
grecheskii (adj.) Greek

grechikha (n.f.) buckwheat
grechnevyi (adj.) buckwheat
grek (n.m) Greek
grekh (n.m.) sin
grelka (n.f.) hot-water bottle
gremet' (v.impf.) thunder
greshit' (v.impf.) sin
greshnyi (adj.) sinful
gresti (v.impf.) row
gresti (v.impf.) rake
gret' (v.impf.) warm
gretskii orekh (adj.-n.m.) walnut
greza (n.f.) dream
grezit' (v.impf.) dream
grib (n.m.) mushroom
grifel' (n.m.) slate-pencil
grim (n.m.) make-up
grimasa (n.f.) grimace
grimirovat' (v.impf.) make up
gripp (n.m.) influenza
griva (n.f.) mane
grivennik (n.m.) ten-kopeck coin
grob (n.m.) coffin
grokhnut'sya (v.pf.) crash
grokhot (n.m.) crash
grom (n.m.) thunder
gromada (n.f.) mass
gromit' (v.impf.) smash
gromkii (adj.) loud
gromkogovoritel' (n.m.) loud speaker
gromoglasnyi (adj.) loud
gromootvod (n.m.) lightning conductor
gromovoi (adj.) thunderous
gromozdit' (v.impf.) heap up
gromozdkii (adj.) cumbersome
gromykhat' (v.impf.) rattle
grosh (n.m.) half-kopeck piece
grossmeister (n.m.) grand chess-master
grot (n.m.) grotto
groza (n.f.) thunderstorm
grozd' (n.f.) cluster
grozit' (v.impf.) threaten
groznyi (adj.) threatening
grozovoi (adj.) storm
grubit' (v.impf.) be rude
grubost' (n.f.) rudeness
grud' (n.f.) breast
gruda (n.f.) heap

grudinka (n.f.) brisket
grudnoi (adj.) breast
grunt (n.m.) soil
gruppa (n.f.) group
grusha (n.f.) pear
grust' (n.f.) sadness
grustit' (v.impf.) be melancholy
grustnyi (adj.) sad
gruz (n.m.) load
gruzchik (n.m.) docker
gruzilo (n.n.) plummet
gruzin (n.m.) Georgian
gruzit' (v.impf.) load
gruznyi (adj.) corpulent
gruzooborot (n.m.) goods turnover
gruzopod"emnost' (n.f.) capacity
gruzovik (n.m.) truck
gryada (n.f.) ridge
gryadka (n.f.) bed
gryadushchii (adj.) coming
gryanut' (v.pf.) break out
gryaz' (n.f.) dirt
gryazi (n.pl.) mud
gryaznyi (adj.) dirty
gryzha (n.f.) hernia
gryznya (n.f.) fight
gryzt' (v.impf.) gnaw
gryzun (n.m.) rodent
guba (n.f.) lip
guba (n.f.) bay
gubernator (n.m.) governor
guberniya (n.f.) province
gubitel'nyi (adj.) destructive
gubka (n.f.) sponge
gubka (n.f.) fungus
gubnoi (adj.) labial
gudenie (n.n.) buzzing
gudet' (v.impf.) buzz
gudok (n.m.) hooter
gudron (n.m.) tar
gul (n.m.) boom, rumble
gulyan'e (n.n.) stroll
gulyash (n.m.) goulash
gumanizm (n.m.) humanism
gumannost' (n.f.) humanity
gummiarabik (n.m.) gum
gumno (n.n.) threshing floor
gur'ba (n.f.) crowd

gurt (n.m.) herd
gus' (n.m.) goose
gusenitsa (n.f.) caterpillar
gusenok (n.m.) gosling
gushcha (n.f.) sediment
gusinyi (adj.) goose
gus'kom (adv.) single file
gustet' (v.impf.) thicken
gustoi (adj.) thick

gusyatina (n.f.) gooseflesh
gutalin (n.m.) shoe polish
guzhevoi (adj.) animal-drawn
gvalt (n.m.) hubbub
gvardeets (n.m.) guardsman
gvardiya (n.f.) guards
gvozd' (n.m.) nail
gvozdika (n.f.) carnation
gvozdika (n.f.) clove

I (И, Й)

i (conj.) and
i. t. d. (i tak dalee) (abbr.) etc. (et cetera)
i. t. p. (i tomu podobnoe) (abbr.) and the like
ibo (conj.) because
ideal (n.m.) ideal
idealizm (n.m.) idealism
ideal'nyi (adj.) ideal
ideinyi (adj.) ideological
ideolog (n.m.) ideologist
ideya (n.f.) idea
idilliya (n.f.) idyll
idioma (n.f.) idiom
idiosinkraziya (n.f.) idiosyncrasy
idiot (n.m.) idiot
idol (n.m.) idol
idti (v.impf.) go
ieroglif (n.m.) hieroglyph
iezuit (n.m.) Jesuit
igla (n.f.) needle
igloterapiya (n.f.) acupuncture
ignorirovat' (v.impf.) ignore
igo (n.n.) yoke
igolka (n.f.) needle
igra (n.f.) play
igrat' (v.impf.) play
igrivyi (adj.) playful
igrok (n.m.) player
igrushka (n.f.) toy
ikat' (v.impf.) hiccup
ikh (p.) them
ikh (p.) their
ikona (n.f.) icon

ikota (n.f.) hiccup
ikra (n.f.) spawn
ikra (n.f.) calf
il (n.m.) silt
ili (conj.) or
illyuminator (n.m.) porthole
illyuminatsiya (n.f.) illumination
illyustratsiya (n.f.) illustration
illyuziya (n.f.) illusion
im (p.) them
imbir' (n.m.) ginger
imenie (n.n.) estate
imeniny (n.pl.) name-day
imenitel'nyi (adj.) nominative
imenno (adv.) exactly
imet' (v.impf.) have
imitatsiya (n.f.) imitation
immigrant (n.m.) immigrant
immunitet (n.m.) immunity
immunobiologiya (n.f.) immunobiology
imperator (n.m.) emperor
imperializm (n.m.) imperialism
imperiya (n.f.) empire
imponirovat' (v.impf.) impress
import (n.m.) import
impotentsiya (n.f.) impotence
improvizatsiya (n.f.) improvisation
impul's (n.m.) impulse
imushchestvo (n.n.) property
imushchii (adj.) propertied
imya (n.n.) name
inoi (adj.) different

inache (adv.) otherwise
indeets (n.m.) Indian (American)
indeks (n.m.) index
indiets (n.m.) Indian (Asian)
individual'nyi (adj.) individual
indoneziets (n.m.) Indonesian
induktsiya (n.f.) induction
indus (n.m.) Hindu
industrializatsiya (n.f.) industrialization
industriya (n.f.) industry
indyuk (n.m.) turkey
inei (n.m.) hoarfrost
in"ektsiya (n.f.) injection
inertnost' (n.f.) inertness
inertsiya (n.f.) inertia
infektsionnyi (adj.) infectious
infektsiya (n.f.) infection
infinitiv (n.m.) infinitive
inflyatsiya (n.f.) inflation
informatsiya (n.f.) information
informbyuro (n.n.) information bureau
informirovat' (v.impf.) inform
infrakrasnyi (adj.) infrared
ingibitor (n.m.) inhibitor
initsialy (n.pl.) initials
initsiativa (n.f.) initiative
inkubator (n.m.) incubator
inkvizitsiya (n.f.) inquisition
innervatsiya (n.f.) innervation
inogda (adv.) sometimes
inogorodnii (adj.) of another town
inorodnyi (adj.) foreign
inoskazatel'nyi (adj.) allegorical
inostranets (n.m.) foreigner
inozemnyi (adj.) foreign
inspektor (n.m.) inspector
inspektsiya (n.f.) inspection
inspirirovat' (v.impf.) inspire
instantsiya (n.f.) instance
instinkt (n.m.) instinct
institut (n.m.) institute
instruktirovat' (v.impf.) instruct
instruktor (n.m.) instructor
instrument (n.m.) instrument
instsenirovat' (v.impf.&pf.) dramatize
integrirovanie (n.n.) integration
intektitsid (n.m.) insecticide
intellekt (n.m.) intellect

intelligentnyi (adj.) cultured
intendant (n.m.) quartermaster
intensivnyi (adj.) intensive
interes (n.m.) interest
internat (n.m.) boarding school
Internatsional (n.m.) the Internationale
internatsionalizm (n.m.) internationalism
internatsional'nyi (adj.) international
internirovat' (v.impf&pf.) intern
interpretatsiya (n.f.) interpretation
interval (n.m.) interval
intervent (n.m.) aggressor
interv'yu (n.n.) interview
intimnyi (adj.) intimate
intonatsiya (n.f.) intonation
intriga (n.f.) intrigue
intsident (n.m.) incident
intuitsiya (n.f.) intuition
invalid (n.m.) invalid
inventar' (n.m.) inventory
inzhener (n.m.) engineer
iod (n.m.) iodine
iodoform (n.m.) iodoform
iog (n.m.) yogi
ion (n.m.) ion
ionosfera (n.f.) ionosphere
iota (n.f.) iota
ippodrom (n.m.) racecourse
iprit (n.m.) mustard gas
iranets (n.m.) Iranian
irlandets (n.m.) Irishman
ironicheskii (adj.) ironical
ironiya (n.f.) irony
irrigatsiya (n.f.) irrigation
ischerpat' (v.pf.) exhaust
ischeznovenie (n.n.) disappearance
ischeznut' (v.pf.) disappear
ischislenie (n.n.) calculation
ishak (n.m.) ass
ishcheika (n.f.) bloodhound
ishias (n.m.) sciatica
isk (n.m.) action
iskalechit' (v.pf.) cripple
iskat' (v.impf.) search
iskazhat' (v.impf.) distort
iskazhenie (n.n.) distortion
iskhod (n.m.) outcome
iskhodit' (v.pf.) proceed

iskhodnyi (adj.) initial
iskhudalyi (adj.) emaciated
isklyuchat' (v.impf.) exclude
isklyuchenie (n.n.) exception
iskolesit' (v.pf.) roam
iskopaemoe (n.n.) fossil
iskorenit' (v.pf.) eradicate
iskosa (adv.) askance
iskoverkat' (v.pf.) deform
iskra (n.f.) spark
iskrennii (adj.) sincere
iskrit'sya (v.impf.) sparkle
iskrivit' (v.pf.) bend
iskromsat' (v.pf.) slash
iskroshit' (v.pf.) crumble
iskupat' (v.pf.) bathe
iskupat' (v.impf.) redeem
iskuplenie (n.n.) redemption
iskushat' (v.impf.) tempt
iskusnyi (adj.) skillful
iskusstvennyi (adj.) artificial
iskusstvo (n.n.) art
islam (n.m.) Islam
islandets (n.m.) Icelander
ispachkat' (v.pf.) soil
ispanets (n.m.) Spaniard
isparenie (n.n.) evaporation
isparina (n.f.) perspiration
isparit'sya (v.pf.) evaporate
ispech' (v.pf.) bake
ispeshchrennyi (adj.) covered with
ispisat' (v.pf.) cover with writing
ispitoi (adj.) haggard
ispodlob'ya (adv.) sullenly
ispodtishka (adv.) stealthily
ispolin (n.m.) giant
ispolkom (n.m.) executive committee
ispolnenie (n.n.) fulfillment
ispolnit' (v.pf.) fulfill
ispolnitel'nyi (adj.) executive
ispol'zovat' (v.pf.) use
isportit' (v.pf.) spoil
ispoved' (n.f.) confession
ispovedovat' (v.impf.) confess
ispravit' (v.pf.) correct
ispravitel'nyi (adj.) correctional
ispravnost' (n.f.) good condition
isprobovat' (v.pf.) try

ispug (n.m.) fright
ispugat' (v.pf.) frighten
ispuskat' (v.impf.) emit
ispytanie (n.n.) trial
ispytannyi (adj.) tried
issledovanie (n.n.) investigation
isstuplenie (n.n.) frenzy
issushit' (v.pf.) dry up
issyakat' (v.impf.) dry up
istechenie (n.n.) expiration
istekat' (v.impf.) expire
istekshii (adj.) past
isterika (n.f.) hysterics
isterzannyi (adj.) disfigured
istets (n.m.) plaintiff
istina (n.f.) truth
istlevat' (v.impf.) decay
istochnik (n.m.) source
istok (n.m.) source
istolkovat' (v.pf.) interpret
istoloch' (v.pf.) pound
istoma (n.f.) languor
istomit'sya (v.pf.) be worn out
istopnik (n.m.) stoker
istorik (n.m.) historian
istoriya (n.f.) history
istoshchat' (v.impf.) exhaust
istoshchenie (n.n.) exhaustion
istratit' (v.pf.) spend
istrebitel' (n.m.) fighter
istrepat' (v.pf.) wear out
istselenie (n.n.) cure
istyazanie (n.n.) torture
istyi (adj.) true
itak (conj.) thus
ital'yanets (n.m.) Italian
itog (n.m.) sum
itogo (adv.) altogether
ittrii (n.m.) yttrium
iva (n.f.) willow
ivolga (n.f.) oriole
iyul' (n.m.) July
iyun' (n.m.) June
iz (prep.) from
izba (n.f.) peasant's house
izba-chital'nya (n.f.) village library
izbalovat' (v.pf.) spoil
izbavit' (v.pf.) save

izbavitel' (n.m.) deliverer
izbegat' (v.impf.) shun
izbegnut' (v.pf.) avoid
izbezhat' (v.pf.) avoid
izbirat' (v.impf.) elect
izbiratel' (n.m.) elector
izbiratel'nyi (adj.) electoral
izbit' (v.pf.) beat up
izbityi (adj.) beaten
izbivat' (v.impf.) beat up
izbranie (n.n.) election
izbrannyi (adj.) selected
izbrat' (v.pf.) choose
izbushka (n.f.) small hut
izbytok (n.m.) abundance
izdaleka (adv.) from afar
izdanie (n.n.) publication
izdat' (v.pf.) publish
izdavat' (v.impf.) publish
izdavna (adv.) long since
izdelie (n.n.) article
izderzhat' (v.pf.) spend
izderzhki (n.pl.) expenses
izdevat'sya (v.impf.) mock
izdevka (n.f.) sneer
izdokhnut' (v.pf.) die
iz"ezdit' (v.pf.) travel all over
izgadit' (v.pf.) befoul
izgib (n.m.) bend
izgladit' (v.pf.) efface
izgnanie (n.n.) exile
izgolodat'sya (v.pf.) starve
izgolov'e (n.n.) headboard
izgonyat' (v.impf.) oust
izgorod' (n.f.) fence
izgotavlivat' (v.impf.) make
izgotovlenie (n.n.) making
izhdivenets (n.m.) dependent
izlagat' (v.impf.) give an account (of)
izlechenie (n.n.) recovery
izlechivat' (v.impf.) cure
izlishek (n.m.) surplus
izlivat' (v.impf.) pour out
izliyanie (n.n.) outpouring
izlomannyi (adj.) broken
izlovchit'sya (v.pf.) contrive
izlozhenie (n.n.) account
izluchat' (v.impf.) radiate

izluchatel' (n.m.) emitter
izluchina (n.f.) bend
izlyublennyi (adj.) favorite
izmazat' (v.pf.) smear
izmel'chit' (v.pf.) chop
izmena (n.f.) treason
izmenit' (v.pf.) change
izmenit' (v.pf.) be unfaithful
izmenchivyi (adj.) changeable
izmenenie (n.n.) change
izmenit'sya (v.pf.) change
izmennik (n.m.) traitor
izmenyat' (v.impf.) change
izmerenie (n.n.) measuring
izmerit' (v.pf.) measure
izmeritel' (n.m.) gauge
izmoroz' (n.f.) hoarfrost
izmozhdennyi (adj.) emaciated
izmuchennyi (adj.) worn out
izmyat' (v.pf.) crush
izmyshlenie (n.n.) fabrication
iznashivat'sya (v.impf.) wear out
iznasilovat' (v.pf.) rape
iznemogat' (v.impf.) be exhausted
iznemoch' (v.pf.) be exhausted
iznezhennyi (adj.) coddled
iznos (n.m.) wear
iznoshennyi (adj.) shabby
iznurit' (v.pf.) exhaust
iznutri (adv.) from within
iznyvat' (v.impf.) pine for
izobilie (n.n.) abundance
izoblichat' (v.impf.) expose
izobrazhat' (v.impf.) represent
izobrazitel'nyi (adj.) graphic
izobresti (v.pf.) invent
izobretatel' (n.m.) inventor
izodrannyi (adj.) torn to shreds
izognutyi (adj.) curved
izolgat'sya (v.pf.) tell lies
izolirovat' (v.imp.&pf.) isolate
izolyator (n.m.) insulator
izomorfizm (n.m.) isomorphism
izorvat' (v.pf.) tear to pieces
izoshchrennyi (adj.) refined
izoterma (n.f.) isotherm
izotermicheskii (adj.) isothermal
izotop (n.m.) isotope

iz-pod (prep.) from under
izraskhodovat' (v.pf.) spend
izrazets (n.m.) tile
izrech' (v.pf.) utter
izrechenie (n.n.) dictum
izredka (adv.) now and then
izrekat' (v.impf.) utter
izrezat' (v.pf.) cut to pieces
izrubit' (v.pf.) hack to pieces
izrugat' (v.pf.) revile
izryadno (adv.) considerably
izryt' (v.pf.) dig up
izuchat' (v.impf.) study
izumlyat' (v.impf.) amaze
izumrud (n.m.) emerald
izurodovat' (v.pf.) disfigure
izuvechit' (v.pf.) cripple
izvayanie (n.n.) statue
izvedat' (v.pf.) experience
izverg (n.m.) monster
izvergat' (v.impf.) throw up
izverzhenie (n.n.) eruption
izveshchat' (v.impf.) inform
izvest' (n.f.) lime
izvestie (n.n.) news
izvestit' (v.pf.) inform
izvestka (n.f.) lime

izvestkovyi (adj.) lime
izvestno (pred.) it is known
izvestnyak (n.m.) limestone
izvilina (n.f.) bend, convolution
izvinenie (n.n.) pardon
izvivat'sya (v.impf.) wind
izvlechenie (n.n.) extraction
izvlekat' (v.impf.) extract
izvne (adv.) from outside
izvodit' (v.impf.) exasperate
izvorachivat'sya (v.impf.) dodge
izvozchik (n.m.) cabman
izvratit' (v.pf.) distort
iz"yan (n.m.) defect
izyashchnyi (adj.) graceful
iz"yat' (v.pf.) confiscate
iz"yatie (n.n.) confiscation
iz"yavit' (v.pf.) express
iz"yavitel'nyi (adj.) indicative (mood)
izyskanie (n.n.) research
izyskannyi (adj.) refined
izyskat' (v.pf.) find
izyskivat' (v.impf.) try to find
izyum (n.m.) raisins
iz-za (prep.) from behind
izzhivat' (v.impf.) overcome
izzhoga (n.f.) heartburn

К (К, Х)

k (prep.) to, toward
kabachok (n.m.) squash
kabala (n.f.) servitude
kaban (n.m.) wild boar
kabel' (n.m.) cable
kabina (n.f.) cabin
kabinet (n.m.) study
kabluk (n.m.) heel
kabotazh (n.m.) cabotage
kachalka (n.f.) rocking chair
kachat' (v.impf.) rock
kacheli (n.pl.) swing
kachestvennyi (adj.) qualitative
kachestvo (n.n.) quality

kachka (n.f.) tossing
kachnut' (v.pf.) rock
kadka (n.f.) tub
kadmii (n.m.) cadmium
kadr (n.m.) still
kadrovyi (adj.) regular
kadry (n.pl.) staff
kadyk (n.m.) Adam's apple
kafe (n.n.) cafe
kafedra (n.f.) pulpit
kaima (n.f.) edging
kak (adv.) how
kak (conj.) as, like
kakao (n.n.) cocoa

kak-nibud' (p.) somehow
kakoi (p.) what, which
kakoi-nibud' (p.) some, any
kakoi-to (p.) some, a kind of
kakov (p.) what
kak-to (adv.) one day, somehow
kalambur (n.m.) pun
kalancha (n.f.) watchtower
kalechit' (v.impf.) cripple
kaleka (n.m.&f.) cripple
kalendar' (n.m.) calendar
kalendarnyi (adj.) calendar
kalenie (n.n.) incandescence
kalibr (n.m.) caliber
kalii (n.m.) potassium
kalitka (n.f.) wicket gate
kal'ka (n.f.) tracing paper
kal'kulyatsiya (n.f.) calculation
kaloriya (n.f.) calorie
kaloshi (n.pl.) galoshes
kal'sony (n.pl.) drawers
kal'tsii (n.m.) calcium
kambii (n.m.) cambium
kamen' (n.m.) stone
kamenistyi (adj.) stony
kamennougol'nyi (adj.) coal
kamennyi (adj.) stone
kamenolomnya (n.f.) quarry
kamenshchik (n.m.) mason
kamera (n.f.) cell
kamernyi (adj.) chamber
kamerton (n.m.) tuning fork
kamfara (n.f.) camphor
kamin (n.m.) fireplace
kamorka (n.f.) closet
kampaniya (n.f.) campaign
kamysh (n.m.) reed
kanadets (n.m.) Canadian
kanal (n.m.) canal
kanareika (n.f.) canary
kanat (n.m.) rope
kanava (n.f.) ditch
kandaly (n.pl.) shackles
kandidat (n.m.) candidate
kanikuly (n.pl.) vacation
kanonerka (n.f.) gunboat
kant (n.m.) piping
kantselyariya (n.f.) office

kantserogenez (n.m.) carcinogenesis
kantserogennyi (adj.) carcinogenic
kanun (n.m.) eve
kanut' (v.pf.) disappear
kanva (n.f.) canvas
kapat' (v.impf.) drop
kapel'diner (n.m.) usher
kapel'ka (n.f.) droplet
kapillyar (n.m.) capillary
kapital (n.m.) capital
kapitalizm (n.m.) capitalism
kapital'nyi (adj.) capital
kapitalovlozhenie (n.n.) investment
kapitan (n.m.) captain
kapitulirovat' (v.impf.&pf.) capitulate
kapkan (n.m.) trap
kaplya (n.f.) drop
kapnut' (v.pf.) drop
kapriz (n.m.) whim
kapron (n.m.) kapron (synthetic fiber)
kapsula (n.f.) capsule
kapusta (n.f.) cabbage
kapyushon (n.m.) hood
kara (n.f.) retribution
karabkat'sya (v.impf.) clamber
karakul' (n.m.) astrakhan
karakuli (n.pl.) scrawl
karamel' (n.f.) caramel
karandash (n.m.) pencil
karantin (n.m.) quarantine
karapuz (n.m.) tot
karat' (v.impf.) punish
karatel'nyi (adj.) punitive
karaul (n.m.) guard
karavai (n.m.) round loaf
karavan (n.m.) caravan
karbid (n.m.) carbide
karbolovyi (adj.) carbolic
karbyurator (n.m.) carburetor
kardiogramma (n.f.) cardiogram
kardiologiya (n.f.) cardiology
karel (n.m.) Karelian
kar'er (n.m.) rapid gallop
kar'er (n.m.) quarry
kar'era (n.f.) career
kareta (n.f.) carriage
karii (adj.) brown
karikatura (n.f.) caricature

karkas (n.m.) framework
karkat' (v.impf.) croak
karlik (n.m.) dwarf
karman (n.m.) pocket
karnaval (n.m.) carnival
karniz (n.m.) cornice
karp (n.m.) carp
karta (n.f.) map
kartavit' (v.impf.) burr
kartech' (n.f.) case shot
kartel' (n.m.) cartel
kartina (n.f.) picture
kartinnyi (adj.) picturesque
kartochka (n.f.) card
kartofel' (n.m.) potatoes
karton (n.m.) cardboard
kartoshka (n.f.) potatoes
kartoteka (n.f.) card index
kartser (n.m.) punishment room
kartuz (n.m.) peaked cap
karusel' (n.f.) merry-go-round
kasatel'naya (n.f.) tangent
kasha (n.f.) gruel
kashel' (n.m.) cough
kashne (n.n.) muffler
kashtan (n.m.) chestnut
kaska (n.f.) helmet
kaskad (n.m.) cascade, stage
kassa (n.f.) booking office
kassatsiya (n.f.) appeal
kassatsionnyi sud (adj.-n.m.) court of appeal
kasseta (n.f.) casette
kassir (n.m.) cashier
kasta (n.f.) caste
kastorovoe maslo (adj.-n.n.) castor oil
kastratsiya (n.f.) castration
kastryulya (n.f.) saucepan
katafalk (n.m.) hearse
kataliz (n.m.) catalysis
katalizator (n.m.) catalyst
katalog (n.m.) catalogue
katanie (n.n.) riding
katar (n.m.) catarrh
katastrofa (n.f.) catastrophe
katat' (v.impf.) take for a ride
kategoricheskii (adj.) categorically
kategoriya (n.f.) category
kater (n.m.) cutter

katet (n.m.) cathetus (side of triangle)
katit'sya (v.impf.) roll
katod (n.m.) cathode
katok (n.m.) skating rink
katolik (n.m.) Catholic (Roman)
katorga (n.f.) hard labor
katushka (n.f.) spool
kauchuk (n.m.) rubber
kavalerist (n.m.) cavalryman
kavaleriya (n.f.) cavalry
kaverznyi (adj.) tricky
kavitatsiya (n.f.) cavitation
kavkazskii (adj.) Caucasian
kavychki (n.pl.) quotation marks
kayat'sya (v.impf.) repent
kayuta (n.f.) cabin
kazak (n.m.) cossack
kazakh (n.m.) Kazakh
kazarma (n.f.) barracks
kazat'sya (v.impf.) seem
kazennyi (adj.) state
kazhdodnevnyi (adj.) daily
kazhdyi (adj.) each
kazhetsya (pred.) it seems
kazn' (n.f.) execution
kazna (n.f.) treasury
kaznit' (v.impf.&pf.) execute
kedr (n.m.) cedar
keks (n.m.) cake
kel'ya (n.f.) cell
kem (p.) who
kenguru (n.m.) kangaroo
kepka (n.f.) cap
keramika (n.f.) ceramics
kerosin (n.m.) paraffin
keta (n.f.) Siberian salmon
khaki (adj.&n.) khaki
khalat (n.m.) dressing gown
khalatnost' (n.f.) negligence
khaltura (n.f.) moonlighting
kham (n.m.) heel
khan (n.m.) khan
khandra (n.f.) spleen
khanzha (n.m.&f.) hypocrite
khanzhestvo (n.n.) hypocrisy
khaos (n.m.) chaos
khaoticheskii (adj.) chaotic
kharakter (n.m.) character

kharakternyi (adj.) characteristic
kharkat' (v.impf.) expectorate
khartiya (n.f.) charter
khata (n.f.) hut
khikhikat' (v.impf.) giggle
khilyi (adj.) feeble
khimchistka (n.f.) dry cleaning
khimik (n.m.) chemist
khimiya (n.f.) chemistry
khina (n.f.) quinine
khiret' (v.impf.) grow feeble
khirurg (n.m.) surgeon
khishchenie (n.n.) plunder
khishchnik (n.m.) beast
khitrit' (v.impf.) be cunning
khitrost' (n.f.) cunning
khizhina (n.f.) hut
khladnokrovie (n.n.) coolness
khlam (n.m.) rubbish
khlebat' (v.impf.) gulp
khlebnut' (v.pf.) take a sip
khleb (n.m.) bread
khlebopechenie (n.n.) baking of bread
khleborodnyi (adj.) grain-growing
khlebozagotovka (n.f.) grain procurement
khlebozavod (n.m.) mechanized bakery
khlestat' (v.impf.) lash
khlev (n.m.) cattle shed
khlopat' (v.impf.) clap
khlopchatobumazhnyi (adj.) cotton
khlopkovodstvo (n.n.) cotton-growing
khlopkovyi (adj.) cotton
khlopnut' (v.pf.) bang
khlopok (n.m.) cotton
khlopotat' (v.impf.) bustle about
khlopoty (n.pl.) trouble
khlop'ya (n.pl.) flakes
khlor (n.m.) chlorine
khlynut' (v.pf.) gush out
khlyst (n.m.) whip
khmel' (n.m.) hop
khmurit'sya (v.impf.) frown
khnykat' (v.impf.) whimper
khobbi (n.n.) hobby
khobot (n.m.) trunk
khod (n.m.) motion
khodataistvo (n.n.) petitioning
khod'ba (n.f.) walking

khodit' (v.impf.) go
khodkii (adj.) salable
khoduli (n.pl.) stilts
khokhot (n.m.) roar of laughter
khokkei (n.m.) hockey
kholera (n.f.) cholera
kholm (n.m.) hill
kholod (n.m.) cold
kholodil'nik (n.m.) refrigerator
kholodno (pred.) it is cold
kholodnyi (adj.) cold
kholostoi (adj.) unmarried
kholst (n.m.) canvas
khomut (n.m.) collar
khor (n.m.) chorus
khorda (n.f.) chord
khorek (n.m.) polecat
khoronit' (v.impf.) bury
khoroshen'kii (adj.) pretty
khoroshen'ko (adv.) thoroughly
khoroshet' (v.impf.) grow prettier
khoroshii (adj.) good
khorosho (adv.) well
khorovod (n.m.) round dance
khory (n.pl.) gallery
khot' (conj.) although
khotet' (v.impf.) want
khotet'sya (v.impf.) want
khotya (conj.) although
khozyaika (n.f.) mistress
khozyain (n.m.) master
khozyaistvennyi (adj.) economic
khozyaistvo (n.n.) economy
khrabrets (n.m.) brave man
khrabrost' (n.f.) bravery
khram (n.m.) temple
khranenie (n.n.) storage
khranit' (v.impf.) keep
khrapet' (v.impf.) snore
khrebet (n.m.) spine
khren (n.m.) horseradish
khrestomatiya (n.f.) reader
khripet' (v.impf.) wheeze
khriplyi (adj.) hoarse
khristianin (n.m.) Christian
khrom (n.m.) chromium
khrom (n.m.) box calf
khromat' (v.impf.) limp

khromoi (adj.) lame
khronicheskii (adj.) chronic
khronika (n.f.) chronicle
khronologiya (n.f.) chronology
khronometr (n.m.) chronometer
khrupkii (adj.) fragile
khrust (n.m.) crunch
khrustal' (n.m.) crystal
khrustalik (n.m.) crystalline lens
khrustet' (v.impf.) crunch
khryashch (n.m.) cartilage
khryukat' (v.impf.) grunt
khudet' (v.impf.) grow thin
khudoi (adj.) thin
khudoi (adj.) bad
khudoi (adj.) torn
khudoshchavyi (adj.) thin
khudozhestvennyi (adj.) artistic
khudozhnik (n.m.) artist
khudshii (adj.) worse
khuligan (n.m.) ruffian
khurma (n.f.) persimmon
khutor (n.m.) farmstead
khuzhe (adj.) worse
khvala (n.f.) praise
khvalit' (v.impf.) praise
khvastat' (v.impf.) boast
khvatat' (v.impf.) snatch
khvatat' (v.impf.) be sufficient
khvatat'sya (v.impf.) snatch
khvatit' (v.pf.) be sufficient
khvatit' (v.pf.) snatch
khvatit'sya (v.pf.) miss
khvoinyi (adj.) coniferous
khvorat' (v.impf.) be ill
khvorost (n.m.) brushwood
khvorostina (n.f.) stick
khvost (n.m.) tail
khvoya (n.f.) needles
kibernetika (n.f.) cybernetics
kichit'sya (v.impf.) boast
kichlivyi (adj.) arrogant
kidat'(sya) (v.impf.) throw
kii (n.m.) cue
kil' (n.m.) keel
kil'ka (n.f.) sprat
kilo (n.n.) kilo
kilogramm (n.m.) kilogram

kilometr (n.m.) kilometer
kilovatt (n.m.) kilowatt
kinematika (n.f.) kinematics
kinematografiya (n.f.) cinematography
kineskop (n.m.) picture tube
kino (n.n.) cinema
kinos"emka (n.f.) filming
kinut' (v.pf.) throw
kinzhal (n.m.) dagger
kiosk (n.m.) kiosk
kipa (n.f.) heap, pile
kiparis (n.m.) cypress
kipenie (n.n.) boiling
kipet' (v.impf.) boil
kipuchii (adj.) boiling
kipyatit' (v.impf.) boil
kipyatok (n.m.) boiling water
kirgiz (n.m.) Kirghiz
kirka (n.f.) pickax
kirpich (n.m.) brick
kisel' (n.m.) kissel (jellied food)
kiset (n.m.) tobacco pouch
kishechnik (n.m.) intestines
kishet' (v.impf.) throng
kishka (n.f.) intestine
kishmya kishet' (v.impf.) teem with
kislorod (n.m.) oxygen
kislotnyi (adj.) acid
kislyi (adj.) sour
kist' (n.f.) brush
kistochka (n.f.) brush
kit (n.m.) whale
kitaets (n.m.) Chinese
kivat' (v.impf.) nod
klad (n.m.) treasure
kladbishche (n.n.) cemetery
kladka (n.f.) laying
kladovaya (n.f.) storeroom
klanyat'sya (v.impf.) bow
klapan (n.m.) valve
klarnet (n.m.) clarinet
klass (n.m.) class
klass (n.m.) classroom
klassicheskii (adj.) classical
klassifitsirovat' (v.impf.) classify
klassik (n.m.) classic
klassovyi (adj.) class
klast' (v.impf.) put

klaviatura (n.f.) keyboard
klavish(a) (n.m.(f)) key
kleenka (n.f.) oilcloth
klei (n.m.) glue
kleikii (adj.) sticky
kleimit' (v.impf.) brand
kleimo (n.n.) brand
kleit' (v.impf.) paste
kleit'sya (v.impf.) stick
klen (n.m.) maple
klepat' (v.impf.) rivet
kleshchi (n.pl.) pincers
kleshnya (n.f.) claw
kletchatka (n.f.) cellulose
kletka (n.f.) cage
kletochnyi (adj.) cellular
klevat' (v.impf.) peck
klever (n.m.) clover
kleveta (n.f.) slander
klich (n.m.) call
klichka (n.f.) nickname
klient (n.m.) client
klika (n.f.) clique
klimaks (n.m.) menopause
klimat (n.m.) climate
klin (n.m.) wedge
klinika (n.f.) hospital
klinok (n.m.) blade
klizma (n.f.) enema
klochok (n.m.) scrap
klok (n.m.) shred
klokotat' (v.impf.) boil
klonit' (v.impf.) bend
klop (n.m.) bedbug
kloun (n.m.) clown
klub (n.m.) club
klub (n.m.) puff
kluben' (n.m.) tuber
klubit'sya (v.impf.) wreathe
klubnika (n.f.) strawberry
klubok (n.m.) ball
klumba (n.f.) flower bed
klyacha (n.f.) jade
klyaksa (n.f.) blot
klyanchit' (v.impf.) beg
klyatva (n.f.) oath
klyauza (n.f.) cavil
klyk (n.m.) fang

klyuch (n.m.) clue
klyuch (n.m.) key
klyuch (n.m.) spring
klyuchitsa (n.f.) collarbone
klyukva (n.f.) cranberry
klyunut' (v.pf.) peck
klyushka (n.f.) hockey stick
klyuv (n.m.) beak
kniga (n.f.) book
knigokhranilishche (n.n.) library
knigopechatanie (n.n.) printing
knizhka (n.f.) book
knizu (adv.) downward
knut (n.m.) whip
knyaz' (n.m.) prince
ko (prep.) to, toward
koalitsiya (n.f.) coalition
kobal't (n.m.) cobalt
kobura (n.f.) holster
kobyla (n.f.) mare
kochan (n.m.) head of cabbage
kochegar (n.m.) stoker
kochenet' (v.impf.) stiffen
kocherga (n.f.) poker
kocheryzhka (n.f.) cabbage stump
kochevat' (v.impf.) wander
kochevnik (n.m.) nomad
kochka (n.f.) hillock
kodeks (n.m.) code
koe-chto (p.) something
koeffitsient (n.m.) coefficient
koe-gde (adv.) somewhere
koe-kak (adv.) anyhow
koe-kakoi (p.) some
koe-kto (p.) somebody
koe-kuda (adv.) somewhere
kofe (n.m.) coffee
kofeinik (n.m.) coffeepot
kofta (n.f.) blouse
kogda (adv.&conj.) when
kogo (p.) who
kogot' (n.m.) claw
koika (n.f.) bunk
koketka (n.f.) coquette
koklyush (n.m.) whooping cough
kokosovyi orekh (adj.-n.m.) coconut
koks (n.m.) coke
kol (n.m.) stake

kolba (n.f.) retort
kolbasa (n.f.) sausage
koldovstvo (n.n.) witchcraft
koldun (n.m.) wizard
kolebanie (n.n.) oscillation
kolechko (n.n.) ringlet
kolenchatyi (adj.) cranked
koleno (n.n.) knee
kolesnitsa (n.f.) chariot
koleso (n.n.) wheel
koleya (n.f.) rut
kolgotki (n.pl.) tights
kolichestvennyi (adj.) quantitative
kolichestvo (n.n.) quantity
kolkhoz (n.m.) kolkhoz
kolkii (adj.) prickly
kollega (n.m.) colleague
kollegiya (n.f.) board
kollektiv (n.m.) collective
kollektivizatsiya (n.f.) collectivization
kollektivnyi (adj.) collective
kollektsioner (n.m.) collector
kollektsiya (n.f.) collection
kolloidnyi (adj.) colloidal
kol'nut' (v.pf.) prick
koloda (n.f.) log
koloda (n.f.) pack
kolodets (n.m.) well
kolodka (n.f.) last
kolokol (n.m.) bell
kolokol'chik (n.m.) bell
kolonializm (n.m.) colonialism
kolonial'nyi (adj.) colonial
kolonist (n.m.) colonist
koloniya (n.f.) colony
kolonizatsiya (n.f.) colonization
kolonka (n.f.) geyser
kolonna (n.f.) column
koloritnyi (adj.) vivid
kolos (n.m.) ear
kolosnik (n.m.) fire bars
kolossal'nyi (adj.) enormous
kolot' (v.impf.) prick
kolot' (v.impf.) chop
kolotit' (v.impf.) beat
kolotyi sakhar (adj.-n.m.) lump sugar
kolpak (n.m.) cap
kol'tsevoi (adj.) circular

kol'tso (n.n.) ring
kolun (n.m.) axe
kolyaska (n.f.) carriage
kolybel' (n.f.) cradle
kolykhat'(sya) (v.impf.) sway
kolyshek (n.m.) peg
kolyuchii (adj.) prickly
kom (n.m.) lump
komanda (n.f.) command
komandir (n.m.) commander
komandirovat' (v.impf.&pf.) dispatch
komandnyi (adj.) commanding
komandovanie (n.n.) command
komanduyushchii (adj.) commander
komar (n.m.) mosquito
komatoznyi (adj.) comatose
kombain (n.m.) combine
kombinat (n.m.) works
kombinezon (n.m.) overalls
kombinirovat' (v.impf.) combine
komediya (n.f.) comedy
komendant (n.m.) commandant
kometa (n.f.) comet
komfort (n.m.) comfort
komichnyi (adj.) comical
komik (n.m.) comedian
komissar (n.m.) commissar
komissariat (n.m.) commissariat
komissionnyi (adj.) commission
komissiya (n.f.) commission
komitet (n.m.) committee
komkat' (v.impf.) crumple
kommentarii (n.m.) commentary
kommercheskii (adj.) commercial
kommuna (n.f.) commune
kommunal'nyi (adj.) communal
kommunar (n.m.) communard
kommunikatsiya (n.f.) communication
kommunist (n.m.) communist
kommunizm (n.m.) communism
kommutator (n.m.) switchboard
komnata (n.f.) room
komod (n.m.) chest of drawers
komok (n.m.) lump
kompaktnyi (adj.) compact
kompaniya (n.f.) company
kompan'on (n.m.) companion
kompas (n.m.) compass

kompensatsiya (n.f.)   compensation
kompetentnyi (adj.)   competent
kompilyatsiya (n.f.)   compilation
kompleks (n.m.)   complex
komplekt (n.m.)   complete set
komplektsiya (n.f.)   build
kompliment (n.m.)   compliment
komponovka (n.f.)   arrangement, layout
kompostirovat' (v.impf.)   punch
kompot (n.m.)   compote
kompozitor (n.m.)   composer
kompress (n.m.)   compress
komprometirovat' (v.impf.)   compromise
kompromiss (n.m.)   compromise
komsomol (n.m.)   Komsomol
komsomol'skii (adj.)   Komsomol (Communist
    youth group)
komu (p.)   who
kon' (n.m.)   horse
konchat'(sya) (v.impf.)   finish
konchik (n.m.)   tip
konchina (n.f.)   death
konchit' (v.pf.)   finish
kondensator (n.m.)   capacitor
kondensatsiya (n.f.)   condensation
konditerskaya (n.f.)   baker's shop
konduktor (n.m.)   conductor
konechno (adv.)   certainly
konechnost' (n.f.)   extremity
konechnyi (adj.)   final
konek (n.m.)   hobby
konets (n.m.)   end
konevodstvo (n.n.)   horse breeding
konferans'e (n.m.)   compere
konferentsiya (n.f.)   conference
konfeta (n.f.)   candy
konfidentsial'nyi (adj.)   confidential
konfiskatsiya (n.f.)   confiscation
konflikt (n.m.)   conflict
konfuz (n.m.)   discomfiture
kongress (n.m.)   congress
konicheskii (adj.)   conic
konina (n.f.)   horseflesh
kon'ki (n.pl.)   skates
kon'kobezhets (n.m.)   skater
konkretizirovat' (v.impf.&pf.)   give concrete
    expression to
konkretnyi (adj.)   concrete

konkurent (n.m.)   competitor
konkurs (n.m.)   competition
konnitsa (n.f.)   cavalry
konnyi (adj.)   horse
konopatit' (v.impf.)   caulk
konoplya (n.f.)   hemp
konservativnyi (adj.)   conservative
konservator (n.m.)   conservative
konservatoriya (n.f.)   conservatory
konservnyi (adj.)   canned
konservy (n.pl.)   canned food
konsilium (n.m.)   consultation
konspekt (n.m.)   summary
konspirativnyi (adj.)   secret
konstanta (n.f.)   constant
konstatirovat' (v.impf.&pf.)   state
konstitutsiya (n.f.)   constitution
konstruktor (n.m.)   designer
konsul (n.m.)   consul
konsul'skii (adj.)   consular
konsul'tant (n.m.)   consultant
kontakt (n.m.)   contact
kontekst (n.m.)   context
kontinent (n.m.)   continent
kontinental'nyi (adj.)   continental
kontingent (n.m.)   quota
kontora (n.f.)   office
kontrabanda (n.f.)   contraband
kontrabas (n.m.)   double bass
kontrakt (n.m.)   contract
kontrast (n.m.)   contrast
kontrataka (n.f.)   counterattack
kontributsiya (n.f.)   contribution
kontrnastuplenie (n.n.)   counteroffensive
kontrol' (n.m.)   control
kontroler (n.m.)   controller
kontrrazvedka (n.f.)   counterintelligence
kontrrevolyutsiya (n.f.)   counterrevolution
kontsentratsiya (n.f.)   concentration
kontseptsiya (n.f.)   conception
kontsern (n.m.)   business concern
kontsert (n.m.)   concert
kontsessiya (n.f.)   concession
kontsovka (n.f.)   conclusion
kontur (n.m.)   contour
kontuzhennyi (adj.)   shell-shocked
konura (n.f.)   kennel
konus (n.m.)   cone

konusoobraznyi (adj.) conical
konveier (n.m.) conveyer
konvektsiya (n.f.) convection
konventsiya (n.f.) convention
konversiya (n.f.) conversion
konvert (n.m.) envelope
konvoi (n.m.) convoy
konvoirovat' (v.impf.) convoy
konvul'siya (n.f.) convulsion
kon'yak (n.m.) cognac
konyukh (n.m.) groom
kon''yunktura (n.f.) situation
konyushnya (n.f.) stable
kooperativ (n.m.) cooperative
kooperatsiya (n.f.) cooperation
kooptirovat' (v.impf.&pf.) co-opt
koordinatsiya (n.f.) coordination
kopat' (v.impf.) dig
kop'e (n.n.) spear
kopeika (n.f.) kopeck
kopilka (n.f.) money box
kopiroval'nyi (adj.) copying
kopirovat' (v.impf.) copy
kopit' (v.impf.) save
kopiya (n.f.) copy
kopna (n.f.) stack
koposhit'sya (v.impf.) swarm
kopot' (n.f.) soot
koptet' (v.impf.) smoke
koptit' (v.impf.) smoke
kopyto (n.n.) hoof
kor' (n.f.) measles
kora (n.f.) bark
korabel (n.m.) shipbuilder
korabl' (n.m.) ship
korablekrushenie (n.n.) shipwreck
korablestroenie (n.n.) shipbuilding
korall (n.m.) coral
korchevat' (v.impf.) root out
korchit' (v.impf.) contort
korchit'sya (v.impf.) writhe
kordon (n.m.) cordon
koreets (n.m.) Korean
koren' (n.m.) root
korenastyi (adj.) stocky
korenit'sya (v.impf.) be rooted in
koreshok (n.m.) rootlet
koridor (n.m.) corridor

korifei (n.m.) coryphaeus
koritsa (n.f.) cinnamon
korka (n.f.) crust
korm (n.m.) forage
korma (n.pl.) stern
kormchii (adj.) helmsman
kormilets (n.m.) breadwinner
kormilitsa (n.f.) wet-nurse
kormit' (v.impf.) feed
kormovoi (adj.) fodder
kormushka (n.f.) trough
korneplod (n.m.) root plant
kornevoi (adj.) root
kornevishche (n.n.) rhizome
korobit' (v.impf.) warp
korobka (n.f.) box
korol' (n.m.) king
koroleva (n.f.) queen
koromyslo (n.n.) yoke
korona (n.f.) crown
koronka (n.f.) crown
koronovat' (v.impf&.pf.) crown
korotat' (v.impf.) pass time
korotkii (adj.) short
korotko (adj.) briefly
korotkometrazhnyi (adj.) short film
korotkovolnovyi (adj.) shortwave
korova (n.f.) cow
korpet' (v.impf.) work hard
korporatsiya (n.f.) corporation
korpus (n.m.) building
korrektirovat' (v.impf.) correct
korrektnyi (adj.) correct
korrektor (n.m.) proofreader
korrespondent (n.m.) correspondent
korroziya (n.f.) corrosion
korruptsiya (n.f.) corruption
korshun (n.m.) vulture
kort (n.m.) court
kortik (n.m.) dirk
koryavyi (adj.) rough
koryst' (n.f.) self-interest
korystnyi (adj.) mercenary
korystolyubivyi (adj.) self-interested
koryto (n.n.) trough
korzina (n.f.) basket
kosa (n.f.) scythe
kosa (n.f.) spit

kosa (n.f.) plait
kosar' (n.m.) haymaker
koshachii (adj.) catlike
koshchunstvo (n.n.) blasphemy
koshelek (n.m.) purse
koshka (n.f.) cat
koshmar (n.m.) nightmare
kosilka (n.f.) lawnmower
kosinus (n.m.) cosine
kosit' (v.impf.) mow
kosit' (v.impf.) squint
kosit'sya (v.impf.) look askance
kosmatyi (adj.) shaggy
kosmetika (n.f.) cosmetics
kosmicheskii (adj.) cosmic
kosmodrom (n.m.) cosmodrome
kosmogoniya (n.f.) cosmogony
kosmonavt (n.m.) cosmonaut
kosmonavtika (n.f.) astronautics
kosmopolit (n.m.) cosmopolitan
kosmos (n.m.) cosmos
kosmy (n.pl.) dishevelled hair
kosnost' (n.f.) stagnation
kosnoyazychnyi (adj.) tongue-tied
kosnut'sya (v.pf.) touch
kosnyi (adj.) stagnant
koso (adv.) sidelong
kosoglazie (n.n.) squint
kosogor (n.m.) slope
kosoi (adj.) slanting
kosolapyi (adj.) clumsy
kost' (n.f.) bone
kostel (n.m.) Polish Roman-Catholic church
koster (n.m.) camp fire
kostistyi (adj.) bony
kostlyavyi (adj.) rawboned
kostochka (n.f.) seed
kostyak (n.m.) skeleton
kostyanoi (adj.) bone
kostyl' (n.m.) crutch
kostyum (n.m.) suit
kosvennyi (adj.) indirect
kosyak (n.m.) jamb
kosynka (n.f.) scare
kot (n.m.) tomcat
kotangens (n.m.) cotangent
kotel (n.m.) boiler
kotel'naya (n.f.) boiler room

kotelok (n.m.) pot
kotenok (n.m.) kitten
kotik (n.m.) fur seal
kotleta (n.f.) cutlet
kotlovan (n.m.) excavation
kotlovina (n.f.) hollow
kotomka (n.f.) knapsack
kotoryi (p.) which
kovannyi (adj.) forged
kovarnyi (adj.) perfidious
kovat' (v.impf.) forge
kover (n.m.) carpet
koverkat' (v.impf.) distort
kovka (n.f.) forging
kovrizhka (n.f.) honey cake
kovsh (n.m.) scoop
kovyl' (n.m.) feather grass
kovylyat' (v.impf) hobble
kovyryat' (v.impf.) pick
koza (n.f.) goat (female)
kozha (n.f.) skin
kozhevennyi (adj.) leather processing
kozhitsa (n.f.) thin skin
kozhura (n.f.) peel
kozly (n.pl.) trestle
kozni (n.pl.) machinations
kozyr' (n.m.) trump
kozyrek (n.m.) peak
kozyrnut' (v.pf.) play one's trump card
kozyryat' (v.impf.) play one's trump card
KPSS (Kommunisticheskaya Partiya Sovetskogo Soyuza) (abbr.) CPSU (Communist Party of the Soviet Union)
krab (n.m.) crab
kradenyi (adj.) stolen
kraeugol'nyi kamen' (adj.-n.m.) cornerstone
krai (n.m.) land
krai (n.m.) edge
kraine (adv.) extremely
krainii (adj.) extreme
krakh (n.m.) crash
krakhmal (n.m.) starch
krakhmal'nyi (adj.) starched
kran (n.m.) faucet
kraniologiya (n.f.) craniology
krapinka (n.f.) spot
krapiva (n.f.) nettle
krasavets (n.m.) handsome man
krashenyi (adj.) painted

krasil'nya (n.f.) dye works
krasit' (v.impf.) color
krasivyi (adj.) beautiful
krasnet' (v.impf.) blush
krasnoarmeets (n.m.) Red Army man
krasnoflotets (n.m.) Red Navy man
krasnogvardeets (n.m.) Red Guard
krasnorechivyi (adj.) eloquent
krasnoshchekii (adj.) red-cheeked
krasnoznamennyi (adj.) holding the Order of
the Red Banner
krasnyi (adj.) red
krasochnyi (adj.) colorful
krasota (n.f.) beauty
krasovat'sya (v.impf.) pose
krast' (v.impf.) steal
krast'sya (v.impf.) sneak
krasyashchii (adj.) dye
krater (n.m.) crater
kratkii (adj.) short
kratkost' (n.f.) brevity
kratkovremennyi (adj.) transitory
kratnoe (n.n.) multiple
krayukha (n.f.) hunk of bread
krazha (n.f.) theft
kredit (n.m.) credit
kreditosposobnyi (adj.) solvent
kreiser (n.m.) cruiser
kreking (n.m.) petroleum cracking process
krem (n.m.) cream
krematorii (n.m.) crematorium
kremen' (n.m.) flint
kreml' (n.m.) Kremlin
kremlevskii (adj.) Kremlin
kremnezem (n.m.) silica
kremnii (n.m.) silicon
kremovyi (adj.) cream-colored
kren (n.m.) list
krep (n.m.) crepe
krepchat' (v.impf.) grow stronger
krepit' (v.impf.) strengthen
krepkii (adj.) strong
kreplenie (n.n.) ski binding
krepnut' (v.impf.) get stronger
krepost' (n.f.) strength
krepost' (n.f.) fortress
krepostnichestvo (n.n.) serfdom
krepostnoi (adj.) fortress

krepostnoi (adj.) serf
kreslo (n.n.) easy chair
krest (n.m.) cross
krest-nakrest (adv.) crisscross
krest'yanin (n.m.) peasant
krichat' (v.impf.) shout
krik (n.m.) shout
kriklivyi (adj.) loud
kriknut' (v.pf.) shout
kriminal'nyi (adj.) criminal
kriogennyi (adj.) cryogenic
kristall (n.m.) crystal
kristallografiya (n.f.) crystallography
kristal'nyi (adj.) crystal clear
kriterii (n.m.) criterion
kritik (n.m.) critic
krivaya (n.f.) curve
krivit' (v.impf.) bend
krivizna (n.f.) curvature
krivlyaka (n.f.) affected person
krivoi (adj.) crooked
krivonogii (adj.) bowlegged
krivotolki (n.pl.) false rumors
krizis (n.m.) crisis
kroika (n.f.) cutting out
kroit' (v.impf.) cut
kroket (n.m.) croquet
krokha (n.f.) crumb
krokhotnyi (adj.) tiny
krokodil (n.m.) crocodile
krol' (n.m.) crawl
krolik (n.m.) rabbit
krolikovodstvo (n.n.) rabbit breeding
krome (prep.) except
kromka (n.f.) edge
kromsat' (v.impf.) shred
krona (n.f.) top
kronshtein (n.m.) bracket
kropotlivyi (adj.) laborious
kroshit' (v.impf.) crumble
kroshka (n.f.) crumb
krot (n.m.) mole
krotkii (adj.) mild
krov' (n.f.) blood
krov (n.m.) shelter
krovat' (n.f.) bed
krovavyi (adj.) bloody
krovel'nyi (adj.) roofing (iron)

krovenosnyi (adj.) circulatory
krovinka (n.f.) drop of blood
krovlya (n.f.) roof
krovnyi (adj.) blood
krovoizliyanie (n.n.) hemorrhage
krovoobrashchenie (n.n.) blood circulation
krovopodtek (n.m.) bruise
krovoprolitie (n.n.) bloodshed
krovotechenie (n.n.) bleeding
krovozhadnyi (adj.) bloodthirsty
krovyanoi (adj.) blood
krucha (n.f.) precipice
krug (n.m.) circle
kruglolitsyi (adj.) round-faced
kruglyi (adj.) round
krugom (adv.) round
krugooborot (n.m.) circulation
krugosvetnyi (adj.) round-the-world
krugovoi (adj.) circular
krugozor (n.m.) outlook
krupa (n.f.) cereals
krupchatka (n.f.) finest flour
krupnyi (adj.) large
krushenie (n.n.) accident
krutit' (v.impf.) turn
krutizna (n.f.) steepness
kruto (adv.) abruptly
krutoi (adj.) steep
kruzhevnoi (adj.) lace
kruzhevo (n.n.) lace
kruzhit' (v.impf.) whirl
kruzhka (n.f.) mug
kruzhok (n.m.) small disk
kryakat' (v.impf.) quack
kryakhtet' (v.impf.) groan
kryazh (n.m.) mountain ridge
krylatyi (adj.) winged
krylo (n.n.) wing
kryl'tso (n.n.) porch
krymskii (adj.) Crimean
krysa (n.f.) rat
krysha (n.f.) roof
kryshka (n.f.) cover
kryt' (v.impf.) cover
kryt'sya (v.impf.) be concealed
kryuchkovatyi (adj.) hooked
kryuchok (n.m.) hook
kryuk (n.m.) hook

kryzhovnik (n.m.) gooseberry
ksendz (n.m.) Polish Catholic priest
ksenon (n.m.) xenon
kstati (adv.) by the way
kto (p.) who
kub (n.m.) cube
kub (n.m.) boiler
kubarem (adv.) head over heels
kubatura (n.f.) volume
kubicheskii (adj.) cubic
kubik (n.m.) brick
kubok (n.m.) goblet
kubometr (n.m.) cubic meter
kucha (n.f.) heap
kucher (n.m.) coachman
kuchka (n.f.) small heap
kuda (adv.) where
kudakhtat' (v.impf.) cackle
kudri (n.pl.) curls
kukarekat' (v.impf.) crow
kukharka (n.f.) cook
kukhnya (n.f.) kitchen
kukla (n.f.) doll
kukolka (n.f.) chrysalis
kukol'nyi (adj.) doll's
kukovat' (v.impf.) cuckoo
kukuruza (n.f.) maize
kukushka (n.f.) cuckoo
kulak (n.m.) fist
kulak (n.m.) kulak
kulek (n.m.) paper bag
kulik (n.m.) sandpiper
kulinarnyi (adj.) culinary
kulisy (n.pl.) wings
kul'minatsionnyi (adj.) culminating
kul't (n.m.) cult
kul'tivirovat' (v.impf.) cultivate
kul'tmassovyi (adj.) educational
kul'trabota (n.f.) cultural and educational
    work
kul'tura (n.f.) culture
kul'turnyi (adj.) cultured
kuluary (n.pl.) lobby
kumach (n.m.) red bunting
kumir (n.m.) idol
kumovstvo (n.n.) nepotism
kumys (n.m.) koumiss (a type of beverage)
kunitsa (n.f.) marten

kupal'nyi (adj.) bathing
kupe (n.n.) compartment
kupets (n.m.) merchant
kupit' (v.pf.) buy
kuplet (n.m.) couplet
kuplya (n.f.) buying
kupol (n.m.) dome
kupon (n.m.) coupon
kuporos (n.m.) vitriol
kurchavyi (adj.) curly
kurd (n.m.) Kurd
kurenie (n.n.) smoking
kur'er (n.m.) messenger
kur'erskii (adj.) express
kurgan (n.m.) burial mound
kurinyi (adj.) hen's
kurit' (v.impf.) smoke
kuritsa (n.f.) hen
kurnosyi (adj.) snub-nosed
kurok (n.m.) cock
kuropatka (n.f.) partidge
kurort (n.m.) spa
kurs (n.m.) course
kursant (n.m.) student
kursirovat' (v.impf.) ply
kursiv (n.m.) italics
kursy (n.pl.) courses
kurtka (n.f.) jacket
kuryashchii (adj.) smoker
kuryatnik (n.m.) hen house
kusat' (v.impf.) bite
kushak (n.m.) sash
kushan'e (n.n.) food

kushetka (n.f.) couch
kuskovoi (adj.) lump
kusok (n.m.) piece
kust (n.m.) bush
kustar' (n.m.) handicraftsman
kustarnik (n.m.) shrubbery
kustarnyi (adj.) handmade
kutat' (v.impf.) wrap oneself up
kuter'ma (n.f.) bustle
kutezh (n.m.) carouse
kutit' (v.impf.) carouse
kutsyi (adj.) docked
kuvyrkat'sya (v.impf.) tumble
kuznechik (n.m.) grasshopper
kuznechnyi (adj.) blacksmith's
kuznets (n.m.) blacksmith
kuznitsa (n.f.) forge
kuzov (n.m.) body
kvadrat (n.m.) square
kvakat' (v.impf.) croak
kvalifikatsiya (n.f.) level of proficiency
kvartal (n.m.) block
kvartet (n.m.) quartet
kvartira (n.f.) flat, apartment
kvarts (n.m.) quartz
kvas (n.m.) kvass
kvashenyi (adj.) sour
kvastsy (n.pl.) alum
kverkhu (adv.) upward
kvitantsiya (n.f.) receipt
kvity (adj.) quits
kvorum (n.m.) quorum

L (Л)

labirint (n.m.) labyrinth
laborant (n.m.) laboratory assistant
laboratoriya (n.f.) laboratory
lachuga (n.f.) hut
lad (n.m.) harmony
ladan (n.m.) incense
ladit' (v.impf.) get on with
ladno (adv.) well

ladon' (n.f.) palm
lad'ya (n.f.) rook
lafet (n.m.) gun carriage
lager' (n.m.) camp
lagernyi (adj.) camp
lai (n.m.) barking
laika (n.f.) husky
laika (n.f.) kid

lak (n.m.)   varnish
lakat' (v.impf.)   lap
lakei (n.m.)   footman
lakirovannyi (adj.)   varnished
lakmusovaya bumaga (adj.-n.f.)   litmus paper
lakomit'sya (v.impf.)   regale
lakonichnyi (adj.)   laconic
lakovyi (adj.)   varnished
lampa (n.f.)   lamp
lan' (n.f.)   doe
landshaft (n.m.)   landscape
landysh (n.m.)   lily of the valley
lapa (n.f.)   paw
lapot' (n.m.)   bast shoe
lapsha (n.f.)   noodles
larek (n.m.)   stall
laringit (n.m.)   laryngitis
laringologiya (n.f.)   laryngology
laska (n.f.)   caress
laskat' (v.impf.)   caress
laskatel'nyi (adj.)   caressing
laskovyi (adj.)   tender
lastik (n.m.)   eraser
lastochka (n.f.)   swallow
latinskii (adj.)   Latin
latun' (n.f.)   brass
latviiskii (adj.)   Latvian
latyn' (n.f.)   Latin
latysh (n.m.)   Lett
laureat (n.m.)   laureate
lava (n.f.)   lava
lavina (n.f.)   avalanche
lavirovat' (v.impf.)   maneuver
lavka (n.f.)   bench
lavka (n.f.)   shop
lavochnik (n.m.)   shopkeeper
lavr (n.m.)   laurel
lavrovyi (adj.)   laurel
layat' (v.impf.)   bark
lazaret (n.m.)   sick quarters
lazeika (n.f.)   loophole
lazer (n.m.)   laser
lazit' (v.impf.)   climb
lazurnyi (adj.)   azure
lazutchik (n.m.)   spy
l'dina (n.f.)   ice floe
lebed' (n.m.)   swan
lebedinyi (adj.)   swan

lebedka (n.f.)   winch
lebezit' (v.impf.)   fawn
lech' (v.pf.)   lie down
lechebnyi (adj.)   therapeutic
lechenie (n.n.)   treatment
led (n.m.)   ice
ledenet' (v.impf.)   freeze
ledenets (n.m.)   fruit-drop
ledenyashchii (adj.)   icy
lednik (n.m.)   glacier
lednik (n.m.)   icehouse
ledokhod (n.m.)   floating ice
ledokol (n.m.)   icebreaker
ledyanoi (adj.)   icy
legal'nyi (adj.)   legal
legavyi (adj.)   pointer
legche (adj.)   easier
legenda (n.f.)   legend
legion (n.m.)   legion
legirovannyi (adj.)   alloyed
legkii (adj.)   light
legko (adv.)   lightly
legkoatlet (n.m.)   athlete
legkoe (n.n.:)   lung
legkomyslennyi (adj.)   light-minded
legkost' (n.f.)   lightness
legkovernyi (adj.)   credulous
legkovesnyi (adj.)   light
legkovoi avtomobil' (adj.-n.m.)   motorcar
legochnyi (adj.)   pulmonary
leiborist (n.m.)   Laborite
leika (n.f.)   watering can
leikimiya (n.f.)   leukemia
leikotsit (n.m.)   leukocyte
leikotsitoz (n.m.)   leukocytosis
leitenant (n.m.)   lieutenant
lekarstvennyi (adj.)   medicinal
leksika (n.f.)   vocabulary
leksikon (n.m.)   vocabulary
lektor (n.m.)   lecturer
lektsiya (n.f.)   lecture
leleyat' (v.impf.)   cherish
lemekh (n.m.)   plowshare
len (n.m.)   flax
len' (n.f.)   laziness
leninets (n.m.)   Leninist
lenit'sya (v.impf.)   be lazy
lenivyi (adj.)   lazy

lenta (n.f.) ribbon
lentyai (n.m.) lazy fellow
lentyainichat' (v.impf.) be idle
leopard (n.m.) leopard
lepeshka (n.f.) flat round cake
lepestok (n.m.) petal
lepet (n.m.) babble
lepit' (v.impf.) model
lepka (n.f.) modelling
les (n.m.) forest
lesa (n.pl.) scaffold
lesa (n.f.) fishing line
leshch (n.m.) bream
lesistyi (adj.) wooded
lesnichestvo (n.n.) forestry
lesnik (n.m.) forester
lesnoi (adj.) forest
lesonasazhdenie (n.n.) afforestation
lesopil'nya (n.f.) sawmill
lesovodstvo (n.n.) forestry
lest' (n.f.) flattery
lestnitsa (n.f.) staircase
lestnyi (adj.) flattering
let (n.m.) flight
leta (n.pl.) years
letal'nyi (adj.) lethal
letat' (v.impf.) fly
letatel'nyi (adj.) flying
letchik (n.m.) pilot
letnyi (adj.) flying
letnii (adj.) summer
leto (n.n.) summer
letopis' (n.f.) chronicle
letoschislenie (n.n.) chronology
letuchest' (n.f.) volatility
letuchii (adj.) flying
letuchka (n.f.) briefing
lev (n.m.) lion
levkoi (n.m.) stock
levsha (n.m.) left-handed person
levyi (adj.) left
levyi (adj.) left-wing
lezhat' (v.impf.) lie
lezt' (v.impf.) climb
lezt' (v.impf.) fall out
lezvie (n.n.) blade
lgat' (v.impf.) lie
l'gota (n.f.) privilege

lgun (n.m.) liar
li (part.) whether
liberalizm (n.m.) liberalism
libo (conj.) or
lichina (n.f.) guise
lichinka (n.f.) larva
lichno (adv.) personally
lichnost' (n.f.) personality
lider (n.m.) leader
lifchik (n.m.) brassiere
lift (n.m.) elevator
liga (n.f.) league
likhach (n.m.) driver
likhoi (adj.) dashing
likhoi (adj.) evil
likhoradka (n.f.) fever
likovanie (n.n.) exultation
likvidatsiya (n.f.) liquidation
liliya (n.f.) lily
lilovyi (adj.) violet
limfa (n.f.) lymph
limit (n.m.) limit
limon (n.m.) lemon
limonad (n.m.) lemonade
limonnyi (adj.) lemon
lineika (n.f.) ruler
lineinyi (adj.) linear
lingvist (n.m.) linguist
liniya (n.f.) line
linovannyi (adj.) lined
linza (n.f.) lens
lipa (n.f.) lime tree
lipkii (adj.) sticky
lipovyi (adj.) lime
lira (n.f.) lyre
lirika (n.f.) lyric poetry
lisa (n.f.) fox
lish' (adv.) only
lish' (conj.) as soon as
lishai (n.m.) lichen
lishat'sya (v.impf.) lose
lishenie (n.n.) deprivation
lishit' (v.pf.) deprive
lishnii (adj.) superfluous
list (n.m.) leaf
list (n.m.) sheet
listopad (n.m.) fall of the leaves
listovka (n.f.) leaflet

listovoi (adj.) sheet
listva (n.f.) foliage
listvennyi (adj.) deciduous
lit' (v.impf.) pour
lit'e (n.n.) casting
liteinaya (n.f.) foundry
literator (n.m.) man of letters
literaturoved (n.m.) specialist in literature
litografiya (n.f.) lithography
litoi (adj.) cast
litovets (n.m.) Lithuanian
litr (n.m.) liter
litsemer (n.m.) hypocrite
litsenziya (n.f.) license
litsevoi (adj.) facade
litso (n.n.) face
lit'sya (v.impf.) pour
liven' (n.m.) downpour
lizat' (v.impf.) lick
l'novodstvo (n.n.) cultivation of flax
l'nut' (v.impf.) cling
l'nyanoi (adj.) flaxen
lob (n.m.) forehead
lodka (n.f.) boat
lodyr' (n.m.) idler
logarifm (n.m.) logarithm
logika (n.f.) logic
logopediya (n.f.) logopedics
logovishche (n.n.) lair
lokaut (n.m.) lockout
lokhanka (n.f.) tub
lokhmatyi (adj.) shaggy
lokhmot'ya (n.pl.) rags
lokomotiv (n.m.) locomotive
lokon (n.m.) curl
lokot' (n.m.) elbow
lom (n.m.) crowbar
lomat' (v.impf.) break
lombard (n.m.) pawnshop
lomit' (v.impf.) ache
lomit'sya (v.impf.) force one's way
lomka (n.f.) breaking
lomkost' (n.f.) brittleness
lomot' (n.m.) hunk
lomota (n.f.) rheumatic pain
lomovoi (adj.) carter
lomtik (n.m.) slice
lono (n.n.) bosom

lopast' (n.f.) blade
lopata (n.f.) spade
lopatka (n.f.) shoulder blade
lopnut' (v.pf.) burst
lopukh (n.m.) burdock
lord (n.m.) lord
los' (n.m.) elk
loshad' (n.f.) horse
loshadinyi (adj.) horse
loshchenyi (adj.) polished
loshchina (n.f.) dell
losk (n.m.) luster
loskut (n.m.) rag
losnit'sya (v.impf.) shine
lososina (n.f.) salmon
lot (n.m.) sounding lead
lotereya (n.f.) lottery
loto (n.n.) lotto
lotochnik (n.m.) peddler
lotok (n.m.) tray
lotsman (n.m.) pilot
lovit' (v.impf.) catch
lovkii (adj.) adroit
lovlya (n.f.) catching
lovushka (n.f.) trap
loyal'nyi (adj.) loyal
loza (n.f.) vine
lozh' (n.f.) lie
lozha (n.f.) box
lozhbina (n.f.) hollow
lozhe (n.n.) couch
lozhit'sya (v.impf.) lie down
lozhka (n.f.) spoon
lozhnyi (adj.) false
lozung (n.m.) slogan
l'stets (n.m.) flatterer
lubok (n.m.) splint
lubok (n.m.) cheap print
luch (n.m.) ray
lucheispuskanie (n.n.) radiation
luchevoi (adj.) radial
luchezarnyi (adj.) radiant
luchina (n.f.) spill
luchistyi (adj.) radiant
luchshe (adj.) better
luchshii (adj.) better, best
ludit' (v.impf.) tin
lug (n.m.) meadow

luk (n.m.)onion
luk (n.m.)bow
lukavyi (adj.)sly
lukovitsa (n.f.)bulb
luna (n.f.)moon
lunatik (n.m.)sleepwalker
lunka (n.f.)hole
lunnyi (adj.)lunar
lunokhod (n.m.)moon rover
lupa (n.f.)magnifying glass
lupit'sya (v.impf.)peel
lushchit' (v.impf.)shell
luza (n.f.)pocket
luzha (n.f.)puddle
luzhaika (n.f.)lawn
l'vinyi (adj.)lion's
lyagat'(sya) (v.impf.)kick
lyagnut' (v.pf.)kick
lyagushka (n.f.)frog
lyamka (n.f.)strap
lyapis (n.m.)silver nitrate
lyapsus (n.m.)blunder
lyazgat' (v.impf.)clank
lyazhka (n.f.)thigh
lyko (n.n.)bast
lyset' (v.impf.)grow bald

lysina (n.f.)bald patch
lyubeznost' (n.f.)courtesy
lyubimets (n.m.)pet
lyubit' (v.impf.)love
lyubitel' (n.m.)amateur
lyuboi (adj.)any
lyubopytnyi (adj.)curious
lyubov' (n.f.)love
lyubovnik (n.m.)lover
lyubovat'sya (v.impf.)admire
lyuboznatel'nyi (adj.)curious
lyubyashchii (adj.)loving
lyudi (n.pl.)people
lyudnyi (adj.)crowded
lyudoed (n.m.)cannibal
lyudskoi (adj.)human
lyuk (n.m.)hatch
lyul'ka (n.f.)cradle
lyuminestsentsiya (n.f.)luminescence
lyustra (n.f.)chandelier
lyutik (n.m.)buttercup
lyutnya (n.f.)lute
lyutyi (adj.)fierce
lyzha (n.f.)ski
lzhivyi (adj.)lying

M (M)

machekha (n.f.)stepmother
machta (n.f.)mast
magazin (n.m.)store
magicheskii (adj.)magic
magistral' (n.f.)main road
magnat (n.m.)magnate
magneto (n.n.)magneto
magneziya (n.f.)magnesia
magnii (n.m.)magnesium
magnit (n.m.)magnet
magnitizm (n.m.)magnetism
magnoliya (n.f.)magnolia
magometanstvo (n.n.)Mohamedanism
mai (n.m.)May
maika (n.f.)t-shirt

maior (n.m.)major
maiskii (adj.)May
mak (n.m.)poppy
makarony (n.pl.)macaroni
makat' (v.impf.)dip
maket (n.m.)model
makh (n.m.)stroke
makhat' (v.impf.)wave
makhinatsiya (n.f.)machination
makhnut' (v.pf.)wave
makhorka (n.f.)coarse tobacco
makhovik (n.m.)flywheel
makhrovyi (adj.)double
makrokosmos (n.m.)macrocosm
maksimal'nyi (adj.)maximum

maksimum (n.m.) maximum
makushka (n.f.) crown
mal (adj.) small
malaets (n.m.) Malayan
malaiskii (adj.) Malay
mal'chik (n.m.) boy
maleishii (adj.) slightest
malen'kii (adj.) little
malina (n.f.) raspberry
malo (adv.) little
malochislennyi (adj.) scanty
malodushie (n.n.) cowardice
malogramotnyi (adj.) semiliterate
maloimushchii (adj.) poor
maloizvestnyi (adj.) little-known
malokrovie (n.n.) anemia
maloletnii (adj.) juvenile
malolitrazhnyi (adj.) economy car
malolyudnyi (adj.) thinly populated
malo-mal'ski (adv.) at all
malo-pomalu (adv.) little by little
maloproduktivnyi (adj.) unproductive
maloroslyi (adj.) undersized
malosoderzhatel'nyi (adj.) empty
malosol'nyi (adj.) lightly salted
malotsennyi (adj.) of little value
malovat (adj.) a little too small
malovazhnyi (adj.) unimportant
maloveroyatnyi (adj.) improbable
malovodnyi (adj.) shallow
maloupotrebitel'nyi (adj.) rare
mal'va (n.f.) hollyhock
malyar (n.m.) house painter
malyariya (n.f.) malaria
malyi (adj.) small
malysh (n.m.) little one
malyutka (n.m.&f.) baby
mama (n.f.) mamma
mamen'ka (n.f.) mamma
mandarin (n.m.) tangerine
mandat (n.m.) mandate
maneken (n.m.) mannequin
manera (n.f.) manner
manery (n.pl.) manners
manevr (n.m.) maneuver
manevrirovat' (v.impf.) maneuver
manevry (n.pl.) maneuvers
manezh (n.m.) manege

manifest (n.m.) manifesto
manifestatsiya (n.f.) demonstration
manikyur (n.m.) manicure
manipulirovat' (v.impf.) manipulate
manishka (n.f.) false shirtfront
manit' (v.impf.) beckon
maniya (n.f.) mania
mankirovat' (v.impf.) neglect
manometr (n.m.) pressure gauge
mantiya (n.f.) robe
manufaktura (n.f.) plant, factory
man'yak (n.m.) maniac
manzheta (n.f.) cuff
marafonskii (adj.) marathon
marat' (v.impf.) make dirty
marganets (n.m.) manganese
margarin (n.m.) margarine
margaritka (n.f.) daisy
marinovannyi (adj.) pickled
marinovat' (v.impf.) pickle
marionetka (n.f.) puppet
marka (n.f.) stamp
markii (adj.) easily soiled
marksist (n.m.) Marxist
marksistsko-leninskii (adj.) Marxist-Leninist
marksizm (n.m.) Marxism
marksizm-leninizm (n.m.) Marxism-
   Leninism
marlya (n.f.) gauze
marmelad (n.m.) fruit jelly
maroder (n.m.) marauder
marsh (n.m.) march
marshal (n.m.) marshal
marshirovat' (v.impf.) march
marshrut (n.m.) route
mart (n.m.) March
martenovskii (adj.) open-hearth
martovskii (adj.) March
martyshka (n.f.) marmoset
mashina (n.f.) machine
mashinal'nyi (adj.) mechanical
mashinist (n.m.) machinist
mashinistka (n.f.) typist
mashinka (n.f.) typewriter
mashinnyi (adj.) machine
mashinostroenie (n.n.) machine building
maska (n.f.) mask
maskarad (n.m.) masquerade

maskirovat' (v.impf.) disguise
maslenitsa (n.f.) Shrovetide
maslenka (n.f.) butter dish
maslina (n.f.) olive
maslo (n.n.) butter
masloboika (n.f.) churn
maslozavod (n.m.) dairy
maslyanistyi (adj.) oily
maslyanyi (adj.) butter
massa (n.f.) mass
massazh (n.m.) massage
masshtab (n.m.) scale
massiv (n.m.) massive
massovka (n.f.) mass meeting
massovyi (adj.) mass
massy (n.pl.) the masses
mast' (n.f.) color
master (n.m.) foreman
masterskaya (n.f.) workshop
masterskii (adj.) masterly
mastika (n.f.) floor polish
mastityi (adj.) venerable
mat (n.m.) checkmate
mat' (n.f.) mother
match (n.m.) match
matematik (n.m.) mathematician
material (n.m.) material
materializm (n.m.) materialism
material'nyi (adj.) material
materik (n.m.) mainland
materinskii (adj.) maternal
materiya (n.f.) matter
materiya (n.f.) cloth
matka (n.f.) uterus
matovyi (adj.) lusterless
matras (n.m.) mattress
matritsa (n.f.) matrix
matros (n.m.) sailor
mavzolei (n.m.) mausoleum
mayachit' (v.impf.) stand out
mayak (n.m.) lighthouse
mayatnik (n.m.) pendulum
maz' (n.f.) ointment
mazat' (v.impf.) oil
mazer (n.m.) maser
mazhor (n.m.) major key (music)
maznya (n.f.) daub
mazok (n.m.) touch
mazut (n.m.) black mineral oil

mchat' (v.impf.) rush along
mebel' (n.f.) furniture
meblirovat' (v.impf.&pf.) furnish
mech (n.m.) sword
mechenyi (adj.) marked
mechet' (n.f.) mosque
mechta (n.f.) dream
med (n.m.) honey
med' (n.f.) copper
medal' (n.f.) medal
medeplavil'nyi (adj.) copper-smelting
medikament (n.m.) medication
meditsina (n.f.) medicine
medlenno (adv.) slowly
medlit' (v.impf.) linger
medlitel'nyi (adj.) slow
mednik (n.m.) coppersmith
mednyi (adj.) copper
medovyi (adj.) honey
medpunkt (n.m.) first aid station
meduza (n.f.) jellyfish
medveditsa (n.f.) she-bear
mekh (n.m.) fur
mekh (n.m.) bellows
mekh (n.m.) wineskin
mekhanik (n.m.) mechanic
mekhanizatsiya (n.f.) mechanization
mekhovoi (adj.) fur
mel (n.m.) chalk
mel' (n.f.) shallow
melankholiya (n.f.) melancholy
melet' (v.impf.) grow shallow
melioratsiya (n.f.) land improvement
mel'kat' (v.impf.) flash
melkii (adj.) small
melkoburzhuaznyi (adj.) petty-bourgeois
mel'kom (adv.) in passing
melkovodnyi (adj.) shallow
mel'nik (n.m.) miller
meloch' (n.f.) change
melochnyi (adj.) petty
melodichnyi (adj.) melodious
melodiya (n.f.) melody
memorial'nyi (adj.) memorial
memuary (n.pl.) memoirs
mena (n.f.) exchange
menee (adv.) less
menovoi (adj.) barter

men'she (adj.) smaller, less
men'shevik (n.m.) menshevik
men'shii (adj.) lesser
men'shinstvo (n.n.) minority
menya (p.) me
menyat' (v.impf.) change
menyu (n.n.) menu
menzurka (n.f.) measuring glass
mera (n.f.) measure
mereshchit'sya (v.impf.) it seems
meridian (n.m.) meridian
merilo (n.n.) standard
merit' (v.impf.) measure
merknut' (v.impf.) grow dim
mernyi (adj.) measured
meropriyatie (n.n.) measure
mertsat' (v.impf.) glimmer
mertvennyi (adj.) deathly
mertvets (n.m.) corpse
mertvyi (adj.) dead
merzavets (n.m.) rascal
merzkii (adj.) vile
merzlyi (adj.) frozen
merzost' (n.f.) nasty thing
meshanina (n.f.) jumble
meshat' (v.impf.) stir
meshat' (v.impf.) disturb
meshat'sya (v.impf.) meddle
meshchanskii (adj.) philistine
meshkat' (v.impf.) linger
meshkovatyi (adj.) baggy
meshok (n.m.) sack
mesivo (n.n.) mash
mest' (n.f.) revenge
mestami (adv.) here and there
mestechko (n.n.) small town
mesti (v.impf.) sweep
mestkom (n.m.) local trade-union committee
mestnost' (n.f.) locality
mesto (n.n.) place
mestoimenie (n.n.) pronoun
mestonakhozhdenie (n.n.) location
mestoprebyvanie (n.n.) abode
mestorozhdenie (n.n.) deposit
mestozhitel'stvo (n.n.) place of residence
mesyachnyi (adj.) monthly
mesyats (n.m.) month
metafizika (n.f.) metaphysics

metafora (n.f.) metaphor
metall (n.m.) metal
metalloid (n.m.) metalloid
metalloobrabatyvayushchii (adj.) metalworking
metallurgicheskii (adj.) metallurgical
metanie (n.n.) throwing
metat' (v.impf.) throw
metel' (n.f.) snowstorm
metelka (n.f.) whisk
meteor (n.m.) meteor
meteorit (n.m.) meteorite
meteorologicheskii (adj.) meteorological
metil (n.m.) methyl
metit' (v.impf.) mark
metit' (v.impf.) aim
metka (n.f.) mark
metkii (adj.) well-aimed
metla (n.f.) broom
metod (n.m.) method
metr (n.m.) meter
metricheskii (adj.) metric
metrika (n.f.) birth certificate
metro (n.n.) subway
metrologiya (n.f.) metrology
metropoliya (n.f.) parent state
mezha (n.f.) boundary path
mezhdometie (n.n.) interjection
mezhdu (adv.) between
mezhdugorodnyi (adj.) trunk line
mezhdunarodnyi (adj.) international
mezhplanetnyi (adj.) interplanetary
mgla (n.f.) haze
mgnovenie (n.n.) instant
mif (n.m.) myth
mig (n.m.) instance
migat' (v.impf.) wink
migom (adv.) in a flash
migratsiya (n.f.) migration
migren' (n.f.) migraine
mikrob (n.m.) microbe
mikrobiologiya (n.f.) microbiology
mikrofon (n.m.) microphone
mikroraion (n.m.) micro-district of a city
mikroskop (n.m.) microscope
mikrovolnovoi (adj.) microwave
mikstura (n.f.) mixture
milen'kii (adj.) pretty

militarizm (n.m.) militarism
militsioner (n.m.) militiaman
militsiya (n.f.) militia
milliard (n.m.) billion
millimetr (n.m.) millimeter
million (n.m.) million
milo (adj.) nice
miloserdie (n.n.) mercy
milost' (n.f.) favor
milostivyi (adj.) gracious
milostynya (n.f.) alms
milovidnyi (adj.) pretty
milya (n.f.) mile
milyi (adj.) nice
mimika (n.f.) facial expression
mimo (adv.) past
mimokhodom (adv.) in passing by
mimoletnyi (adj.) fleeting
mimoza (n.f.) mimosa
mina (n.f.) face
mina (n.f.) mine
mindal' (n.m.) almond
mindal'nyi (adj.) almond
mineral (n.m.) mineral
mineral'nyi (adj.) mineral
mineralogiya (n.f.) mineralogy
miniatyurnyi (adj.) miniature
minimal'nyi (adj.) minimum
minimum (n.m.) minimum
minirovat' (v.impf.) mine
ministerskii (adj.) ministerial
ministr (n.m.) minister
minnyi (adj.) mine
minomet (n.m.) mortar
minonosets (n.m.) torpedo boat
minor (n.m.) minor key
minovat' (v.impf.&pf.) be over
minus (n.m.) minus
minut' (v.pf.) be over
minuta (n.f.) minute
minuvshii (adj.) past
mir (n.m.) world
mir (n.m.) peace
mirit' (v.impf.) reconcile
mirnyi (adj.) peaceful
mirolyubivyi (adj.) peace-loving
mirovoi (adj.) world
mirovozzrenie (n.n.) world outlook

mishen' (n.f.) target
mishura (n.f.) tinsel
miska (n.f.) bowl
missiya (n.f.) mission
misticheskii (adj.) mystical
mistifikatsiya (n.f.) hoax
mistika (n.f.) mysticism
miting (n.m.) meeting
mizernyi (adj.) scanty
mizinets (n.m.) the little finger
mladenets (n.m.) baby
mladshii (adj.) younger
mlechnyi (adj.) milky
mlekopitayushchie (n.pl.) mammals
mne (p.) me
mnenie (n.n.) opinion
mnimyi (adj.) seeming
mnit' (v.impf.) think
mnitel'nyi (adj.) hypochondriac
mnogie (adj.) many
mnogo (adv.) much
mnogochislennyi (adj.) numerous
mnogochlen (n.m.) polynominal
mnogodetnyi (adj.) having many children
mnogoe (n.n.) much
mnogoétazhnyi (adj.) many-storied
mnogogrannyi (adj.) versatile
mnogokaskadnyi (adj.) multistage
mnogokratno (adv.) many times
mnogoletnii (adj.) of long standing
mnogolyudnyi (adj.) crowded
mnogonatsional'nyi (adj.) multinational
mnogoobeshchayushchii (adj.) promising
mnogoobraznyi (adj.) diverse
mnogosemeinyi (adj.) with a large family
mnogoslovnyi (adj.) verbose
mnogoslozhnyi (adj.) polysyllabic
mnogostoronnii (adj.) many-sided
mnogotirazhka (n.f.) factory newspaper
mnogotochie (n.n.) dots
mnogotomnyi (adj.) in many volumes
mnogotsvetnyi (adj.) many-colored
mnogougol'nik (n.m.) polygon
mnogouvazhaemyi (adj.) greatly respected
mnogovekovoi (adj.) centuries-old
mnogoyazychnyi (adj.) polyglot
mnogozhenstvo (n.n.) polygamy
mnogoznachitel'nyi (adj.) meaningful

mnogoznachnyi (adj.)　polysemantic
mnoi (p.)　I, me
mnozhestvennyi (adj.)　plural
mnozhestvo (n.n.)　multitude
mnozhimoe (n.n.)　multiplicand
mobilizovat' (v.impf.&pf.)　mobilize
moch' (v.impf.)　can, be able
moch' (n.f.)　might
mocha (n.f.)　urine
mochalka (n.f.)　wisp
mochevoi puzyr' (adj.-n.m.)　bladder
mochit' (v.impf.)　wet
moda (n.f.)　fashion
model' (n.f.)　model
modelirovanie (n.n.)　simulation
modnyi (adj.)　fashionable
modulyatsiya (n.f.)　modulation
moe (p.)　my, mine
mogila (n.f.)　grave
moguchii (adj.)　powerful
mogushchestvennyi (adj.)　mighty
mogushchestvo (n.n.)　power
moi (n.pl.)　my family
moi (p.)　my, mine
mokh (n.m.)　moss
mokhnatyi (adj.)　hairy
moknut' (v.impf.)　get wet
mokrota (n.f.)　phlegm
mokryi (adj.)　wet
mol (n.m.)　pier
mol' (n.f.)　moth
mol'ba (n.f.)　entreaty
mol'bert (n.m.)　easel
molcha (adv.)　silently
molchat' (v.impf.)　keep silent
moldavanin (n.m.)　Moldavian
molekula (n.f.)　molecule
molekulyarnyi (adj.)　molecular
molibden (n.m.)　molibdenum
molitva (n.f.)　prayer
molnienosnyi (adj.)　swift
molniya (n.f.)　lightning
molochnyi (adj.)　milk
molodet' (v.impf.)　grow younger
molodets (n.m.)　fine fellow
molodezh' (n.f.)　young people
molodnyak (n.m.)　young animals
molodoi (adj.)　young

molodost' (n.f.)　youth
moloko (n.n.)　milk
molokosos (n.m.)　greenhorn
molot (n.m.)　hammer
molot' (v.impf.)　grind
molot'ba (n.f.)　threshing
molotilka (n.f.)　thresher
molotit' (v.impf.)　thresh
molotok (n.m.)　hammer
molozhavyi (adj.)　young looking
molva (n.f.)　rumor
molvit' (v.pf.)　say
moment (n.m.)　moment
monakh (n.m.)　monk
monarkhist (n.m.)　monarchist
monarkhiya (n.f.)　monarchy
monastyr' (n.m.)　cloister
moneta (n.f.)　coin
mongol (n.m.)　Mongol
mongol'skii (adj.)　Mongolian
monografiya (n.f.)　monograph
monolitnyi (adj.)　monolithic
monolog (n.m.)　monologue
monopolist (n.m.)　monopolist
monopoliya (n.f.)　monopoly
monotonnyi (adj.)　monotonous
montazh (n.m.)　assembling
monument (n.m.)　monument
mor (n.m.)　pestilence
moral' (n.f.)　morals
morda (n.f.)　muzzle
more (n.n.)　sea
moreplavanie (n.n.)　navigation
morfologiya (n.f.)　morphology
morg (n.m.)　morgue
morgat' (v.impf.)　blink
morit' (v.impf.)　exterminate
morkov' (n.f.)　carrot
morosit' (v.impf.)　drizzle
moroz (n.m.)　frost
morozhenoe (n.n.)　ice cream
morozoustoichivyi (adj.)　frost resistant
mors (n.m.)　fruit drink
morshchina (n.f.)　wrinkle
morshchit' (v.impf.)　wrinkle
morskoi (adj.)　sea
moryak (n.m.)　sailor
morzh (n.m.)　walrus

moshch' (n.f.) power
moshchenyi (adj.) paved
moshchnost' (n.f.) power
moshennik (n.m.) swindler
moshka (n.f.) midge
moskatel'nyi (adj.) drysalter's
moskovskii (adj.) Moscow
moskvich (n.m.) Muscovite
most (n.m.) bridge
mostit' (v.impf.) pave
mostki (n.pl.) planked footway
mostovaya (n.f.) paved roadway
motat' (v.impf.) wind
motat' (v.impf.) squander
motat'sya (v.impf.) dangle
motiv (n.m.) motive
motok (n.m.) ball
motor (n.m.) motor
motoroller (n.m.) scooter
mototsikl (n.m.) motorcycle
motovstvo (n.n.) squandering
motyga (n.f.) hoe
motylek (n.m.) moth
moya (p.) my, mine
mozg (n.m.) brain
mozhet byt' (adv.) perhaps
mozhno (pred.) it is possible
mozhzhevel'nik (n.m.) juniper
mozolistyi (adj.) horny
mrachnyi (adj.) dark
mrak (n.m.) darkness
mrakobes (n.m.) obscurantist
mramor (n.m.) marble
mshchenie (n.n.) vengeance
mstit' (v.impf.) take revenge
mstitel'nyi (adj.) vindictive
muchenie (n.n.) torment
muchenik (n.m.) martyr
muchit' (v.impf.) torment
muchitel' (n.m.) tormentor
muchnoi (adj.) mealy
mudrenyi (adj.) involved
mudrets (n.m.) sage
mudrit' (v.impf.) complicate matters
    unnecessarily
mudrost' (n.f.) wisdom
mufta (n.f.) muff
muka (n.f.) torment

muka (n.f.) meal
mukha (n.f.) fly
mukhomor (n.m.) toadstool
mul (n.m.) mule
mulat (n.m.) mulatto
mul'tiplikatsionnyi (adj.) animated cartoon
mumiya (n.f.) mummy
mundir (n.m.) uniform
mundshtuk (n.m.) cigarette holder
munitsipal'nyi (adj.) municipal
muravei (n.m.) ant
murlykat' (v.impf.) purr
muskul (n.m.) muscle
musor (n.m.) garbage
mutagen (n.m.) mutagen
mutatsiya (n.f.) mutation
mutit' (v.impf.) stir up
mutnyi (adj.) turbid
muza (n.f.) muse
muzei (n.m.) museum
muzh (n.m.) husband
muzhat'sya (v.impf.) take heart
muzhchina (n.m.) man
muzhestvo (n.n.) courage
muzhskoi (adj.) masculine
muzyka (n.f.) music
my (p.) we
myach (n.m.) ball
myagkii (adj.) soft
myakish (n.m.) soft part (of loaf)
myakot' (n.f.) flesh
myamlit' (v.impf.) mumble
myasistyi (adj.) fleshy
myasnik (n.m.) butcher
myasnoi (adj.) meat
myaso (n.n.) meat
myasorubka (n.f.) meat grinder
myat' (v.impf.) crumple
myata (n.f.) mint
myatezh (n.m.) rebellion
myaukat' (v.impf.) mew
mychat' (v.impf.) moo
mylit' (v.impf.) soap
myl'nitsa (n.f.) soap dish
mylo (n.n.) soap
mys (n.m.) cape
mysh' (n.f.) mouse
myshechnyi (adj.) muscular

myshelovka (n.f.) mousetrap
myshlenie (n.n.) thinking
myshtsa (n.f.) muscle
mysh'yak (n.m.) arsenic
mysl' (n.f.) thought
myslennyi (adj.) mental

myslimyi (adj.) conceivable
myslit' (v.impf.) think
myslitel' (n.m.) thinker
myslyashchii (adj.) intelligent
myt' (v.impf.) wash

N (H)

na (prep.) on, upon
na dnyakh (adv.) the other day, one of these days
na oshchup' (adv.) to the touch
nabaldashnik (n.m.) knob
nabat (n.m.) alarm
nabavit' (v.pf.) add
nabeg (n.m.) raid
nabegat' (v.impf.) run against
nabegat'sya (v.pf.) be tired out with running about
nabekren' (adv.) tilted
nabelo (adv.) clean
naberezhnaya (n.f.) embankment
nabezhat' (v.pf.) run against
nabirat'(sya) (v.impf.) gather
nabityi (adj.) packed
nabivat' (v.impf.) fill
nabivka (n.f.) padding
nablyudatel' (n.m.) observer
naboika (n.f.) heel
nabok (adv.) on one side
nabolevshii (adj.) sore
nabor (n.m.) admission
nabrasyvat' (v.impf.) sketch
nabrasyvat' (v.impf.) throw on
nabrasyvat'sya (v.impf.) attack
nabrat' (v.pf.) gather
nabresti (v.pf.) come cross
nabrosat' (v.pf.) sketch
nabrosit' (v.pf.) throw on
nabrosok (n.m.) sketch
nabukhat' (v.impf.) swell
nabukhnut' (v.pf.) swell
nachal'nik (n.m.) chief

nachal'nyi (adj.) elementary
nachalo (n.n.) beginning
nachal'stvo (n.n.) authorities
nachal'stvuyushchii (adj.) commanding
nachat' (v.pf.) begin
nachatki (n.pl.) rudiments
nacheku (adv.) on the alert
nacherno (adv.) roughly
nachertanie (n.n.) tracing
nachertit' (v.pf.) draw
nachetchik (n.m.) dogmatist
nachinanie (n.n.) undertaking
nachinit' (v.pf.) stuff
nachinka (n.f.) filling
nachislenie (n.n.) extra charge
nachisto (adv.) clean
nachitannyi (adj.) well-read
nad (prep.) over
nadavit' (v.pf.) press
nadbavit' (v.pf.) increase
nadbavlyat' (v.impf.) increase
nadel (n.m.) plot of arable land
nadelat' (v.pf.) make
nadelit' (v.pf.) endow
nadet' (v.pf.) put on
nadevat' (v.impf.) put on
nadeyat'sya (v.impf.) hope
nadezhda (n.f.) hope
nadezhnost' (n.f.) reliability
nadezhnyi (adj.) safe
nadgrobnyi (adj.) grave
nadkostnitsa (n.f.) periosteum
nadkusit' (v.pf.) nibble
nadlezhat' (v.impf.) be required
nadlom (n.m.) fracture

nadmennyi (adj.) arrogant
nado (pred.) must
nadobnost' (n.f.) need
nadoedat' (v.impf.) bore
nadolgo (adv.) for a long time
nadorvat' (v.pf.) tear
nadoumit' (v.pf.) advise
nadpis' (n.f.) inscription
nadpisat' (v.pf.) write
nadrez (n.m.) small cut
nadrugat'sya (v.pf.) treat outrageously
nadryv (n.m.) anguish
nadsmotr (n.m.) supervision
nadstavit' (v.pf.) lengthen
nadstraivat' (v.impf.) build on
nadstroika (n.f.) superstructure
nadumannyi (adj.) farfetched
nadushit' (v.pf.) put scent on
nadut' (v.pf.) inflate
nadutyi (adj.) sulky
naduvatel'stvo (n.n.) cheating
nadvigat' (v.impf.) pull over
nadvinut' (v.pf.) pull over
nadvodnyi (adj.) above water
nadvoe (adv.) in two
nadzemnyi (adj.) above ground
nadziratel' (n.m.) overseer
nadzor (n.m.) supervision
naedat'sya (v.impf.) eat plenty of
naedine (adv.) tete-a-tete
naekhat' (v.pf.) collide
naem (n.m.) hire
naest'sya (v.pf.) eat plenty of
naezdnik (n.m.) horse rider
naezzhat' (v.impf.) come now and then
naftalin (n.m.) naphthalene
nagaika (n.f.) whip
nagibat'sya (v.impf.) stoop
nagishom (adv.) stark naked
naglets (n.m.) insolent fellow
naglost' (n.f.) insolence
naglukho (adv.) tightly
naglyadet'sya (v.pf.) to see enough of
naglyadnyi (adj.) clear
naglyi (adj.) insolent
nagnat' (v.pf.) overtake
nagnetat' (v.impf.) pump
nagnoenie (n.n.) suppuration

nagnut' (v.pf.) bend
nagoi (adj.) nude
nagolo (adv.) closely cropped
nagolovu (adv.) utterly
nagonyai (n.m.) scolding
nagonyat' (v.impf.) overtake
nagorodit' (v.pf.) pile up
nagota (n.f.) nudity
nagotavlivat' (v.impf.) prepare
nagotove (adv.) ready
nagotovit' (v.pf.) prepare
nagovarivat' (v.impf.) slander
nagovorit' (v.pf.) talk
nagrabit' (v.pf.) loot
nagrada (n.f.) reward
nagrevanie (n.n.) heating
nagrevat' (v.impf.) heat
nagromozhdat' (v.impf.) pile up
nagrubit' (v.pf.) speak rudely
nagrudnik (n.m.) bib
nagruzhat' (v.impf.) load
nagruzit' (v.pf.) load
nagruzka (n.f.) loading
nagryanut' (v.pf.) appear unexpectedly
naibolee (adv.) most
naigryvat' (v.impf.) play softly
naikhudshii (adj.) the worst
nailuchshii (adj.) the best
naimenee (adv.) least
naimenovanie (n.n.) name
naimit (n.m.) hireling
naiskosok (adv.) aslant
naiti (v.pf.) find
naitis' (v.pf.) be found
naivnost' (n.f.) naivete
naivysshii (adj.) the highest
naiznanku (adv.) inside out
naizust' (adv.) by heart
nakachat' (v.pf.) pump
nakal (n.m.) incandescence
nakalivat' (v.impf.) heat
nakalyat'sya (v.impf.) become hot
nakalyvat' (v.impf.) pin
nakanune (adv.) on the eve
nakapat' (v.pf.) pour
nakaplivat'(sya) (v.impf) accumulate
nakaz (n.m.) order
nakazanie (n.n.) punishment

nakazyvat' (v.impf.)   punish
nakhal (n.m.)   impudent fellow
nakhlebnik (n.m.)   sponger
nakhlynut' (v.pf.)   overwhelm
nakhmurit'sya (v.pf.)   frown
nakhodit' (v.impf.)   find
nakhodka (n.f.)   find
nakhokhlit'sya (v.pf.)   ruffle up
nakhvatat' (v.pf.)   seize
nakidka (n.f.)   cloak
nakidyvat' (v.impf.)   throw on
nakinut' (v.pf.)   throw on
nakinut'sya (v.pf.)   attack
nakip' (n.f.)   scum
nakladnaya (n.f.)   invoice
nakladyvat' (v.impf.)   put on
nakleika (n.f.)   label
nakleit' (v.pf.)   glue on
naklevyvat'sya (v.impf.)   be afoot
naklon (n.m.)   inclination
naklonenie (n.n.)   mood
naklonit' (v.pf.)   bend
naklonnost' (n.f.)   bent
naklonnyi (adj.)   inclined
nakolot' (v.pf.)   pin
nakolot' (v.pf.)   chop
nakonechnik (n.m.)   tip
nakonets (adv.)   at last
nakopit' (v.pf.)   accumulate
nakoplyat'(sya) (v.impf.)   accumulate
nakormit' (v.pf.)   feed
nakoval'nya (n.f.)   anvil
nakozhnyi (adj.)   skin
nakrakhmalit' (v.pf.)   starch
nakrapyvat' (v.impf.)   trickle
nakrenit'sya (v.pf.)   take a list
nakrest (adv.)   crosswise
nakrichat' (v.pf.)   shout
nakryt' (v.pf.)   cover
nakryvat'sya (v.impf.)   cover oneself
nakupat' (v.impf.)   buy
nakurit' (v.pf.)   fill with smoke
naladit' (v.pf.)   repair
nalagat' (v.impf.)   put on
nalech' (v.pf.)   apply
nalegat' (v.impf.)   apply
nalegke (adv.)   light
nalet (n.m.)   raid

nalet (n.m.)   thin layer
naletat' (v.impf.)   collide
naletchik (n.m.)   raider
nalevo (adv.)   to the left
nalichie (n.n.)   availability
nalichnost' (n.f.)   cash
nalim (n.m.)   burbot (fish)
nalit' (v.pf.)   pour out
nalitoi (adj.)   juicy
nalitso (adv.)   present
nalivat' (v.impf.)   pour out
nalivka (n.f.)   fruit liqueur
nalog (n.m.)   tax
nalogoplatel'shchik (n.m.)   taxpayer
nalovchit'sya (v.pf.)   get the hang of
nalozhennym platezhom (adv.)   cash on delivery
nalozhit' (v.pf.)   put on
nam (p.)   we, us
namachivat' (v.impf.)   moisten
namagnichivanie (n.n.)   magnetization
namatyvat' (v.impf.)   wind
namazat' (v.pf.)   spread
namechat' (v.impf.)   mark
namek (n.m.)   hint
namekat' (v.impf.)   hint
nameren (adj.)   intend
namerenie (n.n.)   intention
namerevat'sya (v.impf.)   intend
nametit' (v.pf.)   outline
nametit' (v.pf.)   fix
nami (p.)   we, us
namochit' (v.pf.)   moisten
namokat' (v.impf.)   get wet
namordnik (n.m.)   muzzle
namorshchit' (v.pf.)   wrinkle
namotat' (v.pf.)   wind
namuchit'sya (v.pf.)   be worn out
namylivat' (v.impf.)   soap
nanesti (v.pf.)   inflict
nanimatel' (n.m.)   employer
nanizat' (v.pf.)   string
nanos (n.m.)   deposit
nanyat' (v.pf.)   rent
naoborot (adv.)   the other way round
naobum (adv.)   at random
naotmash' (adv.)   with the back of the hand
naotrez (adv.)   flatly

napadat' (v.impf.)   attack
napadki (n.pl.)   accusations
napast' (n.f.)   attack
napast' (n.f.)   misfortune
napechatat' (v.impf.)   print
napereboi (adv.)   vying with one another
naperechet (adv.)   all without exception
napered (adv.)   beforehand
naperegonki (adv.)   race
naperekor (adv.)   contrary to
napereves (adv.)   atilt
naperstok (n.m.)   thimble
napev (n.m.)   tune
napikhat' (v.pf.)   cram
napil'nik (n.m.)   file
napirat' (v.impf.)   press
napisat' (v.pf.)   write
napitok (n.m.)   drink
napit'sya (v.pf.)   have something to drink
napivat'sya (v.impf.)   get drunk
naplevat' (v.pf.)   spit
naplyv (n.m.)   influx
napodobie (prep.)   like
napoit' (v.pf.)   to give to drink
napokaz (adv.)   for show
napolnit' (v.pf.)   fill
napolnyat'(sya) (v.impf.)   fill
napolovinu (adv.)   half
napominanie (n.n.)   reminder
napomnit' (v.pf.)   remind
napor (n.m.)   pressure
naposledok (adv.)   at last
napoval (adv.)   outright
naprashivat'sya (v.impf.)   ask for
naprasno (adv.)   in vain
napravit' (v.pf.)   direct
napravo (adv.)   to the right
naprimer (intro.)   for example
naprokat (adv.)   for hire
naprolet (adv.)   on end
naprolom (adv.)   ahead
naprosit'sya (v.pf.)   ask for
naprotiv (adv.)   on the contrary
napryach' (v.pf.)   strain
napryagat' (v.impf.)   strain
napryamik (adv.)   straight
napudrit' (v.pf.)   powder
napugat' (v.pf.)   frighten

napuskat'sya (v.impf.)   fall on
napustit' (v.pf.)   fill
napustit'sya (v.pf.)   fall on
naputat' (v.pf.)   mix up
naputstvie (n.n.)   parting words
napyshchennyi (adj.)   pompous
naraskhvat (adv.)   in great demand
naraspashku (adv.)   unbuttoned
naraspev (adv.)   in a singing voice
narastanie (n.n.)   growing
naravne (adv.)   on a level
narechie (n.n.)   adverb
narechie (n.n.)   dialect
narekanie (n.n.)   censure
narezat' (v.pf.)   cut
narisovat' (v.pf.)   draw
naritsatel'nyi (adj.)   nominal
narkoman (n.m.)   drug addict
narkotik (n.m.)   drug
narkoz (n.m.)   anesthetic
narochityi (adj.)   deliberate
narochno (adv.)   on purpose
narod (n.m.)   people
narodit'sya (v.pf.)   come into being
narodnyi (adj.)   national
narodnokhozyaistvennyi (adj.)   national economic
narodnost' (n.f.)   a nationality
narodonaselenie (n.n.)   population
narost (n.m.)   growth
narozhdat'sya (v.impf.)   come into being
nartsiss (n.m.)   narcissus
narty (n.pl.)   sleigh
narushat' (v.impf.)   violate
narushit' (v.pf.)   violate
naruzhnoe (n.n.)   for external use
naruzhnost' (n.f.)   appearance
naruzhu (adv.)   outside
narvat' (v.pf.)   pick
narvat' (v.pf.)   come to a head (a boil)
narvat'sya (v.pf.)   run into
nary (n.pl.)   plank bed
naryad (n.m.)   attire
naryad (n.m.)   warrant
naryadit'(sya) (v.pf.)   dress up
naryadnyi (adj.)   well dressed
naryadu (adv.)   side by side
naryazhat'(sya) (v.impf.)   dress up

naryv (n.m.) abscess
naryvat'sya (v.impf.) run into
nas (p.) we, us
nasadit' (v.pf.) plant
naschet (prep.) concerning
naschityvat' (v.impf.) number
nasechka (n.f.) incision
nasekomoe (n.n.) insect
naselenie (n.n.) population
naselit' (v.pf.) fill with people
naselyat' (v.impf.) inhabit
nasest (n.m.) roost
nash (p.) our, ours
nashatyrnyi spirt (adj.-n.m.) liquid ammonia
nashchupat' (v.pf.) find
nasheptyvat' (v.impf.) whisper in someone's ear
nashestvie (n.n.) invasion
nashivat' (v.impf.) sew on
nashivka (n.f.) stripe
nashlepat' (v.pf.) slap
nashumet' (v.pf.) make much noise
nasilie (n.n.) violence
nasil'no (adv.) by force
nasilu (adv.) hardly
nasizhennyi (adj.) long occupied
naskakivat' (v.impf.) run into
naskochit' (v.pf.) run into
naskol'ko (adv.) how much
naskoro (adv.) hastily
naskuchit' (v.pf.) bore
naskvoz' (adv.) through
nasladit'sya (v.pf.) enjoy
naslazhdenie (n.n.) delight
nasledie (n.n.) legacy
naslednik (n.m.) heir
nasledstvennost' (n.f.) heredity
nasloenie (n.n.) stratification
nasmekhat'sya (v.impf.) mock
nasmert' (adv.) mortally
nasmeshit' (v.pf.) make laugh
nasmeshka (n.f.) mockery
nasmork (n.m.) cold
nasmotret'sya (v.pf.) see
nasolit' (v.pf.) make things hot
nasos (n.m.) pump
naspekh (adv.) in a hurry
nast (n.m.) snow crust

nastaivat' (v.impf.) insist
nastat' (v.pf.) come
nastavat' (v.impf.) come
nastavit' (v.pf.) aim
nastavlenie (n.n.) admonition
nastavnik (n.m.) mentor
nastezh' (adv.) wide open
nastigat' (v.impf.) overtake
nastilat' (v.impf.) lay
nastoi (n.m.) infusion
nastoichivyi (adj.) persistent
nastol'ko (adv.) so
nastol'nyi (adj.) table
nastorazhivat'sya (v.impf.) prick up one's ears
nastorozhe (adv.) be on the alert
nastorozhit'sya (v.pf.) prick up one's ears
nastoyanie (n.n.) insistence
nastoyashchii (adj.) present
nastoyashchee (n.n.) the present
nastoyat' (v.pf.) insist
nastoyat' (v.pf.) infuse
nastraivat' (v.impf.) tune
nastroenie (n.n.) mood
nastrogo (adv.) strictly
nastroika (n.f.) tuning
nastroit' (v.pf.) tune
nastupat' (v.impf.) come
nastupat' (v.impf.) tread on
nastupat' (v.impf.) attack
nastupatel'nyi (adj.) offensive
nastupit' (v.pf.) come
nastupit' (v.pf.) tread on
nastuplenie (n.n.) coming
nastuplenie (n.n.) offensive
nasturtsiya (n.f.) nasturtium
nasukho (adv.) dry
nasupit'sya (v.pf.) frown
nasushchnyi (adj.) urgent
nasvistyvat' (v.impf.) whistle
nasyp' (n.f.) embankment
nasypat' (v.impf.&pf.) spread
nasyshchat' (v.impf.) saturate
nasyshchennyi (adj.) saturated
nasytit' (v.pf.) satiate
natalkivat'sya (v.impf.) encounter
nataskat' (v.pf.) coach for
nateret' (v.pf.) rub

nateret'sya (v.pf.) rub oneself

naterpet'sya (v.pf.) suffer

natirat' (v. impf.) rub

natisk (n.m.) charge

natknut'sya (v.pf.) run into

natochit' (v.pf.) sharpen

natolknut' (v.pf.) suggest (an idea)

natopit' (v.pf.) heat well

natoshchak (adv.) on an empty stomach

natravit' (v.pf.) set on

natrii (n.m.) sodium

natselivat'sya (v.impf) aim

natsenka (n.f.) extra charge

natsionalizatsiya (n.f.) nationalization

natsionalizm (n.m.) nationalism

natsional'nyi (adj.) national

natsiya (n.f.) nation

natura (n.f.) nature

naturshchik (n.m.) model

natvorit' (v.pf.) do

natyagivat' (v.impf.) stretch

natyanut' (v.pf.) stretch

natyanutyi (adj.) tight

natyazhka (n.f.) stretch

natykat'sya (v.impf.) run into

nauchit' (v.pf.) teach

nauchno-issledovatel'skii (adj.) research

nauchnyi (adj.) scientific

naugad (adv.) at random

nauka (n.f.) science

naushnik (n.m.) headphone

nautek (adv.) headlong

nautro (adv.) the following morning

navaga (n.f.) navaga (fish)

navalit' (v.pf.) heap up

navalivat' (v.impf.) heap up

navar (n.m.) fat

navedat'sya (v.pf.) call on

navedyvat'sya (v.impf.) call on

naveki (adv.) forever

naverkh (adv.) up

naverkhu (adv.) above

naverno(e) (adv.) certainly

navernyaka (adv.) for sure

naverstat' (v.pf.) make up for

naves (n.m.) cover

navesele (adv.) tipsy

naveshchat' (v.impf.) visit

naveshivat' (v.impf.) hang up

navesit' (v.pf.) hang up

navesti (v.pf.) direct

navestit' (v.pf.) visit

navetrennyi (adj.) windward

navevat' (v.impf.) blow

naveyat' (v.pf.) blow

navigatsiya (n.f.) navigation

navisat' (v.impf.) hang over

navisnut' (v.pf.) hang over

navlekat' (v.impf.) bring on

navodchik (n.m.) gunner

navodit' (v.impf.) direct

navodka (n.f.) laying

navodnenie (n.n.) flood

navodnit' (v.pf.) flood

navodyashchii (adj.) leading

navoloka (n.f.) pillowcase

navostrit' (v.pf.) sharpen

navoz (n.m.) manure

navrat' (v.pf.) tell a lie

navryad li (adv.) unlikely

navsegda (adv.) forever

navstrechu (adv.) toward

navyazat' (v.pf.) force upon

navyazchivyi (adj.) obtrusive

navyazyvat'(sya) (v.impf.) force (oneself) upon

navyk (n.m.) skill

navykat(e) (adv.) protruding

navylet (adv.) through

nav'yuchivat' (v.impf.) load

navznich (adv.) on one's back

nazad (adv.) back

nazavtra (adv.) the next day

nazem' (adv.) to the ground

nazemnyi (adj.) ground

nazhat' (v.pf.) press

nazhdak (n.m.) emery

nazhim (n.m.) pressure

nazhit' (v.pf.) acquire

nazhiva (n.f.) profit

nazhivat'(sya) (v.impf.) make a fortune

nazidanie (n.n.) edification

nazlo (adv.) spite

naznachat' (v. impf.) fix

naznachit' (v.pf.) fix

nazoilivyi (adj.) importunate

nazrevat' (v.impf.) come to a head

nazvanie (n.n.) name
nazyvat' (v.impf.) call
ne (part.) not
neakkuratnost' (n.f.) carelessness
nebesnyi (adj.) celestial
neblagodarnyi (adj.) ungrateful
neblagonadezhnyi (adj.) unreliable
neblagopoluchnyi (adj.) unfortunate
neblagopriyatnyi (adj.) unfavorable
neblagorazumnyi (adj.) imprudent
neblagovidnyi (adj.) unseemly
neblagozhelatel'nyi (adj.) malevolent
neblagozvuchnyi (adj.) discordant
nebo (n.n.) palate
nebo (n.n.) sky
nebogatyi (adj.) poor
nebol'shoi (adj.) small
neboskreb (n.m.) skyscraper
nebosvod (n.m.) firmament
nebrezhnyi (adj.) careless
nebylitsa (n.f.) imaginary story
nebyvalyi (adj.) unprecedented
nechayanno (adv.) unintentionally
nechego (p.) there is nothing
nechego (p.) there is no need
nechelovecheskii (adj.) superhuman
nechem (p.) there is nothing
nechestnyi (adj.) dishonest
nechetkii (adj.) illegible
nechetnyi (adj.) odd
nechistoplotnyi (adj.) dirty
nechistoty (n.pl.) sewage
nechistyi (adj.) unclean
nechlenorazdel'nyi (adj.) inarticulate
nechto (p.) something
nechuvstvitel'nyi (adj.) insensitive
nedalekii (adj.) near
nedal'novidnyi (adj.) shortsighted
nedarom (adv.) not without reason
nedavnii (adj.) recent
nedavno (adj.) lately
nedeistvitel'nyi (adj.) invalid
nedelikatnyi (adj.) indelicate
nedelimyi (adj.) indivisible
nedel'nyi (adj.) weekly
nedelya (n.f.) week
nedistsiplinirovannyi (adj.) undisciplined
nedobrokachestvennyi (adj.) of poor quality

nedobrosovestnyi (adj.) unconscientious
nedobrozhelatel'nyi (adj.) malevolent
nedobryi (adj.) unkind
nedochet (n.m.) deficit
nedoedanie (n.n) malnutrition
nedogadlivyi (adj.) slow-witted
nedoglyadet' (v.pf.) overlook
nedoimki (n.pl.) arrears
nedokonchennyi (adj.) unfinished
nedolgo (adv.) not long
nedolgovechnyi (adj.) short-lived
nedolyublivat' (v.impf.) dislike
nedomoganie (n.n.) indisposition
nedomolvka (n.f.) reservation
nedomyslie (n.n.) thoughtlessness
nedonosok (n.m.) premature baby
nedootsenivat' (v.impf.) underestimate
nedopustimyi (adj.) inadmissible
nedorazumenie (n.n.) misunderstanding
nedorod (n.m.) poor harvest
nedorogoi (adj.) inexpensive
nedoschitat'sya (v.pf.) be short of
nedosmotr (n.m.) oversight
nedosmotret' (v.pf.) overlook
nedostacha (n.f.) deficit
nedostat' (v.pf.) lack
nedostatochnost' (n.f.) insufficiency
nedostatok (n.m.) lack
nedostavat' (v.impf.) lack
nedostavlennyi (adj.) undelivered
nedostizhimyi (adj.) unattainable
nedostoinyi (adj.) unworthy
nedostovernyi (adj.) doubtful
nedostupnyi (adj.) inaccessible
nedosug (n.m.) have no time
nedosyagaemyi (adj.) unattainable
nedotroga (n.m.&f.) a touchy person
nedouchka (n.m.&f.) a half-educated person
nedoumenie (n.n.) perplexity
nedoumennyi (adj.) puzzled
nedoumevat' (v.impf.) be puzzled
nedoverie (n.n.) distrust
nedoves (n.m.) short weight
nedovol'nyi (adj.) discontented
nedozvolennyi (adj.) unlawful
nedra (n.pl.) depths
nedrug (n.m.) enemy
nedruzhelyubnyi (adj.) unfriendly

nedug (n.m.) illness
nedurno (adv.) not bad
nedvizhimost' (n.f.) real estate
nedvusmyslennyi (adj.) unequivocal
nedyuzhinnyi (adj.) outstanding
neestestvennyi (adj.) unnatural
neétichnyi (adj.) unethical
neft' (n.f.) oil
neftekhimiya (n.f.) petroleum chemistry
nefteprovod (n.m.) pipeline
nega (n.f.) bliss
negativ (n.m.) negative
negde (adv.) nowhere
negibkii (adj.) inflexible
neglasnyi (adj.) private
neglubokii (adj.) shallow
neglupyi (adj.) sensible
negodnost' (n.f.) unfitness
negodovanie (n.n.) indignation
negodyai (n.m.) villain
negostepriimnyi (adj.) inhospitable
negr (n.m.) Negro
negramotnost' (n.f.) illiteracy
negrityanskii (adj.) Negro
neilon (n.m.) nylon
neimenie (n.n.) absence
neimovernyi (adj.) incredible
neimushchii (adj.) poor
neirologiya (n.f.) neurology
neischerpaemyi (adj.) inexhaustible
neischislimyi (adj.) incalculable
neiskrennii (adj.) insincere
neiskushennyi (adj.) not versed in
neiskusnyi (adj.) unskillful
neispolnenie (n.n.) non-execution
neispravimyi (adj.) incorrigible
neispravnost' (n.f.) disrepair
neissyakaemyi (adj.) inexhaustible
neistoshchimyi (adj.) inexhaustible
neistovstvo (n.n.) frenzy
neitralizatsiya (n.f.) neutralization
neitralitet (n.m.) neutrality
neitral'nyi (adj.) neutral
neitron (n.m.) neutron
neizbezhnyi (adj.) inevitable
neizdannyi (adj.) unpublished
neizgladimyi (adj.) indelible
neizlechimyi (adj.) incurable

neizmennyi (adj.) invariable
neizmerimyi (adj.) immeasurable
neizvedannyi (adj.) unexplored
neizvestnost' (n.f.) uncertainty
nekhoroshii (adj.) bad
nekhorosho (adv.) badly
nekhotya (adv.) unwillingly
nekhvatka (n.f.) shortage
nekii (p.) a certain
nekogo (p.) there is nobody to
nekompetentnyi (adj.) incompetent
nekomu (p.) there is nobody to
nekompetentnyi (adj.) incompetent
nekomu (p.) there is nobody to
nekotoryi (p.) some
nekrasivyi (adj.) plain
nekrolog (n.m.) obituary
nekstai (adv.) inopportunely
nekto (p.) someone
nekuda (adv.) nowhere
nekul'turnyi (adj.) uneducated
nekuryashchii (adj.) nonsmoking
nekvalifitsirovannyi (adj.) unskilled
neladno (adv.) wrong
nelady (n.pl.) discord
nelegal'nyi (adj.) illegal
nelepost' (n.f.) absurdity
nelovkii (adj.) awkward
nelyubeznyi (adj.) unkind
nelyubimyi (adj.) unloved
nelyubov' (n.f.) dislike
nelyudimyi (adj.) unsociable
nel'zya (adv.) it is impossible
nemalo (adv.) not a little
nemalyi (adj.) considerable
nemedlenno (adv.) immediately
nemet' (v.impf.) grow numb
nemetall (n.m.) nonmetal
nemets (n.m.) German
nemetskii (adj.) German
nemiloserdnyi (adj.) unmerciful
nemilost' (n.f.) disgrace
neminuemyi (adj.) inevitable
nemka (n.f.) German woman
nemnogie (adj.) few
nemnogo (adv.) some, a little
nemnogochislennyi (adj.) not numerous
nemnogoslovnyi (adj.) terse

nemnozhko (adv.)　some, a little

nemodnyi (adj.)　unfashionable

nemoi (adj.)　mute

nemolodoi (adj.)　elderly

nemoshchnyi (adj.)　feeble

nemota (n.f.)　dumbness

nemudreno (adj.)　no wonder

nemyslimyi (adj.)　inconceivable

nenadezhnyi (adj.)　insecure

nenadobnost' (n.f.)　uselessness

nenadolgo (adv.)　not for long

nenaglyadnyi (adj.)　beloved

nenapadenie (n.n.)　nonaggression

nenarushimyi (adj.)　sacred

nenastnyi (adj.)　foul

nenasytnyi (adj.)　insatiable

nenavidet' (v. impf.)　hate

nenavist' (n.f.)　hatred

nenormal'nyi (adj.)　abnormal

nenuzhnyi (adj.)　unnecessary

neobdumannyi (adj.)　hasty

neobespechennyi (adj.)　without means

neobitaemyi (adj.)　uninhabited

neobkhodimost' (n.f.)　necessity

neobosnovannyi (adj.)　groundless

neoboznachennyi (adj.)　not indicated

neobozrimyi (adj.)　boundless

neobrabotannyi (adj.)　raw

neobratimost' (n.f.)　irreversibility

neobrazovannyi (adj.)　uneducated

neobshchitel'nyi (adj.)　unsociable

neobuchennyi (adj.)　untrained

neobuzdannyi (adj.)　unbridled

neob"yasnimyi (adj.)　inexplicable

neob"yatnyi (adj.)　immense

neobyazatel'nyi (adj.)　optional

neobychnyi (adj.)　unusual

neobyknovennyi (adj.)　extraordinary

neodnokratno (adv.)　repeatedly

neodnorodnost' (n.f.)　heterogeneity

neodnoznachnost' (n.f.)　ambiguity

neodobrenie (n.n.)　disapproval

neodushevlennyi (adj.)　inanimate

neofitsial'nyi (adj.)　unofficial

neogranichennyi (adj.)　unlimited

neokhota (n.f.)　reluctance

neokhotno (adv.)　unwillingly

neokonchatel'nyi (adj.)　inconclusive

neokonchennyi (adj.)　unfinished

neopisuemyi (adj.)　indescribable

neoplachennyi (adj.)　unpaid

neopravdannyi (adj.)　unjustified

neopredelennyi (adj.)　indefinite

neoproverzhimyi (adj.)　incontestable

neopryatnyi (adj.)　untidy

neopublikovannyi (adj.)　unpublished

neopytnost' (n.f.)　inexperience

neorganicheskii (adj.)　inorganic

neoshchutimyi (adj.)　imperceptible

neoslabnyi (adj.)　assiduous

neosmotritel'nyi (adj.)　imprudent

neosnovatel'nyi (adj.)　unfounded

neosporimyi (adj.)　indisputable

neostorozhnyi (adj.)　careless

neosushchestvimyi (adj.)　impracticable

neosvedomlennyi (adj.)　ill-informed

neosyazaemyi (adj.)　intangible

neot"emlemyi (adj.)　inalienable

neotesannyi (adj.)　uncouth

neotkuda (adv.)　from nowhere

neotlozhnyi (adj.)　urgent

neotluchno (adv.)　constantly

neotrazimyi (adj.)　irresistible

neotsenimyi (adj.)　invaluable

neotstupnyi (adj.)　persistent

neotvratimyi (adj.)　inevitable

neotvyaznyi (adj.)　persistent

neozhidanno (adv.)　unexpectedly

neparnyi (adj.)　unpaired

nepartiinyi (adj.)　nonparty

neperedavaemyi (adj.)　inexpressible

neperekhodnyi (adj.)　intransitive

neperevodimyi (adj.)　untranslatable

neplatel'shchik (n.m.)　defaulter

neplatezh (n.m.)　nonpayment

neplodorodnyi (adj.)　infertile

nepobedimyi (adj.)　invincible

nepochatyi (adj.)　untouched

nepochtitel'nyi (adj.)　disrespectful

nepodaleku (adv.)　not far away

nepodatlivyi (adj.)　stubborn

nepodchinenie (n.n.)　insubordination

nepoddel'nyi (adj.)　genuine

nepodkhodyashchii (adj.)　unsuitable

nepodkupnyi (adj.)　incorruptible

nepodobayushchii (adj.)　unseemly

nepodrazhaemyi (adj.) inimitable
nepodvizhnost' (n.f.) immobility
nepogoda (n.f.) foul weather
nepogreshimyi (adj.) infallible
nepokhozhii (adj.) unlike
nepokolebimyi (adj.) steadfast
nepokornyi (adj.) unruly
nepokrytyi (adj.) uncovered
nepoladki (n.pl.) defects
nepolnotsennyi (adj.) defective
nepolnyi (adj.) incomplete
nepolyarizovannyi (adj.) nonpolarized
nepomernyi (adj.) exorbitant
neponimanie (n.n.) incomprehension
neponyatlivyi (adj.) slow-witted
nepopravimyi (adj.) irreparable
neporyadochnyi (adj.) dishonorable
neporyadok (n.m.) disorder
neposeda (n.m.&f.) fidget
neposil'nyi (adj.) beyond one's strength
neposledovatel'nyi (adj.) inconsistent
neposlushanie (n.n.) disobedience
neposlushnyi (adj.) disobedient
neposredstvennyi (adj.) direct
nepostizhimyi (adj.) inconceivable
nepostoyannyi (adj.) changeable
nepostoyanstvo (n.n.) inconsistency
neposvyashchennyi (adj.) uninitiated
nepovinovenie (n.n.) disobedience
nepovorotlivyi (adj.) clumsy
nepovtorimyi (adj.) unique
nepozvolitel'nyi (adj.) impermissible
nepraktichnyi (adj.) impractical
nepravda (n.f.) untruth
nepravdopodobnyi (adj.) incredible
nepravil'nyi (adj.) irregular
nepravomochnyi (adj.) incompetent
nepravota (n.f.) error
nepravyi (adj.) unjust
nepredel'nyi (adj.) nonlimiting
nepredubezhdennyi (adj.) unprejudiced
nepredusmotritel'nyi (adj.) improvident
nepredvidennyi (adj.) unforeseen
nepreklonnyi (adj.) uncompromising
neprelozhnyi (adj.) immutable
nepremenno (adv.) certainly
nepreodolimyi (adj.) unsurmountable
nepreryvnost' (n.f.) continuity

nepreryvnyi (adj.) nonstop
neprevzoidennyi (adj.) unsurpassed
neprichastnyi (adj.) not implicated
nepriemlemyi (adj.) unacceptable
nepriglyadnyi (adj.) unattractive
neprigodnyi (adj.) unfit
neprikhotlivyi (adj.) undemanding
neprikosnovennyi (adj.) inviolable
neprikrashennyi (adj.) unvarnished
neprilichnyi (adj.) indecent
neprimenimyi (adj.) inapplicable
neprimirimyi (adj.) irreconcilable
neprinuzhdennyi (adj.) natural
neprisposoblennyi (adj.) not suited
nepristoinyi (adj.) obscene
nepristupnyi (adj.) impregnable
nepritvornyi (adj.) unfeigned
neprityazatel'nyi (adj.) unpretentious
neprivetlivyi (adj.) unfriendly
neprivlekatel'nyi (adj.) unattractive
neprivychnyi (adj.) unaccustomed to
nepriyatel' (n.m.) enemy
nepriyatnyi (adj.) unpleasant
nepriyazn' (n.f.) hostility
nepriyaznennyi (adj.) hostile
neprochnyi (adj.) fragile
neprodolzhitel'nyi (adj.) of short duration
neproduktivnyi (adj.) unproductive
neprodumannyi (adj.) insufficiently
  considered
neproglyadnyi (adj.) pitch-dark
neproizvoditel'nyi (adj.) unproductive
neprokhodimyi (adj.) impassable
neprolaznyi (adj.) impassable
nepromokaemyi (adj.) waterproof
nepronitsaemyi (adj.) impenetrable
neproizvol'nyi (adj.) involuntary
neproportsional'nyi (adj.) disproportionate
neproshennyi (adj.) unasked, unbidden
neprostitel'nyi (adj.) unpardonable
neproverennyi (adj.) unverified
neprovodnik (n.m.) nonconductor
neprozrachnyi (adj.) opaque
nerabochii (adj.) nonworking
nerabotosposobnyi (adj.) disabled
neradivyi (adj.) negligent
neraschetlivyi (adj.) wasteful
neraspolozhenie (n.n.) disinclination

nerasshcheplyaemyi (adj.) nonfissionable
neravenstvo (n.n.) inequality
neravnomernost' (n.f.) irregularity
neravnyi (adj.) unequal
nerazberikha (n.f.) confusion
nerazborchivyi (adj.) unscrupulous
nerazdel'nyi (adj.) indivisible
nerazgovorchivyi (adj.) taciturn
nerazlichimyi (adj.) indiscernible
nerazluchnyi (adj.) inseparable
nerazreshennyi (adj.) unsolved
nerazreshimyi (adj.) insoluble
nerazryvnyi (adj.) indissoluble
nerazumnyi (adj.) unwise
nerazvityi (adj.) undeveloped
nereal'nyi (adj.) unreal
neredko (adv.) not infrequently
nereguliruemyi (adj.) nonadjustable
neregulyarnyi (adj.) irregular
nereshitel'nost' (n.f.) indecision
nerovnyi (adj.) unequal
nerushimyi (adj.) inviolable
nerv (n.m.) nerve
neryakha (n.m.&f.) sloven
nerzhaveyushchii (adj.) noncorrosive
nesamostoyatel'nyi (adj.) not independent
nesbytochnyi (adj.) unrealizable
neschastlivyi (adj.) unfortunate
neschastnyi (adj.) unhappy
neschetnyi (adj.) innumerable
nesderzhannyi (adj.) unrestrained
nes"edobnyi (adj.) inedible
neser'eznyi (adj.) not serious
nesesser (n.m.) dressing case
nesgibaemyi (adj.) inflexible
nesgoraemyi (adj.) incombustible
nesgovorchivyi (adj.) intractable
neshchadnyi (adj.) unmerciful
neshutochnyi (adj.) serious
nesimmetrichnost' (n.f.) assymetry
neskladnyi (adj.) awkward
nesklonyaemyi (adj.) indeclinable
neskol'ko (adv.) several
neskol'ko (adv.) somewhat
neskonchaemyi (adj.) interminable
neskromnyi (adj.) immodest
neslozhnyi (adj.) simple
neslykhannyi (adj.) unheard of

neslyshnyi (adj.) inaudible
nesmetnyi (adj.) innumerable
nesmolkaemyi (adj.) incessant
nesmotrya (prep.) in spite of
nesnosnyi (adj.) unbearable
nesoblyudenie (n.n.) nonobservance
nesoglasie (n.n.) disagreement
nesoglasovannyi (adj.) uncoordinated
nesoizmerimyi (adj.) incommensurable
nesokrushimyi (adj.) indestructible
nesomnenno (adv.) undoubtedly
nesoobraznyi (adj.) incompatible
nesootvetstvie (n.n.) discrepancy
nesorazmernyi (adj.) disproportionate
nesostoyatel'nyi (adj.) unsound
nesovershennoletnii (adj.) underage
nesovershennyi (adj.) imperfect
nesovmestimyi (adj.) incompatible
nesoznatel'nyi (adj.) irresponsible
nespelyi (adj.) unripe
nespokoinyi (adj.) restless
nesposobnyi (adj.) incapable
nespravedlivost' (n.f.) injustice
nesprosta (adv.) not without purpose
nesravnimyi (adj.) incomparable
nesterpimyi (adj.) unbearable
nesti (v.impf.) carry
nestis' (v.impf.) rush
nestis' (v.impf.) lay eggs
nestoikii (adj.) unstable
nestroevoi (adj.) noncombatant
nestroinyi (adj.) discordant
nesudokhodnyi (adj.) unnavigable
nesushchaya (n.f.) carrier
nesushchestvennyi (adj.) unessential
nesvarenie (n.n.) indigestion
nesvedushchii (adj.) ignorant
nesvezhii (adj.) not fresh
nesvoevremennyi (adj.) inopportune
nesvyaznyi (adj.) incoherent
net (part.) no, not
netaktichnyi (adj.) tactless
neterpenie (n.n.) impatience
neterpimyi (adj.) intolerant
netochnyi (adj.) inaccurate
netrebovatel'nyi (adj.) undemanding
netrezvyi (adj.) intoxicated
netronutyi (adj.) untouched

netrudosposobnyi (adj.) disabled
netrudovoi (adj.) unearned
netselesoobraznyi (adj.) purposeless
netsenzurnyi (adj.) unprintable
netverdyi (adj.) unsteady
neubeditel'nyi (adj.) unconvincing
neuch (n.m.&f.) ignoramus
neuchtivyi (adj.) impolite
neudacha (n.f.) failure
neuderzhimyi (adj.) irrepressible
neudobnyi (adj.) uncomfortable
neudovletvorennost' (n.f.) dissatisfaction
neudovletvoritel'nyi (adj.) unsatisfactory
neudovol'stvie (n.n.) displeasure
neugomonnyi (adj.) restless
neuklonnyi (adj.) steady
neuklyuzhii (adj.) clumsy
neukroshchennyi (adj.) untamed
neukrotimyi (adj.) indomitable
neulovimyi (adj.) elusive
neumelyi (adj.) unskillful
neumerennyi (adj.) immoderate
neumestnyi (adj.) inappropriate
neumolimyi (adj.) inexorable
neumyshlennyi (adj.) unintentional
neuplata (n.f.) nonpayment
neupotrebitel'nyi (adj.) not in use
neupravlyaemyi (adj.) uncontrolled
neuravnoveshennyi (adj.) unbalanced
neurochnyi (adj.) unusual
neurozhai (n.m.) crop failure
neuryaditsa (n.f.) confusion
neuspekh (n.m.) failure
neuspevaemost' (n.f.) poor progress
neustoichivyi (adj.) unsteady
neustoika (n.f.) forfeit
neustrashimyi (adj.) fearless
neustupchivyi (adj.) unyielding
neusypnyi (adj.) indefatigable
neuteshnyi (adj.) inconsolable
neutolimyi (adj.) unquenchable
neutomimyi (adj.) indefatigable
neuvazhenie (n.n.) disrespect
neuverennost' (n.f.) uncertainty
neuvyadaemyi (adj.) unfading
neuvyazka (n.f.) hitch
neuyazvimyi (adj.) invulnerable
neuyutnyi (adj.) indeed

neuzheli (part.) quarrelsome
neuzhivchivyi (adj.) uncomfortable
neuznavaemyi (adj.) unrecognizable
nevazhnyi (adj.) unimportant
nevdaleke (adv.) not far off
nevedenie (n.n.) ignorance
nevedomyi (adj.) unknown
neverie (n.n.) disbelief
nevernyi (adj.) incorrect
neveroyatnyi (adj.) incredible
neveruyushchii (adj.) unbeliever
neveselyi (adj.) joyless
nevesomost' (n.f.) weightlessness
nevesta (n.f.) bride
nevestka (n.f.) daughter-in-law
nevezha (n.m.&F.) boor
nevezhda (n.m.) ignoramus
nevezhlivyi (adj.) rude
nevidannyi (adj.) unprecedented
nevidimyi (adj.) invisible
nevinnyi (adj.) innocent
nevinovnyi (adj.) not guilty
nevkusnyi (adj.) unpalatable
nevmenyaemyi (adj.) insane
nevmeshatel'stvo (n.n.) noninterference
nevmogotu (adv.) unbearable
nevnimanie (n.n.) inattention
nevnyatnyi (adj.) indistinct
nevod (n.m.) seine
nevodnyi (adj.) nonaqueous
nevolit' (v.impf.) force
nevol'nyi (adj.) involuntary
nevolya (n.f.) captivity
nevoobrazimyi (adj.) unimaginable
nevooruzhennyi (adj.) unarmed
nevospitannyi (adj.) ill-bred
nevozdelannyi (adj.) untilled
nevozderzhannyi (adj.) unrestrained
nevozmozhnost' (n.f.) impossibility
nevozmutimyi (adj.) imperturbable
nevozvratimyi (adj.) irrevocable
nevpopad (adv.) out of place
nevralgiya (n.f.) neuralgia
nevrasteniya (n.f.) neurasthenia
nevrazumitel'nyi (adj.) unintelligible
nevredimyi (adj.) unharmed
nevropatologiya (n.f.) neuropathology
nevyazkii (adj.) inviscid

nevyderzhannyi (adj.) unrestrained
nevygodnyi (adj.) disadvantageous
nevynosimyi (adj.) intolerable
nevypolnenie (n.n.) nonfulfillment
nevypolnimyi (adj.) impracticable
nevyrazimyi (adj.) inexpressible
nevyrazitel'nyi (adj.) inexpressive
nevysokii (adj.) low
nevyyasnennyi (adj.) obscure
nevzgoda (n.f.) adversity
nevziraya (adv.) regardless
nevznachai (adv.) quite unexpectedly
nevzrachnyi (adj.) unattractive
nevzyskatel'nyi (adj.) undemanding
neyarkii (adj.) not bright
neyasnyi (adj.) vague
neyavka (n.f.) absence
nezabudka (n.f.) forget-me-not
nezabvennyi (adj.) unforgettable
nezabyvaemyi (adj.) unforgettable
nezachem (adv.) no need
nezadacha (n.f.) bad luck
nezadolgo (adv.) shortly
nezakonchennyi (adj.) unfinished
nezakonnyi (adj.) illegal
nezamenimyi (adj.) irreplaceable
nezametnyi (adj.) imperceptible
nezamyslovatyi (adj.) simple
nezapamyatnyi (adj.) immemorial
nezapyatnannyi (adj.) stainless
nezaraznyi (adj.) noncontagious
nezashchishchennyi (adj.) unprotected
nezasluzhennyi (adj.) unmerited
nezateilivyi (adj.) plain
nezatukhayushchii (adj.) sustained
nezauryadnyi (adj.) uncommon
nezavidnyi (adj.) unenviable
nezavisimost' (n.f.) independence
nezavisyashchii (adj.) independent
nezdorovyi (adj.) unhealthy
nezemnoi (adj.) unearthly
nezhdannyi (adj.) unexpected
nezhelanie (n.n.) unwillingness
nezhenatyi (adj.) unmarried
nezhenka (n.m.&f.) mollycoddle
nezhiloi (adj.) uninhabited
nezhit' (v.impf.) coddle
nezhiznennyi (adj.) impracticable

nezhnost' (n.f.) tenderness
nezlobivyi (adj.) mild
neznachitel'nyi (adj.) insignificant
neznakomyi (adj.) unknown
neznanie (n.n.) ignorance
nezrelyi (adj.) unripe
nezrimyi (adj.) invisible
nezvanyi (adj.) uninvited
nezyblemyi (adj.) firm
ni...ni (conj.) neither/nor
nichego (p.) nothing
nichei (p.) nobody's
nichem (p.) nothing
nichkom (adv.) prone
nichto (p.) nothing
nichtozhnost' (n.f.) insignificance
nichut' (adv.) not in the least
nich'ya (n.f.) draw
nigde (adv.) nowhere
nikak (adv.) by no means
nikakoi (p.) no
nikchemnyi (adj.) good-for-nothing
nikel' (n.m.) nickel
nikelirovannyi (adj.) nickel-plated
nikem (p.) nobody
nikogda (adv.) never
nikogo (p.) nobody
nikomu (p.) nobody
nikotin (n.m.) nicotine
nikto (p.) nobody
nikuda (adv.) nowhere
nimalo (adv.) not at all
niobii (n.m.) niobium, columbium
niotkuda (adv.) from nowhere
nisha (n.f.) niche
nishchenskii (adj.) miserable
nishcheta (n.f.) poverty
nishchii (adj.) poverty-stricken
nishchii (n.m.) beggar
niskhodyashchii (adj.) descending
niskol'ko (adv.) not in the least
nispadat' (v.impf.) fall
nisprovergat' (v.impf.) overthrow
nit' (n.f.) thread
nitka (n.f.) thread
nitrat (n.m.) nitrate
nitrit (n.m.) nitrite
nits (adv.) . face downward

niva (n.f.) cornfield
niz (n.m.) bottom
nizhe (adj.) lower
nizhepodpisavshiisya (adj.) the undersigned
nizheprivedennyi (adj.) undermentioned
nizhnii (adj.) lower
nizkii (adj.) low
nizko (adj.) low
nizkopoklonstvo (n.n.) servility
nizkoprobnyi (adj.) of low standard
nizkoroslyi (adj.) undersized
nizmennost' (n.f.) lowland
nizost' (n.f.) baseness
nizov'e (n.n.) the lower reaches
nizovoi (adj.) local
nizshii (adj.) lower
nizvergat' (v.impf.) overthrow
no (conj.) but
noch' (n.f.) night
nochevat' (v.impf.) spend the night
nochnik (n.m.) night-light
nochnoi (adj.) night
noga (n.f.) foot, leg
nogot' (n.m.) nail
nol' (n.m.) zero
nomer (n.m.) number
nominal'nyi (adj.) nominal
nora (n.f.) hole
nord (n.m.) north
norka (n.f.) mink
norma (n.f.) quota
normal'nyi (adj.) normal
normirovanie (n.n.) rationing
norvezhets (n.m.) Norwegian
nos (n.m.) nose
nosha (n.f.) burden
nosik (n.m.) spout
nosilki (n.pl.) stretcher
nosil'shchik (n.m.) porter
nosit' (v.impf.) carry
nositel' (n.m.) carrier
nosok (n.m.) sock
nosorog (n.m.) rhinoceros
nosovoi (adj.) nasal
nota (n.f.) note
notarial'nyi (adj.) notarial
notarius (n.m.) notary
notatsiya (n.f.) reprimand

noty (n.pl.) music
novator (n.m.) innovator
noveishii (adj.) newest
novella (n.f.) short story
noven'kii (adj.) brand new
novizna (n.f.) novelty
novobrachnye (n.pl.) newly married couple
novobranets (n.m.) recruit
novogodnii (adj.) New Year's
novolunie (n.n.) new moon
novomodnyi (adj.) new-fangled
novopribyvshii (adj.) newly arrived
novorozhdennyi (adj.) newborn
novosel (n.m.) new settler
novosel'e (n.n.) housewarming
novost' (n.f.) news
novostroika (n.f.) new building
novovvedenie (n.n.) innovation
novshestvo (n.n.) innovation
novyi (adj.) new
noyabr' (n.m.) November
nozdrevatyi (adj.) porous
nozdrya (n.f.) nostril
nozh (n.m.) knife
nozhik (n.m.) knife
nozhka (n.f.) leg
nozhnitsy (n.pl.) scissors
nozhnoi (adj.) foot
nozhny (n.pl.) sheath
nrav (n.m.) disposition
nravit'sya (v.impf.) please
nravouchenie (n.n.) lecture
nravstvennost' (n.f.) morals
nravy (n.pl.) customs
nu (part.) now, then, come on
nudnyi (adj.) tedious
nukleatsiya (n.f.) nucleation
nul' (n.m.) nought
numeratsiya (n.f.) numeration
numizmat (n.m.) numismatist
nutro (n.n.) inside
nuzhda (n.f.) need
nuzhdat'sya (v.impf.) be in need
nuzhnyi (adj.) necessary
nyanchit' (v.impf.) nurse
nyan'ka (n.f.) nurse
nyanya (n.f.) nurse
nyne (adv.) at present

nyryat' (v.impf.) dive
nyt' (v.impf.) complain
nyt'e (n.n.) moaning

nytik (n.m.) whiner
nyuans (n.m.) nuance
nyukh (n.m.) scent

O (O)

o (prep.) of, about
o (interj.) oh
oazis (n.m.) oasis
ob (prep.) of, about
oba (num.) both
obagrit' (v.pf.) crimson
obaldevat' (v.impf.) be stupefied
obankrotit'sya (v.pf.) go bankrupt
obayanie (n.n.) charm
obdavat' (v.impf.) pour over
obdelat' (v.pf.) arrange
obdelit' (v.pf.) deprive
obdirat' (v.impf.) skin
obdumannyi (adj.) deliberate
obdumat' (v.pf.) consider
obdut' (v.pf.) blow on
obduvat' (v.impf.) blow on
obduvka (n.f.) air-cooling
obe (num.) both
obed (n.m.) dinner
ob"edat'sya (v.impf.) overeat
ob"edenie (n.n.) be delicious
ob"edinenie (n.n.) unification
ob"edki (n.pl.) leavings
obednevshii (adj.) impoverished
ob"ekhat' (v.pf.) go round
ob"ekt (n.m.) object
ob"ektiv (n.m.) object-lens
ob"ektivnyi (adj.) objective
obelit' (v.pf.) whitewash
ob"em (n.m.) volume
ob"emistyi (adj.) capacious
oberech'(sya) (v.pf.) guard oneself
oberegat' (v.impf.) guard
obernut' (v.pf.) wrap up
obernut'sya (v.pf.) turn round
obertka (n.f.) wrapper
obeschestit' (v.pf.) dishonor

obeshchanie (n.n.) promise
obeskrovit' (v.pf.) bleed white
obeskurazhit' (v.pf.) discourage
obespechenie (n.n.) security
obespechit' (v.pf.) provide, ensure
obessilet' (v.pf.) break down
obessmertit' (v.pf.) immortalize
obestsenenie (n.n.) depreciation
obestsvetit' (v.impf.) discolor
ob"est'sya (v.pf.) overeat
obet (n.m.) vow
obezbolivanie (n.n.) anesthesia
ob"ezd (n.m.) diversion
obezdolennyi (adj.) deprived
obezlichivat' (v.impf.) depersonalize
obezobrazit' (v.pf.) disfigure
obezopasit' (v.pf.) protect
obezoruzhivat' (v.impf.) disarm
obezumet' (v.pf.) go mad
obezvozhivanie (n.n.) dehydration
obezvredit' (v.pf.) render harmless
obez'yana (n.f.) monkey
obezzarazhivanie (n.n.) disinfection
ob"ezzhat' (v.impf.) travel
obgladyvat' (v.impf.) gnaw
obgonyat' (v.impf.) leave behind
obgorat' (v.impf.) burn
obida (n.f.) offense
obidchivyi (adj.) touchy
obidet' (v.pf.) offend
obidnyi (adj.) offensive
obikhod (n.m.) mode of life
obilie (n.n.) abundance
obirat' (v.impf.) pick
obit' (v.pf.) cover, pad
obitaemyi (adj.) inhabited
obitatel' (n.m.) inhabitant
obivat' (v.impf.) cover, pad

obivka (n.f.) upholstering
obizhat'(sya) (v.impf.) offend (be offended)
obizhennyi (adj.) offended
obkhod (n.m.) round
obkhodit'sya (v.impf.) do without
obkhoditel'nyi (adj.) urbane
obkhozhdenie (n.n.) behavior
obkhvatit' (v.pf.) embrace
obkladyvat' (v.impf.) cover, tax
obkom (n.m.) regional committee
obkradyvat' (v.impf.) rob
oblachnost' (n.f.) clouds
obladanie (n.n.) possession
oblagat' (v.impf.) cover, tax
oblagorazhivat' (v.impf.) ennoble
oblako (n.n.) cloud
oblamyvat' (v.impf.) break off
oblaskat' (v.pf.) caress
oblast' (n.f.) region
oblastnoi (adj.) regional
oblatka (n.f.) capsule
oblava (n.f.) raid
oblech' (v.pf.) clothe, invest
obledenelyi (adj.) ice-covered
oblegat' (v.impf.) fit closely
oblegchat' (v.impf.) make lighter, relieve
oblekat'(sya) (v.impf.) take the form
oblenit'sya (v.pf.) grow lazy
oblepit' (v.pf.) cling
obletat' (v.impf.) fly round
oblezlyi (adj.) shabby
oblezt' (v.pf.) peel off
oblichat' (v.impf.) expose
oblichitel'hyi (adj.) denunciatory
obligatsiya (n.f.) bond
oblik (n.m.) appearance
oblit' (v.pf.) douse
oblitsevat' (v.pf.) face
oblivanie (n.n.) dousing
oblizat' (v.pf.) lick
oblizyvat'sya (v.impf.) lick one's lips
oblokachivat'sya (v.impf.) lean on one's elbows
oblomat' (v.pf.) break off
oblomok (n.m.) fragment
oblozhenie (n.n.) taxation
oblozhka (n.f.) cover
obluchenie (n.n.) irradiation

oblupit' (v.pf.) shell
oblyset' (v.pf.) grow bald
oblyubovat' (v.pf.) take a fancy to
obmakhivat' (v.impf.) brush away
obmakhivat'sya (v.impf.) fan oneself
obmakhnut' (v.pf.) brush away
obmakivat' (v.impf.) dip
obman (n.m.) fraud
obmanchivyi (adj.) deceptive
obmanut' (v.pf.) deceive
obmatyvat' (v.impf.) wind round
obmazat' (v.pf.) coat
obmelenie (n.n.) drying up
obmen (n.m.) exchange
obmen veshchestv (n.m.) metabolism
obmenyat' (v.pf.) barter
obmer (n.m.) measurement
obmerit' (v.pf.) measure
obmesti (v.pf.) dust
obmetat' (v.impf.) overcast
obmolachivat' (v.impf.) thresh
obmolot (n.m.) threshing
obmolvit'sya (v.pf.) make a slip
obmorok (n.m.) faint
obmorozhennyi (adj.) frostbitten
obmotat' (v.pf.) wind round
obmotka (n.f.) winding, coil
obmotki (n.pl.) puttees
obmozgovat' (v.pf.) think over
obmundirovanie (n.n.) uniform
obmyakat' (v.impf.) become soft
obmyvat' (v.impf.) wash
obnadezhit' (v.pf.) reassure
obnaglet' (v.pf.) grow impudent
obnarodovat' (v.impf. & pf.) promulgate
obnaruzhivat'(sya) (v.impf.) discover, display
obnazhat' (v.impf.) bare
obnesti (v.pf.) enclose
obnimat'(sya) (v.impf.) embrace
obnishchanie (n.n.) destitution
obnosit' (v.impf.) enclose
obnoski (n.pl.) cast-off clothes
obnovit' (v.pf.) renew
obnovka (n.f.) new dress
obnovlennyi (adj.) renewed
obnyat' (v.pf.) embrace
obnyukhat' (v.pf.) sniff round

obo (prep.)   of, about
obobrat' (v.pf.)   pick
obobshchenie (n.n.)   generalization
obobshchestvit' (v.pf.)   nationalize
obobshchit' (v.pf.)   generalize
obod (n.m.)   rim
obodrat' (v.pf.)   skin
obodrenie (n.n.)   encouragement
obogashchenie (n.n.)   separation, concentration
obogatit' (v.pf.)   enrich
obognat' (v.pf.)   leave behind
obognut' (v.pf.)   walk round
obogret' (v.pf.)   warm up
obogrevat'(sya) (v.impf.)   warm up
oboi (n.pl.)   wallpaper
oboima (n.f.)   cartridge clip
oboishchik (n.m.)   upholsterer
oboiti (v.pf.)   go round
obokrast' (v.pf.)   rob
obolochka (n.f.)   casing, membrane, layer
obol'shchat' (v.impf.)   seduce
obol'stitel' (n.m.)   seducer
oboltus (n.m.)   blockhead
obomlet' (v.pf.)   be stupefied
obonyanie (n.n.)   sense of smell
oborachivat'(sya) (v.impf.)   turn round
oborka (n.f.)   flounce
oborona (n.f.)   defense
oboronosposobnost' (n.f.)   defense capability
oboronyat' (v.impf.)   defend
oborot (n.m.)   revolution, turnover
oborotnyi (adj.)   reverse
oborudovanie (n.n.)   equipment
oborvanets (n.m.)   ragamuffin
oborvannyi (adj.)   ragged
oborvat' (v.pf.)   break off
obosnovanie (n.n.)   basis
obosnovannyi (adj.)   well-founded
obosnovat'sya (v.pf.)   settle
obosobit' (v.pf.)   separate
obostrenie (n.n.)   sharpening, aggravation
oboyudnyi (adj.)   mutual
oboyudoostryi (adj.)   double-edged
oboz (n.m.)   transport
obozhanie (n.n.)   adoration
obozhestvlyat' (v.impf.)   idolize
obozlit' (v.pf.)   make angry

oboznachat' (v.impf.)   mean
oboznachit' (v.pf.)   mark
obozrevatel' (n.m.)   reviewer
obozvat' (v.pf.)   call
obrabatyvat' (v.impf.)   cultivate
obrabotka (n.f.)   cultivation, processing
obradovat' (v.pf.)   make glad
obrashchat' (v.impf.)   turn, pay attention
obrashchenie (n.n.)   address, appeal
obrastat' (v.impf.)   become overgrown
obratimost' (n.f.)   reversibility
obratit' (v.pf.)   turn
obratnyi (adj.)   reverse, opposite
obraz (n.m.)   form, image
obrazchik (n.m.)   sample
obrazets (n.m.)   example
obraznyi (adj.)   figurative
obrazovanie (n.n.)   education
obrazovanie (n.n.)   formation
obrazovannyi (adj.)   educated
obrazovat' (v.pf.)   form
obrazovyvat'(sya) (v.impf.)   form
obraztsovyi (adj.)   model
obrazumit' (v.pf.)   bring to reason
obrech' (v.pf.)   condemn
obrechennyi (adj.)   condemned
obrekat' (v.impf.)   condemn
obremenyat' (v.impf.)   burden
obrez (n.m.)   edge
obrezat' (v.impf.)   cut off
obrisovat' (v.pf.)   describe
obrok (n.m.)   tax
obronit' (v.pf.)   let fall
obrosshii (adj.)   overgrown
obrubat' (v.impf.)   chop off
obrubok (n.m.)   stump
obruch (n.m.)   hoop
obrugat' (v.pf.)   swear
obrushivat'sya (v.impf.)   collapse
obryad (n.m.)   ceremony
obryuzglyi (adj.)   fat and flabby
obryv (n.m.)   precipice
obryvat'(sya) (v.impf.)   break off
obryvistyi (adj.)   steep
obryvok (n.m.)   scrap
obryzgat' (v.pf.)   splash
obschitat' (v.pf.)   cheat, shortchange
obshchityvat'sya (v.impf.)   miscalculate

obsemenenie (n.n.) dissemination
observatoriya (n.f.) observatory
obsharivat' (v.impf.) rummage
obshchat'sya (v.impf.) associate
obshchedostupnyi (adj.) available
obshcheizvestnyi (adj.) well-known
obshchenarodnyi (adj.) public
obshchenie (n.n.) association
obshcheobrazovatel'nyi (adj.) providing
 general education
obshcheprinyatyi (adj.) generally accepted
obshchesoyuznyi (adj.) All-Union
obshchestvennost' (n.f.) the public
obshchestvo (n.n.) society
obshcheupotrebitel'nyi (adj.) in general use
obshchezhitie (n.n.) hostel
obshchii (adj.) common, general
obshchina (n.f.) community
obshchitel'nyi (adj.) sociable
obshchnost' (n.f.) community
obshirnyi (adj.) vast
obshit' (v.pf.) panel
obshivat' (v.impf.) sew
obshivka (n.f.) edging
obshlag (n.m.) cuff
obsledovanie (n.n.) inspection
obsluzhivanie (n.n.) service
obsokhnut' (v.pf.) dry
obstanovka (n.f.) furniture
obstanovka (n.f.) conditions
obstavit' (v.pf.) furnish
obstoyat' (v.impf.) be, get on
obstoyatel'nyi (adj.) reliable
obstoyatel'stvo (n.n.) circumstance
obstrel (n.m.) fire
obstrelivat' (v.impf.) fire
obstrogat' (v.pf.) plane
obstruktsiya (n.f.) obstruction
obstupat' (v.impf.) surround
obsudit' (v.pf.) discuss
obsykhat' (v.impf.) dry
obsypat' (v.pf.) strew
obtachivat' (v.impf.) grind, turn, machine
obtekaemyi (adj.) streamlined
obtekanie (n.n.) flow pattern
obteret'(sya) (v.pf.) wipe, sponge
obtesat' (v.pf.) plane
obtiranie (n.n.) sponging

obtochit' (v.pf.) turn, machine
obtrepannyi (adj.) shabby
obtrepat' (v.pf.) fray
obturator (n.m.) obturator
obtyagivat' (v.impf.) cover, fit
obtyanut' (v.pf.) cover
obuchat' (v.impf.) give training
obuglivanie (n.n.) carbonization
obukh (n.m.) butt
oburevat' (v.impf.) overwhelm
obuslovit' (v.pf.) stipulate
obut' (v.pf.) put on shoes
obuv' (n.f.) footwear
obuvat'(sya) (v.impf.) put on shoes
obuvnoi (adj.) shoe, footwear
obuza (n.f.) burden
obuzdat' (v.pf.) bridle
obuzit' (v.pf.) make tight
obval (n.m.) collapse
obvalyat' (v.pf.) roll
obvarit' (v.pf.) scald
obvarivat'(sya) (v.impf.) scald (oneself)
obveshivat' (v.impf.) give short weight
obvesit' (v.pf.) give short weight
obvesti (v.pf.) outline
obvetrennyi (adj.) weather-beaten
obvetshalyi (adj.) decayed
obvinenie (n.n.) accusation
obvinyat' (v.impf.) accuse
obvisat' (v.impf.) sag
obvit' (v.pf.) entwine
obvivat'(sya) (v.impf.) wind round
obvodit' (v.impf.) outline
obvodnenie (n.n.) irrigation
obvorozhitel'nyi (adj.) enchanting
obvyazat' (v.pf.) tie
ob"yasnenie (n.n.) explanation
ob"yasnyat'sya (v.impf.) explain
ob"yatie (n.n.) embrace
ob"yavit' (v.pf.) declare
obyazannost' (n.f.) duty
obyazat' (v.pf.) oblige
obyazatel'nyi (adj.) compulsory
obyazyvat' (v.impf.) commit
obychai (n.m.) custom
obydennyi (adj.) ordinary
obygrat' (v.pf.) win
obyknovenie (n.n.) habit

obysk (n.m.)   search
obyskivat' (v.impf.)   search
obyvatel' (n.m.)   philistine
obzavestis' (v.pf.)   provide oneself with
obzhalovanie (n.n.)   appeal
obzhech' (v.pf.)   burn
obzhig (n.m.)   roasting, kilning, baker
obzhit' (v.pf.)   render habitable
obzhora (n.m.&f.)   glutton
obzor (n.m.)   survey
obzyvat' (v.impf.)   call
ochag (n.m.)   hearth
ocharovanie (n.n.)   charm
ocharovat' (v.pf.)   charm
ochen' (adj.)   very
ocherchivat' (v.impf.)   outline
ochered' (n.f.)   turn, line
ocherednoi (adj.)   next
ocherk (n.m.)   essay
ochernit' (v.pf.)   slander
ocherstvet' (v.pf.)   harden
ochertanie (n.n.)   outline
ochertit' (v.pf.)   outline, trace
ochertya (adv.)   headlong
ocheski (n.pl.)   combings
ochevidets (n.m.)   eyewitness
ochevidnyi (adj.)   obvious
ochinit' (v.pf.)   sharpen
ochishchat'(sya) (v.impf.)   clean, refine
ochistitel' (n.m.)   purifier
ochistka (n.f.)   cleaning, refining
ochistki (n.pl.)   peelings
ochki (n.pl.)   glasses
ochko (n.n.)   point
ochnut'sya (v.pf.)   regain consciousness
ochutit'sya (v.pf.)   find oneself
oda (n.f.)   ode
odarennyi (adj.)   gifted
odarit'(v.pf.)   endow
odekolon (n.m.)   eau-de-cologne
odelit' (v.pf.)   apportion
odergivat' (v.impf.)   pull down
odernut' (v.pf.)   pull down
oderzhat' verkh (v.pf.)   gain the upper hand
oderzhimyi (adj.)   possessed
odet' (v.pf.)   dress
odevat'(sya) (v.impf.)   dress
odeyalo (n.n.)   blanket

odeyanie (n.n.)   garment
odezhda (n.f.)   clothes
odichavshii (adj.)   gone wild
odin (num.)   one
odinakovyi (adj.)   identical
odinnadtsat' (num.)   eleven
odinochestvo (n.n.)   solitude
odinochnyi (adj.)   individual
odinokii (adj.)   lonely
odioznyi (adj.)   odious
odna (num.)   one
odnako (adv.)   however
odnazhdy (adv.)   once
odnoatomnyi (adj.)   monoatomic
odnobortnyi (adj.)   single-breasted
odnodnevnyi (adj.)   one-day
odnoétazhnyi (adj.)   one-storied building
odnofamilets (n.m.)   namesake
odnoiménnyi (adj.)   of the same name
odnoklassnik (n.m.)   classmate
odnokletochnyi (adj.)   unicellular
odnokoleinyi (adj.)   single-track
odnokursnik (n.m.)   classmate
odnoletki (n.pl.)   of the same age
odnomestnyi (adj.)   single-seater
odnoobraznyi (adj.)   monotonous
odnorodnyi (adj.)   homogeneous
odnoslozhnyi (adj.)   monosyllabic
odnostoronnii (adj.)   one-sided
odnotsvetnyi (adj.)   one-color
odnovremennyi (adj.)   simultaneous
odnoznachnyi (adj.)   synonymous
odnozvuchnyi (n.f.)   monotonous
odobrenie (n.n.)   approval
odobryat' (v.impf.)   approval
odolevat (v.impf.)   overcome
odolzhenie (n.n.)   favor
odryakhlet' (v.pf.)   become decrepit
odukhotvoryat' (v.impf.)   inspire
odumat'sya (v.pf.)   think better of
odur' (n.f.)   stupor
odurachit' (v.pf.)   makes a fool of
odurelyi (adj.)   stupid
odurmanivat' (v.impf.)   stupefy
oduryayushchii (adj.)   overpowering, heavy
odushevit' (v.pf.)   animate
odushevlyat'(sya) (v.impf.)   animate
odutlovatyi (adj.)   puffy

oduvanchik (n.m.) dandelion
odyshka (n.f.) short breath
ofitser (n.m.) officer
ofitsial'nyi (adj.) official
ofitsiant (n.m.) waiter
ofitsioz (n.m.) semiofficial organ
oformit' (v.pf.) draw up, register
ogarok (n.m.) candle end
ogibat' (v.impf.) walk round
oglashat' (v.impf.) announce
oglasit' (v.pf.) announce
oglaska (n.f.) publicity
oglavlenie (n.n.) contents
ogloblya (n.f.) shaft
oglokhnut' (v.pf.) become deaf
oglushit' (v.pf.) deafen, stun
oglyadet' (v.pf.) take a look
oglyadyvat' (v.impf.) examine, inspect
oglyanut'sya (v.pf.) look back
ognemet (n.m.) flamethrower
ognennyi (adj.) fiery
ogneopasnyi (adj.) inflammable
ognestrel'nyi (adj.) firearms
ognetushitel' (n.m.) fire extinguisher
ogneupor (n.m.) refractory
ogneupornyi (adj.) fireproof
ogolennyi (adj.) bare
ogolit' (v.pf.) bare
ogoltelyi (adj.) wild
ogolyat'(sya) (v.impf.) strip
ogon' (n.m.) fire, flame
ogonek (n.m.) little light
ogorazhivat'(sya) (v.impf.) fence in
ogorchat' (v.impf.) grieve
ogorod (n.m.) kitchen garden
ogorodit' (v.pf.) fence in
ogorodnik (n.m.) truck farmer
ogoroshit' (v.pf.) dumbfound
ogovarivat' (v.impf.) slander, stipulate
ogovorit' (v.pf.) slander, stipulate
ogovorka (n.f.) stipulation
ograbit' (v.pf.) rob
ograda (n.f.) fence
ogranichenie (n.n.) limitation, restriction
ogromnyi (adj.) huge
ogrubelyi (adj.) coarsened
ogryzat'sya (v.impf.) snap
ogryzok (n.m.) stump, cob

ogul'nyi (adj.) indiscriminate
ogurets (n.m.) cucumber
okaimlyat' (v.impf.) border
okamenelost' (n.f.) fossil
okanchivat'(sya) (v.impf.) finish
okapyvat'sya (v.impf.) entrench oneself
okayannyi (adj.) devil
okazat' (v.pf.) render, show
okazat'sya (v.pf.) prove to be
okaziya (n.f.) opportunity
okazyvat'sya (v.impf.) prove to be
okean (n.m.) ocean
okh (interj.) oh!
okhapka (n.f.) armful
okhat' (v.impf.) sigh
okhladevat' (v.impf.) become cold
okhmelet' (v.pf.) become tight
okhnut' (v.pf.) sigh
okhota (n.f.) hunting
okhota (n.f.) wish
okhotit'sya (v.impf.) hunt
okhotnichii (adj.) hunting
okhotnik (n.m.) hunter
okhotnik (n.m.) volunteer
okhotno (adv.) willingly
okhra (n.f.) ochre
okhrana (n.f.) guard
okhripnut' (v.pf.) become hoarse
okhvat (n.m.) scope
okidyvat' (v.impf.) cast around
okis' (n.f.) oxide
okislenie (n.n.) oxidation
okislitel' (n.m.) oxidant, oxidizer, oxidizing
  agent
okkupatsiya (n.f.) occupation
oklad (n.m.) salary scale
okleivat' (v.impf.) paste
oklevetat' (v.pf.) slander
oklikat' (v.impf.) call
okno (n.n.) window
oko (n.n.) eye
okochenet' (v.pf.) become stiff
okolachivat'sya (v.impf.) loiter
okoldovat' (v.pf.) bewitch
okolevat' (v.impf.) die
okol'nyi (adj.) roundabout
okolo (adv.) near
okolysh (n.m.) cap-band

okonchanie (n.n.) finishing
okonchit' (v.pf.) finish
okonnyi (adj.) window
okop (n.m.) trench
okorok (n.m.) ham
okoshko (n.n.) window
okostenelyi (adj.) ossified
okovat' (v.pf.) strap with metal
okovy (n.pl.) fetters
okraina (n.f.) suburb
okrashivat' (v.impf.) paint
okrasit' (v.pf.) paint
okrepnut' (v.pf.) grow strong
okrestnost' (n.f.) environs
okrik (n.m.) shout
okrovavlennyi (adj.) bloodstained
okrug (n.m.) district
okruglit' (v.pf.) round off
okruzhat' (v.impf.) surround
okruzhnoi (adj.) district
okruzhnost' (n.f.) circumference
okrylit' (v.pf.) inspire
oktan (n.m.) octane
oktava (n.f.) octave
oktyabr' (n.m.) October
okuchivat' (v.impf.) earth up
okulyar (n.m.) eyepiece, eyeglass, ocular
okun' (n.m.) perch
okunat' (v.impf.) plunge
okupit'sya (v.pf.) pay, be worth while
okurivat' (v.impf.) fumigate
okurok (n.m.) cigarette butt
okutat' (v.pf.) wrap up
olad'ya (n.f.) thick pancake
oledenelyi (adj.) frozen
olifa (n.f.) linseed oil
oligarkhiya (n.f.) oligarchy
olimpiada (n.f.) Olympiad
olimpiiskii (adj.) Olympic
olitsetvoryat' (v.impf.) personify
oliva (n.f.) olive
ol'kha (n.f.) alder
olovo (n.n.) tin
om (n.m.) ohm
omertvenie (n.n.) necrosis
omerzenie (n.n.) loathing
omlet (n.m.) omelette
omolozhenie (n.n.) rejuvenation

omonim (n.m.) homonym
omrachit' (v.pf.) darken
omut (n.m.) pool
omyvat' (v.impf.) wash
on (p.) he
ona (p.) she
onemet' (v.pf.) become dumb
oni (p.) they
onkologiya (n.f.) oncology
ono (p.) it
opadat' (v.impf.) fall
opala (n.f.) disgrace
opalit' (v.pf.) singe
opasat'sya (v.impf.) fear
opaska (n.f.) caution
opasnost' (n.f.) danger
opast' (v.pf.) fall
opazdyvat' (v.impf.) be late
opechalit' (v.pf.) grieve
opechatka (n.f.) misprint
opechatat' (v.pf.) seal
opechatyvat' (v.impf.) seal
opeka (n.f.) guardianship
opera (n.f.) opera
operabil'nyi (adj.) operable
operativnyi (adj.) surgical, active
operator (n.m.) operator
operedit' (v.pf.) outstrip
operenie (n.n.) plumage
operet'sya (v.pf.) lean on
operetta (n.f.) operetta
operezhenie (n.n.) advance, advancing, lead
operirovat' (v.impf.) operate
operit'sya (v.pf.) grow up
opernyi (adj.) opera
operyat'sya (v.impf.) grow up
opeshit' (v.pf.) be taken back
opilki (n.pl.) sawdust
opirat'sya (v.impf.) lean on
opis' (n.f.) list
opisanie (n.n.) description
opisat' (v.pf.) describe
opiska (n.f.) error
opisyvat' (v.impf.) describe
opium (n.m.) opium
oplakivat' (v.impf.) mourn
oplata (n.f.) payment
opleukha (n.f.) slap in the face

oplevat' (v.pf.) spit
oplodotvorenie (n.n.) fertilization
oploshnost' (n.f.) blunder
oplot (n.m.) stronghold
opokhmelit'sya (v.pf.) take a hair of the dog
  that bit you
opolchenie (n.n.) home guard
opolchit'sya (v.pf.) be up in arms
opolzen' (n.m.) landslide
opomnit'sya (v.pf.) collect oneself
opora (n.f.) support
oporochit' (v.pf.) defame
oporozhnit' (v.pf.) empty
oposhlit' (v.pf.) debase
opovestit' (v.pf.) notify
opoyasat' (v.pf.) girdle
opozdat' (v.pf.) be late, miss
opoznavat' (v.impf.) identify
opozorit' (v.pf.) disgrace
opponent (n.m.) opponent
opportunizm (n.m.) opportunism
oppozitsiya (n.f.) opposition
oprashivat' (v.impf.) question
oprava (n.f.) setting, rim
opravdanie (n.n.) justification
opravdat' (v.pf.) justify
opravdyvat'(sya) (v.impf.) justify (oneself)
opravit' (v.pf.) tidy
opravlyat'sya (v.impf.) recover
opredelenie (n.n.) definition
opredelennyi (adj.) definite
opredelit' (v.pf.) define
opredelitel' (n.m.) determinant
oprokidyvat'(sya) (v.impf.) overturn
oprokinut' (v.pf.) overturn
oprometchivost' (n.f.) rashness
opromet'yu (adv.) headlong
opros (n.m.) interrogation
oprotestovat' (v.pf.) protest
oprotivet' (v.pf.) become repulsive
oprovergat' (v.impf.) refute
opryatnyi (adj.) tidy
opryskivat' (v.impf.) sprinkle
opticheskii (adj.) optical
optika (n.f.) optics
optimizm (n.m.) optimism
optom (adv.) wholesale
optovyi (adj.) wholesale

opublikovanie (n.n.) publication
opukhat' (v.impf.) swell
opukhol' (n.f.) swelling
opushka (n.f.) edge of forest
opuskat'(sya) (v.impf.) be lowered, sink
opustet' (v.pf.) become empty
opustit' (v.pf.) lower
opustoshat' (v.impf.) devastate
oputat' (v.pf.) entangle
opyat' (adv.) again
opylenie (n.n.) pollination
opyt (n.m.) experiment
oranzhereya (n.f.) hothouse
oranzhevyi (adj.) orange
orat' (v.impf.) yell
orator (n.m.) orator
orava (n.f.) gang
orbita (n.f.) orbit
orda (n.f.) horde
orden (n.m.) order
ordenonosets (n.m.) holder of an order
order (n.m.) warrant
ordinarets (n.m.) orderly
ordinata (n.f.) ordinate
orekh (n.m.) nut
orel (n.m.) eagle
oreol (n.m.) halo
oreshnik (n.m.) nut grove
orfograficheskii (adj.) orthographical
organ (n.m.) organ
organicheskii (adj.) organic
organizatsiya (n.f.) organization
organizm (n.m.) organism
organizovannyi (adj.) organized
orgiya (n.f.) orgy
orientatsiya (n.f.) orientation
original (n.m.) original
orkestr (n.m.) orchestra
orlinyi (adj.) aquiline
ornament (n.m.) ornament
orobet' (v.pf.) be abashed
oroshat' (v.impf.) irrigate
orudie (n.n.) tool
orudiinyi (adj.) gun
orudovat' (v.impf.) handle
oruzhie (n.n.) weapon, arms
os' (n.f.) axis, axle
osa (n.f.) wasp

osada (n.f.) siege
osadit' (v.pf.) besiege
osadit' (v.pf.) check
osadki (n.pl.) precipitation
osadnyi (adj.) siege
osadok (n.m.) sediment
osanka (n.f.) bearing
osazhdat' (v.impf.) besiege
osazhdat'sya (v.impf.) precipitate
osazhdenie (n.n.) settling, deposition, sedimentation
osazhivat' (v.impf.) check
oschastlivit' (v.pf.) make happy
osechka (n.f.) misfire
osedanie (n.n.) settling
osedlat' (v.pf.) saddle
osedlyi (adj.) non-nomadic
osekat'sya (v.impf.) stop short
osel (n.m.) donkey
oselok (n.m.) whetstone
osen' (n.f.) autumn
osenit' (v.pf.) occur
osennii (adj.) autumn
osenyat' (v.impf.) occur
osest' (v.pf.) settle
osetin (n.m.) Osset
osetrina (n.f.) sturgeon
oshchetinit'sya (v.pf.) bristle up
oshchipat' (v.pf.) pluck
oshchupat' (v.pf.) touch
oshchup'yu (adv.) groping
oshchushchenie (n.n.) sensation
oshchutimyi (adj.) tangible
oshchutit' (v.pf.) feel
osheinik (n.m.) collar
oshelomit' (v.pf.) stun
oshibat'sya (v.impf.) make mistakes
oshibka (n.f.) mistake
oshparit' (v.pf.) scald
oshtrafovat' (v.pf.) fine
oshtukaturit' (v.pf.) plaster
osilit' (v.pf.) overpower
osina (n.f.) aspen
osinyi (adj.) hornet
osipnut' (v.pf.) grow hoarse
osirotet' (v.pf.) become an orphan
oskalit' (v.pf.) snarl
oskandalit'sya (v.pf.) fall into disgrace

oskolok (n.m.) splinter
oskorbitel'nyi (adj.) insulting
oskorblenie (n.n.) insult
oskvernenie (n.n.) profanation
oskvernit' (v.pf.) profane
oslabevat' (v.impf.) grow weak
oslabit' (v.pf.) relax
oslablenie (n.n.) weakening, abatement, reduction
oslepit' (v.pf.) blind
oslepnut' (v.pf.) get blind
oslozhnenie (n.n.) complication
oslushat'sya (v.pf.) disobey
oslyshat'sya (v.pf.) misunderstand
osmatrivat'sya (v.impf.) look around
osmeivat' (v.impf.) ridicule
osmelet' (v.pf.) become bold
osmelivat'sya (v.impf.) dare
osmeyat' (v.pf.) ridicule
osmotr (n.m.) examination
osmotret' (v.pf.) examine
osmotritel'nost' (n.f.) circumspection
osmyslit' (v.pf.) comprehend
osnastit' (v.pf.) rig
osnastka (n.f.) rigging
osnova (n.f.) basis
osnovanie (n.n.) foundation
osnovat' (v.pf.) found
osnovatel' (n.m.) founder
osnovatel'nyi (adj.) solid
osnovnoi (adj.) principal
osnovopolozhnik (n.m.) founder
osnovyvat' (v.impf.) found
osoba (n.f.) person
osobennost' (n.f.) peculiarity
osobnyak (n.m.) mansion
osobnyakom (adv.) aloof
osobo (adv.) particularly
osoka (n.f.) sedge
osoznat' (v.pf.) realize
ospa (n.f.) smallpox
osparivat' (v.impf.) dispute
osramit' (v.pf.) disgrace
ostal'noe (n.n.) the rest
ostanavlivat'(sya) (v.impf.) stop
ostanki (n.pl.) remains
ostanovit' (v.pf.) stop, interrupt
ostanovka (n.f.) stop

ostatochnyi (adj.) residual
ostatok (n.m.) remainder
ostat'sya (v.pf.) remain
ostavat'sya (v.impf.) remain
ostavlyat' (v.impf.) leave
osteklit' (v.pf.) glaze
ostepenit'sya (v.pf.) settle down
osteregat'sya (v.impf.) beware
ostoichivost' (n.f.) stability
ostolbenet' (v.pf.) be dumbfounded
ostorozhnost' (n.f.) care
ostov (n.m.) framework
ostrich' (v.pf.) cut
ostrie (n.n.) point
ostrigat' (v.impf.) cut
ostrit' (v.impf.) make witty remarks
ostrokonechnyi (adj.) pointed
ostrota (n.f.) sharpness
ostrota (n.f.) witticism
ostroumie (n.n.) wit
ostrov (n.m.) island
ostryi (adj.) sharp
ostudit' (v.pf.) cool
ostupat'sya (v.impf.) stumble
ostyvat' (v.impf.) become cold
osudit' (v.pf.) blame
osunut'sya (v.pf.) become thin
osushat' (v.impf.) drain
osushchestvit' (v.pf.) accomplish
osvaivat'sya (v.impf.) feel at home
osvedomit' (v.pf.) inform
osvedomitel' (n.m.) informer
osveshchat' (v.impf.) light up
osveshchenie (n.n.) illumination
osvetit' (v.pf.) light up
osvezhat' (v.impf.) refresh
osvidetel'stvovanie (n.n.) examination
osvistat' (v.pf.) hiss
osvobodit' (v.pf.) set free
osvoboditel' (n.m.) liberator
osvobozhdat' (v.impf.) release
osvoenie (n.n.) development
osvoit' (v.pf.) master
osyazaemyi (adj.) tangilbe
osyazatel'nyi (adj.) tactile
osypat' (v.impf.) cover
osypat'sya (v.pf.) fall
ot (prep.) from

otaplivat' (v.impf.) heat
otbavit' (v.pf.) take away
otbegat' (v.impf.) run off
otbirat' (v.impf.) take away
otbit' (v.pf.) repulse
otbivat' (v.impf.) repulse
otblesk (n.m.) reflection
otboi (n.m.) retreat
otboinyi molotok (adj.-n.m.) pneumatic drill
otbor (n.m.) selection
otborochnyi (adj.) selection
otbrasyvat' (v.impf.) throw away
otbrosy (n.pl.) refuse
otbyt' (v.pf.) leave
otbyvat' (v.impf.) leave
otchaivat'sya (v.impf.) despair
otchasti (adv.) partly
otchayanie (n.n.) despair
otchayat'sya (v.pf.) despair
otchego (adv.) why
otchestvo (n.n.) patronymic
otchet (n.m.) account
otchetlivyi (adj.) distinct
otchetnost' (n.f.) bookkeeping
otchim (n.m.) stepfather
otchislenie (n.n.) deduction
otchislit' (v.pf.) deduct
otchitat' (v.pf.) reprimand
otchitat'sya (v.pf.) report
otchityvat' (v.impf.) reprimand
otchityvat'sya (v.impf.) report
otchizna (n.f.) native country
otchuzhdat' (v.impf.) alienate
otdacha (n.f.) return
otdalenie (n.n.) removal
otdalit' (v.pf.) remove
otdat' (v.pf.) give back
otdat'sya (v.pf.) give oneself to
otdavat' (v.impf.) give back
otdavit' (v.pf. .) crush
otdel (n.m.) department
otdelat' (v.pf.) trim
otdelat'sya (v.pf.) get rid of
otdelenie (n.n.) separation
otdelitel' (n.m.) separator
otdelka (n.f.) finishing
otdel'nyi (adj.) separate
otdelyat'(sya) (v.impf.) separate

otdelyvat' (v.impf.) trim
otdelyvat'sya (v.impf.) get rid of
otdergivat' (v.impf.) draw back
otdirat' (v.impf.) tear off
otdokhnut' (v.pf.) rest
otdushina (n.f.) air hole
otdykh (n.m.) rest
otdyshat'sya (v.pf.) recover one's breath
otech' (v.pf.) swell
otecheskii (adj.) fatherly
otechestvennyi (adj.) native
otechestvo (n.n.) mother country
otek (n.m.) edema
otekat' (v.impf.) swell
ot"ekhat' (v.pf.) drive off
otelit'sya (v.pf.) calve
otets (n.m.) father
ot"ezd (n.m.) departure
otgadat' (v.pf.) guess
otgibat' (v.impf.) turn back
otgladit' (v.pf.) iron
otglagol'nyi (adj.) verbal
otgolosok (n.m.) echo
otgonyat' (v.impf.) drive away
otgorazhivat' (v.impf.) partition off
otgovarivat'sya (v.impf.) excuse oneself
otgovorit' (v.pf.) dissuade
otgovorka (n.f.) pretext
otgryzat' (v.impf.) bite off
otit (n.m.) otitis
otkachat' (v.pf.) pump out
otkalyvat'(sya) (v.impf.) break off
otkapyvat' (v.impf.) dig up
otkarmlivat' (v.impf.) fatten
otkashlivat'sya (v.impf.) clear one's throat
otkatit' (v.pf.) roll away
otkaz (n.m.) refusal, failure
otkharkivat' (v.impf.) expectorate
otkhlebnut' (v.pf.) take a gulp
otkhlynut' (v.pf.) rush back
otkhod (n.m.) departure
otkhodit' (v.impf.) move away
otkhody (n.pl.) waste
otkidnoi (adj.) folding
otkidyvat'sya (v.impf.) lean back
otkinut' (v.pf) throw away
otkladyvat' (v.impf.) lay aside
otklanyat'sya (v.pf.) take one's leave

otkleit'sya (v.pf.) come unfastened
otklik (n.m.) response
otkliknut'sya (v.pf.) respond
otklonenie (n.n.) deflection, deviation
otklyuchat' (v.impf.) disconnect, cut off, de-energize
otkolot' (v.pf.) chop off
otkolotit' (v.pf.) beat up
otkopat' (v.pf) dig up
otkormit' (v.pf.) fatten
otkormlennyi (adj.) fat
otkos (n.m.) slope
otkrepit' (v.pf.) unfasten
otkrovennyi (adj.) frank
otkryt' (v.pf.) open
otkrytie (n.n.) discovery
otkrytka (n.f.) postcard
otkryvat'(sya) (v.impf.) open
otkuda (adv.) where from
otkuporivat' (v.impf.) uncork
otkusit' (v.pf.) bite off
otlagatel'stvo (n.n.) delay
otlamyvat'(sya) (v.impf.) break off
otlepit' (v.pf.) unstick
otlet (n.m.) takeoff
otletat' (v.impf.) fly away
otlichat' (v.impf.) differ
otlichie (n.n.) difference, distinction
otlichnik (n.m.) excellent student
otlichnyi (adj.) excellent
otlit' (v.pf.) pour off
otliv (n.m.) low tide
otlivat' (v.impf.) pour off
otlivka (n.f.) casting, founding
otlogii (adj.) sloping
otlomat'(sya) (v.pf.) break off
otlomit'(sya) (v.pf.) break off
otlozhenie (n.n.) deposit
otlozhit' (v.pf.) lay aside
otlozhnoi (adj.) turn-down
otluchat'sya (v.impf.) absent oneself
otluchka (n.f.) absence
otlynivat' (v.impf.) shirk
otmakhivat'sya (v.impf.) brush off
otmalchivat'sya (v.impf.) keep silent
otmechat' (v.impf.) mark
otmel' (n.f.) shallow
otmena (n.f.) abolition, repeal

otmenit' (v.pf.)   abolish
otmeret' (v.pf.)   die off
otmerit' (v.pf.)   measure off
otmesti (v.pf.)   sweep away
otmestka (n.f.)   revenge
otmetat' (v.impf.)   sweep away
otmetit' (v.pf.)   mark
otmezhevat'sya (v.pf.)   dissociate oneself
otmiranie (n.n.)   dying off
otmorazhivat' (v.impf.)   be frostbitten
otmychka (n.f.)   master key
otmyvat' (v.impf.)   wash off
otnekivat'sya (v.impf.)   repeatedly refuse
otnesti (v.pf.)   take (to)
otnimat'sya (v.impf.)   be paralyzed
otnoshenie (n.n.)   ratio, rate
otnoshenie (n.n.)   treatment
otnosit' (v.impf.)   take (to)
otnositel'nyi (adj.)   relative
otnosit'sya (v.impf.)   treat
otnyat' (v.pf.)   take away
otnyne (adv.)   from now on
otnyud' (adv.)   not in the least
otobrat' (v.pf.)   take away
otobrazhenie (n.n.)   reflection
otodrat' (v.pf.)   move aside
otodvigat'(sya) (v.impf.)   move aside
otodvinut' (v.pf.)   move aside
otognat' (v.pf.)   drive away
otognut' (v.pf.)   bend back
otogret' (v.pf.)   warm
otogrevat'(sya) (v.impf.)   warm oneself
otoiti (v.pf.)   move away
otomstit' (v.pf.)   revenge oneself on
otopit' (v.pf.)   heat
otoropet' (v.pf.)   be struck dumb
otorvannost' (n.f.)   alienation
otorvat' (v.pf.)   tear off
otoshchat' (v.pf.)   be emaciated
otoslat' (v.pf.)   send off
otovsyudu (adv.)   from everywhere
otozhdestvlyat' (v.impf.)   identify
otozvat' (v.pf.)   take aside
otpadat' (v.impf.)   fall off
otparyvat'(sya) (v.impf.)   rip off, come off
otpast' (v.pf.)   fall off
otpechatat' (v.pf.)   imprint
otperet' (v.pf.)   unlock

otperet'sya (v.pf.)   be unlocked
otperet'sya (v.pf.)   deny
otpikhivat' (v.impf.)   push away
otpilivat' (v.impf.)   saw off
otpiranie (n.n.)   unlocking
otpirat' (v.impf.)   open
otpiratel'stvo (n.n.)   denial
otpirat'sya (v.impf.)   deny
otpit' (v.pf.)   take a drink
otpivat' (v.impf.)   take a drink
otplata (n.f.)   repayment
otplytie (n.n.)   departure
otplyvat' (v.impf.)   sail
otpolzat' (v.impf.)   crawl away
otpor (n.m.)   rebuff
otporot' (v.pf.)   rip off
otpoved' (n.f.)   reproof
otprashivat'sya (v.impf.)   ask for leave
otpravit' (v.pf)   send
otpravitel' (n.m.)   sender
otpravit'sya (v.pf.)   set off
otpravlenie (n.n.)   dispatch
otpravlenie (n.n.)   performance
otpravlyat' (v.impf.)   send
otpravnoi (adj.)   starting
otprazdnovat' (v.pf.)   celebrate
otpryagat' (v.impf.)   unharness
otpryanut' (v.pf.)   recoil
otprygivat' (v.impf.)   jump back
otprysk (n.m.)   offspring
otpugivat' (v.impf.)   frighten
otpusk (n.m.)   leave, vacation
otpustit' (v.pf.)   release
otrabatyvat' (v.impf.)   work
otrabotat' (v.pf.)   work
otrada (n.f.)   pleasure
otrasl' (n.f.)   branch
otrastat' (v.impf.)   grow
otrava (n.f.)   poison
otravlyayushchee veshchestvo (adj.-n.n.)
  toxic agent
otrazhat' (v.impf.)   reflect, repulse
otrazhatel' (n.m.)   reflector, repeller, deflector
otrazit' (v.pf.)   reflect, repulse
otrechenie (n.n.)   renunciation
otrech'sya (v.pf.)   go back on
otrekat'sya (v.impf.)   renounce
otrekomendovat' (v.pf.)   introduce

otrep'ya (n.pl.) rags
otreshat'sya (v.impf.) renounce
otrez (n.m.) length
otrezat' (v.impf.) cut off
otrezok (n.m.) piece
otrezvit' (v.pf.) sober
otritsanie (n.n.) negation
otritsat' (v.impf.) deny
otrochestvo (n.n.) adolescence
otrod'e (n.n.) spawn
otrogi (n.pl.) spurs
otrostok (n.m.) shoot
otrubat' (v.impf.) cut off
otrubi (n.pl.) bran
otrubit' (v.pf.) cut off
otryadit' (v.pf.) detach
otryad (n.m.) detachment
otryakhivat'(sya) (v.impf.) shake off
otryakhnut' (v.pf.) shake off
otryv (n.m.) isolation
otryvistyi (adj.) abrupt
otryvok (n.m.) fragment
otryzhka (n.f.) belch
otsarapat' (v.pf.) scratch
otschitat' (v.pf.) count
otsebyatina (n.f.) ad libbing
otsechenie (n.n.) severance
otseivat'(sya) (v.impf.) sift
otsek (n.m.) compartment
otsekat' (v.impf.) cut off
otsenivat' (v.impf.) value
otsenshchik (n.m.) appraiser
otsepenet' (v.pf.) grow numb
otsepit' (v.pf.) surround
otsev (n.m.) sifting out
otseyat' (v.pf.) sift
otshatnut'sya (v.pf.) recoil
otshchepenets (n.m.) renegade
otshel'nik (n.m.) hermit
otshutit'sya (v.pf.) parry with a jest
otshvyrivat' (v.impf.) fling away
otsinkovannyi (adj.) galvanized
otskakivat' (v.impf.) jump away
otsluzhit' (v.pf.) serve
otsovetovat' (v.pf.) dissuade
otsrochit' (v.pf.) postpone
otstaivat' (v.impf.) defend
otstaivat'sya (v.impf.) settle

otstalost' (n.f.) backwardness
otstat' (v.pf.) fall behind
otstavanie (n.n.) lag
otstavit' (v.pf.) set aside
otstegivat'(sya) (v.impf.) unfasten
otstegnut' (v.pf.) unfasten
otstoyat' (v.pf.) be away
otstoyat' (v.pf.) defend
otstoyat'sya (v.pf.) settle
otstraivat' (v.impf.) finish building
otstranenie (n.n.) pushing aside
otstrelivat'sya (v.impf.) return fire
otstrigat' (v.impf.) cut off
otstroit' (v.pf.) finish building
otstupat' (v.impf.) step back
otstupat'sya (v.impf.) give up
otstupit' (v.pf.) step back
otstupit'sya (v.pf.) give up
otstuplenie (n.n.) retreat
otstupnik (n.m.) apostate
otstupnoe (n.n.) indemnity
otstupya (adv.) away
otsutstvie (n.n.) absence
otsvechivat' (v.impf.) shine
otsylat' (v.impf.) send off
otsypat' (v.pf.) pour out
otsyret' (v.pf.) become damp
otsyuda (adv.) from here
ottachivat' (v.impf.) sharpen
ottaivat' (v.impf.) thaw out
ottalkivanie (n.n.) repulsion
ottalkivat' (v.impf.) push away
ottayat' (v.pf.) thaw out
ottenit' (v.pf.) shade
ottenok (n.m.) shade
ottenyat' (v.impf.) shade
ottepel' (n.f.) thaw
ottesnit' (v.pf.) drive back
ottisk (n.m.) impression
ottochit' (v.pf.) sharpen
ottogo (adv.) that is why
ottolknut' (v.pf.) push away
ottopyrivat'sya (v.impf.) stick out
ottorzhenie (n.n.) rejection
ottsepit' (v.pf.) unhook
ottsovskii (adj.) paternal
ottsvesti (v.pf.) fade
ottuda (adv.) from there

ottyagivat' (v.impf.) delay

otuchat'sya (v.impf.) lose the habit

otuchit' (v.pf.) break a habit

otupenie (n.n.) dull stupor

otupet' (v.pf.) be in a stupor

otutyuzhit' (v.pf.) iron

otvadit' (v.pf.) drive off

otvaga (n.f.) bravery

otval (n.m.) dump

otvalivat'sya (v.impf.) fall off

otvar (n.m.) broth

otvazhnyi (adj.) fearless

otvechat' (v.impf.) answer

otvedat' (v.pf.) try

otverdevanie (n.n.) solidification

otverdevat' (v.impf.) harden

otvergat' (v.impf.) reject

otvernut' (v.pf.) unscrew

otverstie (n.n.) opening

otvertet'sya (v.pf.) get out of something

otvertka (n.f.) screwdriver

otverzhennyi (adj.) outcast

otves (n.m.) plummet

otveshivat' (v.impf.) weigh

otvesit' (v.pf.) weigh

otvesnyi (adj.) plumb

otvesti (v.pf.) lead

otvet (n.m.) answer

otvetchik (n.m.) defendant

otvetit' (v.pf.) answer

otvetstvennost' (n.f.) responsibility

otvetvlenie (n.n.) branch

otvezti (v.pf.) take away

otvilivat' (v.impf.) dodge

otvintit' (v.pf.) unscrew

otvisat' (v.impf.) hang down

otvlech' (v.pf.) distract

otvlekat' (v.impf.) distract

otvod (n.m.) objection

otvoevat' (v.pf.) win back

otvorachivat'(sya) (v.impf.) turn away

otvorit' (v.pf.) open

otvorot (n.m.) lapel

otvoryat'(sya) (v.impf.) open

otvozit' (v.impf.) take away

otvratit' (v.pf.) avert

otvratitel'nyi (adj.) disgusting

otvyazat' (v.pf.) untie

otvyazyvat'sya (v.impf.) come untied

otvykat' (v.impf.) lose the habit

ot"yavlennyi (adj.) thorough

otygrat'sya (v.pf.) revenge oneself on

otyskat' (v.pf.) find

otyskivat' (v.impf.) look for

otzhig (n.m.) annealing

otzhimat' (v.impf.) wring out

otzhit' (v.pf.) become obsolete

otzhivat' (v.impf.) become obsolete

otzhivshii (adj.) obsolete

otzvuk (n.m.) echo

otzyv (n.m.) reference

otzyvchivyi (adj.) sympathetic

oval'nyi (adj.) oval

ovatsiya (n.f.) ovation

ovchina (n.f.) sheepskin

ovdovet' (v.pf.) become a widow

ovechii (adj.) sheep

oves (n.m.) oats

ovin (n.m.) barn

ovladevat' (v.impf.) take possession

ovod (n.m.) gadfly

ovoshchi (n.pl.) vegetables

ovrag (n.m.) ravine

ovsyanka (n.f.) oatmeal

ovtsa (n.f.) sheep

ovtsevodstvo (n.n.) sheepbreeding

ozabochennost' (n.f.) preoccupation

ozadachit' (v.pf.) perplex

ozaglavit' (v.pf.) give a title

ozarit' (v.pf.) light up

ozdorovit' (v.pf.) make healthier

ozero (n.n.) lake

ozherel'e (n.n.) necklace

ozhestochat' (v.impf.) embitter

ozhidanie (n.n.) expectation

ozhirenie (n.n.) obesity

ozhit' (v.pf.) revive

ozhivat' (v.impf.) revive

ozhivit' (v.pf.) resuscitate

ozhizhenie (n.n.) liquefying

ozhog (n.m.) burn

ozimye (n.pl.) winter crops

ozirat'sya (v.impf.) look round

ozlobit' (v.pf.) embitter

oznachat' (v.impf.) signify

oznakomit' (v.pf.) acquaint

oznamenovat' (v.pf.) mark
oznob (n.m.) shiver
ozon (n.m.) ozone
ozonirovanie (n.n.) ozonization

ozornik (n.m.) mischievous child
ozveret' (v.pf.) become brutalized
ozyabnyt' (v.pf.) be cold

P (П)

pa (n.n.) step
pachka (n.f.) bundle
pachkat' (v.impf.) soil
padal' (n.f.) carrion
padat' (v.impf.) fall
padcheritsa (n.f.) stepdaughter
padenie (n.n.) fall
padezh (n.m.) loss of cattle
padezh (n.m.) case
padkii (adj.) greedy
paek (n.m.) ration
pafos (n.m.) pathos
pagubnyi (adj.) pernicious
pai (n.m.) share
paket (n.m.) packet
pakh (n.m.) groin
pakhar' (n.m.) plowman
pakhat' (v.impf.) plow
pakhnut' (v.impf.) smell
pakhota (n.f.) plowed land
pakhuchii (adj.) fragrant
paklya (n.f.) tow
pakost' (n.f.) filth
pakovat' (v.impf.) pack
pakt (n.m.) pact
palach (n.m.) hangman
palata (n.f.) chamber
palatka (n.f.) tent
pal'ba (n.f.) firing
palets (n.m.) finger
palisadnik (n.m.) small front garden
palit' (v.impf.) burn
palit' (v.impf.) fire
palitra (n.f.) palette
palka (n.f.) stick
pal'ma (n.f.) palm tree
palochka (n.f.) stick, bacillus

palomnik (n.m.) pilgrim
pal'to (n.n.) overcoat
paluba (n.f.) deck
palyashchii (adj.) scorching
pamyat' (n.f.) memory
pamyatnik (n.m.) monument
pamyatnyi (adj.) memorable
panel' (n.f.) pavement, panel, board
panicheskii (adj.) panicky
panika (n.f.) panic
paniker (n.m.) alarmist
panikhida (n.f.) service for the dead
panorama (n.f.) panorama
pansion (n.m.) boarding school
pantera (n.f.) panther
pantsir' (n.m.) armor
papa (n.m.) daddy
papirosa (n.f.) cigarette
papka (n.f.) file
paporotnik (n.m.) fern
par (n.m.) steam
par (n.m.) fallow
para (n.f.) pair
parabola (n.f.) parabola
parad (n.m.) parade
paradnyi (adj.) gala
paradoks (n.m.) paradox
parafin (n.m.) paraffin
paragraf (n.m.) paragraph
paralich (n.m.) paralysis
paralizovat' (v.pf.) paralyze
parallaks (n.m.) parallax
parallel' (n.f.) parallel
parapet (n.m.) parapet
parashyut (n.m.) parachute
parazit (n.m.) parasite
parcha (n.f.) brocade

paren' (n.m.) fellow
parenie (n.n.) soaring
parfyumeriya (n.f.) perfumery
pari (n.n.) bet
parik (n.m.) wig
parikmakher (n.m.) hairdresser
parirovat' (v.impf.&pf.) parry
parit' (v.impf.) soar
parit' (v.impf.) steam
paritet (n.m.) parity
park (n.m.) park
parket (n.m.) parquet
parlament (n.m.) parliament
parlamenter (n.m.) truce envoy
parnik (n.m.) hotbed
parnishka (n.m.) boy
parnoi (adj.) fresh
parnyi (adj.) twin
parodiya (n.f.) parody
parokhod (n.m.) steamer
paroksizm (n.m.) paroxysm
parol' (n.m.) password
parom (n.m.) ferry
paroobrazovanie (n.m.) vaporization
parotit (n.m.) parotiditis
parovoi (adj.) steam
parovoz (n.m.) locomotive
parta (n.f.) desk
partaktiv (n.m.) party activists
parter (n.m.) front orchestra seats
partiets (n.m.) party member
partiinost' (n.f.) party membership
partiinyi (adj.) party
partitura (n.f.) score
partiya (n.f.) party
partiya (n.f.) part, batch
partizan (n.m.) partisan
partner (n.m.) partner
partorg (n.m.) party organizer
parus (n.m.) sail
parusina (n.f.) canvas
parusnyi (adj.) sailing
paseka (n.f.) apiary
pashnya (n.f.) field
pashtet (n.m.) pâté
paskha (n.f.) Easter
pasmurnyi (adj.) cloudy
pasovat' (v.impf.) pass

pasport (n.m.) passport
passazhir (n.m.) passenger
passivnyi (adj.) passive
past' (v.pf.) fall
past' (n.f.) mouth
pasta (n.f.) paste
pastbishche (n.n.) pasture
pasterizatsiya (n.f.) pasteurization
pasti (v.impf.) herd
pastis' (v.impf.) graze
pastukh (n.m.) shepherd
pasynok (n.m.) stepson
patefon (n.m.) phonograph
patent (n.m.) patent
patoka (n.f.) treacle
patriarkh (n.m.) patriarch
patriot (n.m.) patriot
patron (n.m.) cartridge
patrul' (n.m.) patrol
patsient (n.m.) patient
patsifist (n.m.) pacifist
pauk (n.m.) spider
pautina (n.f.) cobweb
pauza (n.f.) pause
pavil'on (n.m.) pavilion
pavlin (n.m.) peacock
pavodok (n.m.) spring floods
payal'nik (n.m.) soldering iron
payasnichat' (v.impf.) play the buffoon
payat' (v.impf.) solder
payats (n.m.) clown
payusnaya ikra (adj.-n.f.) pressed caviar
paz (n.m.) groove, slot, notch
pchela (n.f.) bee
pchel'nik (n.m.) apiary
pech' (n.f.) stove
pech' (v.impf.) bake
pechal' (n.f.) sorrow
pechalit' (v.impf.) grieve
pechat' (n.f.) seal
pechat' (n.f.) the press
pechatat' (v.impf.) print
pechatnyi (adj.) printed
pechen' (n.f.) liver
pechen'e (n.n.) cookies
pechenka (n.f.) liver
pechenyi (adj.) baked
pechka (n.f.) stove

pedagog (n.m.) teacher
pedal' (n.f.) pedal
pedant (n.m.) pedant
p'edestal (n.m.) pedestal
pegii (adj.) piebald
peizazh (n.m.) landscape
pekar' (n.m.) baker
pekarnya (n.f.) bakery
pekhota (n.f.) infantry
peklo (n.n.) scorching heat
pelena (n.f.) cover
pelenat' (v.impf.) swaddle, wrap
pelengator (n.m.) direction finder
pelenki (n.pl.) swaddling clothes
pelikan (n.m.) pelican
pel'meni (n.pl.) dumplings
pemza (n.f.) pumice
pen' (n.m.) stump
pena (n.f.) foam
penal (n.m.) pencil case
penie (n.n.) singing
penistyi (adj.) foamy
penit'sya (v.impf.) foam
penka (n.f.) skin
pen'ka (n.f.) hemp
pensioner (n.m.) pensioner
pensiya (n.f.) pension
pensne (n.n.) pince-nez
penya (n.f.) fine
penyat' (v.impf.) reproach
pepel (n.m.) ashes
pepel'nitsa (n.f.) ashtray
pepel'nyi (adj.) ashy
perchatka (n.f.) glove
perebegat' (v.impf.) run across
perebezhka (n.f.) bound
perebirat' (v.impf.) sort out
perebirat'sya (v.impf.) get over, move
perebit' (v.pf.) break
perebit' (v.pf.) interrupt
perebivat' (v.impf.) interrupt
pereboi (n.m.) stoppage
pereborka (n.f.) partition, overhaul
pereborot' (v.pf.) overcome
pereborshchit' (v.pf.) overdo
perebranka (n.f.) wrangle
perebrasyvat' (v.impf.) throw over
perebrasyvat'sya (v.impf.) exchange

perebrat' (v.pf.) sort out
perebrat'sya (v.pf.) get over, move
perebrosit' (v.pf.) throw over
perebrosit'sya (v.pf.) exchange
perebroska (n.f.) transference
perechen' (n.m.) list
perecherkivat' (v.impf.) cross out
perechest' (v.pf.) read
perechislenie (n.n.) enumeration
perechislit' (v.pf.) enumerate
perechit' (v.impf.) talk back
perechitat' (v.pf.) read
perechityvat' (v.impf.) read
perechnitsa (n.f.) pepperbox
pered (prep.) in front of
pered (n.m.) front
peredacha (n.f.) broadcast, gear
peredat' (v.pf.) pass, broadcast
peredatchik (n.m.) transmitter
peredatochnyi (adj.) transmission
peredavat' (v.impf.) pass, broadcast
peredel (n.m.) repartition
peredelat' (v.pf.) alter
peredergivat' (v.impf.) cheat, distort
perednii (adj.) front
perednik (n.m.) apron
perednyaya (n.f.) hall
peredokhnut' (v.pf.) take a rest
peredovik (n.m.) exemplary worker
peredovitsa (n.f.) editorial
peredovoi (adj.) advanced
peredraznivat' (v.impf.) mimic
peredryaga (n.f.) scrape
peredumat' (v.pf.) change one's mind
peredvigat'(sya) (v.impf.) move
peredvinut' (v.pf.) move
peredyshka (n.f.) respite
pereékzamenovka (n.f.) reexamination
pereezd (n.m.) passage, moving
pereezd (n.m.) crossing
pereformirovat' (v.pf.) re-form
peregib (n.m.) bend
pereglyadyvat'sya (v.impf.) exchange
  glances
peregnat' (v.pf.) leave behind
peregnat' (v.pf.) distill
peregnoi (n.m.) humus
peregnut' (v.pf.) bend

peregon (n.m.) stage
peregonka (n.f.) distillation
peregonyat' (v.impf.) leave behind, distill
peregorat' (v.impf.) burn
peregorazhivat' (v.impf.) partition off
peregorodit' (v.pf.) partition off
peregorodka (n.f.) partition
peregovorit' (v.pf.) discuss
peregovory (n.pl.) negotiations
peregrev (n.m.) overheating
peregrevat' (v.impf.) overheat
peregruppirovat' (v.pf.) regroup
peregruzhat' (v.impf.) overload
peregruzka (n.f.) overload
peregryzat' (v.impf.) gnaw through
pereimenovat' (v.pf.) rename
pereiti (v.pf.) cross
pereizbirat' (v.pf.) reelect
pereizdavat' (v.impf.) republish
perekarmlivat' (v.impf.) overfeed
perekhitrit' (v.pf.) outwit
perekhod (n.m.) passage, crossing
perekhodyashchii (adj.) transitory
perekidyvat' (v.impf.) throw over
perekis' (n.f.) peroxide
perekisat' (v.impf.) turn sour
perekladina (n.f.) cross beam
perekladyvat' (v.impf.) move, transfer, shift
pereklichka (n.f.) roll call
pereklikat'sya (v.impf.) shout to one another
pereklyuchat' (v.impf.) switch
pereklyuchatel' (n.m.) switch, commutator
perekochevat' (v.pf.) move
perekormit' (v.pf.) overfeed
perekoshennyi (adj.) distorted
perekosit'sya (v.pf.) become distorted
perekovat' (v.pf.) remold
perekraivat' (v.impf.) reshape
perekreshchivat'sya (v.impf.) cross
perekrestnyi (adj.) cross
perekrestok (n.m.) crossroads
perekrichat' (v.pf.) shout down
perekroit' (v.pf.) reshape
perekrytie (n.n.) overlap, span, ceiling
perekupat' (v.impf.) buy secondhand
perekusit' (v.pf.) bite through
perekvalifikatsiya (n.f.) retraining
perelagat' (v.impf.) move

perelamyvat' (v.impf.) break to pieces
perelet (n.m.) flight
pereletat' (v.impf.) fly over
pereletnyi (adj.) flying
perelezat' (v.impf.) climb over
perelistat' (v.pf) leaf through
perelit' (v.pf.) pour
perelitsevat' (v.pf.) turn
perelivanie (n.n.) transfusion
perelom (n.m.) fracture
perelozhit' (v.pf.) move, transfer
peremalyvat' (v.impf.) grind
peremanivat' (v.impf.) win over
peremena (n.f.) change
peremennaya (n.f.) variable
peremeshat' (v.pf.) mix
peremeshchat' (v.impf.) move
peremeshivat'sya (v.impf.) get mixed
peremestit' (v.pf.) move
peremezhat'sya (v.impf.) intermit
peremigivat'sya (v.impf.) wink
peremirie (n.n.) armistice
peremogat' (v.impf.) try to overcome
peremolot' (v.pf.) grind
peremychka (n.f.) cofferdam
perenapryagat'sya (v.pf.) overstrain oneself
perenaselenie (n.n.) overpopulation
perenesti (v.pf.) transfer, postpone
perenesti (v.pf.) go through
perenestis' (v.pf.) be carried away
perenimat' (v.impf.) take over
perenochevat' (v.pf.) spend the night
perenos (n.m.) transfer
perenosit' (v.impf.) transfer, go through
perenositsa (n.f.) bridge of the nose
perenosit'sya (v.impf.) be carried away
perenoska (n.f.) porterage
perenosnyi (adj.) portable
perenumerovat' (v.pf.) number
perenyat' (v.pf.) take over
pereoborudovanie (n.n.) reequipment
pereobuchenie (n.n.) retraining
pereodetyi (adj.) disguised
pereodevanie (n.n.) disguise
pereosvidetel'stvovanie (n.n.)
  reexamination
pereotsenit' (v.pf.) overestimate
pereotsenivat' (v.impf.) overestimate

pereotsenka (n.f.) overestimation
perepachkat' (v.pf.) make dirty
perepechatat' (v.pf.) reprint
perepelka (n.f.) quail
perepilivat' (v.impf.) saw
perepis' (n.f.) census
perepisat' (v.pf.) copy
perepiska (n.f.) typing, correspondence
pereplavit' (v.pf.) smelt
pereplesti (v.pf.) bind
pereplet (n.m.) book cover
perepletat'(sya) (v.impf.) interweave
perepletchik (n.m.) bookbinder
perepodgotovit' (v.pf.) retrain
perepolnennyi (adj.) overcrowded
perepolokh (n.m.) alarm
perepolzat' (v.impf.) crawl over
pereponka (n.f.) membrane
pereprava (n.f.) crossing
pereprodat' (v.pf.) resell
pereproizvodstvo (n.n.) overproduction
pereprygnut' (v.pf.) jump over
perepugat' (v.pf.) frighten
pereputat' (v.pf.) entangle, confuse
pereput'e (n.n.) crossroads
pererabatyvat' (v.impf.) process
pererabotat' (v.pf.) process
pereraschet (n.m.) recalculation
pereraskhod (n.m.) overdraft
pereraspredelenie (n.n.) redistribution
pererastanie (n.n.) overgrowing
pereregistratsiya (n.f.) re-registration
perereshat' (v.impf.) change one's mind
pererezat' (v.impf.) cut
pererodit'sya (v.pf.) degenerate
pererozhdenie (n.n.) degeneration
pererubat' (v.impf.) cut
perervat' (v.pf.) break
pereryv (n.m.) interruption
peresadit' (v.pf.) transplant
peresadka (n.f.) transplantation, grafting
peresalivat' (v.impf.) oversalt
peresazhivat' (v.impf.) transplant
pereschitat' (v.pf.) count over again
pereschityvat' (v.impf.) count
peresech'(sya) (v.pf.) cross, intersect
peresechenie (n.n.) intersection
peresekat'(sya) (v.impf.) intersect

pereselenets (n.m.) settlor
peresest' (v.pf.) take another seat
pereshagnut' (v.pf.) step over
pereshchegolyat' (v.impf.) outdo
peresheek (n.m.) isthmus
peresheptyvat'sya (v.impf.) whisper
peresilivat' (v.impf.) overpower
pereskakivat' (v.impf.) jump over
pereskaz (n.m.) retelling
pereslat' (v.pf.) send
peresmatrivat' (v.impf.) reconsider
peresmotr (n.m.) revision
peresmotret' (v.pf.) reconsider
peresokhnut' (v.pf.) dry up
peresolit' (v.pf.) oversalt
perespelyi (adj.) overripe
peresporit' (v.pf.) out-argue
peresprashivat' (v.impf.) ask again
peressorit'sya (v.pf.) quarrel
perestarat'sya (v.pf.) overdo
perestat' (v.pf.) stop
perestavat' (v.impf.) stop
perestavit' (v.pf.) rearrange
perestradat' (v.pf.) have suffered
perestraivat'(sya) (v.impf.) reform
perestrelka (n.f.) skirmish
perestroika (n.f.) rebuilding
perestroit' (v.pf.) rebuild
perestupat' (v.impf.) cross
peresudy (n.pl.) idle gossip
peresykhat' (v.impf.) dry up
peresylat' (v.impf.) send
peresylka (n.f.) sending
peresyshchenie (n.n.) oversaturation
peretasovat' (v.pf.) reshuffle
peretashchit' (v.pf.) drag over
peretaskivat' (v.impf.) drag over
pereteret' (v.pf.) fray through
peretopit' (v.pf.) melt down
perets (n.m.) pepper
peretyagivat' (v.impf.) tip the scales
pereubedit' (v.pf.) dissuade
pereulok (n.m.) side street
pereustroistvo (n.n.) reorganization
pereutomlenie (n.n.) overstrain
pereval (n.m.) mountain pass
perevalit' (v.pf.) cross
perevalivat'sya (v.pf.) waddle

perevarit' (v.pf.) digest
perevarivat' (v.impf.) digest
perevarivat' (v.impf.) overdo
perevernut' (v.pf.) turn over
perevertyvat' (v.impf.) turn over
pereves (n.m.) preponderance
pereveshivat' (v.impf.) outweigh
perevesit' (v.pf.) outweigh
perevesti (v.pf.) transfer
perevestis' (v.pf.) be transferred
perevestis' (v.pf.) disappear
perevezti (v.pf.) transport
perevirat' (v.impf.) misinterpret
perevod (n.m.) translation
perevodchik (n.m.) translator
perevodit'sya (v.impf.) be transferred
perevodnoi (adj.) transfer
perevodnyi (adj.) in translation
perevooruzhat' (v.impf.) rearm
perevoplotit'sya (v.pf.) be reincarnated
perevorachivat'(sya) (v.impf.) turn over
perevorot (n.m.) revolution
perevospitanie (n.n.) reeducation
perevoz (n.m.) transport
perevozka (n.f.) transport
perevrat' (v.pf.) misinterpret
perevyaz' (n.f.) shoulder belt
perevyazat' (v.pf.) tie up, bandage
perevyazka (n.f.) bandaging
perevybornyi (adj.) electoral
perevybory (n.pl.) election
perevypolnenie (n.n.) overfulfillment
perevypolnit' (v.pf.) overfulfill
perezaryadit' (v.pf.) reload
perezharit' (v.pf.) overdo
perezhdat' (v.pf.) wait until something is over
perezhevyvat' (v.impf.) chew
perezhidat' (v.impf.) wait
perezhit' (v.pf.) experience
perezhitok (n.m.) survival
perezhivanie (n.n.) experience
perezimovat' (v.pf.) spend the winter
perezrelyi (adj.) overripe
pergament (n.m.) parchment
periferiya (n.f.) periphery, provinces
perigastrit (n.m.) perigastritis
perikardit (n.m.) pericarditis
perila (n.pl.) banisters

perimetr (n.m.) perimeter
perina (n.f.) feather bed
period (n.m.) period
periodicheskii (adj.) periodic
periodichnost' (n.f.) periodicity, frequency
periodika (n.f.) periodicals
periskop (n.m.) periscope
perkhot' (n.f.) dandruff
perlamutr (n.m.) mother-of-pearl
perlon (n.m.) perlon (synthetic fiber)
perlovyi (adj.) pearl barley
pernatyi (adj.) feathered
pero (n.n.) feather
perochinnyi nozh (adj.-n.m.) penknife
perpendikulyar (n.m.) perpendicular
perron (n.m.) platform
pers (n.m.) Persian
persik (n.m.) peach
persona (n.f.) person
personal (n.m.) personnel
personal'nyi (adj.) personal
personazh (n.m.) character
perspektiva (n.f.) perspective
persten' (n.m.) ring
pervenets (n.m.) firstborn
pervichnyi (adj.) primary
pervobytnyi (adj.) primitive
pervoistochnik (n.m.) primary source
pervoklassnyi (adj.) first-class
pervokursnik (n.m.) freshman
pervomaiskii (adj.) May Day
pervonachal'nyi (adj.) primary
pervosortnyi (adj.) of the best quality
pervostepennyi (adj.) paramount
pervyi (adj.) first
pes (n.m.) dog
p'esa (n.f.) play
peschanik (n.m.) sandstone
peschinka (n.f.) grain of sand
pesets (n.m.) polar fox
peshchera (n.f.) cave
peshekhod (n.m.) pedestrian
peshii (adj.) unmounted
peshka (n.f.) pawn
peshkom (adv.) on foot
pesn' (n.f.) song
pesochnyi (adj.) sand
pesok (n.m.) sand

pessimist (n.m.) pessimist
pestik (n.m.) pistil
pestrota (n.f.) diversity of colors
pestryi (adj.) variegated
pet' (v.impf.) sing
petlitsa (n.f.) buttonhole
petlya (n.f.) loop
petrografiya (n.f.) petrography
petrushka (n.m.) Punch
petrushka (n.f.) parsley
petukh (n.m.) cock
pevchii (adj.) singing
pevets (n.m.) singer
pianino (n.n.) piano
pichkat' (v.impf.) stuff
pidzhak (n.m.) coat
pika (n.f.) lance
pikantnyi (adj.) piquant
piket (n.m) picket
pikhta (n.f.) silver fir
piki (n.pl.) spades
pikirovat' (v.impf.) dive
pikirovat'sya (v.impf.) altercate
pikiruyushchii (adj.) diving
piknik (n.m.) picnic
pila (n.f.) saw
pilomaterial (n.m.) shaped timber
pilot (n.m.) pilot
pilyulya (n.f.) pill
pingvin (n.m.) penguin
pintset (n.m.) pincers
pion (n.m.) peony
pioner (n.m.) pioneer
pipetka (n.f.) dropper
pir (n.m.) feast
piramida (n.f.) pyramid
pirat (n.m.) pirate
pirog (n.m.) pie
pirovat' (v.impf.) feast
pirozhnoe (n.n.) fancy cake
pisaka (n.f.) scribbler
pisar' (n.m.) clerk
pisat' (v.impf.) write
pisatel' (n.m.) writer
pischaya bumaga (adj.-n.f.) writing paper
pischebumazhnyi (adj.) stationery
pishcha (n.f.) food
pishchat' (v.impf.) squeak

pishchevarenie (n.n.) digestion
pishchevod (n.m.) gullet
pishchevoi (adj.) food
pishushchaya mashinka (adj.-n.f.) typewriter
pisk (n.m.) squeak
pis'mennyi (adj.) writing, written
pis'mo (n.n.) letter
pis'monosets (n.m.) mailman
pistolet (n.m.) pistol
piston (n.m.) percussion cap
pit' (v.impf.) drink
pitanie (n.n.) nutrition
pitatel' (n.m.) feeder, feeding device
pit'e (n.n.) drink
pitomets (n.m.) pupil
pitomnik (n.m.) nursery
piton (n.m.) python
pivnaya (n.f.) tavern
pivo (n.n.) beer
piyavka (n.f.) leech
pizhama (n.f.) pajamas
plach (n.m.) weeping
plagiat (n.m.) plagiarism
plakat (n.m.) poster
plakat' (v.impf.) weep
plaksa (n.f.) crybaby
plamennyi (adj.) fiery
plamya (n.n.) flame
plan (n.m.) plan
planer (n.m.) glider
planeta (n.f.) planet
planirovanie (n.n.) planning
planirovanie (n.n.) gliding
planirovat' (v.impf.) plan
planirovat' (v.impf.) glide
planka (n.f.) plank
planomernyi (adj.) systematic
planovyi (adj.) planned
plantatsiya (n.f.) plantation
plashch (n.m.) raincoat
plashmya (adv.) prone
plast (n.m.) layer, stratum
plasticheskii (adj.) plastic
plastinka (n.f.) plate, record
plastmassa (n.f.) plastic
plastyr' (n.m.) plaster
plata (n.f.) payment
plat'e (n.n.) dress

platel'shchik (n.m.)　payer
platezh (n.m.)　payment
platezhesposobnyi (adj.)　solvent
platforma (n.f.)　platform
platina (n.f.)　platinum
platit' (v.impf.)　pay
platnyi (adj.)　paid
plato (n.n.)　plateau
platok (n.m.)　shawl, handkerchief
platsdarm (n.m.)　bridgehead
platsenta (n.f.)　placenta
platskarta (n.f.)　reserved seat ticket
plavanie (n.n.)　swimming
plavat' (v.impf.)　swim
plavil'nyi (adj.)　smelting
plavit' (v.impf.)　smelt
plavkii (adj.)　fusible
plavki (n.pl.)　trunks
plavnik (n.m.)　fin
plavnyi (adj.)　smooth
plavuchii (adj.)　floating
plazma (n.f.)　plasma
plebistsit (n.m.)　plebiscite
plecho (n.n.)　shoulder
pled (n.m.)　rug
plemennoi (adj.)　pedigree
plemya (n.n.)　tribe
plemyannik (n.m.)　nephew
plen (n.m.)　captivity
plenarnyi (adj.)　plenary
plenitel'nyi (adj.)　fascinating
plenka (n.f.)　film
plennik (n.m.)　prisoner
plenum (n.m.)　plenum
plenyat'sya (v.impf.)　be fascinated
plesen' (n.f.)　mold
plesh' (n.f.)　bald patch
pleshivyi (adj.)　bald
plesk (n.m.)　splash
plesnevet' (v.impf.)　grow moldy
plesti (v.impf.)　plait
plestis' (v.pf.)　drag oneself
plet' (n.f.)　lash
pleten' (n.m.)　fence
pletenyi (adj.)　wicker
plevatel'nitsa (n.f.)　spittoon
plevok (n.m.)　spittle
plevrit (n.m.)　pleurisy

plita (n.f.)　plate, stove
plitka (n.f.)　plate, stove, tile
plod (n.m.)　fruit, fetus
plodit'sya (v.impf.)　propagate
plodorodie (n.n.)　fertility
plodotvornyi (adj.)　fruitful
plodovityi (adj.)　prolific
plodovodstvo (n.n.)　fruit growing
plokhoi (adj.)　bad, poor
plomba (n.f.)　filling
ploshchad' (n.f.)　area
ploshchadka (n.f.)　ground
ploskii (adj.)　flat
ploskogor'e (n.n.)　plateau
ploskogubtsy (n.pl.)　pliers
ploskost' (n.f.)　plane
plot' (n.f.)　flesh
plot (n.m.)　raft
plotina (n.f.)　dam
plotnik (n.m.)　carpenter
plotnost' (n.f.)　density
plotoyadnyi (adj.)　carnivorous
plovets (n.m.)　swimmer
plug (n.m.)　plow
plut (n.m.)　cheat
plutat' (v.impf.)　stray
plutovat' (v.impf.)　cheat
plyasat' (v.impf.)　dance
plyaska (n.f.)　dance
plyazh (n.m.)　beach
plyt' (v.impf.)　swim
plyunut' (v.pf.)　spit
plyus (n.m.)　plus
plyush (n.m.)　plush
plyushch (n.m.)　ivy
pnevmaticheskii (adj.)　pneumatic
pnevmoniya (n.f.)　pneumonia
po-bratski (adv.)　fraternally
po-delovomu (adv.)　in a businesslike manner
po-druzheski (adv.)　in a friendly way
po-moemu (adv.)　in my opinion
po-nashemu (adv.)　in our opinion
po-nastoyashchemu (adv.)　properly
po-novomu (adv.)　in a new fashion
po-prezhnemu (adv.)　as usual
po-russki (adv.)　in Russian
po-staromu (adv.)　as before
po-svoemu (adv.)　in one's own way

po-tovarishcheski (adv.) as a comrade
po-tvoemu (adv.) in your opinion
po-vashemu (adv.) in your opinion
po-vidimomu (adv.) obviously
pobaivat'sya (v.impf.) be afraid
pobeda (n.f.) victory
pobedonosnyi (adj.) victorious
pobeg (n.m.) flight
pobeg (n.m.) sprout
pobelet' (v.pf.) turn pale
pobelit' (v.pf.) whitewash
poberezh'e (n.n.) seacoast
pobezhat' (n.pf.) run
pobezhdat' (v.impf.) win
pobirat'sya (v.impf.) beg
pobit' (v.pf.) beat
poblagodarit' (v.pf.) thank
poblazhka (n.f.) indulgence
poblednet' (v.pf.) grow pale
pobleknut' (v.pf.) wither
poblizosti (adv.) hereabout(s)
pobochnyi (adj.) side, secondary
poboi (n.pl.) beating
pobornik (n.m.) champion
poborot' (v.pf.) overcome
pobrit'(sya) (v.pf.) shave oneself
pobudit' (v.pf.) impel
pobuditel' (n.m.) stimulus
pobyvat' (v.pf.) be, visit
pobyvka (n.f.) leave
pochechnyi (adv.) renal, nephric
pochem (adv.) how much
pochemu (adv.) why
pochemu-libo (adv.) for some reason or other
pocherk (n.m.) handwriting
pochernet' (v.pf.) turn black
pocherpnut' (v.pf.) derive
pochesat'(sya) (v.pf.) scratch
pochest' (n.f.) honor
pochet (n.m.) honor
pochin (n.m.) initiative
pochinit' (v.pf.) repair
pochinka (n.f.) repair
pochit' (v.pf.) rest
pochitanie (n.n.) respect
pochitat' (v.impf.) honor
pochitat' (v.pf.) read
pochka (n.f.) bud

pochka (n.f.) kidney
pochta (n.f.) mail
pochtenie (n.n.) respect
pochti (adv.) nearly
pochtit' (v.pf.) honor
pochtitel'nyi (adj.) respectful
pochtovyi (adj.) postal, mail
pochudit'sya (v.pf.) seem
pochuvstvovat' (v.pf.) feel
pochva (n.f.) soil
pod (prep.) under
podacha (n.f.) presenting
podachka (n.f.) sop
podagra (n.f.) gout
podarit' (v.pf.) give as a present
podarok (n.m.) present, gift
podat' (v.pf.) give
podat' (n.f.) tax
podatel' (n.m.) applicant
podatlivyi (adj.) pliant
podat'sya (v.pf.) move
podaval'shchitsa (n.f.) waitress
podavat' (v.impf.) give, serve
podavit' (v.pf.) suppress
podavit'sya (v.pf.) choke
podavlenie (n.n.) suppression
podavlennost' (n.f.) depression
podavlyat' (v.impf.) suppress
podavno (adv.) so much the more
podbadrivat' (v.impf.) encourage
podbegat' (v.impf.) run up
podbirat' (v.impf.) pick up
podbirat'sya (v.impf.) steal up to
podbit' (v.pf.) line
podbivat' (v.impf.) line
podbochenivat'sya (v.impf.) place one's
  arms akimbo
podbodrit' (v.pf.) encourage
podbor (n.m.) selection
podborodok (n.m.) chin
podbrasyvat' (v.impf.) throw up
podchas (adv.) now and again
podcherkivat' (v.impf.) emphasize
podchinenie (n.n.) subordination
poddakivat' (v.impf.) echo
poddannyi (adj.) subject
poddat'sya (v.pf.) give in
poddavat'sya (v.impf.) give in

poddelat' (v.pf.)   counterfeit
podderzhat' (v.pf)   support
podderzhivat' (v.impf.)   keep up
poddraznivat' (v.impf.)   tease
podduvalo (n.n.)   ash pit
podeistvovat' (v.pf.)   have an effect
pod"ekhat' (v.pf.)   drive up
podelat' (v.pf.)   do
podelit' (v.pf.)   share
podelka (n.f.)   handmade article
pod"em (n.m.)   ascent
pod"emnyi kran (adj.-n.m.)   crane
podergivat'sya (v.impf.)   twitch
podernut'sya (v.pf.)   be covered with a thin
film of
poderzhannyi (adj.)   secondhand, used
podeshevet' (v.pf.)   become cheaper
pod"ezd (n.m.)   porch
pod"ezzhat' (v.pf.)   drive up
podgibat' (v.impf.)   bend
podglyadet' (v.pf.)   peep
podgonka (n.f.)   matching, adjustment, fitting
podgonyat' (v.impf.)   urge on
podgorat' (v.impf.)   get burned
podgotovitel'nyi (adj.)   preparatory
podkapyvat'(sya) (v.impf.)   dig under
podkaraulivat' (v.impf.)   lie in wait
podkarmlivat' (v.impf.)   feed
podkashivat'sya (v.impf.)   give way
podkatit' (v.pf.)   roll
podkhalim (n.m.)   bootlicker
podkhod (n.m.)   approach
podkhodyashchii (adj.)   suitable
podkhvatit' (v.pf.)   take
podkidyvat' (v.impf.)   throw up
podkladka (n.f.)   lining
podkladyvat' (v.impf.)   put under
podkleivat' (v.impf.)   paste
podkop (n.m.)   underground passage
podkorka (n.f.)   subcortex
podkormit' (v.pf.)   feed
podkosit'sya (v.pf.)   give way
podkova (n.f.)   horseshoe
podkozhnyi (adj.)   hypodermic
podkradyvat'sya (v.impf.)   steal up to
podkrashivat'(sya) (v.impf.)   put on makeup
podkrast'sya (v.pf.)   steal up to
podkrepit' (v.pf.)   strengthen

podkup (n.m.)   bribery
podkupat' (v.impf.)   bribe
podlamyvat'sya (v.impf.)   break
podlazhivat'sya (v.impf.)   make up to
podle (adv.)   near
podlets (n.m.)   villain
podlezhashchee (n.n.)   subject
podlezhat' (v.impf.)   be subject to
podlinnik (n.m.)   original
podlit' (v.pf.)   pour
podlivat' (v.impf.)   pour
podlivka (n.f.)   sauce
podliza (n.f.)   toady
podlog (n.m.)   forgery
podlomit'sya (v.pf.)   break
podlost' (n.f.)   meanness
podlozhit' (v.pf.)   put under
podlozhnyi (adj.)   false
podmaster'e (n.m.)   apprentice
podmazat' (v.pf.)   grease
podmechat' (v.impf.)   notice
podmena (n.f.)   substitution
podmeshat' (v.pf.)   mix in
podmetat' (v.impf.)   sweep
podmetit' (v.pf.)   notice
podmetka (n.f.)   sole
podmigivat' (v.impf.)   wink
podmochennyi (adj.)   wet
podmoga (n.f.)   help
podmokat' (v.impf.)   get wet
podmorazhivat' (v.impf.)   freeze
podmostki (n.pl.)   scaffolding
podmyshka (n.f.)   armpit
podmyvat' (v.impf.)   wash
podnesti (v.pf.)   bring
podnevol'nyi (adj.)   dependent
podnimat' (v.impf.)   lift
podnos (n.m.)   tray
podnoshenie (n.n.)   presentation
podnosit' (v.impf.)   bring
podnovit' (v.pf.)   renovate
podnozhie (n.n.)   foot
podnozhka (n.f.)   step
podnozhnyi korm (adj.-n.m.)   pasture
podnyat' (v.pf.)   lift
podobat' (v.impf.)   become
podobie (n.n.)   similarity
podobostrastie (n.n.)   servility

podobrat' (v.pf.) pick up
podobrat'sya (v.pf.) steal up (to)
pododeyal'nik (n.m.) quilt cover
pododvigat' (v.impf.) push up
podognat' (v.pf.) urge on
podognut' (v.pf.) bend
podogrevat' (v.impf.) warm up
podogrevatel' (n.m.) heater
podoinik (n.m.) milk pail
podoiti (v.pf.) approach
podokhnut' (v.pf.) die
podokhodnyi (adj.) income
podokonnik (n.m.) windowsill
podol (n.m.) hem
podolgu (adv.) for hours
podonki (n.pl.) dregs
podopleka (n.f.) hidden motive
podorozhat' (v.pf.) become more expensive
podorozhnik (n.m.) plantain
podorvat' (v.pf.) blow up
podoshva (n.f.) sole
podoslat' (v.pf.) send for a purpose
podospet' (v.pf.) come in time
podostlat' (v.pf.) spread under
podotchetnyi (adj.) accountable
podotdel (n.m.) section
podozhdat' (v.pf.) wait
podozrevat' (v.impf.) suspect
podozvat' (v.pf.) call up
podpadat' (v.impf.) fall under
podpaivat' (v.impf.) make drunk
podpast' (v.pf.) fall under
podperet' (v.pf.) prop up
podpevala (n.m.&f.) yes-man
podpilivat' (v.impf.) saw, file
podpirat' (v.impf.) prop up
podpis' (n.f.) signature
podpisat' (v.pf.) sign
podpiska (n.f.) subscription
podpisyvat'sya (v.impf.) subscribe
podpoit' (v.pf.) make drunk
podpol'e (n.n.) the underground
podpolkovnik (n.m.) lieutenant colonel
podporka (n.f.) prop
podprygivat' (v.impf.) jump up
podpuskat' (v.impf.) allow to approach
podrastat' (v.impf.) grow up
podrasti (v.pf.) grow up

podrat'sya (v.pf.) come to blows
podrazdelenie (n.n.) subdivision
podrazhanie (n.n.) imitation
podrazumevat' (v.impf.) imply
podrezat' (v.impf.) cut
podrobnyi (adj.) detailed
podrostok (n.m.) teenager
podrovnyat' (v.pf.) trim
podrubat' (v.impf.) hem
podruchnyi (n.m.) apprentice
podruga (n.f.) friend
podruzhit'sya (v.pf.) make friends
podryad (adv.) one after another
podryad (n.m.) contract
podryt' (v.pf.) dig
podryv (n.m.) undermining
podryvat' (v.impf.) dig
podryvat' (v.impf.) blow up
podryvnoi (adj.) sapping
podsazhivat'sya (v.impf.) sit down
podsest' (v.pf.) sit down
podshefnyi (adj.) under the patronage
podshipnik (n.m.) bearing
podshit' (v.pf.) hem
podshivat' (v.impf.) hem
podskakivat' (v.impf.) jump up
podskazat' (v.pf.) prompt
podslepovatyi (adj.) weak sighted
podslushat' (v.pf.) overhear
podsmatrivat' (v.impf.) spy
podsmeivat'sya (v.impf.) make fun of
podsmotret' (v.pf.) spy
podsnezhnik (n.m.) snowdrop
podsobnyi (adj.) subsidiary
podsoedinenie (n.n.) connection, junction
podsolnechnik (n.m.) sunflower
podsovyvat' (v.impf.) put under
podsoznatel'nyi (adj.) subconscious
podspor'e (n.n.) help
podstakannik (n.m.) glass holder
podstantsiya (n.f.) substation
podstavit' (v.pf.) place under
podstavnoi (adj.) false
podsteregat' (v.impf.) lie in wait
podstilat' (v.impf.) spread under
podstraivat' (v.impf.) arrange
podstrekat' (v.impf.) instigate
podstrelit' (v.pf.) wound

podstrich' (v.pf.) cut
podstrigat'sya (v.impf.) have one's hair cut
podstrochnyi (adj.) word-for-word
podstroit' (v.pf.) arrange
podstup (n.m.) approach
podsudimyi (adj.) the accused
podsudnyi (adj.) under the jurisdiction of
podsunut' (v.pf.) put under
podsvechnik (n.m.) candlestick
podsykhat' (v.impf.) dry
podsylat' (v.impf.) send for a purpose
podtachivat' (v.impf.) sharpen
podtalkivat' (v.impf.) give a shove
podtasovat' (v.pf.) garble
podtochit' (v.pf.) sharpen
podtolknut' (v.pf.) give a shove
podtrunivat' (v.impf.) tease
podtsepit' (v.pf.) hook
podtverdit' (v.pf.) confirm
podtyagivat'sya (v.impf.) catch up
podtyanut' (v.pf.) pull up
podtyazhki (n.pl.) suspenders
poduchit' (v.pf.) learn
podumat' (v.pf.) think
podushka (n.f.) pillow
podval (n.m.) basement
podvergat'sya (v.impf.) undergo
podvergnut' (v.pf.) subject
podveshivat' (v.impf.) hang up
podvesit' (v.pf.) hang up
podvesti (v.pf.) bring up
podvezti (v.pf.) give a ride
podvig (n.m.) exploit
podvigat'(sya) (v.impf.) move
podvinut' (v.pf.) move
podvizat'sya (v.impf.) pursue an occupation
podvizhnoi (adj.) mobile
podvizhnost' (n.f.) agility
podvizhnyi (adj.) active
podvlastnyi (adj.) dependent on
podvoda (n.f.) cart
podvodit' (v.pf.) bring up
podvodnik (n.m.) submariner
podvodnyi (adj.) submarine
podvokh (n.m.) trick
podvorotnya (n.f.) gateway
podvoz (n.m.) transport
podvyazat' (v.pf.) tie up

podvyazka (n.f.) suspender
podvyazyvat' (v.impf.) tie up
podvypivshii (adj.) tipsy
podymat'sya (v.impf.) rise
podyshat' (v.pf.) breathe
podyskat' (v.pf.) find
podyskivat' (v.impf.) look for
podytozhivat' (v.impf.) sum up
podzadorit' (v.pf.) egg on
podzagolovok (n.m.) subtitle
podzashchitnyi (adj.) client
podzemel'e (n.n.) cave
podzemnyi (adj.) underground
podzharivat'(sya) (v.impf.) roast
podzhat' (v.pf.) draw in
podzhech' (v.pf.) set on fire
podzheludochnyi (adj.) pancreatic
podzhidat' (v.impf.) wait
podzhigat' (v.impf.) set on fire
podzhigatel' (n.m.) arsonist
podzhimat' (v.impf.) draw in
podzhog (n.m.) arson
podzornaya truba (adj.-n.f.) spyglass
podzyvat' (v.impf.) call
poedinok (n.m.) duel
poekhat' (v.pf.) go
poéma (n.f.) poem
poest' (v.pf.) eat
poét (n.m.) poet
poétomu (adv.) therefore
poezd (n.m.) train
poezdka (n.f.) journey
poéziya (n.f.) poetry
pogashat' (v.impf.) extinguish
pogasit' (v.pf.) extinguish
pogasnut' (v.pf.) go out
pogibat' (v.impf.) perish
pogibshii (adj.) killed
pogladit' (v.pf.) caress
pogloshchenie (n.n.) absorption
poglotit' (v.pf.) absorb
poglyadyvat' (v.impf.) look
pognat' (v.pf.) drive
pognat'sya (v.pf.) run after
pogoda (n.f.) weather
pogolov'e (n.n.) number of livestock
pogolovno (adv.) all without exception
pogon (n.m.) shoulder strap

pogonshchik (n.m.) driver
pogonya (n.f.) pursuit
pogovorka (n.f.) saying
pogranichnik (n.m.) frontier guard
pogreb (n.m.) cold cellar
pogrebal'nyi (adj.) funeral
pogremushka (n.f.) rattle
pogreshnost' (n.f.) error
pogret'(sya) (v.pf.) warm up
pogruzhat' (v.impf.) load
pogruzit' (v.pf.) load
pogruzit' (v.pf.) immerse
pogruzka (n.f.) loading
pogryazat' (v.impf.) be stuck in
pogubit' (v.pf.) ruin
pogulyat' (v.pf.) take a walk
poilo (n.n.) swill
poimat' (v.pf.) catch
poimenno (adv.) by name
poisk (n.m.) search
poistine (adv.) indeed
poit' (v.impf.) give to drink
poiti (v.pf.) go
poka (adv.) while
pokachat' (v.pf.) rock
pokachivat' (v.impf.) rock
pokachnut' (v.pf.) shake
pokatyi (adj.) sloping
pokayanie (n.n.) confession
pokayat'sya (v.pf.) confess
pokaz (n.m.) show
pokazanie (n.n.) deposition
pokazat' (v.pf.) show
pokazat'sya (v.pf.) show oneself
pokazatel' (n.m.) index, coefficient, factor
pokaznoi (adj.) for show
pokazyvat' (v.impf.) show
pokhitit' (v.pf.) steal
pokhlebka (n.f.) soup
pokhlopat' (v.pf.) pat
pokhmel'e (n.n.) hangover
pokhod (n.m.) campaign
pokhodit' (v.impf.) resemble
pokhodka (n.f.) gait
pokhodnyi (adj.) mobile
pokhoronit' (v.pf.) bury
pokhorony (n.pl.) funeral
pokhot' (n.f.) lust

pokhozhdenie (n.n.) adventure
pokhozhii (adj.) similar
pokhudet' (v.pf.) lose weight
pokhvala (n.f.) praise
pokhval'nyi (adj.) praiseworthy
pokhvastat'(sya) (v.pf.) boast
pokidat' (v.impf.) abandon
pokladistyi (adj.) compliant
poklazha (n.f.) load
poklep (n.m.) slander
poklon (n.m.) bow
poklonenie (n.n.) worship
poklonit'sya (n.pf.) bow
poklonnik (n.m.) admirer
poklonyat'sya (v.impf.) worship
poklyast'sya (v.pf.) swear
pokoi (n.m.) rest
pokoi (n.m.) room
pokoinik (n.m.) the deceased
pokoinyi (adj.) calm
pokoinyi (adj.) the deceased
pokoit'sya (v.impf.) lie
pokolebat' (v.pf.) shake
pokolenie (n.n.) generation
pokolotit' (v.pf.) give a thrashing
pokonchit' (v.pf.) finish
pokorenie (n.n.) conquest
pokorit'sya (v.impf.) submit
pokornost' (n.f.) submission
pokorobit'(sya) (v.pf.) warp
pokos (n.m.) mowing
pokosit'sya (v.impf.) look askance
pokrasit' (v.pf.) paint
pokrasnet' (v.pf.) blush
pokrazha (n.f.) theft
pokrikivat' (v.impf.) shout
pokroi (n.m.) cut
pokrov (n.m.) cover, coating
pokrovitel' (n.m.) patron
pokryshka (n.f.) cover
pokrytie (n.n.) covering
pokryvalo (n.n.) counterpane
pokupat' (v.impf.) buy
pokupatel' (n.m.) buyer
pokupka (n.f.) purchase
pokushat'sya (v.impf.) attempt
pol (n.m.) floor
pol (n.m.) sex

pola (n.f.) flap of a coat
poladit' (v.pf.) come to an understanding
polagat' (v.impf.) think
polchasa (n.m.) half hour
polchishche (n.n.) horde
polden' (n.m.) noon
pole (n.n.) field
polemika (n.f.) controversy
polemizirovat' (v.impf.) argue with
poleno (n.n.) log
poles'e (n.n.) woodlands
polet (n.m.) flight
poletet' (v.pf.) fly
poleznyi (adj.) useful
polgoda (n.m.) half year
poliartrit (n.m.) polyarthritis
poligon (n.m.) firing range
poligrafiya (n.f.) polygraphy
poliklinika (n.f.) polyclinic
polimer (n.m.) polymer
polinyalyi (adj.) faded
polinyat' (v.pf.) fade
polirovat' (v.impf.) polish
polit' (v.pf.) pour
politekhnicheskii (adj.) polytechnic
politicheskii (adj.) political
politika (n.f.) politics
politkruzhok (n.m.) political study group
politrabotnik (n.m.) political worker
politseiskii (n.m.) policeman
politsiya (n.f.) police
polivat' (v.impf.) pour, water
polivka (n.f.) watering
polk (n.m.) regiment
polka (n.f.) shelf
polka (n.f.) weeding
pol'ka (n.f.) Pole
pol'ka (n.f.) polka
polkovnik (n.m.) colonel
polkovodets (n.m.) military leader
polkovoi (adj.) regimental
polnet' (v.impf.) put on weight
polno (adv.) enough
polno (adv.) plenty, full
polnoch' (n.f.) midnight
polnokrovnyi (adj.) full-blooded
polnolunie (n.n.) full moon
polnomochie (n.n.) power

polnopravnyi (adj.) enjoying full rights
polnost'yu (adv.) completely
polnota (n.f.) completeness
polnotsennyi (adj.) of full value
polnovlastnyi (adj.) sovereign
polnyi (adj.) full
polnym-polno (adv.) chock-full
polog (n.m.) curtains
pologii (adj.) sloping
polomka (n.f.) breakdown
polosa (n.f.) strip
polosatyi (adj.) strip
poloskanie (n.n.) rinsing
polost' (n.f.) cavity
polot' (v.impf.) weed
polotentse (n.n.) towel
poloter (n.m.) floor polisher
polotnishche (n.n.) width
polotno (n.n.) linen
polovik (n.m.) mat
polovina (n.f.) half
polovod'e (n.n.) spring flood
polovoi (adj.) floor
polovoi (adj.) sexual
polozhenie (n.n.) position
polozhim ((col.)) assuming that
polozhit' (v.pf.) place
polozhitel'nyi (adj.) positive
poloz'ya (n.pl.) runners
pol'skii (adj.) Polish
pol'stit' (v.pf.) flatter
poltora (num.) one and a half
poltseny ((col)) half price
polubotinki (n.pl.) walking shoes
poluchat' (v.impf.) receive
poluchit' (v.pf.) receive
poluchka (n.f.) pay
poludennyi (adj.) midday
polufabrikat (n.m.) half-finished product
polugodie (n.n.) half-year
polugodovalyi (adj.) six-month-old
polugolyi (adj.) half naked
polugramotnyi (adj.) semiliterate
polukrug (n.m.) semicircle
polumera (n.f.) half measure
polumertvyi (adj.) half dead
polumesyats (n.m.) half-moon
polumrak (n.m.) semidarkness

poluoborot (n.m.) half turn
poluostrov (n.m.) peninsula
poluotkrytyi (adj.) half open
poluprovodnik (n.m.) semiconductor
polusharie (n.n.) hemisphere
polushubok (n.m.) half-length coat
polusonnyi (adj.) half asleep
polustanok (n.m.) flag stop (for a train)
polut'ma (n.f.) semidarkness
polyak (n.m.) Pole
polyana (n.f.) clearing
polyarizatsiya (n.f.) polarization
polyarnost' (n.f.) polarity
polyarnyi (adj.) arctic
polyn' (n.f.) wormwood
polyubit' (v.pf.) fall in love
polyubovnyi (adj.) amicable
polyus (n.m.) pole
pol'za (n.f.) use
polzat' (v.impf.) crawl
polzkom (adv.) crawling
pol'zovanie (n.n.) use
pol'zovat'sya (v.impf.) make use of
pomada (n.f.) pomade
pomakhat' (v.pf.) wave
pomakhivat' (v.impf.) swing
pomalen'ku (adv.) little by little
pomalkivat' (v.impf.) hold one's tongue
pomarka (n.f.) blot
pomazok (n.m.) brush
pomchat'sya (v.pf.) dart off
pomechat' (v.impf.) mark
pomekha (n.f.) obstacle
pomenyat'(sya) (v.pf.) change, exchange
pomerit' (v.pf.) measure
pomerit'sya (v.pf.) measure, compare
pomerknut' (v.pf.) grow dim
pomes' (n.f.) hybrid
pomeshannyi (adj.) crazy
pomeshat' (v.pf.) stir
pomeshat' (v.pf.) prevent
pomeshat'sya (v.pf.) go mad
pomeshchat' (v.impf.) place
pomeshchik (n.m.) landlord
pomeshivat' (v.impf.) stir
pomest'e (n.n.) estate
pomestit' (v.pf.) place
pomestitel'nyi (adj.) spacious

pomesyachnyi (adj.) monthly
pomet (n.m.) dung
pomet (n.m.) litter
pometit' (v.pf.) mark
pomidor (n.m.) tomato
pomilovanie (n.n.) pardon
pomimo (prep.) beside
pominat' (v.impf.) mention
pominutno (adv.) every minute
pomirit' (v.pf.) reconcile
pomnit' (v.impf.) remember
pomnozhit' (v.pf.) multiply
pomoch' (v.pf.) help
pomogat' (v.impf.) help
pomoi (n.pl.) slops
pomoinyi (adj.) garbage
pomol (n.m.) grinding
pomolodet' (v.pf.) look younger
pomolvka (n.f.) engagement
pomoshch' (n.f.) help
pomoshchnik (n.m.) helper
pomost (n.m.) platform
pompa (n.f.) pump
pompa (n.f.) pomp
pomutnenie (n.n.) clouding
pomyanut' (v.pf.) mention
pomyatyi (adj.) crumpled
pomykat' (v.impf.) order about
pomysel (n.m.) thought
ponadeyat'sya (v.pf.) hope
ponadobit'sya (v.pf.) become necessary
ponaprasnu (adv.) in vain
ponaslyshke (adv.) by hearsay
ponedel'nik (n.m.) Monday
ponemnogu (adv.) little by little
ponesti (v.pf.) carry
ponevole (adv.) against one's will
ponikat' (v.impf.) droop
ponimanie (n.n.) understanding
ponizhat'(sya) (v.impf.) lower
ponizhenie (n.n.) drop
ponizit' (v.pf) lower
ponos (n.m.) diarrhea
ponoshennyi (adj.) shabby
ponosit' (v.pf.) carry, wear
ponosit' (v.impf.) abuse
ponravit'sya (v.pf.) like
pontonnyi (adj.) pontoon

ponudit' (v.pf.) compel
ponukat' (v.impf.) urge on
ponurit' (v.pf.) hang
ponyat' (v.pf.) understand
ponyatie (n.n.) notion
ponyukhat' (v.pf.) smell
poobedat' (v.pf.) have dinner
poobeshchat' (v.pf.) promise
poocheredno (adv.) in turn
poodal' (adv.) further off
poodinochke (adv.) one at a time
pooshchrenie (n.n.) encouragement
popadanie (n.n.) scoring a hit
poparno (adv.) in pairs
popast' (v.pf.) get, hit
popechenie (n.n.) care
poperechnik (n.m.) diameter
poperek (adv.) across
poperemenno (adv.) in turn
popirat' (v.impf.) trample
poplakat' (v.pf.) shed tears
poplatit'sya (v.pf.) pay
poplavok (n.m.) float
popoika (n.f.) drinking bout
popolam (adv.) in half
popolnenie (n.n.) reinforcement
popolnit' (v.pf.) replenish
popoludni (adv.) in the afternoon
popolunochi (adv.) after midnight
popolznovenie (n.n.) feeble effort
popona (n.f.) horse blanket
poprat' (v.pf.) trample
popravit' (v.pf.) repair
popravka (n.f.) correction, adjustment
poprekat' (v.impf.) reproach
popreki (n.pl.) nagging
popreknut' (v.pf.) reproach
poprishche (n.n.) field
poprobovat' (v.pf.) try
poproshaika (n.m.&f.) beggar
poprosit' (v.pf.) ask
poprostu (adv.) simply
popugai (n.m.) parrot
populyarnyi (adj.) popular
popustitel'stvo (n.n.) connivance
popustu (adv.) in vain
poputno (adv.) in passing
popyatnyi (adj.) backward

popytat' (v.pf.) try
popytka (n.f.) attempt
pora (n.f.) pore
pora (n.f.) time
porabotit' (v.pf.) enslave
poradovat'sya (v.pf.) be pleased
poranit' (v.pf.) wound
poran'she (adv.) earlier
poravnyat'sya (v.pf.) draw level
porazhat'sya (v.impf.) be surprised
porazhenie (n.n.) defeat
porazit' (v.pf.) strike, hit
porcha (n.f.) damage
porez (n.m.) cut
poristyi (adj.) porous
poritsanie (n.n.) reproach
porkhat' (v.impf.) flutter
porochnyi (adj.) vicious
poroda (n.f.) breed
poroda (n.f.) rock
porodistyi (adj.) pedigree
porodit' (v.pf.) give birth
porodnit'sya (v.pf.) become related
porog (n.m.) threshhold
poroi (adv.) now and then
porok (n.m.) vice
porokh (n.m.) gunpowder
porosenok (n.m.) suckling pig
poroshok (n.m.) powder
porosl' (n.f.) young growth
porot' (v.impf.) whip
porot' (v.impf.) undo
porovnu (adv.) equally
porozhdat' (v.impf.) give birth
porozhnii (adv.) empty
porozhnyak (n.m.) empty stock
porozn' (adv.) separately
porshen' (n.m.) piston
port (n.m.) port
portativnyi (adj.) portable
port'era (n.f.) drapery
portfel' (n.m.) briefcase
portit' (v.impf.) spoil
portnoi (n.m.) tailor
portovyi (adj.) port
portret (n.m.) portrait
portsigar (n.m.) cigarette case
portsiya (n.f.) portion

portugalets (n.m.) Portuguese
portvein (n.m.) port
portyanka (n.f.) foot binding
poruchat' (v.impf.) entrust
poruchit'sya (v.pf.) vouch
porugannyi (adj.) desecrated
porugat'sya (v.pf.) quarrel
poruka (n.f.) bail
porvat' (v.pf.) tear, break
poryadkovyi (adj.) ordinal
poryadochnyi (adj.) honest
poryadok (n.m.) order
poryv (n.m.) gust
poryvat' (v.impf.) tear, break
poryvat'sya (v.impf.) try
poryvistyi (adj.) gusty
posadit' (v.pf.) plant
posadka (n.f.) planting, embarkation
posadochnyi (adj.) landing
poschastlivit'sya (v.pf.) be lucky
poschitat' (v.pf.) count
posedet' (v.pf.) become gray
poselenets (n.m.) settlor
poselit' (v.pf.) settle
poselok (n.m.) settlement
poselyat'(sya) (v.impf.) settle
poseshchaemost' (n.f.) attendance
posetitel' (n.m.) visitor
posev (n.m.) sowing
poseyat' (v.pf.) sow
poshatnut' (v.pf.) shake
poshchada (n.f.) mercy
poshchechina (n.f.) slap in the face
poshchupat' (v.pf.) feel
poshivka (n.f.) sewing
poshlina (n.f.) duty
poshlost' (n.f.) platitude
poshtuchnyi (adj.) by the piece
posil'nyi (adj.) within one's powers
posinet' (v.pf.) turn blue
poskol'ku (conj.) since
poskol'znut'sya (v.pf.) slip
poslanets (n.m.) messenger
poslanie (n.n.) message
poslannik (n.m.) envoy
poslat' (v.pf.) send
posle (adv.) afterward
poslednii (adj.) last

posledovat' (v.pf.) follow
posledovatel' (n.m.) follower
posledovatel'no (adv.) in series
posledstvie (n.n.) consequence
posleduyushchii (adj.) following
posleobedennyi (adj.) after dinner
posleslovie (n.n.) epilogue
poslevoennyi (adj.) postwar
poslezavtra (adv.) day after tomorrow
poslovitsa (n.f.) proverb
poslushanie (n.n.) obedience
poslushat'(sya) (v.pf.) obey
poslushnyi (adj.) obedient
posluzhit' (v.pf.) serve
posluzhnoi (adj.) service
poslyshat'sya (v.pf.) be heard
posmatrivat' (v.impf.) glance
posmeivat'sya (v.impf.) chuckle
posmertnyi (adj.) posthumous
posmeshishche (n.n.) laughingstock
posmet' (v.pf.) dare
posmeyat'sya (v.pf.) laugh
posmotret' (v.pf.) look
posobie (n.n.) benefit
posobnik (n.m.) accomplice
posol (n.m.) ambassador
posolit' (v.pf.) salt
posol'stvo (n.n.) embassy
pospat' (v.pf.) get some sleep
pospeshit' (v.pf.) hurry
pospeshnyi (adj.) prompt
pospet' (v.pf.) be in time
pospet' (v.pf.) ripen
pospevat' (v.impf.) be in time
pospevat' (v.impf.) ripen
posredi (adv.) in the midst
posredine (adv.) in the middle
posrednik (n.m.) mediator
posredstvennyi (adj.) mediocre
posredstvom (adv.) by means of
possorit'(sya) (v.pf.) quarrel
post (n.m.) post, position
postanovit' (v.pf.) decree
postanovka (n.f.) organization
postanovlenie (n.n.) resolution
postarat'sya (v.pf.) try
postaret' (v.pf.) grow old
postavit' (v.pf.) put

postavka (n.f.) delivery
postel' (n.f.) bed
postepenno (adv.) gradually
postich' (v.pf.) comprehend
postigat' (v.impf.) comprehend
postilat' (v.impf.) spread
postlat' (v.pf.) spread
postnyi (adj.) Lenten
postoi (n.m.) billeting
postol'ku (conj.) insofar as
postoronit'sya (v.pf.) step aside
postoronnii (adj.) strange
postoyannyi (adj.) constant
postoyanstvo (n.n.) constancy
postoyat' (v.pf.) stand up
postradat' (v.pf.) suffer
postradavshii (adj.) victim
postroenie (n.n.) construction
postromka (n.f.) trace
postuchat'(sya) (v.pf.) knock
postulat (n.m.) postulate
postup' (n.f.) step
postupat' (v.impf.) act
postupatel'nyi (adj.) progressive
postupit'sya (v.pf.) waive
postuplenie (n.n.) entering
postupok (n.m.) action
postydnyi (adj.) shameful
posuda (n.f.) dishes
posvetit' (v.pf.) illuminate
posvistyvat' (v.impf.) whistle
posvyatit' (v.pf.) devote
posyagat' (v.impf.) encroach
posylat' (v.impf.) send
posylka (n.f.) package
posyl'nyi (n.m.) messenger
posypat' (v.impf.) powder
pot (n.m.) sweat
potainoi (adj.) secret
potakat' (v.impf.) indulge
potasovka (n.f.) brawl
potekha (n.f.) fun
potemki (n.pl.) the dark
potemnet' (v.pf.) grow dark
potentsial (n.m.) potential
potentsiometr (n.m.) potentiometer
poteplet' (v.pf.) grow warmer
poterpet' (v.pf.) suffer

poterya (n.f.) loss
poteshnyi (adj.) amusing
potesnit'sya (v.pf.) make room
potet' (v.impf.) sweat
potikhon'ku (adv.) silently
potirat' (v.impf.) rub
potnyi (adj.) sweaty
potok (n.m.) flow, flux, current
potolok (n.m.) ceiling
potolstet' (v.pf.) grow fat
potom (adv.) later, afterward
potomok (n.m.) descendant
potomu (adv.) that is why
potonut' (v.pf.) drown, sink
potop (n.m.) deluge
potopit' (v.pf.) sink
potrebitel' (n.m.) consumer
potreblenie (n.n.) consumption
potrebnost' (n.f.) requirements
potrepannyi (adj.) worn
potreskat'sya (v.pf.) crack
potreskivat' (v.impf.) crackle
potrokha (n.pl.) pluck
potrudit'sya (v.pf.) work
potryasat' (v.impf.) shake, shock
potselovat'(sya) (v.pf.) kiss
potselui (n.m.) kiss
potugi (n.pl.) labor
potukhat' (v.impf.) go out
potupit' (v.pf.) cast down
potushit' (v.pf.) turn off, extinguish
potusknet' (v.pf.) grow dim
potvorstvovat' (v.impf.) connive
potyagivat'sya (v.impf.) stretch oneself
potyanut' (v.pf.) pull
potyanut'sya (v.pf.) stretch oneself
pouchitel'nyi (adj.) instructive
poumnet' (v.pf.) grow wiser
povadit'sya (v.pf.) get the habit
povalit' (v.pf.) throw down
povalit' (v.pf.) throng
povalit'sya (v.pf.) fall down
poval'nyi (adj.) mass
povar (n.m.) cook
povarennyi (adj.) culinary
povedenie (n.n.) conduct
povelevat' (v.impf.) command
povelitel'nyi (adj.) imperative

pover'e (n.n.)   popular belief
poverennyi (adj.)   attorney
povergat' (v.impf.)   throw down
poverit' (v.pf.)   believe
poverka (n.f.)   checking, roll call
poverkh (adv.)   over
poverkhnost' (n.f.)   surface
poverkhnostnyi (adj.)   superficial
povernut' (v.pf.)   turn
poveselet' (v.pf.)   cheer up
povesit' (v.pf.)   hang
povest' (n.f.)   story
povestka (n.f.)   summons
povestvovanie (n.n.)   narration
povetrie (n.n.)   epidemic
povezti (v.pf.)   carry
povezti (v.pf.)   be in luck
povidat' (v.pf.)   see
povidlo (n.n.)   jam
povinnost' (n.f.)   duty
povinovat'sya (v.impf.)   obey
povisnut' (v.pf.)   hang
povlech' (v.pf.)   entail
povliyat' (v.pf.)   influence
povod (n.m.)   cause
povod (n.m.)   rein
povorachivat'(sya) (v.impf.)   turn
povorot (n.m.)   turn
povozka (n.f.)   horse-drawn vehicle
povredit' (v.pf.)   damage
povremenit' (v.pf.)   wait
povsednevnyi (adj.)   daily
povsemestno (adv.)   everywhere
povyshennyi (adj.)   high
povstanets (n.m.)   rebel
povsyudu (adv.)   far and wide
povtorenie (n.n.)   repetition
povtornyi (adj.)   repeated
povyazat' (v.pf.)   tie
povyazka (n.f.)   bandage
povyazyvat' (v.impf.)   tie
povyshat' (v.impf.)   raise
povysit' (v.pf.)   raise
povysitel'nyi (adj.)   step-up, increasing
povzdorit' (v.pf.)   quarrel
poyas (n.m.)   belt
poyasnenie (n.n.)   explanation
poyasnichnyi (adj.)   lumbar

poyasnitsa (n.f.)   small of the back
poyasnyat' (v.impf.)   explain
poyavit'sya (v.pf.)   appear
poza (n.f.)   pose
pozabotit'sya (v.pf.)   take care
pozadi (adv.)   behind
pozaproshlyi (adj.)   before last
pozavchera (adv.)   day before yesterday
pozavtrakat' (v.pf.)   have breakfast
pozdnii (adj.)   late
pozdorovat'sya (v.pf)   greet
pozdravit' (v.pf.)   congratulate
pozemel'nyi (adj.)   land
pozhalet' (v.pf.)   feel sorry for
pozhalovat'sya (v.pf.)   complain
pozhalui (adv.)   perhaps
pozhaluista (part.)   please
pozhar (n.m.)   fire
pozhat' (v.pf.)   press, shake
pozhat' (v.pf.)   reap
pozhelanie (n.n.)   wish
pozhertvovat' (v.pf.)   sacrifice
pozhiloi (adj.)   elderly
pozhimat' (v.impf.)   press, shake
pozhinat' (v.impf.)   reap
pozhirat' (v.impf.)   devour
pozhitki (n.pl.)   belongings
pozhiva (n.f.)   gain
pozhivit'sya (v.pf.)   profit
pozhiznennyi (adj.)   life
pozitron (n.m.)   positron
pozitsionnyi (adj.)   trench warfare
pozitsiya (n.f.)   position
poznakomit' (v.pf.)   acquaint
poznanie (n.n.)   cognition
poznavat' (v.impf.)   get to know
pozolota (n.f.)   gilding
pozor (n.m.)   disgrace
pozvat' (v.pf.)   call
pozvolenie (n.n.)   permission
pozvolit' (v.pf.)   allow, permit
pozvonit' (v.pf.)   ring
pozvonochnye (n.pl.)   vertebrates
pozvonok (n.m.)   vertebra
pozyv (n.m.)   urge
prababushka (n.f.)   great-grandmother
prachechnaya (n.f.)   laundry
praded (n.m.)   great-grandfather

prakh (n.m.) dust, ashes
praktichnyi (adj.) practical
praktika (n.f.) practice
pravda (n.f.) truth
pravdopodobnyi (adj.) likely
pravil'nyi (adj.) correct
pravilo (n.n.) rule
pravit' (v.impf.) govern
pravitel'stvennyi (adj.) government(al)
pravitel'stvo (n.n.) government
pravlenie (n.n.) government
pravnuk (n.m.) great-grandson
pravo (adv.) really
pravo (n.n.) right
pravomochnyi (adj.) competent
pravonarushitel' (n.m.) delinquent
pravopisanie (n.n.) spelling
pravosudie (n.n.) justice
pravota (n.f.) rightness
pravovoi (adj.) legal
pravyashchii (adj.) ruling
pravyi (adj.) right
pravyi (adj.) right wing
prazdnik (n.m.) holiday
prazdnost' (n.f.) idleness
prebyvanie (n.n.) stay
predanie (n.n.) legend
predannost' (n.f.) loyalty
predat' (v.pf.) commit, betray
predatel' (n.m.) traitor
predat'sya (v.pf.) abandon oneself
predavat' (v.impf.) commit, betray
predavat'sya (v.impf.) abandon oneself
predchuvstvie (n.n.) foreboding
predel (n.m.) limit
predel'nyi (adj.) top
predikativnyi (adj.) predicative
predislovie (n.n.) preface
predlagat' (v.impf.) offer
predlog (n.m.) pretext
predlog (n.m.) preposition
predlozhenie (n.n.) offer, suggestion
predlozhenie (n.n.) sentence
predlozhit' (v.pf.) offer, suggest
predlozhnyi (adj.) prepositional
predmest'e (n.n.) suburb
predmet (n.m.) object
prednamerennyi (adj.) premeditated

prednaznachat' (v.impf.) intend
predok (n.m.) ancestor
predokhranenie (n.n.) protection
predokhranit' (v.pf.) protect
predokhranitel' (n.m.) safety lock
predostavit' (v.pf.) let
predosteregat' (v.impf.) warn
predostorozhnost' (n.f.) precaution
predosuditel'nyi (adj.) reprehensible
predotvratit' (v.pf.) prevent
predpisanie (n.n.) instructions
predpochest' (v.pf.) prefer
predpolagat' (v.impf.) intend
predpolozhenie (n.n.) supposition
predposlednii (adj.) next to last
predposylka (n.f.) premise
predpriimchivyi (adj.) enterprising
predprinimat' (v.impf.) undertake
predprinimatel' (n.m.) employer
predpriyatie (n.n.) enterprise
predrakovyi (adj.) precancerous,
    premalignant
predraspolozhenie (n.n.) predisposition
predrassudok (n.m.) prejudice
predreshat' (v.impf.) predetermine
predsedatel' (n.m.) chairman
predshestvennik (n.m.) predecessor
predskazanie (n.n.) forecast
predsmertnyi (adj.) death
predstat' (v.pf.) appear
predstavat' (v.impf.) appear
predstavit' (v.pf.) present
predstavitel' (n.m.) representative
predstavitel'nyi (adj.) representative
predstavitel'nyi (adj.) impressive
predstavitel'stvo (n.n.) representation
predstavlenie (n.n.) show
predstavlyat' (v.impf.) present
predstoyat' (v.impf.) lie ahead
predubezhdenie (n.n.) prejudice
predupredit' (v.pf.) notify
predupreditel'nost' (n.f.) courtesy
predusmatrivat' (v.impf.) foresee
predusmotritel'nyi (adj.) foreseeing
predvaritel'nyi (adj.) preliminary
predveshchat' (v.impf.) foretell
predvestnik (n.m.) forerunner
predvidet' (v.impf.) foresee

predvkushat' (v.impf.)　anticipate
predvoditel' (n.m.)　leader
predvoskhitit' (v.pf.)　anticipate
predvybornyi (adj.)　preelection
predvzyatyi (adj.)　biased
pred"yavitel' (n.m.)　bearer
predydushchii (adj.)　previous
predznamenovanie (n.n.)　omen
preemnik (n.m.)　successor
preemstvennost' (n.f.)　succession, continuity
prefiks (n.m.)　prefix
pregrada (n.f.)　obstacle
pregradit' (v.pf.)　bar
preimushchestvennyi (adj.)　primary
preimushchestvo (n.n.)　advantage
prekhodyashchii (adj.)　passing
preklonenie (n.n.)　admiration
preklonnyi (adj.)　venerable
preklonyat'sya (v.impf.)　worship
prekrashchenie (n.n.)　cessation
prekrasnyi (adj.)　beautiful
prekratit' (v.pf.)　stop
prelest' (n.f.)　charm
prelestnyi (adj.)　charming
prelomlenie (n.n.)　refraction
prel'shchat'sya (v.impf.)　be attracted
prel'stit' (v.pf.)　be attracted
prelyi (adj.)　rotten
prem'er (n.m.)　prime minister
prem'era (n.f.)　first night
premial'nye (n.pl.)　bonus
premirovat' (v.impf.&pf.)　award a prize
premiya (n.f.)　prize
prenebrech' (v.pf.)　neglect
prenebregat' (v.impf.)　neglect
preniya (n.pl.)　debate
preobladat' (v.impf.)　prevail
preobrazhat'sya (v.impf.)　be transformed
preobrazit' (v.pf.)　transform
preobrazovanie (n.n.)　transformation
preobrazovatel' (n.m.)　transformer, converter
preodolevat' (v.impf.)　get over
preparat (n.m.)　preparation
prepiratel'stvo (n.n.)　altercation
prepodavanie (n.n.)　teaching
prepodnesti (v.pf.)　present
prepyatstvie (n.n.)　obstacle

prerekat'sya (v.impf.)　wrangle
preriya (n.f.)　prairie
prervat' (v.pf.)　interrupt
preryvat' (v.impf.)　interrupt
presekat' (v.impf.)　put an end
presledovanie (n.n.)　persecution
preslovutyi (adj.)　notorious
presmykat'sya (v.impf.)　creep
presmykayushchiesya (n.pl.)　reptiles
presnyi (adj.)　fresh
press (n.m.)　press
pressa (n.f.)　press
press-konferentsiya (n.f.)　press conference
pressovanie (n.n.)　pressing, molding
prestarelyi (adj.)　aged
prestizh (n.m.)　prestige
prestol (n.m.)　throne
prestuplenie (n.n.)　crime
prestupnik (n.m.)　criminal
presytit'sya (v.pf.)　surfeit
pretendent (n.m.)　claimant
pretendovat' (v.impf.)　claim
pretenziya (n.f.)　claim
preterpevat' (v.impf.)　suffer
pretvorit' (v.pf.)　turn into, convert
preumen'shat' (v.impf.)　underestimate
preuspet' (v.pf.)　succeed
preuspevat' (v.impf.)　succeed
preuvelichenie (n.n.)　exaggeration
preventivnyi (adj.)　preventive
prevoskhodit' (v.impf.)　surpass
prevoskhodnyi (adj.)　excellent
prevozmoch' (v.pf.)　overcome
prevoznesti (v.impf.)　praise
prevrashchat'(sya) (v.impf.)　turn into
prevratit' (v.pf.)　turn into
prevratno (adv.)　wrongly
prevysit' (v.pf.)　exceed
prevzoiti (v.pf.)　surpass
prezhde (adv.)　before
prezhdevremennyi (adj.)　premature
prezhnii (adj.)　former
prezident (n.m.)　president
prezidium (n.m.)　presidium
prezirat' (v.impf.)　despise
prezrenie (n.n.)　contempt
prezritel'nyi (adj.)　contemptuous
pri (prep.)　by, at, near

pribavit' (v.pf.) add
pribegat' (v.impf.) come running
pribegat' (v.impf.) resort to
priberegat' (v.impf.) save up
pribezhat' (v.pf.) come running
pribezhishche (n.n.) refuge
pribirat' (v.pf.) put in order
pribit' (v.pf.) fasten
pribivat' (v.impf.) fasten
priblizhat'(sya) (v.impf.) draw near
priblizit' (v.pf.) bring nearer
priblizitel'no (adv.) approximately
priboi (n.m.) surf
pribor (n.m.) device
pribrat' (v.pf.) put in order
pribrezhnyi (adj.) coastal
pribyl' (n.f.) profit
pribytie (n.n.) arrival
pribyvat' (v.impf.) arrive
prichal (n.m.) berth, moorage
prichalivat' (v.impf.) moor
prichastie (n.n.) participle
prichem (conj.) besides
prichesat' (v.pf.) comb
pricheska (n.f.) hairdo
prichina (n.f.) cause
prichinit' (v.pf.) cause
prichislit' (v.pf.) number among
prichitanie (n.n.) lamentation
prichitat'sya (v.impf.) be due
prichuda (n.f.) whim
pridacha (n.f.) addition
pridanoe (n.n.) dowry
pridat' (v.pf.) give
pridatok (n.m.) appendage
pridavat' (v.impf.) add
pridelat' (v.pf.) attach
priderzhivat'sya (v.impf.) hold on to
pridirat'sya (v.impf.) find fault
pridirka (n.f.) cavil
pridrat'sya (v.pf.) find fault
pridumat' (v.pf.) think of
pridvigat'(sya) (v.impf.) draw near
pridvinut' (v.pf.) move up
priekhat' (v.pf.) arrive
priem (n.m.) reception
priem (n.m.) method
priemistost' (n.f.) response

priemlemyi (adj.) acceptable
priemnyi (adj.) reception
priemnaya (n.f.) reception room
priemnik (n.m.) receiver
priezd (n.m.) arrival
priglasitel'nyi (adj.) invitation
priglyadet'sya (v.pf.) examine
prignat' (v.pf.) gather in
prigodit'sya (v.pf.) be useful
prigonka (n.f.) fitting, adjustment
prigonyat' (v.impf.) gather in
prigorat' (v.impf.) burn
prigorod (n.m.) suburb
prigorok (n.m.) hillock
prigorshnya (n.f.) handfull
prigotovit' (v.pf.) prepare
prigotovitel'nyi (adj.) preparatory
prigovor (n.m.) sentence
prigrozit' (v.pf.) threaten
priisk (n.m.) mine
priiti (v.pf.) come
priitis' (v.pf.) have to
prikalyvat' (v.impf.) pin
prikasat'sya (v.impf.) touch
prikaz (n.m.) order
prikhod (n.m.) coming
prikhod (n.m.) receipts
prikhodit' (v.impf.) come
prikhodit'sya (v.impf.) be forced to
prikhodyashchii (adj.) nonresident
prikhot' (n.f.) whim
prikhotlivyi (adj.) whimsical
prikhramyvat' (v.impf.) limp
prikhvaryvat' (v.impf.) be unwell
prikidyvat'sya (v.impf.) pretend
prikinut' (v.pf.) estimate
priklad (n.m.) butt
priklad (n.m.) accessories
prikladnoi (adj.) applied
prikladyvat' (v.impf.) apply
priklyuchenie (n.n.) adventure
prikol (n.m.) stake
prikolachivat' (v.impf.) nail
prikolot' (v.pf.) pin
prikomandirovat' (v.pf.) attach
prikosnovenie (n.n.) touch
prikovat' (v.pf.) chain
prikrasit' (v.pf.) embellish

prikrepit' (v.pf.) fasten
prikrytie (n.n.) cover
prikryvat'sya (v.impf.) cover oneself
prikusit' (v.pf.) bite
priladit' (v.pf.) fit
prilagat' (v.impf.) apply
prilagatel'noe (n.n.) adjective
prilaskat' (v.pf.) caress
prilavok (n.m.) counter
prilech' (v.pf.) lie down
prilegat' (v.impf.) fit closely
prilepit' (v.pf.) stick
priletat' (v.impf.) come flying
prilezhanie (n.n.) diligence
prilezhnyi (adj.) diligent
prilichie (n.n.) decency
prilipanie (n.n.) adhesion
prilit' (v.pf.) rush
priliv (n.m.) high tide
pril'nut' (v.pf.) cling
prilozhenie (n.n.) supplement
primanka (n.f.) bait
primchat'sya (v.pf.) run fast
primechanie (n.n.) note
primenenie (n.n.) application
primer (n.m.) example
primerit' (v.pf.) try on
primernyi (adj.) exemplary
primeryat' (v.impf.) try on
primes' (n.f.) admixture
primeta (n.f.) sign
priminat' (v.impf.) flatten
primirenie (n.n.) reconciliation
primitivnyi (adj.) primitive
primknut' (v.pf.) join
primochka (n.f.) lotion
primorskii (adj.) seaside
primus (n.m.) primus stove
primyat' (v.pf.) flatten
primykat' (v.impf.) adjoin
prinadlezhat' (v.impf.) belong
prinadlezhnosti (n.pl.) accessories
prinesti (v.pf.) bring
prinimat' (v.impf.) receive
prinorovit' (v.pf.) adapt
prinoshenie (n.n.) offering
prinosit' (v.impf.) bring
printsip (n.m.) principle

prinudit' (v.pf.) compel
prinuditel'nyi (adj.) compulsory
prinyatie (n.n.) adoption
priobodrit' (v.pf.) encourage
priobodryat'(sya) (v.impf.) cheer up
priobresti (v.pf.) acquire
priobshchat' (v.impf.) join
priostanavlivat' (v.impf.) suspend
priotvorit' (v.pf.) open slightly
pripadochnyi (adj.) epileptic
pripadok (n.m.) fit
pripasat' (v.impf.) store
pripasy (n.pl.) provisions
pripev (n.m.) refrain
pripisat' (v.impf.) add
pripiska (n.f.) postscript
priplachivat' (v.impf.) pay extra
priplata (n.f.) extra pay
priplod (n.m.) litter
priplyusnut' (v.pf.) flatten
priplyvat' (v.impf.) sail up to
pripodnimat'sya (v.impf.) half rise from a chair
pripodnyat' (v.pf.) raise a little
pripominat' (v.impf.) remember
priprava (n.f.) seasoning
pripryatat' (v.pf.) hide
pripugnut' (v.pf.) intimidate
prirabotok (n.m.) supplementary earnings
prirastat' (v.impf.) adhere
priravnivat' (v.impf.) equate
priroda (n.f.) nature
prirost (n.m.) increase
prirozhdennyi (adj.) innate
priruchat' (v.impf.) tame
prisadka (n.f.) additive
prisazhivat'sya (v.impf.) sit down
prisest' (v.pf.) sit down
prishchemit' (v.pf.) pinch
prishchurivat'sya (v.impf.) squint
prishiblennyi (adj.) dejected
prishivat' (v.impf.) sew on
prishporivat' (v.impf.) spur
priskakat' (v.pf.) come galloping
priskorbnyi (adj.) sorrowful
prislat' (v.pf.) send
prislonit'sya (v.pf.) lean
prisluga (n.f.) servants

prislushat'sya (v.pf.) listen
prismatrivat'sya (v.impf.) look attentively
prismotr (n.m.) care
prismotret' (v.pf.) look after
prisnit'sya (v.pf.) dream
prisoedinenie (n.n.) joining
prisoedinit' (v.pf.) join
prisposobit' (v.pf.) fit, adapt
prisposoblenie (n.n.) adaptation, device, appliance
pristal'nyi (adj.) fixed, intent
pristan' (n.f.) quay
pristat' (v.pf.) land
pristavat' (v.impf.) land
pristavit' (v.pf.) put, lean against
pristavka (n.f.) prefix
pristavlyat' (v.impf.) put, lean against
pristegivat' (v.impf.) buckle
pristraivat'(sya) (v.impf.) find a place
pristrastie (n.n.) liking
pristroika (n.f.) annex
pristroit' (v.pf.) attach, add
pristup (n.m.) assault
pristupat' (v.impf.) begin
pristydit' (v.pf.) shame
prisudit' (v.pf.) sentence, condemn
prisushchii (adj.) habitual
prisutstvie (n.n.) presence
prisvaivat' (v.impf.) appropriate, award
prisvoenie (n.n.) awarding
prisvoenie (n.n.) appropriation
prisvoit' (v.pf.) appropriate
prisvoit' (v.pf.) award
prisyaga (n.f.) oath
prisylat' (v.impf.) send
pritait'sya (v.pf.) hide
pritashchit' (v.pf.) lug in
pritesnenie (n.n.) oppression
pritikhat' (v.impf.) grow quiet
pritok (n.m.) tributary
pritom (conj.) besides
priton (n.m.) haunt
pritornyi (adj.) sickly sweet
pritragivat'sya (v.impf.) touch
pritsel (n.m.) sight
pritsenivat'sya (v.impf.) ask the price
pritsep (n.m.) trailer
pritsepit' (v.pf.) hook

pritupit' (v.pf.) blunt
pritvorit'sya (v.pf.) pretend
pritvornyi (adj.) affected
prityagatel'nyi (adj.) attractive
prityagivat' (v.impf.) attract
prityanut' (v.pf.) attract
prityazanie (n.n.) claim
prityazhatel'nyi (adj.) possessive
prityazhenie (n.n.) attraction
priuchat' (v.impf.) train
priurochit' (v.pf.) time
prival (n.m.) halt
priveredlivyi (adj.) fastidious
priverzhennyi (adj.) devoted
priveshivat' (v.impf.) suspend
privesit' (v.pf.) suspend
privesti (v.pf.) bring, lead, result
privet (n.m.) regards
privezti (v.pf.) bring
prividenie (n.n.) ghost
privilegirovannyi (adj.) privileged
privilegiya (n.f.) privilege
privintit' (v.pf.) screw up
privit' (v.pf.) inoculate
privivat'sya (v.impf.) take
privivka (n.f.) inoculation
privkus (n.m.) touch, flavor
privlech' (v.pf.) attract
privlechenie (n.n.) attraction
privlekat' (v.impf.) attract
privlekatel'nyi (adj.) attractive
privod (n.m.) drive, gear
privodit' (v.impf.) bring, lead, result
privodnoi (adj.) driving
privol'nyi (adj.) free
privoz (n.m.) bringing
privstat' (v.pf.) half rise from a chair
privyaz' (n.f.) leash
privyazannost' (n.f.) attachment
privyazat' (v.pf.) tie
privyazchivyi (adj.) affectionate
privykat' (v.impf.) get used to
priyatel' (n.m.) friend
priyatnyi (adj.) pleasant
priyut (n.m.) asylum
priz (n.m.) prize
prizadumat'sya (v.impf.) become thoughtful
prizemlenie (n.n.) landing

prizhat' (v.pf.) press
prizhimat'(sya) (v.impf.) press oneself
prizhimistyi (adj.) tightfisted
prizma (n.f.) prism
prizmaticheskii (adj.) prismatic
priznak (n.m.) sign
priznanie (n.n.) acknowledgement
priznannyi (adj.) acknowledged
priznat' (v.pf.) acknowledge
priznatel'nyi (adj.) grateful
priznavat'(sya) (v.impf.) confess
prizrak (n.m.) specter
prizvanie (n.n.) vocation
prizvat' (v.pf.) call
prizyv (n.m.) call, appeal
pro (prep.) of, about
proba (n.f.) test, assay
probnyi (adj.) trial
probeg (n.m.) run
probel (n.m.) blank
probirat'sya (v.impf.) make one's way
   through
probirka (n.f.) test tube
probit' (v.pf.) make a hole
probit' (v.pf.) strike
probit'sya (v.pf.) force one's way through
probivat' (v.impf.) punch
probka (n.f.) cork
problema (n.f.) problem
problesk (n.m.) flash
proboi (n.m.) rupture, puncture
proboina (n.f.) hole
proboltat'sya (v.pf.) blurt out
probor (n.m.) parting
probrat'sya (v.pf.) make one's way through
probudit'sya (v.pf.) wake up
proburavit' (v.pf.) bore
probyt' (v.pf.) stay
proch' (adv.) away
prochest' (v.pf.) read
prochii (adj.) other
prochishchat' (v.impf.) clean
prochistit' (v.pf.) clean
prochitat' (v.pf.) read
prochnost' (n.f.) strength, rigidity, durability
prochnyi (adj.) firm
prochuvstvovat' (v.pf.) feel keenly
prodat' (v.pf.) sell

prodavat' (v.impf.) sell
prodavets (n.m.) shop assistant
prodazha (n.f.) sale
prodelat' (v.pf.) do; perform
prodelka (n.f.) trick
prodelyvat' (v.impf.) do, perform
prodergivat' (v.impf.) run through
prodernut' (v.pf.) run through
proderzhat' (v.pf.) hold
prodeshevit' (v.pf.) sell cheap
prodiktovat' (v.pf.) dictate
prodlenie (n.n.) prolongation
prodlit'sya (v.pf.) last
prodolgovatyi (adj.) oblong
prodol'nyi (adj.) longitudinal
prodolzhat' (v.impf.) continue
prodolzhitel'nost' (n.f.) duration
prodovol'stvennyi (adj.) food
prodrognut' (v.pf.) be chilled
produkt (n.m.) product
produktivnost' (n.f.) productivity
produktovyi (adj.) food
produktsiya (n.f.) production
produmat' (v.pf.) think over
prodvigat' (v.impf.) move on
prodvinut' (v.pf.) move on
prodyryavit' (v.pf.) make a hole
proedat' (v.impf.) eat away, corrode
proekhat' (v.pf.) pass
proekt (n.m.) project
proektirovanie (n.n.) designing
proektsiya (n.f.) projection
proest' (v.pf.) eat away, corrode
proezd (n.m.) passage
proezzhat' (v.impf.) pass
proezzhii (adj.) traveler
profan (n.m.) ignoramus
profanatsiya (n.f.) profanation
professional'nyi (adj.) professional
professiya (n.f.) profession
professor (n.m.) professor
profil' (n.m.) profile
profilaktika (n.f.) prophylaxis
profsoyuz (n.m.) trade union
progadat' (v.pf.) miscalculate
progalina (n.f.) glade
proglatyvat' (v.impf.) swallow
proglyadet' (v.pf.) overlook

proglyadyvat' (v.impf.) overlook
prognat' (v.pf.) drive away
prognivat' (v.impf.) be rotten through
prognoz (n.m.) forecast
progolodat'sya (v.pf.) get hungry
progonyat' (v.impf.) drive away
progorat' (v.impf.) burn through
progorklyi (adj.) rancid
progovorit' (v.pf.) say
programma (n.f.) program
progress (n.m.) progress
progressiya (n.f.) progression
progryzat' (v.impf.) gnaw through
progul (n.m.) truancy
progulivat' (v.impf.) shirk work
progul'shchik (n.m.) truant
progulyat' (v.pf.) shirk work
progulyat'sya (v.pf.) go for a walk
proigrat' (v.pf.) lose
proigrysh (n.m.) loss
proiskhodit' (v.impf.) occur
proiskhozhdenie (n.n.) origin
proiski (n.pl.) schemes
proisshestvie (n.n.) incident
proistekat' (v.impf.) result from
proiti (v.pf.) pass
proiznesti (v.pf.) pronounce
proiznoshenie (n.n.) pronunciation
proizoiti (v.pf.) occur
proizvedenie (n.n.) product
proizvesti (v.pf.) make
proizvodit' (v.impf.) produce
proizvoditel'nost' (n.f.) productivity
proizvodnyi (adj.) derivative
proizvodstvennyi (adj.) industrial
proizvodstvo (n.n.) production
proizvol (n.m.) tyranny
proizvol'nyi (adj.) arbitrary
prok (n.m.) gain
prokalyvat' (v.impf.) pierce
prokat (n.m.) rent
prokat (n.m.) rolled metal
prokatit'sya (v.pf.) go for a ride
prokaza (n.f.) leprosy
prokaza (n.f.) mischief
prokhlada (n.f.) coolness
prokhod (n.m.) passage
prokhodimets (n.m.) rascal

prokhodit' (v.impf.) pass
prokhodnoi (adj.) of passage
prokhozhii (adj.) passerby
prokipyatit' (v.pf.) boil
prokisat' (v.impf.) turn sour
prokladka (n.f.) laying, packing
proklamatsiya (n.f.) leaflet
proklinat' (v.impf.) curse
prokolot' (v.pf.) pierce
prokormit' (v.pf.) provide
prokradyvat'sya (v.impf.) steal into
proktologiya (n.f.) proctology
prokuratura (n.f.) prosecutor's office
prokuror (n.m.) public prosecutor
prokutit' (v.pf.) dissipate
prolegat' (v.impf.) lie, run
prolet (n.m.) span
proletarii (n.m.) proletarian
proletariat (n.m.) proletariat
proletat' (v.impf.) fly
prolezat' (v.impf.) penetrate
prolezhen' (n.m.) bedsore
proliferatsiya (n.f.) proliferation
prolit' (v.pf.) spill
proliv (n.m.) strait(s)
prolivat' (v.impf.) spill
prolivnoi (adj.) pouring
prolog (n.m.) prologue
prolom (n.m.) break
prolomat' (v.pf.) break
prolozhit' (v.pf.) lay
promakh (n.m.) miss, blunder
promakhnut'sya (v.pf.) miss
promatyvat' (v.impf.) squander
promchat'sya (v.pf.) rush past
promedlenie (n.n.) delay
promel'knut' (v.pf.) flash
promenyat' (v.pf.) exchange
promerzat' (v.impf.) freeze through
promezhutochnyi (adj.) intermediate
promezhutok (n.m.) interval
promochit' (v.pf.) soak
promokat' (v.impf.) get well
promokatel'nyi (adj.) blotting
promolchat' (v.pf.) keep silent
promolvit' (v.pf.) utter
promotat' (v.pf.) squander
promtovarnyi (adj.) manufactured

promysel (n.m.) trade
promyshlennost' (n.f.) industry
promyslovyi (adj.) producers'
promyvanie (n.n.) washing
pronesti (v.pf.) carry
pronestis' (v.pf.) rush past
pronikat' (v.impf.) penetrate
proniknovennyi (adj.) moving
proniknut' (v.pf.) penetrate
pronitsaemost' (n.f.) permeability
pronitsatel'nyi (adj.) penetrating
pronizat' (v.pf.) pierce
pronosit' (v.impf.) carry
pronosit'sya (v.impf.) rush past
pronyrlivyi (adj.) sly
pronyukhat' (v.pf.) nose out
pronzit' (v.pf.) pierce
pronzitel'nyi (adj.) piercing
propadat' (v.impf.) be missing
propaganda (n.f.) propaganda
propashka (n.f.) cultivation
propast' (v.pf.) precipice
propast' (v.pf.) be missing
propazha (n.f.) loss
propech' (v.pf.) bake well
propekat'(sya) (v.impf.) bake well
propeller (n.m.) propeller
propisat' (v.pf.) prescribe
propiska (n.f.) registration
propisnoi (adj.) capital, commonplace
propitanie (n.n.) subsistence
propitat' (v.pf.) saturate
propityvat'sya (v.impf.) be saturated
proplyvat' (v.impf.) swim
propolka (n.f.) weeding
propoloskat' (v.pf.) rinse
proportsional'nyi (adj.) proportional
proportsiya (n.f.) proportion
propoved' (n.f.) sermon
propovedovat' (v.impf.) preach
propusk (n.m.) permit
propustit' (v.pf.) let pass
prorabatyvat' (v.impf.) study, work
prorastat' (v.impf.) germinate
prorekha (n.f.) rent
prorez (n.m.) slot
prorezat' (v.impf.) cut through
prorezyvanie (n.n.) eruption

prorochestvo (n.n.) prophecy
prorok (n.m.) prophet
proronit' (v.pf.) utter
prorub' (n.f.) ice hole
prorubat' (v.impf.) chop through
prorvat' (v.pf.) break through
proryt' (v.pf.) dig
proryv (n.m.) break
proryvat' (v.impf.) dig
proryvat' (v.impf.) break through
prosachivat'sya (v.impf.) leak
pros'ba (n.f.) request
proschitat'sya (v.pf.) miscalculate
prosed' (n.f.) gray
proseivat' (v.impf.) sift
proseka (n.f.) vista
proselochnyi (adj.) country (road)
proseyat' (v.pf.) sift
proshchai(te) (coll.) good-bye
proshchal'nyi (adj.) parting
proshchat' (v.impf.) pardon
proshchat'sya (v.impf.) take leave
proshchenie (n.n.) forgiveness
proshchupat' (v.pf.) feel
proshedshee (n.n.) the past
proshedshii (adj.) past
proshenie (n.n.) petition
prosheptat' (v.pf.) whisper
proshivka (n.f.) lace insertion
proshloe (n.n.) the past
proshlogodnii (adj.) last year's
prosidet' (v.pf.) sit
prosit' (v.impf.) ask
prositel' (n.m.) applicant
prosiyat' (v.pf.) brighten
proskakivat' (v.impf.) slip past
proskal'zyvat' (v.impf.) slip in
proskochit' (v.pf.) rush by
proslavit'sya (v.pf.) become famous
prosledit' (v.pf.) trace
proslezit'sya (v.pf.) shed a tear
prosloika (n.f.) layer
proslushat' (v.pf.) listen, miss
proslyt' (v.pf.) be reputed
prosmatrivat' (v.impf.) overlook
prosmotret' (v.pf.) overlook
prosmotr (n.m.) examination
prosnut'sya (v.pf.) wake up

proso (n.n.)   millet
prosochit'sya (v.pf.)   leak
prosokhnut' (v.pf.)   get dry
prosokhshii (adj.)   dried
prosovyvat' (v.impf.)   push through
prospat' (v.pf.)   oversleep
prospekt (n.m.)   avenue
prosporit' (v.pf.)   lose a bet
prosrochennyi (adj.)   overdue
prosrochit' (v.pf.)   be overdue
prostak (n.m.)   simpleton
prostenok (n.m.)   pier
prostirat'sya (v.impf.)   stretch
prostit' (v.pf.)   forgive
prostit'sya (v.pf.)   take leave of
prostitutka (n.f.)   prostitute
prosto (adv.)   simply
prostodushnyi (adj.)   simple-hearted
prostoi (n.m.)   standing idle
prostoi (adj.)   simple
prostokvasha (n.f.)   sour milk
prostor (n.m.)   spaciousness
prostoserdechnyi (adj.)   simple-hearted
prostota (n.f.)   simplicity
prostrannyi (adj.)   verbose
prostranstvennyi (adj.)   spatial
prostranstvo (n.n.)   space
prostrelit' (v.pf.)   shoot through
prostuda (n.f.)   cold
prostupok (n.m.)   fault
prostynka (n.f.)   sheet
prosunut' (v.pf.)   push through
prosushchestvovat' (v.pf.)   exist
prosushit' (v.pf.)   dry
prosvechivanie (n.n.)   radioscopy
prosverlit' (v.pf.)   bore
prosveshchat' (v.impf.)   enlighten
prosvet (n.m.)   clear space
prosvetit' (v.pf.)   enlighten
prosvetit' (v.pf.)   X-ray
prosvetitel'nyi (adj.)   instructive
prosvetlenie (n.n.)   enlightenment
prosykhat' (v.impf.)   get dry
prosypat' (v.impf.)   oversleep
prosypat' (v.pf.)   spill
protalkivat' (v.impf.)   push through
protaplivat' (v.impf.)   heat
protaskivat' (v.impf.)   pull through

protech' (v.pf.)   leak
protein (n.m.)   protein
protekat' (v.impf.)   flow
protektor (n.m.)   tread, protector, protective
  cover
protektsiya (n.f.)   influence
proteret' (v.pf.)   wipe
protest (n.m.)   protest
protez (n.m.)   artificial limb
protirat' (v.impf.)   wipe
protiv (prep.)   against
protiven' (n.m.)   roasting pan
protivit'sya (v.impf.)   oppose
protivnik (n.m)   opponent
protivnyi (adj.)   disgusting
protivnyi (adj.)   opposite
protivodeistvie (n.n.)   counteraction
protivoestestvennyi (adj.)   unnatural
protivogaz (n.m.)   gas mask
protivokhimicheskii (adj.)   anti-gas
protivopolozhnost' (n.f.)   contrast
protivopostavlenie (n.n.)   opposition
protivorechie (n.n.)   contradiction
protivostoyanie (n.n.)   opposition
protivostoyat' (v.impf.)   resist
protivotankovyi (adj.)   antitank
protivoves (n.m.)   counterweight
protivovozdushnyi (adj.)   antiaircraft
protivoyadie (n.n.)   antidote
protivozakonnyi (adj.)   illegal
protknut' (v.pf.)   pierce
protochnyi (adj.)   flowing
protokol (n.m.)   minutes
protolkat'sya (v.pf.)   force one's way through
proton (n.m.)   proton
protopit' (v.pf.)   heat
protorennyi (adj.)   beaten
prototip (n.m.)   prototype
protsedit' (v.pf.)   filter
protsedura (n.f.)   procedure, treatment
protsent (n.m.)   percentage
protsess (n.m.)   process, trial
protsessiya (n.f.)   procession
protsezhivat' (v.impf.)   filter
protsvetanie (n.n.)   prosperity
protuberanets (n.m.)   protuberance,
  prominence
protukhnut' (v.pf.)   become foul

protyagivat' (v.impf.) stretch
protyanut' (v.pf.) stretch
protyazhenie (n.n.) extent
protyazhnyi (adj.) drawn-out
protykat' (v.impf.) pierce
prouchit' (v.pf.) teach a lesson
proval (n.m.) failure
provedat' (v.pf.) pay a visit
proverit' (v.pf.) verify
provesti (v.pf.) build, conduct, pass
provetrivat' (v.impf.) air
provezti (v.pf.) transport, carry
provinit'sya (v.pf.) be at fault
provintsial'nyi (adj.) provincial
provintsiya (n.f.) province
proviziya (n.f.) provisions
provod (n.m.) wire
provodimost' (n.f.) conductivity
provodit' (v.pf.) accompany
provodit' (v.impf.) build, conduct, pass
provodka (n.f.) wiring
provodnik (n.m.) guide
provodnik (n.m.) conductor
provody (n.pl.) seeing off
provokatsiya (n.f.) provocation
provoloka (n.f.) wire
provornyi (adj.) quick
provotsirovat' (v.impf.) provoke
provoz (n.m.) transport
provozglasit' (v.pf.) proclaim
provozhat' (v.impf.) accompany
provozit' (v.impf.) transport, carry
proyasnit'sya (v.pf.) clear up
proyavit' (v.pf.) show, display
proyavitel' (n.m.) developer
proza (n.f.) prose
prozevat' (v.pf.) let slip
prozhech' (v.pf.) burn through
prozhektor (n.m.) searchlight
prozhigat' (v.impf.) burn through
prozhit' (v.pf.) live
prozhitochnyi (adj.) sufficient to live on
prozhivat' (v.impf.) live
prozhorlivost' (n.f.) voracity
prozorlivyi (adj.) clearheaded
prozrachnyi (adj.) transparent
prozvat' (v.pf.) nickname
prozvishche (n.n.) nickname

prozyabat' (v.impf.) vegetate
prud (n.m.) pond
prut (n.m.) twig
pruzhina (n.f.) spring
pryad' (n.f.) lock
pryadil'nyi (adj.) spinning
pryalka (n.f.) spinning wheel
pryamo (adv.) straight
pryamodushie (n.n.) frankness
pryamoi (adj.) straight
pryamokishechnyi (adj.) rectal
pryamolineinyi (adj.) straightforward
pryamota (n.f.) directness
pryamougol'nyi (adj.) rectangular
pryanik (n.m.) cake
pryanost' (n.f.) spice
pryast' (v.impf.) spin
pryatat' (v.impf.) hide
pryazha (n.f.) yarn
pryazhka (n.f.) buckle
prygat' (v.impf.) jump
pryt' (n.f.) speed
prytkii (adj.) quick
pryzhok (n.m.) jump
psevdonim (n.m.) pseudonym
pshenitsa (n.f.) wheat
pshennyi (adj.) millet
psheno (n.n.) millet
psikhiatr (n.m.) psychiatrist
psikhiatriya (n.f.) psychiatry
psikhika (n.f.) psyche
psikhoanaliz (n.m.) psychoanalysis
psikholog (n.m.) psychologist
psikhologiya (n.f.) psychology
psikhoz (n.m.) psychosis
ptenets (n.m.) nestling
ptichii (adj.) poultry
ptitsa (n.f.) bird
ptitsevodstvo (n.n.) fowling
publichnyi (adj.) public
publika (n.f.) public
puchina (n.f.) gulf
puchok (n.m.) small bunch
pudra (n.f.) powder
pugalo (n.n.) scarecrow
pugat' (v.impf.) frighten
puglivyi (adj.) fearful
pugovitsa (n.f.) button

puk (n.m.) bunch
pukh (n.m.) down
pukhlyi (adj.) plump
pukhnut' (v.impf.) swell
pukhovka (n.f.) powder puff
pukhovyi (adj.) down
pulemet (n.m.) machine gun
pul's (n.m.) pulse
pul'sirovat' (v.impf.) pulse
pulya (n.f.) bullet
punkt (n.m.) point
punktir (n.m.) dotted line
punktual'nyi (adj.) punctual
punktuatsiya (n.f.) punctuation
puntsovyi (adj.) crimson
pupok (n.m.) navel
pupovina (n.f.) umbilical cord
purga (n.f.) snowstorm
purpur (n.m.) purple
purpurovyi (adj.) purple
pushechnyi (adj.) gun
pushinka (n.f.) fluff
pushistyi (adj.) fluffy
pushka (n.f.) gun
pushnina (n.f.) furs
pusk (n.m.) starting
puskai (part.) let
puskat' (v.impf.) let go
pust' (part.) let
pustet' (v.impf.) become empty
pustit' (v.pf.) let go
pustoi (adj.) empty
pustota (n.f.) emptiness, vacuum
pustovat' (v.impf.) stand empty
pustyak (n.m.) trifle
pustyakovyi (adj.) trifling
pustynnyi (adj.) deserted
pustynya (n.f.) desert
pustyr' (n.m.) waste ground
put' (n.m.) way
putanitsa (n.f.) confusion
putem (adv.) by means of
puteprovod (n.m.) overbridge
puteshestvie (n.n.) journey

putevka (n.f.) permit
putevoditel' (n.m.) guide
putina (n.f.) fishing season
puzyr' (n.m.) bubble
puzyrek (n.m.) phial
pyad' (n.f.) span
pyal'tsy (n.pl.) embroidery frame
p'yanet' (v.impf.) get drunk
p'yanitsa (n.m.&f.) drunkard
pyat' (num.) five
pyata (n.f.) heel
pyatak (n.m.) five-kopeck piece
pyat'desyat (num.) fifty
pyaterka (n.f.) five
pyatero (num.) five
pyatidesyatyi (adj.) fiftieth
pyatikonechnyi (adj.) five-pointed
pyatiletka (n.f.) five-year plan
pyatit'sya (v.impf.) move backwards
pyatiugol'nik (n.m.) pentagon
pyatka (n.f.) heel
pyatnadtsat' (num.) fifteen
pyatnistyi (adj.) spotted
pyatnitsa (n.f.) Friday
pyatno (n.n.) spot
pyatok (n.m.) five
pyat'sot (num.) five hundred
pyatyi (adj.) fifth
pyat'yu (adv.) five times
pykhtet' (v.impf.) pant
pyl' (n.f.) dust
pyl (n.m.) ardor
pylat' (v.impf.) blaze
pylesos (n.m.) vacuum cleaner
pylkii (adj.) ardent
pyl'tsa (n.f.) pollen
pyshnost' (n.f.) splendor
pytat' (v.impf.) torture
pytat'sya (v.impf.) attempt
pytka (n.f.) torture
pytlivyi (adj.) inquisitive
pyupitr (n.m.) music stand
pyure (n.n.) mashed potatoes

R (P)

rab (n.m.) slave
raboche-krest'yanskii (adj.) workers' and peasants'
rabochii (n.m.) worker
rabochii (adj.) working
rabolepie (n.n.) servility
rabota (n.f.) work
rabotnik (n.m.) worker
rabotosposobnost' (n.f.) capacity for work
rabotyashchii (adj.) industrious
rabovladel'cheskii (adj.) slave-owning
rabskii (adj.) slave, servile
rad (adj.) glad
radi (prep.) for the sake of
radiator (n.m.) radiator
radiatsiya (n.f.) radiation
radii (n.m.) radium
radikal (n.m.) radical
radikal'nyi (adj.) radical
radio (n.n.) radio
radioaktivnost' (n.f.) radioactivity
radioélektronika (n.f.) radioelectronics
radiofikatsiya (n.f.) installation of radio
radiologiya (n.f.) radiology
radiotekhnika (n.f.) radio engineering
radioterapiya (n.f.) radiotherapy
radioveshchanie (n.n.) broadcasting
radist (n.m.) radio operator
radius (n.m.) radius
radovat' (v.impf.) make glad
raduga (n.f.) rainbow
radushie (n.n.) cordiality
rai (n.m.) paradise
raikom (n.m.) district committee
raion (n.m.) district
raionnyi (adj.) district
rak (n.m) crayfish
rak (n.m.) cancer
raketa (n.f.) rocket, missile
raketka (n.f.) racket
rakovina (n.f.) shell
rama (n.f.) frame
rampa (n.f.) footlights
rana (n.f.) wound
ranets (n.m.) knapsack

ranit' (v.impf.&pf.) wound
rannii (adj.) early
rano (adv.) early
ran'she (adv.) earlier
rapira (n.f.) foil
raport (n.m.) report
rasa (n.f.) race
raschesat' (v.impf.) comb
rascheska (n.f.) comb
raschesyvat' (v.impf.) comb
raschet (n.m.) calculation
raschishchat' (v.impf.) clear away
raschistit' (v.pf.) clear away
raschlenenie (n.n.) breaking up
rasformirovanie (n.n.) disbandment
raskachat' (v.pf.) swing
raskachivat'(sya) (v.impf.) sway, swing
raskaivat'sya (v.impf.) repent
raskalennyi (adj.) scorching
raskalyat'(sya) (v.impf.) become hot
raskalyvat'(sya) (v.impf.) split
raskapyvat' (v.impf.) dig out
raskat (n.m.) peal
raskatat' (v.pf.) roll
raskayanie (n.n.) remorse
raskhazhivat' (v.impf.) walk up and down
raskhitit' (v.pf.) plunder
raskhititel' (n.m.) plunderer
raskhlyabannyi (adj.) lax
raskhod (n.m.) expenditure
raskhodit'sya (v.impf.) break up
raskhodovat' (v.impf.) spend
raskhokhotat'sya (v.pf.) burst out laughing
raskholazhivat' (v.impf.) dampen one's ardor
raskhotet' (v.pf.) cease to want
raskhozhdenie (n.n.) divergence
raskhvalivat' (v.impf.) praise
raskhvatat' (v.pf.) snatch
raskhvorat'sya (v.pf.) fall ill
raskidyvat' (v.impf.) scatter
raskislenie (n.n.) deoxidation
raskladyvat' (v.impf) lay out
rasklanyat'sya (v.pf.) bow
raskleivat' (v.impf.) paste

raskol (n.m.) split
raskopat' (v.pf.) dig out
raskopki (n.pl.) excavations
raskradyvat' (v.impf.) steal
raskrashivat' (v.impf.) color
raskrasit' (v.pf.) color
raskrasnet'sya (v.pf.) become flushed
raskrast' (v.pf.) steal
raskrepostit' (v.pf.) liberate
raskrichat'sya (v.pf.) shriek
raskritikovat' (v.pf.) criticize
raskroshit' (v.pf.) crumble
raskrutit' (v.pf.) untwist
raskryt' (v.pf.) uncover
raskryvat'(sya) (v.impf.) open, come to light
raskupat' (v.pf.) buy up
raskuporivat' (v.impf.) uncork
raskusit' (v.pf.) bite through
raskusyvat' (v.impf.) bite through
raskvitat'sya (v.pf.) settle accounts
rasovyi (adj.) racial
raspad (n.m.) disintegration
raspakhat' (v.pf.) plow up
raspakhivat' (v.impf.) throw open
raspakovat' (v.pf.) unpack
rasparyvat' (v.impf.) rip up
raspast'sya (v.pf.) disintegrate
raspayat' (v.pf.) unsolder
raspechatat' (v.pf.) open, unseal
raspevat' (v.impf.) sing
raspilivat' (v.impf.) saw up
raspisanie (n.n.) schedule
raspisat'sya (v.pf.) sign
raspiska (n.f.) receipt
raspisnoi (adj.) decorated with painting
raspisyvat'sya (v.impf.) sign
rasplachivat'sya (v.impf.) pay off
rasplakat'sya (v.pf.) burst into tears
rasplastat' (v.pf.) spread
rasplata (n.f.) payment
rasplavit'(sya) (v.pf.) melt
rasplavlyat'(sya) (v.impf.) melt
raspleskat' (v.pf.) splash
rasplesti (v.pf.) untwist
raspletat'(sya) (v.impf.) untwine
rasplodit' (v.pf.) breed
rasplyt'sya (v.pf.) spread
rasplyushchit' (v.pf.) flatten

rasplyvat'sya (v.impf.) spread
rasplyvchatyi (adj.) diffuse
raspolagat' (v.impf.) dispose
raspolozhenie (n.n.) arrangement
raspolzat'sya (v.impf.) crawl
rasporka (n.f.) spacer, stay, spreader
rasporot' (v.pf.) rip up
rasporyadok (n.m.) order
rasporyaditel' (n.m.) manager
rasporyadit'sya (v.pf.) give orders
rasporyazhat'sya (v.impf.) give orders
raspoznavat' (v.impf.) distinguish
rasprava (n.f.) violence
raspravit' (v.pf.) straighten
raspravit'sya (v.pf.) make short work of
raspravlyat' (v.impf.) straighten
raspravlyat'sya (v.impf.) make short work of
raspredelenie (n.n.) distribution
rasprodavat' (v.impf.) have a sale
rasprodazha (n.f.) clearance sale
rasproshchat'sya (v.pf.) take leave
rasprostertyi (adj.) outstretched
rasprostit'sya (v.pf.) take leave of
rasprostranenie (n.n.) circulation
rasprostranennyi (adj.) widespread
rasprya (n.f.) discord
raspryagat' (v.impf.) unharness
raspukhat' (v.impf.) swell
raspukhshii (adj.) swollen
raspushchennyi (adj.) dissolute
raspuskat'(sya) (v.impf.) open, dissolve
raspustit' (v.pf.) dismiss
rasputat' (v.pf.) disentangle
rasput'e (n.n.) crossroads
rasputitsa (n.f.) season of bad roads
rasputnyi (adj.) dissolute
rasputyvat' (v.impf.) disentangle
raspylenie (n.n.) pulverization
raspylitel' (n.m.) sprayer, atomizer
raspylyat'(sya) (v.impf.) pulverize
rassada (n.f.) seedlings
rassadit' (v.pf.) plant
rassadit' (v.pf.) seat
rassadnik (n.m.) nursery
rassasyvat'sya (v.impf.) dissolve
rassazhivat' (v.impf.) seat
rasschitat' (v.pf.) calculate

rasschityvat' (v.impf.)   calculate

rassech' (v.pf.)   cut

rassechenie (n.n.)   dissection

rassedlat' (v.pf.)   unsaddle

rasseivat'sya (v.impf.)   be dispersed

rassekat' (v.impf.)   cleave

rasselenie (n.n.)   settling

rasselina (n.f.)   rift

rasselit' (v.pf.)   settle

rasserdit' (v.pf.)   make angry

rassest'sya (v.pf.)   take seats

rasseyannost' (n.f.)   absentmindedness

rasseyat' (v.pf.)   disperse

rasshatat' (v.pf.)   shake loose

rasshatyvat' (v.impf.)   shake loose

rasshchedrit'sya (v.pf.)   be generous

rasshchelina (n.f.)   crevice

rasshchepit' (v.pf.)   split

rasshevelit' (v.pf.)   stir up

rasshibat' (v.impf.)   hurt, break

rasshifrovat' (v.pf.)   decipher

rasshirenie (n.n.)   expansion

rasshirit' (v.pf.)   widen

rasshiryat'(sya) (v.impf.)   widen

rasshit' (v.pf.)   embroider

rasshivat' (v.impf.)   embroider

rasshnurovat' (v.pf.)   unlace

rasskaz (n.m.)   story

rasslabit' (v.pf.)   weaken

rasslaivat'sya (v.impf.)   become stratified

rassledovanie (n.n.)   investigation

rassledovat' (v.pf.)   investigate

rassloenie (n.n.)   stratification

rasslyshat' (v.pf.)   hear

rassmatrivat' (v.impf.)   examine

rassmeshit' (v.pf.)   make somebody laugh

rassmeyat'sya (v.pf.)   burst out laughing

rassmotrenie (n.n.)   examination

rassokhnut'sya (v.pf.)   crack

rassol (n.m.)   brine

rassorit'sya (v.pf.)   quarrel

rassortirovat' (v.pf.)   sort out

rassosat'sya (v.pf.)   dissolve

rassovat' (v.pf.)   shove about

rassprashivat' (v.impf.)   make inquiries

rassrochit' (v.pf.)   pay by installments

rasstanovka (n.f.)   arrangement

rasstat'sya (v.pf.)   part

rasstavat'sya (v.impf.)   part

rasstavit' (v.pf.)   arrange

rasstegivat'(sya) (v.impf.)   unbutton

rasstegnut' (v.pf.)   undo

rasstilat' (v.impf.)   spread

rasstoyanie (n.n.)   distance

rasstraivat'sya (v.impf.)   be frustrated

rasstrel (n.m.)   shooting

rasstroennyi (adj.)   upset, out of tune

rasstroistvo (n.n.)   disorder, indigestion

rasstupat'sya (v.impf.)   move aside

rassuditel'nost' (n.f.)   sense

rassudok (n.m.)   reason

rassuzhdat' (v.impf.)   reason

rassvesti (v.pf.)   dawn

rassvet (n.m.)   daybreak

rassvirepet' (v.pf.)   grow furious

rassykhat'sya (v.impf.)   crack

rassylat' (v.impf.)   send about

rassylka (n.f.)   distribution

rassypat' (v.pf.)   spill

rassypchatyi (adj.)   short

rastachivat' (v.impf.)   bore

rastalkivat' (v.impf.)   push apart

rastaskat' (v.pf.)   pilfer

rastayat' (v.pf.)   thaw, melt

rastech'sya (v.pf.)   run

rastekat'sya (v.impf.)   run

rastenie (n.n.)   plant

rasteret' (v.pf.)   grind

rasteryannost' (n.f.)   confusion

rasteryat' (v.pf.)   lose

rasterzat' (v.pf.)   tear to pieces

rasti (v.impf.)   grow

rastirat'(sya) (v.impf.)   rub

rastit' (v.impf.)   raise

rastitel'nost' (n.f.)   vegetation

rastitel'nyi (adj.)   vegetable

rastochat' (v.impf.)   waste

rastolkat' (v.pf.)   push apart

rastolkovat' (v.pf.)   explain

rastoloch' (v.pf.)   grind

rastolstet' (v.pf.)   put on weight

rastopit' (v.pf.)   kindle

rastoptat' (v.pf.)   trample

rastorgat' (v.impf.)   dissolve, cancel

rastoropnyi (adj.)   quick

rastorzhenie (n.n.)   dissolution

rastrachivat' (v.impf.) embezzle
rastrata (n.f.) embezzlement
rastravit' (v.pf.) aggravate
rastrepat' (v.pf.) tousle
rastreskat'sya (v.pf.) crack
rastrogat' (v.impf.) move
rastsarapat' (v.pf.) scratch
rastsenivat' (v.impf.) estimate, consider
rastsenka (n.f.) valuation
rastsepit' (v.pf.) unhook
rastseplenie (n.n.) disengaging, uncoupling
rastsvesti (v.pf.) blossom
rastsvet (n.m.) blossoming, prosperity
rastsvetka (n.f.) color arrangement
rastvor (n.m.) solution
rastvor (n.m.) opening
rastvorimost' (n.f.) dissolubility
rastvorit' (v.pf.) dissolve
rastvorit' (v.pf.) open
rastvoritel' (n.m.) solvent
rastvorit'sya (v.pf.) dissolve
rastvorit'sya (v.pf.) open
rastvoryat'(sya) (v.impf.) dissolve
rastyagivat'(sya) (v.impf.) stretch
rastyanut' (v.pf.) stretch, sprain
rastyazhenie (n.n.) stretching, sprain
rastyazhimyi (adj.) elastic
ratifikatsiya (n.f.) ratification
ratsionalizatsiya (n.f.) rationalization
ratsional'nyi (adj.) rational
ravenstvo (n.n.) equality
ravnenie (n.n.) alignment
ravnina (n.f.) plain
ravno (adv.) equally
ravnobedrennyi (adj.) isosceles
ravnodeistvuyushchaya (n.f.) resultant (force)
ravnodenstvie (n.n.) equinox
ravnodushie (n.n.) indifference
ravnomernyi (adj.) even
ravnootstoyashchii (adj.) equidistant
ravnopravie (n.n.) equality of rights
ravnosil'nyi (adj.) of equal strength, be tantamount to
ravnostoronnii (adj.) equilateral
ravnovelikii (adj.) isometric
ravnovesie (n.n.) equilibrium
ravnoznachnyi (adj.) equivalent

ravnyat' (v.impf.) equalize
ravnyi (adj.) equal
raz (n.m.) time
raz (conj.) since
razbaltyvat' (v.impf.) divulge
razbavit' (v.pf.) dilute
razbazarivat' (v.impf.) squander
razbeg (n.m.) running start
razbegat'sya (v.impf.) run, scatter
razbezhat'sya (v.pf.) run, scatter
razbintovat' (v.pf.) remove a bandage
razbiratel'stvo (n.n.) hearing
razbirat'sya (v.impf.) understand
razbit' (v.pf.) break, divide, split
razbityi (adj.) broken
razbivat'(sya) (v.impf.) break, crash
razbivka (n.f.) laying out
razbogatet' (v.pf.) get rich
razboi (n.m.) robbery
razbolet'sya (v.pf.) become ill
razbombit' (v.pf.) bomb
razbor (n.m.) analysis
razborchivyi (adj.) scrupulous
razbornyi (adj.) collapsible
razbrakovka (n.f.) sorting, grading
razbrasyvat' (v.impf.) scatter
razbredat'sya (v.impf.) disperse
razbrosannyi (adj.) scattered
razbrosat' (v.pf.) scatter
razbudit' (v.pf.) wake
razbukhat' (v.impf.) swell
razbushevat'sya (v.pf.) rage
razdacha (n.f.) distribution
razdat' (v.pf.) distribute
razdat'sya (v.pf.) be heard
razdavat' (v.impf.) distribute
razdavat'sya (v.impf.) be heard
razdavit' (v.pf.) crush
razdel (n.m.) division
razdelat'sya (v.pf.) be through with
razdelenie (n.n.) division
razdel'nyi (adj.) separate
razdelyat'(sya) (v.pf.) divide
razdet' (v.pf.) undress
razdevalka (n.f.) cloakroom
razdirat' (v.impf.) tear to pieces
razdobyt' (v.pf.) get
razdol'e (n.n.) expanse

razdor (n.m.) discord
razdosadovat' (v.pf.) vex
razdrazhat' (v.impf.) irritate
razdrazhitel' (n.m.) stimulus, stimulant, irritant
razdraznit' (v.pf.) tease
razdrobit' (v.pf.) break
razdumat' (v.pf.) change one's mind
razdum'e (n.n.) thoughtful mood
razdut' (v.pf.) fan, exaggerate
razduvat'sya (v.impf.) swell
razdvaivat'sya (v.impf.) bifurcate
razdvigat' (v.impf.) move apart
razdvoenie (n.n.) bifurcation
raz"edat' (v.impf.) corrode
raz"edinit' (v.pf.) disconnect
raz"ekhat'sya (v.pf.) separate
razevat' (v.impf.) gape
raz"ezd (n.m.) siding
raz"ezzhat' (v.impf.) drive about
razgadat' (v.pf.) solve
razgadka (n.f.) guessing, answer
razgadyvat' (v.pf.) solve
razgar (n.m.) climax
razgermetizatsiya (n.f.) decompression
razgibat'(sya) (v.impf.) straighten out
razgladit' (v.pf.) smooth out
razglagol'stvovat' (v.impf.) hold forth
razglasit' (v.pf.) divulge
razglyadet' (v.pf.) make out
razglyadyvat' (v.impf.) examine
razgnevannyi (adj.) incensed
razgon (n.m.) start
razgorat'sya (v.impf.) flare up
razgorazhivat' (v.impf.) partition
razgorodit' (v.pf.) partition
razgoryachennyi (adj.) heated
razgoryachit'sya (v.pf.) get excited
razgovarivat' (v.impf.) speak
razgovor (n.m.) conversation
razgrabit' (v.pf.) plunder
razgrafit' (v.pf.) rule
razgranichenie (n.n.) demarcation
razgrebat' (v.impf.) rake
razgrom (n.m.) rout
razgruzhat' (v.impf.) unload
razgruzit' (v.pf.) unload
razgruzka (n.f.) unloading

razgryzat' (v.impf.) bite
razgul (n.m.) revelry
razgulivat' (v.impf.) stroll
razgul'nyi (adj.) dissolute
razgulyat'sya (v.pf.) clear up
razinut' (v.pf.) open
razinya (n.m.&f.) scatterbrain
razitel'nyi (adj.) striking
razlad (n.m.) discord
razlagat' (v.impf.) lay out, corrupt, decompose
razlamyvat' (v.impf.) break up
razlech'sya (v.pf.) sprawl
razlenit'sya (v.pf.) grow lazy
razletat'sya (v.impf.) fly away
razlezat'sya (v.impf.) fall apart
razlichat' (v.impf.) distinguish
razlichie (n.n.) difference
razlit' (v.pf.) spill
razliv (n.m.) flood
razlivka (n.f.) filling, casting
razlomat' (v.pf.) break up
razlomit'(sya) (v.pf.) break
razlozhenie (n.n.) decay
razlozhit' (v.pf.) lay out, corrupt, decompose
razluka (n.f.) separation
razlyubit' (v.pf.) cease to love
razmagnichivat' (v.impf.) demagnetize
razmakh (n.m.) span, scope
razmalyvat' (v.impf.) grind
razmatyvat' (v.impf.) unwind
razmazat' (v.pf.) spread
razmel'chat' (v.impf.) crush into pieces
razmen (n.m.) exchange
razmenyat' (v.pf.) change
razmer (n.m.) dimensions, size
razmerennyi (adj.) measured
razmeshat' (v.pf.) stir
razmeshchat' (v.impf.) accommodate
razmestit' (v.pf.) place
razmetat' (v.pf.) sweep away
razmetit' (v.pf.) mark
razmezhevanie (n.n.) demarcation
razmezhevat'sya (v.pf.) fix bounderies
razminirovat' (v.pf.) clear of mines
razminut'sya (v.pf.) miss
razmnozhat'(sya) (v.impf.) multiply
razmnozhenie (n.n.) reproduction

razmnozhit' (v.pf.) duplicate
razmochit' (v.pf.) soak
razmolot' (v.pf.) grind
razmolvka (n.f.) disagreement
razmotat' (v.pf.) unwind
razmozzhit' (v.pf.) smash
razmyagchat' (v.impf) soften
razmyshlenie (n.n.) reflection
razmyv (n.m.) erosion
raznashivat' (v.impf.) break in
raznesti (v.pf.) carry, deliver, destroy
raznimat' (v.impf.) dismantle
raznitsa (n.f.) difference
raznit'sya (v.impf.) differ
raznoboi (n.m.) lack of coordination
raznoe (n.n.) miscellaneous
raznoglasie (n.n.) discord, discrepancy
raznokalibernyi (adj.) of different calibers
raznokharakternyi (adj.) variegated
raznoobrazie (n.n.) variety
raznorechivyi (adj.) contradictory
raznorodnyi (adj.) heterogeneous
raznoschik (n.m.) peddler
raznosherstnyi (adj.) mixed
raznosit' (v.impf.) carry, destroy
raznosit' (v.pf.) break in
raznost' (n.f.) difference
raznostoronnii (adj.) versatile
raznotsvetnyi (adj.) variegated
raznoves (n.m.) set of weights
raznovidnost' (n.f.) variety
raznuzdannyi (adj.) unbridled
raznyat' (v.pf.) dismantle
raznyi (adj.) different
razoblachat' (v.impf.) expose
razobrat' (v.pf.) take, take apart
razobshchat' (v.impf.) separate
razocharovanie (n.n.) disappointment
razocharovyvat' (v.impf.) disappoint
razodet'sya (v.pf.) dress up
razodrat' (v.pf.) tear to pieces
razognat' (v.pf.) drive away
razognut' (v.pf.) straighten out
razogrevat' (v.impf.) warm up
razoitis' (v.pf.) go away, break up
razom (adv.) at once
razorenie (n.n.) ruin
razoruzhat' (v.impf.) disarm

razorvat' (v.pf.) tear
razoryat' (v.impf.) ruin
razoslat' (v.pf.) send
razostlat' (v.pf.) spread
razozlit' (v.pf.) infuriate
razrabatyvat' (v.impf.) work out, elaborate
razrabotat' (v.pf.) work out, elaborate
razrastat'sya (v.impf.) grow, expand
razrazhat'sya (v.impf.) break out
razreshat'sya (v.impf.) be decided
razreshit' (v.pf.) permit
razrez (n.m.) cut, incision
razroznennyi (adj.) odd
razrubat' (v.impf.) chop up
razrukha (n.f.) ruin
razrushat'sya (v.impf.) go to ruin
razrushit' (v.pf.) destroy
razryad (n.m.) category
razryad (n.m.) discharge
razryadka (n.f.) relaxation
razryazhat' (v.impf.) discharge
razrydat'sya (v.pf.) burst out sobbing
razrykhlit' (v.pf.) loosen
razryt' (v.pf.) dig up
razryv (n.m.) gap
razryvat' (v.impf.) tear
razryvat' (v.impf.) dig up
razryvnoi (adj.) explosive
razubedit' (v.pf.) dissuade
razubezhdat'sya (v.impf.) change one's mind
razuchit'sya (v.pf.) forget
razuchivat' (v.impf.) study
razukrasit' (v.pf.) decorate
razukrupnenie (n.n.) breaking up into smaller units
razum (n.m.) reason
razumeetsya (v.impf.) be understood
razumnyi (adj.) reasonable
razut'sya (v.pf.) take off one's shoes
razuvat'sya (v.impf.) take off one's shoes
razuverit' (v.pf.) dissuade
razuznavat' (v.impf.) make inquiries
razval (n.m.) chaos
razvaliny (n.pl.) ruins
razvalit' (v.pf.) break down
razvalivat'sya (v.impf.) fall to pieces
razve (part.) really
razvedat' (v.pf.) find out

razvedenie (n.n.) breeding
razvedennyi (adj.) divorced
razvedka (n.f.) intelligence
razveivat' (v.impf.) disperse
razvenchat' (v.pf) debunk
razvernut' (v.pf.) unfold, open
razverstka (n.f.) distribution
razvertka (n.f.) scanning
razvertyvat'(sya) (v.impf.) unfold
razveselit' (v.pf.) cheer up
razveshivat' (v.impf) weigh, hang up
razvesistyi (adj.) branching
razvesit' (v.pf.) weigh
razvesit' (v.pf.) hang up
razvesnoi (adj.) sold by weight
razvesti (v.pf.) separate, dilute
razvesti (v.pf.) breed
razvestis' (v.pf.) divorce
razvestis' (v.pf.) multiply
razvetvlenie (n.n.) branching
razvevat'sya (v.impf.) fly
razveyat' (v.impf.) disperse
razvezti (v.pf.) deliver
razvintit' (v.pf) unscrew
razvitie (n.n.) development
razvivat'(sya) (v.impf.) develop
razvlech' (v.pf.) amuse
razvlechenie (n.n.) entertainment
razvod (n.m.) divorce
razvodnoi most (adj.-n.m.) drawbridge
razvolnovat'sya (v.pf.) become agitated
razvorachivat' (v.impf.) unfold
razvozit' (v.impf.) deliver
razvrashchat' (v.impf.) corrupt
razvrat (n.m.) lechery
razvyazat' (v.pf.) untie
razvyazka (n.f.) outcome
razvyaznyi (adj.) familiar
razvyazyvat' (v.impf.) untie
raz"yarennyi (adj.) furious
raz"yasnenie (n.n.) explanation
razygrat' (v.pf.) play
razygryvat'sya (v.impf.) break out, run high
razyskat' (v.pf.) find
razyskivat' (v.impf.) search
razzhalobit' (v.pf.) move to pity
razzhalovat' (v.pf.) demote
razzhat' (v.pf.) unclasp

razzhech' (v.pf.) kindle
razzhevat' (v.pf.) chew
razzhimat' (v.pf.) unclasp
razzhiret' (v.pf.) grow fat
reabilitirovat' (v.impf.&pf.) rehabilitate
reagirovat' (v.impf.) react
reaktivatsiya (n.f.) reactivation
reaktivnost' (n.f.) reactance, reactivity
reaktivnyi (adj.) jet
reaktor (n.m.) reactor
reaktsioner (n.m.) reactionary
reaktsiya (n.f.) reaction
realisticheskii (adj.) realistic
realizatsiya (n.f.) realization
realizm (n.m.) realism
realizovat' (v.pf.) realize
real'nost' (n.f.) reality
rebenok (n.m.) child
rebro (n.n.) rib
rebyata (n.pl.) children
rech' (n.f.) speech
rechka (n.f.) river
redaktirovat' (v.impf.) edit
redaktor (n.m.) editor
redaktsionnyi (adj.) editorial
redaktsiya (n.f.) editorial office
redet' (v.impf.) grow thin
rediska (n.f.) radish
red'ka (n.f.) black radish
redkii (adj.) rare
reduktor (n.m.) reduction gear
referat (n.m.) essay
refleks (n.m.) reflex
reflektor (n.m.) reflector
reflektornyi (adj.) reflex
reforma (n.f.) reform
refractor (n.m.) refractor
regeneratsiya (n.f.) regeneration
registr (n.m.) register
registratsiya (n.f.) registration
reglament (n.m.) regulations
regulirovat' (v.impf.) regulate
regulyarnyi (adj.) regular
reid (n.m.) raid
reid (n.m.) road
reis (n.m.) trip
reka (n.f.) river
reklama (n.f.) advertisement

rekognostsirovka (n.f.) reconnaissance
rekombinatsiya (n.f.) recombination
rekomendovat' (v.impf.&pf.) recommend
rekonstruirovat' (v.impf.&pf.) reconstruct
rekonstruktsiya (n.f.) reconstruction
rekord (n.m.) record
rekvizirovat' (v.impf.&pf.) requisition
rekvizit (n.m.) props
rekvizitsiya (n.f.) requisition
rele (n.n.) relay
rel'ef (n.m.) relief
religioznyi (adj.) religious
religiya (n.f.) religion
rel's (n.m.) rail
remen' (n.m.) belt
remeslennik (n.m.) craftsman
remeslo (n.n.) trade
remont (n.m.) repair
remontno-tekhnicheskii (adj.) maintenance
remontnyi (adj.) repair(ing)
renegat (n.m.) renegade
renta (n.f.) rent
rentabel'nyi (adj.) profitable
rentgen (n.m.) roentgen
rentgenologiya (n.f.) roentgenology
rentgenovskii (adj.) X-ray
reorganizatsiya (n.f.) reorganization
reostat (n.m.) rheostat
repa (n.f.) turnip
reparatsiya (n.f.) reparation
repatriatsiya (n.f.) repatriation
repertuar (n.m.) repertoire
repetirovat' (v.impf.) rehearse
repetitsiya (n.f.) rehearsal
replika (n.f.) remark
reporter (n.m.) reporter
repressiya (n.f.) repression
reproduktor (n.m.) loudspeaker
reproduktsiya (n.f.) reproduction
reputatsiya (n.f.) reputation
reshat' (v.impf.) decide
reshetka (n.f.) lattice
resheto (n.n.) sieve
reshimost' (n.f.) resolution
reshit' (v.pf.) decide
reshitel'nyi (adj.) decisive
resnitsa (n.f.) eyelash
respublika (n.f.) republic

ressora (n.f.) spring
restavratsiya (n.f.) restoration
restoran (n.m.) restaurant
resursy (n.pl.) resources
retirovat'sya (v.impf.&pf.) withdraw
retivyi (adj.) zealous
retsenzent (n.m.) critic
retsenziya (n.f.) review
retsept (n.m.) prescription
retseptor (n.m.) receptor
retsidiv (n.m.) relapse
retushirovat' (v.impf.&pf.) retouch
rev (n.m.) roar
revansh (n.m.) revenge
reverberatsiya (n.f.) reverberation
revers (n.m.) reversing gear
revet' (v.impf.) roar
revizionizm (n.m.) revisionism
revizionnyi (adj.) revision
reviziya (n.f.) inspection
revmatizm (n.m.) rheumatism
revnivyi (adj.) jealous
revnost' (n.f.) jealousy
revnostnyi (adj.) zealous
revol'ver (n.m.) revolver
revolyutsioner (n.m.) revolutionary
revolyutsiya (n.f.) revolution
rezat' (v.impf.) cut
rez'ba (n.f.) carving, thread
rezektsiya (n.f.) resection
rezerv (n.m.) reserve
rezervuar (n.m.) reservoir
rezets (n.m.) chisel
rezhim (n.m.) regime
rezhisser (n.m.) producer
rezidentsiya (n.f.) residence
rezina (n.f.) rubber
rezkii (adj.) sharp
reznoi (adj.) carved
rezolyutsiya (n.f.) resolution
rezonans (n.m.) resonance
rezonnyi (adj.) reasonable
rezul'tat (n.m.) result
rezus (n.m.) Rhesus
rezvit'sya (v.impf.) frisk
rezvyi (adj.) active
rezyumirovat' (v.impf.) summarize
rif (n.m.) reef

riflenyi (adj.) corrugated
rifma (n.f.) rhyme
riga (n.f.) threshing barn
rikoshet (n.m.) ricochet
riksha (n.m.) rickshaw
rimskii (adj.) Roman
ring (n.m.) ring
rinut'sya (v.pf.) rush
ris (n.m.) rice
risk (n.m.) risk
risovanie (n.n.) drawing
risovat'sya (v.impf.) pose
risovyi (adj.) rice
risunok (n.m.) drawing
ritm (n.m.) rhythm
robet' (v.impf.) be timid
robkii (adj.) timid
rod (n.m.) family, genus, gender
rodil'nyi (adj.) maternity
rodina (n.f.) native land
rodinka (n.f.) birthmark
rodit' (v.pf.) give birth
roditel' (n.m.) parent
roditel'nyi (adj.) genitive
roditel'skii (adj.) parental
rodnik (n.m.) spring
rodnoi (adj.) own, native
rodonachal'nik (n.m.) ancestor
rodoslovnyi (adj.) genealogical
rodovoi (adj.) tribal
rodstvennik (n.m.) relation
rodstvennyi (adj.) related
rodstvo (n.n.) relationship
rody (n.pl.) childbirth
rog (n.m.) horn
rogatyi (adj.) horned
rogovoi (adj.) horn
rogozha (n.f.) matting
roi (n.m.) swarm
roit'sya (v.impf.) swarm
rok (n.m.) fate
rol' (n.f.) role
rolik (n.m.) roller
rom (n.m.) rum
roman (n.m.) novel
romans (n.m.) song
romantika (n.f.) romance
romantizm (n.m.) romanticism

romashka (n.f.) ox-eye daisy
romb (n.m.) rhombus
ronyat' (v.impf.) drop
ropot (n.m.) murmur
rosa (n.f.) dew
roscherk (n.m.) flourish
roshcha (n.f.) grove
roskosh' (n.f.) luxury
roskoshnyi (adj.) luxurious
roslyi (adj.) tall
rospis' (n.f.) paintings
rospusk (n.m.) breaking up, dissolution
rossiiskii (adj.) Russian
rosskazni (n.pl.) old wives' tales
rossyp' (n.f.) scattering, placer
rost (n.m.) growth
rostok (n.m.) sprout
rostovshchik (n.m.) moneylender
rot (n.m.) mouth
rota (n.f.) company
rotor (n.m.) rotor
rotozei (n.m.) scatterbrain
rov (n.m) ditch
rovesnik (n.m.) contemporary
rovnyi (adj.) flat
royal' (n.m.) grand piano
roza (n.f.) rose
rozetka (n.f.) socket, receptacle
rozga (n.f.) birch rod
rozh' (n.f.) rye
rozhat' (v.impf.) give birth
rozhdestvo (n.n.) Christmas
rozhenitsa (n.f.) woman in labor
roznitsa (n.f.) retail
rozovyi (adj.) pink
rozygrysh (n.m.) drawing
rozysk (n.m.) search
rtut' (n.f.) mercury
rubanok (n.m.) plane
rubashka (n.f.) shirt
rubets (n.m.) scar
rubezh (n.m.) boundary
rubin (n.m.) ruby
rubishche (n.n.) rags
rubit' (v.impf.) chop
rubka (n.f.) deckhouse
rubka (n.f.) chopping
rubl' (n.m.) ruble

rubrika (n.f.) heading
ruchatel'stvo (n.n.) guarantee
ruchat'sya (v.impf.) warrant
ruchei (n.m.) brook
ruchka (n.f.) handle
ruchnoi (adj.) manual
ruda (n.f.) ore
rudnik (n.m.) mine
rudokop (n.m.) miner
rugan' (n.f.) swearing
rugatel'stvo (n.n.) swearword
ruka (n.f.) hand, arm
rukav (n.m.) sleeve
rukavitsa (n.f.) mitten
rukhlyad' (n.f.) junk
rukhnut' (v.pf.) collapse
rukodelie (n.n.) needlework
rukomoinik (n.m.) water dispenser
rukopashnaya (n.f.) hand to hand fighting
rukopis' (n.f.) manuscript
rukopisnyi (adj.) manuscript
rukopleskanie (n.n.) applause
rukopozhatie (n.n.) handshake
rukovodit' (v.impf.) lead
rukovoditel' (n.m.) leader
rukovodstvo (n.n.) guidance, manual
rukoyatka (n.f.) handle
rul' (n.m.) rudder
rulevoi (adj.) steering
rumyana (n.pl.) rouge
rumyanets (n.m.) color
rumyn (n.m.) Rumanian
rupor (n.m.) mouthpiece
rusalka (n.f.) mermaid
rushit'sya (v.impf.) fall
ruslo (n.n.) riverbed
russkaya (adj.) Russian woman
russkii (adj.) Russian
rusyi (adj.) blond
rutina (n.f.) routine
ruzh'e (n.n.) gun
rvanut'sya (v.pf.) rush

rvat' (v.impf.) tear
rvat' (v.impf.) vomit
rvat'sya (v.impf.) tear
rvenie (n.n.) ardor
rvota (n.f.) vomiting
ryab' (n.f.) ripple
ryabchik (n.m.) hazel hen
ryabina (n.f.) ashberry
ryabit' (v.impf.) ripple
ryaboi (adj.) pockmarked
ryad (n.m.) row
ryadom (adv.) beside
ryadovoi (adj.) private
r'yanyi (adj.) zealous
ryasa (n.f.) cassock
ryavkat' (v.impf.) bellow
ryba (n.f.) fish
rybak (n.m.) fisherman
rybii (adj.) fish
rybnyi (adj.) fish
rybolov (n.m.) fisherman
rybovodstvo (n.n.) fish breeding
rychag (n.m.) lever
rychat' (v.impf.) growl
rydat' (v.impf.) sob
rykhlyi (adj.) crumbly, porous
rylo (n.n.) snout
rynok (n.m.) market
rys' (n.f.) lynx
rys' (n.f.) trot
rysak (n.m.) trotter
ryt' (v.impf.) dig
rytsar' (n.m.) knight
rytsarskii (adj.) chivalrous
rytvina (n.f.) groove
ryumka (n.f.) wineglass
ryzhii (adj.) red
rzhanoi (adj.) rye
rzhat' (v.impf.) neigh
rzhavchina (n.f.) rust
rzhavet' (v.impf.) rust

S (С, Ш, Щ)

s (prep.) with
s (prep.) from
sablya (n.f.) saber
sabotazh (n.m.) sabotage
sachok (n.m.) landing net
sad (n.m.) garden
sadit'sya (v.impf.) sit down
sadok (n.m.) fish pond
sadovnik (n.m.) gardener
sadovod (n.m.) horticulturist
sadovodstvo (n.n.) horticulture
saf'yan (n.m.) morocco leather
saika (n.f.) roll
sakhar (n.m.) sugar
saksofon (n.m.) saxophone
salat (n.m.) lettuce, salad
salazki (n.pl.) sledge
salfetka (n.f.) napkin
sal'nyi (adj.) greasy
salo (n.n.) fat
salyut (n.m.) salute
samets (n.m.) male
samizdat (n.m.) underground press
samka (n.f.) female
samobytnyi (adj.) original
samochuvstvie (n.n.) general state
samodeistvuyushchii (adj.) self-acting,
    automatic
samodel'nyi (adj.) homemade
samoderzhavie (n.n.) autocracy
samodeyatel'nost' (n.f.) amateur
    performance
samodovol'nyi (adj.) self-satisfied
samodur (n.m.) petty tyrant
samokhodnyi (adj.) self-propelled
samokritika (n.f.) self-criticism
samolet (n.m.) aircraft
samolyubivyi (adj.) proud
samomnenie (n.n.) conceit
samonadeyannyi (adj.) presumptuous
samoobladanie (n.n.) self-control
samoobman (n.m.) self-deception
samooborona (n.f.) self-defense
samoobrazovanie (n.n.) self-education
samoobsluzhivanie (n.n.) self-service

samoopredelenie (n.n.) self-determination
samootverzhennost' (n.f.) selflessness
samopisets (n.m.) automatic recorder
samopishushchii (adj.) self-recording
samopozhertvovanie (n.n.) self-sacrifice
samorodok (n.m.) nugget
samosokhranenie (n.n.) self-preservation
samosoznanie (n.n.) self-awareness
samostoyatel'nost' (n.f.) independence
samosud (n.m.) lynching
samotek (n.m.) drift
samotsvet (n.m.) semiprecious stone
samoubiistvo (n.n.) suicide
samouchitel' (n.m.) teach-yourself book
samouchka (n.m.&f.) self-taught person
samounizhenie (n.n.) self-humiliation
samoupravlenie (n.n.) self-government
samoupravstvo (n.n.) arbitrariness
samouverennost' (n.f.) self-confidence
samovar (n.m.) samovar
samovnushenie (n.n.) auto-suggestion
samovol'nyi (adj.) self-willed
samovozgoranie (n.n.) spontaneous
    combustion
samozabvennyi (adj.) selfless
samozashchita (n.f.) self-defense
samozvanets (n.m.) imposter
samyi (adj.) the same, the very
sanatorii (n.m) sanatorium
sandaliya (n.f.) sandal
sani (n.pl.) sleigh
sanitar (n.m.) hospital attendant
sanktsionirovat' (v.impf. &pf.) sanction
sanktsiya (n.f.) sanction
santimetr (n.m.) centimeter
saper (n.m.) sapper
sapfir (n.m.) sapphire
sapog (n.m.) high boot
sapozhnik (n.m.) shoemaker
sarafan (n.m.) sarafan
sarai (n.m.) shed
sarancha (n.f.) locust
sardel'ka (n.f.) sausage
sardina (n.f.) sardine
sarkazm (n.m.) sarcasm

sarkoma (n.f.)   sarcoma
satellit (n.m.)   satellite
satin (n.m.)   sateen
satira (n.f.)   satire
savan (n.m.)   shroud
sazha (n.f.)   soot
sazhat' (v.impf.)   plant
sazhenets (n.m.)   seedling
sbavit' (v.pf.)   reduce
sbegat' (v.pf.)   run
sbegat'sya (v.impf.)   come running
sberech' (v.pf.)   save
sberegatel'nyi (adj.)   saving
sberezhenie (n.n.)   saving
sberkassa (n.f.)   savings bank
sberknizhka (n.f.)   passbook
sbezhat' (v.pf.)   run down
sbit' (v.pf.)   throw down
sbivat'sya (v.impf.)   lose one's way
sbivchivyi (adj.)   confused
sblizhenie (n.n.)   rapprochement
sblizit' (v.pf.)   draw together
sboku (adv.)   from one side
sbor (n.m.)   collection
sborishche (n.n.)   crowd
sborka (n.f.)   assembly
sborki (n.pl.)   gathers
sbornik (n.m.)   collection
sbornyi (adj.)   assembly
sborochnyi (adj.)   assembly
sborshchik (n.m.)   fitter
sbory (n.pl.)   preparations
sbrasyvat' (v.impf.)   throw down
sbrivat' (v.impf.)   shave off
sbrod (n.m.)   riffraff
sbrosit' (v. pf.)   throw down
sbruya (n.f.)   harness
sbyt (n.m.)   sale
sbyt' (v.pf)   get rid
sbyt'sya (v.pf.)   come true
sbyvat' (v.impf.)   get rid
sbyvat'sya (v.impf.)   come true
schast'e (n.n.)   happiness
schastlivyi (adj.)   happy
schest' (v.pf.)   consider
schet (n.m.)   calculation
schetchik (n.m.)   meter, counter
schetchik (n.m.)   teller

schetovod (n.m.)   accountant
schety (n.pl.)   abacus
schishchat' (v.impf.)   clean off
schistit' (v.pf.)   clean off
schitat' (v.impf.)   count
schitat'sya (v.impf.)   consider
schityvanie (n.n.)   read-out
sdacha (n.f.)   lease, surrender, change
sdat' (v.pf.)   hand in
sdavat'(sya) (v.impf.)   surrender
sdavit' (v.pf.)   squeeze
sdavlennyi (adj.)   squeezed
sdelat' (v.pf.)   do, make
sdelka (n.f.)   bargain
sdel'nyi (adj.)   piecework
sdergivat' (v.impf.)   pull off
sdernut' (v.pf.)   pull off
sderzhannost' (n.f.)   restraint
sderzhat' (v.pf.)   restrain
sderzhivat'(sya) (v.impf.)   control oneself
sdirat' (v.impf.)   skin
sdoba (n.f.)   fancy bread
sdokhnut' (v.pf.)   die
sdruzhit'sya (v.pf.)   make friends
sduvat' (v.impf.)   blow away
sdvig (n.m.)   displacement, change
sdvigat'(sya) (v.impf.)   move
sdvinut' (v.pf.)   move
seans (n.m.)   show
sebestoimost' (n.f.)   cost price
sech' (v.impf.)   whip
sechenie (n.n.)   section
sech'sya (v.impf.)   split
s"edat' (v.impf.)   eat
sedet' (v.impf.)   turn gray
sedimentatsiya (n.f.)   sedimentation
sedlat' (v.impf.)   saddle
sedlo (n.n.)   saddle
sed'moi (adj.)   seventh
sedoborodyi (adj.)   graybearded
sedoi (adj.)   gray
sedok (n.m.)   rider
sedovlasyi (adj.)   gray-haired
segment (n.m.)   segment
segodnya (adv.)   today
sei (p.)   this
seichas (adv.)   now
seif (n.m.)   safe

seismologiya (n.f.) seismology

s"ekhat' (v.pf.) go down

sekret (n.m.) secret

sekretar' (n.m.) secretary

sekretnyi (adj.) secret

sekretornyi (adj.) secretory

sekretsiya (n.f.) secretion

seksual'nyi (adj.) sexual

sekta (n.f.) sect

sektor (n.m.) sector

sektsiya (n.f.) section

sekunda (n.f.) second

sel'd' (n.f.) herring

seledka (n.f.) herring

selektsiya (n.f.) selection

selen (n.m.) selenium

selenie (n.n.) village

selezen' (n.m.) drake

selezenka (n.f.) spleen

selitra (n.f.) saltpeter

selit'sya (v.impf.) settle

selo (n.n.) village

sel'skii (adj.) rural

sel'skokhozyaistvennyi (adj.) agricultural

sel'sovet (n.m.) village Soviet

sem' (num.) seven

semafor (n.m.) light signals

semantika (n.f.) semantics

semeinyi (adj.) family

semenit' (v.impf.) mince

semennoi (adj.) seminal

semerka (n.f.) seven

semero (num.) seven

semestr (n.m.) term

semga (n.f.) salmon

semidesyatiletnii (adj.) seventy-year-old

semidesyatyi (adj.) seventieth

semiletnii (adj.) seven-year

seminar (n.m.) seminar

seminariya (n.f.) seminary

s"emka (n.f.) shooting

semnadtsat' (num.) seventeen

s"emshchik (n.m.) tenant

semya (n.n.) seed, semen

sem'ya (n.f.) family

senat (n.m.) senate

seni (n.pl.) inner porch

seno (n.n.) hay

sensatsiya (n.f.) sensation

sentimental'nyi (adj.) sentimental

sentyabr' (n.m.) September

separatnyi (adj.) separate

sera (n.f.) sulphur

serb (n.m.) Serbian

serdechnost' (n.f.) heartiness

serdityi (adj.) angry

serdtse (n.n.) heart

serdtsebienie (n.n.) palpitation

serdtsevina (n.f.) core

serebristyi (adj.) silver

serebro (n.n.) silver

serebryanyi (adj.) silver

seredina (n.f.) middle

serednyak (n.m.) peasant of average means

serenada (n.f.) serenade

serezhka (n.f.) earring

ser'eznyi (adj.) serious

ser'ga (n.f.) earring

seriinyi (adj.) serial

seriya (n.f.) series

sernistyi (adj.) sulfureous

sernyi (adj.) sulfuric

serouglerod (n.m.) carbon disulfide

serovatyi (adj.) grayish

serovodorod (n.m.) hydrogen sulfide

serp (n.m.) sickle

serpovidnyi (adj.) crescent

servirovat' (v.impf.) serve

serviz (n.m.) service

seryi (adj.) gray

serzhant (n.m.) sergeant

sessiya (n.f.) session

sest' (v.pf.) sit down

s"est' (v.pf.) eat

s"estnoi (adj.) food

sestra (n.f.) sister

set' (n.f.) net

setchatka (n.f.) retina

setka (n.f.) netting

setovat' (v.impf.) complain

sev (n.m.) sowing

sever (n.m.) north

severo-vostok (n.m.) northeast

severo-zapad (n.m.) northwest

sevooborot (n.m.) crop rotation

seyalka (n.f.) seed drill

s"ezd (n.m.) congress
s"ezdit' (v.pf.) visit
s"ezhivat'sya (v.impf.) shrink
sezon (n.m.) season
s"ezzhat'sya (v.impf.) assemble
sfabrikovat' (v.pf.) forge
sfera (n.f.) sphere
sfericheskii (adj.) spherical
sfinks (n.m.) sphinx
sformirovat' (v.pf.) form
sformulirovat' (v.pf.) formulate
sfotografirovat' (v.pf.) photograph
sgib (n.m.) bend
sgibat'(sya) (v.impf.) bend down
sgladit' (v.pf.) smooth
sglupit' (v.pf.) do something stupid
sgnit' (v.pf.) rot
sgnoit' (v.pf.) let rot
sgonyat' (v.impf.) drive away
sgoranie (n.n.) combustion
sgorbit'sya (v.pf.) stoop
sgoret' (v.pf.) burn down
sgoryacha (adv.) in a fit of temper
sgovarivat'sya (v.impf.) come to an
    agreement
sgovor (n.m.) collusion
sgovorchivyi (adj.) compliant
sgrebat' (v.impf.) rake up
sgruzhat' (v.impf.) unload
sgushchat'(sya) (v.impf.) thicken
sgustit' (v.pf.) thicken
sgustok (n.m.) clot
shablon (n.m.) pattern
shafran (n.m.) saffron
shag (n.m.) step
shagat' (v.impf.) step
shagom (adv.) at a walking pace
shaiba (n.f.) puck
shaika (n.f.) gang
shaika (n.f.) washbasin
shakal (n.m.) jackal
shakh (n.m.) shah
shakh (n.m.) check
shakhmatist (n.m.) chess player
shakhmatnyi (adj.) chess
shakhmaty (n.pl.) chess
shakhta (n.f.) mine
shal' (n.f.) shawl

shalash (n.m.) cabin
shalit' (v.impf.) be naughty
shal'noi (adj.) wild
shalost' (n.f.) prank
shalovlivyi (adj.) playful
shalun (n.m.) mischievous child
shamkat' (v.impf.) mumble
shans (n.m.) chance
shantazh (n.m.) blackmail
shapka (n.f.) cap
shar (n.m.) ball
sharada (n.f.) charade
sharakhat'sya (v.impf.) shy, start up
sharf (n.m.) scarf
sharik (n.m.) small ball
sharikopodshipnik (n.m.) ball bearing
sharit' (v.impf.) search
sharkat' (v.impf.) shuffle
sharmanka (n.f.) street organ
sharnir (n.m.) hinge
sharovidnyi (adj.) spherical
sharzh (n.m.) caricature
shashka (n.f.) sword
shashki (n.pl.) checkers
shassi (n.n.) chassis
shatat' (v.impf.) sway
shaten (n.m.) brown-haired man
shater (n.m.) tent
shatkii (adj.) unsteady
shchadit' (v.impf.) spare
shchavel' (n.m.) sorrel
shcheben' (n.m.) crushed stone
shchebetat' (v.impf.) chirp
shchedrost' (n.f.) generosity
shchegol' (n.m.) dandy
shchegol (n.m.) goldfinch
shchegol'nut' (v.pf.) show off
shchegolyat' (v.impf.) flaunt
shcheka (n.f.) cheek
shchekolda (n.f.) latch
shchekotat' (v.impf.) tickle
shchekotka (n.f.) tickling
shchel' (n.f.) chink
shchelchok (n.m.) snap
shchelkat' (v.impf.) click
shchelknut' (v.pf.) click
shcheloch' (n.f.) alkali
shchelochnoi (adj.) alkaline

shchelok (n.m.)   alkaline solution

shchenok (n.m.)   puppy

shchepetil'nyi (adj.)   scrupulous

shchepka (n.f.)   chip

shchepotka (n.f.)   pinch

shchetina (n.f.)   bristle

shchetka (n.f.)   brush

shchi (n.pl.)   cabbage soup

shchikolotka (n.f.)   ankle

shchipat' (v.impf.)   pinch

shchipchiki (n.pl.)   tweezers

shchipok (n.m.)   pinch

shchiptsy (n.pl.)   tongs, pincers

shchit (n.m.)   shield

shchitovidnyi (adj.)   thyroid

shchuchii (adj.)   pike

shchuka (n.f.)   pike

shchup (n.m.)   feeler, gauge, dip stick

shchupal'tse (n.n.)   tentacle

shchupat' (v.impf.)   feel

shchuplyi (adj.)   puny

shchurit' (v.impf.)   squint

shedevr (n.m.)   masterpiece

shef (n.m.)   chief

shelest (n.m.)   rustle

shelestet' (v.impf.)   rustle

shelk (n.m.)   silk

shelkovichnyi cherv' (adj.-n.m.)   silkworm

shelkovistyi (adj.)   silky

shelkovyi (adj.)   silk

shelokhnut'sya (v.pf.)   stir

shelukha (n.f.)   peelings

shelushit' (v.impf.)   shell

shepelyavit' (v.impf.)   lisp

shepnut' (v.pf.)   whisper

shepot (n.m.)   whisper

sheptat' (v.impf.)   whisper

sherenga (n.f.)   rank

sherokhovatyi (adj.)   rough

shershavyi (adj.)   rough

sherst' (n.f.)   wool

shest (n.m.)   pole

shest' (num.)   six

shesterka (n.f.)   six

shesternya (n.f.)   gear

shestero (num.)   six

shestidesyatyi (adj.)   sixtieth

shestiletnii (adj.)   six-year-old

shestimesyachnyi (adj.)   six-month

shestiugol'nyi (adj.)   hexagonal

shestnadtsat' (num.)   sixteen

shestnadtsatyi (adj.)   sixteenth

shestoi (adj.)   sixth

shestvie (n.n.)   procession

shevelit' (v.impf.)   move

shevel'nut'(sya) (v.pf.)   move

shevro (n.n.)   kid

sheya (n.f.)   neck

shezlong (n.m.)   chaise lounge

shifr (n.m.)   cipher

shikarnyi (adj.)   smart

shikat' (v.impf.)   hiss

shilo (n.n.)   awl

shina (n.f.)   tire

shinel' (n.f.)   greatcoat

shinkovat' (v.impf.)   chop

ship (n.m.)   thorn

shipet' (v.impf.)   hiss

shipovnik (n.m.)   dog-rose

shipuchii (adj.)   fizzing

shipyashchii (adj.)   sibilant

shirina (n.f.)   breadth

shirit'sya (v.impf.)   widen

shirma (n.f.)   screen

shirokii (adj.)   broad, wide

shiroko (adv.)   widely, broadly

shirokoékrannyi (adj.)   wide-screen

shirokoplechii (adj.)   broad-shouldered

shirokoveshchanie (n.n.)   broadcasting

shirota (n.f.)   width

shishka (n.f.)   cone

shit' (v.impf.)   sew

shkaf (n.m.)   dresser, wardrobe

shkala (n.f.)   scale

shkatulka (n.f.)   box

shkhuna (n.f.)   schooner

shkiper (n.m.)   skipper

shkiv (n.m.)   pulley

shkola (n.f.)   school

shkola-internat (n.m.)   boarding school

shkol'nik (n.m.)   schoolboy

shkura (n.f.)   skin

shkval (n.m.)   squall

shlagbaum (n.m.)   barrier

shlak (n.m.)   slag

shlam (n.m.)   slime, slurry, sludge

shlang (n.m.) hose
shlem (n.m.) helmet
shlepat'sya (v.impf.) fall with a thud
shlepnut' (v.pf.) slap
shlifovat' (v.impf.) grind, polish
shlifovka (n.f.) grinding, polishing
shlyapa (n.f.) hat
shlyupka (n.f.) boat
shlyuz (n.m.) lock
shmel' (n.m.) bumblebee
shmygat' (v.impf.) dart
shnitsel' (n.m.) schnitzel
shnur (n.m.) string
shnyryat' (v.impf.) poke about
shofer (n.m.) driver
shok (n.m.) shock
shokirovat' (v.impf.) shock
shokolad (n.m.) chocolate
shorokh (n.m.) rustle
shorty (n.pl.) shorts
shory (n.pl.) blinders
shosse (n.n.) highway
shotlandets (n.m.) Scot
shotlandtsy (n.pl.) the Scots
shov (n.m.) seam
shovinizm (n.m.) chauvinism
shpaga (n.f.) sword
shpagat (n.m.) string
shpaklevat' (v.impf.) putty
shpala (n.f.) sleeper
shpargalka (n.f.) crib
shpil'ka (n.f.) hairpin
shpinat (n.m.) spinach
shpingalet (n.m.) bolt
shpion (n.m.) spy
shpora (n.f.) spur
shprits (n.m.) syringe
shproty (n.pl.) sprats
shpul'ka (n.f.) spool
shram (n.m.) scar
shrapnel' (n.f.) shrapnel
shrift (n.m.) type
shtab (n.m.) staff
shtabel' (n.m.) stack
shtamp (n.m.) stamp
shtanga (n.f.) bar, weight
shtany (n.pl.) pants
shtapel'nyi (adj.) staple

shtat (n.m.) state
shtat (n.m.) staff
shtativ (n.m.) tripod
shtatnyi (adj.) regular
shtatskii (adj.) civilian
shtempel' (n.m.) stamp
shtempelevat' (v.impf.) stamp
shtepsel' (n.m.) plug
shtift (n.m.) pin, pivot, plug
shtil' (n.m.) calm
shtol'nya (n.f.) gallery
shtopat' (v.impf.) darn, mend
shtopor (n.m.) corkscrew
shtora (n.f.) blind
shtorm (n.m.) storm
shtraf (n.m.) fine
shtreikbrekher (n.m.) strikebreaker
shtrek (n.m.) drift
shtrikh (n.m.) touch
shtuchnyi (adj.) piece
shtuka (n.f.) piece
shtukaturit' (v.impf.) plaster
shturm (n.m.) storm
shturman (n.m.) navigator
shturmovat' (v.impf.) storm
shturval (n.m.) steering wheel
shtyk (n.m.) bayonet
shuba (n.f.) fur coat
shuler (n.m.) card shark
shum (n.m.) noise
shumet' (v.impf.) make noise
shumnyi (adj.) noisy
shumok (n.m.) noise
shumovka (n.f.) skimmer
shurf (n.m.) bore hole
shurin (n.m.) brother-in-law
shurshat' (v.impf.) rustle
shustryi (adj.) bright
shut (n.m.) fool
shutit' (v.impf.) joke
shutka (n.f.) joke
shutochnyi (adj.) comic
shutya (adv.) in jest
shvabra (n.f.) mop
shved (n.m.) Swede
shveinyi (adj.) sewing
shveitsar (n.m.) doorman
shveitsarets (n.m.) Swiss

shveya (n.f.) seamstress

shvyrnut' (v.pf.) fling

sibirskii (adj.) Siberian

sidelka (n.f.) nurse

siden'e (n.n.) seat

sidet' (v.impf.) sit

sidr (n.m.) cider

sidyachii (adj.) sitting, sedentary

sifilis (n.m.) syphilis

sigara (n.f.) cigar

signal (n.m.) signal

sila (n.f.) strength, force, power

silach (n.m.) athlete

silikat (n.m.) silicate

silit'sya (v.impf.) try

sil'nyi (adj.) strong

silok (n.m.) trap

silos (n.m.) silage

silovoi (adj.) power

siluét (n.m.) silhouette

simbioz (n.m.) symbiosis

simfonicheskii (adj.) symphony

simfoniya (n.f.) symphony

simmetriya (n.f.) symmetry

simpatiya (n.f.) liking

simpatizirovat' (v.impf.) sympathize

simptom (n.m.) symptom

simulirovat' (v.impf.) simulate, sham

simvol (n.m.) symbol

simvolizirovat' (v.impf.) symbolize

sinagoga (n.f.) synagogue

sindikat (n.m.) syndicate

sindrom (n.m.) syndrome

sineva (n.f.) dark blue color

sinii (adj.) blue

sin'ka (n.f.) blue

sinkhofazotron (n.m.) synchophasotron

sinkhronizatsiya (n.f.) synchronization

sinod (n.m.) synod

sinonim (n.m.) synonym

sintaksis (n.m.) syntax

sintez (n.m.) synthesis

sinus (n.m.) sine

sinusoida (n.f.) sinusoid

sinyak (n.m.) bruise

siplyi (adj.) hoarse

siren' (n.f.) lilac

sirena (n.f.) siren

sirenevyi (adj.) lilac

sirop (n.m.) syrup

sirota (n.m.&f.) orphan

sistema (n.f.) system

sistematika (n.f.) systematization

sitets (n.m.) printed cotton

sito (n.n.) sieve

sittsevyi (adj.) printed cotton

situatsiya (n.f.) situation

siyanie (n.n.) radiance

sizyi (adj.) dove colored

skachka (n.f.) gallop

skachkoobraznyi (adj.) uneven

skachok (n.m.) jump

skafandr (n.m.) diving suit, space suit

skakat' (v.impf.) jump

skala (n.f.) rock

skalit' (v.impf.) grin

skalka (n.f.) rolling pin

skal'pel' (n.m.) scalpel

skalyvat' (v.impf.) break, pin together

skameechka (n.f.) small bench

skameika (n.f.) bench

skam'ya (n.f.) bench

skandal (n.m.) row, scandal

skaplivat'(sya) (v.impf.) accumulate

skarb (n.m.) goods and chattels

skarednyi (adj.) stingy

skarlatina (n.f.) scarlet fever

skat (n.m.) slope

skatat' (v.pf.) roll up

skatert' (n.f.) tablecloth

skatit' (v.pf.) roll down

skatyvat' (v.impf.) roll up

skatyvat' (v.impf.) roll down

skatyvat'sya (v.impf.) slide down

skazanie (n.n.) legend

skazat' (v.pf.) say

skazitel' (n.m.) storyteller

skazka (n.f.) tale

skazuemoe (n.n.) predicate

skazyvat'sya (v.impf.) tell on

skelet (n.m.) skeleton

skeptik (n.m.) skeptic

skhema (n.f.) scheme

skhitrit' (v.pf.) use cunning

skhlynut' (v.pf.) subside, recede

skhodit' (v.impf.) go down

skhodit' (v.impf.) go, fetch
skhodit'sya (v.impf.) meet, agree
skhodka (n.f.) meeting
skhodni (n.pl.) gangway
skhodnyi (adj.) similar
skholastika (n.f.) scholasticism
skhoronit' (v.pf.) bury
skhozhii (adj.) similar
skhvatit' (v.pf.) catch
skhvatka (n.f.) skirmish
skidka (n.f.) discount
skinut' (v.pf.) throw off
skipetr (n.m.) scepter
skipidar (n.m.) turpentine
skird(a) (n.m.&f.) stack
skisat' (v.pf) turn sour
skitat'sya (v.impf.) wander
sklad (n.m.) storehouse
sklad (n.m.) turn
skladchina (n.f.) clubbing
skladka (n.f.) crease
skladnoi (adj.) folding
skladnyi (adj.) harmonious
skladyvat' (v.impf.) add
skleit' (v.pf.) paste together
skleivat'(sya) (v.impf.) stick together
sklep (n.m.) vault
skleroz (n.m.) sclerosis
sklochnik (n.m.) squabbler
skloka (n.f.) squabble
sklon (n.m.) slope
sklonenie (n.n.) declension
sklonit' (v.pf.) bend, win
sklonnost' (n.f.) inclination
sklonyaemyi (adj.) declinable
sklonyat' (v.impf.) bend, win
sklonyat' (v.impf.) decline
sklonyat'sya (v.impf.) bend, be inclined
sklonyat'sya (v.impf.) be declined
sklyanka (n.f.) vial
skoba (n.f.) cramp
skobka (n.f.) bracket
skoblit' (v.impf.) scrape
skobyanoi (adj.) hardware
skolachivat' (v.impf.) join
skol'ko (adv.) how much, how many
skolot' (v.pf.) break
skolot' (v.pf.) pin together

skol'zhenie (n.n.) sliding
skol'zkii (adj.) slippery
skol'znut' (v.pf.) slip
skomandovat' (v.pf.) command
skombinirovat' (v.pf.) combine
skomkat' (v.pf.) crumple
skonchat'sya (v.pf.) die
skontsentrirovat' (v.pf.) concentrate
skopit' (v.pf.) save
skorbet' (v.impf.) mourn
skorbnyi (adj.) mournful
skoree (adv.) faster
skorlupa (n.f.) shell
skornyak (n.m.) furrier
skoro (adj.) fast, soon
skorogovorka (n.f.) patter
skoroportyashchiisya (adj.) perishable
skoropostizhnyi (adj.) sudden
skorospelyi (adj.) early
skorosshivatel' (n.m.) folder
skorost' (adv.) speed
skorostrel'nyi (adj.) rapid-fire
skorotechnyi (adj.) transient
skorpion (n.m.) scorpion
skoryi (adj.) fast
skosit' (v.pf.) mow
skosit' (v.pf.) squint
skot (n.m.) livestock
skotovod (n.m.) cattle breeder
skotskii (adj.) bestial
skovat' (v.pf.) chain
skovoroda (n.f.) frying pan
skovyvat' (v.impf.) chain
skrasit' (v.pf.) brighten up
skrebok (n.m.) scraper
skrepit' (v.pf.) fasten
skrepka (n.f.) clip
skreplenie (n.n.) fastening, joint
skreshchivat' (v.impf.) cross
skresti (v.impf.) scrape
skrestit' (v.pf.) cross
skrezhet (n.m.) grinding noise
skrip (n.m.) creak
skripach (n.m.) violinist
skripet' (v.impf.) creak
skripka (n.f.) violin
skripnut' (v.pf.) creak
skromnost' (n.f.) modesty

skrutit' (v.pf.) twist
skryaga (n.m.&f.) miser
skryt' (v.pf.) hide
skrytnost' (n.f.) reticence
skrytyi (adj.) hidden
skryvat'(sya) (v.impf.) disappear, hide
skuchat' (v.impf.) be bored
skuchennyi (adj.) dense
skuchnyi (adj.) boring
skudnyi (adj.) scanty
skuka (n.f.) boredom
skula (n.f.) cheekbone
skulit' (v.impf.) whimper
skul'ptor (n.m.) sculptor
skupat' (v.impf.) buy up
skupit'sya (v.impf.) be stingy
skupka (n.f.) buying up
skupoi (adj.) stingy
skupost' (n.f.) stinginess
skupshchik (n.m.) wholesaler
skushat' (v.pf.) eat up
skvazhina (n.f.) well
skver (n.m.) public garden
skvernoslovit' (v.impf.) use foul language
skvernyi (adj.) bad
skvorets (n.m.) starling
skvoz' (prep.) through
skvozit' (v.impf.) show through
skvoznyak (n.m.) draught
slabet' (v.impf.) weaken
slabitel'noe (n.n.) laxative
slabo (adv.) feebly
slabokharakternyi (adj.) weak-willed
slabosil'nyi (adj.) weak
slabost' (n.f.) weakness
slaboumie (n.n.) imbecility
slabovol'nyi (adj.) weak-willed
slabyi (adj.) weak
sladit' (v.pf.) manage
sladkii (adj.) sweet
sladost' (n.f.) sweetness
sladostrastnyi (adj.) voluptuous
slagaemoe (n.n.) addendum
slagayushchaya (n.f.) component
slanets (n.m.) schist
slashchavyi (adj.) sugary
slastena (n.f.) sweet tooth
slasti (n.pl.) candy

slava (n.f.) glory
slavit'sya (v.impf.) be famous
slavnyi (adj.) glorious
slavyanin (n.m.) Slav
slech' (v.pf.) be laid up
sled (n.m.) track, trace
sledit' (v.impf.) watch
sledit' (v.impf.) leave traces
sledom (adv.) after
sledovat' (v.impf.) follow
sledovatel' (n.m.) investigator
sledstvie (n.n.) inquiry
sledstvie (n.n.) consequence
sleduyushchii (adj.) following
slegka (adv.) slightly
slepen' (n.m.) horsefly
slepit' (v.impf.) blind
slepit' (v.pf.) mold
slepit' (v.pf.) paste together
slepnut' (v.impf.) become blind
slepoi (adj.) blind
slepok (n.m.) mold
slepota (n.f.) blindness
slesar' (n.m.) fitter
slesarnyi (adj.) metalworker's
slet (n.m.) rally
sletat' (v.impf.) fly down
sletat'sya (v.impf.) gather
sletet' (v.pf.) fly down
sletet'sya (v.pf.) gather
sleva (adv.) on the left
sleza (n.f.) tear
slezat' (v.impf.) get down
slezhenie (n.n.) tracking
slezhka (n.f.) shadowing
slezit'sya (v.impf.) water
slezotochivyi gaz (adj.-n.m.) tear gas
slichat' (v.impf.) compare
slipat'sya (v.impf.) stick together
slishkom (adv.) too
slit' (v.pf.) pour
slitno (adv.) together
slitok (n.m.) ingot
sliva (n.f.) plum
slivat'(sya) (v.impf.) merge
slivki (n.pl.) cream
sliyanie (n.n.) confluence, merging
sliz' (n.f.) slime, mucus

slizistyi (adj.) slimy, mucous
sloenyi pirog (adj.-n.m.) puff pastry
slog (n.m.) syllable
slog (n.m.) style
sloi (n.m.) layer
sloistyi (adj.) stratified, flaky
slom (n.m.) pulling down
slomat' (v.pf.) break, fracture
slon (n.m.) elephant
slonyat'sya (v.impf.) loiter
slovak (n.m.) Slovak
slovar' (n.m.) dictionary, vocabulary
slovarnyi (adj.) lexical
slovatskii (adj.) Slovakian
slovesnost' (n.f.) literature
slovesnyi (adj.) oral
slovno (adv.) as though
slovo (n.n.) word
slovom (adv.) in short
slovoobrazovanie (n.n.) word-building
slovookhotlivyi (adj.) talkative
slovosochetanie (n.n.) combination of words
slozhenie (n.n.) addition
slozhit' (v.pf.) add
slozhnost' (n.f.) complication
sluchai (n.m.) case, incident, accident
sluchainyi (adj.) accidental
sluchat'sya (v.impf.) happen
sluga (n.m.) servant
slukh (n.m.) hearing
slukhovoi (adj.) acoustic, auditory
slushatel' (n.m.) listener
sluzhashchii (n.m.) employee
sluzhba (n.f.) service
sluzhebnyi (adj.) service, auxiliary
sluzhenie (n.n.) service
slyabing (n.m.) slabbing
slyakot' (n.f.) slush
slyshat' (v.impf.) hear
slyshimost' (n.f.) audibility
slyshno (pred.) one can hear
slyuda (n.f.) mica
slyuna (n.f.) saliva
slyunyavyi (adj.) slobbery
smachivat' (v.impf.) moisten
smakhivat' (v.impf.) brush off
smanivat' (v.impf.) entice
smasterit' (v.pf.) make

smatyvat' (v.impf.) reel
smazat' (v.pf.) grease
smazka (n.f.) lubrication
smekh (n.m.) laughter
smekhotvornyi (adj.) laughable
smel'chak (n.m.) daredevil
smelost' (n.f.) courage
smelyi (adj.) courageous
smena (n.f.) change
smerch (n.m.) whirlwind
smerit' (v.pf.) measure
smerkat'sya (v.impf.) get dark
smert' (n.f.) death
smertel'nyi (adj.) mortal
smertnost' (n.f.) mortality
smes' (n.f.) mixture
smeshannyi (adj.) mixed
smeshchat' (v.impf.) displace, remove
smeshchenie (n.n.) displacement, shift, bias
smeshit' (v.impf.) make laugh
smeshivat' (v.impf.) mix
smesitel' (n.m.) mixer
smesti (v.pf.) sweep away
smestit' (v.pf.) displace, remove
smet' (v.impf.) dare
smeta (n.f.) estimate
smetana (n.f.) sour cream
smetat' (v.impf.) sweep away
smetat' (v.impf.) tack
smetlivost' (n.f.) resourcefulness
smeyat'sya (v.impf.) laugh
smezhnost' (n.f.) contiguity
smezhnyi (adj.) adjacent
smilostivit'sya (v.pf.) have pity
smirenie (n.n.) humility
smirit' (v.pf.) subdue
smirno (adv.) quietly
smiryat'sya (v.impf) submit
smoch' (v.pf.) be able
smochit' (v.pf.) moisten
smola (n.f.) resin
smolchat' (v.pf.) hold one's tongue
smolkat' (v.impf.) grow silent
smorkat'sya (v.impf.) blow one's nose
smorodina (n.f.) currant
smorshchennyi (adj.) wrinkled
smotat' (v.pf.) reel
smotr (n.m.) inspection

smotret' (v.impf.) look

smrad (n.m.) stench

smuglyi (adj.) dark

smushchat'(sya) (v.impf.) be embarrassed

smutit' (v.pf.) confuse

smutnyi (adj.) vague

smyagchat'(sya) (v.impf.) soften

smyat' (v.pf.) crumple

smyatenie (n.n.) confusion

smychka (n.f.) union

smychok (n.m.) bow

smykat'(sya) (v.impf.) close

smyshlenyi (adj.) clever

smysl (n.m.) sense

smyt' (v.pf.) wash off

smyvat'(sya) (v.impf.) wash off

snabdit' (v.pf.) supply

snachala (adv.) at first

snaiper (n.m.) sharpshooter

snaruzhi (adv.) outside

snaryad (n.m.) projectile

snaryadit' (v.pf.) equip

snaryazhat'(sya) (v.impf.) equip oneself

snaryazhenie (n.n.) equipment

snast' (n.f.) rigging

sneg (n.m.) snow

snegir' (n.m.) bullfinch

snegoochistitel' (n.m.) snowplow

snegopad (n.m.) snowfall

snegurochka (n.f.) Snow-Maiden

snesti (v.pf.) take

snesti (v.pf.) lay

snestis' (v.pf.) communicate

snezhinka (n.f.) snowflake

snezhnyi (adj.) snow

snezhok (n.m.) snowball

snimat'sya (v.impf.) photograph

snimok (n.m.) shapshot

sniskat' (v.pf.) win

sniskhoditel'nost' (n.f.) condescension

snit'sya (v.impf.) dream

snizhat'sya (v.impf.) descend

snizit' (v.pf.) lower

snizoiti (v.pf.) condescend

snizu (adv.) from below

snokha (n.f.) daughter-in-law

snop (n.m.) sheaf

snopovyazalka (n.f.) binder

snorovka (n.f.) skill

snosheniya (n.pl.) relations

snosit' (v.impf.) take, pull down

snoska (n.f.) footnote

snosnyi (adj.) bearable

snotvornoe (n.n.) sleeping pill

snova (adv.) again

snovidenie (n.n.) dream

snyat' (v.pf.) take off

snyatie (n.n.) raising, removal

so (prep.) with, from

soavtor (n.m.) coauthor

sobaka (n.f.) dog

sobesednik (n.m.) interlocutor

sobiranie (n.n.) collection

soblazn (n.m.) temptation

soblyudat' (v.impf.) observe

soblyusti (v.pf.) observe

sobol' (n.m.) sable

soboleznovanie (n.n.) condolence

sobor (n.m.) cathedral

sobranie (n.n.) meeting

sobrat' (v.pf.) collect

sobstvennik (n.m.) owner

sobstvenno (adv.) strictly

sobstvennoruchno (adv.) with one's own hand

sobstvennost' (n.f.) property

sobytie (n.n.) event

sochetanie (n.n.) combination

sochinenie (n.n.) composition

sochit'sya (v.impf.) ooze

sochlenenie (n.n.) joint

sochnyi (adj.) juicy

sochuvstvovat' (v.impf.) sympathize

soda (n.f.) soda

sodeistvie (n.n.) assistance

soderzhanie (n.n.) maintenance

soderzhat' (v.impf.) keep

soderzhatel'nyi (adj.) rich in content

soderzhimoe (n.n.) contents

sodoklad (n.m.) co-report

sodrat' (v.pf.) skin

sodrogat'sya (v.impf.) shudder

sodruzhestvo (n.n.) concord

soedinenie (n.n.) junction, combination

soedinennyi (adj.) united

soedinit' (v.impf.) unite

soedinitel'nyi (adj.) connecting

soedinyat'(sya) (v.impf.) unite, combine

soevyi (adj.) soybean

soglashatel' (n.m.) collaborator

soglashat'sya (v.impf.) agree

soglasie (n.n.) consent

soglasno (adv.) according to

soglasnyi (adj.) consonant

soglasnyi (adj.) agreeable

soglasovanie (n.n.) coordination

sognat' (v.pf.) drive away

sognut' (v.pf.) bend

sograzhdane (n.pl.) fellow citizens

sogreshit' (v.pf.) commit a sin

sogret' (v.pf.) warm

sogrevanie (n.n.) warming

soiti (v.pf.) go down

soizmerimyi (adj.) commensurable

sok (n.m.) juice

sokha (n.f.) wooden plow

sokhnut' (v.impf.) dry

sokhranenie (n.n.) preservation

sokhrannost' (n.f.) safety

sokol (n.m.) falcon

sokrashchat'(sya) (v.impf.) reduce, shorten

sokratit' (v.pf.) abbreviate, reduce, cancel

sokrovennyi (adj.) innermost

sokrovishche (n.n.) treasure

sokrushat' (v.impf.) smash

sol' (n.f.) salt

soldat (n.m.) soldier

solen'e (n.n.) food preserved in brine

solenie (n.n.) salting

solenyi (adj.) salt, saline

solgat' (v.pf.) lie

solidarnost' (n.f.) solidarity

solidnost' (n.f.) reliability, solidity

solist (n.m.) soloist

solit' (v.impf.) salt

solnechnyi (adj.) sun, solar

solntse (n.n.) sun

solo (n.n.) solo

soloma (n.f.) straw

solonchaki (n.pl.) salt marshes

solonina (n.f.) corned beef

solonka (n.f.) saltcellar

solovei (n.m.) nightingale

solyanaya kislota (adj.-n.f.) hydrochloric

acid

solyanoi (adj.) salt

somknut' (v.pf.) close

somnenie (n.n.) doubt

somnevat'sya (v.impf.) doubt

son (n.m.) sleep, dream

sonnyi (adj.) sleeping, sleepy

soobrazhat' (v.impf.) think out, consider

soobrazit' (v.pf.) understand, grasp

soobrazitel'nost' (n.f.) quick-wit

soobrazno (adv.) according to

soobrazovat' (v.impf.) conform

soobshcha (adv.) jointly

soobshchat' (v.impf.) inform

soobshchit' (v.pf.) inform

soobshchnik (n.m.) accomplice

soorudit' (v.pf.) erect

sootechestvennik (n.m.) compatriot

sootnoshenie (n.n.) correlation

sootvetstvenno (adv.) accordingly

sopernik (n.m.) rival

sopet' (v.impf.) sniff

sopka (n.f.) hill, mound

soplo (n.n.) nozzle

sopostavit' (v.pf.) compare

soprikasat'sya (v.impf.) come into contact

soprikosnovenie (n.n.) contact

soprikosnut'sya (v.pf.) come into contact

soprotivlenie (n.n.) resistance, resistor

soprovozhdat' (v.impf.) accompany

soputstvovat' (v.impf.) accompany

sor (n.m.) sweepings

soratnik (n.m.) comrade-in-arms

sorazmerit' (v.pf.) regulate, adjust

sorazmeryat' (v.impf.) regulate, adjust

sorevnovanie (n.n.) competition

sorit' (v.impf.) litter

sornyak (n.m.) weed

sorochka (n.f.) shirt

sorok (num.) forty

soroka (n.f.) magpie

sorokovoi (adj.) fortieth

sort (n.m.) sort

sorvanets (n.m.) madcap

sorvat' (v.pf.) tear off, disrupt

sosat' (v.impf.) suck

soschitat' (v.pf.) count

sosed (n.m.) neighbor

sosiska (n.f.)   frankfurter
soska (n.f.)   comforter
soskakivat' (v.impf.)   jump off, come off
soskal'zyvat' (v.impf.)   slip off
soskochit' (v.pf.)   jump off, come off
soskuchit'sya (v.pf.)   miss
soslagatel'nyi (adj.)   subjunctive
soslat' (v.pf.)   exile
soslat'sya (v.pf.)   refer
soslovie (n.n.)   estate
sosluzhivets (n.m.)   colleague
sosna (n.f.)   pine
sosok (n.m.)   nipple
sosredotochennost' (n.f.)   concentration
sostarit'sya (v.pf.)   grow old
sostav (n.m.)   composition
sostavit' (v.pf.)   put together
sostavitel' (n.m.)   compiler, author
sostavlenie (n.n.)   composition, compiling
sostavlyayushchaya (n.f.)   component, constituent
sostoyanie (n.n.)   condition
sostoyanie (n.n.)   fortune
sostoyat' (v.impf.)   be, consist
sostoyatel'nyi (adj.)   well-off
sostradanie (n.n.)   compassion
sostyazanie (n.n.)   contest
sosud (n.m.)   vessel
sosul'ka (n.f.)   icicle
sosushchestvovanie (n.n.)   coexistence
sotnya (n.f.)   a hundred
sotrudnichat' (v.impf.)   collaborate
sotrudnichestvo (n.n.)   cooperation
sotrudnik (n.m.)   employee
sotryasat' (v.impf.)   shake
sotsial-demokrat (n.m.)   Social Democrat
sotsialist (n.m.)   socialist
sotsialisticheskii (adj.)   socialist
sotsializm (n.m.)   socialism
sotsial'nyi (adj.)   social
sotssorevnovanie (n.n.)   socialist emulation
sotsstrakh (n.m.)   social security
soty (n.pl.)   honeycomb
sotyi (adj.)   hundredth
souchastie (n.n.)   partnership
souchenik (n.m.)   schoolmate
sous (n.m.)   sauce
sova (n.f.)   owl

sovat' (v.impf.)   poke
sovershat' (v.impf.)   accomplish
sovershenno (adv.)   absolutely
sovershennoletie (n.n.)   majority
sovershennoletnii (adj.)   of age
sovershennyi (adj.)   perfect
sovershenstvo (n.n.)   perfection
sovershit' (v.pf.)   accomplish
soveshchanie (n.n.)   conference
sovest' (n.f.)   conscience
sovestlivyi (adj.)   conscientious
sovet (n.m.)   Soviet
sovet (n.m.)   council
sovet (n.m.)   advice
sovetchik (n.m.)   adviser
sovetnik (n.m.)   counselor
sovetovat' (v.impf.)   advise
sovetskii (adj.)   Soviet
sovkhoz (n.m.)   state farm
sovladat' (v.pf.)   control
sovmeshchat' (v.impf.)   combine
sovmestimyi (adj.)   compatible
sovmestno (adv.)   jointly
sovok (n.m.)   scoop
sovokupnost' (n.f.)   totality, aggregate
sovpadat' (v.impf.)   coincide, concur
sovpast' (v.pf.)   coincide
sovrashchat' (v.impf.)   seduce
sovrat' (v.pf.)   tell a lie
sovratit' (v.pf.)   seduce
sovremennyi (adj.)   contemporary
sovsem (adv.)   quite
soyuz (n.m.)   union
soyuz (n.m.)   conjunction
soyuznik (n.m.)   ally
sozdanie (n.n.)   creation
sozdavat' (v.impf.)   create
sozertsat' (v.impf.)   contemplate
sozhalet' (v.impf.)   regret
sozhitel' (n.m.)   roommate
sozhzhenie (n.n.)   burning
sozidat' (v.impf.)   create
soznanie (n.n.)   consciousness, awareness
soznavat' (v.impf.)   be conscious of
sozrevanie (n.n.)   ripening
sozrevat' (v.impf.)   ripen
sozvat' (v.pf.)   call, summon
sozvezdie (n.n.)   constellation

sozvonit'sya (v.pf.) make a call
sozvuchie (n.n.) accord
sozyv (n.m.) convocation
spadat' (v.impf.) fall down, subside
spaika (n.f.) soldered joint
spaivat' (v.impf.) make drunk
spaivat' (v.impf.) solder
spalit' (v.pf.) burn
spal'nya (n.f.) bedroom
spartakiada (n.f.) sports festival
sparzha (n.f.) asparagus
spasatel'nyi (adj.) lifesaving
spasenie (n.n.) rescuing
spasibo (part.) thanks
spasitel' (n.m.) rescuer
spast' (v.pf.) fall down
spasti (v.pf.) save, rescue
spat' (v.impf.) sleep
spayannost' (n.f.) unity
spayat' (v.pf.) solder
spazm(a) (n.m.&f.) spasm
spektakl' (n.m.) performance
spektr (n.m.) spectrum
spektrogramma (n.f.) spectrogram
spektrometriya (n.f.) spectrometry
spekulirovat' (v.impf.) speculate
spelyi (adj.) ripe
speredi (adv.) in front
spertyi (adj.) close
sperva (adv.) at first
spes' (n.f.) haughtiness
speshit' (v.impf.) hurry
speshit'sya (v.pf.) dismount
speshka (n.f.) hurry
spesivyi (adj.) haughty
spet' (v.impf.) ripen
spet' (v.pf.) sing
spetsializatsiya (n.f.) specialization
spetsial 'nost' (n.f.) speciality
spetsificheskii (adj.) specific
spetsifikatsiya (n.f.) specification
spetsodezhda (n.f.) work clothes
spetsovka (n.f.) overalls
spichechnyi (adj.) match
spichka (n.f.) match
spikhivat' (v.impf.) push aside
spilivat' (v.impf.) saw down
spina (n.f.) back

spinka (n.f.) back
spinnoi (adj.) spinal
spiral' (n.f.) spiral, coil
spirt (n.m.) alcohol
spisat' (v.pf.) copy
spisok (n.m.) list
spitsa (n.f.) knitting needle
splachivat'(sya) (v.impf.) rally
splav (n.m.) floating
splav (n.m.) alloy
splavit' (v.pf.) float
splavit' (v.pf.) alloy
splavlyat' (v.impf.) float, alloy
splesti (v.pf.) weave
spletat'(sya) (v.impf.) interlace
spletnik (n.m.) gossip
splevyvat' (v.impf.) spit
splochenie (n.n.) rallying
splosh' (adv.) entirely
sploshnoi (adj.) unbroken
splotit'(sya) (v.pf.) rally
splyunut' (v.pf.) spit
splyushchennyi (adj.) flattened out
splyusnutyi (adj.) flattened out
spodvizhnik (n.m.) comrade-in-arms
spoit' (v.pf.) make drink
spokhvatit'sya (v.pf.) remember suddenly
spokoinyi (adj.) quiet
spolaskivat' (v.impf.) rinse
spolna (adv.) completely
spolosnut' (v.pf.) rinse
spolzat' (v.impf.) slip down
spor (n.m.) argument
spora (n.f.) spore
sporit' (v.impf.) argue
sporot' (v.pf.) rip off
sport (n.m.) sport
sportivnyi (adj.) sporting
sportsmen (n.m.) sportsman
sposob (n.m.) way, manner
sposobnost' (n.f.) ability
sposobstvovat' (v.impf.) assist
spotknut'sya (v.pf.) stumble
sprashivat' (v.impf.) ask
sprava (adv.) to the right
spravedlivost' (n.f.) justice
spravedlivyi (adj.) just
spravit' (v.pf.) celebrate

spravit'sya (v.pf.)   inquire
spravka (n.f.)   information, certificate
spravlyat' (v.impf.)   celebrate
spravlyat'sya (v.impf.)   inquire
spravochnik (n.m.)   reference book
sprintsevat' (v.impf.)   syringe
spros (n.m.)   demand
sprosonok (adv.)   half-awake
sprovotsirovat' (v.impf.)   provoke
spryagat' (v.impf.)   conjugate
spryatat' (v.pf.)   hide
sprygivat' (v.impf.)   jump off
spryskivat' (v.impf.)   sprinkle
spugivat' (v.impf.)   frighten off
spusk (n.m.)   descent
spustit' (v.pf.)   lower
spustya (prep.)   after
sputat' (v.pf.)   entangle, confuse
sputnik (n.m.)   traveling companion, sputnik
spyachka (n.f.)   hibernation
sram (n.m.)   shame
srastat'sya (v.impf.)   grow together
sravnenie (n.n.)   comparison
sravnit' (v.pf.)   compare
sravnivat' (v.impf)   level
sravnivat' (v.impf.)   compare
srazhat'sya (v.impf.)   fight
srazu (adv.)   at once
sreda (n.f.)   Wednesday
sreda (n.f.)   environment, medium
sredi (prep.)   among
srednee (n.n.)   mean, average
srednevekovyi (adj.)   medieval
srednii (adj.)   middle
sredstvo (n.n.)   means, remedy
srez (n.m.)   cut
srezat' (v.impf.)   cut off
srisovat' (v.pf.)   copy
srochnyi (adj.)   urgent
srodstvo (n.n.)   affinity
srok (n.m.)   date, term
srovnyat' (v.pf.)   level
srub (n.m.)   framework
sryt' (v.pf.)   level to the ground
sryv (n.m.)   failure
sryvat' (v.impf.)   level to the ground
sryvat' (v.impf.)   tear off
ssadina (n.f.)   abrasion

ssadit' (v.pf.)   help down
sshibat' (v.impf.)   knock down
sshivat' (v.impf.)   sew together
ssora (n.f.)   quarrel
SSSR (abbr.)   USSR
ssuda (n.f.)   loan
ssylat' (v.impf.)   exile
ssylat'sya (v.impf.)   be exiled
ssylat'sya (v.impf.)   be referred
ssylka (n.f.)   exile
ssylka (n.f.)   reference
ssyl'nyi (n.m.)   exile
ssypat' (v.pf.)   pour
stabilizatsiya (n.f.)   stabilization
stabil'nyi (adj.)   stable
stachechnik (n.m.)   striker
stachka (n.f.)   strike
stadion (n.m.)   stadium
stadiya (n.f.)   stage
stado (n.n.)   herd
stakan (n.m.)   glass
stal' (n.f.)   steel
staleliteinyi zavod (adj.-n.m.)   steel foundry
staleplavil'nyi (adj.)   steel smelting
staleprokatnyi (adj.)   steel rolling
stalevar (n.m.)   steel founder
stalkivat'sya (v.impf.)   collide
stameska (n.f.)   chisel
stan (n.m.)   figure
stan (n.m.)   mill
stan (n.m.)   camp
standart (n.m.)   standard
standartnyi (adj.)   standard
staniol' (n.f.)   tinfoil
stankostroenie (n.n.)   machine tool
  construction
stanok (n.m.)   machine tool
stanovit'sya (v.impf.)   become
stanovit'sya (v.impf.)   stand
stantsiya (n.f.)   station
staptyvat' (v.impf.)   wear out
staranie (n.n.)   effort
staratel' (n.m.)   gold digger
staratel'nost' (n.f.)   diligence
starcheskii (adj.)   senile
star'e (n.n.)   old junk
staret' (v.impf.)   grow old

starik (n.m.)   old man
starina (n.f.)   olden times
starit' (v.impf.)   to age
staromodnyi (adj.)   old-fashioned
starost' (n.f.)   old age
starosta (n.m.&f.)   leader
starozhil (n.m.)   old resident
starshii (adj.)   oldest
starshina (n.m.)   sergeant major
starshinstvo (n.n.)   seniority
start (n.m.)   start
starukha (n.f.)   old woman
staryi (adj.)   old
stashchit' (v.pf.)   pull off, steal
staskivat' (v.impf.)   pull off
stat' (v.pf.)   stop
stat' (v.pf.)   begin
stat' (v.pf.)   become
statist (n.m.)   super
statistika (n.f.)   statistics
statnyi (adj.)   well-built
statsionar (n.m.)   hospital
statsionarnyi (adj.)   stationary
stat'sya (v.pf.)   become, happen
statuya (n.f.)   statue
stat'ya (n.f.)   article
stavit' (v.impf.)   put, produce
stavka (n.f.)   rate, stake
stavka (n.f.)   headquarters
stavlennik (n.m.)   protege
stavnya (n.f.)   shutter
staya (n.f.)   flock
stayat' (v.pf.)   melt
stazh (n.m.)   record of service
stearin (n.m.)   tallow
stebel' (n.m.)   stem
stech' (v.pf.)   flow down
stechenie (n.n.)   confluence
steganyi (adj.)   quilted
stegat' (v.impf.)   whip
stegat' (v.impf.)   quilt
stegnut' (v.pf.)   whip
stekat'sya (v.impf.)   join, gather
steklo (n.n.)   glass
steklovolokno (n.n.)   fiberglass
steklyannyi (adj.)   glass
stekol'shchik (n.m.)   glazier
stelit'sya (v.impf.)   drift

stel'ka (n.f.)   innersole
stemnet' (v.pf.)   grow dark
stena (n.f.)   wall
stend (n.m.)   bench, bed, stand
stengazeta (n.f.)   wall newspaper
stennoi (adj.)   wall
stenografirovat' (v.impf.)   take down in
   shorthand
stenogramma (n.f.)   shorthand report
stepen' (n.f.)   degree
stepnoi (adj.)   steppe
sterech' (v.impf.)   watch
stereofonicheskii (adj.)   stereophonic
stereometriya (n.f.)   stereometry
stereoskop (n.m.)   stereoscope
stereotip (n.m.)   stereotype
steret' (v.pf.)   wipe off
sterilizatsiya (n.f.)   sterilization
steril'nyi (adj.)   sterile
sterlyad' (n.f.)   sterlet (fish)
sterpet' (v.pf.)   bear
stertyi (adj.)   effaced
sterzhen' (n.m.)   bar
stesnenie (n.n.)   constraint
stesnit' (v.pf.)   hamper
stesnyat'sya (v.impf.)   feel shy
stetoskop (n.m.)   stethoscope
stezhok (n.m.)   stitch
stikh (n.m.)   verse
stikhat' (v.impf.)   calm down
stikhiinyi (adj.)   elemental
stikhiya (n.f.)   element
stikhnut' (v.pf.)   calm down
stikhoslozhenie (n.n.)   versification
stikhotvorenie (n.n.)   poem
stil' (n.m.)   style
stilisticheskii (adj.)   stylistic
stimul (n.m.)   stimulus
stipendiat (n.m.)   grant holder
stipendiya (n.f.)   grant, scholarship
stiral'naya mashina (adj.-n.f.)   washing
   machine
stirat' (v.impf.)   wipe off
stirat' (v.impf.)   wash
stirat'sya (v.impf.)   be effaced
stirka (n.f.)   washing
stiskivat' (v.impf.)   squeeze
stlat' (v.impf.)   spread

sto (num.)   hundred
stochnyi (adj.)   drain, sewage
stog (n.m.)   stack
stogradusnyi (adj.)   centigrade
stoi (imp.)   stop!
stoika (n.f.)   set
stoika (n.f.)   counter
stoikii (adj.)   firm
stoilo (n.n.)   stall
stoimost' (n.f.)   value
stoimya (adv.)   upright
stoit' (v.impf.)   cost
stoitsizm (n.m.)   stoicism
stok (n.m.)   flowing, sewer
stol (n.m.)   table
stol' (adv.)   so
stolb (n.m.)   pillar, post
stolbets (n.m.)   column
stolbnyak (n.m.)   tetanus
stoletie (n.n.)   century
stolitsa (n.f.)   capital
stolknovenie (n.n.)   collision
stol'ko (adv.)   so much, so many
stolovat'sya (v.impf.)   board
stolovaya (n.f.)   dining room, canteen
stolp (n.m.)   pillar
stolpit'sya (v.pf.)   crowd
stolyar (n.m.)   joiner
stomatologiya (n.f.)   stomatology
stometrovka (n.f.)   100-meter sprint
ston (n.m.)   moan
stop (n.m.)   stop
stopa (n.f.)   foot
stopa (n.f.)   ream
stopka (n.f.)   small glass
stopka (n.f.)   pile
stop-kran (n.m.)   emergency brake
stoprotsentnyi (adj.)   hundred percent
stoptat' (v.pf.)   wear out
storgovat'sya (v.pf.)   strike a bargain
storona (n.f.)   side
storonit'sya (v.impf.)   avoid
storonnik (n.m.)   supporter
storozh (n.m.)   guard
storozhit' (v.impf.)   guard
stoyachii (adj.)   standing, stagnant
stoyanka (n.f.)   stand, stop
stoyat' (v.impf.)   stand, stop

stradalets (n.m.)   sufferer
stradat' (v.impf.)   suffer
stradatel'nyi (adj.)   passive
strakh (n.m.)   fear
strakhkassa (n.f.)   insurance office
strakhovanie (n.n.)   insurance
strana (n.f.)   country
stranitsa (n.f.)   page
strannik (n.m.)   wanderer
strannyi (adj.)   strange, odd
stranstvovat' (v.impf.)   wander
strashit' (v.impf.)   frighten
strashnyi (adj.)   fearful
strast' (n.f.)   passion
strastnyi (adj.)   passionate
strateg (n.m.)   strategist
stratifikatsiya (n.f.)   stratification
stratostat (n.m.)   stratospheric baloon
straus (n.m.)   ostrich
strazha (n.f.)   guard
strekotat' (v.impf.)   chirr
strekoza (n.f.)   dragonfly
strela (n.f.)   arrow
strel'ba (n.f.)   shooting
strelka (n.f.)   pointer
strelkovyi (adj.)   rifle
strelochnik (n.m.)   pointsman, switchman
strelok (n.m.)   marksman
strelyat' (v.impf.)   shoot
stremglav (adv.)   headlong
stremitel'nyi (adj.)   impetuous
stremya (n.n.)   stirrup
stremyanka (n.f.)   stepladder
strich' (v.impf.)   cut
strizhennyi (adj.)   short
strochit' (v.impf.)   stitch
strochka (n.f.)   stitch
strochka (n.f.)   line
strochnaya bukva (adj.-n.f.)   small letter
stroenie (n.n.)   structure
stroevoi (adj.)   building
stroevoi (adj.)   combatant
strofa (n.f.)   stanza
strogat' (v.impf.)   plane
strogii (adj.)   strict
stroi (n.m.)   system
stroika (n.f.)   construction
stroinost' (n.f.)   harmony

stroit' (v.impf.) build
stroitel' (n.m.) builder
stroitel'stvo (n.n.) construction
stroit'sya (v.impf.) be under construction
stroka (n.f.) line
strontsii (adj.) strontium
strop (n.m.) sling
stropilo (n.n.) rafter
stroptivost' (n.f.) obstinacy
struchok (n.m.) pod
struit'sya (v.impf.) stream
struktura (n.f.) structure
struna (n.f.) string
strunnyi (adj.) string
strusit' (v.pf.) lose courage
struya (n.f.) jet
struzhka (n.f.) shaving
stryakhivat' (v.impf.) shake off
stryapat' (v.impf.) cook
stsedit' (v.pf.) strain off
stsena (n.f.) stage, scene
stsenarii (n.m.) screen play
stsenicheskii (adj.) scenic
stsepit' (v.pf.) couple
stsepit'sya (v.pf.) come to grips
stsepka (n.f.) coupling
stseplyat'sya (v.impf.) come to grips
stuchat' (v.impf.) knock
student (n.m.) student
studit' (v.impf.) cool
studiya (n.f.) studio
stuk (n.m.) knock
stuknut' (v.pf.) knock
stul (n.m.) chair
stupat' (v.impf.) step
stupen' (n.f.) step, stage
stupit' (v.pf.) step
stupnya (n.f.) foot
stushevat'sya (v.pf.) be confused
stvol (n.m.) trunk, barrel
stvorka (n.f.) fold
styagivat' (v.impf.) tighten
styanut' (v.pf.) tighten
stychka (n.f.) skirmish
styd (n.m.) shame
stydlivost' (n.f.) shyness
stydno (pred.) shame
styk (n.m.) joint

stynut' (v.impf.) get cool
styuardessa (n.f.) stewardess
subbota (n.f.) Saturday
subbotnik (n.m.) subbotnik
sub"ekt (n.m.) subject
subsidirovat' (v.impf.) subsidize
subsidiya (n.f.) subsidy
substantsiya (n.f.) substance
substrat (n.m.) substrate
subtropicheskii (adj.) subtropical
suchit' (v.impf.) twist
suchkovatyi (adj.) knotty
sud (n.m.) court, trial
sud'ba (n.f.) fate
sudebnyi (adj.) legal
sudimost' (n.f.) previous conviction
sudno (n.n.) ship
sudokhodnyi (adj.) navigable
sudomoika (n.f.) kitchen help
sudoproizvodstvo (n.n.) legal procedure
sudoroga (n.f.) cramp
sudostroenie (n.n.) shipbuilding
sudoverf' (n.f.) shipyard
sud'ya (n.m.) judge
sueta (n.f.) fuss
sueverie (n.n.) superstition
suffiks (n.m.) suffix
sufler (n.m.) prompter
suglinok (n.m.) loamy soil
sugrob (n.m.) snowdrift
sugubo (adv.) especially
suk (n.m.) bough
suka (n.f.) bitch
sukhar' (n.m.) rusk
sukhoi (adj.) dry
sukhoputnyi (adj.) land
sukhoshchavyi (adj.) lean
sukhost' (n.f.) dryness
sukhovei (n.m.) dry wind
sukhozhilie (n.n.) tendon
sukno (n.n.) cloth
sukonnyi (adj.) cloth
sulema (n.f.) corrosive sublimate
sul'fat (n.m.) sulfate
sulit' (v.impf.) promise
sultan (n.m.) sultan
suma (n.f.) bag
sumasbrod (n.m.) madcap

sumasshedshii (adj.) mad
sumatokha (n.f.) bustle
sumbur (n.m.) confusion
sumerki (n.pl.) twilight
sumet' (v.pf.) succeed
sumka (n.f.) bag
summa (n.f.) sum
summator (n.m.) accumulator, adder
sumrachnyi (adj.) gloomy
sumrak (n.m.) dusk
sunduk (n.m.) trunk
sunut'sya (v.pf.) butt in
sup (n.m.) soup
superoblozhka (n.f.) book cover
supovoi (adj.) soup
support (n.m.) rest, saddle, carriage
suprug (n.m.) husband
surguch (n.m.) sealing wax
sur'ma (n.f.) antimony
surovyi (adj.) severe
surrogat (n.m.) substitute
susha (n.f.) land
sushchestvennyi (adj.) essential
sushchestvitel'noe (n.n.) noun
sushchestvo (n.n.) being
sushchestvo (n.n.) essence
sushchestvovanie (n.n.) existence
sushchii (adj.) real
sushchnost' (n.f.) essence
sushenyi (adj.) dried
suslik (n.m.) ground squirrel
suspenziya (n.f.) suspension
sustav (n.m.) joint
sut' (n.f.) essence
sutki (n.pl.) day
sutochnyi (adj.) daily
sutoloka (n.f.) commotion
sutulit'sya (v.impf.) stoop
suverennyi (adj.) sovereign
suzhdenie (n.n.) judgment
suzhenie (n.n.) narrowing
suzhivat'(sya) (v.impf.) narrow
svad'ba (n.f.) wedding
svalivat' (v.impf.) throw down
svalka (n.f.) junkyard
svarit' (v.pf.) cook, weld
svarivat' (v.impf.) weld
svarka (n.f.) welding

svarlivyi (adj.) quarrelsome
svatat' (v.impf.) propose as husband (wife)
svaya (n.f.) pile
svecha (n.f.) candle, spark plug
svechenie (n.n.) luminescence
svedenie (n.n.) information
svedushchii (adj.) experienced
svekla (n.f.) beet
svekor (n.m.) father-in-law
svekrov' (n.f.) mother-in-law
sverchok (n.m.) cricket
svergat' (v.impf.) overthrow
sverit' (v.pf.) check
sverkat' (v.impf.) sparkle
sverkh (prep.) beyond, above, over
sverkh"estestvennyi (adj.) supernatural
sverkhpribyl' (n.f.) superprofit
sverkhprovodimost' (n.f.) superconductivity
sverkhshtatnyi (adj.) supernumerary
sverkhurochnyi (adj.) overtime
sverkhu (adv.) from above, over
sverlit' (v.impf.) drill
sverlo (n.n.) drill
svernut' (v.pf.) roll up
sverstnik (n.m.) contemporary
svertok (n.m.) package
svertyvanie (n.n.) coagulation
sveryat' (v.impf.) check
sveshat' (v.pf.) weigh
sveshivat'(sya) (v.impf.) dangle
svesit' (v.pf.) dangle
svesti (v.pf.) take, reduce
svet (n.m.) light
svet (n.m.) world
svetat' (v.impf.) dawn
svetil'nyi gaz (adj.-n.m.) coal gas
svetilo (n.n.) heavenly body
svetit' (v.impf.) shine
svetlet' (v.impf.) clear up
svetlyachok (n.m.) firefly
svetlyi (adj.) light
svetoch (n.m.) luminary
svetochuvstvitel'nyi (adj.) light sensitive
svetofil'tr (n.m.) light filter
svetofor (n.m.) traffic lights
svetomaskirovka (n.f.) blackout
svetosila (n.f.) illumination
svetotekhnika (n.f.) illuminating engineering

svetovod (n.m.) light guide
svetovoi (adj.) light
svetskii (adj.) secular, worldly
svetyashchiisya (adj.) luminous
svezhest' (n.f.) freshness
svezho (adj.) it is cool
svezti (v.pf.) remove
svidanie (n.n.) date, appointment
svidetel' (n.m.) witness
svidetel'stvo (n.n.) certificate, license
svinar' (n.m.) pig tender
svinarka (n.f.) pig tender
svinarnik (n.m.) pigsty
svinets (n.m.) lead
svinina (n.f.) pork
svinka (n.f.) mumps
svinoi (adj.) pig, pork
svinovodstvo (n.n.) pig breeding
svintsovyi (adj.) lead
svin'ya (n.f.) pig
svirel' (n.f.) pipe
svirepyi (adj.) fierce
svisat' (v.impf.) hang down
svist (n.m.) whistle
svistet' (v.impf.) whistle
svistnut' (v.pf.) whistle
svistok (n.m.) whistle
svit' (v.pf.) twist
svita (n.f.) suite
sviter (n.m.) sweater
svivat' (v.impf.) twist
svoboda (n.f.) freedom
svobodolyubivyi (adj.) freedom-loving
svobodomyslie (n.n.) freethinking
svod (n.m.) arch
svod (n.m.) code
svodchatyi (adj.) arched
svodit' (v.impf.) take, reduce
svodka (n.f.) summary
svodnyi (adj.) summary
svoeobraznyi (adj.) original
svoevol'nyi (adj.) self-willed
svoevremennyi (adj.) opportune
svoistvennyi (adj.) characteristic
svoistvo (n.n.) property
svora (n.f.) pack
svorachivat' (v.impf.) roll up, curtail, turn
svozit' (v.impf.) remove, take

svyashchennyi (adj.) sacred
svyato (adv.) reverently
svyatoi (adj.) holy
svyaz' (n.f.) tie, connection, communication
svyazannyi (adj.) connected
svyazat' (v.pf.) tie, bind
svyazist (n.m.) signaller
svyazka (n.f.) sheaf, bunch, chord, ligament
svyaznyi (adj.) coherent
svyazuyushchii (adj.) binding
svyazyvat'sya (v.impf.) communicate
svykat'sya (v.impf.) get used to
svyshe (prep.) over, beyond
svysoka (adv.) haughtily
sygrat' (v.pf.) play
syn (n.m.) son
syp' (n.f.) rash
sypat' (v.impf.) pour
sypnoi tif (adj.-n.m.) typhus
sypuchii (adj.) friable
syr (n.m.) cheese
syr'e (n.n.) raw material
syrnik (n.m.) cheese pancake
syroi (adj.) damp, raw
syrost' (n.f.) dampness
syrovarnya (n.f.) cheese dairy
syshchik (n.m.) detective
sysknoi (adj.) detective
sytnyi (adj.) nourishing
sytost' (n.f.) satiety
sytyi (adj.) satisfied
syuda (adv.) here
syurpriz (n.m.) surprise
syurtuk (n.m.) frock coat
syusyukat' (v.impf.) lisp
syuzhet (n.m.) topic
syvorotka (n.f.) serum
szadi (adv.) from behind
szhalit'sya (v.pf.) take pity on
szhat' (v.pf.) reap
szhat' (v.pf.) compress
szhatie (n.n.) compression
szhato (adv.) briefly
szhech' (v.pf.) burn down
szhimat' (v.impf.) compress
szhit'sya (v.pf.) get used to
szyvat' (v.impf.) call

T (Т, Ц)

t.e. (abbr.) i.e.
ta (p.) that
tabachnyi (adj.) tobacco
tabak (n.m.) tobacco
tabel' (n.m.) timesheet
tabletka (n.f.) pill
tablitsa (n.f.) table, chart
tabor (n.m.) camp
tabun (n.m.) herd
taburet(ka) (n.m.&f.) stool
tachka (n.f.) wheelbarrow
tadzhik (n.m.) Tadzhik
tafta (n.f.) taffeta
taiga (n.f.) taiga
taikom (adv.) secretly
taim (n.m.) half
taina (n.f.) mystery
tainstvennyi (adj.) mysterious
tait' (v.impf.) conceal
tak (adv.) so
takelazh (n.m.) rigging
takhometr (n.m.) tachometer
takhta (n.f.) ottoman
takoi (adj.) such
takov (p.) such
taksa (n.f.) dachshund
taksa (n.f.) tariff
taksi (n.n.) taxi
takt (n.m.) tact
takt (n.m.) beat (music)
taktichnyi (adj.) tactful
taktika (n.f.) tactics
takzhe (adv.) also
talant (n.m.) talent
talisman (n.m.) talisman
taliya (n.f.) waist
tal'k (n.m.) talc
tallii (n.m.) thallium
talon (n.m.) coupon
talyi (adj.) melted
tam (adv.) there
tamada (n.m.) toastmaster
tamozhennyi (adj.) customs
tanets (n.m.) dance
tangens (n.m.) tangent

tank (n.m.) tank
tankovyi (adj.) armored
tantal (n.m.) tantalum
tantsor (n.m.) dancer
tapochki (n.pl.) slippers
tara (n.f.) package, container
tarakan (n.m.) cockroach
taranit' (v.impf.) ram
tarashchit' (v.impf.) stare
tarelka (n.f.) plate
tarif (n.m.) tariff
tashchit' (v.impf.) drag
taskat' (v.impf.) drag
tasovat' (v.impf.) shuffle
TASS (abbr.) Tass (Telegraph Agency of the
    Soviet Union)
tatarin (n.m.) Tartar
tayanie (n.n.) melting
tayat' (v.impf.) melt
taz (n.m.) basin
taz (n.m.) pelvis
te (p.) those
teatr (n.m.) theater
tech' (v.impf.) flow
tech' (n.f.) leak
techenie (n.n.) current
tekh (p.) those
tekhnicheskii (adj.) technical
tekhnik (n.m.) technician
tekhnika (n.f.) technology, engineering
tekhnikum (n.m.) technical school
tekhnolog (n.m.) technologist
tekhnologicheskii (adj.) technological
tekst (n.m.) text
tekstil'nyi (adj.) textile
tektonika (n.f.) tectonics
tekuchii (adj.) fluid, fluctuating
tekushchii (adj.) current, flowing
telefon (n.m.) telephone
telefon-avtomat (n.m.) public phone
telefonirovat' (v.impf.) telephone
telefonnyi (adj.) telephone
telefonogramma (n.f.) telephone message
telega (n.f.) cart
telegraf (n.m.) telegraph

telegramma (n.f.) telegram
telenok (n.m.) calf
teleskop (n.m.) telescope
telesnyi (adj.) corporal
televidenie (n.n.) television
televizor (n.m.) TV set
telezhka (n.f.) trolley
telit'sya (v.impf.) calve
telka (n.f.) heifer
tellur (n.m.) tellurium
telo (n.n.) body
telokhranitel' (n.m.) bodyguard
teloslozhenie (n.n.) build
telyatina (n.f.) veal
tem (p.) those
tem (conj.) so much the
tema (n.f.) topic
tembr (n.m.) timber
temi (p.) those
temnet' (v.impf.) grow dark
temnitsa (n.f.) dungeon
temno (adj.) dark
temno-sinii (adj.) dark blue
temnota (n.f.) darkness
temnovolosyi (adj.) dark-haired
temnyi (adj.) dark
temp (n.m.) rate, tempo
temperament (n.m.) temperament
temperatura (n.f.) temperature
temya (n.n.) crown
ten' (n.f.) shade, shadow
tendentsioznyi (adj.) tendentious
tendentsiya (n.f.) tendency
tenevoi (adj.) shady
tennis (n.m.) tennis
tenor (n.m.) tenor
tent (n.m.) awning
teorema (n.f.) theorem
teoreticheskii (adj.) theoretical
teoretik (n.m.) theoretician
teoriya (n.f.) theory
teper' (adv.) now
tepereshnii (adj.) present-day
teplet' (v.impf.) grow warm
teplitsa (n.f.) greenhouse
teplo (n.n.) warmth
teplo (adv.) warmly, cordially
teploemkost' (n.f.) heat capacity

teplofikatsiya (n.f.) central heating
teploizolyatsiya (n.f.) heat insulation
teplokhod (n.m.) motor vessel
teploobmen (n.m.) heat exchange
teplota (n.f.) warmth, heat
teplotekhnika (n.f.) heat engineering
teplotsentral' (n.f.) heating plant
teplovoi (adj.) thermal
teplyi (adj.) warm
terapevt (n.m.) physician
terebit' (v.impf.) pull
teret' (v.impf.) rub
terka (n.f.) shredder
termicheskii (adj.) thermal
termin (n.m.) term
termodinamika (n.f.) thermodynamics
termometr (n.m.) thermometer
termos (n.m.) thermos
termostat (n.m.) thermostat
termoyadernyi (adj.) thermonuclear
ternistyi (adj.) thorny
terpelivyi (adj.) patient
terpenie (n.n.) patience
terpet' (v.impf.) suffer, bear
terpimost' (n.f.) tolerance
terpkii (adj.) tart
terrasa (n.f.) terrace
territorial'nyi (adj.) territorial
territoriya (n.f.) territory
terror (n.m.) terror
teryat' (v.impf.) lose
terzanie (n.n.) torment
tes (n.m.) battens
tesat' (v.impf.) hew
tesemka (n.f.) tape
teshcha (n.f.) mother-in-law
teshit' (v.impf.) amuse
tes'ma (n.f.) tape
tesnit' (v.impf.) press
tesnota (n.f.) narrowness
test' (n.m.) father-in-law
testo (n.n.) dough
teterka (n.f.) gray hen
tetka (n.f.) aunt
tetrad' (n.f.) notebook
tetya (n.f.) aunt
tezis (n.m.) thesis
tezka (n.m.&f.) namesake

tif (n.m.)   typhus
tigel' (n.m.)   crucible
tigr (n.m.)   tiger
tik (n.m.)   ticking
tik (n.m.)   tic
tikan'e (n.n.)   tick
tikhii (adj.)   quiet
tikho (adv.)   quietly
tikhookeanskii (adj.)   Pacific
til'da (n.f.)   tilde
tina (n.f.)   slime
tip (n.m.)   type
tipografiya (n.f.)   printing house
tir (n.m.)   shooting gallery
tiran (n.m.)   tyrant
tirazh (n.m.)   circulation
tire (n.n.)   dash
tishina (n.f.)   quiet
tiskat' (v.impf.)   squeeze
tiski (n.pl.)   vice
tisnenie (n.n.)   stamping
titan (n.m.)   titanium
titanicheskii (adj.)   titanic
titul (n.m.)   title
titul'nyi list (adj.-n.m.)   title page
tkach (n.m.)   weaver
tkan' (n.f.)   cloth
tkanyi (adj.)   woven
tkat' (v.impf.)   weave
tkatskii (adj.)   weaving
tknut' (v.pf.)   poke
tlenie (n.n.)   smouldering
tlet' (v.impf.)   smoulder
t'ma (n.f.)   darkness
to (p.)   that
to (adv.)   then
tochil'nyi kamen' (adj.-n.m.)   whetstone
tochit' (v.impf.)   sharpen
tochit' (v.impf.)   gnaw
tochka (n.f.)   point, period
tochno (adv.)   exactly
tochno (conj.)   as though
tochnost' (n.f.)   exactness
toch'-v-toch' (adv.)   exactly
togda (adv.)   then
togo (p.)   that
tok (n.m.)   current
tokar' (n.m.)   turner

tokarnyi stanok (adj.-n.m.)   lathe
toksicheskii (adj.)   toxic
toksikologiya (n.f.)   toxicology
tolcheya (n.f.)   crush
tolchok (n.m.)   push
tolk (n.m.)   sense
tolkat' (v.impf.)   push
tolknut' (v.pf.)   push
tol'ko (adv.)   only
tolkom (adv.)   plainly
tolkotnya (n.f.)   crush
tolkovanie (n.n.)   interpretation
tolkovyi (adj.)   intelligible
toloch' (v.impf.)   pound
tolokno (n.n.)   oatmeal
tolpa (n.f.)   crowd
tolshchina (n.f.)   thickness
tolstet' (v.impf.)   grow stout
tolstokozhii (adj.)   thick-skinned
tolstyi (adj.)   thick
tom (n.m.)   volume
tomat (n.m.)   tomato paste
tomit' (v.impf.)   exhaust
tomitel'nyi (adj.)   wearisome
tomnyi (adj.)   languid
tomu (p.)   that
ton (n.m.)   tone
tonkii (adj.)   thin
tonkost' (n.f.)   thinness
tonna (n.f.)   ton
tonnel' (n.m.)   tunnel
tonut' (v.impf.)   drown, sink
topat' (v.impf.)   stamp
topit' (v.impf.)   heat
topit' (v.impf.)   melt
topit' (v.impf.)   drown
topit'sya (v.impf.)   burn
topit'sya (v.impf.)   drown oneself
topit'sya (v.impf.)   melt
topka (n.f.)   heating, furnace
topkii (adj.)   swampy
toplenyi (adj.)   melted
toplivo (n.n.)   fuel
topnut' (v.pf.)   stamp
topografiya (n.f.)   topography
topol' (n.m.)   poplar
topologiya (n.f.)   topology
topor (n.m.)   axe

topot (n.m.) tramp
toptat' (v.impf) trample down
torchat' (v.impf.) stick out
torf (n.m.) peat
torg (n.m.) haggle
torgovat' (v.impf.) trade, deal in
torgovets (n.m.) merchant
torgovlya (n.f.) trade
torgpred (n.m.) trade representative
torii (n.m.) thorium
tormoshit' (v.impf.) worry
tormoz (n.m.) brake
tormozhenie (n.n.) braking
toropit' (v.impf.) hurry
torpeda (n.f.) torpedo
tort (n.m.) cake
torzhestvennyi (adj.) solemn
torzhestvo (n.n.) celebration
toshchii (adj.) lean
toshnit' (v.impf.) feel sick
toshnota (n.f.) nausea
toska (n.f.) melancholy
tost (n.m.) toast
tot (p.) that
totchas (adv.) immediately
tovar (n.m.) wares
tovarishch (n.m.) comrade
tovarnyi (adj.) goods
tovaroobmen (n.m.) barter
tozhdestvennyi (adj.) identical
tozhdestvo (n.n.) identity
tozhe (adv.) also
traditsionnyi (adj.) traditional
traditsiya (n.f.) tradition
traektoriya (n.f.) trajectory
trafaret (n.m.) stencil
tragediya (n.f.) tragedy
tragicheskii (adj.) tragic
tragik (n.m.) tragedian
trakt (n.m.) highway
traktat (n.m.) treatise
traktir (n.m.) inn
traktor (n.m.) tractor
traktorostroenie (n.n.) tractor building
traktovat' (v.impf.) interpret
trambovat' (v.impf.) ram
tramplin (n.m.) ski jump, springboard
tramvai (n.m.) streetcar

transatlanticheskii (adj.) transatlantic
transformirovat' (v.impf.) transform
transgressiya (n.f.) transgression
transheya (n.f.) trench
transkriptsiya (n.f.) transcription
translirovat' (v.impf.) broadcast
transmissiya (n.f.) transmission
transport (n.m.) transport
transporter (n.m.) conveyer
tranzit (n.m.) transit
trap (n.m.) ladder
trapetsiya (n.f.) trapezium
trapeza (n.f.) meal
trassa (n.f.) route
trata (n.f.) expense
trauler (n.m.) trawler
traur (n.m.) mourning
trava (n.f.) grass
travit' (v.impf.) hunt
travit' (v.impf.) exterminate
travlya (n.f.) hunting
travma (n.f.) trauma
travoyadnyi (adj.) herbivorous
travyanistyi (adj.) grassy
trebovat' (v.impf.) demand
trefy (n.pl.) clubs
trekhdnevnyi (adj.) three-day
trekhétazhnyi (adj.) three-story
trekhgodichnyi (adj.) three-year
trekhgrannyi (adj.) trihedral
trekhletnii (adj.) three-year
trekhmestnyi (adj.) three-seater
trekhmesyachnyi (adj.) three-month
trekhsmennyi (adj.) three-shift
trekhtsvetnyi (adj.) three-colored
trekhvalentnyi (adj.) trivalent
trel' (n.f.) trill
trenazher (n.m.) simulator
trener (n.m.) coach
trenie (n.n.) friction
trenirovat' (v.impf.) coach
trenoga (n.f.) tripod
trepat' (v.impf.) tousle, flutter
trepet (n.m.) trembling
treshchat' (v.impf.) crack
treshchina (n.f.) crack
tresk (n.m.) cracking
treska (n.f.) cod

treskat'sya (v.impf.) crack
treskotnya (n.f.) rattle
tresnut' (v.pf.) crack
trest (n.m.) trust
treteiskii sud (adj.-n.m.) court of arbitration
tretichnyi (adj.) tertiary
tretii (adj.) third
tretirovat' (v.impf.) slight
treugol'nik (n.m.) triangle
trevoga (n.f.) alarm
trezvost' (n.f.) sobriety
tri (num.) three
tribuna (n.f.) rostrum
tribunal (n.m.) tribunal
tridtsat' (num.) thirty
tridtsatyi (adj.) thirtieth
trigonometriya (n.f.) trigonometry
triko (n.n.) tights
trilogiya (n.f.) trilogy
trinadtsat' (num.) thirteen
trinadtsatyi (adj.) thirteenth
trio (n.n.) trio
trista (num.) three hundred
triumf (n.m.) triumph
trizhdy (adv.) three times
troe (num.) three
troekratnyi (adj.) threefold
trofei (n.m.) trophy
trogatel'nyi (adj.) touching
trogat'sya (v.impf.) start
troika (n.f.) three
troinoi (adj.) triple
troistvennyi (adj.) tripartite
trolleibus (n.m.) trolley
tron (n.m.) throne
tronut' (v.pf.) touch
tropa (n.f.) path
tropicheskii (adj.) tropical
tropik (n.m.) tropic
tropinka (n.f.) path
troposfera (n.f.) troposphere
tros (n.m.) rope
trostnik (n.m.) reed
trostochka (n.f.) walking stick
trotuar (n.m.) sidewalk
truba (n.f.) pipe, trumpet
trubach (n.m.) trumpeter
trubka (n.f.) tube, receiver

trubochist (n.m.) chimney sweep
truboprovod (n.m.) pipeline
trud (n.m.) labor, work
trudit'sya (v.impf.) work, toil
trudno (adj.) difficult
trudnost' (n.f.) difficulty
trudolyubivyi (adj.) industrious
trudoden' (n.m.) work day
trudosposobnost' (n.f.) capacity for work
trudovoi (adj.) working
trudyashchiisya (adj.) working
trup (n.m.) corpse
truppa (n.f.) company
trus (n.m.) coward
trushchoba (n.f.) slum
trusiki (n.pl.) shorts
trusit' (v.impf.) fear
truslivyi (adj.) cowardly
trusost' (n.f.) cowardice
trusy (n.pl.) shorts
truzhenik (n.m.) toiler
tryakhnut' (v.pf.) give a jolt
tryapka (n.f.) rag
tryasina (n.f.) quagmire
tryaska (n.f.) jolting
tryasti (v.impf.) shake
tryuk (n.m.) trick
tryum (n.m.) hold
tsaplya (n.f.) heron
tsar' (n.m.) tsar
tsarapat' (v.impf.) scratch
tsarit' (v.impf.) reign
tsarizm (n.m.) tsarism
tsarstvo (n.n.) kingdom
tsedit' (v.impf) filter
tsekh (n.m.) shop
tsel' (n.f.) purpose, target
tselebnyi (adj.) curative
tselesoobraznyi (adj.) expedient
tseleustremlennyi (adj.) purposeful
tselikom (adv.) entirely
tselina (n.f.) virgin soil
tselit' (v.impf.) aim
tsellofan (n.m.) cellophane
tsellyuloza (n.f.) cellulose
tsel'nometalicheskii (adj.) all-metal
tseloe (n.n.) the whole
tselomudrie (n.n.) chastity

tselost' (n.f.) safety
tselovat' (v.impf.) kiss
tselyi (adj.) whole
tsement (n.m.) cement
tsena (n.f.) price
tsenit' (v.impf.) value
tsennost' (n.f.) value
tsentner (n.m.) 100 kilograms
tsentr (n.m.) center
tsentralizatsiya (n.f.) centralization
tsentralizm (n.m.) centralism
tsentral'nyi (adj.) central
tsentrifuga (n.f.) centrifuge
tsentrobezhnyi (adj.) centrifugal
tsentrostremitel'nyi (adj.) centripetal
tsenz (n.m.) qualification
tsenzura (n.f.) censorship
tsep' (n.f.) chain
tsepenet' (v.impf.) grow torpid
tsepkii (adj.) tenacious
tseplyat'sya (v.impf.) cling
tsepnoi (adj.) chain
tsepochka (n.f.) chain
tseremoniya (n.f.) ceremony
tserii (n.m.) cerium
tserkov' (n.f.) church
tserkovnyi (adj.) church
tshchatel'nyi (adj.) careful
tshchedushnyi (adj.) puny
tshcheslavie (n.n.) vanity
tshchetnyi (adj.) vain
tsianid (n.m.) cyanide
tsiferblat (n.m.) dial, face
tsifra (n.f.) figure
tsifrovoi (adj.) in figures
tsikl (n.m.) cycle
tsiklon (n.m.) cyclone
tsikorii (n.m.) chicory
tsilindr (n.m.) cylinder
tsinizm (n.m.) cynicism
tsinga (n.f.) scurvy
tsink (n.m.) zinc
tsinovka (n.f.) mat
tsirk (n.m.) circus
tsirkul' (n.m.) compass
tsirkulirovat' (v.impf.) circulate
tsirkulyar (n.m.) circular
tsirkulyatsiya (n.f.) circulation

tsisterna (n.f.) tank
tsitadel' (n.f.) citadel
tsitata (n.f.) quotation
tsitologiya (n.f.) cytology
tsitrusovye (n.pl.) citrus plants
tsivilizatsiya (n.f.) civilization
tsokan'e (n.n.) clatter
tsokol' (n.m.) plinth
tsukat (n.m.) candied fruit
tsvesti (v.impf.) bloom
tsvet (n.m.) color
tsvet (n.m.) prime
tsvetnik (n.m.) flower garden
tsvetnoi (adj.) color
tsvetochnyi (adj.) flower
tsvetok (n.m.) flower
tsvetovodstvo (n.n.) floriculture
tsvetushchii (adj.) blossoming
tsvety (n.pl.) flowers
tsygan (n.m.) Gypsy
tsyplenok (n.m.) chicken
tsypochki (n.pl.) tiptoe
tualet (n.m.) dress, toilet
tuberkulez (n.m.) tuberculosis
tucha (n.f.) cloud
tuchnyi (adj.) obese
tuda (adv.) there
tuflya (n.f.) shoe
tugoi (adj.) tight
tugoplavkii (adj.) refractory
tukhlyi (adj.) rotten
tukhnut' (v.impf.) go out
tukhnut' (v.impf.) rot
tulovishche (n.n.) trunk
tulup (n.m.) sheepskin coat
tuman (n.m.) mist, fog
tumannost' (n.f.) nebula
tumba (n.f.) stone
tundra (n.f.) tundra
tuneyadets (n.m.) parasite
tunnel' (n.m.) tunnel
tupik (n.m.) blind alley
tupitsa (n.m.&f.) dunce
tupoi (adj.) blunt, obtuse
tupost' (n.f.) bluntness, dullness
tupoumie (n.n.) stupidity
tur (n.m.) round
turbina (n.f.) turbine

turbulentnost' (n.f.) turbulence
turetskii (adj.) Turkish
turizm (n.m.) tourism
turkmen (n.m.) Turkmen
turnir (n.m.) tournament
turok (n.m.) Turk
tush' (n.f.) india ink
tush (n.m.) flourish
tusha (n.f.) carcass
tushenka (n.f.) canned meat
tushenyi (adj.) stewed
tushevat' (v.impf.) shade
tushit' (v.impf.) extinguish
tushit' (v.impf.) stew
tusklyi (adj.) dim
tut (adv.) here
tuz (n.m.) ace
tuzemnyi (adj.) native
tuzhurka (n.f.) jacket
tvar' (n.f.) creature
tverdet' (v.impf.) harden
tverdit' (v.impf.) repeat
tverdost' (n.f.) hardness
tverdyi (adj.) hard
tverdynya (n.f.) stronghold
tvoi (p.) your
tvorcheskii (adj.) creative
tvorenie (n.n.) creation
tvorit' (v.impf.) create
tvoritel'nyi (adj.) instrumental
tvorog (n.m.) cottage cheese
ty (p.) you

tyaga (n.f.) draft, traction
tyagach (n.m.) prime mover
tyagat'sya (v.impf.) measure one's strength
tyagostnyi (adj.) burdensome
tyagotenie (n.n.) gravitation
tyagotit' (v.impf.) be a burden
tyaguchii (adj.) viscous
tyanut' (v.impf.) pull
tyanut'sya (v.impf.) drag, stretch
tyazhba (n.f.) litigation
tyazhelo (adv.) heavily
tyazheloranenyi (adj.) severely wounded
tyazhelovesnyi (adj.) ponderous
tyazhelyi (adj.) heavy
tyazhest' (n.f.) weight, gravity
tychinka (n.f.) stamen
tykat' (v.impf.) poke
tykva (n.f.) pumpkin
tyl (n.m.) rear
tyn (n.m.) paling
tysyacha (num.) thousand
tysyacheletie (n.n.) millenium
tysyachnyi (adj.) thousandth
tyubik (n.m.) tube
tyufyak (n.m.) mattress
tyuk (n.m.) package
tyul' (n.m.) tulle
tyulen' (n.m.) seal
tyul'pan (n.m.) tulip
tyur'ma (n.f.) prison
tyuremnyi (adj.) prison
tyurkskii (adj.) Turkic

U (У)

u (prep.) at, by, with
ubavit' (v.pf.) diminish
ubavlenie (n.n.) decrease
ubavlyat'(sya) (v.impf.) decrease
ubayukat' (v.pf.) lull
ubedit' (v.pf.) convince
ubegat' (v.impf.) run away
uberech' (v.pf.) guard
uberegat'(sya) (v.impf.) protect oneself

ubezhat' (v.pf.) run away
ubezhdat' (v.impf.) convince
ubezhishche (n.n.) refuge
ubiistvo (n.n.) murder
ubiistvennyi (adj.) deadly
ubiistvo (n.n.) murder
ubirat' (v.impf.) remove, decorate
ubityi (adj.) killed
ubivat' (v.impf.) kill

ubogii (adj.) poor
uboi (n.m.) slaughter
ubor (n.m.) attire
uboristyi (adj.) close
uborka (n.f.) harvesting, cleaning
ubornaya (n.f.) toilet
uborochnyi (adj.) harvesting
uborshchitsa (n.f.) cleaner
ubranstvo (n.n.) decoration
ubrat' (v.pf.) remove, decorate
ubyl' (n.f.) decrease
ubyt' (v.pf.) decrease
ubytok (n.m.) loss
ubyvat' (v.impf.) decrease
uchashchat'sya (v.impf.) become more frequent
uchashchiisya (n.m.) student
uchast' (n.f.) fate
uchastit'sya (v.pf.) become more frequent
uchastlivyi (adj.) sympathetic
uchastnik (n.m.) participant
uchastok (n.m.) lot
uchastvovat' (v.impf.) participate
ucheba (n.f.) studies
uchebnyi (adj.) educational
uchenie (n.n.) studies
uchenik (n.m.) student
uchenost' (n.f.) learning
uchest' (v.pf.) take into consideration
uchet (n.m.) calculation
uchetchik (n.m.) record keeper
uchetnyi (adj.) registration
uchilishche (n.n.) secondary school
uchinit' (v.pf.) make, commit
uchit' (v.impf.) teach, learn
uchitel' (n.m.) teacher
uchityvat' (n.impf.) take into consideration
uchredit' (v.pf.) establish
uchtivyi (adj.) civil
udacha (n.f.) success
udal' (n.f.) boldness
udalenie (n.n.) removal, extraction
udalyat'(sya) (v.impf.) remove, retire
udar (n.m.) blow
udarenie (n.n.) accent
udarit' (v.pf.) strike
udaryat'(sya) (v.impf.) hit
udat'sya (v.pf.) be a success

udav (n.m.) boa constrictor
udavat'sya (v.impf.) be a success
udavit' (v.pf.) strangle
udel (n.m.) density
udelit' (v.pf) give, spare
udel'nyi ves (adj.-n.m.) specific gravity
udelyat' (v.impf.) give, spare
uderzh (n.m.) restraint
uderzhanie (n.n.) deduction
uderzhivat'(sya) (v.impf.) hold back, refrain
udeshevit' (v.pf.) reduce the price
udila (n.pl.) bit
udilishche (n.n.) fishing rod
udirat' (v.pf.) run away
udit' (v.impf.) fish
udivit' (v.pf.) astonish
udlinenie (n.n.) lengthening
udobnyi (adj.) comfortable
udobovarimyi (adj.) digestible
udobrenie (n.n.) fertilizer
udobrit' (v.pf.) fertilize
udobstvo (n.n.) comfort
udochka (n.f.) fishing rod
udoi (n.m.) yield of milk
udostaivat'(sya) (v.impf.) be honored
udostoit' (v.pf.) honor
udostoverenie (n.n.) certificate
udostoverit' (v.pf.) certify
udosuzhit'sya (v.pf.) find time for
udovletvorenie (n.n.) satisfaction
udovletvorit' (v.pf.) satisfy
udovol'stvie (n.n.) pleasure
udovol'stvovat'sya (v.impf.) be satisfied
udrat' (v.pf.) run away
udruchat' (v.impf.) depress
udruchennyi (adj.) depressed
udruzhit' (v.pf.) do someone a service
udushat' (v.impf.) suffocate
udush'e (n.n.) suffocation
udushlivyi (adj.) suffocating
udvaivat'(sya) (v.impf.) double
udvoenie (n.n.) doubling
udvoennyi (adj.) doubled
uedinenie (n.n.) solitude
uezzhat' (v.impf.) go away
ugadat' (v.pf.) guess
ugar (n.m.) carbon monoxide
ugasanie (n.n.) dying away

ugasat' (v.impf.)   die away
uglekop (n.m.)   miner
uglerod (n.m.)   carbon
uglevod (n.m.)   carbohydrate
uglevodorod (n.m.)   hydrocarbon
uglovatyi (adj.)   angular
uglovoi (adj.)   corner
uglubit' (v.pf.)   deepen
uglublenie (n.n.)   deepening
uglublyat' (v.impf.)   deepen
ugnat' (v.pf.)   drive away
ugnat'sya (v.pf.)   keep pace with
ugnetatel' (n.m.)   oppressor
ugodit' (v.pf.)   please
ugodit' (v.pf.)   hit
ugodlivyi (adj.)   officious
ugol' (n.m.)   coal
ugol (n.m.)   corner
ugol'nik (n.m.)   set square
ugol'nyi (adj.)   coal
ugolok (n.m.)   corner
ugolovnyi (adj.)   criminal
ugomonit' (v.pf.)   calm
ugonyat' (v.impf.)   drive away
ugor' (n.m.)   blackhead
ugor' (n.m.)   eel
ugoshchenie (n.n.)   refreshments
ugostit' (v.pf.)   entertain, treat
ugovarivat'(sya) (v.impf.)   agree, arrange
ugovor (n.m.)   agreement
ugozhdat' (v.impf.)   please
ugroza (n.f.)   threat
ugrozhat' (v.impf.)   threaten
ugryumyi (adj.)   sullen
ugryzenie (n.n.)   remorse
uima (n.f.)   lots
uiti (v.pf.)   go away
ukachat' (v.pf.)   rock to sleep
ukatat' (v.pf.)   roll
ukaz (n.m.)   decree
ukazanie (n.n.)   instructions
ukazat' (v.pf.)   indicate
ukazka (n.f.)   order, pointer
ukazyvat' (v.impf.)   indicate
ukha (n.f.)   fish soup
ukhab (n.m.)   bump
ukhazhivat' (v.impf.)   nurse
ukhishchrenie (n.n.)   device

ukhitrit'sya (v.pf.)   contrive
ukhmyl'nut'sya (v.pf.)   grin
ukho (n.n.)   ear
ukhod (n.m.)   departure
ukhod (n.m.)   care
ukhodit' (v.impf.)   go away
ukhudshenie (n.n.)   deterioration
ukhudshit' (v.pf.)   make worse
ukhvatit' (v.pf.)   catch
uklad (n.m.)   way of life, structure
ukladka (n.f.)   packing, setting, laying
uklon (n.m.)   gradient, deviation
uklyuchina (n.f.)   rowlock
ukol (n.m.)   prick
ukomplektovat' (v.pf.)   complete
ukor (n.m.)   reproach
ukorachivat' (v.impf.)   shorten
ukorenit'sya (v.pf.)   take root
ukoriznennyi (adj.)   reproachful
ukorotit' (v.pf.)   shorten
ukoryat' (v.impf.)   reproach
ukradkoi (adv.)   stealthily
ukrainets (n.m.)   Ukrainian
ukrashat' (v.impf.)   decorate
ukrasit' (v.pf.)   decorate
ukrast' (v.pf.)   steal
ukrepit' (v.pf.)   strengthen
ukromnyi (adj.)   secluded
ukrop (n.m.)   dill
ukrotitel' (n.m.)   tamer
ukrupnenie (n.n.)   consolidation
ukryt' (v.pf.)   cover up
ukrytie (n.n.)   shelter
ukryvatel'stvo (n.n.)   concealment
uksus (n.m.)   vinegar
ukus (n.m.)   bite
ukutat' (v.pf.)   wrap up
uladit' (v.pf.)   settle
ulamyvat' (v.impf.)   prevail
ulavlivat' (v.impf.)   catch
ulazhivat' (v.impf.)   settle
ulech'sya (v.pf.)   lie down
ulei (n.m.)   hive
uletat' (v.impf.)   fly away
uletuchit'sya (v.pf.)   evaporate
ulichat' (v.impf.)   prove someone guilty
ulichnyi (adj.)   street
ulika (n.f.)   evidence

ulitka (n.f.) snail
ulitsa (n.f.) street
uliznut' (v.pf.) slip away
ulomat' (v.pf.) prevail
ulov (n.m.) catch
ulovimyi (adj.) perceptible
ulovka (n.f.) trick
ulozhit' (v.pf.) lay
ul'timatum (n.m.) ultimatum
ul'trafioletovyi (adj.) ultraviolet
ul'trazvukovoi (adj.) supersonic
uluchit' (v.pf.) find
uluchshat'(sya) (v.impf.) improve
uluchshit' (v.pf.) improve
ulybat'sya (v.impf.) smile
ulybka (n.f.) smile
um (n.m.) mind
umalchivat' (v.impf.) suppress
umalishennyi (adj.) mad
umalit' (v.pf.) belittle
umalyat' (v.impf.) belittle
umchat'sya (v.pf.) whirl away
umelyi (adj.) skillful
umenie (n.n.) skill
umen'shaemoe (n.n.) minuend
umen'shat'sya (v.impf.) decrease
umen'shit' (v.pf.) diminish
umerennost' (n.f.) moderation
umeret' (v.pf.) die
umerit' (v.pf.) moderate
umershchvlenie (n.n.) killing
umershii (adj.) dead
umertvit' (v.pf.) kill
umeryat' (v.impf.) moderate
umestit'sya (v.pf.) find room
umestnyi (adj.) pertinent
umet' (v.impf.) be able
umilenie (n.n.) tenderness
umirat' (v.impf.) die
umnet' (v.impf) grow wiser
umnozhenie (n.n.) multiplication
umnozhit' (v.pf.) increase
umnyi (adj.) clever
umolchat' (v.pf.) suppress
umolit' (v.pf.) move by entreaties
umolkat' (v.impf.) become silent
umolyat' (v.impf.) implore
umopomeshatel'stvo (n.n.) madness

umoritel'nyi (adj.) incredibly funny
umozaklyuchenie (n.n.) deduction
umstvennyi (adj.) mental
umudrennyi (adj.) wise
umudrit'sya (v.pf.) contrive
umysel (n.m.) design
umyshlennyi (adj.) deliberate
umyt' (v.pf.) wash
umyvanie (n.n.) washing
unasledovat' (v.pf.) inherit
unavozhivat' (v.impf.) manure
unesti (v.pf.) take away
unichtozhenie (n.n.) destruction
unichtozhit' (v.pf.) destroy
unifitsirovat' (v.impf.&pf.) unify
unimat'(sya) (v.impf.) calm, soothe, stop
unitaz (n.m.) toilet bowl
universal'nyi (adj.) universal
universitet (n.m.) university
unizhat' (v.impf.) humiliate
unizhennyi (adj.) humble
unizit' (v.pf.) humiliate
unizitel'nyi (adj.) humiliating
unosit' (v.impf.) take away
unyat' (v.pf.) calm, soothe
unylyi (adj.) downcast
unynie (n.n.) low spirits
unyvat' (v.impf.) dejected
upadok (n.m.) decline
upakovat' (v.pf.) pack
upast' (v.pf.) fall
uperet'sya (v.pf.) resist
upitannyi (adj.) well-fed
uplata (n.f.) payment
uplotnenie (n.n.) consolidation, packing,
  sealing
uplyvat' (v.impf.) swim away, sail away
upodobit'sya (v.pf.) become like
upoenie (n.n.) ecstasy
upolnomochennyi (n.m.) representative
upolzat' (v.impf.) crawl away
upominanie (n.n.) mention
upomyanut' (v.pf.) mention
upomyanutyi (adj.) above-mentioned
upor (n.m.) stress, stop, support
upornyi (adj.) persistent
uporstvovat' (v.impf.) persist
uporyadochennyi (adj.) well-regulated

upotrebit' (v.pf.) use
uprashivat' (v.impf.) beg
upravdom (n.m.) house-manager
upravit'sya (v.pf.) manage
upravlenie (n.n.) management
uprazdnit' (v.pf.) abolish
uprazhnenie (n.n.) exercise
uprek (n.m.) reproach
uprekat' (v.impf.) reproach
uprochit' (v.pf.) strengthen
uproshchat' (v.impf.) simplify
uprosit' (v.pf.) prevail
uprostit' (v.pf.) simplify
uprugii (adj.) elastic
uprugost' (n.f.) elasticity
upryamyi (adj.) obstinate
upryatat' (v.pf.) hide
upryazh' (n.f.) harness
upryazhka (n.f.) team
upushchenie (n.n.) omission
upuskat' (v.impf.) miss
ura (interj.) hurrah!
uragan (n.m.) hurricane
uran (n.m.) uranium
uravnenie (n.n.) equation
uravnitel'nyi (adj.) leveling
uravnivat' (v.impf.) equalize
uravnovesit' (v.pf.) balance
uravnyat' (v.pf.) equalize
uregulirovat' (v.pf.) regulate
urezat' (v.impf.) cut down
urna (n.f.) urn
urochnyi (adj.) fixed
urod (n.m.) monster
urodit'sya (v.pf.) ripen
urodlivyi (adj.) ugly
urok (n.m.) lesson
urologiya (n.f.) urology
uron (n.m.) losses
uronit' (v.pf.) drop
uroven' (n.m.) level
urozhai (n.m.) crop
urozhenets (n.m.) native
urvat' (v.pf.) snatch
uryvat' (v.impf.) snatch
uryvkami (adv.) by fits and starts
usad'ba (n.f.) farmstead
usadit' (v.pf.) seat

usadit' (v.pf.) plant
usatyi (adj.) with a moustache
usazhivat' (v.impf.) seat
usazhivat'sya (v.impf.) take a seat
useivat' (v.impf.) strew
userdie (n.n.) zeal
usest'sya (v.pf.) take a seat
useyannyi (adj.) strewn
ushchel'e (n.n.) gorge
ushchemit' (v.pf.) pinch, infringe
ushcherb (n.m.) damage
ushchipnut' (v.pf.) pinch
ushib (n.m.) injury
ushko (n.n.) eye
ushnoi (adj.) ear
usidchivost' (n.f.) perseverance
usidet' (v.pf.) remain seated
usik (n.m.) antenna
usilenie (n.n.) intensification
usilennyi (adj.) intensified
usilie (n.n.) force, stress, effort
usilivat'(sya) (v.impf.) intensify
uskakat' (v.pf.) gallop away
uskol'zat' (v.impf.) slip away
uskorenie (n.n.) acceleration
uskorit' (v.pf.) accelerate
usladit' (v.pf.) delight
uslavlivat'sya (v.impf.) arrange
usledit' (v.pf.) keep an eye on
uslovie (n.n.) condition
uslovnyi (adj.) conditional
uslozhnenie (n.n.) complication
usluga (n.f.) service
usluzhit' (v.pf.) do someone a service
usluzhlivyi (adj.) obliging
uslykhat' (v.pf.) hear
usmatrivat' (v.impf.) perceive
usmekhat'sya (v.impf.) smile
usmeshka (n.f.) smile
usmirenie (n.n.) pacification
usmotrenie (n.n.) discretion
usnut' (v.pf.) fall asleep
usomnit'sya (v.pf.) doubt
usovershenstvovat' (v.pf.) improve
uspekh (n.m.) success
uspeshnyi (adj.) successful
uspet' (v.pf.) have time for
uspevaemost' (n.f.) progress

uspokaivat'(sya) (v.impf.) calm down
uspokoenie (n.n.) peace
uspokoit' (v.pf.) calm, soothe
ustalost' (n.f.) fatigue
ustanavlivat' (v.impf.) install
ustanovit' (v.pf.) put, establish
ustanovka (n.f.) mounting
ustarelyi (adj.) obsolete
ustat' (v.pf.) get tired
ustav (n.m.) charter
ustavat' (v.impf.) get tired
ustavit' (v.pf.) arrange
ustavit'sya (v.pf.) stare
ust'e (n.n.) mouth
ustnyi (adj.) oral
ustoi (n.pl.) foundations
ustoichivost' (n.f.) stability
ustoyat' (v.pf.) keep balance
ustraivat'(sya) (v.impf.) settle
ustranit' (v.pf) remove
ustrashat' (v.impf.) frighten
ustremit' (v.pf.) direct
ustritsa (n.f.) oyster
ustroistvo (n.n.) arrangement, device
ustroit' (v.pf.) arrange
ustup (n.m.) projection
ustupat' (v.impf.) yield, cede
ustupka (n.f.) concession
ustydit'sya (v.pf.) be ashamed
usugubit' (v.pf.) aggravate
usvaivat' (v.impf.) master, adopt
usvoenie (n.n.) mastering, adoption
usvoit' (v.pf.) master, adopt
usy (n.pl.) moustaches
usynovit' (v.pf.) adopt
usypat' (v.pf.) strew
usypit' (v.pf.) put to sleep
utaivat' (v.impf.) conceal
utaptyvat' (v.impf.) trample down
utaskivat' (v.impf.) carry off
utech' (v.pf.) flow away, escape
utechka (n.f.) leakage
utekat' (v.impf.) flow away, escape
uteret' (v.pf.) wipe
uterpet' (v.pf.) restrain oneself
uteryat' (v.pf.) lose
utes (n.m.) rock
uteshat'(sya) (v.impf.) console oneself

uteshit' (v.pf.) comfort
utikhat' (v.impf.) die away
utilitarnyi (adj.) utilitarian
utilizatsiya (n.f.) utilization
util'syr'e (n.n.) waste
utirat' (v.impf.) wipe
utka (n.f.) duck
utknut' (v.pf.) bury
utochnenie (n.n.) elaboration
utolit' (v.pf.) satisfy, quench
utolshchenie (n.n.) thickening
utolyat' (v.impf.) satisfy, quench
utomit' (v.pf.) tire
utomlenie (n.n.) fatigue
utonchennost' (n.f.) refinement
utonut' (v.pf.) be drowned
utopat' (v.impf.) be drowned, wallow in
utopit' (v.pf.) drown, sink
utopiya (n.f.) utopia
utoplennik (n.m.) drowned man
utoptat' (v.pf.) trample down
utrambovat' (v.pf.) ram
utrata (n.f.) loss
utratit' (v.pf.) lose
utrennii (adj.) morning
utrirovat' (v.impf.&pf.) exaggerate
utro (n.n.) morning
utroba (n.f.) womb
utroit' (v.pf.) treble
utrom (adv.) in the morning
utruzhdat' (v.impf.) trouble
utselet' (v.pf.) remain intact
utsepit'sya (v.pf.) catch hold of
utvar' (n.f.) utensils
utverditel'nyi (adj.) affirmative
utyug (n.m.) iron
uvazhaemyi (adj.) respected
uvazhitel'nyi (adj.) valid
uvechit' (v.impf.) mutilate
uvedomit' (v.pf) inform
uvekovechit' (v.pf.) immortalize
uvelichenie (n.n.) increase
uvelichivat' (v.impf.) increase, enlarge
uvenchat' (v.pf.) crown
uverenie (n.n.) assurance
uverennost' (n.f.) confidence
uverit' (v.pf.) assure
uvernut'sya (v.pf.) evade

uvertka (n.f.) evasion
uvertyura (n.f.) overture
uveryat' (v.impf.) assure
uveselenie (n.n.) amusement
uveshat' (v.pf.) hang with
uveshchevat' (v.impf.) admonish
uvesistyi (adj.) ponderous
uvesti (v.pf.) take away
uvezti (v.pf.) take away
uvidat'(sya) (v.impf.) meet
uvidet' (v.pf.) see
uvilivat' (v.impf.) evade
uvlazhnyat' (v.impf.) moisten
uvlech' (v.pf.) carry away, fascinate
uvlechenie (n.n.) enthusiasm, passion
uvlekatel'nyi (adj.) fascinating
uvlekayushchiisya (adj.) enthusiastic
uvodit' (v.impf.) take away
uvolit' (v.pf.) dismiss
uvol'nenie (n.n.) discharge
uvol'nitel'naya (n.f.) leave
uvol'nyat'(sya) (v.impf.) leave one's job
uvozit' (v.impf.) take away
uvy (interj.) alas!
uvyadat' (v.impf.) fade
uvyadshii (adj.) withered
uvyanut' (v.pf.) fade
uvyazat' (v.pf.) tie up, coordinate
uvyazat' (v.pf.) stick in
uvyaznut' (v.pf.) stick in
uvyazyvat' (v.impf.) tie up, coordinate

uyasnit' (v.pf.) understand
uyazvimyi (adj.) vulnerable
uyut (n.m.) coziness
uzakonit' (v.pf.) legalize
uzbek (n.m.) Uzbek
uzda (n.f.) bridle
uzel (n.m.) knot, ganglion
uzh (n.m.) grass snake
uzh (adv.) already, really
uzhalit' (v.pf.) sting
uzhas (n.m.) horror
uzhasnut'sya (v.pf.) be horrified
uzhasnyi (adj.) terrible
uzhe (adv.) already
uzhenie (n.n.) fishing, angling
uzhimka (n.f.) grimace
uzhin (n.m.) supper
uzhit'sya (v.pf.) live together, get on
uzhivat'sya (v.impf.) live together, get on
uzhivchivyi (adj.) easy to get on with
uzkii (adj.) narrow, tight
uzkokoleinyi (adj.) narrow-gauge
uzlovatyi (adj.) knotty
uzlovoi (adj.) main
uznavat' (v.impf.) learn, find out
uznik (n.m.) prisoner
uzor (n.m.) pattern
uzost' (n.f.) narrowness
uzurpirovat' (v.impf.&pf.) usurp
uzy (v.pl.) bonds

V (В)

v (prep.) in, at, into
vaflya (n.f.) wafer
vagon (n.m.) railway car
vagonetka (n.f.) trolley
vagonovozhatyi (adj.) driver
vagon-restoran (n.m.) dining car
vakansiya (n.f.) vacancy
vakhta (n.f.) watch
vaksa (n.f.) shoe polish
vaktsina (n.f.) vaccine

vakuum (n.m.) vacuum
val (n.m.) mound
val (n.m.) shaft
val (n.m.) roller
valenki (n.pl.) felt boots
valentnost' (n.f.) valence
valet (n.m.) knave
valik (n.m.) bolster, cylinder
valit' (v.impf.) throw down
valovoi (adj.) gross

val's (n.m.) waltz

valyat' (v.impf.) drag along, roll

valyuta (n.f.) currency

vanadii (n.m.) vanadium

vandal (n.m.) vandal

vanil' (n.f.) vanilla

vanna (n.f.) bath

var (n.m.) pitch

varen'e (n.n.) jam

varenyi (adj.) boiled

varezhki (n.pl.) mittens

variant (n.m.) version

varit' (v.impf.) boil

varka (n.f.) cooking

varvar (n.m.) barbarian

vash (p.) your, yours

vasilek (n.m.) cornflower

vassal (n.m.) vassal

vata (n.f.) cotton wool

vataga (n.f.) gang

vaterliniya (n.f.) waterline

vatin (n.m.) wadding

vatnik (n.m.) quilted jacket

vatnyi (adj.) wadded

vatrushka (n.f.) cheesecake

vatt (n.m.) watt

vayanie (n.n.) sculpture

vaza (n.f.) vase

vazelin (n.m.) vaseline

vazhnichat' (v.impf.) put on airs

vazhnyi (adj.) important

vbegat' (v.impf.) run in

vbirat' (v.impf.) absorb

vbit' (v.pf.) drive in

vbivat' (v.impf.) drive in

vblizi (adv.) nearby

vchera (adv.) yesterday

vchetvero (adv.) four times

vchitat'sya (v.pf.) read attentively

vdal' (adv.) into the distance

vdaleke (adv.) in the distance

vdavat'sya (v.impf.) jut out, go into

vdavit' (v.pf.) press in

vdesyatero (adv.) ten times

vdet' (v.pf.) put into

vdevat' (v.impf.) put into

vdobavok (adv.) in addition

vdogonku (adv.) in pursuit of

vdokhnovit' (v.pf.) inspire

vdokhnut' (v.pf.) inhale

vdol' (prep.) along

vdolbit' (v.pf.) drum

vdova (n.f.) widow

vdrebezgi (adv.) to pieces

vdrug (adv.) suddenly

vdumat'sya (v.pf.) think over

vdut' (v.pf.) blow in

vduvat' (v.impf.) blow in

vdvigat' (v.impf.) push in

vdvoe (adv.) double, twice

vdvoem (adv.) both, together

vdvoine (adv.) double

vdykhat' (v.impf.) inhale

vecher (n.m.) evening

vecherinka (n.f.) party

vechernii (adj.) evening

vecherom (adv.) in the evening

vechnost' (n.f.) eternity

vedat' (v.impf.) be in charge

v"edat'sya (v.impf.) eat into

vedenie (n.n.) authority

vedenie (n.n.) conduct

ved'ma (n.f.) witch

vedomost' (n.f.) list, register

vedomstvo (n.n.) department

vedro (n.n.) bucket

vedushchii (adj.) leading

veer (n.m.) fan

vegetarianets (n.m.) vegetarian

vek (n.m.) century

vekha (n.f.) landmark

veko (n.n.) eyelid

vekovoi (adj.) ancient

veksel' (n.m.) promisary note

vektor (n.m.) vector

velet' (v.impf.) order

velichestvennyi (adj.) majestic

velichie (n.n.) grandeur

velichina (n.f.) quantity

velikan (n.m.) giant

velikii (adj.) great

velikodushie (n.n.) generosity

velikolepnyi (adj.) magnificent

velosiped (n.m.) bicycle

vena (n.f.) vein

venericheskii (adj.) venereal

venets (n.m.) crown

vengerskii (adj.) Hungarian

vengr (n.m.) Hungarian

venik (n.m.) broom

venok (n.m.) wreath

venoznyi (adj.) venous

ventil' (n.m.) valve

ventilyatsiya (n.f.) ventilation

vera (n.f.) faith

veranda (n.f.) verandah

verba (n.f.) pussy willow

verblyud (n.m.) camel

verbovat' (v.impf.) recruit

verenitsa (n.f.) row

veresk (n.m.) heather

verevka (n.f.) rope

verf' (n.f.) shipyard

verit' (v.impf.) believe

veritel'naya gramota (adj.-n.f.) credentials

verkh (adv.) top

verkhom (adv.) on horseback

verkhov'e (n.n.) upper reaches

verkhovnyi (adj.) supreme

verkhushka (n.f.) top

vermishel' (n.f.) vermicelli

verno (adv.) correctly

verno (adv.) probably

vernost' (n.f.) correctness

vernut' (v.pf.) return

vernyi (adj.) correct

veroispovedanie (n.n.) religion

verolomnyi (adj.) treacherous

veroterpimost' (n.f.) toleration

verovanie (n.n.) creed

veroyatnost' (n.f.) probability

vershina (n.f.) summit

versiya (n.f.) version

verstak (n.m.) joiner's bench

verstat' (v.impf.) make up into pages

verstka (n.f.) imposing

vertel (n.m.) spit

vertet' (v.impf.) turn around

vertikal'nyi (adj.) vertical

vertolet (n.m.) helicopter

veruyushchii (adj.) religious

ves' (p.) all

ves (n.m.) weight

vesel'e (n.n.) fun

veselit' (v.impf.) amuse

veselo (adv.) gaily

veselost' (n.f.) gaiety

vesennii (adj.) spring

veshalka (n.f.) coat hanger

veshat' (v.impf.) hang

veshat' (v.impf.) weigh

veshch' (n.f.) thing

veshchestvennyi (adj.) material

veshchestvo (n.n.) substance

vesit' (v.impf.) weigh

veslo (n.n.) oar

ves'ma (adv.) highly

vesna (n.f.) spring

vesnushka (n.f.) freckle

vest' (n.f.) news

vesti (v.impf.) conduct, lead

vestnik (n.m.) herald

vestovoi (adj.) orderly

vesy (n.pl.) scales

vetchina (n.f.) ham

veter (n.m.) wind

veteran (n.m.) veteran

veterinar (n.m.) veterinary

veterok (n.m.) breeze

vetka (n.f.) branch

vetkhii (adj.) old, dilapidated

v'etnamets (n.m.) Vietnamese

veto (n.n.) veto

vetochka (n.f.) twig

vetrenyi (adj.) windy

vetryanaya ospa (adj.-n.f.) chicken pox

vetryanoi (adj.) wind powered

vetv' (n.f.) branch

vetvistyi (adj.) branchy

veyalka (n.f.) winnowing machine

veyanie (n.n.) winnowing

veyanie (n.n.) breath, trend

veyat' (v.impf.) winnow

veyat' (v.impf.) blow

v"ezd (n.m.) entrance, drive

vezde (adv.) everywhere

vezhlivyi (adj.) polite

vezti (v.impf.) carry, drive

vezti (v.impf.) have luck

v"ezzhat' (v.impf.) enter, drive in

vglub' (adv.) deep

vglyadet'sya (v.pf.) peer

vgonyat' (v.impf.)　drive in
vibrator (n.m.)　vibrator, oscillator
vibratsiya (n.f.)　vibration
vid (n.m.)　appearance
vid (n.m.)　kind, species
vid (n.m.)　aspect
videnie (n.n.)　vision
videt' (v.impf.)　see
vidimo (adv.)　apparently
vidimost' (n.f.)　visibility
vidnet'sya (v.impf.)　be visible
vidnyi (adj.)　visible, eminent
vidoizmenenie (n.n.)　modification
vidovoi (adj.)　specific
vika (n.f.)　vetch
vikhr' (n.m.)　whirlwind
vilka (n.f.)　fork, plug
vily (n.pl.)　pitchfork
vilyat' (v.impf.)　wag
vina (n.f.)　guilt, fault
vinegret (n.m.)　Russian salad
vinil (n.m.)　vinyl
vinit' (v.impf.)　blame
vinitel'nyi (adj.)　accusative
vinnyi (adj.)　wine
vino (n.n.)　wine
vinodelie (n.n.)　wine making
vinograd (n.m.)　grapes
vinovatyi (adj.)　guilty
vinovnik (n.m.)　culprit
vint (n.m.)　screw
vintovka (n.f.)　rifle
vintovoi (adj.)　spiral
violonchel' (n.f.)　cello
violonchelist (n.m.)　cellist
virtuoz (n.m.)　virtuoso
virulentnost' (n.f.)　virulence
virus (n.m.)　virus
virusologiya (n.f.)　virology
viselitsa (n.f.)　gallows
viset' (v.impf.)　hang
vishnevyi (adj.)　cherry
vishnya (n.f.)　cherry
viskoza (n.f.)　rayon
vismut (n.m.)　bismuth
visok (n.m.)　temple
visyachii (adj.)　hanging
vit' (v.impf.)　weave

vitamin (n.m.)　vitamin
vitat' (v.impf.)　soar
vitrina (n.f.)　shopwindow
vitse-admiral (n.m.)　vice admiral
vivisektsiya (n.f.)　vivisection
viza (n.f.)　visa
vizg (n.m.)　squeal
vizirovat' (v.impf.)　visa
vizit (n.m.)　visit
vizual'nyi (adj.)　visual
vkatit' (v.pf.)　roll in
vkhod (n.m.)　entrance
vkhodit' (v.impf.)　enter
vkhodnoi (adj.)　entrance
vklad (n.m.)　deposit, contribution
vkladchik (n.m.)　depositor
vkladka (n.f.)　inset
vkleivat' (v.impf.)　paste in
vklinit'sya (v.pf.)　be wedged in
vklyuchat'sya (v.impf.)　join
vklyuchenie (n.n.)　inclusion
vklyuchit' (v.pf.)　include, turn on
vkolachivat' (v.impf.)　drive in
vkolotit' (v.pf.)　drive in
vkonets (adv.)　utterly
vkopannyi (adj.)　dug in
vkorenivshiisya (adj.)　rooted
vkos' (adv.)　aslant
vkradchivyi (adj.)　ingratiating
vkradyvat'sya (v.impf.)　steal in
vkrattse (adv.)　briefly
vkrutuyu (adv.)　hard-boiled
vkus (n.m.)　taste
vlachit' (v.impf.)　drag
vladelets (n.m.)　owner
vladet' (v.impf.)　own
vladychestvo (n.n.)　dominion
vlaga (n.f.)　moisture
vlagalishche (n.n.)　vagina
vlamyvat'sya (v.impf.)　break in
vlast' (n.f.)　power
vlast' (n.f.)　authority, rule
vlastnyi (adj.)　imperious
vlastvovat' (v.impf.)　hold sway over
vlazhnost' (n.f.)　humidity
vlech' (v.impf.)　attract
vlechenie (n.n.)　inclination
vletat' (v.impf.)　fly in

vlevo (adv.) to the left
vlezat' (v.impf.) climb in
vlivanie (n.n.) infusion
vlivat' (v.impf.) pour in
vliyanie (n.n.) influence
V.L.K.S.M. (abbr.) Leninist Young
   Communist League of the Soviet Union
vlomit'sya (v.pf.) break in
vlozhit' (v.pf.) put in
vlyubit'sya (v.pf.) fall in love
vmenyaemost' (n.f.) sanity
vmenyat' (v.impf.) regard, impute
vmeshat'sya (v.pf.) intervene
vmeshchat' (v.impf.) contain
vmeste (adv.) together
vmestimost' (n.f.) capacity
vmesto (prep.) instead of
vmig (adv.) in a moment
vnachale (adv.) at first
vnaem (adv.) hire
vne (prep.) out of, outside
vnedrenie (n.n.) inculcation, application
vneocherednoi (adj.) extraordinary
vneshkol'nyi (adj.) extracurricular
vneshne (adv.) outwardly
vneshnii (adj.) outward, external
vneshtatnyi (adj.) not on permanent staff
vnesti (v.pf.) carry in
vnezapnyi (adj.) sudden
vnich'yu (adv.) in a draw
vnikat' (v.impf.) investigate thoroughly
vnimanie (n.n.) attention
vnimatel'nyi (adj.) attentive
vniz (adv.) down
vnizu (adv.) below
vnosit' (v.impf.) carry in
vnov' (adv.) again
vnuchka (n.f.) granddaughter
vnuk (n.m.) grandson
vnushat' (v.impf.) suggest, imspire
vnutr' (adv.) in, inside
vnutrennii (adj.) inside, internal
vnutrennosti (n.pl.) internal organs
vnutri (adv.) inside, within
vnutrivennyi (adj.) intravenous
vnutrividovoi (adj.) intraspecific
vnutriyadernyi (adj.) intranuclear
vnyatnyi (adj.) distinct

vo (prep.) in, at, into
vobrat' (v.pf.) absorb
voda (n.f.) water
vodevil' (n.m.) vaudeville
vodit' (v.impf.) lead
voditel' (n.m.) driver
voditel'stvo (n.n.) leadership
vodit'sya (v.impf.) be found, associate with
vodka (n.f.) vodka
vodnyi (adj.) water, aquatic, aqueous
vodoboyazn' (n.f.) hydrophobia
vodoem (n.m.) reservoir
vodoizmeshchenie (n.n.) displacement
vodokachka (n.f.) pump house
vodokhranilishche (n.n.) reservoir
vodolaz (n.m.) diver
vodolechenie (n.n.) hydropathy
vodonepronitsaemyi (adj.) watertight
vodopad (n.m.) waterfall
vodopoi (n.m.) watering place
vodoprovod (n.m.) water pipe
vodorazdel (n.m.) watershed
vodorod (n.m.) hydrogen
vodorosl' (n.f.) seaweed
vodostochnyi (adj.) drain
vodostoikii (adj.) water-resistant
vodovorot (n.m.) whirlpool
vodruzhat' (v.impf.) raise
vodvorit' (v.pf.) install
vodyanistyi (adj.) watery, insipid
vodyanka (n.f.) dropsy
vodyanoi (adj.) water, aquatic
voedino (adv.) together
voenachal'nik (n.m.) military leader
voenizatsiya (n.f.) militarization
voenkom (n.m.) military commissar
voennoobyazannyi (n.m.) reservist
voennoplennyi (n.m.) prisoner of war
voenno-polevoi sud (adj.-n.m.) court-martial
voennosluzhashchii (n.m.) serviceman
voenno-vozdushnyi (adj.) air force
voennyi (adj.) military
voevat' (v.impf.) be at war
vognat' (v.pf.) drive in
vognutyi (adj.) concave
voi (n.m.) howl
voilok (n.m.) felt
voin (n.m.) warrior

voina (n.f.) war
voinstvennyi (adj.) warlike
voiska (n.pl.) troops
voisko (n.n.) army
voiti (v.pf.) enter
vokal'nyi (adj.) vocal
vokrug (adv.) round
vokzal (n.m.) railroad station
vol (n.m.) ox
volchii (adj.) wolfish
volchok (n.m.) top
volchonok (n.m.) wolf cub
voldyr' (n.m.) blister
voleibol (n.m.) volleyball
volei-nevolei (adv.) willy-nilly
volevoi (adj.) strong-willed
vol'fram (n.m.) tungsten
volk (n.m.) wolf
volna (n.f.) wave
volnenie (n.n.) agitation, unrest
volnistyi (adj.) wavy
vol'no (adv.) at ease
vol'nonaemnyi (adj.) civilian
volnoobraznyi (adj.) undulating
vol'noslushatel' (n.m.) external student
vol'nost' (n.f.) liberty
volnovat' (v.impf.) agitate, worry
volnovod (n.m.) waveguide
volnuyushchii (adj.) exciting
volochit' (v.impf.) drag
volokita (n.f.) procrastination
voloknistyi (adj.) fibrous
volokno (n.n.) fiber
volos (n.m.) hair
volshebnik (n.m.) magician
vol't (n.m.) volt
volya (n.f.) will
von' (n.f.) stench
von (adv.) out
von (part.) there
vonzat' (v.impf.) thrust
voobrazhaemyi (adj.) imaginary
voobrazit' (v.pf.) imagine
voobshche (adv.) in general
voochiyu (adv.) with one's own eyes
voodushevit' (v.impf.) inspire
vooruzhenie (n.n.) armaments
vooruzhat' (v.impf.) arm

vo-pervykh (adv.) firstly
vopit' (v.impf.) shout
vopiyushchii (adj.) crying
vopl' (n.m.) wail
voplotit' (v.pf.) embody
vopreki (prep.) in spite of
vopros (n.m.) question
vor (n.m.) thief
vorchanie (n.n.) grumbling
vorkovat' (v.impf.) coo
vorobei (n.m.) sparrow
vorochat' (v.impf.) turn
vorokh (n.m.) heap
voron (n.m.) raven
vorona (n.f.) crow
voronka (n.f.) funnel
voronoi (adj.) black
voroshit' (v.impf.) turn over
vorot (n.m.) collar
vorot (n.m.) windlass
vorota (n.pl.) gate
vorotnik (n.m.) collar
vorovat' (v.impf.) steal
vors (n.m.) pile
vorvat'sya (v.pf.) burst into
vosem' (num.) eight
vosemnadtsat' (num.) eighteen
vosh' (n.f.) louse
vosk (n.m.) wax
voskhititel'nyi (adj.) delightful
voskhod (n.m.) rise
voskhishchat' (v.impf.) delight
voskhozhdenie (n.n.) ascent
voskhvalyat' (v.impf.) praise
voskliknut' (v.pf.) exclaim
voskovoi (adj.) waxen
voskresat' (v.impf.) be resurrected
voskresen'e (n.n.) Sunday
voskresit' (v.pf.) resuscitate
vos'merka (n.f.) the eight
vos'michasovoi (adj.) eight-hour
vos'midesyatyi (adj.) eightieth
vos'miugol'nyi (adj.) octagonal
vos'moi (adj.) eighth
vospalenie (n.n.) inflammation
vospevat' (v.impf.) hymn
vospitanie (n.n.) education
vosplamenit' (v.pf.) ignite, inflame

vospolnit' (v.pf.)   fill up
vospol'zovat'sya (v.pf.)   make use
vospominanie (n.n.)   recollection
vosprepyatstvovat' (v.pf.)   hinder
vospretit' (v.pf.)   forbid
vospriimchivyi (adj.)   receptive, susceptible
vosproizvedenie (n.n.)   reproduction
vosprotivit'sya (v.pf.)   oppose
vospryanut' (v.pf.)   take heart
vossoedinenie (n.n.)   reunion
vosstanavlivat' (v.impf.)   restore
vosstanie (n.n.)   rising
vosstanovit' (v.pf.)   restore
vosstat' (v.pf.)   rise
vosstavat' (v.impf.)   rise
vostochnyi (adj.)   eastern, oriental
vostok (n.m.)   east, orient
vostorg (n.m.)   delight
vostorzhennyi (adj.)   enthusiastic
vostorzhestvovat' (v.pf.)   triumph
vostrebovanie (n.n.)   claiming
vosvoyasi (adv.)   back home
vot (part.)   here, there
votknut' (v.pf.)   thrust in
votsarit'sya (v.impf.)   reign
votum (n.m.)   vote
vovlekat' (v.impf.)   involve
vo-vremya (adv.)   in time
vovsyu (adv.)   with might and main
vo-vtorykh (adv.)   secondly
voyaka (n.m.)   fighter
voyuyushchii (adj.)   belligerent
voz (n.m.)   cart
vozbudimost' (n.f.)   excitability
vozbudit' (v.pf.)   excite
vozbuditel' (n.m.)   stimulus
vozbuzhdat'sya (v.impf.)   get excited
vozbu.·hdenie (n.n.)   excitation
vozchik (n.m.)   carter
vozdavat' (v.impf.)   render
vozdeistvie (n.n.)   influence
vozdelat' (v.pf.)   cultivate
vozderzhanie (n.n.)   abstention
vozderzhannyi (adj.)   abstentious
vozderzhat'sya (v.pf.)   abstain
vozderzhavshiisya (n.m.)   abstainer
vozdukh (n.m.)   air
vozdukhonepronitsaemyi (adj.)   airtight

vozdukhoplavanie (n.n.)   aeronautics
vozdukhoprovod (n.m.)   air duct
vozdushnyi (adj.)   air
vozdvigat' (v.impf.)   erect
vozglas (n.m.)   exclamation
vozglavit' (v.pf.)   be at the head of
vozhatyi (n.m.)   leader
vozhd' (n.m.)   leader
vozhzhi (n.pl.)   reins
vozit' (v.impf.)   carry, drive
vozit'sya (v.impf.)   take much trouble over
vozlagat' (v.impf.)   lay upon
vozle (prep.)   beside
vozlozhit' (v.pf.)   lay upon
vozlyublennyi (adj.)   beloved
vozmestit' (v.pf.)   compensate
vozmezdie (n.n.)   retribution
vozmozhnost' (n.f.)   possibility
vozmushchenie (n.n.)   disturbance
vozmutit' (v.pf.)   anger
vozmutitel'nyi (adj.)   scandalous
vozmuzhalost' (n.f.)   maturity
voznagradit' (v.pf.)   reward
voznenavidet' (v.pf.)   conceive hatred for
voznikat' (v.impf.)   arise
vozniknovenie (n.n.)   origin
vozniknut' (v.pf.)   arise
voznya (n.f.)   fuss
vozobnovit' (v.pf.)   renew
vozrast (n.m.)   age
vozrastanie (n.n.)   growth
vozrasti (v.pf.)   grow
vozrazhat' (v.impf.)   object
vozrazit' (v.pf.)   object
vozrodit' (v.pf.)   revive
vozvelichivat' (v.impf.)   exalt
vozvesti (v.pf.)   erect
vozvrashchat'(sya) (v.impf.)   return
vozvrat (n.m.)   return
vozvyshennyi (adj.)   elevated
vozvysit' (v.pf.)   raise
vozzrenie (n.n.)   opinion
vozzvanie (n.n.)   appeal
vozzvat' (v.pf.)   appeal
vpadat' (v.impf.)   flow into
vpadina (n.f.)   cavity
vpalyi (adj.)   hollow
vpast' (v.pf.)   fall into

vpechatlenie (n.n.) impression
vpered (adv.) forward
vperedi (adv.) in front
vperemeshku (adv.) in confusion
vperemezhku (adv.) alternately
vperit' (v.pf.) fix
vpervye (adv.) first
vpikhivat' (v.impf.) push in
vpitat' (v.pf.) absorb
vpit'sya (v.impf.) dig into
vpityvat'(sya) (v.impf.) soak in
vpivat'sya (v.impf.) dig into
vplav' (adv.) swimming across
vplesti (v.pf.) plait (into)
vplot' do (adv.) right up to
vplotnuyu (adv.) close
vpolgolosa (adv.) in undertones
vpolne (adv.) quite
vpolzat' (v.impf.) crawl in
vpopykhakh (adv.) in a hurry
vporu (adv.) fit
vposledstvii (adv.) afterward
vpot'makh (adv.) in the dark
vprave (pred.) have a right
vpravit' (v.pf.) set
vpravo (adv.) to the right
vpred' (adv.) henceforth
vprochem (conj.) however
vprogolod' (adv.) starving
vprok (adv.) for future use
vpryagat' (v.impf.) harness
vprygivat' (v.impf.) jump
vpryskivanie (n.n.) injection
vpuskat' (v.impf.) admit
vpustuyu (adv.) to no purpose
vputat' (v.pf.) involve
vputyvat'sya (v.impf.) meddle
vrach (n.m.) physician
vrachebnyi (adj.) medical
vrag (n.m.) enemy
vran'e (n.n.) lies
vrashchat' (v.impf.) revolve
vrasplokh (adv.) unawares
vrassypnuyu (adv.) in all directions
vrastat' (v.impf.) grow inward
vrat' (v.impf.) lie
vratar' (n.m.) goalkeeper
vrazbrod (adv.) in all directions

vrazhda (n.f.) enmity
vrazheskii (adj.) hostile
vrazrez (adv.) contrary
vrazumitel'nyi (adj.) intelligible
vred (n.m.) harm
vreditel' (n.m.) vermin
vrednyi (adj.) bad
vremennyi (adj.) temporary
vremya (n.n.) time
vremyaischislenie (n.n.) calendar
vremyapreprovozhdenie (n.n.) pastime
vrezat'sya (v.pf.) cut into
vrode (prep.) like
vroven' (adv.) level with
vroz' (adv.) apart
vrozhdennyi (adj.) innate
vruchat' (v.impf.) deliver
vrun (n.m.) liar
vryad li (adv.) unlikely
vryvat'sya (v.impf.) burst into
vsadit' (v.pf.) stick into
vsadnik (n.m.) rider
vsasyvat' (v.impf.) suck in
vse (p.) all
vse (p.) whole
vse eshche (adv.) still
vsegda (adv.) always
vsego (adv.) in all
vselenie (n.n.) installation
vselennaya (n.f.) universe
vselit' (n.pf.) move in
vsemerno (adv.) in every possible way
vsemirnyi (adj.) universal
vsemogushchii (adj.) omnipotent
vsenarodnyi (adj.) nationwide
vseobshchii (adj.) general
vsepobezhdayushchii (adj.) all-conquering
vser'ez (adv.) in earnest
vserossiiskii (adj.) All-Russian
vsesil'nyi (adj.) omnipotent
vsesoyuznyi (adj.) All-Union
vsestoronnii (adj.) all-around,
    comprehensive
vse-taki (part.) nevertheless
vsetselo (adv.) entirely
vsevozmozhnyi (adj.) of every kind
vshit' (v.pf.) sew in
vshivat' (v.impf.) sew in

vshivyi (adj.) lice infested

vskach' (adv.) at a gallop

vskakivat' (v.impf.) jump up

vskapyvat' (v.impf.) dig

vskarabkat'sya (v.pf.) climb

vskarmlivat' (v.impf.) nurse

vskhlipyvat' (v.impf.) sob

vskhodit' (v.impf.) ascend, rise, sprout

vskhody (n.pl.) young growth

vskidyvat' (v.impf.) toss up

vskipat' (v.pf.) boil

vskipyatit' (v.pf.) boil

vskochit' (v.pf.) jump up

vskolykhnut' (v.pf.) stir

vskol'z' (adv.) casually

vskopat' (v.pf.) dig

vskore (adv.) soon after

vskormit' (v.pf.) nurse

vskrikivat' (v.impf.) cry out

vskryt' (v.pf.) open, unseal

vskrytie (n.n.) dissection

vskryvat' (v.impf.) reveal

vsled (adv.) after

vsledstvie (prep.) because of

vslepuyu (adv.) blindly

vslukh (adv.) aloud

vslushat'sya (v.pf.) listen attentively

vsmatrivat'sya (v.impf.) peer

vsmyatku (adv.) soft-boiled

vsosat' (v.pf.) suck in

vsovyvat' (v.impf.) put in

vspakhat' (v.pf.) plow

vspashka (n.f.) plowing

vspenivat'sya (v.impf.) froth

vsplesk (n.m.) splash

vsplesnut' (v.pf.) splash

vsplyvat' (v.pf.) come to the surface

vsposhit' (v.pf.) startle

vspominat'(sya) (v.impf.) recollect

vspomnit' (v.pf.) recollect

vspomogatel'nyi (adj.) auxiliary

vsporkhnut' (v.pf.) take wing

vspotet' (v.pf.) sweat

vsprygivat' (v.impf.) jump up

vspryskivanie (n.n.) injection

vspryskivat' (v.impf.) sprinkle

vspugivat' (v.impf.) frighten away

vspykhivat' (v.impf.) burst into flame

vspyl'chivost' (n.f.) hot temper

vspylit' (v.pf.) flare up

vspyshka (n.f.) flare

vstat' (v.pf.) get up

vstavanie (n.n.) rising

vstavat' (v.impf.) get up

vstavit' (v.impf.) put in

vstrecha (n.f.) meeting

vstrechnyi (adj.) proceeding from the opposite direction

vstrepenut'sya (v.pf.) start

vstretit' (v.pf.) meet

vstrevozhit' (v.pf.) alarm

vstryakhivat' (v.impf.) shake up

vstryaska (n.f.) shaking

vstupat' (v.impf.) join

vstupat'sya (v.impf.) stand up for

vstupit' (v.pf.) join

vstupit'sya (v.pf.) stand up for

vstupitel'nyi (adj.) introductory

vstuplenie (n.n.) entry

vsunut' (v.pf.) put in

vsya (p.) all

vsyacheski (adv.) in every way

vsyakii (adj.) any

vsypat' (v.impf.) pour into

vsyudu (adv.) everywhere

vtaine (adv.) secretly

vtalkivat' (v.impf.) push in

vtaptyvat' (v.impf.) trample down

vtaskivat' (v.impf.) drag

v techenie (prep.) during

vtekat' (v.impf.) flow in

vteret' (v.pf.) rub in

vtikhomolku (adv.) surreptitiously

vtirat'sya (v.impf.) insinuate oneself

vtiskivat' (v.impf.) squeeze in

vtolknut' (v.pf.) push in

vtolkovat' (v.pf.) make one understand

vtoptat' (v.pf.) trample down

vtorgat'sya (v.impf.) invade

vtorichnyi (adj.) second, secondary

vtorit' (v.impf.) echo

vtornik (n.m.) Tuesday

vtoroe (n.n.) second course

vtoroi (adj.) second

vtorokursnik (n.m.) sophomore

vtoropyakh (adv.) in a hurry

vtorostepennyi (adj.) secondary

vtroe (adv.) three times

vtroem (adv.) all three

vtsepit'sya (v.pf.) get hold of

VTSSPS (abbr.) All-Union Central Council of Trade Unions

vtyagivat'sya (v.impf.) get used to

vtyanut' (v.pf.) draw in

vtyanut'sya (v.pf.) get used to

vtykat' (v.impf.) stick in

vual' (n.f.) veil

vul'garnyi (adj.) vulgar

vulkan (n.m.) volcano

vulkanizatsiya (n.f.) vulcanization, curing

vunderkind (n.m.) infant prodigy

vuz (n.m.) college

vvalit'sya (v.pf.) tumble in

vvalivat'sya (v.impf.) tumble in

vvedenie (n.n.) introduction

vverit' (v.pf.) entrust

vverkh (adv.) upward

vvernut' (v.pf.) put in

vveryat' (v.impf.) entrust

vvesti (v.pf.) introduce

vvezti (v.pf.) import

vvidu (prep.) in view of

vvintit' (v.pf.) screw in

vvodit' (v.impf.) introduce

vvodnyi (adj.) introductory

vvoz (n.m.) import

vvyazat'sya (v.pf.) get involved in

vvys' (adv.) upward

vy (p.) you

vyalit' (v.impf.) dry-cure

vyalyi (adj.) slack

vyanut' (v.impf.) wither

vyaz (n.m.) elm

vyazanie (n.n.) knitting

vyazanka (n.f.) bundle

vyazat' (v.impf.) tie up, knit

vyazat'sya (v.impf.) tally with

vyazhushchii (adj.) astringent

vyazkii (adj.) viscous

vyazkost' (n.f.) viscosoty

vybaltyvat' (v.impf.) let out

vybegat' (v.impf.) run out

vybirat' (v.impf.) elect, choose

vybirat'sya (v.impf.) get out

vybit' (v.pf.) beat out

vybivat'sya (v.impf.) be exhausted

vyboltat' (v.pf.) let out

vybor (n.m.) choice

vybornyi (adj.) election

vybory (n.pl.) election

vybrasyvat' (v.impf.) discard

vybrat' (v.pf.) elect, choose

vybrat'sya (v.pf.) get out

vybrit' (v.pf.) shave

vybrosit' (v.pf.) throw out

vybyvat' (v.impf.) leave, quit

vycherkivat' (v.impf.) strike out

vycherpat' (v.pf.) scoop dry

vychest' (v.pf.) deduct

vychet (n.m.) deduction

vychishchat' (v.impf.) clean

vychislenie (n.n.) calculation

vychislit' (v.pf.) calculate

vychistit' (v.pf.) clean

vychitaemoe (n.n.) subtrahend

vychitanie (n.n.) subtraction

vychitat' (v.impf.) deduct

vychurnyi (adj.) pretentious

vydacha (n.f.) issuing

vydalblivat' (v.impf.) hollow out

vydat' (v.pf.) give out, issue

vydavat' (v.impf.) give (out, away), issue

vydavat'sya (v.impf.) protrude

vydavit' (v.pf.) press out

vydayushchiisya (adj.) outstanding

vydelenie (n.n.) secretion

vydelit' (v.pf.) distinguish

vydelka (n.f.) manufacture

vydelyat' (v.impf.) distinguish

vydelyvat' (v.impf.) make

vydergivat' (v.impf.) pull out

vydernut' (v.pf.) pull out

vyderzhannyi (adj.) self-restrained

vyderzhivat' (v.impf.) stand, bear

vyderzhka (n.f.) excerpt

vyderzhka (n.f.) self-control

vydokhnut' (v.pf.) breathe out

vydolbit' (v.pf) hollow out

vydra (n.f.) otter

vydumat' (v.pf.) invent

vydumyvat' (v.impf.) invent

vydvigat'(sya) (v.impf.) move out, advance

vydvinut' (v.pf.)   move out, advance
vydykhat'(sya) (v.impf.)   breathe out
vyekhat' (v.pf.)   leave
vyemka (n.f.)   hollow
vyezd (n.m.)   departure
vyezzhat' (v.impf.)   leave
vygadat' (v.pf.)   gain
vygibat' (v.impf.)   curve
vygladit' (v.pf.)   iron
vyglyadet' (v.impf.)   look
vyglyadyvat' (v.impf.)   look out
vygnat' (v.pf.)   drive out
vygoda (n.f.)   profit
vygon (n.m.)   pasture land
vygonyat' (v.impf.)   drive out
vygorat' (v.impf.)   burn down
vygorazhivat' (v.impf.)   fence off, shield
vygoret' (v.pf.)   burn down
vygorodit' (v.pf.)   fence off, shield
vygovarivat' (v.impf.)   reprimand
vygovor (n.m.)   accent, reprimand
vygovorit' (v.impf.)   articulate, reserve
vygruzhat' (v.impf.)   unload
vygruzka (n.f.)   unloading
vyigrat' (v.pf.)   win
vyigrysh (n.m.)   prize
vyiti (v.pf.)   go out
vykachat' (v.pf.)   pump out
vykalyvat' (v.impf.)   thrust out, put out
vykapyvat' (v.impf.)   dig out
vykarmlivat' (v.impf.)   bring up
vykazat' (v.pf.)   show
vykhazhivat' (v.impf.)   pull through (an illness)
vykhlopotat' (v.pf.)   obtain
vykhod (n.m.)   exit
vykhodets (n.m.)   emigrant, of some origin
vykhodit' (v.pf.)   tend
vykhodit' (v.impf.)   go out
vykhodka (n.f.)   trick
vykhodnoi (adj.)   day-off
vykholennyi (adj.)   well-groomed
vykhvatit' (v.pf.)   snatch
vykidysh (n.m.)   miscarriage
vykidyvat' (v.impf.)   throw out
vykinut' (v.pf)   throw out
vykladyvat' (v.impf.)   lay out

vyklikat' (v.impf.)   call out
vyklyuchatel' (n.m.)   switch
vyklyuchit' (v.pf.)   turn off
vykolachivat' (v.impf.)   knock out
vykolot' (v.pf.)   thrust out, put out
vykopat' (v.pf.)   dig out
vykorchevat' (v.pf.)   root out
vykormit' (v.pf.)   bring up, rear
vykovat' (v.pf.)   forge
vykraivat' (v.impf.)   cut out
vykrasit' (v.pf.)   paint, dye
vykrik (n.m.)   cry
vykrikivat' (v.impf.)   cry out
vykroit' (v.pf.)   cut out
vykruchivat'sya (v.impf.)   extricate oneself
vykrutit' (v.pf.)   unscrew
vykup (n.m.)   ransom
vykupat' (v.impf.)   redeem
vykupat' (v.pf.)   bathe
vykurivat' (v.impf.)   smoke out
vylamyvat' (v.impf.)   break out
vylavlivat' (v.impf.)   fish out
vylazka (n.f.)   sally, rush forward
vylechit' (v.pf.)   cure
vylechivat'(sya) (v.impf.)   be cured
vylepit' (v.pf.)   model
vylet (n.m.)   flight
vyletat' (v.impf.)   fly out
vylezat' (v.impf.)   climb out
vylit' (v.pf.)   pour out
vylivat'sya (v.impf.)   run out
vylomat' (v.pf.)   break out
vylovit' (v.pf.)   fish out
vylozhit' (v.pf.)   lay out
vylupit'sya (v.pf.)   hatch
vymachivat' (v.impf.)   drench
vymalivat' (v.impf.)   beg
vymanivat' (v.impf.)   lure out
vymazat' (v.pf.)   smear
vymenivat' (v.impf.)   exchange
vymeret' (v.pf.)   die out, become extinct
vymerzat' (v.impf.)   freeze
vymeshchat' (v.impf.)   retaliate, vent
vymesti (v.pf.)   sweep
vymestit' (v.pf.)   retaliate, vent
vymetat' (v.impf.)   sweep
vymirat' (v.impf.)   die out, become extinct
vymochit' (v.pf.)   drench

vymogat' (v.impf.) extort
vymokat' (v.impf.) be drenched
vymolit' (v.pf.) obtain by entreaties
vymolvit' (v.pf.) utter
vymostit' (v.pf.) pave
vympel (n.m.) pennant
vymya (n.n.) udder
vymysel (n.m.) fiction
vymyshlennyi (adj.) invented
vymyt'(sya) (v.pf.) wash
vynesti (v.pf.) carry out, endure
vynimat' (v.impf.) take out
vynosit' (v.impf.) carry out, endure
vynoslivost' (n.f.) endurance
vynudit' (v.pf.) force
vynut' (v.pf.) take out
vynyrnut' (v.pf.) emerge
vypad (n.m.) attack
vypadat' (v.impf.) fall out
vypalyvat' (v.impf.) weed out
vyparivanie (n.n.) evaporation
vyparivat' (v.impf.) evaporate
vypast' (v.pf.) fall out
vypekat' (v.impf.) bake
vypilivat' (v.impf.) saw out
vypisyvat' (v.impf.) write out
vypit' (v.pf.) drink
vypivat' (v.impf.) drink
vypivka (n.f.) drinking
vyplachivat' (v.impf.) pay
vyplata (n.f.) payment
vyplavit' (v.pf.) smelt
vypleskivat' (v.impf.) splash out
vyplevyvat' (v.impf.) spit out
vyplyunut' (v.pf.) spit out
vyplyvat' (v.impf.) swim out
vypolnenie (n.n.) execution, fulfillment
vypolnit' (v.pf.) execute, fulfill
vypoloskat' (v.pf.) rinse out
vypolot' (v.pf.) weed out
vypolzat' (v.impf.) crawl out
vyprashivat' (v.impf.) beg
vypravit' (v.pf.) correct
vypravka (n.f.) bearing
vyprovazhivat' (v.impf.) show the door to
vyprovodit' (v.pf.) show the door to
vypryagat' (v.impf.) unharness
vypryamit' (v.pf.) straighten

vypryamitel' (n.m.) rectifier
vypryamlyat' (v.impf.) straighten
vyprygivat' (v.impf.) jump out
vypuklost' (n.f.) prominence
vypusk (n.m.) output
vypusknik (n.m.) graduate
vypusknoi (adj.) exhaust
vypustit' (v.pf.) let out
vyputat'sya (v.pf.) extricate oneself
vypytat' (v.pf.) extract information
vypytyvat' (v.impf.) extract information
vyrabatyvat' (v.impf.) manufacture
vyrabotka (n.f.) output
vyrastat' (v.impf.) grow
vyrastit' (v.pf.) bring up, raise
vyravnivat' (v.impf.) smooth out
vyrazhat' (v.impf.) express
vyrazhennyi (adj.) expressed
vyrazit' (v.pf.) express
vyrazitel'nyi (adj.) expressive
vyrez (n.m.) cut
vyrezat' (v.impf.) cut out
vyrezka (n.f.) clipping
vyrezyvat' (v.impf.) cut out
vyrisovyvat'sya (v.impf.) stand out, be
    visible
vyrodit'sya (v.pf.) degenerate
vyronit' (v.pf.) drop
vyrovnyat' (v.pf.) smooth out
vyrozhdenie (n.n.) degeneration
vyrubat' (v.impf.) cut down
vyruchat' (v.impf.) help out
vyruchit' (v.pf.) help out
vyrugat' (v.pf.) scold
vyrvat' (v.pf.) pull out
vyrvat'sya (v.pf.) break away (loose)
vyryt' (v.pf.) dig
vyryvat' (v.impf.) dig
vyryvat' (v.impf.) pull out
vyryvat'sya (v.impf.) break away (loose)
vys' (n.f.) height
vysadit' (v.pf.) disembark, transplant
vysasyvat' (v.impf.) suck out
vysazhivat'(sya) (v.impf.) disembark
vysech' (v.pf.) cut
vysech' (v.pf.) whip
vysekat' (v.impf.) cut
vyselenie (n.n.) eviction

vyselit' (v.pf.) evict
vyshe (adj.) higher
vysheupomyanutyi (adj.) above-mentioned
vyshina (v.f.) height
vyshit' (v.pf.) embroider
vyshivanie (n.n.) embroidery
vyshka (n.f.) tower
vyshvyrnut' (v.pf.) hurl out
vysidet' (v.pf.) remain, hatch
vysit'sya (v.impf.) rise
vyskablivat' (v.impf.) scrape out
vyskakivat' (v.impf.) jump out
vyskal'zyvat' (v.impf.) slip out
vyskazat' (v.pf.) express an opinion
vyskazyvanie (n.n.) opinion, statement
vyskoblit' (v.pf.) scrape out
vyskochit' (v.pf.) jump out
vyskol'znut' (v.pf.) slip out
vyslat' (v.pf.) dispatch, exile
vysledit' (v.pf.) track down
vysluga (n.f.) period of service
vyslushat' (v.pf.) hear, listen, sound
vysluzhivat'sya (v.impf.) gain promotion
vysmeivat' (v.impf.) ridicule
vysmorkat'sya (v.pf.) blow one's nose
vysokhnut' (v.pf.) dry up
vysokii (adj.) high, tall
vysoko (adv.) high
vysokokachestvennyi (adj.) high-quality
vysokokvalifitsirovannyi (adj.) highly
    qualified
vysokomerie (n.n.) arrogance
vysokomolekulyarnyi (adj.) high-molecular
vysokoparnyi (adj.) pompous
vysokovol'tnyi (adj.) high-voltage
vysosat' (v.pf.) suck out
vysota (n.f.) height
vysotnyi (adj.) high-altitude
vysovyvat'(sya) (v.impf.) hang out
vyspat'sya (v.pf.) have a good sleep
vysshii (adj.) higher
vystavit' (v.pf.) bring out, display
vystavka (n.f.) exhibition
vystavlyat' (v.impf.) bring out, display
vystirat' (v.pf.) wash
vystradat' (v.pf.) suffer
vystraivat' (v.impf.) draw up
vystrel (n.m.) shot

vystroit' (v.pf.) build
vystroit' (v.pf.) draw up
vystup (n.m.) projection
vystupat' (v.impf.) come forward, perform
vystuplenie (n.n.) march, statement,
    performance
vysunut' (v.pf.) put out
vysushit' (v.pf.) dry
vysverlivat' (v.impf.) drill
vysykhat' (v.impf.) dry up
vysylat' (v.impf.) dispatch, exile
vysylka (n.f.) dispatch, exile
vysypat' (v.pf.) pour out
vysypat'sya (v.pf.) spill out
vysypat'sya (v.impf.) have a good sleep
vyt' (v.impf.) howl
vytalkivat' (v.impf.) push out
vytarashchit' (v.pf.) stare
vytaskivat' (v.impf.) drag out
vytech' (v.pf.) flow out
vytekat' (v.impf.) flow out, follow
vyteret' (v.pf.) wipe
vytesnit' (v.pf.) force out
vytirat'(sya) (v.impf.) dry oneself
vytkat' (v.pf.) weave
vytolknut' (v.pf.) push out
vytryasti (v.pf.) shake out
vytsarapat' (v.pf.) scratch out
vytsvesti (v.pf.) fade
vytyagivat'(sya) (v.impf.) stretch
vytyanyt' (v.pf.) stretch
vytyazhka (n.f.) extract
vyuchit' (v.pf.) teach, learn
v'yuchnoe zhivotnoe (adj.-n.n.) beast of
    burden
vyudit' (v.pf.) fish out
v'yuga (n.f.) snowstorm
v'yushchiisya (adj.) curly, climbing
vyvalit' (v.pf.) empty
vyvalivat'sya (v.impf.) fall out
vyvarivat' (v.impf.) boil down
vyvedat' (v.pf.) extract information
vyverit' (v.pf.) verify
vyvernut' (v.pf.) unscrew
vyvernut'sya (v.pf.) wriggle out
vyvertyvat' (v.impf.) unscrew
vyveryat' (v.impf.) verify
vyveshivat' (v.impf.) hang out

vyvesit' (v.pf.) hang out
vyveska (n.f.) signboard
vyvesti (v.impf.) take out, withdraw
vyvetrivanie (n.n.) weathering
vyvezti (v.pf.) take out, withdraw
vyvikh (n.m.) dislocation
vyvintit' (v.pf.) screw out
vyvod (n.m.) withdrawal, conclusion
vyvodit'sya (v.impf.) disappear
vyvodok (n.m.) brood
vyvolakivat' (v.impf.) drag out
vyvorachivat' (v.impf.) screw out
vyvoz (n.m.) export
vyyasnenie (n.n.) clarification
vyyasnit' (v.pf.) make clear, ascertain
vyyavit' (v.pf.) reveal
vyzdoravlivat' (v.impf.) recover
vyzdorovlenie (n.n.) recovery
vyzhat' (v.pf.) squeeze out
vyzhdat' (v.pf.) wait for
vyzhech' (v.pf.) burn out
vyzhidat' (v.impf.) wait for
vyzhigat' (v.impf.) burn out
vyzhimat' (v.impf.) squeeze out
vyzhit' (v.pf.) survive
vyzhivat' (v.impf.) survive
vyzov (n.m.) call, summons
vyzubrit' (v.pf.) learn by heart
vyzvat' (v.pf.) call, summon
vyzyvat'sya (v.impf.) volunteer
vyzyvayushchii (adj.) defiant
vzaimnost' (n.f.) reciprocity
vzaimodeistvie (n.n.) interaction
vzaimoisklyuchayushchii (adj.) incompatible
vzaimootnoshenie (n.n.) relation
vzaimopomoshch' (n.f.) mutual aid
vzaimosvyaz' (n.f.) correlation
vzamen (prep.) in exchange for
vzaperti (adv.) locked up
vzbalmoshnyi (adj.) unbalanced
vzbaltyvat' (v.impf.) shake up
vzbegat' (v.impf.) run up
vzbeshennyi (adj.) furious
vzbesit' (v.pf.) infuriate
vzbirat'sya (v.impf.) climb
vzbit' (v.pf.) beat up
vzbivat' (v.impf.) beat up
vzboltat' (v.pf.) shake up

vzbudorazhit' (v.pf.) disturb
vzbuntovat'sya (v.pf.) revolt
vzdergivat' (v.impf.) jerk up
vzdernut' (v.pf.) jerk up
vzdokh (n.m.) sigh
vzdor (n.m.) nonsense
vzdorozhat' (v.pf.) rise in price
vzdragivat' (v.impf.) start
vzdremnut' (v.pf.) take a nap
vzdrognut' (v.pf.) start
vzdumat' (v.pf.) take it into one's head
vzdut' (v.pf.) inflate
vzdutie (n.n.) swelling
vzduvat' (v.impf.) inflate
vzdykhat' (v.impf.) sigh
vz"eroshit' (v.pf.) tousle
vzglyad (n.m.) glance
vzglyanut' (v.pf.) glance
vzgromozdit'sya (v.pf.) clamber upon
vzimat' (v.impf.) levy
vzirat' (v.impf.) look
vzlamyvat' (v.impf.) break open
vzlet (n.m.) takeoff
vzletat' (v.impf.) take off
vzlom (n.m.) breaking open
vzmakh (n.m.) stroke
vzmakhivat' (v.impf.) flap, wave
vzmor'e (n.n.) seashore
vznos (n.m.) payment
vznuzdat' (v.pf.) bridle
vzobrat'sya (v.pf.) climb
vzoiti (v.pf.) ascend
vzor (n.m.) look
vzorvat' (v.pf.) blow up
vzroslyi (adj.) adult
vzryv (n.m.) explosion
vzryvatel' (n.m.) fuse
vzryvchatyi (adj.) explosive
vzvalivat' (v.impf.) load
vzves' (n.f.) suspension
vzveshivat' (v.impf.) weigh
vzvesit' (v.pf.) weigh
vzvesti (v.pf.) raise
vzvintit' (v.pf.) work up
vzvit'sya (v.pf.) fly up
vzvivat'sya (v.impf.) fly up
vzvizgivat' (v.impf.) squeak
vzvod (n.m.) platoon

vzvodit' (v.impf.) raise
vzvodnyi (n.m.) platoon commander
vzvolnovannyi (adj.) excited
vzyat' (v.pf.) take
vzyatie (n.n.) seizure
vzyatka (n.f.) bribe

vzyatochnichestvo (n.n.) graft
vzyskanie (n.n.) penalty
vzyskat' (v.pf.) exact
vzyskatel'nyi (adj.) exacting
vzyvat' (v.impf.) appeal

Y · (Ы, Ю, Я)

ya (p.) I
yablochnyi (adj.) apple
yabloko (n.n.) apple
yablonya (n.f.) apple tree
yacheika (n.f.) cell
yachmen' (n.m.) barley
yachmen' (n.m.) sty
yad (n.m.) poison
yadernyi (adj.) nuclear
yadovityi (adj.) poisonous
yadro (n.n.) kernel, nucleus
yagnenok (n.m.) lamb
yagoda (n.f.) berry
yagoditsa (n.f.) buttock
yaichnitsa (n.f.) fried eggs
yaichnyi (adj.) egg
yaitso (n.n.) egg
yakhta (n.f.) yacht
yakoby (conj.) as if
yakor' (n.m.) anchor
yakut (n.m.) Yakut
yalik (n.m.) yawl
yama (n.f.) pit
yamochka (n.f.) dimple
yantar' (n.m.) amber
yanvar' (n.m.) January
yaponets (n.m.) Japanese
yarkii (adj.) bright
yarlyk (n.m.) label
yarmarka (n.f.) fair
yarmo (n.n.) yoke
yarost' (n.f.) fury
yarostnyi (adj.) furious
yarovoi (adj.) spring crop
yarus (n.m.) circle

yaryi (adj.) ardent
yasen' (n.m.) ash tree
yashcheritsa (n.f.) lizard
yashchik (n.m.) box
yashchur (n.m.) foot-and-mouth disease
yasli (n.pl.) crib
yasli (n.pl.) nursery school
yasno (adv.) clearly
yasnyi (adj.) clear
yastreb (n.m.) hawk
yastva (n.pl.) viands, food
yavit'sya (v.pf.) appear
yavka (n.f.) appearance
yavlenie (n.n.) phenomenon
yavlyat'sya (v.impf.) appear
yavnyi (adj.) obvious
yazva (n.f.) ulcer
yazvitel'nyi (adj.) biting
yazychnik (n.m.) pagan
yazyk (n.m.) tongue
yazyk (n.m.) language
yazykoznanie (n.n.) linguistics
yubilei (n.m.) jubilee
yubka (n.f.) skirt
yug (n.m.) south
yugo-vostochnyi (adj.) southeast
yugo-vostok (n.m.) southeast
yugo-zapad (n.m.) southwest
yugo-zapadnyi (adj.) southwest
yumor (n.m.) humor
yunga (n.m.) boy
yunosha (n.m.) youth
yunost' (n.f.) youth
yunyi (adj.) youthful
yuridicheskii (adj.) law

yuriskonsul't (n.m.) legal adviser
yurist (n.m.) lawyer
yurta (n.f.) yurta, animal skin hut
yustirovka (n.f.) adjustment, alignment
yustitsiya (n.f.) justice

yutit'sya (v.impf.) be cooped up
yuvelir (n.m.) jeweler
yuzhanin (n.m.) southerner
yuzhnyi (adj.) south

Z (З, Ж)

za (prep.) behind, beyond, after
zaballotirovat' (v.pf.) blackball
zabastovat' (v.pf.) go on strike
zabastovka (n.f.) strike
zabava (n.f.) amusement
zabeg (n.m.) heat
zabegat' (v.pf.) drop in
zaberemenet' (v.pf.) conceive
zabintovat' (v.pf.) bandage
zabirat' (v.impf.) take away
zabirat'sya (v.impf.) climb
zabit' (v.pf.) drive in
zabit'sya (v.pf.) hide
zabit'sya (v.pf.) begin to beat
zabityi (adj.) downtrodden
zabivat' (v.impf.) drive in
zabivat'sya (v.impf.) hide
zabiyaka (n.m.&f.) bully
zablagorassudit'sya (v.pf.) think fit
zablagovremenno (adv.) in good time
zablestet' (v.pf.) shine
zabludit'sya (v.pf.) get lost
zabluzhdat'sya (v.impf.) be mistaken
zaboi (n.m.) face
zabolevaemost' (n.f.) sick rate
zabolevat' (v.impf.) fall ill
zabor (n.m.) fence
zabota (n.f.) care
zabrakovat' (v.pf.) reject
zabrasyvat' (v.impf.) throw
zabrat' (v.pf.) take away
zabrat'sya (v.pf.) climb
zabresti (v.pf.) wander
zabronirovat' (v.pf.) reserve
zabrosat' (v.pf.) throw
zabrosit' (v.pf.) throw, neglect

zabryzgat' (v.pf.) bespatter
zabvenie (n.n.) oblivion
zabyt'e (n.n.) unconsciousness
zabyt'sya (v.pf.) doze off, forget oneself
zabytyi (adj.) forgotten
zabyvat' (v.impf.) forget
zabyvat'sya (v.impf.) doze off, forget oneself
zabyvchivyi (adj.) forgetful
zachastuyu (adv.) often
zachatie (n.n.) conception
zachem (adv.) why
zacherkivat' (v.impf.) strike out
zacherpnut' (v.pf.) scoop up
zacherstvet' (v.pf.) become stale
zachet (n.m.) test
zachinshchik (n.m.) instigator
zachislit' (v.pf.) include
zachitat'sya (v.pf.) get absorbed in a book
zad (n.m.) back, behind
zadabrivat' (v.impf.) cajole
zadacha (n.f.) problem
zadanie (n.n.) assignment
zadarivat' (v.impf.) load with presents
zadat' (v.pf.) set, ask
zadatki (n.pl.) potentialities
zadatok (n.m.) deposit
zadavit' (v.pf.) crush
zadelat' (v.pf.) do up, close up
zadergivat' (v.impf.) draw
zadernut' (v.pf.) draw
zaderzhanie (n.n.) detention
zaderzhat' (v.pf.) detain
zaderzhka (n.f.) delay, retardation
zadet' (v.pf.) touch
zadevat' (v.impf.) touch
zadira (n.m.&f.) bully

zadnii (adj.) back
zadnik (n.m.) back
zadobrit' (v.pf.) cajole
zadokhnut'sya (v.pf.) suffocate
zadolgo (adv.) long before
zadolzhat' (v.pf.) owe money
zadolzhennost' (n.f.) debts
zadom (adv.) backward
zador (n.m.) ardor
zadrat' (v.pf.) tear to pieces
zadremat' (v.pf.) doze off
zadrozhat' (v.pf.) begin to tremble
zadumat' (v.pf.) plan
zadumat'sya (v.pf.) muse, be lost in thought
zadushevnyi (adj.) cordial
zadushit' (v.pf.) strangle
zadut' (v.pf.) blow out
zaduvat' (v.impf.) blow out
zadvigat' (v.impf.) push into
zadvizhka (n.f.) bolt
zadvorki (n.pl.) backyard
zadykhat'sya (v.impf.) suffocate
zaekhat' (v.pf.) call in
zaem (n.m.) loan
zaezdit' (v.pf.) overwork
zaezzhat' (v.impf.) call in
zafiksirovat' (v.pf.) fix
zagadat' (v.pf.) think of
zagadka (n.f.) riddle
zagar (n.m.) suntan
zagib (n.m.) bend
zagladit' (v.pf.) iron, press
zaglavie (n.n.) title
zaglokhnut' (v.pf.) die away
zaglushat' (v.impf.) drown, deaden
zaglyaden'e (n.n.) lovely sight
zaglyadyvat' (v.impf.) look in
zaglyanut' (v.pf.) look in
zagnat' (v.pf.) drive in, tire out
zagnivanie (n.n.) rotting, decay
zagnut' (v.pf.) bend
zagolovok (n.m.) title
zagon (n.m.) enclosure
zagonyat' (v.impf.) drive in, tire out
zagorat' (v.impf.) get suntanned
zagorat'sya (v.impf.) catch fire
zagorazhivat' (v.impf.) fence in
zagorelyi (adj.) suntanned

zagoret'sya (v.pf.) catch fire
zagorodit' (v.pf.) fence in
zagorodka (n.f.) fence
zagorodnyi (adj.) country
zagotavlivat' (v.impf.) prepare
zagovarivat' (v.impf.) start talking
zagovor (n.m.) conspiracy
zagovorit' (v.pf.) start talking
zagovorshchik (n.m.) conspirator
zagranichnyi (adj.) foreign
zagrazhdenie (n.n.) obstruction
zagrebat' (v.impf.) rake up
zagrimirovat' (v.pf.) make up
zagrivok (n.m.) nape
zagromozhdat' (v.impf.) encumber
zagrubelyi (adj.) coarsened
zagrustit' (v.pf.) become sad
zagruzhat' (v.impf.) load
zagruzka (n.f.) load
zagryaznenie (n.n.) pollution
zagryzat' (v.impf.) bite to death
zags (n.m.) registry office
zagubit' (v.pf.) ruin
zagulyat' (v.pf.) go on a spree
zagustet' (v.pf.) get thick
zagvozdka (n.f.) snag
zaigryvat' (v.impf.) flirt
zaika (n.m.&f.) stammerer
zaimoobrazno (adv.) on credit
zaimstvovat' (v.impf.) borrow
zainteresovannyi (adj.) interested
zainteresovat' (v.pf.) interest
zaiskivat' (v.impf.) make up to
zaiti (v.pf.) drop in
zakabalit' (v.pf.) enslave
zakal (n.m.) tempering
zakalyat' (v.impf.) temper
zakalyvat' (v.impf.) slaughter, stab
zakanchivat'(sya) (v.impf.) finish
zakapat' (v.pf.) bespatter
zakapyvat' (v.impf.) bury
zakashlyat'sya (v.pf.) have a fit of coughing
zakat (n.m.) sunset
zakatat' (v.pf.) roll up
zakatit' (v.pf.) roll under
zakatyvat' (v.impf.) roll up
zakatyvat' (v.impf.) roll under
zakayat'sya (v.pf.) forswear

zakaz (n.m.) order
zakhlebnut'sya (v.pf.) choke
zakhlestnut' (v.pf.) fasten, flow over
zakhlopnut' (v.pf.) bang
zakhlopyvat'sya (v.impf.) close with a bang
zakhod (n.m.) sunset
zakhokhotat' (v.pf.) burst out laughing
zakholustnyi (adj.) out-of-the-way
zakhotet' (v.pf.) wish
zakhudalyi (adj.) shabby
zakhvat (n.m.) seizure
zakhvatchik (n.m.) invader
zakhvatnicheskii (adj.) aggressive
zakhvorat' (v.pf.) fall ill
zakidat' (v.pf.) scatter
zakidyvat' (v.impf.) scatter
zakidyvat' (v.impf.) throw
zakinut' (v.pf.) throw
zakipat' (v.impf.) begin to boil
zakis' (n.f.) protoxide
zakisat' (v.impf.) turn sour
zaklad (n.m.) pawning
zakladka (n.f.) laying
zakladka (n.f.) bookmark
zakladnaya (n.f.) mortgage
zakladyvat' (v.impf.) mortgage
zakleimit' (v.pf.) brand
zakleit' (v.pf.) glue up
zakleivat' (v.impf.) glue up
zaklepka (n.f.) rivet
zaklinanie (n.n.) incantation
zaklyatyi (adj.) mortal
zaklyuchat' (v.impf.) conclude
zaklyuchat'sya (v.impf.) consist of
zaklyuchenie (n.n.) conclusion
zakochenet' (v.pf.) become numb
zakolachivat' (v.impf.) board up
zakoldovannyi (adj.) enchanted
zakolka (n.f.) hairpin
zakolot' (v.pf.) slaughter
zakolotit' (v.pf.) board up
zakon (n.m.) law
zakonchennyi (adj.) complete
zakonchit' (v.pf.) finish
zakonodatel'stvo (n.n.) legislation
zakonomernost' (n.f.) conformity with laws
  of nature
zakonoproekt (n.m.) bill

zakopat' (v.pf.) bury
zakopchennyi (adj.) smoky
zakoptelyi (adj.) smoky
zakorenelyi (adj.) inveterate
zakosnelyi (adj.) obdurate
zakoulok (n.m.) back street
zakovat' (v.pf.) put in irons
zakradyvat'sya (v.impf.) steal in
zakrashivat' (v.impf.) paint over
zakrasit' (v.pf.) paint over
zakrast'sya (v.pf.) steal in
zakrepit' (v.pf.) fasten
zakrepitel' (n.m.) fixing agent
zakrepostit' (v.pf.) enslave
zakrichat' (v.pf.) cry out
zakroishchik (n.m.) cutter
zakrom (n.m.) corn bin
zakruglenie (n.n.) curve
zakrutit' (v.pf.) twirl
zakruzhit'sya (v.pf.) whirl
zakryakhtet' (v.pf.) groan
zakrytie (n.n.) closing
zakryvat'(sya) (v.pf.) close
zakudakhtat' (v.pf.) cackle
zakulisnyi (adj.) backstage
zakupat' (v.impf.) purchase
zakupka (n.f.) purchase
zakuporivat' (v.impf.) stop up
zakurivat' (v.impf.) light up a cigarette
zakusit' (v.pf.) have a snack
zakuska (n.f.) snack
zakutat' (v.pf.) bundle up
zakutyvat' (v.impf.) bundle up
zakvaska (n.f.) ferment
zal (n.m.) hall
zaladit' (v.pf.) take to
zalayat' (v.pf.) begin to bark
zalechivat' (v.impf.) heal
zaleganie (n.n.) bed, seam
zalepit' (v.pf.) close up, paste up
zaletat' (v.impf.) fly into
zalezat' (v.impf.) climb
zalezh' (n.f.) deposit
zalezhat'sya (v.pf.) lie too long
zalit'(sya) (v.pf.) flood, pour
zaliv (n.m.) bay
zalivat' (v.impf.) flood, pour
zalog (n.m.) pledge, deposit

zalog (n.m.) voice
zalozhit' (v.pf.) pawn, mortgage
zalozhit' (v.pf.) lay a foundation
zalozhnik (n.m.) hostage
zalp (n.m.) salvo
zamakhivat'sya (v.impf.) threaten
zamalchivat' (v.impf.) hush up
zamanivat' (v.impf.) lure
zamashki (n.pl.) manners
zamaskirovat' (v.pf.) disguise
zamazat' (v.pf.) paint over, dirty
zamazyvat' (v.impf.) paint over, dirty
zamechanie (n.n.) remark
zamechatel'nyi (adj.) remarkable
zamedlenie (n.n.) slowing down, deceleration
zamedlit' (v.pf.) slow down
zamena (n.f.) substitution
zamenimyi (adj.) replaceable
zamenitel' (n.m.) substitute
zameret' (v.pf.) stand still
zamerit' (v.pf.) measure
zamertvo (adv.) like one dead
zameryat' (v.impf.) measure
zamerzat' (v.impf.) freeze
zameshat' (v.pf.) mix up
zameshatel'stvo (n.n.) confusion
zameshchat' (v.impf.) act for, fill in for
zameshivat' (v.impf.) mix up
zameshivat' (v.impf.) knead
zameshkat'sya (v.pf.) tarry
zamesit' (v.pf.) knead
zamesti (v.pf.) sweep up, cover up
zamestit' (v.pf.) act for, fill in for
zamestitel' (n.m.) assistant
zametat' (v.impf.) sweep up, cover up
zametit' (v.pf.) notice, remark
zametnyi (adj.) visible
zaminka (n.f.) hitch
zamirat' (v.impf.) stand still
zamknutost' (n.f.) reticence
zamknut'sya (v.pf.) close, become reserved
zamochit' (v.pf.) soak
zamok (n.m.) lock
zamolchat' (v.pf.) grow silent
zamolkat' (v.impf.) grow silent
zamolvit' (v.pf.) put in a word for
zamorazhivat' (v.impf.) freeze

zamorozki (n.pl.) early frosts
zamorysh (n.m.) weakling
zamsha (n.f.) suede
zamuchit' (v.pf.) torture to death
zamurovat' (v.pf.) brick up
zamusolennyi (adj.) bedraggled
zamuzhestvo (n.n.) marriage
zamyat' (v.pf.) hush up
zamykanie (n.n.) short circuit
zamykat' (v.impf.) lock
zamysel (n.m.) intention
zamyshlyat' (v.impf.) plan
zamyslit' (v.pf.) plan
zamyslovatyi (adj.) intricate
zanaves (n.m.) curtain
zanavesit' (v.impf.) curtain
zanesti (v.pf.) bring
zanimat' (v.impf.) borrow, occupy
zanimatel'nyi (adj.) entertaining
zanimat'sya (v.impf.) be engaged in
zanoschivyi (adj.) arrogant
zanosit' (v.impf.) raise
zanosy (n.pl.) snowdrifts
zanovo (adv.) anew
zanoza (n.f.) splinter
zanyat' (v.pf.) borrow
zanyat' (v.pf.) occupy
zanyatie (n.n.) occupation
zanyatie (n.n.) seizure
zanyatnyi (adj.) amusing
zanyato (adj.) engaged
zanyatoi (adj.) busy
zaochnik (n.m.) external student
zaodno (adv.) in concert
zaokeanskii (adj.) overseas
zaostrennyi (adj.) pointed
zapachkat' (v.pf.) make dirty
zapad (n.m.) west
zapadnyi (adj.) west, western
zapaivat' (v.impf.) solder
zapakh (n.m.) smell
zapakhivat'sya (v.pf.) wrap oneself up in
zapakovat' (v.pf.) pack
zapal (n.m.) fuse
zapal (n.m.) heaves
zapal'chivyi (adj.) quick-tempered
zapas (n.m.) supply
zapashka (n.f.) plowing

zapasnoi (adj.) emergency, spare
zapasti (v.pf.) store
zapayat' (v.pf.) solder
zapazdyvanie (n.n.) lag, delay
zapazdyvat' (v.impf.) be late
zapech' (v.pf.) bake (in)
zapechatat' (v.pf.) seal up
zapechatlevat' (v.impf.) impress
zapechatyvat' (v.impf.) seal up
zapekanka (n.f.) baked pudding
zapelenat' (v.pf.) swaddle
zaperet' (v.pf.) lock
zapet' (v.pf.) start singing
zapevala (n.m.) leading singer
zapikhat' (v.pf.) push (in)
zapinat'sya (v.impf.) hesitate
zapirat' (v.impf.) lock up
zapiratel'stvo (n.n.) denial
zapis' (n.f.) entry, recording
zapisat' (v.pf.) write down
zapiska (n.f.) note
zapiski (n.pl.) notes, memoirs
zapit' (v.pf.) drink something down
zapivat' (v.impf.) drink something down
zaplakannyi (adj.) tear-stained
zaplata (n.f.) patch
zaplatit' (v.pf.) pay
zaplesnevelyi (adj.) moldy
zaplesti (v.pf.) braid
zapletat'sya (v.impf.) falter, be unsteady
zaplombirovat' (v.pf.) seal, fill
zaplyvat' (v.impf.) swim
zapnut'sya (v.pf.) hesitate
zapodozrit' (v.pf.) suspect
zapoi (n.m.) hard drinking
zapolnit' (v.pf.) fill
zapolzat' (v.impf.) creep in
zapominanie (n.n.) memory, storage
zapominat'(sya) (v.impf.) remember
zapomnit' (v.pf.) remember
zaponka (n.f.) cuff link
zapor (n.m.) constipation
zapor (n.m.) bolt
zaporoshit' (v.pf.) powder with snow
zapotelyi (adj.) misted
zapoved' (n.f.) commandment
zapovednik (n.m.) nature preserve
zapozdalyi (adj.) belated

zaprashivat' (v.impf.) make inquiries
zapravila (n.m.) boss
zapravit' (v.pf.) tuck in, fill up
zapravochnyi (adj.) filling
zapreshchat' (v.impf.) forbid
zapret (n.m.) ban
zaprikhodovat' (v.pf.) credit the account
zaprokidyvat' (v.impf.) throw back
zapros (n.m.) inquiry
zaprosto (adv.) without ceremony
zaprotokolirovat' (v.pf.) enter in the record
zapruda (n.f.) dam
zapryach' (v.pf.) harness
zapryagat' (v.impf.) harness
zapryatat' (v.pf.) hide away
zapryazhka (n.f.) team
zapugat' (v.pf.) intimidate
zapushchennyi (adj.) neglected
zapuskat' (v.impf.) launch, neglect
zapustelyi (adj.) desolate
zapustit' (v.pf.) launch, neglect
zaputannyi (adj.) involved
zapyast'e (n.n.) wrist
zapyataya (n.f.) comma
zapyatnat' (v.pf.) stain
zapykhat'sya (v.pf.) be out of breath
zapylit' (v.pf.) cover with dust
zarabatyvat' (v.impf.) earn
zarabotnaya plata (adj.-n.f.) wages
zarabotok (n.m.) earnings
zaranee (adv.) beforehand
zarastat' (v.impf.) be overgrown
zaraza (n.f.) infection
zarazhat' (v.impf.) infect
zarech'sya (v.pf.) make a vow not to
zaregistrirovat' (v.pf.) register
zarekat'sya (v.impf.) make a vow not to
zarekomendovat' (v.pf.) prove oneself
zarevo (n.n.) glow
zarezat' (v.pf.) slaughter
zarisovka (n.f.) sketch
zarnitsa (n.f.) summer lightning
zarodit' (v.pf.) engender
zarodysh (n.m.) embryo
zarok (n.m.) pledge
zarosli (n.pl.) overgrowth
zarozhdenie (n.n.) conception, origin
zarplata (n.f.) wages

zarubat' (v.impf.) kill with an axe
zarubit' (v.pf.) kill with an axe
zarubezhnyi (adj.) foreign
zarubka (n.f.) notch
zarubtsevat'sya (v.pf.) cicatrize
zaruchat'sya (v.pf.) enlist
zarya (n.f.) dawn
zaryabit' (v.pf.) dazzle
zaryad (n.m.) charge
zaryazhat' (v.impf.) load
zaryazhennyi (adj.) charged
zarychat' (v.pf.) roar
zarydat' (v.pf.) sob
zaryt' (v.pf.) bury
zaryvat' (v.impf.) bury
zarzhavet' (v.pf.) become rusty
zarzhavlennyi (adj.) rusty
zasada (n.f.) ambush
zasadit' (v.pf.) plant
zasakharennyi (adj.) candied
zasalivat' (v.impf.) salt
zasalivat' (v.impf.) stain with grease
zasasyvat' (v.impf.) suck in
zasedanie (n.n.) meeting
zaselennyi (adj.) populated
zasest' (v.pf.) settle
zasevat' (v.impf.) sow
zaseyat' (v.pf.) sow
zashatat'sya (v.pf.) stagger
zashchishchat' (v.impf.) defend
zashchita (n.f.) defense
zashivat' (v.impf.) sew up
zashnurovat' (v.pf.) lace up
zashtopat' (v.pf.) mend
zashumet' (v.pf.) make noise
zasidet'sya (v.pf.) sit up late
zasil'e (n.n.) preponderance
zaskrezhetat' (v.pf.) grind
zaskripet' (v.pf.) creak
zaslonka (n.f.) lid
zaslonyat' (v.impf.) shield
zasluga (n.f.) merit
zaslushat' (v.pf.) hear
zasmeyat' (v.pf.) scoff
zasmolit' (v.pf.) pitch
zasnut' (v.pf.) fall asleep
zasokhnut' (v.pf.) wither
zasol (n.m.) salting

zasolit' (v.pf.) salt
zasorenie (n.n.) obstruction
zasosat' (v.pf.) suck in
zasov (n.m.) bolt
zasovyvat' (v.impf.) shove in
zaspannyi (adj.) sleepy
zaspat'sya (v.pf.) oversleep
zasporit' (v.pf.) argue
zastarelyi (adj.) chronic
zastat' (v.pf.) find
zastava (n.f.) picket, post
zastavat' (v.impf.) find
zastavit' (v.pf.) make, compel
zastavit' (v.pf.) block, cram
zastavlyat' (v.impf.) compel, block
zastegnut' (v.pf.) button up
zasteklit' (v.pf.) glaze
zastenchivyi (adj.) shy
zastenok (n.m.) torture chamber
zastezhka (n.f.) fastening
zastigat' (v.impf.) catch
zastilat' (v.impf.) cover
zastoi (n.m.) stagnation
zastraivat' (v.impf.) build
zastrakhovat' (v.pf.) insure
zastrelit' (v.pf.) shoot
zastrel'shchik (n.m.) pioneer
zastrevat' (v.impf.) get stuck
zastroit' (v.pf.) build
zastryat' (v.pf.) get stuck
zastudit' (v.pf.) expose to cold
zastup (n.m.) spade
zastupat'sya (v.impf.) intercede
zastupnik (n.m.) defender
zastyvat' (v.impf.) congeal
zasuchivat' (v.impf.) roll up
zasukha (n.f.) drought
zasunut' (v.pf.) shove in
zasushivat' (v.impf.) dry
zasvetit'sya (v.pf.) light up
zasvetlo (adv.) before nightfall
zasvidetel'stvovat' (v.pf.) testify
zasykhat' (v.impf.) wither
zasylat' (v.impf.) send
zasypat' (v.pf.) fill in
zasypat' (v.impf.) fall asleep
zataennyi (adj.) secret, repressed
zataplivat' (v.impf.) make the fire

zatashchit' (v.pf.)   drag off
zataskannyi (adj.)   hackneyed
zatech' (v.pf.)   become numb
zateilivyi (adj.)   ingenious
zatekat' (v.impf.)   become numb
zatem (adv.)   then
zatemnenie (n.n.)   blackout
zatemno (adv.)   before dawn
zatemnyat' (v.impf.)   darken
zateret' (v.pf.)   rub out
zateryat' (v.pf.)   misplace
zatevat' (v.impf.)   up to
zateya (n.f.)   scheme
zatikhat' (v.impf.)   calm down
zatirat' (v.impf.)   rub out
zatish'e (n.n.)   calm
zatkhlyi (adj.)   musty
zatknut' (v.pf.)   stop up, plug
zatmevat' (v.impf.)   eclipse
zato (conj.)   but
zatochat' (v.impf.)   imprison
zatolkat' (v.pf.)   push into
zatonut' (v.pf.)   sink
zatopit' (v.pf.)   make the fire
zatopit' (v.pf.)   flood
zatoptat' (v.pf.)   trample down
zator (n.m.)   jam
zatormozit' (v.pf.)   brake
zatovarivanie (n.n.)   overstock
zatragivat' (v.impf.)   affect
zatrata (n.f.)   expenditure
zatratit' (v.pf.)   spend
zatravit' (v.pf.)   hunt down
zatrebovat' (v.pf.)   request
zatronut' (v.pf.)   affect
zatrudnenie (n.n.)   difficulty
zatsepit' (v.pf.)   hook
zatseplyat' (v.impf.)   hook
zatsvesti (v.pf.)   blossom
zatukhanie (n.n.)   attenuation
zatumanit'sya (v.pf.)   grow dim
zatushevat' (v.pf.)   shade in
zatverdenie (n.n.)   callosity, solidification
zatverdit' (v.pf.)   learn by heart
zatvor (n.m.)   lock
zatvorit' (v.pf.)   close
zatyagivat' (v.impf.)   tighten
zatyanut' (v.pf.)   tighten

zatyanut' (v.pf.)   begin to sing
zatyanut'sya (v.pf.)   be delayed
zatyazhka (n.f.)   delaying
zatykat' (v.pf.)   stop up
zatylok (n.m.)   back of the head
zaunyvnyi (adj.)   mournful
zauryadnyi (adj.)   mediocre
zavalivat' (v.impf.)   block up
zavarivat' (v.impf.)   make
zavedenie (n.n.)   institution
zavedomo (adv.)   wittingly
zavedovat' (v.impf.)   manage
zaveduyushchii (n.m.)   manager
zaverbovat' (v.pf.)   recruit
zaverit' (v.pf.)   assure
zavernut' (v.pf.)   wrap up, turn
zavershat' (v.impf.)   complete
zavertet'sya (v.pf.)   spin round
zavertyvat' (v.impf.)   wrap up
zaveryat' (v.impf.)   assure
zavesa (n.f.)   screen
zaveshchanie (n.n.)   will
zaveshivat' (v.impf.)   cover
zavesti (v.pf.)   start
zavesti (v.pf.)   buy, get hold of
zavesti (v.pf.)   bring, take
zavet (n.m.)   precept
zavezti (v.pf.)   deliver, drop off
zavidovat' (v.impf.)   envy
zavintit' (v.pf.)   screw up
zaviset' (v.impf.)   depend
zavist' (n.f.)   envy
zavistlivyi (adj.)   envious
zavit' (v.pf.)   wave, curl
zavitoi (adj.)   curled
zavitok (n.m.)   curl
zavivat'(sya) (v.impf.)   have one's hair set
zavivka (n.f.)   wave
zavkom (n.m.)   factory committee
zavladevat' (v.impf.)   take possession of
zavlekat' (v.impf.)   entice
zavod (n.m.)   factory
zavod (n.m.)   winding mechanism
zavodit' (v.impf.)   bring, get, start
zavodnoi (adj.)   clockwork
zavodoupravlenie (n.n.)   factory management
zavodskoi (adj.)   factory

zavoevanie (n.n.) conquest
zavorachivat' (v.impf.) wrap up, turn
zavozit' (v.impf.) leave, drop off
zavsegdatai (n.m.) habitue
zavtra (adv.) tomorrow
zavtrak (n.m.) breakfast
zavtrashnii (adj.) tomorrow
zavyanut' (v.pf.) fade
zavyaz' (n.f.) ovary
zavyazat' (v.pf.) tie up
zavyazka (n.f.) string
zavyaznut' (v.pf.) get stuck
zavyazyvat' (v.impf.) tie up
zavyvat' (v.impf.) howl
zavzyatyi (adj.) inveterate
zayadlyi (adj.) inveterate
zayats (n.m.) hare
zayavit' (v.pf.) declare
zayavka (n.f.) claim
zayavlenie (n.n.) declaration, application
zazelenet' (v.pf.) turn green
zazemlenie (n.n.) earthing
zazevat'sya (v.pf.) gape
zazhat' (v.pf.) squeeze
zazhech' (v.pf.) set fire
zazhigalka (n.f.) lighter
zazhiganie (n.n.) ignition
zazhigatel'nyi (adj.) incendiary
zazhim (n.m.) clamp
zazhit' (v.pf.) begin to live
zazhit' (v.pf.) heal
zazhitochnyi (adj.) prosperous
zazhivat' (v.impf.) heal
zazhivo (adv.) alive
zazhmurit' (v.pf.) narrow one's eyes
zaznavat'sya (v.impf.) give oneself airs
zazubrit' (v.pf.) jag, notch
zazubrit' (v.pf.) cram
zazvonit' (v.pf.) ring
zazvuchat' (v.pf.) sound
zdanie (n.n.) building
zdes' (adv.) here
zdorovat'sya (v.impf.) greet
zdorov'e (n.n.) health
zdorovo (adv.) well done
zdorovyi (adj.) healthy
zdravitsa (n.f.) toast
zdravnitsa (n.f.) health resort

zdravo (adv.) soundly
zdravookhranenie (n.n.) public health
zdravyi (adj.) sensible
zebra (n.f.) zebra
zelen' (n.f.) verdure
zelenet' (v.impf.) turn green
zelenyi (adj.) green
zemel'nyi (adj.) land
zemlecherpalka (n.f.) dredge
zemledelets (n.m.) farmer
zemlekop (n.m.) unskilled worker
zemlemer (n.m.) land surveyor
zemletryasenie (n.n.) earthquake
zemleustroistvo (n.n.) land-use regulations
zemlevladelets (n.m.) landowner
zemlistyi (adj.) earthy
zemlya (n.f.) land
zemlyak (n.m.) fellow countryman
zemlyanika (n.f.) wild strawberries
zemlyanka (n.f.) dugout
zemlyanoi (adj.) earth, earthen
zemnoi (adj.) earthly
zemnovodnye (n.pl.) amphibia
zenit (n.m.) zenith
zenitnyi (adj.) antiaircraft
zenitsa (n.f.) pupil
zerkalo (n.n.) mirror
zernistyi (adj.) granular
zerno (n.n.) grain
zev (n.m.) pharynx
zevaka (n.m.) idler
zhaba (n.f.) toad
zhaba (n.f.) quinsy
zhabry (n.pl.) gills
zhadnyi (adj.) greedy
zhaket (n.m.) jacket
zhal' (pred.) pity
zhalet' (v.impf.) feel sorry for
zhalit' (v.impf.) sting
zhalkii (adj.) pitiful
zhalo (n.n.) sting
zhaloba (n.f.) complaint
zhalost' (n.f.) pity
zhalostlivyi (adj.) compassionate
zhalovan'e (n.n.) salary
zhalovat'sya (v.impf.) complain
zhandarm (n.m.) gendarme
zhanr (n.m.) genre

zhar (n.m.) heat, fever

zhara (n.f.) heat

zharenyi (adj.) fried

zhargon (n.m.) jargon

zharkii (adj.) hot

zharkoe (n.n.) roast meat

zharoponizhayushchii (adj.) antipyretic

zharostoikost' (n.f.) heat resistance

zharovnya (n.f.) brazier

zhasmin (n.m.) jasmin

zhat' (v.impf.) squeeze

zhat' (v.impf.) reap

zhatva (n.f.) harvest

zhavoronok (n.m.) skylark

zhazhda (n.f.) thirst

zhe (part.) and, as to, but

zhech' (v.impf.) burn

zhelanie (n.n.) wish

zhelat' (v.impf.) wish

zhelatel'nyi (adj.) desirable

zhelatin (n.m.) gelatine

zhelch' (n.f.) bile

zhelchnyi (adj.) bilious

zhele (n.n.) jelly

zheleza (n.f.) gland

zhelezistyi (adj.) ferriferous

zheleznodorozhnyi (adj.) railroad

zheleznyi (adj.) iron

zhelezo (n.n.) iron

zhelezobeton (n.m.) reinforced concrete

zhelob (n.m.) chute

zheltet' (v.impf.) grow yellow

zheltok (n.m.) yolk

zheltukha (n.f.) jaundice

zheltyi (adj.) yellow

zhelud' (n.m.) acorn

zheludok (n.m.) stomach

zhemannyi (adj.) affected

zhemchug (n.m.) pearl

zhena (n.f.) wife

zhenikh (n.m.) bridegroom

zhenit' (v.impf.) marry

zhenshchina (n.f.) woman

zhenskii (adj.) female

zhenstvennyi (adj.) womanly

zherd' (n.f.) pole

zherebenok (n.m.) foal

zherlo (n.n.) mouth

zhernov (n.m.) millstone

zhertva (n.f.) sacrifice, victim

zhest' (n.f.) tin

zhest (n.m.) gesture

zhestkii (adj.) hard

zhestokii (adj.) cruel

zheton (n.m.) token

zhevat' (v.impf.) chew

zhezl (n.m.) baton

zhguchii (adj.) burning

zhgut (n.m.) tourniquet

zhidkii (adj.) liquid

zhila (n.f.) sinew, vein

zhil'e (n.n.) dwelling

zhilet (n.m.) waistcoat

zhilets (n.m.) tenant

zhilishche (n.n.) dwelling

zhilistyi (adj.) sinewy

zhilka (n.f.) vein

zhiloi (adj.) dwelling

zhilploshchad' (n.f.) dwelling space

zhir (n.m.) fat

zhiret' (v.impf.) grow fat

zhirnyi (adj.) fat

zhit' (v.impf.) live

zhiteiskii (adj.) worldly

zhitel' (n.m.) inhabitant

zhitnitsa (n.f.) granary

zhito (n.n.) corn

zhiv'em (adv.) alive

zhivitel'nyi (adj.) invigorating

zhivo (adv.) vividly, promptly

zhivoi (adj.) living, alive

zhivopis' (n.f.) painting

zhivopisets (n.m.) painter

zhivopisnyi (adj.) picturesque

zhivost' (n.f.) animation

zhivot (n.m.) stomach

zhivotnoe (n.n.) animal

zhivotnovodstvo (n.n.) stockbreeding

zhivotnyi (adj.) animal

zhivotrepeshchushchii (adj.) burning, vital

zhivuchii (adj.) hardly

zhizn' (n.f.) life

zhiznedeyatel'nost' (n.f.) vital activity

zhiznennyi (adj.) of life, vital

zhizneopisanie (n.n.) biography

zhizneradostnyi (adj.) cheerful

zhiznesposobnyi (adj.) viable
zhmurit'sya (v.impf.) squint
zhmurki (n.pl.) blindman's buff
zhmykhi (n.pl.) oil cake
zhneika (n.f.) reaper
zhnets (n.m.) reaper
zhrebii (n.m.) lot
zhrets (n.m.) priest
zhuk (n.m.) beetle
zhulik (n.m.) swindler
zhul'nichat' (v.impf.) cheat
zhuravl' (n.m.) crane
zhurchat' (v.impf.) ripple
zhurit' (v.impf.) reprove
zhurnal (n.m.) journal, magazine
zhutkii (adj.) terrible
zhuzhzhat' (v.impf.) buzz
zhvachka (n.f.) cud
zhyuri (n.n.) jury
zigzag (n.m.) zigzag
zigzagoobraznyi (adj.) zigzag
zima (n.f.) winter
zimnii (adj.) winter
zimoi (adv.) in winter
zimovat' (v.impf.) hibernate
zlaki (n.pl.) cereals
zlit' (v.impf.) anger, irritate
zlo (n.n.) evil
zlo (adv.) maliciously
zloba (n.f.) spite
zlobodnevnyi (adj.) burning, urgent
zlodei (n.m.) villain
zlodeyanie (n.n.) atrocity
zloi (adj.) wicked
zlokachestvennyi (adj.) malignant
zlonamerennyi (adj.) malicious
zlopamyatnyi (adj.) full of rancor
zlopoluchnyi (adj.) ill-started
zloradnyi (adj.) gloating
zloslovie (n.n.) malicious gossip
zlost' (n.f.) malice
zlostnyi (adj.) malicious
zloumyshlennik (n.m.) malefactor
zloupotrebit' (v.pf.) abuse
zloupotreblenie (n.n.) abuse
zloveshchii (adj.) ominous
zlovonie (n.n.) stench
zlovrednyi (adj.) vicious

zmei (n.m.) kite
zmeinyi (adj.) snake's
zmeya (n.f.) snake
znachenie (n.n.) meaning
znachit' (v.impf.) mean, signify
znachitel'nyi (adj.) considerable, important
znachok (n.m.) badge
znak (n.m.) sign, symbol
znakomit' (v.impf.) acquaint
znamenatel' (n.m.) denominator
znamenatel'nyi (adj.) significant
znamenitost' (n.f.) celebrity
znamenosets (n.m.) standard-bearer
znamenovat' (v.impf.) mark, signify
znamya (n.n.) banner
znanie (n.n.) knowledge
znat' (v.impf.) know
znatnyi (adj.) distinguished
znatok (n.m.) expert
znayushchii (adj.) learned
znobit' (v.impf.) feel feverish
znoi (n.m.) intense heat
zob (n.m.) goiter
zodchii (n.m.) architect
zola (n.f.) ashes
zolotistyi (adj.) golden
zolotnik (n.m.) slide, valve
zoloto (n.n.) gold
zolotonosnyi (adj.) gold-bearing
zolotopromyshlennost' (n.f.) gold industry
zolotukha (n.f.) scrofula
zolovka (n.f.) sister-in-law
zona (n.f.) zone
zond (n.m.) probe
zont (n.m.) umbrella
zoolog (n.m.) zoologist
zoopark (n.m.) zoo
zorkii (adj.) sharp-sighted, alert
zov (n.m.) call
zrachok (n.m.) pupil
zrelishche (n.n.) spectacle
zrelost' (n.f.) maturity
zrenie (n.n.) sight
zret' (v.impf.) ripen
zritel' (n.m.) spectator
zrya (adv.) to no purpose
zryachii (adj.) sighted
zub (n.m.) tooth

zubchatyi (adj.) cogged
zubets (n.m.) tooth, cog
zubnoi (adj.) tooth, dental
zubochistka (n.f.) toothpick
zubovrachebnyi (adj.) dental
zubrit' (v.impf.) cram
zud (n.m.) itch
zvanie (n.n.) rank
zvanyi (adj.) formal
zvat' (v.impf.) call
zvenet' (v.impf.) ring
zven'evoi (n.m.) team leader
zveno (n.n.) link
zver' (n.m.) beast
zverinets (n.m.) menagerie
zverskii (adj.) brutal
zvezda (n.f.) star
zvezdnyi (adj.) starry

zvon (n.m.) ringing
zvonkii (adj.) ringing
zvuchat' (v.impf.) sound
zvuchnyi (adj.) resonant
zvuk (n.m.) sound
zvukoizolyatsiya (n.f.) soundproofing
zvukonepronitsaemyi (adj.) soundproof
zvukoulavlivatel' (n.m.) sound locator
zvukovoi (adj.) sound
zvukozapis' (n.f.) sound recording
zvyakat' (v.impf.) jingle
zyab' (n.f.) plowland
zyabkii (adj.) sensitive to cold
zyabnut' (v.impf.) suffer from cold
zyat' (n.m.) son-in-law
zyb' (n.f.) ripple
zybkii (adj.) unsteady
zychnyi (adj.) loud

ENGLISH-RUSSIAN SECTION

A (A)

abacus schety (n.pl.)
abandon pokidat' (v.impf.)
abandon oneself predat'sya (v.pf.)
　　predavat'sya (v.impf.)
abandoned broshennyi (adj.)
abashed, to be orobet' (v.pf.)
abatement oslablenie (n.n.)
abbot abbat (n.m.)
abbreviate sokratit' (v.pf.)
ABC-book bukvar' (n.m.)
abdominal bryushnoi (adj.)
aberration aberratsiya (n.f.)
ability sposobnost' (n.f.)
Abkhazian abkhazets (n.m.)
able, to be moch' (v.impf.)
　　smoch' (v.pf.)
　　umet' (v.impf.)
abnormal nenormal'nyi (adj.)
abode mestoprebyvanie (n.n.)
abolish otmenit' (v.pf.)
　　uprazdnit' (v.pf.)
abolition otmena (n.f.)
aboriginal aborigen (n.m.)
abortion abort (n.m.)
about o (prep.)
　　ob (prep.)
　　obo (prep.)
　　pro (prep.)
above naverkhu (adv.)
　　sverkh (prep.)
above, from sverkhu (adv.)
above ground nadzemnyi (adj.)
above mentioned upomyanutyi (adj.)
　　vysheupomyanutyi (adj.)
above water nadvodnyi (adj.)
abrasion ssadina (n.f.)
abrupt otryvistyi (adj.)
abruptly kruto (adv.)
abscess gnoinik (n.m.)
　　naryv (n.m.)
abscissa abstsissa (n.f.)
absence neimenie (n.n.)
　　neyavka (n.f.)
　　otluchka (n.f.)
　　otsutstvie (n.n.)

absent oneself otluchat'sya (v.impf.)
absentmindedness rasseyannost' (n.f.)
absolute absolyutnyi (adj.)
absolutely sovershenno (adv.)
absorb poglotit' (v.pf.)
　　vbirat' (v.impf.)
　　vobrat' (v.pf.)
　　vpitat' (v.pf.)
absorption absorbtsiya (n.f.)
　　pogloshchenie (n.n.)
abstain vozderzhat'sya (v.pf.)
abstainer vozderzhavshiisya (n.m.)
abstention vozderzhanie (n.n.)
abstentious vozderzhannyi (adj.)
abstract abstraktnyi (adj.)
　　annotatsiya (n.f.)
abstractionism abstraktsionizm (n.m.)
absurdity absurd (n.m.)
　　nelepost' (n.f.)
abundance izbytok (n.m.)
　　izobilie (n.n.)
　　obilie (n.n.)
abuse ponosit' (v.impf.)
　　zloupotrebit' (v.pf.)
　　zloupotreblenie (n.n.)
abusive brannyi (adj.)
abyss bezdna (n.f.)
acacia akatsiya (n.f.)
academician akademik (n.m.)
academy akademiya (n.f.)
accelerate uskorit' (v.pf.)
acceleration uskorenie (n.n.)
accent aktsent (n.m.)
　　udarenie (n.n.)
　　vygovor (n.m.)
acceptable priemlemyi (adj.)
accepted, generally obshcheprinyatyi (adj.)
access dostup (n.m.)
accessible dostupnyi (adj.)
accessories priklad (n.m.)
　　prinadlezhnosti (n.pl.)
accident avariya (n.f.)
　　krushenie (n.n.)
　　sluchai (n.m.)
accidental sluchainyi (adj.)

acclimatize oneself akklimatizirovat'sya (v.impf.)
accommodate razmeshchat' (v.impf.)
accompany akkompanirovat' (v.impf.)
  dovesti (v.pf.)
  dovodit' (v.impf.)
  provodit' (v.pf.)
  provozhat' (v.impf.)
  soprovozhdat' (v.impf.)
  soputstvovat' (v.impf.)
accomplice posobnik (n.m.)
  soobshchnik (n.m.)
accomplish osushchestvit' (v.pf.)
  sovershat' (v.impf.)
  sovershit' (v.pf.)
accord sozvuchie (n.n.)
according to soglasno (adv.)
  soobrazno (adv.)
accordingly sootvetstvenno (adv.)
accordion akkordeon (n.m.)
  garmonika (n.f.)
accordion, bayan bayan (n.m.)
accordion player garmonist (n.m.)
account izlozhenie (n.n.)
  otchet (n.m.)
account, to credit the zaprikhodovat' (v.pf.)
account of, to give an izlagat' (v.impf.)
accountable podotchetnyi (adj.)
accountant schetovod (n.m.)
accounts, to settle raskvitat'sya (v.pf.)
accumulate nakaplivat'(sya) (v.impf)
  nakopit' (v.pf.)
  nakoplyat'(sya) (v.impf.)
  skaplivat'(sya) (v.impf.)
accumulator akkumulyator (n.m.)
accusation obvinenie (n.n.)
accusations napadki (n.pl.)
accusative vinitel'nyi (adj.)
accuse obvinyat' (v.impf.)
accused, the podsudimyi (adj.)
ace tuz (n.m.)
ache lomit' (v.impf.)
achievement dostizhenie (n.n.)
acid kislotnyi (adj.)
acid, amino aminokislota (n.f.)
acknowledge priznat' (v.pf.)
acknowledged priznannyi (adj.)
acknowledgement priznanie (n.n.)

acorn zhelud' (n.m.)
acoustic slukhovoi (adj.)
acoustics akustika (n.f.)
acquaint oznakomit' (v.pf.)
  poznakomit' (v.pf.)
  znakomit' (v.impf.)
acquire nazhit' (v.pf.)
  priobresti (v.pf.)
acrobat akrobat (n.m.)
across cherez (prep.)
  poperek (adv.)
act akt (n.m.)
  deistvovat' (v.impf.)
  postupat' (v.impf.)
act for zameshchat' (v.impf.)
  zamestit' (v.pf.)
acting deistvuyushchii (adj.)
action aktsiya (n.f.)
  isk (n.m.)
  postupok (n.m.)
activate aktivizirovat' (v.impf.&pf.)
active aktivnyi (adj.)
  operativnyi (adj.)
  podvizhnyi (adj.)
  rezvyi (adj.)
active members, most aktiv (n.m.)
activists, party partaktiv (n.m.)
activity aktivnost' (n.f.)
activity, vital zhiznedeyatel'nost' (n.f.)
actor akter (n.m.)
actress aktrisa (n.f.)
actually deistvitel'no (adv.)
acupuncture igloterapiya (n.f.)
ad-libbing otsebyatina (n.f.)
Adam's apple kadyk (n.m.)
adapt prinorovit' (v.pf.)
  prisposobit' (v.pf.)
adaptation prisposoblenie (n.n.)
add dobavit' (v.pf.)
  nabavit' (v.pf.)
  pribavit' (v.pf.)
  pridavat' (v.impf.)
  pripisat' (v.impf.)
  pristroit' (v.pf.)
  skladyvat' (v.impf.)
  slozhit' (v.pf.)
addendum slagaemoe (n.n.)
adder gadyuka (n.f.)

addict, drug narkoman (n.m.)
adding machine summator (n.m.)
addition dopolnenie (n.n.)
    pridacha (n.f.)
    slozhenie (n.n.)
addition, in vdobavok (adv.)
additional dopolnitel'nyi (adj.)
additional payment doplata (n.f.)
additive prisadka (n.f.)
address adres (n.m.)
    obrashchenie (n.n.)
adhere prirastat' (v.impf.)
adherent edinomyshlennik (n.m.)
adhesion prilipanie (n.n.)
adjacent smezhnyi (adj.)
adjective prilagatel'noe (n.n.)
adjoin primykat' (v.impf.)
adjust sorazmerit' (v.pf.)
    sorazmeryat' (v.impf.)
adjustment podgonka (n.f.)
    popravka (n.f.)
    prigonka (n.f.)
    yustirovka (n.f.)
administrative administrativnyi (adj.)
administrator administrator (n.m.)
admiral admiral (n.m.)
admiral, vice vitse-admiral (n.m.)
admiration preklonenie (n.n.)
admire lyubovat'sya (v.impf.)
admirer poklonnik (n.m.)
admission nabor (n.m.)
admit dopuskat' (v.impf.)
    dopustit' (v.pf.)
    vpuskat' (v.impf.)
admixture primes' (n.f.)
admonish uveshchevat' (v.impf.)
admonition nastavlenie (n.n.)
adolescence otrochestvo (n.n.)
adopt usvaivat' (v.impf.)
    usvoit' (v.pf.)
    usynovit' (v.pf.)
adoption prinyatie (n.n.)
    usvoenie (n.n.)
adoration obozhanie (n.n.)
adroit lovkii (adj.)
adult vzroslyi (adj.)
advance operezhenie (n.n.)
    vydvigat'(sya') (v.impf.)

    vydvinut' (v.pf.)
advanced peredovoi (adj.)
advancing operezhenie (n.n.)
advantage preimushchestvo (n.n.)
adventure avantyura (n.f.)
    pokhozhdenie (n.n.)
    priklyuchenie (n.n.)
adverb narechie (n.n.)
adversity nevzgoda (n.f.)
advertisement reklama (n.f.)
advice sovet (n.m.)
advise nadoumit' (v.pf.)
    sovetovat' (v.impf.)
adviser sovetchik (n.m.)
adviser, legal yuriskonsul't (n.m.)
Adzhar adzharets (n.m.)
aerated gazirovannyi (adj.)
aerial antenna (n.f.)
aeronautics vozdukhoplavanie (n.n.)
aesthetics éstetika (n.f.)
afar, from izdaleka (adv.)
affair delo (n.n.)
affect zatragivat' (v.impf.)
    zatronut' (v.pf.)
affected pritvornyi (adj.)
    zhemannyi (adj.)
affected person krivlyaka (n.f.)
affectionate privyazchivyi (adj.)
affinity srodstvo (n.n.)
affirmative utverditel'nyi (adj.)
afforestation lesonasazhdenie (n.n.)
Afghan afganets (n.m.)
afoot, to be naklevyvat'sya (v.impf.)
afraid, to be boyat'sya (v.impf.)
    pobaivat'sya (v.impf.)
after sledom (adv.)
    spustya (prep.)
    vsled (adv.)
    za (prep.)
after dinner posleobedennyi (adj.)
after midnight popolunochi (adv.)
afternoon, in the popoludni (adv.)
afterward posle (adv.)
    potom (adv.)
    vposledstvii (adv.)
again opyat' (adv.)
    snova (adv.)
    vnov' (adv.)

against protiv (prep.)
against one's will ponevole (adv.)
age starit' (v.impf.)
   vozrast (n.m.)
age, of sovershennoletnii (adj.)
age, of the same odnoletki (n.pl.)
aged prestarelyi (adj.)
agent agent (n.m.)
agent, fixing zakrepitel' (n.m.)
agent, oxidizing okislitel' (n.m.)
agent, toxic otravlyayushchee veshchestvo
   (adj.-n.n.)
aggravate rastravit' (v.pf.)
   usugubit' (v.pf.)
aggravation obostrenie (n.n.)
aggregate sovokupnost' (n.f.)
aggression agressiya (n.f.)
aggressive agressivnyi (adj.)
   zakhvatnicheskii (adj.)
aggressor intervent (n.m.)
agility podvizhnost' (n.f.)
agitate agitirovat' (v.impf.)
   volnovat' (v.impf.)
agitated, to become razvolnovat'sya (v.pf.)
agitation volnenie (n.n.)
agony agoniya (n.f.)
agrarian agrarnyi (adj.)
agree skhodit'sya (v.impf.)
   soglashat'sya (v.impf.)
   ugovarivat'(sya) (v.impf.)
agreeable soglasnyi (adj.)
agreement dogovor (n.m.)
   ugovor (n.m.)
agreement, to come to an sgovarivat'sya
   (v.impf.)
agreement, to reach dogovarivat'sya
   (v.impf.)
   dogovorit'sya (v.pf.)
agricultural sel'skokhozyaistvennyi (adj.)
agricultural biology agrobiologiya (n.f.)
agronomist agronom (n.m.)
agrotechnics agrotekhnika (n.f.)
ah akh (interj.)
ahead naprolom (adv.)
ahead of schedule dosrochno (adv.)
aid, mutual vzaimopomoshch' (n.f.)
aide ad"yutant (n.m.)
aim metit' (v.impf.)

   nastavit' (v.pf.)
   natselivat'sya (v.impf)
   tselit' (v.impf.)
aimless bestsel'nyi (adj.)
air provetrivat' (v.impf.)
   vozdukh (n.m.)
   vozdushnyi (adj.)
air duct vozdukhoprovod (n.m.)
air force voenno-vozdushnyi (adj.)
air hole otdushina (n.f.)
airbase aviabaza (n.f.)
air-cooling obduvka (n.f.)
aircraft aviatsionnyi (adj.)
   samolet (n.m.)
airless bezvozdushnyi (adj.)
airnavigation aéronavigatsiya (n.f.)
airplane aéroplan (n.m.)
airport aérodrom (n.m.)
airs, to give oneself zaznavat'sya (v.impf.)
airs, to put on vazhnichat' (v.impf.)
airtight vozdukhonepronitsaemyi (adj.)
alarm nabat (n.m.)
   perepolokh (n.m.)
   trevoga (n.f.)
   vstrevozhit' (v.pf.)
alarm clock budil'nik (n.m.)
alarmist paniker (n.m.)
alas! uvy (interj.)
Albanian albanets (n.m.)
album al'bom (n.m.)
albumen belok (n.m.)
albuminous belkovyi (adj.)
alcohol spirt (n.m.)
alcoholism alkogolizm (n.m.)
alder ol'kha (n.f.)
alert zorkii (adj.)
alert, on the nacheku (adv.)
alert, to be on the nastorozhe (adv.)
algebra algebra (n.f.)
algorithm algoritm (n.m.)
alien chuzhdyi (adj.)
   chuzhoi (adj.)
alien land chuzhbina (n.f.)
alienate otchuzhdat' (v.impf.)
alienation otorvannost' (n.f.)
alignment ravnenie (n.n.)
   yustirovka (n.f.)
alimony alimenty (n.pl.)

alive zazhivo (adv.)
   zhiv'em (adv.)
   zhivoi (adj.)
alkali shcheloch' (n.f.)
alkaline shchelochnoi (adj.)
alkaline solution shchelok (n.m.)
all ves' (p.)
   vse (p.)
   vsya (p.)
all, at malo-mal'ski (adv.)
all four chetveren'ki (n.pl.)
all hands on deck avral (n.m.)
all three vtroem (adv.)
all without exception naperechet (adv.)
   pogolovno (adv.)
all-around vsestoronnii (adj.)
all-conquering vsepobezhdayushchii (adj.)
allegorical inoskazatel'nyi (adj.)
allegory allegoriya (n.f.)
alley, blind tupik (n.m.)
all-metal tsel'nometalicheskii (adj.)
allow pozvolit' (v.pf.)
allow to approach podpuskat' (v.impf.)
alloy splav (n.m.)
   splavit' (v.pf.)
   splavlyat' (v.impf.)
alloyed legirovannyi (adj.)
All-Russian vserossiiskii (adj.)
All-Union obshchesoyuznyi (adj.)
   vsesoyuznyi (adj.)
All-Union Central Council of Trade Unions
     VTSSPS (abbr.)
ally soyuznik (n.m.)
almanac al'manakh (n.m.)
almond mindal' (n.m.)
   mindal'nyi (adj.)
alms milostynya (n.f.)
along vdol' (prep.)
aloof osobnyakom (adv.)
aloud vslukh (adv.)
alphabet alfavit (n.m.)
   azbuka (n.f.)
alpine al'piiskii (adj.)
already uzh (adv.)
   uzhe (adv.)
also takzhe (adv.)
   tozhe (adv.)
alter peredelat' (v.pf.)

altercate pikirovat'sya (v.impf.)
altercation prepiratel'stvo (n.n.)
alternately vperemezhku (adv.)
alternation cheredovanie (n.n.)
although khot' (conj.)
   khotya (conj.)
altogether itogo (adv.)
alum kvastsy (n.pl.)
aluminum alyuminii (n.m.)
always vsegda (adv.)
amateur diletant (n.m.)
   lyubitel' (n.m.)
amateur flying club aéroklub (n.m.)
amateur performance samodeyatel'nost'
   (n.f.)
amaze izumlyat' (v.impf.)
ambassador posol (n.m.)
amber yantar' (n.m.)
ambiguity neodnoznachnost' (n.f.)
ambiguous dvusmyslennyi (adj.)
ambition chestolyubie (n.n.)
ambitious chestolyubivyi (adj.)
ambivalent dvoistvennyi (adj.)
ambush zasada (n.f.)
American amerikanets (n.m.)
amicable polyubovnyi (adj.)
amino acid aminokislota (n.f.)
ammonia ammiak (n.m.)
ammonia, liquid nashatyrnyi spirt (adj.-n.m.)
ammunition boepripasy (n.pl.)
amnesty amnistiya (n.f.)
among sredi (prep.)
amoral amoral'nyi (adj.)
ampere amper (n.m.)
amphibia zemnovodnye (n.pl.)
amphitheater amfiteatr (n.m.)
amplitude amplituda (n.f.)
amputation amputatsiya (n.f.)
amuse razvlech' (v.pf.)
   teshit' (v.impf.)
   veselit' (v.impf.)
amusement uveselenie (n.n.)
   zabava (n.f.)
amusing poteshnyi (adj.)
   zanyatnyi (adj.)
anachronism anakhronizm (n.m.)
analog analog (n.m.)
analogy analogiya (n.f.)

analysis analiz (n.m.)
   razbor (n.m.)
analytic analiticheskii (adj.)
anarchism anarkhizm (n.m.)
anarchy anarkhiya (n.f.)
   bezvlastie (n.n.)
anatomist anatom (n.m.)
anatomy anatomiya (n.f.)
ancestor predok (n.m.)
   rodonachal'nik (n.m.)
anchor yakor' (n.m.)
ancient drevnii (adj.)
   vekovoi (adj.)
and i (conj.)
   zhe (part.)
and the like i.t.p. (i tomu podobnoe) (abbr.)
anemia malokrovie (n.n.)
anesthesia obezbolivanie (n.n.)
anesthetic narkoz (n.m.)
anew zanovo (adv.)
angel angel (n.m.)
anger gnev (n.m.)
   vozmutit' (v.pf.)
   zlit' (v.impf.)
angling uzhenie (n.n.)
Anglo-Saxon anglosaksonskii (adj.)
angry serdityi (adj.)
angry, to make obozlit' (v.pf.)
   rasserdit' (v.pf.)
anguish nadryv (n.m.)
angular uglovatyi (adj.)
animal zhivotnoe (n.n.)
   zhivotnyi (adj.)
animal, baby detenysh (n.m.)
animal-drawn guzhevoi (adj.)
animals, young molodnyak (n.m.)
animate odushevit' (v.pf.)
   odushevlyat'(sya) (v.impf.)
animated cartoon mul'tiplikatsionnyi (adj.)
animation zhivost' (n.f.)
ankle shchikolotka (n.f.)
annealing otzhig (n.m.)
annex pristroika (n.f.)
anniversary godovshchina (n.f.)
anniversary, twentieth dvadtsatiletie (n.n.)
announce oglashat' (v.impf.)
   oglasit' (v.pf.)
announcement anons (n.m.)

announcer diktor (n.m.)
annoy dosazhdat' (v.impf.)
annoyance dosada (n.f.)
annual ezhegodnyi (adj.)
   godichnyi (adj.)
annul annulirovat' (v.impf.&pf.)
anode anod (n.m.)
anomaly anomaliya (n.f.)
anonymous anonimnyi (adj.)
   bezymyannyi (adj.)
another, one after podryad (adv.)
answer otvechat' (v.impf.)
   otvet (n.m.)
   otvetit' (v.pf.)
   razgadka (n.f.)
ant muravei (n.m.)
antagonism antagonizm (n.m.)
antenna usik (n.m.)
anthracite antratsit (n.m.)
antiaircraft protivovozdushnyi (adj.)
   zenitnyi (adj.)
antibiotic antibiotik (n.m.)
anticipate predvkushat' (v.impf.)
   predvoskhitit' (v.pf.)
antidote protivoyadie (n.n.)
anti-fascist antifashist (n.m.)
anti-gas protivokhimicheskii (adj.)
anti-imperialist antiimperialisticheskii (adj.)
anti-military antimilitaristicheskii (adj.)
antimony sur'ma (n.f.)
anti-national antinarodnyi (adj.)
antipathy antipatiya (n.f.)
antipyretic zharoponizhayushchii (adj.)
antiquary antikvar (n.m.)
antique antichnyi (adj.)
anti-religious antireligioznyi (adj.)
anti-Semitism antisemitizm (n.m.)
antisocial antiobshchestvennyi (adj.)
anti-Soviet antisovetskii (adj.)
antitank protivotankovyi (adj.)
anti-war antivoennyi (adj.)
antonym antonim (n.m.)
anvil nakoval'nya (n.f.)
any lyuboi (adj.)
   vsyakii (adj.)
anyhow koe-kak (adv.)
anything chto-libo (p.)
apart vroz' (adv.)

apartment kvartira (n.f.)

apartment management domoupravlenie (n.n.)

apathetic apatichnyi (adj.)

apathy apatiya (n.f.)

aphorism aforizm (n.m.)

apiary paseka (n.f.)
> pchel'nik (n.m.)

apogee apogei (n.m.)

apolitical apolitichnyi (adj.)

apostate otstupnik (n.m.)

apostrophe apostrof (n.m.)

apotheosis apofeoz (n.m.)

apparently vidimo (adv.)

appeal apellirovat' (v.pf.)
> kassatsiya (n.f.)
> obrashchenie (n.n.)
> obzhalovanie (n.n.)
> prizyv (n.m.)
> vozzvanie (n.n.)
> vozzvat' (v.pf.)
> vzyvat' (v.impf.)

appear poyavit'sya (v.pf.)
> predstat' (v.pf.)
> predstavat' (v.impf.)
> yavit'sya (v.pf.)
> yavlyat'sya (v.impf.)

appear as figurirovat' (v.impf.)

appear unexpectedly nagryanut' (v.pf.)

appearance naruzhnost' (n.f.)
> oblik (n.m.)
> vid (n.m.)
> yavka (n.f.)

appendage pridatok (n.m.)

appendicitis appenditsit (n.m.)

appetite appetit (n.m.)

applaud aplodirovat' (v.impf.)

applause rukopleskanie (n.n.)

apple yablochnyi (adj.)
> yabloko (n.n.)

apple tree yablonya (n.f.)

appliance prisposoblenie (n.n.)

applicant podatel' (n.m.)
> prositel' (n.m.)

application primenenie (n.n.)
> vnedrenie (n.n.)
> zayavlenie (n.n.)

applied prikladnoi (adj.)

apply nalech' (v.pf.)
> nalegat' (v.impf.)
> prikladyvat' (v.impf.)
> prilagat' (v.impf.)

appointment svidanie (n.n.)

apportion odelit' (v.pf.)

appraiser otsenshchik (n.m.)

apprentice podmaster'e (n.m.)
> podruchnyi (n.m.)

approach blizit'sya (v.impf.)
> podkhod (n.m.)
> podoiti (v.pf.)
> podstup (n.m.)

approach, allow to podpuskat' (v.impf.)

appropriate prisvaivat' (v.impf.)
> prisvoit' (v.pf.)

appropriation assignovanie (n.n.)
> prisvoenie (n.n.)

approval odobrenie (n.n.)

approve odobryat' (v.impf.)

approximately priblizitel'no (adv.)

apricot abrikos (n.m.)

April aprel' (n.m.)

apron fartuk (n.m.)
> perednik (n.m.)

aquarium akvarium (n.m.)

aquatic vodnyi (adj.)
> vodyanoi (adj.)

aqueous vodnyi (adj.)

aquiline orlinyi (adj.)

Arab arab (n.m.)

arable land, plot of nadel (n.m.)

arbiter arbitr (n.m.)

arbitrariness samoupravstvo (n.n.)

arbitrary proizvol'nyi (adj.)

arc duga (n.f.)

arch arka (n.f.)
> svod (n.m.)

archaeologist arkheolog (n.m.)

archaeology arkheologiya (n.f.)

archaism arkhaizm (n.m.)

arched svodchatyi (adj.)

archipelago arkhipelag (n.m.)

architect arkhitektor (n.m.)
> zodchii (n.m.)

archives arkhiv (n.m.)

arctic arkticheskii (adj.)
> *(cont'd)*

polyarnyi (adj.)
ardent pylkii (adj.)
   yaryi (adj.)
ardor pyl (n.m.)
   rvenie (n.n.)
   zador (n.m.)
ardor, to dampen somebody's
     raskholazhivat' (v.impf.)
area ploshchad' (n.f.)
arena arena (n.f.)
Argentinian argentinets (n.m.)
argue sporit' (v.impf.)
   zasporit' (v.pf.)
argue with polemizirovat' (v.impf.)
argument argument (n.m.)
   dovod (n.m.)
   spor (n.m.)
aria ariya (n.f.)
arid bezvodnyi (adj.)
arise voznikat' (v.impf.)
   vozniknut' (v.pf.)
aristocrat aristokrat (n.m.)
arithmetic arifmetika (n.f.)
arm ruka (n.f.)
   vooruzhat' (v.impf.)
armaments vooruzhenie (n.n.)
Armenian armyanin (n.m.)
   armyanskii (adj.)
armful okhapka (n.f.)
armistice peremirie (n.n.)
armless bezrukii (adj.)
armor bronirovat' (v.impf.)
   bronya (n.f.)
   pantsir' (n.m.)
armored bronirovannyi (adj.)
   tankovyi (adj.)
armored car bronevik (n.m.)
armored train bronepoezd (n.m.)
armor-piercing broneboinyi (adj.)
armpit podmyshka (n.f.)
arms oruzhie (n.n.)
arms akimbo, to place one's
     podbochenivat'sya (v.impf.)
arms, coat of gerb (n.m.)
arms, to be up in opolchit'sya (v.pf.)
army armeiskii (adj.)
   armiya (n.f.)
   voisko (n.n.)

aroma aromat (n.m.)
arrange obdelat' (v.pf.)
   podstraivat' (v.impf.)
   podstroit' (v.pf.)
   rasstavit' (v.pf.)
   ugovarivat'(sya) (v.impf.)
   uslavlivat'sya (v.impf.)
   ustavit' (v.pf.)
   ustroit' (v.pf.)
arrangement komponovka (n.f.)
   raspolozhenie (n.n.)
   rasstanovka (n.f.)
   ustroistvo (n.n.)
arrears nedoimki (n.pl.)
arrest arest (n.m.)
arrival pribytie (n.n.)
   priezd (n.m.)
arrive pribyvat' (v.impf.)
   priekhat' (v.pf.)
arrive at dodumat'sya (v.pf.)
arrived, newly novopribyvshii (adj.)
arrogance gonor (n.m.)
   vysokomerie (n.n.)
arrogant kichlivyi (adj.)
   nadmennyi (adj.)
   zanoschivyi (adj.)
arrow strela (n.f.)
arsenal arsenal (n.m.)
arsenic mysh'yak (n.m.)
arson podzhog (n.m.)
arsonist podzhigatel' (n.m.)
art iskusstvo (n.n.)
artel artel' (n.f.)
artery arteriya (n.f.)
artesian artezianskii (adj.)
article chlen (n.m.)
   izdelie (n.n.)
   stat'ya (n.f.)
article, handmade podelka (n.f.)
article, satirical fel'eton (n.m.)
articulate chlenorazdel'nyi (adj.)
   vygovorit' (v.impf.)
articulation diktsiya (n.f.)
artificial iskusstvennyi (adj.)
artificial limb protez (n.m.)
artillery artilleriiskii (adj.)
   artilleriya (n.f.)
artilleryman artillerist (n.m.)

artist   artist (n.m.)
    khudozhnik (n.m.)
artistic   khudozhestvennyi (adj.)
artless   beskhitrostnyi (adj.)
arts, graphic   grafika (n.f.)
as   kak (conj.)
as a comrade   po-tovarishcheski (adv.)
as before   po-staromu (adv.)
as if   budto (conj.)
    yakoby (conj.)
as soon as   lish' (conj.)
as though   slovno (adv.)
    tochno (conj.)
as to   zhe (part.)
as usual   po-prezhnemu (adv.)
ascend   vskhodit' (v.impf.)
    vzoiti (v.pf.)
ascent   pod"em (n.m.)
    voskhozhdenie (n.n.)
ascertain   vyyasnit' (v.pf.)
ascetic   asket (n.m.)
ash pit   podduvalo (n.n.)
ash tree   yasen' (n.m.)
ashamed, to be   ustydit'sya (v.pf.)
ashberry   ryabina (n.f.)
ashes   pepel (n.m.)
    prakh (n.m.)
    zola (n.f.)
ashtray   pepel'nitsa (n.f.)
ashy   pepel'nyi (adj.)
Asian   aziatskii (adj.)
ask   poprosit' (v.pf.)
    prosit' (v.impf.)
    sprashivat' (v.impf.)
    zadat' (v.pf.)
ask again   peresprashivat' (v.impf.)
ask for   naprashivat'sya (v.impf.)
    naprosit'sya (v.pf.)
ask for leave   otprashivat'sya (v.impf.)
ask the price   pritsenivat'sya (v.impf.)
askance   iskosa (adv.)
aslant   naiskosok (adv.)
    vkos' (adv.)
asleep, half   polusonnyi (adj.)
asleep, to fall   usnut' (v.pf.)
    zasnut' (v.pf.)
    zasypat' (v.impf.)
asparagus   sparzha (n.f.)

aspect   vid (n.m.)
aspen   osina (n.f.)
asphalt   asfal't (n.m.)
ass   ishak (n.m.)
assault   pristup (n.m.)
assay   proba (n.f.)
assemble   s"ezzhat'sya (v.impf.)
assembling   montazh (n.m.)
assembly   assambleya (n.f.)
    sborka (n.f.)
    sbornyi (adj.)
    sborochnyi (adj.)
assets   aktiv (n.m.)
assiduous   neoslabnyi (adj.)
assignment   zadanie (n.n.)
assimilate   assimilirovat'sya (v.impf.&pf.)
assist   sposobstvovat' (v.impf.)
assistance   sodeistvie (n.n.)
assistant   assistent (n.m.)
    zamestitel' (n.m.)
assistant, laboratory   laborant (n.m.)
assistant, medical   fel'dsher (n.m.)
assistant, shop   prodavets (n.m.)
associate   obshchat'sya (v.impf.)
associate with   vodit'sya (v.impf.)
association   assotsiatsiya (n.f.)
    obshchenie (n.n.)
assortment   assortiment (n.m.)
assuming that   polozhim ((col.))
assumption   dopushchenie (n.n.)
assurance   aplomb (n.m.)
    uverenie (n.n.)
assure   uverit' (v.pf.)
    uveryat' (v.impf.)
    zaverit' (v.pf.)
    zaveryat' (v.impf.)
assymetry   nesimmetrichnost' (n.f.)
aster   astra (n.f.)
asteroid   asteroid (n.m.)
asthma   astma (n.f.)
astonish   udivit' (v.pf.)
astrakhan   karakul' (n.m.)
astringent   vyazhushchii (adj.)
astronaut   astronavt (n.m.)
astronautics   kosmonavtika (n.f.)
astronomer   astronom (n.m.)
astrophysicist   astrofizik (n.m.)
asylum   priyut (n.m.)

asymmetry asimmetriya (n.f.)
at pri (prep.)
  u (prep.)
  v (prep.)
  vo (prep.)
at a gallop vskach' (adv.)
at a walking pace shagom (adv.)
at all malo-mal'ski (adv.)
at all, not nimalo (adv.)
at ease vol'no (adv.)
at fault, to be provinit'sya (v.pf.)
at first snachala (adv.)
  sperva (adv.)
  vnachale (adv.)
at last nakonets (adv.)
  naposledok (adv.)
at once razom (adv.)
  srazu (adv.)
at present nyne (adv.)
at random naobum (adv.)
  naugad (adv.)
at the head of, to be vozglavit' (v.pf.)
at war, to be voevat' (v.pf.)
atavism atavizm (n.m.)
atheism ateizm (n.m.)
atheist bezbozhnik (n.m.)
athlete atlet (n.m.)
  legkoatlet (n.m.)
  silach (n.m.)
atilt napereves (adv.)
atlas atlas (n.m.)
atmosphere atmosfera (n.f.)
atom atom (n.m.)
atomic atomnyi (adj.)
atomizer raspylitel' (n.m.)
atrocity zlodeyanie (n.n.)
atrophy atrofirovat'sya (v.impf.&pf.)
attach pridelat' (v.pf.)
  prikomandirovat' (v.pf.)
  pristroit' (v.pf.)
attache attashe (n.m.)
attachment privyazannost' (n.f.)
attack ataka (n.f.)
  nabrasyvat'sya (v.impf.)
  nakinut'sya (v.pf.)
  napadat' (v.impf.)
  napast' (n.f.)
  nastupat' (v.impf.)

  vypad (n.m.)
attempt pokushat'sya (v.impf.)
  popytka (n.f.)
  pytat'sya (v.impf.)
attendance poseshchaemost' (n.f.)
attendant, hospital sanitar (n.m.)
attention vnimanie (n.n.)
attentive vnimatel'nyi (adj.)
attenuation zatukhanie (n.n.)
attic cherdak (n.m.)
attire naryad (n.m.)
  ubor (n.m.)
attorney poverennyi (adj.)
attorney, power of doverennost' (n.f.)
attract prityagivat' (v.impf.)
  prityanut' (v.pf.)
  privlech' (v.pf.)
  privlekat' (v.impf.)
  vlech' (v.impf.)
attracted, to be prel'shchat'sya (v.impf.)
  prel'stit' (v.pf.)
attraction prityazhenie (n.n.)
  privlechenie (n.n.)
attractive prityagatel'nyi (adj.)
  privlekatel'nyi (adj.)
attribute atribut (n.m.)
auction auktsion (n.m.)
audibility slyshimost' (n.f.)
auditory slukhovoi (adj.)
August avgust (n.m.)
aunt tetka (n.f.)
  tetya (n.f.)
Australian avstraliets (n.m.)
Austrian avstriets (n.m.)
authenticity dostovernost' (n.f.)
author avtor (n.m.)
  sostavitel' (n.m.)
authorities nachal'stvo (n.n.)
authority avtoritet (n.m.)
  vedenie (n.n.)
  vlast' (n.f.)
autobiography avtobiografiya (n.f.)
autocracy samoderzhavie (n.n.)
autogenous avtogennyi (adj.)
autograph avtograf (n.m.)
automatic avtomaticheskii (adj.)
  samodeistvuyushchii (adj.)
automatic block system avtoblokirovka (n.f.)

automatic machine   avtomat (n.m.)
automatic recorder   samopisets (n.m.)
automation   avtomatizatsiya (n.f.)
automobile   avtomobil' (n.m.)
automobile works   avtozavod (n.m.)
autonomy   avtonomiya (n.f.)
auto-suggestion   samovnushenie (n.n.)
autumn   osen' (n.f.)
    osennii (adj.)
auxiliary   sluzhebnyi (adj.)
    vspomogatel'nyi (adj.)
availability   nalichie (n.n.)
available   obshchedostupnyi (adj.)
avalanche   lavina (n.f.)
avenue   alleya (n.f.)
    prospekt (n.m.)
average   srednee (n.n.)
avert   otvratit' (v.pf.)
aviation   aviatsiya (n.f.)
avitaminosis   avitaminoz (n.m.)
avoid   chuzhdat'sya (v.impf.)
    izbegnut' (v.pf.)
    izbezhat' (v.pf.)

    storonit'sya (v.impf.)
award   prisvaivat' (v.impf.)
    prisvoit' (v.pf.)
award a prize   premirovat' (v.impf.&pf.)
awarding   prisvoenie (n.n.)
awareness   soznanie (n.n.)
away   doloi (adv.)
    otstupya (adv.)
    proch' (adv.)
away, to be   otstoyat' (v.pf.)
awkward   nelovkii (adj.)
    neskladnyi (adj.)
awl   shilo (n.n.)
awning   tent (n.m.)
axe   kolun (n.m.)
    topor (n.m.)
axe, to kill with an   zarubat' (v.impf.)
    zarubit' (v.pf.)
axiom   aksioma (n.f.)
axis   os' (n.f.)
axle   os' (n.f.)
Azerbaijanian   azerbaidzhanets (n.m.)
azure   lazurnyi (adj.)

B (Б)

babble   lepet (n.m.)
baby   malyutka (n.m.&f.)
    mladenets (n.m.)
baby animal   detenysh (n.m.)
baby, premature   nedonosok (n.m.)
bacillus   batsilla (n.f.)
    palochka (n.f.)
back   nazad (adv.)
    spina (n.f.)
    spinka (n.f.)
    zad (n.m.)
    zadnii (adj.)
    zadnik (n.m.)
back home   vosvoyasi (adv.)
back of the head   zatylok (n.m.)
back, on one's   navznich (adv.)
back, small of the   poyasnitsa (n.f.)
back street   zakoulok (n.m.)

background   fon (n.m.)
backstage   zakulisnyi (adj.)
backward   popyatnyi (adj.)
    zadom (adv.)
backwardness   otstalost' (n.f.)
backwoods   glush' (n.f.)
backyard   zadvorki (n.pl.)
bacteriologist   bakteriolog (n.m.)
bacteriology   bakteriologiya (n.f.)
bacterium   bakteriya (n.f.)
bad   giblyi (adj.)
    khudoi (adj.)
    nekhoroshii (adj.)
    plokhoi (adj.)
    skvernyi (adj.)
    vrednyi (adj.)
bad luck   nezadacha (n.f.)
bad, not   nedurno (adv.)

badge znachok (n.m.)
badger barsuk (n.m.)
badly bol'no (adv.)
   durno (adv.)
   nekhorosho (adv.)
bag suma (n.f.)
   sumka (n.f.)
bag, paper kulek (n.m.)
baggy meshkovatyi (adj.)
bail poruka (n.f.)
bait primanka (n.f.)
bake ispech' (v.pf.)
   pech' (v.impf.)
   vypekat' (v.impf.)
bake in zapech' (v.pf.)
bake well propech' (v.pf.)
   propekat'(sya) (v.impf.)
baked pechenyi (adj.)
baked pudding zapekanka (n.f.)
baker pekar' (n.m.)
baker's shop bulochnaya (n.f.)
   konditerskaya (n.f.)
bakery pekarnya (n.f.)
bakery, mechanized khlebozavod (n.m.)
baking obzhig (n.m.)
baking of bread khlebopechenie (n.n.)
balalaika balalaika (n.f.)
balance balans (n.m.)
   uravnovesit' (v.pf.)
balance, to keep ustoyat' (v.pf.)
balcony balkon (n.m.)
bald pleshivyi (adj.)
bald patch lysina (n.f.)
   plesh' (n.f.)
bald, to grow lyset' (v.impf.)
   oblyset' (v.pf.)
Balkan balkanskii (adj.)
ball bal (n.m.)
   klubok (n.m.)
   motok (n.m.)
   myach (n.m.)
   shar (n.m.)
ball bearing sharikopodshipnik (n.m.)
ball, small sharik (n.m.)
ballad ballada (n.f.)
ballast ballast (n.m.)
ballet balet (n.m.)
ballet dancer balerina (n.f.)

ballistics ballistika (n.f.)
balloon, stratospheric stratostat (n.m.)
Baltic baltiiskii (adj.)
bamboo bambuk (n.m.)
ban zapret (n.m.)
banana banan (n.m.)
bandage bint (n.m.)
   perevyazat' (v.pf.)
   povyazka (n.f.)
   zabintovat' (v.pf.)
bandage, to remove a razbintovat' (v.pf.)
bandaging perevyazka (n.f.)
bandit bandit (n.m.)
bang khlopnut' (v.pf.)
   zakhlopnut' (v.pf.)
bang, to close with a zakhlopyvat'sya
   (v.impf.)
banisters perila (n.pl.)
bank bank (n.m.)
bank, state gosbank (n.m.)
banker bankir (n.m.)
bankrupt bankrot (n.m.)
bankrupt, to go obankrotit'sya (v.pf.)
banner znamya (n.n.)
banquet banket (n.m.)
bar brusok (n.m.)
   pregradit' (v.pf.)
   shtanga (n.f.)
   sterzhen' (n.m.)
barbarian varvar (n.m.)
bare obnazhat' (v.impf.)
   ogolennyi (adj.)
   ogolit' (v.pf.)
barefoot bosikom (adv.)
bargain sdelka (n.f.)
bargain, to strike a storgovat'sya (v.pf.)
barge barzha (n.f.)
baritone bariton (n.m.)
barium barii (n.m.)
bark kora (n.f.)
   layat' (v.impf.)
bark, to begin to zalayat' (v.pf.)
barking lai (n.m.)
barley yachmen' (n.m.)
barley, pearl perlovyi (adj.)
barn ovin (n.m.)
barn, threshing riga (n.f.)
barometer barometr (n.m.)

barrack barak (n.m.)
barracks kazarma (n.f.)
barrel bochka (n.f.)
   stvol (n.m.)
barricade barrikada (n.f.)
barrier bar'er (n.m.)
   shlagbaum (n.m.)
bars, fire kolosnik (n.m.)
barter menovoi (adj.)
   obmenyat' (v.pf.)
   tovaroobmen (n.m.)
base baza (n.f.)
based on, to be bazirovat'sya (v.impf.)
basement podval (n.m.)
baseness nizost' (n.f.)
Bashkir bashkir (n.m.)
basin taz (n.m.)
basis bazis (n.m.)
   obosnovanie (n.n.)
   osnova (n.f.)
basket korzina (n.f.)
basketball basketbol (n.m.)
bas-relief barel'ef (n.m.)
bass bas (n.m.)
bass, double kontrabas (n.m.)
bast lyko (n.n.)
bast shoe lapot' (n.m.)
batch partiya (n.f.)
bath vanna (n.f.)
bathe iskupat' (v.pf.)
   vykupat' (v.pf.)
bathhouse banya (n.f.)
bathing kupal'nyi (adj.)
bathysphere batisfera (n.f.)
baton zhezl (n.m.)
battalion batal'on (n.m.)
battens tes (n.m.)
battery batareya (n.f.)
battle bitva (n.f.)
   boi (n.m.)
battleship bronenosets (n.m.)
bay bukhta (n.f.)
   gnedoi (adj.)
   guba (n.f.)
   zaliv (n.m.)
bayan accordion bayan (n.m.)
bayonet shtyk (n.m.)
be byt' (v.impf.)

   byvat' (v.impf.)
   est' (v.pres.)
   obstoyat' (v.impf.)
   pobyvat' (v.pf.)
   sostoyat' (v.impf.)
beach plyazh (n.m.)
beads biser (n.m.)
   busy (n.pl.)
beak klyuv (n.m.)
beam balka (n.f.)
   brus (n.m.)
beam, cross perekladina (n.f.)
bean bob (n.m.)
bean, haricot fasol' (n.f.)
bear sterpet' (v.pf.)
   vyderzhivat' (v.impf.)
bearable snosnyi (adj.)
beard boroda (n.f.)
bearded borodatyi (adj.)
bearer pred"yavitel' (n.m.)
bearing osanka (n.f.)
   podshipnik (n.m.)
   vypravka (n.f.)
beast khishchnik (n.m.)
   zver' (n.m.)
beast of burden v'yuchnoe zhivotnoe
   (adj.-n.n.)
beat bit' (v.impf.)
   kolotit' (v.impf.)
   pobit' (v.pf.)
beat (music) takt (n.m.)
beat out vybit' (v.pf.)
beat, to begin to zabit'sya (v.pf.)
beat up izbit' (v.pf.)
   izbivat' (v.impf.)
   otkolotit' (v.pf.)
   vzbit' (v.pf.)
   vzbivat' (v.impf.)
beaten bityi (adj.)
   izbityi (adj.)
   protorennyi (adj.)
beating poboi (n.pl.)
beautiful krasivyi (adj.)
   prekrasnyi (adj.)
beauty krasota (n.f.)
beaver bober (n.m.)
   bobrovyi (adj.)
because ibo (conj.)

because of vsledstvie (prep.)

beckon manit' (v.impf.)

become delat'sya (v.impf.)
    podobat' (v.impf.)
    stanovit'sya (v.impf.)
    stat' (v.pf.)
    stat'sya (v.pf.)

bed gryadka (n.f.)
    krovat' (n.f.)
    postel' (n.f.)
    stend (n.m.)
    zaleganie (n.n.)

bed, double dvuspal'nyi (adj.)

bed, feather perina (n.f.)

bedbug klop (n.m.)

bedraggled zamusolennyi (adj.)

bedroom spal'nya (n.f.)

bedsore prolezhen' (n.m.)

bee pchela (n.f.)

beech buk (n.m.)

beef govyadina (n.f.)

beef, corned solonina (n.f.)

beer pivo (n.n.)

beet svekla (n.f.)

beetle zhuk (n.m.)

before prezhde (adv.)

before dawn zatemno (adv.)

before last pozaproshlyi (adj.)

before nightfall zasvetlo (adv.)

beforehand napered (adv.)
    zaranee (adv.)

befoul izgadit' (v.pf.)

beg klyanchit' (v.impf.)
    pobirat'sya (v.impf.)
    uprashivat' (v.impf.)
    vymalivat' (v.impf.)
    vyprashivat' (v.impf.)

beggar nishchii (n.m.)
    poproshaika (n.m.&f.)

begin nachat' (v.pf.)
    pristupat' (v.impf.)
    stat' (v.pf.)

beginning nachalo (n.n.)

behavior obkhozhdenie (n.n.)

behind pozadi (adv.)
    za (prep.)
    zad (n.m.)

behind, from iz-za (prep.)

    szadi (adv.)

being sushchestvo (n.n.)

being, human chelovek (adj.)

being, to come into narodit'sya (v.pf.)
    narozhdat'sya (v.impf.)

belated zapozdalyi (adj.)

belch otryzhka (n.f.)

Belgian bel'giets (n.m.)

belief, popular pover'e (n.n.)

believe poverit' (v.pf.)
    verit' (v.impf.)

belittle umalit' (v.pf.)
    umalyat' (v.impf.)

bell kolokol (n.m.)
    kolokol'chik (n.m.)

belligerent voyuyushchii (adj.)

bellow ryavkat' (v.impf.)

bellows mekh (n.m.)

belong prinadlezhat' (v.impf.)

belongings pozhitki (n.pl.)

beloved nenaglyadnyi (adj.)
    vozlyublennyi (adj.)

below vnizu (adv.)

below, from snizu (adv.)

belt poyas (n.m.)
    remen' (n.m.)

belt, shoulder perevyaz' (n.f.)

beluga sturgeon beluga (n.f.)

bench lavka (n.f.)
    skam'ya (n.f.)
    skameika (n.f.)
    stend (n.m.)

bench, joiner's verstak (n.m.)

bench, small skameechka (n.f.)

bend gnut' (v.impf.)
    iskrivit' (v.pf.)
    izgib (n.m.)
    izluchina (n.f.)
    izvilina (n.f.)
    klonit' (v.impf.)
    krivit' (v.impf.)
    nagnut' (v.pf.)
    naklonit' (v.pf.)
    peregib (n.m.)
    peregnut' (v.pf.)
    podgibat' (v.impf.)
    podognut' (v.pf.)
    sgib (n.m.)

sklonit' (v.pf.)
sklonyat' (v.impf.)
sklonyat'sya (v.impf.)
sognut' (v.pf.)
zagib (n.m.)
zagnut' (v.pf.)
bend back otognut' (v.pf.)
bend down sgibat'(sya) (v.impf.)
benefactor blagodetel' (n.m.)
beneficial blagotvornyi (adj.)
benefit posobie (n.n.)
benevolent blagosklonnyi (adj.)
dobrozhelatel'nyi (adj.)
bent naklonnost' (n.f.)
benzine benzin (n.m.)
beret beret (n.m.)
berry yagoda (n.f.)
berth prichal (n.m.)
beryllium berillii (n.m.)
beside pomimo (prep.)
ryadom (adv.)
vozle (prep.)
besides prichem (conj.)
pritom (conj.)
besiege osadit' (v.pf.)
osazhdat' (v.impf.)
bespatter zabryzgat' (v.pf.)
zakapat' (v.pf.)
best luchshii (adj.)
best, the nailuchshii (adj.)
bestial skotskii (adj.)
bet pari (n.n.)
bet, to lose a prosporit' (v.pf.)
beta rays beta luchi (n.pl.)
betray predat' (v.pf.)
predavat' (v.impf.)
better luchshe (adj.)
luchshii (adj.)
better of, to think odumat'sya (v.pf.)
between mezhdu (adv.)
beware osteregat'sya (v.impf.)
bewitch okoldovat' (v.pf.)
beyond sverkh (prep.)
svyshe (prep.)
za (prep.)
beyond one's strength neposil'nyi (adj.)
bias smeshchenie (n.n.)
biased predvzyatyi (adj.)

bib nagrudnik (n.m.)
bible bibliya (n.f.)
bibliography bibliografiya (n.f.)
bicycle velosiped (n.m.)
bifurcate razdvaivat'sya (v.impf.)
bifurcation razdvoenie (n.n.)
big bol'shoi (adj.)
bilateral dvustoronnii (adj.)
bilberry chernika (n.f.)
bilberry, red brusnika (n.f.)
bile zhelch' (n.f.)
bilious zhelchnyi (adj.)
bill afisha (n.f.)
zakonoproekt (n.m.)
bill, ten-ruble desyatka (n.f.)
billeting postoi (n.m.)
billiards bil'yard (n.m.)
billion milliard (n.m.)
bin, corn zakrom (n.m.)
binary dvoichnyi (adj.)
bind pereplesti (v.pf.)
svyazat' (v.pf.)
binder snopovyazalka (n.f.)
binding svyazuyushchii (adj.)
binding, foot portyanka (n.f.)
binding, ski kreplenie (n.n.)
binominal binom (n.m.)
dvuchlen (n.m.)
biochemistry biokhimiya (n.f.)
biography biografiya (n.f.)
zhizneopisanie (n.n.)
biology biologiya (n.f.)
biology, agricultural agrobiologiya (n.f.)
bionics bionika (n.f.)
biophysics biofizika (n.f.)
biopsy biopsiya (n.f.)
bipolar dvupolyusnyi (adj.)
birch bereza (n.f.)
birch rod rozga (n.f.)
bird ptitsa (n.f.)
bird cherry tree cheremukha (n.f.)
birth certificate metrika (n.f.)
birth, to give porodit' (v.pf.)
porozhdat' (v.impf.)
rodit' (v.pf.)
rozhat' (v.impf.)
birthmark rodinka (n.f.)
bisector bissektrisa (n.f.)

bisexual dvupolyi (adj.)
bishop episkop (n.m.)
bismuth vismut (n.m.)
bit udila (n.pl.)
bitch suka (n.f.)
bite kusat' (v.impf.)
   prikusit' (v.pf.)
   razgryzat' (v.impf.)
   ukus (n.m.)
bite off otgryzat' (v.impf.)
   otkusit' (v.pf.)
bite through perekusit' (v.pf.)
   raskusit' (v.pf.)
   raskusyvat' (v.impf.)
bite to death zagryzat' (v.impf.)
biting yazvitel'nyi (adj.)
bitter gor'kii (adj.)
bitter taste gorech' (n.f.)
bitter, to taste gorchit' (v.impf.)
black chernyi (adj.)
   voronoi (adj.)
black earth chernozem (n.m.)
black mineral oil mazut (n.m.)
black radish red'ka (n.f.)
Black Sea chernomorskii (adj.)
black, to turn chernet' (v.impf.)
   pochernet' (v.pf.)
blackball zaballotirovat' (v.pf.)
blackberry ezhevika (n.f.)
blacken chernit' (v.impf.)
blackhead ugor' (n.m.)
blackmail shantázh (n.m.)
blackout svetomaskirovka (n.f.)
   zatemnenie (n.n.)
black-skinned chernokozhii (adj.)
blacksmith kuznets (n.m.)
blacksmith's kuznechnyi (adj.)
bladder mochevoi puzyr' (adj.-n.m.)
blade klinok (n.m.)
   lezvie (n.n.)
   lopast' (n.f.)
blade, shoulder lopatka (n.f.)
blame osudit' (v.pf.)
   vinit' (v.impf.)
blank probel (n.m.)
blanket odeyalo (n.n.)
blanket, horse popona (n.f.)
blasphemy koshchunstvo (n.n.)

blast furnace domennyi (adj.)
   domna (n.f.)
blaze pylat' (v.impf.)
bleach belit' (v.impf.)
bleed white obeskrovit' (v.pf.)
bleeding krovotechenie (n.n.)
bless blagoslovit' (v.pf.)
blind oslepit' (v.pf.)
   shtora (n.f.)
   slepit' (v.impf.)
   slepoi (adj.)
blind alley tupik (n.m.)
blindman's buff zhmurki (n.pl.)
blind, to become slepnut' (v.impf.)
blind, to get oslepnut' (v.pf.)
blinders shory (n.pl.)
blindly vslepuyu (adv.)
blindness slepota (n.f.)
blink morgat' (v.impf.)
bliss blazhenstvo (n.n.)
   nega (n.f.)
blister voldyr' (n.m.)
bloc blok (n.m.)
block blok (n.m.)
   churban (n.m.)
   glyba (n.f.)
   kvartal (n.m.)
   zastavit' (v.pf.)
   zastavlyat' (v.impf.)
block signalling blokirovka (n.f.)
block system, automatic avtoblokirovka
   (n.f.)
block up zavalivat' (v.impf.)
blockade blokada (n.f.)
blockhead bolvan (n.m.)
   oboltus (n.m.)
blond belokuryi (adj.)
   rusyi (adj.)
blood krov' (n.f.)
   krovnyi (adj.)
   krovyanoi (adj.)
blood circulation krovoobrashchenie (n.n.)
blood, drop of krovinka (n.f.)
bloodhound ishcheika (n.f.)
bloodshed krovoprolitnyi (adj.)
bloodstained okrovavlennyi (adj.)
bloodthirsty krovozhadnyi (adj.)
bloody krovavyi (adj.)

bloom tsvesti (v.impf.)

blossom rastsvesti (v.pf.)

  zatsvesti (v.pf.)

blossoming rastsvet (n.m.)

  tsvetushchiĭ (adj.)

blot klyaksa (n.f.)

  pomarka (n.f.)

blotting promokatel'nyi (adj.)

blouse bluza (n.f.)

  kofta (n.f.)

blow dunut' (v.pf.)

  dut' (v.impf.)

  navevat' (v.impf.)

  naveyat' (v.pf.)

  udar (n.m.)

  veyat' (v.impf.)

blow away sduvat' (v.impf.)

blow in vdut' (v.pf.)

  vduvat' (v.impf.)

blow on obdut' (v.pf.)

  obduvat' (v.impf.)

blow one's nose smorkat'sya (v.impf.)

  vysmorkat'sya (v.pf.)

blow out zadut' (v.pf.)

  zaduvat' (v.impf.)

blow up podorvat' (v.pf.)

  podryvat' (v.impf.)

  vzorvat' (v.pf.)

blows, to come to podrat'sya (v.pf.)

blue goluboi (adj.)

  sin'ka (n.f.)

  sinii (adj.)

blue color, dark sineva (n.f.)

blue, dark temno-sinii (adj.)

blue, to turn posinet' (v.pf.)

blunder lyapsus (n.m.)

  oploshnost' (n.f.)

  promakh (n.m.)

blunt pritupit' (v.pf.)

  tupoi (adj.)

bluntness tupost' (n.f.)

blurt out proboltat'sya (v.pf.)

blush krasnet' (v.impf.)

  pokrasnet' (v.pf.)

boa constrictor udav (n.m.)

boar, wild zemlyanika (n.f.)

board doska (n.f.)

  kollegiya (n.f.)

  panel' (n.f.)

  stolovat'sya (v.impf.)

board up zakolachivat' (v.impf.)

  zakolotit' (v.pf.)

boarding school internat (n.m.)

  pansion (n.m.)

  shkola-internat (n.m.)

boast khvastat' (v.impf.)

  kichit'sya (v.impf.)

  pokhvastat'(sya) (v.pf.)

boat lodka (n.f.)

  shlyupka (n.f.)

boat, torpedo minonosets (n.m.)

body kuzov (n.m.)

  telo (n.n.)

body, heavenly svetilo (n.n.)

bodyguard telokhranitel' (n.m.)

boil furunkul (n.m.)

  kipet' (v.impf.)

  kipyatit' (v.impf.)

  klokotat' (v.impf.)

  prokipyatit' (v.pf.)

  varit' (v.impf.)

  vskipat' (v.pf.)

  vskipyatit' (v.pf.)

boil down vyvarivat' (v.impf.)

boil, to begin to zakipat' (v.impf.)

boiled varenyi (adj.)

boiler kotel (n.m.)

  kub (n.m.)

boiler room kotel'naya (n.f.)

boiling kipenie (n.n.)

  kipuchii (adj.)

boiling water kipyatok (n.m.)

bold, to become osmelet' (v.pf.)

boldness udal' (n.f.)

Bolshevik bol'shevik (n.m.)

bolster valik (n.m.)

bolt bolt (n.m.)

  shpingalet (n.m.)

  zadvizhka (n.f.)

  zapor (n.m.)

  zasov (n.m.)

bomb bomba (n.f.)

  razbombit' (v.pf.)

bomb shelter bomboubezhishche (n.n.)

bombard bombardirovat' (v.impf.)

bomber bombardirovshchik (n.m.)

bond obligatsiya (n.f.)
bonds uzy (v.pl.)
bone kost' (n.f.)
  kostyanoi (adj.)
bonus premial'nye (n.pl.)
bony kostistyi (adj.)
book kniga (n.f.)
  knizhka (n.f.)
book cover perplet (n.m.)
  superoblozhka (n.f.)
book, reference spravochnik (n.m.)
book, to get absorbed in a zachitat'sya (v.pf.)
bookbinder perepletchik (n.m.)
bookcase étazherka (n.f.)
booking office kassa (n.f.)
bookkeeper bukhgalter (n.m.)
bookkeeping otchetnost' (n.f.)
booklet broshyura (n.f.)
bookmark zakladka (n.f.)
bookseller, secondhand bukinist (n.m.)
boom gul (n.m.)
boor nevezha (n.m.&f.)
boot, high sapog (n.m.)
boot, top of a golenishche (n.n.)
bootblack chistil'shchik (n.m.)
bootlicker podkhalim (n.m.)
boots, felt burki (n.pl.)
  valenki (n.pl.)
border granitsa (n.f.)
  okaimlyat' (v.impf.)
bore burit' (v.impf.)
  nadoedat' (v.impf.)
  naskuchit' (v.pf.)
  proburavit' (v.pf.)
  prosverlit' (v.pf.)
  rastachivat' (v.impf.)
bore hole shurf (n.m.)
bored, to be skuchat' (v.impf.)
boredom skuka (n.f.)
boric bornyi (adj.)
boring burovoi (adj.)
  skuchnyi (adj.)
borrow zaimstvovat' (v.impf.)
  zanimat' (v.impf.)
  zanyat' (v.pf.)
bosom lono (n.n.)
boss zapravila (n.m.)
botany botanika (n.f.)

both oba (num.)
  obe (num.)
  vdvoem (adv.)
bottle butylka (n.f.)
  flakon (n.m.)
bottle, hot-water grelka (n.f.)
bottom dno (n.n.)
  niz (n.m.)
bottom, to the donizu (adv.)
bottomless bezdonnyi (adj.)
bough suk (n.m.)
boulevard bul'var (n.m.)
bound perebezhka (n.f.)
boundaries, to fix razmezhevat'sya (v.pf.)
boundary rubezh (n.m.)
boundary path mezha (n.f.)
boundless bezbrezhnyi (adj.)
  bezgranichnyi (adj.)
  neobozrimyi (adj.)
bouquet buket (n.m.)
bourgeois burzhua (n.m.)
  burzhuaznyi (adj.)
bout, drinking popoika (n.f.)
bow bant (n.m.)
  klanyat'sya (v.impf.)
  luk (n.m.)
  poklon (n.m.)
  poklonit'sya (n.pf.)
  rasklanyat'sya (v.pf.)
  smychok (n.m.)
bowl miska (n.f.)
bowl, toilet unitaz (n.m.)
bowlegged krivonogii (adj.)
box budka (n.f.)
  korobka (n.f.)
  lozha (n.f.)
  shkatulka (n.f.)
  yashchik (n.m.)
box calf khrom (n.m.)
boxing boks (n.m.)
boy mal'chik (n.m.)
  parnishka (n.m.)
  yunga (n.m.)
boycott boikot (n.m.)
bracelet braslet (n.m.)
bracing bodryashchii (adj.)
bracket kronshtein (n.m.)
  skobka (n.f.)

bragging bakhval'stvo (n.n.)
braid zaplesti (v.pf.)
brain mozg (n.m.)
brainless bezgolovyi (adj.)
    bezmozglyi (adj.)
brake tormoz (n.m.)
    zatormozit' (v.pf.)
braking tormozhenie (n.n.)
bran otrubi (n.pl.)
branch otrasl' (n.f.)
    otvetvlenie (n.n.)
    vetka (n.f.)
    vetv' (n.f.)
branch office filial (n.m.)
branching razvesistyi (adj.)
    razvetvlenie (n.n.)
branchy vetvistyi (adj.)
brand kleimit' (v.impf.)
    kleimo (n.n.)
    zakleimit' (v.pf.)
brand new noven'kii (adj.)
brass latun' (n.f.)
brassiere byustgal'ter (n.m.)
    lifchik (n.m.)
brave man khrabrets (n.m.)
bravery khrabrost' (n.f.)
    otvaga (n.f.)
brawl potasovka (n.f.)
brazier zharovnya (n.f.)
Brazilian brazilets (n.m.)
breach bresh' (n.f.)
bread khleb (n.m.)
bread, baking of khlebopechenie (n.n.)
bread, fancy sdoba (n.f.)
bread, hunk of krayukha (n.f.)
breadwinner kormilets (n.m.)
breadth shirina (n.f.)
break lomat' (v.impf.)
    perebit' (v.pf.)
    perervat' (v.pf.)
    podlamyvat'sya (v.impf.)
    podlomit'sya (v.pf.)
    porvat' (v.pf.)
    poryvat' (v.pf.)
    prolom (n.m.)
    prolomat' (v.pf.)
    proryv (n.m.)
    rasshibat' (v.impf.)

    razbit' (v.pf.)
    razbivat'(sya) (v.impf.)
    razdrobit' (v.pf.)
    razlomit'(sya) (v.pf.)
    skalyvat' (v.impf.)
    skolot' (v.pf.)
    slomat' (v.pf.)
break a habit otuchit' (v.pf.)
break away vyrvat'sya (v.pf.)
    vyryvat'sya (v.impf.)
break down obessilet' (v.pf.)
    razvalit' (v.pf.)
break in raznashivat' (v.impf.)
    raznosit' (v.pf.)
    vlamyvat'sya (v.impf.)
    vlomit'sya (v.pf.)
break off oblamyvat' (v.impf.)
    oblomat' (v.pf.)
    oborvat' (v.pf.)
    obryvat'(sya) (v.impf.)
    otkalyvat'(sya) (v.impf.)
    otlamyvat'(sya) (v.impf.)
    otlomat'(sya) (v.pf.)
    otlomit'(sya) (v.pf.)
break open vzlamyvat' (v.impf.)
break out gryanut' (v.pf.)
    razrazhat'sya (v.impf.)
    razygryvat'sya (v.impf.)
    vylamyvat' (v.impf.)
    vylomat' (v.pf.)
break through prorvat' (v.pf.)
    proryvat' (v.impf.)
break to pieces perelamyvat' (v.impf.)
break up raskhodit'sya (v.impf.)
    razlamyvat' (v.impf.)
    razlomat' (v.pf.)
    razoitis' (v.pf.)
breakdown polomka (n.f.)
breakfast zavtrak (n.m.)
breakfast, to have pozavtrakat' (v.pf.)
breaking lomka (n.f.)
breaking open vzlom (n.m.)
breaking up raschlenenie (n.n.)
    rospusk (n.m.)
breaking up into smaller units
      razukrupnenie (n.n.)
bream leshch (n.m.)
breast grud' (n.f.)
      (cont'd)

grudnoi (adj.)
breath dunovenie (n.n.)
   veyanie (n.n.)
breath, short odyshka (n.f.)
breath, to be out of zapykhat'sya (v.pf.)
breath, to recover one's otdyshat'sya (v.pf.)
breathe dyshat' (v.impf.)
   podyshat' (v.pf.)
breathe out vydokhnut' (v.pf.)
   vydykhat'(sya) (v.impf.)
breathing dykhanie (n.n.)
breed poroda (n.f.)
   rasplodit' (v.pf.)
   razvesti (v.pf.)
breeder, cattle skotovod (n.m.)
breeding razvedenie (n.n.)
breeding, horse konevodstvo (n.n.)
breeding, pig svinovodstvo (n.n.)
breeding, rabbit krolikovodstvo (n.n.)
breeze veterok (n.m.)
brevity kratkost' (n.f.)
bribe podkupat' (v.impf.)
   vzyatka (n.f.)
bribery podkup (n.m.)
brick kirpich (n.m.)
   kubik (n.m.)
brick up zamurovat' (v.pf.)
bride nevesta (n.f.)
bridegroom zhenikh (n.m.)
bridge most (n.m.)
bridge of the nose perenositsa (n.f.)
bridgehead platsdarm (n.m.)
bridle obuzdat' (v.pf.)
   uzda (n.f.)
   vznuzdat' (v.pf.)
briefcase portfel' (n.m.)
briefing letuchka (n.f.)
briefly korotko (adj.)
   szhato (adv.)
   vkrattse (adv.)
brigade brigada (n.f.)
bright shustryi (adj.)
   yarkii (adj.)
bright, not neyarkii (adj.)
brighten prosiyat' (v.pf.)
brighten up skrasit' (v.pf.)
brilliant genial'nyi (adj.)
brine rassol (n.m.)

brine, food preserved in solen'e (n.n.)
bring podnesti (v.pf.)
   podnosit' (v.impf.)
   prinesti (v.pf.)
   prinosit' (v.impf.)
   privesti (v.pf.)
   privezti (v.pf.)
   privodit' (v.impf.)
   zanesti (v.pf.)
   zavesti (v.pf.)
   zavodit' (v.impf.)
bring nearer priblizit' (v.pf.)
bring on navlekat' (v.impf.)
bring out vystavit' (v.pf.)
   vystavlyat' (v.impf.)
bring to reason obrazumit' (v.pf.)
bring up podvesti (v.pf.)
   podvodit' (v.pf.)
   vykarmlivat' (v.impf.)
   vykormit' (v.pf.)
   vyrastit' (v.pf.)
bringing privoz (n.m.)
brisket grudinka (n.f.)
bristle shchetina (n.f.)
   oshchetinit'sya (v.pf.)
British britanskii (adj.)
brittleness lomkost' (n.f.)
broad shirokii (adj.)
broadcast peredacha (n.f.)
   peredat' (v.pf.)
   peredavat' (v.impf.)
   translirovat' (v.impf.)
broadcasting radioveshchanie (n.n.)
   shirokoveshchanie (n.n.)
broadly shiroko (adv.)
broad-shouldered shirokoplechii (adj.)
brocade parcha (n.f.)
broken izlomannyi (adj.)
   razbityi (adj.)
bromine brom (n.m.)
bronchitis bronkhit (n.m.)
bronchus bronkh (n.m.)
bronze bronza (n.f.)
brooch broshka, brosh' (n.f.)
brood vyvodok (n.m.)
brook ruchei (n.m.)
broom metla (n.f.)
   venik (n.m.)

broth bul'on (n.m.)
    otvar (n.m.)
brother brat (n.m.)
brother-in-law shurin (n.m.)
brotherly bratskii (adj.)
brown karii (adj.)
brown-haired man shaten (n.m.)
bruise krovopodtek (n.m.)
    sinyak (n.m.)
brush kist' (n.f.)
    kistochka (n.f.)
    pomazok (n.m.)
    shchetka (n.f.)
brush away obmakhivat' (v.impf.)
    obmakhnut' (v.pf.)
brush off otmakhivat'sya (v.impf.)
    smakhivat' (v.impf.)
brushwood khvorost (n.m.)
brutal zverskii (adj.)
brutalized, to become ozveret' (v.pf.)
bubble puzyr' (n.m.)
bucket bad'ya (n.f.)
    vedro (n.n.)
buckle pristegivat' (v.impf.)
    pryazhka (n.f.)
buckwheat grechikha (n.f.)
    grechnevyi (adj.)
bud buton (n.m.)
    pochka (n.f.)
budget byudzhet (n.m.)
buffalo buivol (n.m.)
buffer bufer (n.m.)
buffoon, to play the payasnichat' (v.impf.)
bugle gorn (n.m.)
build komplektsiya (n.f.)
    provesti (v.pf.)
    provodit' (v.impf.)
    stroit' (v.impf.)
    teloslozhenie (n.n.)
    vystroit' (v.pf.)
    zastraivat' (v.impf.)
    zastroit' (v.pf.)
build on nadstraivat' (v.impf.)
builder stroitel' (n.m.)
building korpus (n.m.)
    stroevoi (adj.)
    zdanie (n.n.)
building, new novostroika (n.f.)

building, to finish otstraivat' (v.impf.)
    otstroit' (v.pf.)
building, tractor traktorostroenie (n.n.)
bulb lukovitsa (n.f.)
Bulgarian bolgarin (n.m.)
bull byk (n.m.)
bulldog bul'dog (n.m.)
bulldozer bul'dozer (n.m.)
bullet pulya (n.f.)
bulletin byulleten' (n.m.)
bullfinch snegir' (n.m.)
bully zabiyaka (n.m.&f.)
    zadira (n.m.&f.)
bumblebee shmel' (n.m.)
bump ukhab (n.m.)
bunch puk (n.m.)
    svyazka (n.f.)
bunch, small puchok (n.m.)
bundle pachka (n.f.)
    vyazanka (n.f.)
bundle up zakutat' (v.pf.)
    zakutyvat' (v.impf.)
bungler golovotyap (n.m.)
bunk koika (n.f.)
bunting, red kumach (n.m.)
burbot (fish) nalim (n.m.)
burden bremya (n.n.)
    nosha (n.f.)
    obremenyat' (v.impf.)
    obuza (n.f.)
burden, beast of v'yuchnoe zhivotnoe
    (adj.-n.n.)
burden, to be a tyagotit' (v.impf.)
burdensome tyagostnyi (adj.)
burdock lopukh (n.m.)
bureau byuro (n.n.)
bureau, information informbyuro (n.n.)
bureaucrat byurokrat (n.m.)
burial mound kurgan (n.m.)
Burmese birmanets (n.m.)
burn goret' (v.impf.)
    obgorat' (v.impf.)
    obzhech' (v.pf.)
    ozhog (n.m.)
    palit' (v.impf.)
    peregorat' (v.impf.)
    prigorat' (v.impf.)
    spalit' (v.pf.)
    (cont'd)

topit'sya (v.impf.)
zhech' (v.impf.)

burn down sgoret' (v.pf.)
szhech' (v.pf.)
vygorat' (v.impf.)
vygoret' (v.pf.)

burn out dogorat' (v.impf.)
vyzhech' (v.pf.)
vyzhigat' (v.impf.)

burn through progorat' (v.impf.)
prozhech' (v.pf.)
prozhigat' (v.impf.)

burned, to get podgorat' (v.impf.)

burner gorelka (n.f.)

burning gar' (n.f.)
gorenie (n.n.)
sozhzhenie (n.n.)
zhguchii (adj.)
zhivotrepeshchushchii (adj.)
zlobodnevnyi (adj.)

burnt gorelyi (adj.)

burr kartavit' (v.impf.)

burst lopnut' (v.pf.)

burst into vorvat'sya (v.pf.)
vryvat'sya (v.impf.)

burst into flame vspykhivat' (v.impf.)

burst into tears rasplakat'sya (v.pf.)

burst out laughing raskhokhotat'sya (v.pf.)
rassmeyat'sya (v.pf.)
zakhokhotat' (v.pf.)

burst out sobbing razrydat'sya (v.pf.)

bury khoronit' (v.impf.)
pokhoronit' (v.pf.)
skhoronit' (v.pf.)
utknut' (v.pf.)
zakapyvat' (v.impf.)
zakopat' (v.pf.)
zaryt' (v.pf.)
zaryvat' (v.impf.)

bus avtobus (n.m.)

bush kust (n.m.)

business delo (n.n.)

business concern kontsern (n.m.)

businesslike delovoi (adj.)

businesslike manner, in a po-delovomu (adv.)

businessman delets (n.m.)

bust byust (n.m.)

bustle begotnya (n.f.)
kuter'ma (n.f.)
sumatokha (n.f.)

bustle about khlopotat' (v.impf.)

busy zanyatoi (adj.)

but no (conj.)
zato (conj.)
zhe (part.)

butcher myasnik (n.m.)

butt bodat' (v.impf.)
obukh (n.m.)
priklad (n.m.)

butt in sunut'sya (v.pf.)

butter maslo (n.n.)
maslyanyi (adj.)

buttercup lyutik (n.m.)

butter dish maslenka (n.f.)

butterfly babochka (n.f.)

buttock yagoditsa (n.f.)

button pugovitsa (n.f.)

button up zastegnut' (v.pf.)

buttonhole petlitsa (n.f.)

buy kupit' (v.pf.)
nakupat' (v.impf.)
pokupat' (v.impf.)
zavesti (v.pf.)

buy secondhand perekupat' (v.impf.)

buy up raskupat' (v.pf.)
skupat' (v.impf.)

buyer pokupatel' (n.m.)

buying kuplya (n.f.)

buying up skupka (n.f.)

buzz gudet' (v.impf.)
zhuzhzhat' (v.impf.)

buzzing gudenie (n.n.)

by pri (prep.)
u (prep.)

by fits and starts uryvkami (adv.)

by force nasil'no (adv.)

by hearsay ponaslyshke (adv.)

by heart naizust' (adv.)

by means of posredstvom (adv.)
putem (adv.)

by name poimenno (adv.)

by no means nikak (adv.)

by the piece poshtuchnyi (adj.)

by the way kstati (adv.)

Byelorussian belorus (n.m.)

C (Ч)

cabbage kapusta (n.f.)
cabbage, head of kochan (n.m.)
cabbage soup shchi (n.pl.)
cabbage stump kocheryzhka (n.f.)
cabin kabina (n.f.)
   kayuta (n.f.)
   shalash (n.m.)
cable kabel' (n.m.)
cabman izvozchik (n.m.)
cabotage kabotazh (n.m.)
cackle kudakhtat' (v.impf.)
   zakudakhtat' (v.pf.)
cadmium kadmii (n.m.)
cafe kafe (n.n.)
cage kletka (n.f.)
cajole zadabrivat' (v.impf.)
   zadobrit' (v.pf.)
cake keks (n.m.)
   pryanik (n.m.)
   tort (n.m.)
cake, fancy pirozhnoe (n.n.)
cake, flat round lepeshka (n.f.)
cake, honey kovrizhka (n.f.)
cake, sponge biskvit (n.m.)
calcium kal'tsii (n.m.)
calculate rasschitat' (v.pf.)
   rasschityvat' (v.impf.)
   vychislit' (v.pf.)
calculation ischislenie (n.n.)
   kal'kulyatsiya (n.f.)
   raschet (n.m.)
   schet (n.m.)
   uchet (n.m.)
   vychislenie (n.n.)
calendar kalendar' (n.m.)
   kalendarnyi (adj.)
   vremyaischislenie (n.n.)
calf ikra (n.f.)
   telenok (n.m.)
caliber kalibr (n.m.)
calibers, of different raznokalibernyi (adj.)
calico, unbleached byaz' (n.f.)
call dozvonit'sya (v.pf.)
   klich (n.m.)
   nazyvat' (v.impf.)

   obozvat' (v.pf.)
   obzyvat' (v.impf.)
   oklikat' (v.impf.)
   podzyvat' (v.impf.)
   pozvat' (v.pf.)
   prizvat' (v.pf.)
   prizyv (n.m.)
   sozvat' (v.pf.)
   szyvat' (v.impf.)
   vyzov (n.m.)
   vyzvat' (v.pf.)
   zov (n.m.)
   zvat' (v.impf.)
call in zaekhat' (v.pf.)
   zaezzhat' (v.impf.)
call on navedat'sya (v.pf.)
   navedyvat'sya (v.impf.)
call out vyklikat' (v.impf.)
call, to make a sozvonit'sya (v.pf.)
call up podozvat' (v.pf.)
calligraphy chistopisanie (n.n.)
callosity, solidification zatverdenie (n.n.)
calm pokoinyi (adj.)
   shtil' (n.m.)
   ugomonit' (v.pf.)
   unimat'(sya) (v.impf.)
   unyat' (v.pf.)
   uspokoit' (v.pf.)
   zatish'e (n.n.)
calm down stikhat' (v.impf.)
   stikhnut' (v.pf.)
   uspokaivat'(sya) (v.impf.)
   zatikhat' (v.impf.)
calorie kaloriya (n.f.)
calve otelit'sya (v.pf.)
   telit'sya (v.impf.)
cambium kambii (n.m.)
cambric batist (n.m.)
camel verblyud (n.m.)
camera fotoapparat (n.m.)
camp lager' (n.m.)
   lagernyi (adj.)
   stan (n.m.)
   tabor (n.m.)
camp fire koster (n.m.)

campaign kampaniya (n.f.)
   pokhod (n.m.)
camphor kamfara (n.f.)
can banka (n.f.)
   bidon (n.m.)
   moch' (v.impf.)
can, watering leika (n.f.)
Canadian kanadets (n.m.)
canal kanal (n.m.)
canary kanareika (n.f.)
cancel rastorgat' (v.impf.)
   sokratit' (v.pf.)
cancer rak (n.m.)
candidate kandidat (n.m.)
candidate, to be a ballotirovat'sya (v.impf.)
candied zasakharennyi (adj.)
candied fruit tsukat (n.m.)
candle svecha (n.f.)
candle end ogarok (n.m.)
candlestick podsvechnik (n.m.)
candy konfeta (n.f.)
   slasti (n.pl.)
canned konservnyi (adj.)
canned food konservy (n.pl.)
canned meat tushenka (n.f.)
cannibal lyudoed (n.m.)
canoe baidarka (n.f.)
   cheln (n.m.)
   chelnok (n.m.)
canteen stolovaya (n.f.)
canvas kanva (n.f.)
   kholst (n.m.)
   parusina (n.f.)
cap kepka (n.f.)
   kolpak (n.m.)
   shapka (n.f.)
cap, peaked furazhka (n.f.)
   kartuz (n.m.)
cap, percussion piston (n.m.)
capacious emkii (adj.)
   ob"emistyi (adj.)
capacitor kondensator (n.m.)
capacity gruzopod"emnost' (n.f.)
   vmestimost' (n.f.)
capacity for work rabotosposobnost' (n.f.)
   trudosposobnost' (n.f.)
capacity, heat teploemkost' (n.f.)
cap-band okolysh (n.m.)

cape mys (n.m.)
capillary kapillyar (n.m.)
capital kapital (n.m.)
   kapital'nyi (adj.)
   propisnoi (adj.)
   stolitsa (n.f.)
capitalism kapitalizm (n.m.)
capitulate kapitulirovat' (v.impf.&pf.)
capsule kapsula (n.f.)
   oblatka (n.f.)
captain kapitan (n.m.)
captivity nevolya (n.f.)
   plen (n.m.)
car, armored bronevik (n.m.)
car, dining vagon-restoran (n.m.)
car, railway vagon (n.m.)
carafe grafin (n.m.)
caramel karamel' (n.f.)
caravan karavan (n.m.)
carbide karbid (n.m.)
carbohydrate uglevod (n.m.)
carbolic karbolovyi (adj.)
carbon uglerod (n.m.)
carbon disulfide serouglerod (n.m.)
carbon monoxide ugar (n.m.)
carbonization obuglivanie (n.n.)
carburetor karbyurator (n.m.)
carcass tusha (n.f.)
carcinogenesis kantserogenez (n.m.)
carcinogenic kantserogennyi (adj.)
card kartochka (n.f.)
card index kartoteka (n.f.)
card shark shuler (n.m.)
cardboard karton (n.m.)
cardiogram kardiogramma (n.f.)
cardiology kardiologiya (n.f.)
care ostorozhnost' (n.f.)
   popechenie (n.n.)
   prismotr (n.m.)
   ukhod (n.m.)
   zabota (n.f.)
care, to take berech' (v.impf.)
   pozabotit'sya (v.pf.)
career kar'era (n.f.)
carefree bezzabotnyi (adj.)
careful berezhnyi (adj.)
   tshchatel'nyi (adj.)
careless bespechnyi (adj.)

nebrezhnyi (adj.)

neostorozhnyi (adj.)

carelessness neakkuratnost' (n.f.)

caress laska (n.f.)

laskat' (v.impf.)

oblaskat' (v.pf.)

pogladit' (v.pf.)

prilaskat' (v.pf.)

caressing laskatel'nyi (adj.)

caricature karikatura (n.f.)

sharzh (n.m.)

carnation gvozdika (n.f.)

carnival karnaval (n.m.)

carnivorous plotoyadnyi (adj.)

carouse kutezh (n.m.)

kutit' (v.impf.)

carp karp (n.m.)

carpenter plotnik (n.m.)

carpet kover (n.m.)

carriage ékipazh (n.m.)

kareta (n.f.)

kolyaska (n.f.)

support (n.m.)

carriage, gun lafet (n.m.)

carried away, to be perenestis' (v.pf.)

perenosit'sya (v.impf.)

carrier nesushchaya (n.f.)

nositel' (n.m.)

carrion padal' (n.f.)

carrot morkov' (n.f.)

carry nesti (v.impf.)

nosit' (v.impf.)

ponesti (v.pf.)

ponosit' (v.pf.)

povezti (v.pf.)

pronesti (v.pf.)

pronosit' (v.impf.)

provezti (v.pf.)

provozit' (v.impf.)

raznesti (v.pf.)

raznosit' (v.impf.)

vezti (v.impf.)

vozit' (v.impf.)

carry away uvlech' (v.pf.)

carry in vnesti (v.pf.)

vnosit' (v.impf.)

carry off utaskivat' (v.impf.)

carry out vynesti (v.pf.)

vynosit' (v.impf.)

carry to donesti (v.pf.)

cart podvoda (n.f.)

telega (n.f.)

voz (n.m.)

cartel kartel' (n.m.)

carter lomovoi (adj.)

vozchik (n.m.)

cartilage khryashch (n.m.)

cartoon, animated mul'tiplikatsionnyi (adj.)

cartridge patron (n.m.)

cartridge case gil'za (n.f.)

cartridge clip oboima (n.f.)

carved reznoi (adj.)

carving rez'ba (n.f.)

cascade kaskad (n.m.)

case padezh (n.m.)

case, dressing nesesser (n.m.)

case, incident sluchai (n.m.)

case of drawing instruments gotoval'nya
(n.f.)

case shot kartech' (n.f.)

casette kasseta (n.f.)

cash nalichnost' (n.f.)

cash on delivery nalozhennym platezhom
(adv.)

cashier kassir (n.m.)

casing obolochka (n.f.)

cassock ryasa (n.f.)

cast litoi (adj.)

cast around okidyvat' (v.impf.)

cast down potupit' (v.pf.)

cast down, to be unyvat' (v.impf.)

cast iron chugun (n.m.)

caste kasta (n.f.)

casting lit'e (n.n.)

otlivka (n.f.)

cast-off clothes obnoski (n.pl.)

castor bobrik (n.m.)

castor oil kastorovoe maslo (adj.-n.n.)

castration kastratsiya (n.f.)

casually vskol'z' (adv.)

cat koshka (n.f.)

catalogue katalog (n.m.)

catalysis kataliz (n.m.)

catalyst katalizator (n.m.)

catarrh katar (n.m.)

catastrophe katastrofa (n.f.)

catch   lovit' (v.impf.)
    poimat' (v.pf.)
    skhvatit' (v.pf.)
    ukhvatit' (v.pf.)
    ulavlivat' (v.impf.)
    ulov (n.m.)
    zastigat' (v.impf.)
catch fire   zagorat'sya (v.impf.)
    zagoret'sya (v.pf.)
catch hold of   utsepit'sya (v.pf.)
catch up   dognat' (v.pf.)
    dogonyat' (v.impf.)
    podtyagivat'sya (v.impf.)
catching   lovlya (n.f.)
categorically   kategoricheskii (adj.)
category   kategoriya (n.f.)
    razryad (n.m.)
caterpillar   gusenitsa (n.f.)
cathedral   sobor (n.m.)
cathetus (side of triangle)   katet (n.m.)
cathode   katod (n.m.)
Catholic (Roman)   katolik (n.m.)
catlike   koshachii (adj.)
cattle breeder   skotovod (n.m.)
cattle, loss of   padezh (n.m.)
cattle shed   khlev (n.m.)
Caucasian   kavkazskii (adj.)
caulk   konopatit' (v.impf.)
cause   povod (n.m.)
    prichina (n.f.)
    prichinit' (v.pf.)
caustic   edkii (adj.)
caution   opaska (n.f.)
cavalry   kavaleriya (n.f.)
    konnitsa (n.f.)
cavalryman   kavalerist (n.m.)
cave   peshchera (n.f.)
    podzemel'e (n.n.)
caviar, pressed   payusnaya ikra (adj.-n.f.)
cavil   klyauza (n.f.)
    pridirka (n.f.)
cavitation   kavitatsiya (n.f.)
cavity   polost' (n.f.)
    vpadina (n.f.)
cease to love   razlyubit' (v.pf.)
cease to want   raskhotet' (v.pf.)
cedar   kedr (n.m.)
cede   ustupat' (v.impf.)

ceiling   perekrytie (n.n.)
    potolok (n.m.)
celebrate   chestvovat' (v.impf.)
    otprazdnovat' (v.pf.)
    spravit' (v.pf.)
    spravlyat' (v.impf.)
celebration   torzhestvo (n.n.)
celebrity   znamenitost' (n.f.)
celestial   nebesnyi (adj.)
cell   kamera (n.f.)
    kel'ya (n.f.)
    yacheika (n.f.)
cell, photoelectric   fotoelement (n.m.)
cellar, cold   pogreb (n.m.)
cellist   violonchelist (n.m.)
cello   violonchel' (n.f.)
cellophane   tsellofan (n.m.)
cellular   kletochnyi (adj.)
cellulose   kletchatka (n.f.)
    tsellyuloza (n.f.)
cement   tsement (n.m.)
cemetery   kladbishche (n.n.)
censorship   tsenzura (n.f.)
censure   narekanie (n.n.)
census   perepis' (n.f.)
center   tsentr (n.m.)
centigrade   stogradusnyi (adj.)
centimeter   santimetr (n.m.)
central   tsentral'nyi (adj.)
central heating   teplofikatsiya (n.f.)
centralism   tsentralizm (n.m.)
centralization   tsentralizatsiya (n.f.)
centrifugal   tsentrobezhnyi (adj.)
centrifuge   tsentrifuga (n.f.)
centripetal   tsentrostremitel'nyi (adj.)
centuries-old   mnogovekovoi (adj.)
century   stoletie (n.n.)
    vek (n.m.)
ceramics   keramika (n.f.)
cereals   krupa (n.f.)
    zlaki (n.pl.)
ceremony   obryad (n.m.)
    tseremoniya (n.f.)
ceremony, without   zaprosto (adv.)
cerium   tserii (n.m.)
certain, a   nekii (p.)
certainly   konechno (adv.)
    naverno(e) (adv.)

nepremenno (adv.)	**chaos** khaos (n.m.)
certificate attestat (n.m.)	razval (n.m.)
spravka (n.f.)	**chaotic** khaoticheskii (adj.)
svidetel'stvo (n.n.)	**chapel** chasovnya (n.f.)
udostoverenie (n.n.)	**chapter** glava (n.f.)
certificate, birth metrika (n.f.)	**character** kharakter (n.m.)
certify udostoverit' (v.pf.)	personazh (n.m.)
cessation prekrashchenie (n.n.)	**characteristic** kharakternyi (adj.)
chain prikovat' (v.pf.)	svoistvennyi (adj.)
skovat' (v.pf.)	**charade** sharada (n.f.)
skovyvat' (v.impf.)	**charge** natisk (n.m.)
tsep' (n.f.)	zaryad (n.m.)
tsepnoi (adj.)	**charge, extra** nachislenie (n.n.)
tsepochka (n.f.)	natsenka (n.f.)
chair stul (n.m.)	**charge, free of** besplatnyi (adj.)
chair, easy kreslo (n.n.)	**charge, to be in** vedat' (v.impf.)
chair, rocking kachalka (n.f.)	**charged** zaryazhennyi (adj.)
chairman predsedatel' (n.m.)	**chariot** kolesnitsa (n.f.)
chaise lounge shezlong (n.m.)	**charity** blagotvoritel'nost' (n.f.)
chalk mel (n.m.)	**charm** obayanie (n.n.)
chamber kamernyi (adj.)	ocharovanie (n.n.)
palata (n.f.)	ocharovat' (v.pf.)
chamber, gas dushegubka (n.f.)	prelest' (n.f.)
chamber, pressure barokamera (n.f.)	**charming** prelestnyi (adj.)
chamber, torture zastenok (n.m.)	**chart** diagramma (n.f.)
champion chempion (n.m.)	tablitsa (n.f.)
pobornik (n.m.)	**charter** khartiya (n.f.)
championship chempionat (n.m.)	ustav (n.m.)
chance shans (n.m.)	**chassis** shassi (n.n.)
chandelier lyustra (n.f.)	**chastity** tselomudrie (n.n.)
change izmenenie (n.n.)	**chatter** boltat' (v.impf.)
izmenit' (v.pf.)	**chatterbox** boltun (n.m.)
izmenit'sya (v.pf.)	**chauvinism** shovinizm (n.m.)
izmenyat' (v.impf.)	**cheap** deshevyi (adj.)
meloch' (n.f.)	**cheap print** lubok (n.m.)
menyat' (v.impf.)	**cheap, to sell** prodeshevit' (v.pf.)
peremena (n.f.)	**cheaper, to become** podeshevet' (v.pf.)
razmenyat' (v.pf.)	**cheaply** deshevo (adv.)
sdacha (n.f.)	**cheaply, very** bestsenok (n.m.)
sdvig (n.m.)	**cheat** obschitat' (v.pf.)
smena (n.f.)	peredergivat' (v.impf.)
change, exchange pomenyat'(sya) (v.pf.)	plut (n.m.)
change one's mind peredumat' (v.pf.)	plutovat' (v.impf.)
perereshat' (v.impf.)	zhul'nichat' (v.impf.)
razdumat' (v.pf.)	**cheating** naduvatel'stvo (n.n.)
razubezhdat'sya (v.impf.)	**check** chek (n.m.)
changeable izmenchivyi (adj.)	osadit' (v.pf.)
nepostoyannyi (adj.)	osazhivat' (v.impf.)
	(cont'd)

shakh (n.m.)
sverit' (v.pf.)
sveryat' (v.impf.)
checkers shashki (n.pl.)
checking, roll call poverka (n.f.)
checkmate mat (n.m.)
cheek shcheka (n.f.)
cheekbone skula (n.f.)
cheer up poveselet' (v.pf.)
priobodryat'(sya) (v.impf.)
razveselit' (v.pf.)
cheerful zhizneradostnyi (adj.)
cheerfulness bodrost' (n.f.)
cheerless bezotradnyi (adj.)
cheese syr (n.m.)
cheese, cottage tvorog (n.m.)
cheese dairy syrovarnya (n.f.)
cheese pancake syrnik (n.m.)
cheesecake vatrushka (n.f.)
chemist khimik (n.m.)
chemistry khimiya (n.f.)
chemistry, petroleum neftekhimiya (n.f.)
chemist's apteka (n.f.)
cherish leleyat' (v.impf.)
cherry chereshnya (n.f.)
vishnevyi (adj.)
vishnya (n.f.)
cherry tree, bird cheremukha (n.f.)
chess shakhmatnyi (adj.)
shakhmaty (n.pl.)
chess master, grand grossmeister (n.m.)
chess player shakhmatist (n.m.)
chest of drawers komod (n.m.)
chestnut kashtan (n.m.)
chew perezhevyvat' (v.impf.)
razzhevat' (v.pf.)
zhevat' (v.impf.)
chicken tsyplenok (n.m.)
chicken pox vetryanaya ospa (adj.-n.f.)
chicory tsikorii (n.m.)
chief glavnyi (adj.)
nachal'nik (n.m.)
shef (n.m.)
child ditya (n.n.)
rebenok (n.m.)
child, mischievous ozornik (n.m.)
shalun (n.m.)
childbirth rody (n.pl.)

childless bezdetnyi (adj.)
children deti (n.pl.)
detvora (n.pl.)
rebyata (n.pl.)
children, having many mnogodetnyi (adj.)
Chilean chiliets (n.m.)
chiliiskii (adj.)
chilled, to be prodrognut' (v.pf.)
chimney sweep trubochist (n.m.)
chin podborodok (n.m.)
china farfor (n.m.)
Chinese kitaets (n.m.)
chink shchel' (n.f.)
chip shchepka (n.f.)
chirp chirikat' (v.impf.)
shchebetat' (v.impf.)
chirr strekotat' (v.impf.)
chisel doloto (n.n.)
rezets (n.m.)
stameska (n.f.)
chivalrous rytsarskii (adj.)
chlorine khlor (n.m.)
chock-full polnym-polno (adv.)
chocolate shokolad (n.m.)
chocolate ice éskimo (n.n.)
choice vybor (n.m.)
choke davit'sya (v.impf.)
podavit'sya (v.pf.)
zakhlebnut'sya (v.pf.)
cholera kholera (n.f.)
choose izbrat' (v.pf.)
vybirat' (v.impf.)
vybrat' (v.pf.)
chop izmel'chit' (v.pf.)
kolot' (v.impf.)
nakolot' (v.pf.)
rubit' (v.impf.)
shinkovat' (v.impf.)
chop off obrubat' (v.impf.)
otkolot' (v.pf.)
chop through prorubat' (v.impf.)
chop up razrubat' (v.impf.)
chopping rubka (n.f.)
chord akkord (n.m.)
khorda (n.f.)
svyazka (n.f.)
chorus khor (n.m.)
Christian khristianin (n.m.)

Christmas rozhdestvo (n.n.)
chromium khrom (n.m.)
chronic khronicheskii (adj.)
  zastarelyi (adj.)
chronicle khronika (n.f.)
  letopis' (n.f.)
chronology khronologiya (n.f.)
  letoschislenie (n.n.)
chronometer khronometr (n.m.)
chrysalis kukolka (n.f.)
chuckle posmeivat'sya (v.impf.)
church tserkov' (n.f.)
  tserkovnyi (adj.)
church, Polish Roman Catholic kostel (n.m.)
churn masloboika (n.f.)
chute zhelob (n.m.)
Chuvash chuvash (n.m.)
cicatrize zarubtsevat'sya (v.pf.)
cider sidr (n.m.)
cigar sigara (n.f.)
cigarette papirosa (n.f.)
cigarette butt okurok (n.m.)
cigarette case portsigar (n.m.)
cigarette holder mundshtuk (n.m.)
cigarette, to light up a zakurivat' (v.impf.)
cinema kino (n.n.)
cinematography kinematografiya (n.f.)
cinnamon koritsa (n.f.)
cipher shifr (n.m.)
circle krug (n.m.)
  yarus (n.m.)
circuit, short zamykanie (n.n.)
circular kol'tsevoi (adj.)
  krugovoi (adj.)
  tsirkulyar (n.m.)
circulate tsirkulirovat' (v.impf.)
circulation krugooborot (n.m.)
  rasprostranenie (n.n.)
  tirazh (n.m.)
  tsirkulyatsiya (n.f.)
circulation, blood krovoobrashchenie (n.n.)
circulatory krovenosnyi (adj.)
circumcision obrezanie (n.n.)
circumference okruzhnost' (n.f.)
circumspection osmotritel'nost' (n.f.)
circumstance obstoyatel'stvo (n.n.)
circus tsirk (n.m.)
cistern bak (n.m.)

citadel tsitadel' (n.f.)
citizen grazhdanin (n.m.)
citizens, fellow sograzhdane (n.pl.)
citizenship grazhdanstvo (n.n.)
citrus plants tsitrusovye (n.pl.)
city, micro-district of a mikroraion (n.m.)
civil grazhdanskii (adj.)
  uchtivyi (adj.)
civilian shtatskii (adj.)
  vol'nonaemnyi (adj.)
civilization tsivilizatsiya (n.f.)
claim pretendovat' (v.impf.)
  pretenziya (n.f.)
  prityazanie (n.n.)
  zayavka (n.f.)
claimant pretendent (n.m.)
claiming vostrebovanie (n.n.)
clamber karabkat'sya (v.impf.)
clamber up vzgromozdit'sya (v.pf.)
clamp zazhim (n.m.)
clank bryatsat' (v.impf.)
  lyazgat' (v.impf.)
clap khlopat' (v.impf.)
clarification vyyasnenie (n.n.)
clarinet klarnet (n.m.)
class klass (n.m.)
  klassovyi (adj.)
classic klassik (n.m.)
classical klassicheskii (adj.)
classify klassifitsirovat' (v.impf.)
classless besklassovyi (adj.)
classmate odnoklassnik (n.m.)
  odnokursnik (n.m.)
classroom klass (n.m.)
clatter tsokan'e (n.n.)
claw kleshnya (n.f.)
  kogot' (n.m.)
clay glina (n.f.)
  glinyanyi (adj.)
clean chistit' (v.impf.)
  chistoplotnyi (adj.)
  chistyi (adj.)
  nabelo (adv.)
  nachisto (adv.)
  ochishchat'(sya) (v.impf.)
  prochishchat' (v.impf.)
  prochistit' (v.pf.)
  vychishchat' (v.impf.)
  (cont'd)

vychistit' (v.pf.)

clean off schishchat' (v.impf.)
   schistit' (v.pf.)

cleaner uborshchitsa (n.f.)

cleaning ochistka (n.f.)
   uborka (n.f.)

cleaning, dry khimchistka (n.f.)

cleanliness chistota (n.f.)

cleanly chisto (adv.)

clear chetkii (adj.)
   naglyadnyi (adj.)
   yasnyi (adj.)

clear away raschishchat' (v.impf.)
   raschistit' (v.pf.)

clear of mines razminirovat' (v.pf.)

clear one's throat otkashlivat'sya (v.impf.)

clear space prosvet (n.m.)

clear, to make vyyasnit' (v.pf.)

clear up proyasnit'sya (v.pf.)
   razgulyat'sya (v.pf.)
   svetlet' (v.impf.)

clearance sale rasprodazha (n.f.)

clearheaded prozorlivyi (adj.)

clearing polyana (n.f.)

clearly yasno (adv.)

cleave rassekat' (v.impf.)

clergy dukhovenstvo (n.n.)

clerk pisar' (n.m.)

clever smyshlenyi (adj.)
   umnyi (adj.)

click shchelkat' (v.impf.)
   shchelknut' (v.pf.)

client klient (n.m.)
   podzashchitnyi (adj.)

climate klimat (n.m.)

climax razgar (n.m.)

climb lazit' (v.impf.)
   lezt' (v.impf.)
   vskarabkat'sya (v.pf.)
   vzbirat'sya (v.impf.)
   vzobrat'sya (v.pf.)
   zabirat'sya (v.impf.)
   zabrat'sya (v.pf.)
   zalezat' (v.impf.)

climb in vlezat' (v.impf.)

climb out vylezat' (v.impf.)

climb over perelezat' (v.impf.)

climbing v'yushchiisya (adj.)

cling l'nut' (v.impf.)
   oblepit' (v.pf.)
   pril'nut' (v.pf.)
   tseplyat'sya (v.impf.)

clink glasses chokat'sya (v.impf.)

clip skrepka (n.f.)

clipping vyrezka (n.f.)

clique klika (n.f.)

cloak nakidka (n.f.)

cloak, felt burka (n.f.)

cloakroom garderob (n.m.)
   razdevalka (n.f.)

clock, alarm budil'nik (n.m.)

clockwork zavodnoi (adj.)

cloister monastyr' (n.m.)

close smykat'(sya) (v.impf.)
   somknut' (v.pf.)
   spertyi (adj.)
   uboristyi (adj.)
   vplotnuyu (adv.)
   zakryvat'(sya) (v.pf.)
   zatvorit' (v.pf.)

close up zadelat' (v.pf.)
   zalepit' (v.pf.)

close with a bang zakhlopyvat'sya (v.impf.)

closely cropped nagolo (adv.)

closeness dukhota (n.f.)

closet kamorka (n.f.)

closing zakrytie (n.n.)

clot sgustok (n.m.)

cloth materiya (n.f.)
   sukno (n.n.)
   sukonnyi (adj.)
   tkan' (n.f.)

cloth, thick drap (n.m.)

clothe oblech' (v.pf.)

clothes odezhda (n.f.)

clothes, cast-off obnoski (n.pl.)

clothes, swaddling pelenki (n.pl.)

clothes, work spetsodezhda (n.f.)

cloud oblako (n.n.)
   tucha (n.f.)

clouding pomutnenie (n.n.)

cloudless bezoblachnyi (adj.)

clouds oblachnost' (n.f.)

cloudy pasmurnyi (adj.)

clove gvozdika (n.f.)

clover klever (n.m.)

clown kloun (n.m.)
    payats (n.m.)
club klub (n.m.)
club, amateur flying aeroklub (n.m.)
clubbing skladchina (n.f.)
clubs trefy (n.pl.)
clue klyuch (n.m.)
clumsy kosolapyi (adj.)
    nepovorotlivyi (adj.)
    neuklyuzhii (adj.)
cluster grozd' (n.f.)
coach trener (n.m.)
    trenirovat' (v.impf.)
coach for nataskat' (v.pf.)
coachman kucher (n.m.)
coagulation svertyvanie (n.n.)
coal kamennougol'nyi (adj.)
    ugol' (n.m.)
    ugol'nyi (adj.)
coal gas svetil'nyi gaz (adj.-n.m.)
coalition koalitsiya (n.f.)
coarse tobacco makhorka (n.f.)
coarsened ogrubelyi (adj.)
    zagrubelyi (adj.)
coast beregovoi (adj.)
coastal pribrezhnyi (adj.)
coat obmazat' (v.pf.)
    pidzhak (n.m.)
coat, flap of a pola (n.f.)
coat, frock syurtuk (n.m.)
coat, fur shuba (n.f.)
coat hanger veshalka (n.f.)
coat of arms gerb (n.m.)
coat, sheepskin tulup (n.m.)
coating pokrov (n.m.)
coauthor soavtor (n.m.)
cob ogryzok (n.m.)
cobalt kobal't (n.m.)
cobblestone bulyzhnik (n.m.)
cobweb pautina (n.f.)
cock kurok (n.m.)
    petukh (n.m.)
cockroach tarakan (n.m.)
cocoa kakao (n.n.)
coconut kokosovyi orekh (adj.-n.m.)
cod treska (n.f.)
coddle nezhit' (v.impf.)
coddled iznezhennyi (adj.)

code kodeks (n.m.)
    svod (n.m.)
coefficient koeffitsient (n.m.)
    pokazatel' (n.m.)
coexistence sosushchestvovanie (n.n.)
coffee kofe (n.m.)
coffeepot kofeinik (n.m.)
cofferdam peremychka (n.f.)
coffin grob (n.m.)
cog zubets (n.m.)
cogged zubchatyi (adj.)
cognac kon'yak (n.m.)
cognition poznanie (n.n.)
coherent svyaznyi (adj.)
coil spiral' (n.f.)
coin moneta (n.f.)
coin, ten-kopeck grivennik (n.m.)
coincide sovpadat' (v.impf.)
    sovpast' (v.pf.)
coke koks (n.m.)
cold kholod (n.m.)
    kholodnyi (adj.)
    nasmork (n.m.)
    prostuda (n.f.)
cold, it is kholodno (pred.)
cold, sensitive to zyabkii (adj.)
cold, to be ozyabnyt' (v.pf.)
cold, to become okhladevat' (v.impf.)
    ostyvat' (v.impf.)
cold, to expose to zastudit' (v.pf.)
cold, to suffer from zyabnut' (v.impf.)
collaborate sotrudnichat' (v.impf.)
collaborator soglashatel' (n.m.)
collapse obrushivat'sya (v.impf.)
    obval (n.m.)
    rukhnut' (v.pf.)
collapsible razbornyi (adj.)
collar khomut (n.m.)
    osheinik (n.m.)
    vorot (n.m.)
    vorotnik (n.m.)
collarbone klyuchitsa (n.f.)
colleague kollega (n.m.)
    sosluzhivets (n.m.)
collect sobrat' (v.pf.)
collect oneself opomnit'sya (v.pf.)
collection kollektsiya (n.f.)
    sbor (n.m.)
    (cont'd)

sbornik (n.m.)

sobiranie (n.n.)

collective kollektiv (n.m.)

kollektivnyi (adj.)

collectivization kollektivizatsiya (n.f.)

collector kollektsioner (n.m.)

college vuz (n.m.)

collide naekhat' (v.pf.)

naletat' (v.impf.)

stalkivat'sya (v.impf.)

collision stolknovenie (n.n.)

colloidal kolloidnyi (adj.)

collusion sgovor (n.m.)

colon dvoetochie (n.n.)

colonel polkovnik (n.m.)

colonial kolonial'nyi (adj.)

colonialism kolonializm (n.m.)

colonist kolonist (n.m.)

colonization kolonizatsiya (n.f.)

colony koloniya (n.f.)

color krasit' (v.impf.)

mast' (n.f.)

raskrashivat' (v.impf.)

raskrasit' (v.pf.)

rumyanets (n.m.)

tsvet (n.m.)

tsvetnoi (adj.)

color arrangement rastsvetka (n.f.)

color, dark blue sineva (n.f.)

color-blindness dal'tonizm (n.m.)

colorful krasochnyi (adj.)

colorless bestsvetnyi (adj.)

colors, diversity of pestrota (n.f.)

columbium niobii (n.m.)

column grafa (n.f.)

kolonna (n.f.)

stolbets (n.m.)

comatose komatoznyi (adj.)

comb chesat' (v.impf.)

greben' (n.m.)

grebenka (n.f.)

prichesat' (v.pf.)

raschesat' (v.impf.)

rascheska (n.f.)

raschesyvat' (v.impf.)

combatant stroevoi (adj.)

combination sochetanie (n.n.)

soedinenie (n.n.)

combine kombain (n.m.)

kombinirovat' (v.impf.)

skombinirovat' (v.pf.)

soedinyat'(sya) (v.impf.)

sovmeshchat' (v.impf.)

combings ocheski (n.pl.)

combustion sgoranie (n.n.)

combustion, spontaneous samovozgoranie (n.n.)

come nastat' (v.pf.)

nastavat' (v.impf.)

nastupat' (v.impf.)

nastupit' (v.pf.)

priiti (v.pf.)

prikhodit' (v.impf.)

come cross nabresti (v.pf.)

come forward vystupat' (v.impf.)

come in time podospet' (v.pf.)

come into being narodit'sya (v.pf.)

narozhdat'sya (v.impf.)

come into contact soprikasat'sya (v.impf.)

soprikosnut'sya (v.pf.)

come now and then naezzhat' (v.impf.)

come off otparyvat'(sya) (v.impf.)

soskakivat' (v.impf.)

soskochit' (v.pf.)

come on nu (part.)

come running pribegat' (v.impf.)

pribezhat' (v.pf.)

sbegat'sya (v.impf.)

come to a head (a boil) narvat' (v.pf.)

come to an agreement sgovarivat'sya (v.impf.)

come to an understanding poladit' (v.pf.)

come to blows podrat'sya (v.pf.)

come to grips stsepit'sya (v.pf.)

stseplyat'sya (v.impf.)

come to light raskryvat'(sya) (v.impf.)

come to the surface vsplyvat' (v.pf.)

come true sbyt'sya (v.pf.)

sbyvat'sya (v.impf.)

comedian komik (n.m.)

comedy komediya (n.f.)

comet kometa (n.f.)

comfort komfort (n.m.)

udobstvo (n.n.)

uteshit' (v.pf.)

comfortable blagoustroennyi (adj.)

udobnyi (adj.)
comforter soska (n.f.)
comic shutochnyi (adj.)
comical komichnyi (adj.)
coming gryadushchii (adj.)
nastuplenie (n.n.)
prikhod (n.m.)
comma zapyataya (n.f.)
command komanda (n.f.)
komandovanie (n.n.)
povelevat' (v.impf.)
skomandovat' (v.pf.)
commandant komendant (n.m.)
commander komandir (n.m.)
komanduyushchii (adj.)
commander in chief
glavnokomanduyushchii (n.m.)
commander, platoon vzvodnyi (n.m.)
commanding komandnyi (adj.)
nachal'stvuyushchii (adj.)
commandment zapoved' (n.f.)
commensurable soizmerimyi (adj.)
commentary kommentarii (n.m.)
commercial kommercheskii (adj.)
commissar komissar (n.m.)
commissar, military voenkom (n.m.)
commissariat komissariat (n.m.)
commission komissionnyi (adj.)
komissiya (n.f.)
commission, state planning gosplan (n.m.)
commit obyazyvat' (v.impf.)
predat' (v.pf.)
predavat' (v.impf.)
uchinit' (v.pf.)
commit a sin sogreshit' (v.pf.)
committee komitet (n.m.)
committee, district raikom (n.m.)
committee, executive ispolkom (n.m.)
committee, factory zavkom (n.m.)
committee, local trade-union mestkom
(n.m.)
committee, regional obkom (n.m.)
common obshchii (adj.)
commonplace banal'nyi (adj.)
propisnoi (adj.)
commotion sutoloka (n.f.)
communal kommunal'nyi (adj.)
communard kommunar (n.m.)

commune kommuna (n.f.)
communicate snestis' (v.pf.)
svyazyvat'sya (v.impf.)
communication kommunikatsiya (n.f.)
svyaz' (n.f.)
communism kommunizm (n.m.)
communist kommunist (n.m.)
community obshchina (n.f.)
obshchnost' (n.f.)
commutator pereklyuchatel' (n.m.)
compact kompaktnyi (adj.)
companion kompan'on (n.m.)
company kompaniya (n.f.)
rota (n.f.)
truppa (n.f.)
compare pomerit'sya (v.pf.)
slichat' (v.impf.)
sopostavit' (v.pf.)
sravnit' (v.pf.)
sravnivat' (v.impf.)
comparison sravnenie (n.n.)
compartment kupe (n.n.)
otsek (n.m.)
compass kompas (n.m.)
tsirkul' (n.m.)
compassion sostradanie (n.n.)
compassionate zhalostlivyi (adj.)
compatible sovmestimyi (adj.)
compatriot sootechestvennik (n.m.)
compel ponudit' (v.pf.)
prinudit' (v.pf.)
zastavit' (v.pf.)
zastavlyat' (v.impf.)
compensate vozmestit' (v.pf.)
compensation kompensatsiya (n.f.)
compere konferans'e (n.m.)
competent kompetentnyi (adj.)
pravomochnyi (adj.)
competition konkurs (n.m.)
sorevnovanie (n.n.)
competitor konkurent (n.m.)
compilation kompilyatsiya (n.f.)
compiler sostavitel' (n.m.)
compiling sostavlenie (n.n.)
complain nyt' (v.impf.)
pozhalovat'sya (v.pf.)
setovat' (v.impf.)
zhalovat'sya (v.impf.)

complaint zhaloba (n.f.)
complete dodelat' (v.pf.)
   ukomplektovat' (v.pf.)
   zakonchennyi (adj.)
   zavershat' (v.impf.)
complete set komplekt (n.m.)
completely dochista (adv.)
   polnost'yu (adv.)
   spolna (adv.)
completeness polnota (n.f.)
completion dovershenie (n.n.)
complex kompleks (n.m.)
compliant pokladistyi (adj.)
   sgovorchivyi (adj.)
complicate matters unnecessarily mudrit'
   (v.impf.)
complication oslozhnenie (n.n.)
   slozhnost' (n.f.)
   uslozhnenie (n.n.)
compliment kompliment (n.m.)
component slagayushchaya (n.f.)
   sostavlyayushchaya (n.f.)
composer kompozitor (n.m.)
composition sochinenie (n.n.)
   sostav (n.m.)
   sostavlenie (n.n.)
compote kompot (n.m.)
comprehend osmyslit' (v.pf.)
   postich' (v.pf.)
   postigat' (v.impf.)
comprehensive vsestoronnii (adj.)
compress kompress (n.m.)
   szhat' (v.pf.)
   szhimat' (v.impf.)
compression szhatie (n.n.)
compromise komprometirovat' (v.impf.)
   kompromiss (n.m.)
compulsory obyazatel'nyi (adj.)
   prinuditel'nyi (adj.)
computer, electronic elektronno
   vychislitel'naya mashina (n.f.)
comrade tovarishch (n.m.)
comrade, as a po-tovarishcheski (adv.)
comrade-in-arms soratnik (n.m.)
   spodvizhnik (n.m.)
concave vognutyi (adj.)
conceal tait' (v.impf.)
   utaivat' (v.impf.)

concealed, to be kryt'sya (v.impf.)
concealment ukryvatel'stvo (n.n.)
conceit samomnenie (n.n.)
conceivable myslimyi (adj.)
conceive zaberemenet' (v.pf.)
conceive hatred for voznenavidet' (v.pf.)
concentrate skontsentrirovat' (v.pf.)
concentration kontsentratsiya (n.f.)
   obogashchenie (n.n.)
   sosredotochennost' (n.f.)
conception kontseptsiya (n.f.)
   zachatie (n.n.)
   zarozhdenie (n.n.)
concerning naschet (prep.)
concert kontsert (n.m.)
concert, in zaodno (adv.)
concession kontsessiya (n.f.)
   ustupka (n.f.)
conclude zaklyuchat' (v.impf.)
conclusion kontsovka (n.f.)
   vyvod (n.m.)
   zaklyuchenie (n.n.)
concord sodruzhestvo (n.n.)
concrete beton (n.m.)
   konkretnyi (adj.)
concrete mixer betonomeshalka (n.f.)
concrete, reinforced zhelezobeton (n.m.)
concur sovpadat' (v.impf.)
condemn obrech' (v.pf.)
   obrekat' (v.impf.)
   prisudit' (v.pf.)
condemned obrechennyi (adj.)
condensation kondensatsiya (n.f.)
condescend snizoiti (v.pf.)
condescension sniskhoditel'nost' (n.f.)
condition sostoyanie (n.n.)
   uslovie (n.n.)
condition, good ispravnost' (n.f.)
conditional uslovnyi (adj.)
condition obstanovka (n.f.)
condolence soboleznovanie (n.n.)
conduct povedenie (n.n.)
   provesti (v.pf.)
   provodit' (v.impf.)
   vedenie (n.n.)
   vesti (v.impf.)
conductivity provodimost' (n.f.)
conductivity, electrical elektroprovodnost' (n.f.)

conductor dirizher (n.m.)
    konduktor (n.m.)
    provodnik (n.m.)
conductor, lightning gromootvod (n.m.)
cone konus (n.m.)
    shishka (n.f.)
conference konferentsiya (n.f.)
    soveshchanie (n.n.)
conference, press press-konferentsiya (n.f.)
confess ispovedovat' (v.impf.)
    pokayat'sya (v.pf.)
    priznavat'(sya) (v.impf.)
confession ispoved' (n.f.)
    pokayanie (n.n.)
confidence uverennost' (n.f.)
confidential konfidentsial'nyi (adj.)
confirm podtverdit' (v.pf.)
confiscate iz"yat' (v.pf.)
confiscation iz"yatie (n.n.)
    konfiskatsiya (n.f.)
conflict konflikt (n.m.)
confluence sliyanie (n.n.)
    stechenie (n.n.)
conform soobrazovat' (v.impf.)
confuse pereputat' (v.pf.)
    smutit' (v.pf.)
    sputat' (v.pf.)
confused sbivchivyi (adj.)
confused, to be stushevat'sya (v.pf.)
confusion nerazberikha (n.f.)
    neuryaditsa (n.f.)
    putanitsa (n.f.)
    rasteryannost' (n.f.)
    smyatenie (n.n.)
    sumbur (n.m.)
    zameshatel'stvo (n.n.)
confusion, in vperemeshku (adv.)
congeal zastyvat' (v.impf.)
congratulate pozdravit' (v.pf.)
congress kongress (n.m.)
    s"ezd (n.m.)
conic konicheskii (adj.)
conical konusoobraznyi (adj.)
coniferous khvoinyi (adj.)
conjugal brachnyi (adj.)
conjugate spryagat' (v.impf.)
conjunction soyuz (n.m.)

connected svyazannyi (adj.)
connecting soedinitel'nyi (adj.)
connection podsoedinenie (n.n.)
    svyaz' (n.f.)
connivance popustitel'stvo (n.n.)
connive potvorstvovat' (v.impf.)
conquest pokorenie (n.n.)
    zavoevanie (n.n.)
conscience sovest' (n.f.)
conscientious dobrosovestnyi (adj.)
    sovestlivyi (adj.)
conscious of, to be soznavat' (v.impf.)
consciousness soznanie (n.n.)
consciousness, to regain ochnut'sya (v.pf.)
consent soglasie (n.n.)
consequence posledstvie (n.n.)
    sledstvie (n.n.)
conservative konservativnyi (adj.)
    konservator (n.m.)
conservatory konservatoriya (n.f.)
consider obdumat' (v.pf.)
    rastsenivat' (v.impf.)
    schest' (v.pf.)
    schitat'sya (v.impf.)
    soobrazhat' (v.impf.)
considerable nemalyi (adj.)
    znachitel'nyi (adj.)
considerably izryadno (adv.)
consideration, to take into uchest' (v.pf.)
    uchityvat'
      (v.impf.)
considered, insufficiently neprodumannyi
    (adj.)
consist of zaklyuchat'sya (v.impf.)
console oneself uteshat'(sya) (v.impf.)
consolidation ukrupnenie (n.n.)
    uplotnenie (n.n.)
consonant soglasnyi (adj.)
conspiracy zagovor (n.m.)
conspirator zagovorshchik (n.m.)
constancy postoyanstvo (n.n.)
constant konstanta (n.f.)
    postoyannyi (adj.)
constantly neotluchno (adv.)
constellation sozvezdie (n.n.)
constipation zapor (n.m.)
constituent sostavlyayushchaya (n.f.)
constitution konstitutsiya (n.f.)

constraint stesnenie (n.n.)
constrictor, boa udav (n.m.)
construction postroenie (n.n.)
    stankostroenie (n.n.)
    stroika (n.f.)
    stroitel'stvo (n.n.)
construction, to be under stroit'sya (v.impf.)
consul konsul (n.m.)
consular konsul'skii (adj.)
consultant konsul'tant (n.m.)
consultation konsilium (n.m.)
consumer potrebitel' (n.m.)
consumption chakhotka (n.f.)
    potreblenie (n.n.)
contact kontakt (n.m.)
    soprikosnovenie (n.n.)
contact, to come into soprikasat'sya (v.impf.)
    soprikosnut'sya (v.pf.)
contain vmeshchat' (v.impf.)
container tara (n.f.)
contemplate sozertsat' (v.impf.)
contemporary rovesnik (n.m.)
    sovremennyi (adj.)
    sverstnik (n.m.)
contempt prezrenie (n.n.)
contemptuous prezritel'nyi (adj.)
content dovol'nyi (adj.)
content, rich in soderzhatel'nyi (adj.)
content, to be dovol'stvovat'sya (v.impf.)
contents oglavlenie (n.n.)
    soderzhimoe (n.n.)
contest sostyazanie (n.n.)
context kontekst (n.m.)
contiguity smezhnost' (n.f.)
continent kontinent (n.m.)
continental kontinental'nyi (adj.)
continue dlit'sya (v.impf.)
    prodolzhat' (v.impf.)
continuity nepreryvnost' (n.f.)
    preemstvennost' (n.f.)
continuous bespreryvnyi (adj.)
contort korchit' (v.impf.)
contour kontur (n.m.)
contraband kontrabanda (n.f.)
contract kontrakt (n.m.)
    podryad (n.m.)
contradiction protivorechie (n.n.)
contradictory raznorechivyi (adj.)

contrary vrazrez (adv.)
contrary, on the naprotiv (adv.)
contrary to naperekor (adv.)
contrast kontrast (n.m.)
    protivopolozhnost' (n.f.)
contribution kontributsiya (n.f.)
    vklad (n.m.)
contrive izlovchit'sya (v.pf.)
    ukhitrit'sya (v.pf.)
    umudrit'sya (v.pf.)
control kontrol' (n.m.)
    sovladat' (v.pf.)
control oneself sderzhivat'(sya) (v.impf.)
controller dispetcher (n.m.)
    kontroler (n.m.)
controversy polemika (n.f.)
convection konvektsiya (n.f.)
convention konventsiya (n.f.)
conversation beseda (n.f.)
    razgovor (n.m.)
conversion konversiya (n.f.)
convert pretvorit' (v.pf.)
converter preobrazovatel' (n.m.)
conveyer konveier (n.m.)
    transporter (n.m.)
conviction, previous sudimost' (n.f.)
convince ubedit' (v.pf.)
    ubezhdat' (v.impf.)
convocation sozyv (n.m.)
convolution izvilina (n.f.)
convoy konvoi (n.m.)
    konvoirovat' (v.impf.)
convulsion konvul'siya (n.f.)
coo vorkovat' (v.impf.)
cook kukharka (n.f.)
    povar (n.m.)
    stryapat' (v.impf.)
    svarit' (v.pf.)
cookies pechen'e (n.n.)
cooking varka (n.f.)
cool ostudit' (v.pf.)
    studit' (v.impf.)
cool, it is svezho (adj.)
cool, to get stynut' (v.impf.)
coolness khladnokrovie (n.n.)
    prokhlada (n.f.)
cooped up, to be yutit'sya (v.impf.)
cooperation kooperatsiya (n.f.)

sotrudnichestvo (n.n.)

cooperative kooperativ (n.m.)

co-opt kooptirovat' (v.impf.&pf.)

coordinate uvyazat' (v.pf.)
uvyazyvat' (v.impf.)

coordination koordinatsiya (n.f.)
soglasovanie (n.n.)

coordination, lack of raznoboi (n.m.)

copper med' (n.f.)
mednyi (adj.)

copper-smelting medeplavil'nyi (adj.)

coppersmith mednik (n.m.)

copy kopirovat' (v.impf.)
kopiya (n.f.)
perepisat' (v.pf.)
spisat' (v.pf.)
srisovat' (v.pf.)

copy, rough chernovik (n.m.)

copying kopiroval'nyi (adj.)

coquette koketka (n.f.)

coral korall (n.m.)

cord, umbilical pupovina (n.f.)

cordial zadushevnyi (adj.)

cordiality radushie (n.n.)

cordially teplo (adv.)

cordon kordon (n.m.)

core serdtsevina (n.f.)

co-report sodoklad (n.m.)

cork probka (n.f.)

corkscrew shtopor (n.m.)

corn zhito (n.n.)

corn bin zakrom (n.m.)

corned beef solonina (n.f.)

corner uglovoi (adj.)
ugol (n.m.)
ugolok (n.m.)

cornerstone kraeugol'nyi kamen' (adj.-n.m.)

cornfield niva (n.f.)

cornflower vasilek (n.m.)

cornice karniz (n.m.)

corporal telesnyi (adj.)

corporal, lance efreitor (n.m.)

corporation korporatsiya (n.f.)

corpse mertvets (n.m.)
trup (n.m.)

corpulent dorodnyi (adj.)
gruznyi (adj.)

correct ispravit' (v.pf.)

korrektirovat' (v.impf.)
korrektnyi (adj.)
pravil'nyi (adj.)
vernyi (adj.)
vypravit' (v.pf.)

correction popravka (n.f.)

correctional ispravitel'nyi (adj.)

correctly verno (adv.)

correctness vernost' (n.f.)

correlation sootnoshenie (n.n.)
vzaimosvyaz' (n.f.)

correspondence perepiska (n.f.)

correspondent korrespondent (n.m.)

corresponding member chlen korrespondent (n.m.)

corridor koridor (n.m.)

corrode proedat' (v.impf.)
proest' (v.pf.)
raz"edat' (v.impf.)

corrosion korroziya (n.f.)

corrosive sublimate sulema (n.f.)

corrugated gofrirovannyi (adj.)
riflenyi (adj.)

corrupt razlagat' (v.impf.)
razlozhit' (v.pf.)
razvrashchat' (v.impf.)

corruption korruptsiya (n.f.)

coryphaeus korifei (n.m.)

cosine kosinus (n.m.)

cosmetics kosmetika (n.f.)

cosmic kosmicheskii (adj.)

cosmodrome kosmodrom (n.m.)

cosmogony kosmogoniya (n.f.)

cosmonaut kosmonavt (n.m.)

cosmopolitan kosmopolit (n.m.)

cosmos kosmos (n.m.)

cossack kazak (n.m.)

cost stoit' (v.impf.)

cost, prime sebestoimost' (n.f.)

cotangent kotangens (n.m.)

cottage cheese tvorog (n.m.)

cottage, summer dacha (n.f.)

cotton bumazhnyi (adj.)
khlopchatobumazhnyi (adj.)
khlopkovyi (adj.)
khlopok (n.m.)

cotton, printed sitets (n.m.)
sittsevyi (adj.)

cotton wool vata (n.f.)
cotton-growing khlopkovodstvo (n.n.)
couch kushetka (n.f.)
   lozhe (n.n.)
cough kashel' (n.m.)
cough, whooping koklyush (n.m.)
council sovet (n.m.)
counselor sovetnik (n.m.)
count graf (n.m.)
   otschitat' (v.pf.)
   pereschityvat' (v.impf.)
   poschitat' (v.pf.)
   schitat' (v.impf.)
   soschitat' (v.pf.)
count over again pereschitat' (v.pf.)
counter prilavok (n.m.)
   schetchik (n.m.)
   stoika (n.f.)
counteraction protivodeistvie (n.n.)
counterattack kontrataka (n.f.)
counterfeit poddelat' (v.pf.)
counterintelligence kontrrazvedka (n.f.)
counteroffensive kontrnastuplenie (n.n.)
counterpane pokryvalo (n.n.)
counterrevolution kontrrevolyutsiya (n.f.)
counterweight protivoves (n.m.)
countess grafinya (n.f.)
countless beschislennyi (adj.)
country strana (n.f.)
   zagorodnyi (adj.)
country, mother otechestvo (n.n.)
country, native otchizna (n.f.)
country (road) proselochnyi (adj.)
countryman, fellow zemlyak (n.m.)
couple cheta (n.f.)
   stsepit' (v.pf.)
couple, newly married novobrachnye (n.pl.)
couplet kuplet (n.m.)
couplets, sung chastushki (n.pl.)
coupling stsepka (n.f.)
coupon kupon (n.m.)
   talon (n.m.)
courage muzhestvo (n.n.)
   smelost' (n.f.)
courage, to lose strusit' (v.impf.)
courageous smelyi (adj.)
course kurs (n.m.)

course, second vtoroe (n.n.)
courses kursy (n.pl.)
court dvor (n.m.)
   dvortsovyi (adj.)
   kort (n.m.)
   sud (n.m.)
court of appeal kassatsionnyi sud (adj.-n.m.)
court of arbitration treteiskii sud (adj.-n.m.)
courtesy predupreditel'nost' (n.f.)
court-martial voenno-polevoi sud (adj.-n.m.)
cousin dvoyurodnyi (adj.)
cover chekhol (n.m.)
   futlyar (n.m.)
   kryshka (n.f.)
   kryt' (v.impf.)
   nakryt' (v.pf.)
   naves (n.m.)
   obit' (v.pf.)
   obivat' (v.impf.)
   oblozhka (n.f.)
   obtyanut' (v.pf.)
   osypat' (v.impf.)
   pelena (n.f.)
   pokrov (n.m.)
   pokryshka (n.f.)
   prikrytie (n.n.)
   zastilat' (v.impf.)
   zaveshivat' (v.impf.)
cover oneself nakryvat'sya (v.impf.)
   prikryvat'sya (v.impf.)
cover up ukryt' (v.pf.)
   zamesti (v.pf.)
   zametat' (v.impf.)
covered with ispeshchrennyi (adj.)
covered with a thin film of, to be
      podernut'sya (v.pf.)
covering pokrytie (n.n.)
cow korova (n.f.)
coward trus (n.m.)
cowardice malodushie (n.n.)
   trusost' (n.f.)
cowardly truslivyi (adj.)
coziness uyut (n.m.)
CPSU (Communist Party of the Soviet Union)
   KPSS (Kommunisticheskaya Partiya
   Sovetskogo Soyuza) (abbr.)
crab krab (n.m.)

crack potreskat'sya (v.pf.)
    rassokhnut'sya (v.pf.)
    rassykhat'sya (v.impf.)
    rastreskat'sya (v.pf.)
    treshchat' (v.impf.)
    treshchina (n.f.)
    treskat'sya (v.impf.)
    tresnut' (v.pf.)
cracking tresk (n.m.)
cracking process, petroleum kreking (n.m.)
crackle potreskivat' (v.impf.)
cradle kolybel' (n.f.)
    lyul'ka (n.f.)
craftsman remeslennik (n.m.)
cram napikhat' (v.pf.)
    zastavit' (v.pf.)
    zazubrit' (v.pf.)
    zubrit' (v.impf.)
cramp skoba (n.f.)
    sudoroga (n.f.)
cranberry klyukva (n.f.)
crane pod"emnyi kran (adj.-n.m.)
    zhuravl' (n.m.)
craniology kraniologiya (n.f.)
crank chudak (n.m.)
cranked kolenchatyi (adj.)
crash grokhnut'sya (v.pf.)
    grokhot (n.m.)
    krakh (n.m.)
    razbivat'(sya) (v.impf.)
crater krater (n.m.)
crawl krol' (n.m.)
    polzat' (v.impf.)
    raspolzat'sya (v.impf.)
crawl away otpolzat' (v.impf.)
    upolzat' (v.impf.)
crawl in vpolzat' (v.impf.)
crawl out vypolzat' (v.impf.)
crawl over perepolzat' (v.impf.)
crawling polzkom (adv.)
crayfish rak (n.m)
crazy pomeshannyi (adj.)
creak skrip (n.m.)
    skripet' (v.impf.)
    skripnut' (v.pf.)
    zaskripet' (v.pf.)
cream krem (n.m.)

    slivki (n.pl.)
cream, sour smetana (n.f.)
cream-colored kremovyi (adj.)
crease skladka (n.f.)
create sozdavat' (v.impf.)
    sozidat' (v.impf.)
    tvorit' (v.impf.)
creation sozdanie (n.n.)
    tvorenie (n.n.)
creative tvorcheskii (adj.)
creature tvar' (n.f.)
creatures, fellow blizhnie (n.pl.)
credentials veritel'naya gramota (adj.-n.f.)
credit kredit (n.m.)
credit, letter of akkreditiv (n.m.)
credit, on zaimoobrazno (adv.)
credit the account zaprikhodovat' (v.pf.)
credulous legkovernyi (adj.)
creed verovanie (n.n.)
creep presmykat'sya (v.impf.)
creep in zapolzat' (v.impf.)
crematorium krematorii (n.m.)
crepe krep (n.m.)
crescent serpovidnyi (adj.)
crevice rasshchelina (n.f.)
crew ékipazh (n.m.)
crib shpargalka (n.f.)
    yasli (n.pl.)
cricket sverchok (n.m.)
crime prestuplenie (n.n.)
Crimean krymskii (adj.)
criminal kriminal'nyi (adj.)
    prestupnik (n.m.)
    ugolovnyi (adj.)
crimson obagrit' (v.pf.)
    puntsovyi (adj.)
cripple iskalechit' (v.pf.)
    izuvechit' (v.pf.)
    kalechit' (v.impf.)
    kaleka (n.m.&f.)
crisis krizis (n.m.)
crisscross krest-nakrest (adv.)
criterion kriterii (n.m.)
critic kritik (n.m.)
    retsenzent (n.m.)
criticize raskritikovat' (v.pf.)
croak karkat' (v.impf.)

kvakat' (v.impf.)
crocodile krokodil (n.m.)
crooked krivoi (adj.)
crop urozhai (n.m.)
crop failure neurozhai (n.m.)
crop rotation sevooborot (n.m.)
crop, spring yarovoi (adj.)
crops, winter ozimye (n.pl.)
croquet kroket (n.m.)
cross krest (n.m.)
    pereiti (v.pf.)
    perekreshchivat'sya (v.impf.)
    perekrestnyi (adj.)
    peresech'(sya) (v.pf.)
    perestupat' (v.impf.)
    perevalit' (v.pf.)
    skreshchivat' (v.impf.)
    skrestit' (v.pf.)
cross beam perekladina (n.f.)
cross out perecherkivat' (v.impf.)
crossing pereezd (n.m.)
    perekhod (n.m.)
    pereprava (n.f.)
crossroads perekrestok (n.m.)
    pereput'e (n.n.)
    rasput'e (n.n.)
crosswise nakrest (adv.)
crow kukarekat' (v.impf.)
    vorona (n.f.)
crowbar lom (n.m.)
crowd gur'ba (n.f.)
    sborishche (n.n.)
    stolpit'sya (v.pf.)
    tolpa (n.f.)
crowded lyudnyi (adj.)
    mnogolyudnyi (adj.)
crown korona (n.f.)
    koronka (n.f.)
    koronovat' (v.impf&.pf.)
    makushka (n.f.)
    temya (n.n.)
    uvenchat' (v.pf.)
    venets (n.m.)
crucible tigel' (n.m.)
cruel zhestokii (adj.)
cruiser kreiser (n.m.)
crumb krokha (n.f.)

kroshka (n.f.)
crumble iskroshit' (v.pf.)
    kroshit' (v.impf.)
    raskroshit' (v.pf.)
crumbly rykhlyi (adj.)
crumple komkat' (v.impf.)
    myat' (v.impf.)
    skomkat' (v.pf.)
    smyat' (v.pf.)
crumpled pomyatyi (adj.)
crunch khrust (n.m.)
    khrustet' (v.impf.)
crush davka (n.f.)
    drobit' (v.impf.)
    izmyat' (v.pf.)
    otdavit' (v.pf.)
    razdavit' (v.pf.)
    tolcheya (n.f.)
    tolkotnya (n.f.)
    zadavit' (v.pf.)
crush into pieces razmel'chat' (v.impf.)
crushed stone shcheben' (n.m.)
crust gorbushka (n.f.)
    korka (n.f.)
crutch kostyl' (n.m.)
cry vykrik (n.m.)
cry out vskrikivat' (v.impf.)
    vykrikivat' (v.impf.)
    zakrichat' (v.pf.)
crybaby plaksa (n.f.)
crying vopiyushchii (adj.)
cryogenic kriogennyi (adj.)
crystal khrustal' (n.m.)
    kristall (n.m.)
crystal clear kristal'nyi (adj.)
crystalline lens khrustalik (n.m.)
crystallography kristallografiya (n.f.)
cub, wolf volchonok (n.m.)
cube kub (n.m.)
cubic kubicheskii (adj.)
cubic meter kubometr (n.m.)
cuckoo kukovat' (v.impf.)
    kukushka (n.f.)
cucumber ogurets (n.m.)
cud zhvachka (n.f.)
cudgel dubina (n.f.)
cue kii (n.m.)

cuff manzheta (n.f.)
　　obshlag (n.m.)
cuff link zaponka (n.f.)
culinary kulinarnyi (adj.)
　　povarennyi (adj.)
culminating kul'minatsionnyi (adj.)
culprit vinovnik (n.m.)
cult kul't (n.m.)
cultivate kul'tivirovat' (v.impf.)
　　obrabatyvat' (v.impf.)
　　vozdelat' (v.pf.)
cultivation obrabotka (n.f.)
　　propashka (n.f.)
cultivation of flax l'novodstvo (n.n.)
cultural and educational work kul'trabota
　　　(n.f.)
culture kul'tura (n.f.)
culture, physical fizkul'tura (n.f.)
cultured intelligentnyi (adj.)
　　kul'turnyi (adj.)
cumbersome gromozdkii (adj.)
cunning khitrost' (n.f.)
cunning, to be khitrit' (v.impf.)
cunning, to use skhitrit' (v.pf.)
cup chashka (n.f.)
curative tselebnyi (adj.)
cure istselenie (n.n.)
　　izlechivat' (v.impf.)
　　vylechit' (v.pf.)
cured, to be vylechivat'(sya) (v.impf.)
curing vulkanizatsiya (n.f.)
curious lyubopytnyi (adj.)
　　lyuboznatel'nyi (adj.)
curl lokon (n.m.)
　　zavit' (v.pf.)
　　zavitok (n.m.)
curled zavitoi (adj.)
curls kudri (n.pl.)
curly kurchavyi (adj.)
　　v'yushchiisya (adj.)
currant smorodina (n.f.)
currency valyuta (n.f.)
current potok (n.m.)
　　techenie (n.n.)
　　tekushchii (adj.)
　　tok (n.m.)
curse proklinat' (v.impf.)

curtail svorachivat' (v.impf.)
curtain zanaves (n.m.)
　　zanavesit' (v.impf.)
curtains polog (n.m.)
curvature krivizna (n.f.)
curve krivaya (n.f.)
　　vygibat' (v.impf.)
　　zakruglenie (n.n.)
curved izognutyi (adj.)
custom obychai (n.m.)
customs nravy (n.pl.)
　　tamozhennyi (adj.)
cut kroit' (v.impf.)
　　narezat' (v.pf.)
　　ostrich' (v.pf.)
　　ostrigat' (v.impf.)
　　pererezat' (v.impf.)
　　pererubat' (v.impf.)
　　podrezat' (v.impf.)
　　podstrich' (v.pf.)
　　pokroi (n.m.)
　　porez (n.m.)
　　rassech' (v.pf.)
　　razrez (n.m.)
　　rezat' (v.impf.)
　　srez (n.m.)
　　strich' (v.impf.)
　　vyrez (n.m.)
　　vysech' (v.pf.)
　　vysekat' (v.impf.)
cut down urezat' (v.impf.)
　　vyrubat' (v.impf.)
cut into vrezat'sya (v.pf.)
cut off obrezat' (v.impf.)
　　otklyuchat' (v.impf.)
　　otrezat' (v.impf.)
　　otrubat' (v.impf.)
　　otrubit' (v.pf.)
　　otsekat' (v.impf.)
　　otstrigat' (v.impf.)
　　srezat' (v.impf.)
cut out vykraivat' (v.impf.)
　　vykroit' (v.pf.)
　　vyrezat' (v.impf.)
　　vyrezyvat' (v.impf.)
cut, small nadrez (n.m.)
cut through prorezat' (v.impf.)

cut to pieces　izrezat' (v.pf.)
cutlet　kotleta (n.f.)
cutter　kater (n.m.)
　　zakroishchik (n.m.)
cutthroat　golovorez (n.m.)
cutting out　kroika (n.f.)
cyanide　tsianid (n.m.)
cybernetics　kibernetika (n.f.)
cycle　tsikl (n.m.)

cyclone　tsiklon (n.m.)
cylinder　ballon (n.m.)
　　tsilindr (n.m.)
　　valik (n.m.)
cynicism　tsinizm (n.m.)
cypress　kiparis (n.m.)
cytology　tsitologiya (n.f.)
Czech　chekh (n.m.)
　　cheshskii (adj.)

D　(Д)

dachshund　taksa (n.f.)
daddy　papa (n.m.)
dagger　kinzhal (n.m.)
dahlia　georgin (n.m.)
daily　dnevnoi (adj.)
　　ezhednevno (adv.)
　　kazhdodnevnyi (adj.)
　　povsednevnyi (adj.)
　　sutochnyi (adj.)
dairy　maslozavod (n.m.)
dairy, cheese　syrovarnya (n.f.)
daisy　margaritka (n.f.)
daisy, ox-eye　romashka (n.f.)
dam　damba (n.f.)
　　plotina (n.f.)
　　zapruda (n.f.)
damage　porcha (n.f.)
　　povredit' (v.pf.)
　　ushcherb (n.m.)
damp　syroi (adj.)
damp, to become　otsyret' (v.pf.)
dampen one's ardor　raskholazhivat' (v.impf.)
dampness　syrost' (n.f.)
dance　khorovod (n.m.)
　　plyasat' (v.impf.)
　　plyaska (n.f.)
　　tanets (n.m.)
dancer　tantsor (n.m.)
dancer, ballet　balerina (n.f.)
dandelion　oduvanchik (n.m.)
dandruff　perkhot' (n.f.)
dandy　frant (n.m.)

　　shchegol' (n.m.)
danger　opasnost' (n.f.)
dangle　boltat'sya (v.impf.)
　　motat'sya (v.impf.)
　　sveshivat'(sya) (v.impf.)
　　svesit' (v.pf.)
Danish　datskii (adj.)
dare　derzat' (v.impf.)
　　derznut' (v.pf.)
　　osmelivat'sya (v.impf.)
　　posmet' (v.pf.)
　　smet' (v.impf.)
daredevil　smel'chak (n.m.)
daring　derznovennyi (adj.)
dark　mrachnyi (adj.)
　　smuglyi (adj.)
　　temno (adj.)
　　temnyi (adj.)
dark, in the　vpot'makh (adv.)
dark, the　potemki (n.pl.)
dark, to get　smerkat'sya (v.impf.)
dark, to grow　potemnet' (v.pf.)
　　stemnet' (v.pf.)
　　temnet' (v.impf.)
darken　omrachit' (v.pf.)
　　zatemnyat' (v.impf.)
dark-haired　temnovolosyi (adj.)
dark-haired man　bryunet (n.m.)
darkness　mrak (n.m.)
　　t'ma (n.f.)
　　temnota (n.f.)
darn　shtopat' (v.impf.)

dart shmygat' (v.impf.)
dart off pomchat'sya (v.pf.)
Darwinism darvinizm (n.m.)
dash tire (n.n.)
dashing likhoi (adj.)
data dannye (n.pl.)
date data (n.f.)
    datirovat' (v.impf.)
    finik (n.m.)
    srok (n.m.)
    svidanie (n.n.)
dative datel'nyi (adj.)
daub maznya (n.f.)
daughter dochka (n.f.)
daughter-in-law nevestka (n.f.)
    snokha (n.f.)
dawn rassvesti (v.pf.)
    svetat' (v.impf.)
    zarya (n.f.)
dawn, before zatemno (adv.)
day den' (n.m.)
    dnevnoi (adj.)
    sutki (n.pl.)
day after tomorrow poslezavtra (adv.)
day before yesterday pozavchera (adv.)
day, the next nazavtra (adv.)
day, the other na dnyakh (adv.)
daybreak rassvet (n.m.)
day-off vykhodnoi (adj.)
days, one of these na dnyakh (adv.)
daytime, in the dnem (adv.)
dazzle zaryabit' (v.pf.)
dead dokhlyi (adj.)
    mertvyi (adj.)
    umershii (adj.)
dead, half polumertvyi (adj.)
dead, like one zamerto (adv.)
dead, service for the panikhida (n.f.)
deaden zaglushat' (v.impf.)
deadly ubiistvennyi (adj.)
deaf, the glukhie (n.collect.)
deaf, to become oglokhnut' (v.pf.)
deaf, to grow glokhnut' (v.impf.)
deafen oglushit' (v.pf.)
deaf-mute glukhonemoi (adj.)
deafness glukhota (n.f.)
deal in torgovat' (v.impf.)
dean dekan (n.m.)

death konchina (n.f.)
    predsmertnyi (adj.)
    smert' (n.f.)
death, torture to zamuchit' (v.pf.)
deathly mertvennyi (adj.)
debase oposhlit' (v.pf.)
debate debaty (n.pl.)
    preniya (n.pl.)
debit debet (n.m.)
debt dolg (n.m.)
debtor dolzhnik (n.m.)
debts zadolzhennost' (n.f.)
debunk razvenchat' (v.pf)
debut debyut (n.m.)
decade desyatiletie (n.n.)
decay istlevat' (v.impf.)
    razlozhenie (n.n.)
    zagnivanie (n.n.)
decayed obvetshalyi (adj.)
deceased, the pokoinik (n.m.)
    pokoinyi (adj.)
deceive obmanut' (v.pf.)
deceleration zamedlenie (n.n.)
December dekabr' (n.m.)
decency prilichie (n.n.)
deceptive obmanchivyi (adj.)
decide reshat' (v.impf.)
    reshit' (v.pf.)
decided, to be razreshat'sya (v.impf.)
deciduous listvennyi (adj.)
decimal desyatichnyi (adj.)
decipher rasshifrovat' (v.pf.)
decisive reshitel'nyi (adj.)
deck paluba (n.f.)
deck, all hands on avral (n.m.)
deckhouse rubka (n.f.)
declaration deklaratsiya (n.f.)
    zayavlenie (n.n.)
declare ob"yavit' (v.pf.)
    zayavit' (v.pf.)
declension sklonenie (n.n.)
declinable sklonyaemyi (adj.)
decline sklonyat' (v.impf.)
    upadok (n.m.)
declined, to be sklonyat'sya (v.impf.)
decompose razlagat' (v.impf.)
    razlozhit' (v.pf.)
decompression razgermetizatsiya (n.f.)

decontamination degazatsiya (n.f.)
   dezaktivatsiya (n.f.)
decorate razukrasit' (v.pf.)
   ubirat' (v.impf.)
   ubrat' (v.pf.)
   ukrashat' (v.impf.)
   ukrasit' (v.pf.)
decorated with painting raspisnoi (adj.)
decoration ubranstvo (n.n.)
decrease ubavlenie (n.n.)
   ubavlyat'(sya) (v.impf.)
   ubyl' (n.f.)
   ubyt' (v.pf.)
   ubyvat' (v.impf.)
   umen'shat'sya (v.impf.)
decree dekret (n.m.)
   postanovit' (v.pf.)
   ukaz (n.m.)
decrepit dryakhlyi (adj.)
decrepit, to become odryakhlet' (v.pf.)
deduct otchislit' (v.pf.)
   vychest' (v.pf.)
   vychitat' (v.impf.)
deduction otchislenie (n.n.)
   uderzhanie (n.n.)
   umozaklyuchenie (n.n.)
   vychet (n.m.)
deed, good blagodeyanie (n.n.)
de-energize otklyuchat' (v.impf.)
deep besprobudnyi (adj.)
   glubokii (adj.)
   vglub' (adv.)
deepen uglubit' (v.impf.)
   uglublyat' (v.impf.)
deepening uglublenie (n.n.)
deeply gluboko (adv.)
defame oporochit' (v.pf.)
defaulter neplatel'shchik (n.m.)
defeat porazhenie (n.n.)
defect brak (n.m.)
   defekt (n.m.)
   iz"yan (n.m.)
defective nepolnotsennyi (adj.)
defects nepoladki (n.pl.)
defend oboronyat' (v.impf.)
   otstaivat' (v.impf.)
   otstoyat' (v.pf.)
   zashchishchat' (v.impf.)

defendant otvetchik (n.m.)
defender zastupnik (n.m.)
defense oborona (n.f.)
   zashchita (n.f.)
defense capability oboronosposobnost' (n.f.)
defenseless bezzashchitnyi (adj.)
defiant vyzyvayushchii (adj.)
deficit defitsit (n.m.)
   nedochet (n.m.)
   nedostacha (n.f.)
define opredelit' (v.pf.)
definite opredelennyi (adj.)
definition opredelenie (n.n.)
deflection otklonenie (n.n.)
deflector otrazhatel' (n.m.)
deform iskoverkat' (v.pf.)
degenerate pererodit'sya (v.pf.)
   vyrodit'sya (v.pf.)
degeneration pererozhdenie (n.n.)
   vyrozhdenie (n.n.)
degree gradus (n.m.)
   stepen' (n.f.)
dehydration obezvozhivanie (n.n.)
dehydrogenation degidrirovanie (n.n.)
dejected prishiblennyi (adj.)
   unyvat' (v.impf.)
delay otlagatel'stvo (n.n.)
   ottyagivat' (v.impf.)
   promedlenie (n.n.)
   zaderzhka (n.f.)
   zapazdyvanie (n.n.)
delayed, to be zatyanut'sya (v.pf.)
delaying zatyazhka (n.f.)
delegation delegatsiya (n.f.)
deliberate demonstrativnyi (adj.)
   narochityi (adj.)
   obdumannyi (adj.)
   umyshlennyi (adj.)
delicious, to be ob"edenie (n.n.)
delight naslazhdenie (n.n.)
   usladit' (v.pf.)
   voskhishchat' (v.impf.)
   vostorg (n.m.)
delightful voskhititel'nyi (adj.)
delinquent pravonarushitel' (n.m.)
delirium bred (n.m.)
deliver dostavit' (v.pf.)
   dostavlyat' (v.impf.)

raznesti (v.pf.)
razvezti (v.pf.)
razvozit' (v.impf.)
vruchat' (v.impf.)
zavezti (v.pf.)
deliverer izbavitel' (n.m.)
delivery postavka (n.f.)
dell loshchina (n.f.)
deluge potop (n.m.)
demagnetize razmagnichivat' (v.impf.)
demagogue demagog (n.m.)
demand spros (n.m.)
trebovat' (v.impf.)
demand, in great naraskhvat (adv.)
demarcation demarkatsionnyi (adj.)
razgranichenie (n.n.)
razmezhevanie (n.n.)
demilitarization demilitarizatsiya (n.f.)
demobilization demobilizatsiya (n.f.)
democracy demokratiya (n.f.)
democrat demokrat (n.m.)
demon bes (n.m.)
demonstration demonstratsiya (n.f.)
manifestatsiya (n.f.)
demonstrative demonstrativnyi (adj.)
demoralization demoralizatsiya (n.f.)
demote razzhalovat' (v.pf.)
den berloga (n.f.)
denial otpiratel'stvo (n.n.)
zapiratel'stvo (n.n.)
denominator znamenatel' (n.m.)
dense dremuchii (adj.)
skuchennyi (adj.)
density plotnost' (n.f.)
udel (n.m.)
dental zubnoi (adj.)
zubovrachebnyi (adj.)
denunciation donos (n.m.)
denunciatory oblichitel'hyi (adj.)
deny otperet'sya (v.pf.)
otpirat'sya (v.impf.)
otritsat' (v.impf.)
deoxidation raskislenie (n.n.)
department fakul'tet (n.m.)
otdel (n.m.)
vedomstvo (n.n.)
departure ot''ezd (n.m.)
otkhod (n.m.)

otplytie (n.n.)
ukhod (n.m.)
vyezd (n.m.)
depend zaviset' (v.impf.)
dependent izhdivenets (n.m.)
podnevol'nyi (adj.)
dependent on podvlastnyi (adj.)
depersonalize obezlichivat' (v.impf.)
deposit mestorozhdenie (n.n.)
nanos (n.m.)
otlozhenie (n.n.)
vklad (n.m.)
zadatok (n.m.)
zalezh' (n.f.)
zalog (n.m.)
deposition osazhdenie (n.n.)
pokazanie (n.n.)
depositor vkladchik (n.m.)
depot depo (n.n.)
depreciation amortizatsiya (n.f.)
obestsenenie (n.n.)
depress udruchat' (v.impf.)
depressed udruchennyi (adj.)
depressing gnetushchii (adj.)
depression depressiya (n.f.)
podavlennost' (n.f.)
deprivation lishenie (n.n.)
deprive lishit' (v.pf.)
obdelit' (v.pf.)
deprived obezdolennyi (adj.)
deprived of rights bespravnyi (adj.)
depth glub' (n.f.)
glubina (n.f.)
depths nedra (n.pl.)
deputy deputat (n.m.)
derivative proizvodnyi (adj.)
derive pocherpnut' (v.pf.)
dermatology dermatologiya (n.f.)
descend snizhat'sya (v.impf.)
descendant potomok (n.m.)
descending niskhodyashchii (adj.)
descent spusk (n.m.)
describe obrisovat' (v.pf.)
opisat' (v.pf.)
opisyvat' (v.impf.)
description opisanie (n.n.)
desecrated porugannyi (adj.)
desert pustynya (n.f.)

deserted pustynnyi (adj.)
design umysel (n.m.)
designer konstruktor (n.m.)
designing proektirovanie (n.n.)
desirable zhelatel'nyi (adj.)
desk parta (n.f.)
desolate zapustelyi (adj.)
despair otchaivat'sya (v.impf.)
    otchayanie (n.n.)
    otchayat'sya (v.pf.)
despise prezirat' (v.impf.)
despot despot (n.m.)
dessert desert (n.m.)
destitution obnishchanie (n.n.)
destroy raznesti (v.pf.)
    raznosit' (v.impf.)
    razrushit' (v.pf.)
    unichtozhit' (v.pf.)
destroyer ésminets (n.m.)
destruction unichtozhenie (n.n.)
destructive gubitel'nyi (adj.)
detach otryadit' (v.pf.)
detachment otryad (n.m.)
detail detal' (n.f.)
detailed podrobnyi (adj.)
detain zaderzhat' (v.pf.)
detective syshchik (n.m.)
    sysknoi (adj.)
detention zaderzhanie (n.n.)
deterioration ukhudshenie (n.n.)
determinant opredelitel' (n.m.)
deuterium deiterii (n.m.)
devaluation deval'vatsiya (n.f.)
devastate opustoshat' (v.impf.)
develop razvivat'(sya) (v.impf.)
developer proyavitel' (n.m.)
development osvoenie (n.n.)
    razvitie (n.n.)
deviation otklonenie (n.n.)
    deviatsiya (n.f.)
    uklon (n.m.)
device apparat (n.m.)
    pribor (n.m.)
    prisposoblenie (n.n.)
    ukhishchrenie (n.n.)
    ustroistvo (n.n.)
devil chert (n.m.)
    d'yavol (n.m.)

    okayannyi (adj.)
devote posvyatit' (v.pf.)
devoted priverzhennyi (adj.)
devour pozhirat' (v.impf.)
dew rosa (n.f.)
diabetes diabet (n.m.)
diagnosis diagnoz (n.m.)
diagonal diagonal' (n.f.)
diagram diagramma (n.f.)
dial tsiferblat (n.m.)
dialect dialekt (n.m.)
    narechie (n.n.)
dialectics dialektika (n.f.)
dialogue dialog (n.m.)
diameter diametr (n.m.)
    poperechnik (n.m.)
diamond almaz (n.m.)
    bril'yant (n.m.)
diamonds bubny (n.pl.)
diaphragm diafragma (n.f.)
diarrhea ponos (n.m.)
diary dnevnik (n.m.)
dictate diktovat' (v.impf.)
    prodiktovat' (v.pf.)
dictation diktant (n.m.)
dictator diktator (n.m.)
dictatorship diktatura (n.f.)
dictionary slovar' (n.m.)
dictum izrechenie (n.n.)
die izdokhnut' (v.pf.)
    okolevat' (v.impf.)
    podokhnut' (v.pf.)
    sdokhnut' (v.pf.)
    skonchat'sya (v.pf.)
    umeret' (v.pf.)
    umirat' (v.impf.)
die away ugasat' (v.impf.)
    utikhat' (v.impf.)
    zaglokhnut' (v.pf.)
die off otmeret' (v.pf.)
die out vymeret' (v.pf.)
    vymirat' (v.impf.)
diesel dizel' (n.m.)
diet dieta (n.f.)
differ otlichat' (v.impf.)
    raznit'sya (v.impf.)
difference otlichie (n.n.)
    razlichie (n.n.)

raznitsa (n.f.)
raznost' (n.f.)
different inoi (adj.)
raznyi (adj.)
differential differentsial (n.m.)
differentiate differentsirovat' (v.impf.)
difficult trudno (adj.)
difficulty trudnost' (n.f.)
zatrudnenie (n.n.)
diffuse rasplyvchatyi (adj.)
diffusion diffuziya (n.f.)
dig kopat' (v.impf.)
podryt' (v.pf.)
podryvat' (v.impf.)
proryt' (v.pf.)
proryvat' (v.impf.)
ryt' (v.impf.)
vskapyvat' (v.impf.)
vskopat' (v.pf.)
vyryt' (v.pf.)
vyryvat' (v.impf.)
dig into vpit'sya (v.impf.)
vpivat'sya (v.impf.)
dig out raskapyvat' (v.impf.)
raskopat' (v.pf.)
vykapyvat' (v.impf.)
vykopat' (v.pf.)
dig under podkapyvat'(sya) (v.impf.)
dig up izryt' (v.pf.)
otkapyvat' (v.impf.)
otkopat' (v.pf)
razryt' (v.pf.)
razryvat' (v.impf.)
digest perevarit' (v.pf.)
perevarivat' (v.impf.)
digestible udobovarimyi (adj.)
digestion pishchevarenie (n.n.)
dignity dostoinstvo (n.n.)
dilapidated vetkhii (adj.)
diligence prilezhanie (n.n.)
staratel'nost' (n.f.)
diligent prilezhnyi (adj.)
dill ukrop (n.m.)
dilute razbavit' (v.pf.)
razvesti (v.pf.)
dim tusklyi (adj.)
dim, to grow merknut' (v.impf.)
pomerknut' (v.pf.)

potusknet' (v.pf.)
zatumanit'sya (v.pf.)
dimensions razmer (n.m.)
diminish ubavit' (v.pf.)
umen'shit' (v.pf.)
dimple yamochka (n.f.)
dining car vagon-restoran (n.m.)
dining room stolovaya (n.f.)
dinner obed (n.m.)
dinner, after posleobedennyi (adj.)
dinner, to have poobedat' (v.pf.)
diode diod (n.m.)
dip makat' (v.impf.)
obmakivat' (v.impf.)
dip stick shchup (n.m.)
diphtheria difterit (n.m.)
diphthong diftong (n.m.)
diploma diplom (n.m.)
diplomat diplomat (n.m.)
direct besperesadochnyi (adj.)
napravit' (v.pf.)
navesti (v.pf.)
navodit' (v.impf.)
neposredstvennyi (adj.)
ustremit' (v.pf.)
direction finder pelengator (n.m.)
direction, proceeding from the opposite
vstrechnyi (adj.)
directions, in all vrassypnuyu (adv.)
vrazbrod (adv.)
directness pryamota (n.f.)
director direktor (n.m.)
dirigible dirizhabl' (n.m.)
dirk kortik (n.m.)
dirt gryaz' (n.f.)
dirty gryaznyi (adj.)
nechistoplotnyi (adj.)
zamazat' (v.pf.)
zamazyvat' (v.impf.)
dirty, to make marat' (v.impf.)
perepachkat' (v.pf.)
zapachkat' (v.pf.)
disabled nerabotosposobnyi (adj.)
netrudosposobnyi (adj.)
disadvantageous nevygodnyi (adj.)
disagreement nesoglasie (n.n.)
razmolvka (n.f.)
disappear devat'(sya) (v.impf.)
(cont'd)

ischeznut' (v.pf.)
kanut' (v.pf.)
perevestis' (v.pf.)
skryvat'(sya) (v.impf.)
vyvodit'sya (v.impf.)
disappearance ischeznovenie (n.n.)
disappoint razocharovyvat' (v.impf.)
disappointment razocharovanie (n.n.)
disapproval neodobrenie (n.n.)
disarm obezoruzhivat' (v.impf.)
razoruzhat' (v.impf.)
disbandment rasformirovanie (n.n.)
disbelief neverie (n.n.)
discard vybrasyvat' (v.impf.)
discharge razryad (n.m.)
razryazhat' (v.impf.)
uvol'nenie (n.n.)
discipline distsiplina (n.f.)
discolor obestsvetit' (v.impf.)
discomfiture konfuz (n.m.)
disconnect otklyuchat' (v.impf.)
raz"edinit' (v.pf.)
discontented nedovol'nyi (adj.)
discord nelady (n.pl.)
rasprya (n.f.)
razdor (n.m.)
razlad (n.m.)
raznoglasie (n.n.)
discordant neblagozvuchnyi (adj.)
nestroinyi (adj.)
discount skidka (n.f.)
discourage obeskurazhit' (v.pf.)
discover obnaruzhivat'(sya) (v.impf.)
discovery otkrytie (n.n.)
discredit diskreditirovat' (v.impf.&pf.)
discrepancy nesootvetstvie (n.n.)
raznoglasie (n.n.)
discretion usmotrenie (n.n.)
discrimination diskriminatsiya (n.f.)
discuss obsudit' (v.pf.)
peregovorit' (v.pf.)
discussion diskussiya (n.f.)
disease, foot-and-mouth yashchur (n.m.)
disembark vysadit' (v.pf.)
vysazhivat'(sya) (v.impf.)
disengaging rastseplenie (n.n.)
disentangle rasputat' (v.pf.)
rasputyvat' (v.impf.)

disfigure izurodovat' (v.pf.)
obezobrazit' (v.pf.)
disfigured isterzannyi (adj.)
disgrace nemilost' (n.f.)
opala (n.f.)
opozorit' (v.pf.)
osramit' (v.pf.)
pozor (n.m.)
disgrace, to fall into oskandalit'sya (v.pf.)
disguise maskirovat' (v.impf.)
pereodevanie (n.n.)
zamaskirovat' (v.pf.)
disguised pereodetyi (adj.)
disgusting otvratitel'nyi (adj.)
protivnyi (adj.)
dish blyudo (n.n.)
dish, soap myl'nitsa (n.f.)
dishes posuda (n.f.)
dishonest nechestnyi (adj.)
dishonor obeschestit' (v.pf.)
dishonorable beschestnyi (adj.)
neporyadochnyi (adj.)
dishwater burda (n.f.)
disinclination neraspolozhenie (n.n.)
disinfection dezinfektsiya (n.f.)
obezzarazhivanie (n.n.)
disintegrate raspast'sya (v.pf.)
disintegration raspad (n.m.)
disinterested beskorystnyi (adj.)
disk disk (n.m.)
disk, small kruzhok (n.m.)
dislike nedolyublivat' (v.impf.)
nelyubov' (n.f.)
dislocation vyvikh (n.m.)
dismantle raznimat' (v.impf.)
raznyat' (v.pf.)
dismiss raspustit' (v.pf.)
uvolit' (v.pf.)
dismount speshit'sya (v.pf.)
disobedience neposlushanie (n.n.)
nepovinovenie (n.n.)
disobedient neposlushnyi (adj.)
disobey oslushat'sya (v.pf.)
disorder besporyadok (n.m.)
neporyadok (n.m.)
rasstroistvo (n.n.)
disorganized bezalabernyi (adj.)
dispatch komandirovat' (v.impf.&pf.)

otpravlenie (n.n.)
vyslat' (v.pf.)
vysylat' (v.impf.)
vysylka (n.f.)
dispensary ambulatoriya (n.f.)
dispanser (n.m.)
dispenser, water rukomoinik (n.m.)
disperse rasseyat' (v.pf.)
razbredat'sya (v.impf.)
razveivat' (v.impf.)
razveyat' (v.impf.)
dispersed, to be rasseivat'sya (v.impf.)
dispersion dispersiya (n.f.)
displace smeshchat' (v.impf.)
smestit' (v.pf.)
displacement sdvig (n.m.)
smeshchenie (n.n.)
vodoizmeshchenie (n.n.)
display obnaruzhivat'(sya) (v.impf.)
proyavit' (v.pf.)
vystavit' (v.pf.)
vystavlyat' (v.impf.)
displeasure neudovol'stvie (n.n.)
dispose raspolagat' (v.impf.)
disposition nrav (n.m.)
disproportionate neproportsional'nyi (adj.)
nesorazmernyi (adj.)
disputation disput (n.m.)
dispute osparivat' (v.impf.)
disrepair neispravnost' (n.f.)
disrespect neuvazhenie (n.n.)
disrespectful nepochtitel'nyi (adj.)
disrupt sorvat' (v.pf.)
dissatisfaction neudovletvorennost' (n.f.)
dissect anatomirovat' (v.impf.)
dissection rassechenie (n.n.)
vskrytie (n.n.)
dissemination obsemenenie (n.n.)
dissipate prokutit' (v.pf.)
dissociate oneself otmezhevat'sya (v.pf.)
dissolubility rastvorimost' (n.f.)
dissolute besputnyi (adj.)
raspushchennyi (adj.)
rasputnyi (adj.)
razgul'nyi (adj.)
dissolution rastorzhenie (n.n.)
rospusk (n.m.)
dissolve raspuskat'(sya) (v.impf.)

rassasyvat'sya (v.impf.)
rassosat'sya (v.pf.)
rastorgat' (v.impf.)
rastvorit' (v.pf.)
rastvorit'sya (v.pf.)
rastvoryat'(sya) (v.impf.)
dissonance dissonans (n.m.)
dissuade otgovorit' (v.pf.)
otsovetovat' (v.pf.)
pereubedit' (v.pf.)
razubedit' (v.pf.)
razuverit' (v.pf.)
distance dal' (n.f.)
dal'nost' (n.f.)
distantsiya (n.f.)
rasstoyanie (n.n.)
distance, in the vdaleke (adv.)
distance, into the vdal' (adv.)
distant dal'nii (adj.)
distill peregnat' (v.pf.)
peregonyat' (v.impf.)
distillation peregonka (n.f.)
distilled distillirovannyi (adj.)
distinct otchetlivyi (adj.)
vnyatnyi (adj.)
distinction otlichie (n.n.)
distinguish raspoznavat' (v.impf.)
razlichat' (v.impf.)
vydelit' (v.pf.)
vydelyat' (v.impf.)
distinguished znatnyi (adj.)
distort iskazhat' (v.impf.)
izvratit' (v.pf.)
koverkat' (v.impf.)
peredergivat' (v.impf.)
distorted perekoshennyi (adj.)
distorted, to become perekosit'sya (v.pf.)
distortion iskazhenie (n.n.)
distract otvlech' (v.pf.)
otvlekat' (v.impf.)
distribute razdat' (v.pf.)
razdavat' (v.impf.)
distribution raspredelenie (n.n.)
rassylka (n.f.)
razdacha (n.f.)
razverstka (n.f.)
district okrug (n.m.)
okruzhnoi (adj.)
(cont'd)

raion (n.m.)
raionnyi (adj.)
district committee raikom (n.m.)
distrust nedoverie (n.n.)
disturb bespokoit' (v.impf.)
budorazhit' (v.impf.)
meshat' (v.impf.)
vzbudorazhit' (v.pf.)
disturbance vozmushchenie (n.n.)
ditch kanava (n.f.)
rov (n.m)
ditch, irrigation aryk (n.m.)
dive nyryat' (v.impf.)
pikirovat' (v.impf.)
diver vodolaz (n.m.)
divergence raskhozhdenie (n.n.)
diverse mnogoobraznyi (adj.)
diversion ob"ezd (n.m.)
divide delit' (v.impf.)
razbit' (v.pf.)
razdelyat'(sya) (v.pf.)
dividend delimoe (n.n.)
diving pikiruyushchii (adj.)
diving suit skafandr (n.m.)
division delenie (n.n.)
diviziya (n.f.)
razdel (n.m.)
razdelenie (n.n.)
divisor delitel' (n.m.)
divorce razvestis' (v.pf.)
razvod (n.m.)
divorced razvedennyi (adj.)
divulge razbaltyvat' (v.impf.)
razglasit' (v.pf.)
dizziness golovokruzhenie (n.n.)
do delat' (v.impf.)
natvorit' (v.pf.)
podelat' (v.pf.)
prodelat' (v.pf.)
prodelyvat' (v.impf.)
sdelat' (v.pf.)
son (n.m.)
do someone a service udruzhit' (v.pf.)
usluzhit' (v.pf.)
do something stupid sglupit' (v.pf.)
do up zadelat' (v.pf.)
do with det' (v.pf.)
do without obkhodit'sya (v.impf.)

dock dok (n.m.)
docked kutsyi (adj.)
docker doker (n.m.)
gruzchik (n.m.)
doctor doktor (n.m.)
doctrine doktrina (n.f.)
document dokument (n.m.)
dodge izvorachivat'sya (v.impf.)
otvilivat' (v.impf.)
doe lan' (n.f.)
dog pes (n.m.)
sobaka (n.f.)
dogma dogma (n.f.)
dogmatist nachetchik (n.m.)
dog-rose shipovnik (n.m.)
doll kukla (n.f.)
dollar dollar (n.m.)
doll's kukol'nyi (adj.)
dolphin del'fin (n.m.)
dome kupol (n.m.)
domestic domashnii (adj.)
dominant dominanta (n.f.)
domination gospodstvo (n.n.)
dominion dominion (n.m.)
vladychestvo (n.n.)
donkey osel (n.m.)
donor donor (n.m.)
door dver' (n.f.)
doorman shveitsar (n.m.)
dose doza (n.f.)
dots mnogotochie (n.n.)
dotted line punktir (n.m.)
double dvoinik (n.m.)
dvoinoi (adj.)
dvoyakii (adj.)
makhrovyi (adj.)
udvaivat'(sya) (v.impf.)
vdvoe (adv.)
vdvoine (adv.)
double bass kontrabas (n.m.)
double-bed dvuspal'nyi (adj.)
double-breasted dvubortnyi (adj.)
doubled udvoennyi (adj.)
double-dealer dvurushnik (n.m.)
double-edged oboyudoostryi (adj.)
double-faced dvulichnyi (adj.)
doubling udvoenie (n.n.)
doubt somnenie (n.n.)

somnevat'sya (v.impf.)
usomnit'sya (v.pf.)
doubtful nedostovernyi (adj.)
dough testo (n.n.)
douse oblit' (v.pf.)
dousing oblivanie (n.n.)
dove-colored sizyi (adj.)
down pukh (n.m.)
pukhovyi (adj.)
vniz (adv.)
down, to get slezat' (v.impf.)
down with doloi (adv.)
downcast unylyi (adj.)
downpour liven' (n.m.)
downtrodden zabityi (adj.)
downward knizu (adv.)
dowry pridanoe (n.n.)
doze dremat' (v.impf.)
doze off zabyt'sya (v.pf.)
zabyvat'sya (v.impf.)
zadremat' (v.pf.)
dozen dyuzhina (n.f.)
draft chertezh (n.m.)
skvoznyak (n.m.)
tyaga (n.f.)
drag tashchit' (v.impf.)
taskat' (v.impf.)
tyanut'sya (v.impf.)
vlachit' (v.impf.)
volochit' (v.impf.)
vtaskivat' (v.impf.)
drag along valyat' (v.impf.)
drag off zatashchit' (v.pf.)
drag oneself plestis' (v.pf.)
drag out vytaskivat' (v.impf.)
vyvolakivat' (v.impf.)
drag over peretashchit' (v.pf.)
peretaskivat' (v.impf.)
dragon drakon (n.m.)
dragonfly strekoza (n.f.)
drain osushat' (v.impf.)
stochnyi (adj.)
vodostochnyi (adj.)
drainage drenazh (n.m.)
drake selezen' (n.m.)
drama drama (n.f.)
dramatize instsenirovat' (v.impf.&pf.)
drapery port'era (n.f.)

draw chertit' (v.impf.)
nachertit' (v.pf.)
narisovat' (v.pf.)
nich'ya (n.f.)
zadergivat' (v.impf.)
zadernut' (v.pf.)
draw back otdergivat' (v.impf.)
draw in podzhat' (v.pf.)
podzhimat' (v.impf.)
vtyanut' (v.pf.)
draw, in a vnich'yu (adv.)
draw level poravnyat'sya (v.pf.)
draw near priblizhat'(sya) (v.impf.)
pridvigat'(sya) (v.impf.)
draw together sblizit' (v.pf.)
draw up oformit' (v.pf.)
vystraivat' (v.impf.)
vystroit' (v.pf.)
drawbridge razvodnoi most (adj.-n.m.)
drawers kal'sony (n.pl.)
drawers, chest of komod (n.m.)
drawing cherchenie (n.n.)
risovanie (n.n.)
risunok (n.m.)
rozygrysh (n.m.)
drawn-out protyazhnyi (adj.)
dream greza (n.f.)
grezit' (v.impf.)
mechta (n.f.)
prisnit'sya (v.pf.)
snit'sya (v.impf.)
snovidenie (n.n.)
dreamer fantazer (n.m.)
dredge zemlecherpalka (n.f.)
dregs podonki (n.pl.)
drench vymachivat' (v.impf.)
vymochit' (v.pf.)
drenched, to be vymokat' (v.impf.)
dress odet' (v.pf.)
odevat'(sya) (v.impf.)
plat'e (n.n.)
tualet (n.m.)
dress, new obnovka (n.f.)
dress up naryadit'(sya) (v.pf.)
naryazhat'(sya) (v.impf.)
razodet'sya (v.pf.)
dresser shkaf (n.m.)
dressing case nesesser (n.m.)

dressing gown khalat (n.m.)
dried prosokhshii (adj.)
   sushenyi (adj.)
drift dreif (n.m.)
   samotek (n.m.)
   shtrek (n.m.)
   stelit'sya (v.impf.)
drill sverlit' (v.impf.)
   sverlo (n.n.)
   vysverlivat' (v.impf.)
drill, pneumatic otboinyi molotok (adj.-n.m.)
drill, seed seyalka (n.f.)
drilling burenie (n.n.)
drink napitok (n.m.)
   pit' (v.impf.)
   pit'e (n.n.)
   vypit' (v.pf.)
   vypivat' (v.impf.)
drink, fruit mors (n.m.)
drink something down zapit' (v.pf.)
   zapivat' (v.impf.)
drink, to give to napoit' (v.pf.)
   poit' (v.impf.)
   spoit' (v.pf.)
drink, to have something to napit'sya (v.pf.)
drink, to take a otpit' (v.pf.)
   otpivat' (v.impf.)
drink up dopit' (v.pf.)
   dopivat' (v.impf.)
drinking vypivka (n.f.)
drinking bout popoika (n.f.)
drinking, hard zapoi (n.m.)
drive ekhat' (v.impf.)
   ezda (n.f.)
   ezdit' (v.impf.)
   gnat' (v.impf.)
   gonyat' (v.impf.)
   pognat' (v.pf.)
   privod (n.m.)
   v"ezd (n.m.)
   vezti (v.impf.)
   vozit' (v.impf.)
drive about raz"ezzhat' (v.impf.)
drive away otgonyat' (v.impf.)
   otognat' (v.pf.)
   prognat' (v.pf.)
   progonyat' (v.impf.)
   razognat' (v.pf.)

   sgonyat' (v.impf.)
   sognat' (v.pf.)
   ugnat' (v.pf.)
   ugonyat' (v.impf.)
drive back ottesnit' (v.pf.)
drive in v"ezzhat' (v.impf.)
   vbit' (v.pf.)
   vbivat' (v.impf.)
   vgonyat' (v.impf.)
   vkolachivat' (v.impf.)
   vkolotit' (v.pf.)
   vognat' (v.pf.)
   zabit' (v.pf.)
   zabivat' (v.impf.)
   zagnat' (v.pf.)
   zagonyat' (v.impf.)
drive off ot"ekhat' (v.pf.)
   otvadit' (v.pf.)
drive out vygnat' (v.pf.)
   vygonyat' (v.impf.)
drive up pod"ekhat' (v.pf.)
   pod"ezzhat' (v.pf.)
driver likhach (n.m.)
   pogonshchik (n.m.)
   shofer (n.m.)
   vagonovozhatyi (adj.)
   voditel' (n.m.)
driving dvizhushchii (adj.)
   privodnoi (adj.)
drizzle morosit' (v.impf.)
droop ponikat' (v.impf.)
drop kapat' (v.impf.)
   kaplya (n.f.)
   kapnut' (v.pf.)
   ponizhenie (n.n.)
   ronyat' (v.impf.)
   uronit' (v.pf.)
   vyronit' (v.pf.)
drop a line cherknut' (v.pf.)
drop in zabegat' (v.pf.)
   zaiti (v.pf.)
drop of blood krovinka (n.f.)
drop off zavezti (v.pf.)
   zavozit' (v.impf.)
droplet kapel'ka (n.f.)
dropper pipetka (n.f.)
dropsy vodyanka (n.f.)
drought zasukha (n.f.)

drown potonut' (v.pf.)
    tonut' (v.impf.)
    topit' (v.impf.)
    utopit' (v.pf.)
    zaglushat' (v.impf.)
drown oneself topit'sya (v.impf.)
drowned man utoplennik (n.m.)
drowned, to be utonut' (v.pf.)
    utopat' (v.impf.)
drowsiness dremota (n.f.)
drug narkotik (n.m.)
drug addict narkoman (n.m.)
drug store apteka (n.f.)
drum baraban (n.m.)
    vdolbit' (v.pf.)
drunk, to get napivat'sya (v.impf.)
    p'yanet' (v.impf.)
drunk, to make podpaivat' (v.impf.)
    podpoit' (v.pf.)
    spaivat' (v.impf.)
drunkard p'yanitsa (n.m.&f.)
dry dosukha (adv.)
    nasukho (adv.)
    obsokhnut' (v.pf.)
    obsykhat' (v.impf.)
    podsykhat' (v.impf.)
    prosushit' (v.pf.)
    sokhnut' (v.impf.)
    sukhoi (adj.)
    vysushit' (v.pf.)
    zasushivat' (v.impf.)
dry cleaning khimchistka (n.f.)
dry oneself vytirat'(sya) (v.impf.)
dry, to get prosokhnut' (v.pf.)
    prosykhat' (v.impf.)
dry up issushit' (v.pf.)
    issyakat' (v.impf.)
    peresokhnut' (v.pf.)
    peresykhat' (v.impf.)
    vysokhnut' (v.pf.)
    vysykhat' (v.impf.)
dry wind sukhovei (n.m.)
dry-cure vyalit' (v.impf.)
drying up obmelenie (n.n.)
dryness sukhost' (n.f.)
drysalter's moskatel'nyi (adj.)
duck utka (n.f.)
duck, eider gagachii (adj.)

due dolzhnyi (adj.)
due, to be prichitat'sya (v.impf.)
duel duél' (n.f.)
    poedinok (n.m.)
duet duét (n.m.)
dug in vkopannyi (adj.)
dugout blindazh (n.m.)
    zemlyanka (n.f.)
dull stupor otupenie (n.n.)
dullness tupost' (n.f.)
duma duma (n.f.)
dumb besslovesnyi (adj.)
dumb, to be struck otoropet' (v.pf.)
dumb, to become onemet' (v.pf.)
dumbbells ganteli (n.pl.)
dumbfound ogoroshit' (v.pf.)
dumbfounded, to be ostolbenet' (v.pf.)
dumbness nemota (n.f.)
dump otval (n.m.)
dumplings pel'meni (n.pl.)
dunce tupitsa (n.m.&f.)
dune dyuna (n.f.)
dung pomet (n.m.)
dungeon temnitsa (n.f.)
duplicate dublikat (n.m.)
    dublirovat' (v.impf.)
    razmnozhit' (v.pf.)
durability prochnost' (n.f.)
duration prodolzhitel'nost' (n.f.)
duration, of long dolgovremennyi (adj.)
duration, of short neprodolzhitel'nyi (adj.)
during v techenie (prep.)
dusk sumrak (n.m.)
dust obmesti (v.pf.)
    prakh (n.m.)
    pyl' (n.f.)
dust, to cover with zapylit' (v.pf.)
Dutch gollandets (n.m.)
duty obyazannost' (n.f.)
    poshlina (n.f.)
    povinnost' (n.f.)
duty-free besposhlinnyi (adj.)
dwarf karlik (n.m.)
dwelling zhil'e (n.n.)
    zhilishche (n.n.)
    zhiloi (adj.)
dwelling space zhilploshchad' (n.f.)
dye krasyashchii (adj.)
    (cont'd)

vykrasit' (v.pf.)
dye works krasil'nya (n.f.)
dying away ugasanie (n.n.)
dying off otmiranie (n.n.)
dynamic dinamicheskii (adj.)
dynamics dinamika (n.f.)

dynamite dinamit (n.m.)
dynamo dinamo-mashina (n.f.)
dynasty dinastiya (n.f.)
dysentery dizenteriya (n.f.)
dyspepsia dispepsiya (n.f.)

E　(Е, Ё, Э)

each kazhdyi (adj.)
eagle orel (n.m.)
eagle owl filin (n.m.)
ear kolos (n.m.)
　　ukho (n.n.)
　　ushnoi (adj.)
earlier poran'she (adv.)
　　ran'she (adv.)
early rannii (adj.)
　　rano (adv.)
　　skorospelyi (adj.)
early frosts zamorozki (n.pl.)
earn zarabatyvat' (v.impf.)
earnest, in vser'ez (adv.)
earnings zarabotok (n.m.)
earnings, supplementary prirabotok (n.m.)
earring ser'ga (n.f.)
　　serezhka (n.f.)
ears, to prick up one's nastorazhivat'sya
　　(v.impf.)
　　nastorozhit'sya (v.pf.)
ears, to reach one's donestis' (v.pf.)
earth zemlyanoi (adj.)
earth, black chernozem (n.m.)
earth up okuchivat' (v.impf.)
earthen zemlyanoi (adj.)
earthenware, glazed fayans (n.m.)
earthing zazemlenie (n.n.)
earthly zemnoi (adj.)
earthquake zemletryasenie (n.n.)
earthy zemlistyi (adj.)
ease, at vol'no (adv.)
easel mol'bert (n.m.)
easier legche (adj.)
easily soiled markii (adj.)

east vostok (n.m.)
Easter paskha (n.f.)
eastern vostochnyi (adj.)
easy chair kreslo (n.n.)
easy to get on with uzhivchivyi (adj.)
eat est' (v.impf.)
　　poest' (v.pf.)
　　s"edat' (v.impf.)
　　s"est' (v.pf.)
eat away proedat' (v.impf.)
　　proest' (v.pf.)
eat into v"edat'sya (v.impf.)
eat plenty of naedat'sya (v.impf.)
　　naest'sya (v.pf.)
eat up skushat' (v.pf.)
eater edok (n.m.)
eating, to finish doedat' (v.pf.)
　　doest' (v.pf.)
eau de cologne odekolon (n.m.)
eccentric ékstsentrichnyi (adj.)
echelon éshelon (n.m.)
echo ékho (n.n.)
　　otgolosok (n.m.)
　　otzvuk (n.m.)
　　poddakivat' (v.impf.)
　　vtorit' (v.impf.)
eclipse zatmevat' (v.impf.)
economic ékonomicheskii (adj.)
　　khozyaistvennyi (adj.)
economic, national
　　narodnokhozyaistvennyi (adj.)
economics ékonomika (n.f.)
economize ékonomit' (v.impf.)
economy ékonomiya (n.f.)
　　khozyaistvo (n.n.)

economy car malolitrazhnyi (adj.)

ecstasy ékstaz (n.m.)
    upoenie (n.n.)

edema otek (n.m.)

edge krai (n.m.)
    kromka (n.f.)
    obrez (n.m.)

edge of forest opushka (n.f.)

edging kaima (n.f.)
    obshivka (n.f.)

edification nazidanie (n.n.)

edit redaktirovat' (v.impf.)

editor redaktor (n.m.)

editorial peredovitsa (n.f.)
    redaktsionnyi (adj.)

editorial office redaktsiya (n.f.)

educated obrazovannyi (adj.)

education obrazovanie (n.n.)
    vospitanie (n.n.)

education, providing general
    obshcheobrazovatel'nyi (adj.)

educational kul'tmassovyi (adj.)
    uchebnyi (adj.)

eel ugor' (n.m.)

efface izgladit' (v.pf.)

effaced stertyi (adj.)

effaced, to be stirat'sya (v.impf.)

effect effekt (n.m.)

effect, to have an podeistvovat' (v.pf.)

effective effektivnyi (adj.)

efficiency, fighting boesposobnost' (n.f.)

efficient del'nyi (adj.)

effort staranie (n.n.)
    usilie (n.n.)

effort, feeble popolznovenie (n.n.)

egg yaichnyi (adj.)
    yaitso (n.n.)

egg on podzadorit' (v.pf.)

eggs, fried glazun'ya (n.f.)
    yaichnitsa (n.f.)

eggs, to lay nestis' (v.impf.)

Egyptian egipetskii (adj.)

eider duck gagachii (adj.)

eight vosem' (num.)

eight, the vos'merka (n.f.)

eighteen vosemnadtsat' (num.)

eighth vos'moi (adj.)

eight-hour vos'michasovoi (adj.)

eightieth vos'midesyatyi (adj.)

elaborate razrabatyvat' (v.impf.)
    razrabotat' (v.impf.)

elaboration utochnenie (n.n.)

elastic élastichnyi (adj.)
    rastyazhimyi (adj.)
    uprugii (adj.)

elasticity uprugost' (n.f.)

elbow lokot' (n.m.)

elbows, to lean on one's oblokachivat'sya
    (v.impf.)

elderly nemolodoi (adj.)
    pozhiloi (adj.)

elect izbirat' (v.impf.)
    vybirat' (v.impf.)
    vybrat' (v.pf.)

election izbranie (n.n.)
    perevybory (n.pl.)
    vybornyi (adj.)
    vybory (n.pl.)

elector izbiratel' (n.m.)

electoral izbiratel'nyi (adj.)
    perevybornyi (adj.)

electric élektricheskii (adj.)

electric floor polisher élektropoloter (n.m.)

electric locomotive élektrovoz (n.m.)

electric motor élektrodvigatel' (n.m.)

electric power station élektrostantsiya (n.f.)

electrical conductivity élektroprovodnost'
    (n.f.)

electrical energy élektroenergiya (n.f.)

electrical engineer élektrotekhnik (n.m.)

electrician élektromonter (n.m.)

electrify élektrifitsirovat' (v.impf.&pf.)

electrode élektrod (n.m.)

electron élektron (n.m.)

electronic computer élektronno-vychislitel'naya
    mashina (n.f.)

electronics élektronika (n.f.)

elegant élegantnyi (adj.)

element élement (n.m.)
    stikhiya (n.f.)

elemental stikhiinyi (adj.)

elementary élementarnyi (adj.)
    nachal'nyi (adj.)

elephant slon (n.m.)

elevated vozvyshennyi (adj.)

elevator élevator (n.m.)
    (cont'd)

lift (n.m.)
eleven odinnadtsat' (num.)
elk los' (n.m.)
elm vyaz (n.m.)
eloquent krasnorechivyi (adj.)
elusive neulovimyi (adj.)
emaciated iskhudalyi (adj.)
izmozhdennyi (adj.)
emaciated, to be otoshchat' (v.pf.)
emancipation émansipatsiya (n.f.)
embalm bal'zamirovat' (v.impf.)
embankment naberezhnaya (n.f.)
nasyp' (n.f.)
embarkation posadka (n.f.)
embarrassed, to be smushchat'(sya) (v.impf.)
embassy posol'stvo (n.n.)
embellish prikrasit' (v.pf.)
embezzle rastrachivat' (v.impf.)
embezzlement rastrata (n.f.)
embitter ozhestochat' (v.impf.)
ozlobit' (v.pf.)
emblem émblema (n.f.)
embody voplotit' (v.pf.)
embrace ob"yatie (n.n.)
obkhvatit' (v.pf.)
obnimat'(sya) (v.impf.)
obnyat' (v.pf.)
embrasure ambrazura (n.f.)
embroider rasshit' (v.pf.)
rasshivat' (v.impf.)
vyshit' (v.pf.)
embroidery vyshivanie (n.n.)
embroidery frame pyal'tsy (n.pl.)
embryo zarodysh (n.m.)
emerald izumrud (n.m.)
emerge vynyrnut' (v.pf.)
emergency avariinyi (adj.)
zapasnoi (adj.)
emergency brake stop-kran (n.m.)
emery nazhdak (n.m.)
emigrant émigrant (n.m.)
vykhodets (n.m.)
eminent vidnyi (adj.)
emit ispuskat' (v.impf.)
emitter izluchatel' (n.m.)
emotion émotsiya (n.f.)
emotional émotsional'nyi (adj.)
emperor imperator (n.m.)

emphasize podcherkivat' (v.impf.)
empire imperiya (n.f.)
empiriocriticism émpiriokrititsizm (n.m.)
employee sluzhashchii (n.m.)
sotrudnik (n.m.)
employer nanimatel' (n.m.)
predprinimatel' (n.m.)
emptiness pustota (n.f.)
empty bessoderzhatel'nyi (adj.)
malosoderzhatel'nyi (adj.)
oporozhnit' (v.pf.)
porozhnii (adv.)
pustoi (adj.)
vyvalit' (v.pf.)
empty stock porozhnyak (n.m.)
empty stomach, on an natoshchak (adv.)
empty, to become opustet' (v.pf.)
pustet' (v.impf.)
empty, to stand pustovat' (v.impf.)
enamel émal' (n.f.)
enamelled émalirovannyi (adj.)
enchanted zakoldovannyi (adj.)
enchanting obvorozhitel'nyi (adj.)
enclose obnesti (v.pf.)
obnosit' (v.impf.)
enclosure zagon (n.m.)
encore bis (interj.)
encounter natalkivat'sya (v.impf.)
encourage podbadrivat' (v.impf.)
podbodrit' (v.pf.)
priobodrit' (v.pf.)
encouragement obodrenie (n.n.)
pooshchrenie (n.n.)
encroach posyagat' (v.impf.)
encumber zagromozhdat' (v.impf.)
encyclopedia éntsiklopediya (n.f.)
end final (n.m.)
konets (n.m.)
end, on naprolet (adv.)
end, to put an presekat' (v.impf.)
endless beskonechnyi (adj.)
bezyskhodnyi (adj.)
endow nadelit' (v.pf.)
odarit' (v.pf.)
endurance vynoslivost' (n.f.)
endure vynesti (v.pf.)
vynosit' (v.impf.)
enema klizma (n.f.)

enemy   nedrug (n.m.)
   nepriyatel' (n.m.)
   vrag (n.m.)
energetic   énergichnyi (adj.)
energy   énergiya (n.f.)
energy, electrical   elektroenergiya (n.f.)
engaged   zanyato (adj.)
engaged in, to be   zanimat'sya (v.impf.)
engagement   pomolvka (n.f.)
engender   zarodit' (v.pf.)
engineer   inzhener (n.m.)
engineer, electrical   elektrotekhnik (n.m.)
engineering   tekhnika (n.f.)
engineering, heat   teplotekhnika (n.f.)
engineering, hydraulic   gidrotekhnika (n.f.)
engineering, illuminating   svetotekhnika (n.f.)
engineering, power   energetika (n.f.)
engineering, radio   radiotekhnika (n.f.)
engineering, solar power   gelioenergetika
   (n.f.)
English   angliiskii (adj.)
Englishman   anglichanin (n.m.)
engrave   gravirovat' (v.impf.)
engraver   graver (n.m.)
engraving   gravyura (n.f.)
enjoy   nasladit'sya (v.pf.)
enlarge   uvelichivat' (v.impf.)
enlighten   prosveshchat' (v.impf.)
   prosvetit' (v.pf.)
enlightenment   prosvetlenie (n.n.)
enlist   zaruchat'sya (v.pf.)
enmity   vrazhda (n.f.)
ennoble   oblagorazhivat' (v.impf.)
enormous   kolossal'nyi (adj.)
enough   polno (adv.)
enrich   obogatit' (v.pf.)
ensemble   ansambl' (n.m.)
enslave   porabotit' (v.pf.)
   zakabalit' (v.pf.)
   zakrepostit' (v.pf.)
ensure   obespechit' (v.pf.)
entail   povlech' (v.pf.)
entangle   oputat' (v.pf.)
   pereputat' (v.pf.)
   sputat' (v.pf.)
enter   v"ezzhat' (v.impf.)
   vkhodit' (v.impf.)
   voiti (v.pf.)

enter in the record   zaprotokolirovat' (v.pf.)
entering   postuplenie (n.n.)
enterprise   predpriyatie (n.n.)
enterprising   predpriimchivyi (adj.)
entertain   ugostit' (v.pf.)
entertaining   zanimatel'nyi (adj.)
entertainment   razvlechenie (n.n.)
enthusiasm   éntuziazm (n.m.)
   uvlechenie (n.n.)
enthusiastic   uvlekayushchiisya (adj.)
   vostorzhennyi (adj.)
entice   smanivat' (v.impf.)
   zavlekat' (v.impf.)
entirely   splosh' (adv.)
   tselikom (adv.)
   vsetselo (adv.)
entrance   v"ezd (n.m.)
   vkhod (n.m.)
   vkhodnoi (adj.)
entreaties, to move by   umolit' (v.pf.)
entreaties, to obtain by   vymolit' (v.pf.)
entreaty   mol'ba (n.f.)
entrench oneself   okapyvat'sya (v.impf.)
entrust   poruchat' (v.impf.)
   vverit' (v.pf.)
   vveryat' (v.impf.)
entry   vstuplenie (n.n.)
   zapis' (n.f.)
entwine   obvit' (v.pf.)
enumerate   perechislit' (v.pf.)
enumeration   perechislenie (n.n.)
envelope   konvert (n.m.)
envious   zavistlivyi (adj.)
environment   sreda (n.f.)
environs   okrestnost' (n.f.)
envoy   poslannik (n.m.)
envy   zavidovat' (v.impf.)
   zavist' (n.f.)
enzyme   ferment (n.m.)
epic   épicheskii (adj.)
   épopeya (n.f.)
epidemic   épidemiya (n.f.)
   povetrie (n.n.)
epidemiology   épidemiologiya (n.f.)
epigram   épigramma (n.f.)
epigraph   épigraf (n.m.)
epileptic   pripadochnyi (adj.)
epilogue   épilog (n.m.)
   (cont'd)

posleslovie (n.n.)
episode épizod (n.m.)
epitaph épitafiya (n.f.)
epithet épitet (n.m.)
epoch épokha (n.f.)
epos épos (n.m.)
equal ravnyi (adj.)
equality ravenstvo (n.n.)
equality of rights ravnopravie (n.n.)
equalize ravnyat' (v.impf.)
uravnivat' (v.impf.)
uravnyat' (v.pf.)
equally porovnu (adv.)
ravno (adv.)
equate priravnivat' (v.impf.)
equation uravnenie (n.n.)
equator ékvator (n.m.)
equidistant ravnootstoyashchii (adj.)
equilateral ravnostoronnii (adj.)
equilibrium ravnovesie (n.n.)
equinox ravnodenstvie (n.n.)
equip ékipirovat' (v.impf.&pf.)
snaryadit' (v.pf.)
equip oneself snaryazhat'(sya) (v.impf.)
equipment oborudovanie (n.n.)
snaryazhenie (n.n.)
equipment, military amunitsiya (n.f.)
equivalent ékvivalent (n.m.)
ravnoznachnyi (adj.)
era éra (n.f.)
eradicate iskorenit' (v.pf.)
eraser lastik (n.m.)
erect soorudit' (v.pf.)
vozdvigat' (v.impf.)
vozvesti (v.pf.)
ermine gornostai (n.m.)
erosion razmyv (n.m.)
erotic éroticheskii (adj.)
error nepravota (n.f.)
opiska (n.f.)
pogreshnost' (n.f.)
erudition éruditsiya (n.f.)
eruption izverzhenie (n.n.)
prorezyvanie (n.n.)
escalator éskalator (n.m.)
escape utech' (v.pf.)
utekat' (v.impf.)
escort éskort (n.m.)

Eskimo éskimos (n.m.)
especially sugubo (adv.)
essay ocherk (n.m.)
referat (n.m.)
essence éssentsiya (n.f.)
sushchestvo (n.n.)
sushchnost' (n.f.)
sut' (n.f.)
essential sushchestvennyi (adj.)
establish uchredit' (v.pf.)
ustanovit' (v.pf.)
estate imenie (n.n.)
pomest'e (n.n.)
soslovie (n.n.)
estimate prikinut' (v.pf.)
rastsenivat' (v.impf.)
smeta (n.f.)
Estonian éstonets (n.m.)
etc. (et cetera) i.t.d. (i tak dalee) (abbr.)
eternity vechnost' (n.f.)
ether éfir (n.m.)
ethical étichnyi (adj.)
ethics étika (n.f.)
ethnography étnografiya (n.f.)
etiquette étiket (n.m.)
etymology étimologiya (n.f.)
eugenics evgenika (n.f.)
Europe Evropa (n.f.)
evacuation évakuatsiya (n.f.)
evade uvernut'sya (v.pf.)
uvilivat' (v.impf.)
evaporate isparit'sya (v.pf.)
uletuchit'sya (v.pf.)
vyparivat' (v.impf.)
evaporation isparenie (n.n.)
vyparivanie (n.n.)
evasion uvertka (n.f.)
eve kanun (n.m.)
eve, on the nakanune (adv.)
even chetnyi (adj.)
dazhe (part.)
ravnomernyi (adj.)
evening vecher (n.m.)
vechernii (adj.)
evening, in the vecherom (adv.)
event sobytie (n.n.)
every minute ezheminutno (adv.)
pominutno (adv.)

everywhere povsemestno (adv.)
  vezde (adv.)
  vsyudu (adv.)
everywhere, from otovsyudu (adv.)
evict vyselit' (v.pf.)
eviction vyselenie (n.n.)
evidence ulika (n.f.)
evil likhoi (adj.)
  zlo (n.n.)
evolutionary évolyutsionnyi (adj.)
exact vzyskat' (v.pf.)
exacting vzyskatel'nyi (adj.)
exactly imenno (adv.)
  toch'-v-toch' (adv.)
  tochno (adv.)
exactness tochnost' (n.f.)
exaggerate razdut' (v.pf.)
  utrirovat' (v.impf.&pf.)
exaggerated dutyi (adj.)
exaggeration preuvelichenie (n.n.)
exalt vozvelichivat' (v.impf.)
examination ékzamen (n.m.)
  osmotr (n.m.)
  osvidetel'stvovanie (n.n.)
  prosmotr (n.m.)
  rassmotrenie (n.n.)
examine ékzamenovat' (v.impf.)
  oglyadyvat' (v.impf.)
  osmotret' (v.pf.)
  priglyadet'sya (v.pf.)
  rassmatrivat' (v.impf.)
  razglyadyvat' (v.impf.)
examiner ékzamenator (n.m.)
example obrazets (n.m.)
  primer (n.m.)
example, for naprimer (intro.)
exasperate izvodit' (v.impf.)
excavation kotlovan (n.m.)
excavations raskopki (n.pl.)
excavator ékskavator (n.m.)
exceed prevysit' (v.pf.)
excellent otlichnyi (adj.)
  prevoskhodnyi (adj.)
except krome (prep.)
exception isklyuchenie (n.n.)
excerpt vyderzhka (n.f.)
excess beschinstvo (n.n.)
  ékstsess (n.m.)

excessive chrezmernyi (adj.)
exchange birzha (n.f.)
  mena (n.f.)
  obmen (n.m.)
  perebrasyvat'sya (v.impf.)
  perebrosit'sya (v.pf.)
  pomenyat'(sya) (v.pf.)
  promenyat' (v.pf.)
  razmen (n.m.)
  vymenivat' (v.impf.)
exchange for, in vzamen (prep.)
exchange glances pereglyadyvat'sya
  (v.impf.)
exchange, heat teploobmen (n.m.)
excitability vozbudimost' (n.f.)
excitation vozbuzhdenie (n.n.)
excite vozbudit' (v.pf.)
excited vzvolnovannyi (adj.)
excited, to get razgoryachit'sya (v.pf.)
  vozbuzhdat'sya (v.impf.)
excitement azart (n.m.)
exciting volnuyushchii (adj.)
exclaim voskliknut' (v.pf.)
exclamation vozglas (n.m.)
exclude isklyuchat' (v.impf.)
excursion ékskursiya (n.f.)
excuse oneself otgovarivat'sya (v.impf.)
execute kaznit' (v.impf.&pf.)
  vypolnit' (v.pf.)
execution kazn' (n.f.)
  vypolnenie (n.n.)
executive ispolnitel'nyi (adj.)
executive committee ispolkom (n.m.)
exemplary primernyi (adj.)
exercise uprazhnenie (n.n.)
exhaust ischerpat' (v.pf.)
  istoshchat' (v.impf.)
  iznurit' (v.pf.)
  tomit' (v.impf.)
  vypusknoi (adj.)
exhausted, to be iznemoch' (v.pf.)
  iznemogat' (v.impf.)
  vybivat'sya (v.impf.)
exhaustion istoshchenie (n.n.)
exhibit éksponat (n.m.)
exhibition vystavka (n.f.)
exile izgnanie (n.n.)
  soslat' (v.pf.)
  (cont'd)

ssyl'nyi (n.m.)

ssylat' (v.impf.)

ssylka (n.f.)

vyslat' (v.pf.)

vysylat' (v.impf.)

vysylka (n.f.)

exiled, to be ssylat'sya (v.impf.)

exist prosushchestvovat' (v.pf.)

existence bytie (n.n.)

sushchestvovanie (n.n.)

exit vykhod (n.m.)

exorbitant nepomernyi (adj.)

expand razrastat'sya (v.impf.)

expanse razdol'e (n.n.)

expansion rasshirenie (n.n.)

expectation ozhidanie (n.n.)

expectorate kharkat' (v.impf.)

otkharkivat' (v.impf.)

expedient tselesoobraznyi (adj.)

expedition ékspeditsiya (n.f.)

expenditure raskhod (n.m.)

zatrata (n.f.)

expense trata (n.f.)

expenses izderzhki (n.pl.)

expensive dorogoi (adj.)

expensive, to become more podorozhat'
(v.pf.)

experience izvedat' (v.pf.)

perezhit' (v.pf.)

perezhivanie (n.n.)

experienced svedushchii (adj.)

experiment éksperiment (n.m.)

opyt (n.m.)

expert ékspert (n.m.)

znatok (n.m.)

expiration istechenie (n.n.)

expire istekat' (v.impf.)

explain ob"yasnyat'sya (v.impf.)

poyasnyat' (v.impf.)

rastolkovat' (v.pf.)

explanation ob"yasnenie (n.n.)

poyasnenie (n.n.)

raz"yasnenie (n.n.)

exploit ékspluatirovat' (v.impf.)

podvig (n.m.)

explosion vzryv (n.m.)

explosive razryvnoi (adj.)

vzryvchatyi (adj.)

explosive, high fugasnyi (adj.)

export éksport (n.m.)

vyvoz (n.m.)

expose izoblichat' (v.impf.)

oblichat' (v.impf.)

razoblachat' (v.impf.)

expose to cold zastudit' (v.pf.)

exposition ékspozitsiya (n.f.)

express iz"yavit' (v.pf.)

kur'erskii (adj.)

vyrazhat' (v.impf.)

vyrazit' (v.pf.)

express an opinion vyskazat' (v.pf.)

expressed vyrazhennyi (adj.)

expression, facial mimika (n.f.)

expression to, to give concrete

konkretizirovat' (v.impf. & pf.)

expressive vyrazitel'nyi (adj.)

expropriate ékspropriirovat' (v.impf.&pf.)

extent protyazhenie (n.n.)

exterminate morit' (v.impf.)

travit' (v.impf.)

external vneshnii (adj.)

external student vol'noslushatel' (n.m.)

zaochnik (n.m.)

external use, for naruzhnoe (n.n.)

exterritorial éksterritorial'nyi (adj.)

extinct, to become vymeret' (v.pf.)

vymirat' (v.impf.)

extinguish gasit' (v.impf.)

pogashat' (v.impf.)

pogasit' (v.pf.)

potushit' (v.pf.)

tushit' (v.impf.)

extinguisher, fire ognetushitel' (n.m.)

extort vymogat' (v.impf.)

extra charge nachislenie (n.n.)

natsenka (n.f.)

extra pay priplata (n.f.)

extra, to pay priplachivat' (v.impf.)

extract izvlekat' (v.impf.)

vytyazhka (n.f.)

extract information vypytat' (v.pf.)

vypytyvat' (v.impf.)

vyvedat' (v.pf.)

extraction izvlechenie (n.n.)

udalenie (n.n.)

extracurricular vneshkol'nyi (adj.)

extraordinary chrezvychainyi (ajd.)
  neobyknovennyi (adj.)
  vneocherednoi (adj.)
extravagant ékstravagantnyi (adj.)
extreme krainii (adj.)
extremely kraine (adv.)
extremity konechnost' (n.f.)
extricate oneself vykruchivat'sya (v.impf.)
  vyputat'sya (v.pf.)
exultation likovanie (n.n.)
eye glaz (n.m.)
  glaznoi (adj.)

oko (n.n.)
ushko (n.n.)
eye on, to keep an usledit' (v.pf.)
eyebrow brov' (n.f.)
eyeglass okulyar (n.m.)
eyelash resnitsa (n.f.)
eyelid veko (n.n.)
eyepiece okulyar (n.m.)
eyes, to narrow one's zazhmurit' (v.pf.)
eyes, with one's own voochiyu (adv.)
eyewitness ochevidets (n.m.)

F (Ф)

fable basnya (n.f.)
fabrication izmyshlenie (n.n.)
fabulous basnoslovnyi (adj.)
facade fasad (n.m.)
  litsevoi (adj.)
face litso (n.n.)
  mina (n.f.)
  oblitsevat' (v.pf.)
  tsiferblat (n.m.)
  zaboi (n.m.)
face downward nits (adv.)
faceted granenyi (adj.)
facial expression mimika (n.f.)
fact fakt (n.m.)
faction fraktsiya (n.f.)
factional fraktsionnyi (adj.)
factor faktor (n.m.)
  pokazatel' (n.m.)
factory fabrichnyi (adj.)
  fabrika (n.f.)
  manufaktura (n.f.)
  zavod (n.m.)
  zavodskoi (adj.)
factory committee zavkom (n.m.)
factory management zavodoupravlenie (n.n.)
factory newspaper mnogotirazhka (n.f.)
fade ottsvesti (v.pf.)
  polinyat' (v.pf.)
  uvyadat' (v.impf.)

uvyanut' (v.pf.)
vytsvesti (v.pf.)
zavyanut' (v.pf.)
faded bleklyi (adj.)
  polinyalyi (adj.)
failure neudacha (n.f.)
  neuspekh (n.m.)
  otkaz (n.m.)
  proval (n.m.)
  sryv (n.m.)
failure, crop neurozhai (n.m.)
faint obmorok (n.m.)
fair yarmarka (n.f.)
fair-haired man blondin (n.m.)
fairway farvater (n.m.)
fairy feya (n.f.)
faith vera (n.f.)
fakir fakir (n.m.)
falcon sokol (n.m.)
fall nispadat' (v.impf.)
  opadat' (v.impf.)
  opast' (v.pf.)
  osypat'sya (v.pf.)
  padat' (v.impf.)
  padenie (n.n.)
  past' (v.pf.)
  rushit'sya (v.impf.)
  upast' (v.pf.)
fall apart razlezat'sya (v.impf.)

fall asleep usnut' (v.pf.)
  zasnut' (v.pf.)
  zasypat' (v.impf.)
fall behind otstat' (v.pf.)
fall down povalit'sya (v.pf.)
  spadat' (v.impf.)
  spast' (v.pf.)
fall ill raskhvorat'sya (v.pf.)
  zabolevat' (v.impf.)
  zakhvorat' (v.pf.)
fall in love polyubit' (v.pf.)
  vlyubit'sya (v.pf.)
fall in price deshevet' (v.impf.)
fall into vpast' (v.pf.)
fall into disgrace oskandalit'sya (v.pf.)
fall of the leaves listopad (n.m.)
fall off otpadat' (v.impf.)
  otpast' (v.pf.)
  otvalivat'sya (v.impf.)
fall on napuskat'sya (v.impf.)
  napustit'sya (v.pf.)
fall out lezt' (v.impf.)
  vypadat' (v.impf.)
  vypast' (v.pf.)
  vyvalivat'sya (v.impf.)
fall, to let obronit' (v.pf.)
fall to pieces razvalivat'sya (v.impf.)
fall to someone's lot dostavat'sya (v.impf.)
fall under podpadat' (v.impf.)
  podpast' (v.pf.)
fall with a thud shlepat'sya (v.impf.)
fallow par (n.m.)
false fal'shivyi (adj.)
  lozhnyi (adj.)
  podlozhnyi (adj.)
  podstavnoi (adj.)
false rumors krivotolki (n.pl.)
false shirtfront manishka (n.f.)
falsify fal'sifitsirovat' (v.impf.)
falsity fal'sh' (n.f.)
falter zapletat'sya (v.impf.)
familiar razvyaznyi (adj.)
family blizkie (n.pl.)
  rod (n.m.)
  sem'ya (n.f.)
  semeinyi (adj.)
family, my moi (n.pl.)
family, with a large mnogosemeinyi (adj.)

famous, to be slavit'sya (v.impf.)
famous, to become proslavit'sya (v.pf.)
fan bolel'shchik (n.m.)
  razdut' (v.pf.)
  veer (n.m.)
fan oneself obmakhivat'sya (v.impf.)
fanatic fanatik (n.m.)
fanaticism fanatizm (n.m.)
fancy to, to take a oblyubovat' (v.pf.)
fang klyk (n.m.)
fantastic fantasticheskii (adj.)
fantasy fantaziya (n.f.)
far dalekii (adj.)
far and wide povsyudu (adv.)
far away, not nepodaleku (adv.)
far off daleko (adv.)
far off, not nevdaleke (adv.)
farce fars (n.m.)
farfetched nadumannyi (adj.)
farm ferma (n.f.)
farm, state sovkhoz (n.m.)
farmer fermer (n.m.)
  zemledelets (n.m.)
farmer, truck ogorodnik (n.m.)
farmhand batrak (n.m.)
farmstead khutor (n.m.)
  usad'ba (n.f.)
farsighted dal'novidnyi (adj.)
  dal'nozorkii (adj.)
fascinate uvlech' (v.pf.)
fascinated, to be plenyat'sya (v.impf.)
fascinating charuyushchii (adj.)
  plenitel'nyi (adj.)
  uvlekatel'nyi (adj.)
fascism fashizm (n.m.)
fashion fason (n.m.)
  moda (n.f.)
fashion, in a new po-novomu (adv.)
fashionable feshenebel'nyi (adj.)
  modnyi (adj.)
fast bystrodeistvuyushchii (adj.)
  skoro (adj.)
  skoryi (adj.)
fasten pribit' (v.pf.)
  pribivat' (v.impf.)
  prikrepit' (v.pf.)
  skrepit' (v.pf.)
  zakhlestnut' (v.pf.)

zakrepit' (v.pf.)

fastening skreplenie (n.n.)

zastezhka (n.f.)

faster skoree (adv.)

fastidious priveredlivyi (adj.)

fat navar (n.m.)

otkormlennyi (adj.)

salo (n.n.)

zhir (n.m.)

zhirnyi (adj.)

fat and flabby obryuzglyi (adj.)

fat, to grow potolstet' (v.pf.)

razzhiret' (v.pf.)

zhiret' (v.impf.)

fatal fatal'nyi (adj.)

fatalism fatalizm (n.m.)

fate dolya (n.f.)

rok (n.m.)

sud'ba (n.f.)

uchast' (n.f.)

father otets (n.m.)

father-in-law svekor (n.m.)

fatherly otecheskii (adj.)

fatigue ustalost' (n.f.)

utomlenie (n.n.)

fatten otkarmlivat' (v.impf.)

otkormit' (v.pf.)

faucet kran (n.m.)

fault prostupok (n.m.)

vina (n.f.)

fault, to be at provinit'sya (v.pf.)

fault, to find pridirat'sya (v.impf.)

pridrat'sya (v.pf.)

faultless bezoshibochnyi (adj.)

fauna fauna (n.f.)

favor milost' (n.f.)

odolzhenie (n.n.)

favorable blagopriyatnyi (adj.)

favorite baloven' (n.m.)

izlyublennyi (adj.)

fawn lebezit' (v.impf.)

fear boyazn' (n.f.)

opasat'sya (v.impf.)

strakh (n.m.)

trusit' (v.impf.)

fearful puglivyi (adj.)

strashnyi (adj.)

fearless besstrashnyi (adj.)

neustrashimyi (adj.)

otvazhnyi (adj.)

feast pir (n.m.)

pirovat' (v.impf.)

feather pero (n.n.)

feather bed perina (n.f.)

feather grass kovyl' (n.m.)

feathered pernatyi (adj.)

February fevral' (n.m.)

federal federal'nyi (adj.)

federation federatsiya (n.f.)

federative federativnyi (adj.)

fee gonorar (n.m.)

feeble khilyi (adj.)

nemoshchnyi (adj.)

feeble effort popolznovenie (n.n.)

feeble, to grow khiret' (v.impf.)

feebly slabo (adv.)

feed kormit' (v.impf.)

nakormit' (v.pf.)

podkarmlivat' (v.impf.)

podkormit' (v.pf.)

feeder pitatel' (n.m.)

feel oshchutit' (v.pf.)

pochuvstvovat' (v.pf.)

poshchupat' (v.pf.)

proshchupat' (v.pf.)

shchupat' (v.impf.)

feel at home osvaivat'sya (v.impf.)

feel feverish znobit' (v.impf.)

feel keenly prochuvstvovat' (v.pf.)

feel shy stesnyat'sya (v.impf.)

feel sick toshnit' (v.impf.)

feel sorry for pozhalet' (v.pf.)

zhalet' (v.impf.)

feeler shchup (n.m.)

feigned delannyi (adj.)

fellow paren' (n.m.)

fellow citizens sograzhdane (n.pl.)

fellow countryman zemlyak (n.m.)

fellow creatures blizhnie (n.pl.)

fellow, fine molodets (n.m.)

fellow, impudent nakhal (n.m.)

fellow, insolent naglets (n.m.)

fellow, lazy lentyai (n.m.)

felt fetr (n.m.)

voilok (n.m.)

felt boots burki (n.pl.)

(cont'd)

valenki (n.pl.)
felt cloak burka (n.f.)
female samka (n.f.)
zhenskii (adj.)
fence izgorod' (n.f.)
ograda (n.f.)
pleten' (n.m.)
zabor (n.m.)
zagorodka (n.f.)
fence in ogorazhivat'(sya) (v.impf.)
ogorodit' (v.pf.)
zagorazhivat' (v.impf.)
zagorodit' (v.pf.)
fence off vygorazhivat' (v.impf.)
vygorodit' (v.pf.)
fencing fekhtovanie (n.n.)
ferment brodit' (v.impf.)
zakvaska (n.f.)
fermentation brozhenie (n.n.)
fermentatsiya (n.f.)
fern paporotnik (n.m.)
ferriferous zhelezistyi (adj.)
ferry parom (n.m.)
fertility plodorodie (n.n.)
fertilization oplodotvorenie (n.n.)
fertilize udobrit' (v.pf.)
fertilizer udobrenie (n.n.)
fester gnoit'sya (v.impf.)
festival festival' (n.m.)
festival, sports spartakiada (n.f.)
fetch skhodit' (v.impf.)
fetish fetish (n.m.)
fetters okovy (n.pl.)
fetus plod (n.m.)
feudal feodal'nyi (adj.)
feudal lord feodal (n.m.)
fever likhoradka (n.f.)
zhar (n.m.)
fever, scarlet skarlatina (n.f.)
feverish, to feel znobit' (v.impf.)
few nemnogie (adj.)
fiasco fiasko (n.n.)
fiber volokno (n.n.)
fiberglass steklovolokno (n.n.)
fibrous voloknistyi (adj.)
fiction belletristika (n.f.)
fiktsiya (n.f.)
vymysel (n.m.)

fictitious fiktivnyi (adj.)
fidget ёrzat' (v.impf.)
neposeda (n.m.&f.)
field pashnya (n.f.)
pole (n.n.)
poprishche (n.n.)
field glasses binokl' (n.m.)
field marshal fel'dmarshal (n.m.)
fierce lyutyi (adj.)
svirepyi (adj.)
fiery ognennyi (adj.)
plamennyi (adj.)
fifteen pyatnadtsat' (num.)
fifth pyatyi (adj.)
fiftieth pyatidesyatyi (adj.)
fifty pyat'desyat (num.)
fight bit'sya (v.impf.)
bor'ba (n.f.)
borot'sya (v.impf.)
draka (n.f.)
drat'sya (v.impf.)
gryznya (n.f.)
srazhat'sya (v.impf.)
fighter borets (n.m.)
istrebitel' (n.m.)
voyaka (n.m.)
fighting boevoi (adj.)
fighting efficiency boesposobnost' (n.f.)
fighting, hand to hand rukopashnaya (n.f.)
figurative figural'nyi (adj.)
obraznyi (adj.)
figure figura (n.f.)
stan (n.m.)
tsifra (n.f.)
figure skater figurist (n.m.)
figured figurnyi (adj.)
figures, in tsifrovoi (adj.)
file napil'nik (n.m.)
papka (n.f.)
podpilivat' (v.impf.)
file, single gus'kom (adv.)
fill nabivat' (v.impf.)
napolnit' (v.pf.)
napolnyat'(sya) (v.impf.)
napustit' (v.pf.)
zaplombirovat' (v.pf.)
zapolnit' (v.pf.)
fill in zasypat' (v.pf.)

fill in for   zameshchat' (v.impf.)
   zamestit' (v.pf.)
fill up   vospolnit' (v.pf.)
   zapravit' (v.pf.)
fill with people   naselit' (v.pf.)
fill with smoke   nakurit' (v.pf.)
filling   nachinka (n.f.)
   plomba (n.f.)
   razlivka (n.f.)
   zapravochnyi (adj.)
filling station   benzokolonka (n.f.)
film   fil'm (n.m.)
   plenka (n.f.)
film, short   korotkometrazhnyi (adj.)
filming   kinos"emka (n.f.)
filter   fil'tr (n.m.)
   protsedit' (v.pf.)
   protsezhivat' (v.impf.)
   tsedit' (v.impf)
filter, light   svetofil'tr (n.m.)
filth   pakost' (n.f.)
fin   plavnik (n.m.)
final   konechnyi (adj.)
finance   finansirovat' (v.impf.)
financial   finansovyi (adj.)
find   izyskat' (v.pf.)
   naiti (v.pf.)
   nakhodit' (v.impf.)
   nakhodka (n.f.)
   nashchupat' (v.pf.)
   otyskat' (v.pf.)
   podyskat' (v.pf.)
   razyskat' (v.pf.)
   uluchit' (v.pf.)
   zastat' (v.pf.)
   zastavat' (v.impf.)
find a place   pristraivat'(sya) (v.impf.)
find fault   pridirat'sya (v.impf.)
   pridrat'sya (v.pf.)
find oneself   ochutit'sya (v.pf.)
find out   doiskat'sya (v.pf.)
   razvedat' (v.pf.)
   uznavat' (v.impf.)
find out, to try to   dopytyvat'sya (v.impf.)
find room   umestit'sya (v.pf.)
find time for   udosuzhit'sya (v.pf.)
find, to try to   izyskivat' (v.impf.)
fine   oshtrafovat' (v.pf.)

   penya (n.f.)
   shtraf (n.m.)
fine fellow   molodets (n.m.)
finger   palets (n.m.)
finger, the little   mizinets (n.m.)
finish   dochitat' (v.pf.)
   dokanchivat' (v.impf.)
   dokonchit' (v.pf.)
   finish (n.m.)
   konchat'(sya) (v.impf.)
   konchit' (v.pf.)
   okanchivat'(sya) (v.impf.)
   okonchit' (v.pf.)
   pokonchit' (v.pf.)
   zakanchivat'(sya) (v.impf.)
   zakonchit' (v.pf.)
finish building   otstraivat' (v.impf.)
   otstroit' (v.pf.)
finish eating   doedat' (v.pf.)
   doest' (v.pf.)
finish off   dobit' (v.pf.)
   dobivat' (v.impf.)
finish playing   doigrat' (v.pf.)
   doigryvat' (v.impf.)
finish talking   dogovarivat' (v.impf)
   dogovorit' (v.pf.)
finish writing   dopisat' (v.pf.)
finishing   okonchanie (n.n.)
   otdelka (n.f.)
Finn   finn (n.m.)
fir   el' (n.f.)
   elovyi (adj.)
fir, silver   pikhta (n.f.)
fir tree   elka (n.f.)
fire   obstrel (n.m.)
   obstrelivat' (v.impf.)
   ogon' (n.m.)
   palit' (v.impf.)
   pozhar (n.m.)
fire bars   kolosnik (n.m.)
fire, camp   koster (n.m.)
fire extinguisher   ognetushitel' (n.m.)
fire, return   otstrelivat'sya (v.impf.)
fire, to catch   zagorat'sya (v.impf.)
   zagoret'sya (v.pf.)
fire, to make the   zataplivat' (v.impf.)
   zatopit' (v.pf.)
fire, to set   zazhech' (v.pf.)

fire, to set on podzhech' (v.pf.)
    podzhigat' (v.impf.)
firearms ognestrel'nyi (adj.)
firebrand goloveshka (n.f.)
firefly svetlyachok (n.m.)
fireplace kamin (n.m.)
fireproof ogneupornyi (adj.)
firewood drova (n.pl.)
fireworks feierverk (n.m.)
firing pal'ba (n.f.)
firing range poligon (n.m.)
firm firma (n.f.)
    nezyblemyi (adj.)
    prochnyi (adj.)
    stoikii (adj.)
firmament nebosvod (n.m.)
first pervyi (adj.)
    vpervye (adv.)
first aid station medpunkt (n.m.)
first, at snachala (adv.)
    sperva (adv.)
    vnachale (adv.)
first floor bel'etazh (n.m.)
first night prem'era (n.f.)
firstborn pervenets (n.m.)
first-class pervoklassnyi (adj.)
firstly vo-pervykh (adv.)
fish ryba (n.f.)
    rybii (adj.)
    rybnyi (adj.)
    udit' (v.impf.)
fish breeding rybovodstvo (n.n.)
fish lure blesna (n.f.)
fish out vylavlivat' (v.impf.)
    vylovit' (v.pf.)
    vyudit' (v.pf.)
fish pond sadok (n.m.)
fish soup ukha (n.f.)
fisherman rybak (n.m.)
    rybolov (n.m.)
fishing uzhenie (n.n.)
fishing line lesa (n.f.)
fishing rod udilishche (n.n.)
    udochka (n.f.)
fishing season putina (n.f.)
fist kulak (n.m.)
fit godnyi (adj.)
    obtyagivat' (v.impf.)

priladit' (v.pf.)
    pripadok (n.m.)
    prisposobit' (v.pf.)
    vporu (adv.)
fit closely oblegat' (v.impf.)
    prilegat' (v.impf.)
fit of coughing, to have a zakashlyat'sya
    (v.pf.)
fit of temper, in a sgoryacha (adv.)
fits and starts, by uryvkami (adv.)
fitter sborshchik (n.m.)
    slesar' (n.m.)
fitting podgonka (n.f.)
    prigonka (n.f.)
five pyat' (num.)
    pyaterka (n.f.)
    pyatero (num.)
    pyatok (n.m.)
five hundred pyat'sot (num.)
five times pyat'yu (adv.)
five-kopeck piece pyatak (n.m.)
five-pointed pyatikonechnyi (adj.)
five-year plan pyatiletka (n.f.)
fix fiksirovat' (v.impf.)
    nametit' (v.pf.)
    naznachat' (v. impf.)
    naznachit' (v.pf.)
    vperit' (v.pf.)
    zafiksirovat' (v.pf.)
fix boundaries razmezhevat'sya (v.pf.)
fixed pristal'nyi (adj.)
    urochnyi (adj.)
fixing agent zakrepitel' (n.m.)
fizzing shipuchii (adj.)
flag flag (n.m.)
flag stop (for a train) polustanok (n.m.)
flagpole drevko (n.n.)
flakes khlop'ya (n.pl.)
flaky sloistyi (adj.)
flame ogon' (n.m.)
    plamya (n.n.)
flame, to burst into vspykhivat' (v.impf.)
flamethrower ognemet (n.m.)
flank flang (n.m.)
flannel flanel' (n.f.)
flap vzmakhivat' (v.impf.)
flap of a coat pola (n.f.)
flare vspyshka (n.f.)

flare up razgorat'sya (v.impf.)
   vspylit' (v.pf.)
flash blesnut' (v.pf.)
   mel'kat' (v.impf.)
   problesk (n.m.)
   promel'knut' (v.pf.)
flash, in a migom (adv.)
flask flyaga (n.f.)
flat bemol' (n.m.)
   ploskii (adj.)
   rovnyi (adj.)
flat round cake lepeshka (n.f.)
flatly naotrez (adv.)
flatten priminat' (v.impf.)
   primyat' (v.pf.)
   priplyusnut' (v.pf.)
   rasplyushchit' (v.pf.)
flattened out splyushchennyi (adj.)
   splyusnutyi (adj.)
flatter pol'stit' (v.pf.)
flatterer l'stets (n.m.)
flattering lestnyi (adj.)
flattery lest' (n.f.)
flaunt shchegolyat' (v.impf.)
flavor privkus (n.m.)
flax len (n.m.)
flax, cultivation of l'novodstvo (n.n.)
flaxen l'nyanoi (adj.)
flea blokha (n.f.)
fleet flot (n.m.)
fleeting mimoletnyi (adj.)
flesh myakot' (n.f.)
   plot' (n.f.)
fleshy myasistyi (adj.)
flexible gibkii (adj.)
flight begstvo (n.n.)
   let (n.m.)
   perelet (n.m.)
   pobeg (n.m.)
   polet (n.m.)
   vylet (n.m.)
fling shvyrnut' (v.pf.)
fling away otshvyrivat' (v.impf.)
flint kremen' (n.m.)
flirt zaigryvat' (v.impf.)
flirtation flirt (n.m.)
float poplavok (n.m.)
   splavit' (v.pf.)

   splavlyat' (v.impf.)
floating plavuchii (adj.)
   splav (n.m.)
floating ice ledokhod (n.m.)
flock staya (n.f.)
floe, ice l'dina (n.f.)
flood navodnenie (n.n.)
   navodnit' (v.pf.)
   razliv (n.m.)
   zalit'(sya) (v.pf.)
   zalivat' (v.impf.)
   zatopit' (v.pf.)
flood, spring polovod'e (n.n.)
floods, spring pavodok (n.m.)
floor étazh (n.m.)
   pol (n.m.)
   polovoi (adj.)
floor, first bel'etazh (n.m.)
floor polish mastika (n.f.)
floor polisher poloter (n.m.)
floor polisher, electric elektropoloter (n.m.)
floor, threshing gumno (n.n.)
flora flora (n.f.)
floriculture tsvetovodstvo (n.n.)
flotation flotatsiya (n.f.)
flounce oborka (n.f.)
flour, finest krupchatka (n.f.)
flourish roscherk (n.m.)
   tush (n.m.)
flow obtekanie (n.n.)
   potok (n.m.)
   protekat' (v.impf.)
   tech' (v.impf.)
flow away utech' (v.pf.)
   utekat' (v.impf.)
flow down stech' (v.pf.)
flow in vtekat' (v.impf.)
flow into vpadat' (v.impf)
flow out vytech' (v.pf.)
   vytekat' (v.impf.)
flow over zakhlestnut' (v.pf.)
flow pattern obtekanie (n.n.)
flower tsvetochnyi (adj.)
   tsvetok (n.m.)
flower bed klumba (n.f.)
flower garden tsvetnik (n.m.)
flowers tsvety (n.pl.)

flowing protochnyi (adj.)
   stok (n.m.)
   tekushchii (adj.)
fluctuating tekuchii (adj.)
flue dymokhod (n.m.)
fluently beglo (adv.)
fluff pushinka (n.f.)
fluffy pushistyi (adj.)
fluid tekuchii (adj.)
fluorescence fluorestsentsiya (n.f.)
fluorination ftorirovanie (n.n.)
fluorine ftor (n.m)
flushed, to become raskrasnet'sya (v.pf.)
flute fleita (n.f.)
flutter porkhat' (v.impf.)
   trepat' (v.impf.)
flux flyus (n.m.)
   potok (n.m.)
fly letat' (v.impf.)
   mukha (n.f.)
   poletet' (v.pf.)
   proletat' (v.impf.)
   razvevat'sya (v.impf.)
fly away otletat' (v.impf.)
   razletat'sya (v.impf.)
   uletat' (v.impf.)
fly down sletat' (v.impf.)
   sletet' (v.pf.)
fly in vletat' (v.impf.)
fly into zaletat' (v.impf.)
fly out vyletat' (v.impf.)
fly over pereletat' (v.impf.)
fly round obletat' (v.impf.)
fly up vzvit'sya (v.pf.)
   vzvivat'sya (v.impf.)
flying letatel'nyi (adj.)
   letnyi (adj.)
   letuchii (adj.)
   pereletnyi (adj.)
flying club, amateur aeroklub (n.m.)
flying, to come priletat' (v.impf.)
flywheel makhovik (n.m.)
foal zherebenok (n.m.)
foam pena (n.f.)
   penit'sya (v.impf.)
foamy penistyi (adj.)
focus fokus (n.m.)
fodder furazh (n.m.)

   kormovoi (adj.)
fog tuman (n.m.)
foil fol'ga (n.f.)
   rapira (n.f.)
fold stvorka (n.f.)
folder skorosshivatel' (n.m.)
folding otkidnoi (adj.)
   skladnoi (adj.)
foliage listva (n.f.)
folio foliant (n.m.)
folklore fol'klor (n.m.)
follow posledovat' (v.pf.)
   sledovat' (v.impf.)
   vytekat' (v.impf.)
follower posledovatel' (n.m.)
following posleduyushchii (adj.)
   sleduyushchii (adj.)
folly dur' (n.f.)
food eda (n.f.)
   kushan'e (n.n.)
   pishcha (n.f.)
   pishchevoi (adj.)
   prodovol'stvennyi (adj.)
   produktovyi (adj.)
   s"estnoi (adj.)
   yastva (n.pl.)
food, canned konservy (n.pl.)
food preserved in brine solen'e (n.n.)
fool dura (n.f.)
   shut (n.m.)
fool of, to make a odurachit' (v.pf.)
foolhardy bedovyi (adj.)
foot noga (n.f.)
   nozhnoi (adj.)
   podnozhie (n.n.)
   stopa (n.f.)
   stupnya (n.f.)
foot binding portyanka (n.f.)
foot, on peshkom (adv.)
foot-and-mouth disease yashchur (n.m.)
football futbol (n.m.)
football shoes butsy (n.pl.)
footlights rampa (n.f.)
footman lakei (n.m.)
footnote snoska (n.f.)
footway, planked mostki (n.pl.)
footwear obuv' (n.f.)
   obuvnoi (adj.)

for dlya (prep.)
for a long time nadolgo (adv.)
for example naprimer (intro.)
for external use naruzhnoe (n.n.)
for future use vprok (adv.)
for hire naprokat (adv.)
for hours podolgu (adv.)
for show napokaz (adv.)
    pokaznoi (adj.)
for some reason or other pochemu-libo (adv.)
for sure navernyaka (adv.)
for the sake of radi (prep.)
for two weeks dvukhnedel'nyi (adj.)
forage korm (n.m.)
forbid vospretit' (v.pf.)
    zapreshchat' (v.impf.)
force forsirovat' (v.impf.)
    nevolit' (v.impf.)
    sila (n.f.)
    usilie (n.n.)
    vynudit' (v.pf.)
force, by nasil'no (adv.)
force one's way lomit'sya (v.impf.)
force one's way through probit'sya (v.pf.)
    protolkat'sya (v.pf.)
force out vytesnit' (v.pf.)
force upon navyazat' (v.pf.)
force oneself upon navyazyvat'(sya)
    (v.impf.)
forced to, to be prikhodit'sya (v.impf.)
ford brod (n.m.)
foreboding predchuvstvie (n.n.)
forecast predskazanie (n.n.)
    prognoz (n.m.)
forehead lob (n.m.)
foreign chuzhezemnyi (adj.)
    inorodnyi (adj.)
    inozemnyi (adj.)
    zagranichnyi (adj.)
    zarubezhnyi (adj.)
foreigner inostranets (n.m.)
foreman desyatnik (n.m.)
    master (n.m.)
forerunner predvestnik (n.m.)
foresee predusmatrivat' (v.impf.)
    predvidet' (v.impf.)
foreseeing predusmotritel'nyi (adj.)
forest les (n.m.)

    lesnoi (adj.)
forest, edge of opushka (n.f.)
forest, pine bor (n.m.)
forester lesnik (n.m.)
forestry lesnichestvo (n.n.)
    lesovodstvo (n.n.)
foretell predveshchat' (v.impf.)
forever naveki (adv.)
    navsegda (adv.)
forfeit neustoika (n.f.)
forge kovat' (v.impf.)
    kuznitsa (n.f.)
    sfabrikovat' (v.pf.)
    vykovat' (v.pf.)
forged kovannyi (adj.)
forgery podlog (n.m.)
forget razuchit'sya (v.pf.)
    zabyvat' (v.impf.)
forget oneself zabyt'sya (v.pf.)
    zabyvat'sya (v.impf.)
forgetful zabyvchivyi (adj.)
forget-me-not nezabudka (n.f.)
forging kovka (n.f.)
forgive prostit' (v.pf.)
forgiveness proshchenie (n.n.)
forgotten zabytyi (adj.)
fork vilka (n.f.)
fork, tuning kamerton (n.m.)
form anketa (n.f.)
    blank (n.m.)
    forma (n.f.)
    formirovat' (v.impf.)
    obraz (n.m.)
    obrazovat' (v.pf.)
    obrazovyvat'(sya) (v.impf.)
    sformirovat' (v.pf.)
form, to take the oblekat'(sya) (v.impf.)
formal zvanyi (adj.)
formalism formalizm (n.m.)
formality formal'nost' (n.f.)
formation formatsiya (n.f.)
    obrazovanie (n.n.)
former byvshii (adj.)
    prezhnii (adj.)
formless besformennyi (adj.)
formula formula (n.f.)
formulate sformulirovat' (v.pf.)
forswear zakayat'sya (v.pf.)

fort   fort (n.m.)
fortieth   sorokovoi (adj.)
fortress   krepost' (n.f.)
    krepostnoi (adj.)
fortune   sostoyanie (n.n.)
fortune, to make a   nazhivat'(sya) (v.impf.)
fortune-teller   gadalka (n.f.)
forty   sorok (num.)
forward   vpered (adv.)
forward, to come   vystupat' (v.impf.)
fossil   iskopaemoe (n.n.)
    okamenelost' (n.f.)
foul   gadit' (v.impf.)
    nenastnyi (adj.)
foul language, to use   skvernoslovit' (v.impf.)
foul, to become   protukhnut' (v.pf.)
foul weather   nepogoda (n.f.)
found   osnovat' (v.pf.)
    osnovyvat' (v.impf.)
found, to be   naitis' (v.pf.)
    vodit'sya (v.impf.)
foundation   fundament (n.m.)
    osnovanie (n.n.)
foundation, to lay a   zalozhit' (v.pf.)
foundations   ustoi (n.pl.)
founder   osnovatel' (n.m.)
    osnovopolozhnik (n.m.)
founding   otlivka (n.f.)
foundry   liteinaya (n.f.)
foundry (mill), steel   staleliteinyi zavod
    (adj.-n.m.)
fountain   fontan (n.m.)
fountain pen   avtoruchka (n.f.)
four   chetverka (n.f.)
    chetvero (num.)
    chetyre (num.)
four, all   chetveren'ki (n.pl.)
four times   vchetvero (adv.)
four-footed   chetveronogii (n.m.)
four-seater   chetyrekhmestnyi (adj.)
four-storied   chetyrekhétazhnyi (adj.)
fourteen   chetyrnadtsat' (num.)
fourth   chetvertyi (adj.)
four-year   chetyrekhletnii (adj.)
fowling   ptitsevodstvo (n.n.)
fox   lisa (n.f.)
fox, polar   pesets (n.m.)
fox, silver   cherno-buryi (adj.)

fox-trot   fokstrot (n.m.)
foyer   foie (n.n.)
fraction   drob' (n.f.)
fracture   nadlom (n.m.)
    perelom (n.m.)
    slomat' (v.pf.)
fragile   khrupkii (adj.)
    neprochnyi (adj.)
fragment   fragment (n.m.)
    oblomok (n.m.)
    otryvok (n.m.)
fragrance   blagoukhanie (n.n.)
fragrant   dushistyi (adj.)
    pakhuchii (adj.)
frame   rama (n.f.)
frame, embroidery   pyal'tsy (n.pl.)
framework   karkas (n.m.)
    ostov (n.m.)
    srub (n.m.)
frank   otkrovennyi (adj.)
frankfurter   sosiska (n.f.)
frankness   pryamodushie (n.n.)
fraternally   po-bratski (adv.)
fraud   obman (n.m.)
fraught   chrevatyi (adj.)
fray   obtrepat' (v.pf.)
fray through   pereteret' (v.pf.)
freckle   vesnushka (n.f.)
free   darovoi (adj.)
    privol'nyi (adj.)
free of charge   besplatnyi (adj.)
free, to set   osvobodit' (v.pf.)
freedom   svoboda (n.f.)
freedom-loving   svobodolyubivyi (adj.)
freethinking   svobodomyslie (n.n.)
freeze   ledenet' (v.impf.)
    podmorazhivat' (v.impf.)
    vymerzat' (v.impf.)
    zamerzat' (v.impf.)
    zamorazhivat' (v.impf.)
freeze through   promerzat' (v.impf.)
freight   frakht (n.m.)
French   frantsuzskii (adj.)
    frantsuzy (n.pl.)
Frenchman   frantsuz (n.m.)
frenzy   isstuplenie (n.n.)
    neistovstvo (n.n.)
frequency   chastota (n.f.)

periodichnost' (n.f.)

frequency-modulated chastotno
modulirovannyi (adj.)

frequent chastyi (adj.)

frequent, to become more uchashchat'sya
(v.impf.)
uchastit'sya (v.pf.)

fresco freska (n.f.)

fresh parnoi (adj.)
presnyi (adj.)

fresh, not nesvezhii (adj.)

freshman pervokursnik (n.m.)

freshness svezhest' (n.f.)

friable sypuchii (adj.)

friction trenie (n.n.)

Friday pyatnitsa (n.f.)

fried zharenyi (adj.)

fried eggs glazun'ya (n.f.)
yaichnitsa (n.f.)

friend drug (n.m.)
podruga (n.f.)
priyatel' (n.m.)

friendly druzhnyi (adj.)

friendly way, in a po-druzheski (adv.)

friends, to be druzhit' (v.impf.)

friends, to make podruzhit'sya (v.pf.)
sdruzhit'sya (v.pf.)

friendship druzhba (n.f.)

fright ispug (n.m.)

frighten ispugat' (v.pf.)
napugat' (v.pf.)
otpugivat' (v.impf.)
perepugat' (v.pf.)
pugat' (v.impf.)
strashit' (v.impf.)
ustrashat' (v.impf.)

frighten away vspugivat' (v.impf.)

frighten off spugivat' (v.impf.)

fringe bakhroma (n.f.)

frisk rezvit'sya (v.impf.)

frivolous frivol'nyi (adj.)

frock coat syurtuk (n.m.)

frog lyagushka (n.f.)

from iz (prep.)
ot (prep.)
s (prep.)
so (prep.)

from above sverkhu (adv.)

from afar izdaleka (adv.)

from behind iz-za (prep.)
szadi (adv.)

from below snizu (adv.)

from everywhere otovsyudu (adv.)

from here otsyuda (adv.)

from now on otnyne (adv.)

from nowhere neotkuda (adv.)
niotkuda (adv.)

from one side sboku (adv.)

from outside izvne (adv.)

from there ottuda (adv.)

from under iz-pod (prep.)

from within iznutri (adv.)

front front (n.m.)
pered (n.m.)
perednii (adj.)

front, in speredi (adv.)
vperedi (adv.)

front of, in pered (prep.)

front orchestra seats parter (n.m.)

frontier guard pogranichnik (n.m.)

front-line soldier frontovik (n.m.)

frost moroz (n.m.)

frost resistant morozoustoichivyi (adj.)

frostbitten obmorozhennyi (adj.)

frostbitten, to be otmorazhivat' (v.impf.)

frosts, early zamorozki (n.pl.)

froth vspenivat'sya (v.impf.)

frown khmurit'sya (v.impf.)
nakhmurit'sya (v.pf.)
nasupit'sya (v.pf.)

frozen merzlyi (adj.)
oledenelyi (adj.)

fruit frukt (n.m.)
plod (n.m.)

fruit, candied tsukat (n.m.)

fruit drink mors (n.m.)

fruit growing plodovodstvo (n.n.)

fruit jelly marmelad (n.m.)

fruit liqueur nalivka (n.f.)

fruit-drop ledenets (n.m.)

fruitful plodotvornyi (adj.)

frustrated, to be rasstraivat'sya (v.impf.)

frying pan skovoroda (n.f.)

fuel goryuchee (n.n.)
toplivo (n.n.)

fugitive beglets (n.m.)

fulfill ispolnit' (v.pf.)
   vypolnit' (v.pf.)
fulfillment ispolnenie (n.n.)
   vypolnenie (n.n.)
full polno (adv.)
   polnyi (adj.)
full house anshlag (n.m.)
full moon polnolunie (n.n.)
full of holes dyryavyi (adj.)
full of rancor zlopamyatnyi (adj.)
full-blooded polnokrovnyi (adj.)
fumes chad (n.m.)
fumigate okurivat' (v.impf.)
fun potekha (n.f.)
   vesel'e (n.n.)
fun of, to make podsmeivat'sya (v.impf.)
function funktsionirovat' (v.impf.)
   funktsiya (n.f.)
fund fond (n.m.)
funeral pogrebal'nyi (adj.)
   pokhorony (n.pl.)
fungicide fungitsid (n.m.)
fungus gubka (n.f.)
funicular funikuler (n.m.)
funnel voronka (n.f.)
funny, incredibly umoritel'nyi (adj.)
fur mekh (n.m.)
   mekhovoi (adj.)
fur coat shuba (n.f.)
fur seal kotik (n.m.)
furious raz"yarennyi (adj.)

   vzbeshennyi (adj.)
   yarostnyi (adj.)
furious, to grow rassvirepet' (v.pf.)
furnace gorn (n.m.)
   topka (n.f.)
furnace, blast domennyi (adj.)
   domna (n.f.)
furnish meblirovat' (v.impf.&pf.)
   obstavit' (v.pf.)
furniture mebel' (n.f.)
   obstanovka (n.f.)
furore furor (n.m.)
furrier skornyak (n.m.)
furrow borozda (n.f.)
furs pushnina (n.f.)
further dal'neishii (adj.)
   dal'she (adj.)
   dalee (adv.)
further off poodal' (adv.)
fury yarost' (n.f.)
fuse vzryvatel' (n.m.)
   zapal (n.m.)
fuselage fyuzelyazh (n.m.)
fusible plavkii (adj.)
fuss sueta (n.f.)
   voznya (n.f.)
futile bezrezul'tatnyi (adj.)
future budushchee (n.n.)
   budushchii (adj.)
future use, for vprok (adv.)

G (Г)

gadfly ovod (n.m.)
gaiety veselost' (n.f.)
gaily veselo (adv.)
gain pozhiva (n.f.)
   prok (n.m.)
   vygadat' (v.pf.)
gain promotion vysluzhivat'sya (v.impf.)
gain the upper hand oderzhat' verkh (v.pf.)
gait pokhodka (n.f.)
gaiters getry (n.pl.)

gala paradnyi (adj.)
gallery galereya (n.f.)
   galerka (n.f.)
   khory (n.pl.)
   shtol'nya (n.f.)
gallery, shooting tir (n.m.)
galley-proof granka (n.f.)
gallium gallii (n.m.)
gallop galop (n.m.)
   skachka (n.f.)

gallop, at a vskach' (adv.)
gallop away uskakat' (v.pf.)
gallop, rapid kar'er (n.m.)
galloping, to come priskakat' (v.pf.)
gallows viselitsa (n.f.)
galoshes galoshi (n.pl.)
    kaloshi (n.pl.)
galvanic gal'vanicheskii (adj.)
galvanized otsinkovannyi (adj.)
galvanizing gal'vanizatsiya (n.f.)
game dich' (n.f.)
gamma radiation gamma-izluchenie (n.n.)
gang banda (n.f.)
    orava (n.f.)
    shaika (n.f.)
    vataga (n.f.)
ganglion uzel (n.m.)
gangrene gangrena (n.f.)
gangway skhodni (n.pl.)
gap razryv (n.m.)
gape razevat' (v.impf.)
    zazevat'sya (v.pf.)
garage avtobaza (n.f.)
    garazh (n.m.)
garbage musor (n.m.)
    pomoinyi (adj.)
garble podtasovat' (v.pf.)
garden sad (n.m.)
garden, kitchen ogorod (n.m.)
garden, public skver (n.m.)
garden, small front palisadnik (n.m.)
gardener sadovnik (n.m.)
garland girlyanda (n.f.)
garlic chesnok (n.m.)
garment odeyanie (n.n.)
garnet granat (n.m.)
garnish garnir (n.m.)
garrison garnizon (n.m.)
gas gaz (n.m.)
    gazovyi (adj.)
gas chamber dushegubka (n.f.)
gas generator gazogenerator (n.m.)
gas main gazoprovod (n.m.)
gas mask protivogaz (n.m.)
gas shelter gazoubezhishche (n.n.)
gas, tear slezotochivyi gaz (adj.-n.m.)
gaseous gazoobraznyi (adj.)
gasp akhnut' (v.pf.)

gastritis gastrit (n.m.)
gate vorota (n.pl.)
gateway podvorotnya (n.f.)
gather nabirat'(sya) (v.impf.)
    nabrat' (v.pf.)
    sletat'sya (v.impf.)
    sletet'sya (v.pf.)
    stekat'sya (v.impf.)
gather in prignat' (v.pf.)
    prigonyat' (v.impf.)
gathers sborki (n.pl.)
gauge izmeritel' (n.m.)
    shchup (n.m.)
gauge, pressure manometr (n.m.)
gauze marlya (n.f.)
gear peredacha (n.f.)
    privod (n.m.)
    shesternya (n.f.)
gear, reduction reduktor (n.m.)
gear, reversing revers (n.m.)
gelatine zhelatin (n.m.)
gendarme zhandarm (n.m.)
gender rod (n.m.)
genealogical rodoslovnyi (adj.)
genealogy genealogiya (n.f.)
general general (n.m.)
    general'nyi (adj.)
    obshchii (adj.)
    vseobshchii (adj.)
general education, providing
    obshcheobrazovatel'nyi (adj.)
general, in voobshche (adv.)
general state samochuvstvie (n.n.)
general use, in obshcheupotrebitel'nyi (adj.)
generalissimo generalissimus (n.m.)
generalization obobshchenie (n.n.)
generalize obobshchit' (v.pf.)
generally accepted obshcheprinyatyi (adj.)
generation pokolenie (n.n.)
generator generator (n.m.)
generator, gas gazogenerator (n.m.)
generosity shchedrost' (n.f.)
    velikodushie (n.n.)
generous, to be rasshchedrit'sya (v.pf.)
genesis genezis (n.m.)
genetics genetika (n.f.)
genitive roditel'nyi (adj.)
genius genii (n.m.)

genre   zhanr (n.m.)

gentleman   barin (n.m.)
   gospodin (n.m.)

genuine   nepoddel'nyi (adj.)

genus   rod (n.m.)

geochemistry   geokhimiya (n.f.)

geographer   geograf (n.m.)

geological survey   geologorazvedka (n.f.)

geologist   geolog (n.m.)

geomagnetism   geomagnetizm (n.m.)

geometry   geometriya (n.f.)

geophysical   geofizicheskii (adj.)

Georgian   gruzin (n.m.)

geranium   geran' (n.f.)

German   germanskii (adj.)
   nemets (n.m.)
   nemetskii (adj.)

German woman   nemka (n.f.)

germinate   prorastat' (v.impf.)

gesture   zhest (n.m.)

get   popast' (v.pf.)
   razdobyt' (v.pf.)
   zavodit' (v.impf.)

get hold of   razdobyt' (v.pf.)

get on   obstoyat' (v.impf.)
   uzhit'sya (v.pf.)
   uzhivat'sya (v.impf.)

get on with   ladit' (v.impf.)

get on with, easy to   uzhivchivyi (adj.)

get out   vybirat'sya (v.impf.)
   vybrat'sya (v.pf.)

get out of something   otvertet'sya (v.pf.)

get over   perebirat'sya (v.impf.)
   perebrat'sya (v.pf.)
   preodolevat' (v.impf.)

get to   doekhat' (v.pf.)
   doezzhat' (v.pf.)
   naspekh (adv.)

get up   vstat' (v.pf.)
   vstavat' (v.impf.)

get used to   privykat (v.impf.)

geyser   kolonka (n.f.)

ghost   prividenie (n.n.)

giant   gigant (n.m.)
   ispolin (n.m.)
   velikan (n.m.)

giddiness   durnota (n.f.)

gift   dar (n.m.)

podarok (n.m.)

gifted   odarennyi (adj.)

giggle   khikhikat' (v.impf.)

gilding   pozolota (n.f.)

gills   zhabry (n.pl.)

gimlet   burav (n.m.)

ginger   imbir' (n.m.)

girder   ferma (n.f.)

girdle   opoyasat' (v.pf.)

girl   devitsa (n.f.)
   devochka (n.f.)
   devushka (n.f.)

give   dat' (v.pf.)
   davat' (v.impf.)
   podat' (v.pf.)
   podavat' (v.impf.)
   pridat' (v.pf.)
   udelit' (v.pf.)
   udelyat' (v.impf.)

give away   vydavat' (v.impf.)

give back   otdat' (v.pf.)
   otdavat' (v.impf.)

give birth   porodit' (v.pf.)
   porozhdat' (v.impf.)
   rodit' (v.pf.)
   rozhat' (v.impf.)

give in   poddat'sya (v.pf.)
   poddavat'sya (v.impf.)

give oneself to   otdat'sya (v.pf.)

give orders   rasporyazhat'sya (v.impf.)

give out   vydat' (v.pf.)

give up   otstupat'sya (v.impf.)
   otstupit'sya (v.pf.)

give way   podkashivat'sya (v.impf.)
   podkosit'sya (v.pf.)

given   dannyi (adj.)

glacier   gletcher (n.m.)
   lednik (n.m.)

glaciology   glyatsiologiya (n.f.)

glad   rad (adj.)

glad, to make   obradovat' (v.pf.)
   radovat' (v.impf.)

glade   progalina (n.f.)

glance   posmatrivat' (v.impf.)
   vzglyad (n.m.)
   vzglyanut' (v.pf.)

glances, to exchange   pereglyadyvat'sya
   (v.impf.)

gland zheleza (n.f.)

glass stakan (n.m.)

   steklo (n.n.)

   steklyannyi (adj.)

glass holder podstakannik (n.m.)

glass, magnifying lupa (n.f.)

glass, measuring menzurka (n.f.)

glass, small stopka (n.f.)

glasses ochki (n.pl.)

glasses, field binokl' (n.m.)

glasses, to clink chokat'sya (v.impf.)

glaze osteklit' (v.pf.)

   zasteklit' (v.pf.)

glazier stekol'shchik (n.m.)

glib boikii (adj.)

glide planirovat' (v.impf.)

glider planer (n.m.)

gliding planirovanie (n.n.)

glimmer mertsat' (v.impf.)

gloating zloradnyi (adj.)

globe globus (n.m.)

gloomy sumrachnyi (adj.)

glorious slavnyi (adj.)

glory slava (n.f.)

glove perchatka (n.f.)

glow zarevo (n.n)

glucose glyukoza (n.f.)

glue klei (n.m.)

glue on nakleit' (v.pf.)

glue up zakleit' (v.pf.)

   zakleivat' (v.impf.)

glutton obzhora (n.m.&f.)

glycerine glitserin (n.m.)

gnaw glodat' (v.impf.)

   gryzt' (v.impf.)

   obgladyvat' (v.impf.)

   tochit' (v.impf.)

gnaw through peregryzat' (v.impf.)

   progryzat' (v.impf.)

go idti (v.impf.)

   khodit' (v.impf.)

   poekhat' (v.pf.)

   poiti (v.pf.)

   skhodit' (v.impf.)

go away razoitis' (v.pf.)

   uezzhat' (v.impf.)

   uiti (v.pf.)

   ukhodit' (v.impf.)

go back on otrech'sya (v.pf.)

go down s"ekhat' (v.pf.)

   skhodit' (v.impf.)

   soiti (v.pf.)

go into vdavat'sya (v.impf.)

go mad obezumet' (v.pf.)

   pomeshat'sya (v.pf.)

go out gasnut' (v.impf.)

   pogasnut' (v.pf.)

   potukhat' (v.impf.)

   tukhnut' (v.impf.)

   vyiti (v.pf.)

   vykhodit' (v.impf.)

go round ob"ekhat' (v.pf.)

   oboiti (v.pf.)

go through perenesti (v.pf.)

   perenosit' (v.impf.)

goal gol (n.m.)

goalkeeper vratar' (n.m.)

goat (female) koza (n.f.)

goblet bokal (n.m.)

   kubok (n.m.)

God bog (n.m.)

goiter zob (n.m.)

gold zoloto (n.n.)

gold digger staratel' (n.m.)

gold industry zolotopromyshlennost' (n.f.)

gold, pure chervonnyi (adj.)

gold-bearing zolotonosnyi (adj.)

golden zolotistyi (adj.)

goldfinch shchegol (n.m.)

gondola gondola (n.f.)

gone wild odichavshii (adj.)

good dobro (n.n.)

   khoroshii (adj.)

good deed blagodeyanie (n.n.)

good-bye proshchai(te) (coll.)

good-for-nothing nikchemnyi (adj.)

good-natured bezzlobnyi (adj.)

   dobrodushnyi (adj.)

goods tovarnyi (adj.)

goods and chattels skarb (n.m.)

goods turnover gruzooborot (n.m.)

goose gus' (n.m.)

   gusinyi (adj.)

gooseberry kryzhovnik (n.m.)

gooseflesh gusyatina (n.f.)

gorge ushchel'e (n.n.)

gosling   gusenok (n.m.)
gospel   evangelie (n.m.)
gossip   spletnik (n.m.)
gossip, idle   peresudy (n.pl.)
gossip, malicious   zloslovie (n.n.)
Gothic   goticheskii (adj.)
goulash   gulyash (n.m.)
gout   podagra (n.f.)
govern   pravit' (v.impf.)
government   pravitel'stvo (n.n.)
    pravlenie (n.n.)
government(al)   pravitel'stvennyi (adj.)
governor   gubernator (n.m.)
gown, dressing   khalat (n.m.)
grace   gratsiya (n.f.)
graceful   gratsioznyi (adj.)
    izyashchnyi (adj.)
gracious   milostivyi (adj.)
gradient   uklon (n.m.)
grading   razbrakovka (n.f.)
gradually   postepenno (adv.)
graduate   vypusknik (n.m.)
graduation   diplomnyi (adj.)
graft   vzyatochnichestvo (n.n.)
grafting   peresadka (n.f.)
grain   zerno (n.n.)
grain of sand   peschinka (n.f.)
grain procurement   khlebozagotovka (n.f.)
grain-growing   khleborodnyi (adj.)
gram   gramm (n.m.)
grammar   grammatika (n.f.)
granary   zhitnitsa (n.f.)
grand chess master   grossmeister (n.m.)
grand piano   royal' (n.m.)
granddaughter   vnuchka (n.f.)
grandeur   velichie (n.n.)
grandiose   grandioznyi (adj.)
grandmother   babushka (n.f.)
grandson   vnuk (n.m.)
granite   granit (n.m.)
grant   dotatsiya (n.f.)
    stipendiya (n.f.)
grant holder   stipendiat (n.m.)
granular   zernistyi (adj.)
granuloma   granulema (n.f.)
grapes   vinograd (n.m.)
graphic   graficheskii (adj.)
    izobrazitel'nyi (adj.)

graphic arts   grafika (n.f.)
graphite   grafit (n.m.)
grasp   soobrazit' (v.pf.)
grass   trava (n.f.)
grass, feather   kovyl' (n.m.)
grass snake   uzh (n.m.)
grasshopper   kuznechik (n.m.)
grassy   travyanistyi (adj.)
grateful   blagodarnyi (adj.)
    priznatel'nyi (adj.)
gratis   darom (adv.)
gratuitous   bezvozmezdnyi (adj.)
grave   mogila (n.f.)
    nadgrobnyi (adj.)
gravel   gravii (n.m.)
gravitation   gravitatsiya (n.f.)
    tyagotenie (n.n.)
gravity   tyazhest' (n.f.)
gravity, specific   udel'nyi ves (adj.-n.m.)
gray   prosed' (n.f.)
    sedoi (adj.)
    seryi (adj.)
gray hen   teterka (n.f.)
gray, to become   posedet' (v.pf.)
gray, to turn   sedet' (v.impf.)
graybearded   sedoborodyi (adj.)
gray-haired   sedovlasyi (adj.)
grayish   serovatyi (adj.)
grayish-brown   buryi (adj.)
graze   pastis' (v.impf.)
grease   podmazat' (v.pf.)
    smazat' (v.pf.)
grease, to stain with   zasalivat' (v.impf.)
greasy   sal'nyi (adj.)
great   bol'shoi (adj.)
    velikii (adj.)
greatcoat   shinel' (n.f.)
great-grandfather   praded (n.m.)
great-grandmother   prababushka (n.f.)
great-grandson   pravnuk (n.m.)
greediness   alchnost' (n.f.)
greedy   padkii (adj.)
    zhadnyi (adj.)
Greek   grecheskii (adj.)
    grek (n.m)
green   zelenyi (adj.)
green, to turn   zazelenet' (v.pf.)
    zelenet' (v.impf.)

greenhorn molokosos (n.m.)
greenhouse teplitsa (n.f.)
greet pozdorovat'sya (v.pf)
   zdorovat'sya (v.impf.)
grenade granata (n.f.)
grief gore (n.n.)
grieve ogorchat' (v.impf.)
   opechalit' (v.pf.)
   pechalit' (v.impf.)
grimace grimasa (n.f.)
   uzhimka (n.f.)
grin skalit' (v.impf.)
   ukhmyl'nut'sya (v.pf.)
grind molot' (v.impf.)
   obtachivat' (v.impf.)
   peremalyvat' (v.impf.)
   peremolot' (v.pf.)
   rasteret' (v.pf.)
   rastoloch' (v.pf.)
   razmalyvat' (v.impf.)
   razmolot' (v.pf.)
   zaskrezhetat' (v.pf.)
grind, polish shlifovat' (v.impf.)
grinder, meat myasorubka (n.f.)
grinding pomol (n.m.)
   shlifovka (n.f.)
grinding noise skrezhet (n.m.)
grips, to come to stsepit'sya (v.pf.)
   stseplyat'sya (v.impf.)
groan kryakhtet' (v.impf.)
   zakryakhtet' (v.pf.)
grocery bakaleinyi (adj.)
   bakaleya (n.f.)
   gastronomicheskii (adj.)
groin pakh (n.m.)
groom konyukh (n.m.)
groove paz (n.m.)
   rytvina (n.f.)
groping oshchup'yu (adv.)
gross valovoi (adj.)
grotto grot (n.m.)
ground nazemnyi (adj.)
   ploshchadka (n.f.)
ground squirrel suslik (n.m.)
ground, to level to the sryt' (v.pf.)
   sryvat' (v.impf.)
ground, to the nazem' (adv.)
ground, waste pustyr' (n.m.)

groundless bespochvennyi (adj.)
   besprichinnyi (adj.)
   neobosnovannyi (adj.)
group gruppa (n.f.)
grove roshcha (n.f.)
grove, nut oreshnik (n.m.)
grow delat'sya (v.impf.)
   otrastat' (v.impf.)
   rasti (v.impf.)
   razrastat'sya (v.impf.)
   vozrasti (v.pf.)
   vyrastat' (v.impf.)
grow together srastat'sya (v.impf.)
grow up operit'sya (v.pf.)
   operyat'sya (v.impf.)
   podrastat' (v.impf.)
   podrasti (v.pf.)
growing narastanie (n.n.)
growl rychat' (v.impf.)
growth narost (n.m.)
   rost (n.m.)
   vozrastanie (n.n.)
gruel kasha (n.f.)
grumble bryuzzhat' (v.impf.)
grumbler bryuzga (n.m.&f.)
grumbling vorchanie (n.n.)
grunt khryukat' (v.impf.)
guarantee garantirovat' (v.impf.&pf.)
   garantiya (n.f.)
   ruchatel'stvo (n.n.)
guard blyusti (v.impf.)
   karaul (n.m.)
   oberegat' (v.impf.)
   okhrana (n.f.)
   storozh (n.m.)
   storozhit' (v.impf.)
   strazha (n.f.)
   uberech' (v.pf.)
guard, frontier pogranichnik (n.m.)
guard, home opolchenie (n.n.)
guard oneself oberech'(sya) (v.pf.)
guardhouse gauptvakhta (n.f.)
guardianship opeka (n.f.)
guards gvardiya (n.f.)
guardsman gvardeets (n.m.)
guess dogadat'sya (v.pf.)
   dogadka (n.f.)
   otgadat' (v.pf.)
   (cont'd)

ugadat' (v.pf.)
guessing razgadka (n.f.)
guest gost' (n.m.)
guidance rukovodstvo (n.n.)
guide gid (n.m.)
provodnik (n.m.)
putevoditel' (n.m.)
guilt vina (n.f.)
guilty vinovatyi (adj.)
guilty, not nevinovnyi (adj.)
guilty, to prove someone ulichat' (v.impf.)
guise lichina (n.f.)
guitar gitara (n.f.)
gulf puchina (n.f.)
gullet pishchevod (n.m.)
gulp khlebat' (v.impf.)
gulp, to take a otkhlebnut' (v.pf.)
gum desna (n.f.)
gummiarabik (n.m.)

gumboil flyus (n.m.)
gun orudiinyi (adj.)
pushechnyi (adj.)
pushka (n.f.)
ruzh'e (n.n.)
gun carriage lafet (n.m.)
gun, machine pulemet (n.m.)
gunboat kanonerka (n.f.)
gunner navodchik (n.m.)
gunner, submachine avtomatchik (n.m.)
gunpowder porokh (n.m.)
gush out khlynut' (v.pf.)
gust poryv (n.m.)
gusty poryvistyi (adj.)
gymnast gimnast (n.m.)
gynecologist ginekolog (n.m.)
gynecology ginekologiya (n.f.)
gypsum gips (n.m.)
Gypsy tsygan (n.m.)

H

haberdashery galantereya (n.f.)
habit obyknovenie (n.n.)
habit, to break a otuchit' (v.pf.)
habit, to get the povadit'sya (v.pf.)
habit, to lose the otuchat'sya (v.impf.)
otvykat' (v.impf.)
habitable, to render obzhit' (v.pf.)
habitual prisushchii (adj.)
habitue zavsegdatai (n.m.)
hack to pieces izrubit' (v.pf.)
hackneyed zataskannyi (adj.)
haggard ispitoi (adj.)
haggle torg (n.m.)
hail grad (n.m.)
hair volos (n.m.)
hair, dishevelled kosmy (n.pl.)
hairdo pricheska (n.f.)
hairdresser parikmakher (n.m.)
hairpin shpil'ka (n.f.)
zakolka (n.f.)
hairy mokhnatyi (adj.)
half napolovinu (adv.)

polovina (n.f.)
taim (n.m.)
half asleep polusonnyi (adj.)
half dead polumertvyi (adj.)
half hour polchasa (n.m.)
half, in popolam (adv.)
half measure polumera (n.f.)
half naked polugolyi (adj.)
half, one and a poltora (num.)
half price poltseny (col.)
half rise pripodnimat'sya (v.impf.)
privstat' (v.pf.)
half year polgoda (n.m.)
polugodie (n.n.)
half-awake sprosonok (adv.)
half-finished product polufabrikat (n.m.)
half-kopeck piece grosh (n.m.)
half-length coat polushubok (n.m.)
half-moon polumesyats (n.m.)
half-open poluotkrytyi (adj.)
half-turn poluoborot (n.m.)
hall perednyaya (n.f.)

zal (n.m.)
hall, lecture auditoriya (n.f.)
hallucination gallyutsinatsiya (n.f.)
halo oreol (n.m.)
halogen galogen (n.m.)
halt prival (n.m.)
ham okorok (n.m.)
vetchina (n.f.)
hammer molot (n.m.)
molotok (n.m.)
hammock gamak (n.m.)
hamper stesnit' (v.pf.)
hand ruka (n.f.)
hand in sdat' (v.pf.)
hand, to gain the upper oderzhat' verkh
(v.pf.)
hand to hand fighting rukopashnaya (n.f.)
hand, with one's own sobstvennoruchno
(adv.)
hand, with the back of the naotmash' (adv.)
handfull gorst' (n.f.)
prigorshnya (n.f.)
handicraftsman kustar' (n.m.)
handkerchief platok (n.m.)
handle orudovat' (v.impf.)
ruchka (n.f.)
rukoyatka (n.f.)
handmade kustarnyi (adj.)
handmade article podelka (n.f.)
handshake rukopozhatie (n.n.)
handsome man krasavets (n.m.)
handwriting pocherk (n.m.)
hang ponurit' (v.pf.)
povesit' (v.pf.)
povisnut' (v.pf.)
veshat' (v.impf.)
viset' (v.impf.)
hang down otvisat' (v.impf.)
svisat' (v.impf.)
hang of, to get the nalovchit'sya (v.pf.)
hang out vysovyvat'(sya) (v.impf.)
vyveshivat' (v.impf.)
vyvesit' (v.pf.)
hang over navisat' (v.impf.)
navisnut' (v.pf.)
hang up naveshivat' (v.impf.)
navesit' (v.pf.)
podveshivat' (v.impf.)

podvesit' (v.pf.)
razveshivat' (v.impf.)
razvesit' (v.pf.)
hang with uveshat' (v.pf.)
hangar angar (n.m.)
hanger, coat veshalka (n.f.)
hanging visyachii (adj.)
hangman palach (n.m.)
hangover pokhmel'e (n.n.)
happen byvat' (v.impf.)
sluchat'sya (v.impf.)
statsya (v.pf.)
happiness schast'e (n.n.)
happy blagopoluchnyi (adj.)
schastlivyi (adj.)
happy, to make oschastlivit' (v.pf.)
harbor gavan' (n.f.)
hard tverdyi (adj.)
zhestkii (adj.)
hard drinking zapoi (n.m.)
hard labor katorga (n.f.)
hard-boiled vkrutuyu (adv.)
harden ocherstvet' (v.pf.)
otverdevat' (v.impf.)
tverdet' (v.impf.)
hardly edva (adv.)
ele (adv.)
nasilu (adv.)
zhivuchii (adj.)
hardness tverdost' (n.f.)
hardware skobyanoi (adj.)
hare zayats (n.m.)
haricot bean fasol' (n.f.)
harm vred (n.m.)
harmless bezobidnyi (adj.)
bezvrednyi (adj.)
harmless, to render obezvredit' (v.pf.)
harmonious blagozvuchnyi (adj.)
garmonichnyi (adj.)
skladnyi (adj.)
harmonium fisgarmoniya (n.f.)
harmonize garmonirovat' (v.impf.)
harmony garmoniya (n.f.)
lad (n.m.)
stroinost' (n.f.)
harness sbruya (n.f.)
upryazh' (n.f.)
vpryagat' (v.impf.)
(cont'd)

zapryach' (v.pf.)
zapryagat' (v.impf.)
harp arfa (n.f.)
harrow borona (n.f.)
harvest zhatva (n.f.)
harvest, poor nedorod (n.m.)
harvesting uborka (n.f.)
uborochnyi (adj.)
haste gonka (n.f.)
hastily naskoro (adv.)
hasty neobdumannyi (adj.)
hat shlyapa (n.f.)
hatch lyuk (n.m.)
vylupit'sya (v.pf.)
vysidet' (v.pf.)
hate nenavidet' (v. impf.)
hatred nenavist' (n.f.)
hatred for, to conceive voznenavidet' (v.pf.)
haughtily svysoka (adv.)
haughtiness spes' (n.f.)
haughty spesivyi (adj.)
haunt priton (n.m.)
have est' (v.pres.)
imet' (v.impf.)
have to priitis' (v.pf.)
hawk yastreb (n.m.)
hay seno (n.n.)
haymaker kosar' (n.m.)
haze mgla (n.f.)
hazel hen ryabchik (n.m.)
he on (p.)
head glava (n.f.)
golova (n.f.)
golovka (n.f.)
head, back of the zatylok (n.m.)
head of cabbage kochan (n.m.)
head of, to be at the vozglavit' (v.pf.)
head over heels kubarem (adv.)
head, to come to a narvat' (v.pf.)
nazrevat' (v.impf.)
head, to take into one's vzdumat' (v.pf.)
headboard izgolov'e (n.n.)
heading rubrika (n.f.)
headlight fara (n.f.)
headlong nautek (adv.)
ochertya (adv.)
opromet'yu (adv.)
stremglav (adv.)

headphone naushnik (n.m.)
headquarters stavka (n.f.)
heal zalechivat' (v.impf.)
zazhit' (v.pf.)
zazhivat' (v.impf.)
health zdorov'e (n.n.)
health, public zdravookhranenie (n.n.)
health resort zdravnitsa (n.f.)
healthier, to make ozdorovit' (v.pf.)
healthy zdorovyi (adj.)
heap gruda (n.f.)
kipa (n.f.)
kucha (n.f.)
vorokh (n.m.)
heap, small kuchka (n.f.)
heap up gromozdit' (v.impf.)
navalit' (v.pf.)
navalivat' (v.impf.)
hear rasslyshat' (v.pf.)
slyshat' (v.impf.)
uslykhat' (v.pf.)
vyslushat' (v.pf.)
zaslushat' (v.pf.)
hear, one can slyshno (pred.)
heard, to be poslyshat'sya (v.pf.)
razdat'sya (v.pf.)
razdavat'sya (v.impf.)
hearing razbiratel'stvo (n.n.)
slukh (n.m.)
hearsay, by ponaslyshke (adv.)
hearse katafalk (n.m.)
heart serdtse (n.n.)
heart, by naizust' (adv.)
heart, to take muzhat'sya (v.impf.)
vospryanut' (v.pf.)
heartburn izzhoga (n.f.)
hearth ochag (n.m.)
heartiness serdechnost' (n.f.)
heartless besserdechnyi (adj.)
bezdushnyi (adj.)
hearts chervy (n.pl.)
heat nagrevat' (v.impf.)
nakalivat' (v.impf.)
otaplivat' (v.impf.)
otopit' (v.pf.)
protaplivat' (v.impf.)
protopit' (v.pf.)
teplota (n.f.)

topit' (v.impf.)
zabeg (n.m.)
zhar (n.m.)
zhara (n.f.)
heat capacity teploemkost' (n.f.)
heat engineering teplotekhnika (n.f.)
heat exchange teploobmen (n.m.)
heat insulation teploizolyatsiya (n.f.)
heat, intense znoi (n.m.)
heat resistance zharostoikost' (n.f.)
heat, scorching peklo (n.n.)
heat well natopit' (v.pf.)
heated razgoryachennyi (adj.)
heater podogrevatel' (n.m.)
heather veresk (n.m.)
heating nagrevanie (n.n.)
topka (n.f.)
heating, central teplofikatsiya (n.f.)
heating plant teplotsentral' (n.f.)
heavenly body svetilo (n.n.)
heaves zapal (n.m.)
heavily tyazhelo (adv.)
heavy oduryayushchii (adj.)
tyazhelyi (adj.)
hectare ga (n.m.)
gektar (n.m.)
hedgehog ezh (n.m.)
heel kabluk (n.m.)
kham (n.m.)
naboika (n.f.)
pyata (n.f.)
pyatka (n.f.)
heels, head over kubarem (adv.)
hegemony gegemoniya (n.f.)
heifer telka (n.f.)
height vys' (n.f.)
vyshina (v.f.)
vysota (n.f.)
heir naslednik (n.m.)
helicopter vertolet (n.m.)
helium gelii (n.m.)
hell ad (n.m.)
hellish adskii (adj.)
hello allo (interj.)
helmet kaska (n.f.)
shlem (n.m.)
helmsman kormchii (adj.)
help podmoga (n.f.)

podspor'e (n.n.)
pomoch' (v.pf.)
pomogat' (v.impf.)
pomoshch' (n.f.)
help down ssadit' (v.pf.)
help, kitchen sudomoika (n.f.)
help out vyruchat' (v.impf.)
vyruchit' (v.pf.)
helper pomoshchnik (n.m.)
helpless bespomoshchnyi (adj.)
hem podol (n.m.)
podrubat' (v.impf.)
podshit' (v.pf.)
podshivat' (v.impf.)
hemisphere polusharie (n.n.)
hemoglobin gemoglobin (n.m.)
hemolysis gemoliz (n.m.)
hemorrhage krovoizliyanie (n.n.)
hemp konoplya (n.f.)
pen'ka (n.f.)
hen kuritsa (n.f.)
hen, gray teterka (n.f.)
hen, hazel ryabchik (n.m.)
hen house kuryatnik (n.m.)
henceforth vpred' (adv.)
hen's kurinyi (adj.)
her eyu (p.)
herald vestnik (n.m.)
heraldic gerbovyi (adj.)
herbarium gerbarii (n.m.)
herbivorous travoyadnyi (adj.)
herd gurt (n.m.)
pasti (v.impf.)
stado (n.n.)
tabun (n.m.)
here syuda (adv.)
tut (adv.)
vot (part.)
zdes' (adv.)
here, from otsyuda (adv.)
here and there mestami (adv.)
hereabout(s) poblizosti (adv.)
heredity nasledstvennost' (n.f.)
heresy eres' (n.f.)
heretic eretik (n.m.)
hermetically sealed germeticheskii (adj.)
hermit otshel'nik (n.m.)
hernia gryzha (n.f.)

hero geroi (n.m.)

heroism geroizm (n.m.)

heron tsaplya (n.f.)

herring sel'd' (n.f.)
   seledka (n.f.)

hesitate zapinat'sya (v.impf.)
   zapnut'sya (v.pf.)

heterocyclic geterotsiklicheskii (adj.)

heterogeneity neodnorodnost' (n.f.)

heterogeneous raznorodnyi (adj.)

heuristic évristicheskii (adj.)

hew tesat' (v.impf.)

hexagonal shestiugol'nyi (adj.)

hibernate zimovat' (v.impf.)

hibernation spyachka (n.f.)

hiccup ikat' (v.impf.)
   ikota (n.f.)

hidden skrytyi (adj.)

hidden motive podopleka (n.f.)

hide pripryatat' (v.pf.)
   pritait'sya (v.pf.)
   pryatat' (v.impf.)
   skryt' (v.pf.)
   skryvat'(sya) (v.impf.)
   spryatat' (v.pf.)
   upryatat' (v.pf.)
   zabit'sya (v.pf.)
   zabivat'sya (v.impf.)

hide away zapryatat' (v.pf.)

hieroglyph ieroglif (n.m.)

high povyshennyi (adj.)
   vysokii (adj.)
   vysoko (adv.)

high tide priliv (n.m.)

high-altitude vysotnyi (adj.)

higher vyshe (adj.)
   vysshii (adj.)

highest, the naivysshii (adj.)

highlander gorets (n.m.)

highly ves'ma (adv.)

high-molecular vysokomolekulyarnyi (adj.)

high-quality vysokokachestvennyi (adj.)

high-voltage vysokovol'tnyi (adj.)

highway avtostrada (n.f.)
   shosse (n.n.)
   trakt (n.m.)

hill gorka (n.f.)
   kholm (n.m.)

   sopka (n.f.)

hillock bugor (n.m.)
   kochka (n.f.)
   prigorok (n.m.)

him emu (p.)

hinder vosprepyatstvovat' (v.pf.)

Hindu indus (n.m.)

hinge sharnir (n.m.)

hint namek (n.m.)
   namekat' (v.impf.)

hippopotamus begemot (n.m.)

hire naem (n.m.)
   vnaem (adv.)

hire, for naprokat (adv.)

hireling naimit (n.m.)

hiss osvistat' (v.pf.)
   shikat' (v.impf.)
   shipet' (v.impf.)

histology gistologiya (n.f.)

historian istorik (n.m.)

history istoriya (n.f.)

history, natural estestvoznanie (n.n.)

hit popast' (v.pf.)
   porazit' (v.pf.)
   udaryat'(sya) (v.impf.)
   ugodit' (v.pf.)

hit, scoring a popadanie (n.n.)

hitch neuvyazka (n.f.)
   zaminka (n.f.)

hive ulei (n.m.)

hoarfrost inei (n.m.)
   izmoroz' (n.f.)

hoarse khriplyi (adj.)
   siplyi (adj.)

hoarse, to become okhripnut' (v.pf.)

hoarse, to grow osipnut' (v.pf.)

hoax mistifikatsiya (n.f.)

hobble kovylyat' (v.impf)

hobby khobbi (n.n.)
   konek (n.m.)

hockey khokkei (n.m.)

hockey stick klyushka (n.f.)

hoe motyga (n.f.)

hold derzhat' (v.impf.)
   proderzhat' (v.pf.)
   tryum (n.m.)

hold back uderzhivat'(sya) (v.impf)

hold forth razglagol'stvovat' (v.impf.)

hold of, to get vtsepit'sya (v.pf.)
hold on to derzhat'sya (v.impf.)
   priderzhivat'sya (v.impf.)
hold sway over vlastvovat' (v.impf.)
holder, glass podstakannik (n.m.)
holder of an order ordenonosets (n.m.)
hole dyra (n.f.)
   lunka (n.f.)
   nora (n.f.)
   proboina (n.f.)
hole, ice prorub' (n.f.)
hole, to make a probit' (v.pf.)
   prodyryavit' (v.pf.)
holes, full of dyryavyi (adj.)
holiday prazdnik (n.m.)
hollow dolbit' (v.impf.)
   duplo (n.n.)
   kotlovina (n.f.)
   lozhbina (n.f.)
   vpalyi (adj.)
   vyemka (n.f.)
hollow out vydalblivat' (v.impf.)
   vydolbit' (v.pf)
hollyhock mal'va (n.f.)
holster kobura (n.f.)
holy svyatoi (adj.)
home domoi (adv.)
home, back vosvoyasi (adv.)
home guard opolchenie (n.n.)
home, to feel at osvaivat'sya (v.impf.)
homeless bezdomnyi (adj.)
homemade samodel'nyi (adj.)
homeopathy gomeopatiya (n.f.)
homogeneous gomogennyi (adj.)
   odnorodnyi (adj.)
homologue gomolog (n.m.)
homonym omonim (n.m.)
honest poryadochnyi (adj.)
honesty chestnost' (n.f.)
honey med (n.m.)
   medovyi (adj.)
honey cake kovrizhka (n.f.)
honeycomb soty (n.pl.)
honor chest' (n.f.)
   chtit' (v.impf.)
   pochest' (n.f.)
   pochet (n.m.)
   pochitat' (v.impf.)

   pochtit' (v.pf.)
   udostoit' (v.pf.)
honored, to be udostaivat'(sya) (v.impf.)
hood kapyushon (n.m.)
hoof kopyto (n.n.)
hook kryuchok (n.m.)
   kryuk (n.m.)
   podtsepit' (v.pf.)
   pritsepit' (v.pf.)
   zatsepit' (v.pf.)
   zatseplyat' (v.impf.)
hooked kryuchkovatyi (adj.)
hoop obruch (n.m.)
hooter gudok (n.m.)
hop khmel' (n.m.)
hope chayanie (n.n.)
   nadeyat'sya (v.impf.)
   nadezhda (n.f.)
   ponadeyat'sya (v.pf.)
hopeless beznadezhnyi (adj.)
   bezvykhodnyi (adj.)
horde orda (n.f.)
   polchishche (n.n.)
horizon gorizont (n.m.)
hormone gormon (n.m.)
horn rog (n.m.)
   rogovoi (adj.)
horned rogatyi (adj.)
hornet osinyi (adj.)
horny mozolistyi (adj.)
horrified, to be uzhasnut'sya (v.pf.)
horror uzhas (n.m.)
horse kon' (n.m.)
   konnyi (adj.)
   loshad' (n.f.)
   loshadinyi (adj.)
horse blanket popona (n.f.)
horse breeding konevodstvo (n.n.)
horse rider naezdnik (n.m.)
horseback verkhom (adv.)
horse-drawn vehicle povozka (n.f.)
horseflesh konina (n.f.)
horsefly slepen' (n.m.)
horseradish khren (n.m.)
horseshoe podkova (n.f.)
horticulture sadovodstvo (n.n.)
horticulturist sadovod (n.m.)
hose shlang (n.m.)

hospitable gostepriimnyi (adj.)
hospital bol'nichnyi (adj.)
   bol'nitsa (n.f.)
   gospital' (n.m.)
   klinika (n.f.)
   statsionar (n.m.)
hospital attendant sanitar (n.m.)
hostage zalozhnik (n.m.)
hostel obshchezhitie (n.n.)
hostile nepriyaznennyi (adj.)
   vrazheskii (adj.)
hostility nepriyazn' (n.f.)
hot goryachii (adj.)
   goryacho (adv.)
   zharkii (adj.)
hot temper vspyl'chivost' (n.f.)
hot, to become nakalyat'sya (v.impf.)
   raskalyat'(sya) (v.pf.)
hot, to make things nasolit' (v.pf.)
hotbed parnik (n.m.)
hotel gostinitsa (n.f.)
hothouse oranzhereya (n.f.)
hot-water bottle grelka (n.f.)
hound gonchaya (n.f.)
hour chas (n.m.)
hour, half polchasa (n.m.)
hour, hour's chasovoi (adj.)
hourly ezhechasno (adv.)
hours, for podolgu (adv.)
hour's, hour chasovoi (adj.)
house dom (n.m.)
house, full anshlag (n.m.)
house domovyi (adj.)
house painter malyar (n.m.)
house, peasant's izba (n.f.)
house, pump vodokachka (n.f.)
household domovyi (adj.)
house-manager upravdom (n.m.)
housewarming novosel'e (n.n.)
how kak (adv.)
how many skol'ko (adv.)
how much naskol'ko (adv.)
   pochem (adv.)
   skol'ko (adv.)
however odnako (adv.)
   vprochem (conj.)
howl voi (n.m.)
   vyt' (v.impf.)

   zavyvat' (v.impf.)
hubbub gvalt (n.m.)
huge ogromnyi (adj.)
human lyudskoi (adj.)
human being chelovek (n.m.)
human kindness chelovekolyubie (n.n.)
humane chelovechnyi (adj.)
humanism gumanizm (n.m.)
humanity chelovechestvo (n.n.)
   gumannost' (n.f.)
humble unizhennyi (adj.)
humidity vlazhnost' (n.f.)
humiliate unizhat' (v.impf.)
   unizit' (v.pf.)
humiliating unizitel'nyi (adj.)
humility smirenie (n.n.)
humor yumor (n.m.)
hump gorb (n.m.)
humus peregnoi (n.m.)
hundred sto (num.)
hundred, a sotnya (n.f.)
hundred kilograms tsentner (n.m.)
hundred meter sprint stometrovka (n.f.)
hundred percent stoprotsentnyi (adj.)
hundredth sotyi (adj.)
Hungarian vengerskii (adj.)
   vengr (n.m.)
hunger golod (n.m.)
hunger strike golodovka (n.f.)
hungry golodnyi (n.m.)
hungry, to get progolodat'sya (v.pf.)
hunk lomot' (n.m.)
hunk of bread krayukha (n.f.)
hunt okhotit'sya (v.impf.)
   travit' (v.impf.)
hunt down zatravit' (v.pf.)
hunter okhotnik (n.m.)
hunting okhota (n.f.)
   okhotnichii (adj.)
   travlya (n.f.)
hurl out vyshvyrnut' (v.pf.)
hurrah! ura (interj.)
hurricane uragan (n.m.)
hurry pospeshit' (v.pf.)
   speshit' (v.impf.)
   speshka (n.f.)
   toropit' (v.impf.)
hurry, in a vpopykhakh (adv.)

vtoropyakh (adv.)

hurt rasshibat' (v.impf.)

hurts, it bol'no (adv.)

husband muzh (n.m.)

suprug (n.m.)

husband (wife), to propose as svatat'
(v.impf.)

hush up zamalchivat' (v.impf.)

zamyat' (v.pf.)

husky laika (n.f.)

hut khata (n.f.)

khizhina (n.f.)

lachuga (n.f.)

hut, animal skin yurta (n.f.)

hut, small izbushka (n.f.)

hyacinth giatsint (n.m.)

hybrid gibrid (n.m.)

pomes' (n.f.)

hydraulic engineering gidrotekhnika (n.f.)

hydraulics gidravlika (n.f.)

hydrobiology gidrobiologiya (n.f.)

hydrocarbon uglevodorod (n.m.)

hydrochloric acid solyanaya kislota (adj.-n.f.)

solyanaya kislota (adj.-n.f.)

hydrodynamics gidrodinamika (n.f.)

hydroelectric power station gidrostantsiya (n.f.)

hydrogen vodorod (n.m.)

hydrogen sulfide serovodorod (n.m.)

hydrolysis gidroliz (n.m.)

hydropathy vodolechenie (n.n.)

hydrophobia vodoboyazn' (n.f.)

hydroplane gidroplan (n.m.)

hyena giena (n.f.)

hygiene gigiena (n.f.)

hygroscopic gigroskopicheskii (adj.)

hymn gimn (n.m.)

vospevat' (v.impf.)

hyperbole giperbola (n.f.)

hypertension gipertoniya (n.f.)

hypertrophy gipertrofiya (n.f.)

hypnosis gipnoz (n.m.)

hypochondriac mnitel'nyi (adj.)

hypocrisy khanzhestvo (n.n.)

hypocrite khanzha (n.m.&f.)

litsemer (n.m.)

hypodermic podkozhnyi (adj.)

hypotenuse gipotenuza (n.f.)

hypothesis gipoteza (n.f.)

hysterics isterika (n.f.)

I (И, Й)

I mnoi (p.)

ya (p.)

ice led (n.m.)

ice cream morozhenoe (n.n.)

ice, floating ledokhod (n.m.)

ice floe l'dina (n.f.)

ice hole prorub' (n.f.)

icebreaker ledokol (n.m.)

ice-covered obledenelyi (adj.)

icehouse lednik (n.m.)

Icelander islandets (n.m.)

icicle sosul'ka (n.f.)

icing glazur' (n.f.)

icon ikona (n.f.)

icy ledenyashchii (adj.)

ledyanoi (adj.)

icy condition of roads gololeditsa (n.f.)

idea ideya (n.f.)

ideal ideal (n.m.)

ideal'nyi (adj.)

idealism idealizm (n.m.)

identical odinakovyi (adj.)

tozhdestvennyi (adj.)

identify opoznavat' (v.impf.)

otozhdestvlyat' (v.impf.)

identity tozhdestvo (n.n.)

ideological ideinyi (adj.)

ideologist ideolog (n.m.)

idiom idioma (n.f.)

idiosyncrasy idiosinkraziya (n.f.)

idiot idiot (n.m.)

idle gossip peresudy (n.pl.)

idle, standing prostoi (n.m.)
idle, to be lentyainichat' (v.impf.)
idleness bezdel'e (n.n.)
 prazdnost' (n.f.)
idler lodyr' (n.m.)
 zevaka (n.m.)
idol idol (n.m.)
 kumir (n.m.)
idolize obozhestvlyat' (v.impf.)
idyll idilliya (n.f.)
i.e. t.e. (abbr.)
if esli (conj.)
ignite vosplamenit' (v.pf.)
ignition zazhiganie (n.n.)
ignominious besslavnyi (adj.)
ignoramus neuch (n.m.&f.)
 nevezhda (n.m.)
 profan (n.m.)
ignorance nevedenie (n.n.)
 neznanie (n.n.)
ignorant nesvedushchii (adj.)
ignore ignorirovat' (v.impf.)
ill, to be bolet' (v.impf.)
 khvorat' (v.impf.)
ill, to become razbolet'sya (v.pf.)
ill, to fall raskhvorat'sya (v.pf.)
 zabolevat' (v.impf.)
 zakhvorat' (v.pf.)
ill-bred nevospitannyi (adj.)
illegal nelegal'nyi (adj.)
 nezakonnyi (adj.)
 protivozakonnyi (adj.)
illegible nechetkii (adj.)
ill-informed neosvedomlennyi (adj.)
illiteracy negramotnost' (n.f.)
illiterate bezgramotnyi (adj.)
illness bolezn' (n.f.)
 nedug (n.m.)
ill-started zlopoluchnyi (adj.)
illuminate posvetit' (v.pf.)
illuminating engineering svetotekhnika (n.f.)
illumination illyuminatsiya (n.f.)
 osveshchenie (n.n.)
 svetosila (n.f.)
illusion illyuziya (n.f.)
illustration illyustratsiya (n.f.)
image obraz (n.m.)
imaginary voobrazhaemyi (adj.)

imagine voobrazit' (v.pf.)
imbecility slaboumie (n.n.)
imitation imitatsiya (n.f.)
 podrazhanie (n.n.)
immeasurable bezmernyi (adj.)
 neizmerimyi (adj.)
immediately nemedlenno (adv.)
 totchas (adv.)
immemorial nezapamyatnyi (adj.)
immense neob"yatnyi (adj.)
immerse pogruzit' (v.pf.)
immigrant immigrant (n.m.)
immobility nepodvizhnost' (n.f.)
immoderate neumerennyi (adj.)
immodest neskromnyi (adj.)
immoral beznravstvennyi (adj.)
immortal bessmertnyi (adj.)
immortalize obessmertit' (v.pf.)
 uvekovechit' (v.pf.)
immunity immunitet (n.m.)
immunobiology immunobiologiya (n.f.)
immutable neprelozhnyi (adj.)
impartial bespristrastnyi (adj.)
impassable neprokhodimyi (adj.)
 neprolaznyi (adj.)
impassive besstrastnyi (adj.)
impatience neterpenie (n.n.)
impel pobudit' (v.pf.)
impenetrable nepronitsaemyi (adj.)
imperative povelitel'nyi (adj.)
imperceptible neoshchutimyi (adj.)
 nezametnyi (adj.)
imperfect nesovershennyi (adj.)
imperialism imperializm (n.m.)
imperious vlastnyi (adj.)
impermissible nepozvolitel'nyi (adj.)
impersonal bezlichnyi (adj.)
impertinence derzost' (n.f.)
impertinent derzkii (adj.)
imperturbable nevozmutimyi (adj.)
impetuous stremitel'nyi (adj.)
implicated, not neprichastnyi (adj.)
implore umolyat' (v.impf.)
imply podrazumevat' (v.impf.)
impolite neuchtivyi (adj.)
import import (n.m.)
 vvezti (v.pf.)
 vvoz (n.m.)

important vazhnyi (adj.)
   znachitel'nyi (adj.)
importunate nazoilivyi (adj.)
imposing verstka (n.f.)
impossibility nevozmozhnost' (n.f.)
impossible, it is nel'zya (adv.)
imposter samozvanets (n.m.)
impotence impotentsiya (n.f.)
impoverished obednevshii (adj.)
impracticable neosushchestvimyi (adj.)
   nevypolnimyi (adj.)
   nezhiznennyi (adj.)
impractical nepraktichnyi (adj.)
impregnable nepristupnyi (adj.)
impress imponirovat' (v.impf.)
   zapechatlevat' (v.impf.)
impression ottisk (n.m.)
   vpechatlenie (n.n.)
impressive predstavitel'nyi (adj.)
imprint otpechatat' (v.pf.)
imprison zatochat' (v.impf.)
improbable maloveroyatnyi (adj.)
impromptu ékspromt (n.m.)
improve uluchshat'(sya) (v.impf.)
   uluchshit' (v.pf.)
   usovershenstvovat' (v.pf.)
improvement, land melioratsiya (n.f.)
improvident nepredusmotritel'nyi (adj.)
improvisation improvizatsiya (n.f.)
imprudent neblagorazumnyi (adj.)
   neosmotritel'nyi (adj.)
impudent fellow nakhal (n.m.)
impudent, to grow obnaglet' (v.pf.)
impulse impul's (n.m.)
impute vmenyat' (v.impf.)
in v (prep.)
   vnutr' (adv.)
   vo (prep.)
in a hurry naspekh (adv.)
   vpopykhakh (adv.)
   vtoropyakh (adv.)
in a moment vmig (adv.)
in addition vdobavok (adv.)
in all vsego (adv.)
in concert zaodno (adv.)
in confusion vperemeshku (adv.)
in earnest vser'ez (adv.)
in every way vsyacheski (adv.)

in exchange for vzamen (prep.)
in front speredi (adv.)
   vperedi (adv.)
in front of pered (prep.)
in general voobshche (adv.)
in good time zablagovremenno (adv.)
in jest shutya (adv.)
in love, to fall polyubit' (v.pf.)
   vlyubit'sya (v.pf.)
in my opinion po-moemu (adv.)
in order to chtoby (conj.)
in passing mel'kom (adv.)
   poputno (adv.)
in spite of nesmotrya (prep.)
   vopreki (prep.)
in time vo-vremya (adv.)
in turn poocheredno (adv.)
   poperemenno (adv.)
in vain naprasno (adv.)
   ponaprasnu (adv.)
   popustu (adv.)
in view of vvidu (prep.)
inaccessible nedostupnyi (adj.)
inaccurate netochnyi (adj.)
inaction bezdeistvie (n.n.)
inadmissible nedopustimyi (adj.)
inalienable neot"emlemyi (adj.)
inanimate neodushevlennyi (adj.)
inapplicable neprimenimyi (adj.)
inappropriate neumestnyi (adj.)
inarticulate nechlenorazdel'nyi (adj.)
inattention nevnimanie (n.n.)
inaudible neslyshnyi (adj.)
incalculable neischislimyi (adj.)
incandescence kalenie (n.n.)
   nakal (n.m.)
incantation zaklinanie (n.n.)
incapable nesposobnyi (adj.)
incendiary zazhigatel'nyi (adj.)
incense ladan (n.m.)
incensed razgnevannyi (adj.)
incessant nesmolkaemyi (adj.)
incessantly bez umolku (adv.)
incident intsident (n.m.)
   proisshestvie (n.n.)
   sluchai (n.m.)
incision nasechka (n.f.)
   razrez (n.m.)

inclination naklon (n.m.)
    sklonnost' (n.f.)
    vlechenie (n.n.)
inclined naklonnyi (adj.)
inclined, to be sklonyat'sya (v.impf.)
include vklyuchit' (v.pf.)
    zachislit' (v.pf.)
inclusion vklyuchenie (n.n.)
incoherent bessvyaznyi (adj.)
    nesvyaznyi (adj.)
incombustible nesgoraemyi (adj.)
income dokhod (n.m.)
    podokhodnyi (adj.)
incommensurable nesoizmerimyi (adj.)
incomparable bespodobnyi (adj.)
    nesravnimyi (adj.)
incompatible nesoobraznyi (adj.)
    nesovmestimyi (adj.)
    vzaimoisklyuchayushchii
      (adj.)
incompetent nekompetentnyi (adj.)
    nepravomochnyi (adj.)
incomplete nepolnyi (adj.)
incomprehension neponimanie (n.n.)
inconceivable nemyslimyi (adj.)
    nepostizhimyi (adj.)
inconclusive neokonchatel'nyi (adj.)
inconsistency nepostoyanstvo (n.n.)
inconsistent neposledovatel'nyi (adj.)
inconsolable bezuteshnyi (adj.)
    neuteshnyi (adj.)
incontestable neoproverzhimyi (adj.)
incorrect nevernyi (adj.)
incorrigible neispravimyi (adj.)
incorruptible nepodkupnyi (adj.)
increase nadbavit' (v.pf.)
    nadbavlyat' (v.impf.)
    prirost (n.m.)
    umnozhit' (v.pf.)
    uvelichenie (n.n.)
    uvelichivat' (v.impf.)
increasing povysitel'nyi (adj.)
incredible neimovernyi (adj.)
    nepravdopodobnyi (adj.)
    neveroyatnyi (adj.)
incubator inkubator (n.m.)
inculcation vnedrenie (n.n.)
incurable neizlechimyi (adj.)

indecent neprilichnyi (adj.)
indecision nereshitel'nost' (n.f.)
indeclinable nesklonyaemyi (adj.)
indeed neuyutnyi (adj.)
    poistine (adv.)
indefatigable neusypnyi (adj.)
    neutomimyi (adj.)
indefinite bessrochnyi (adj.)
    neopredelennyi (adj.)
indelible neizgladimyi (adj.)
indelicate nedelikatnyi (adj.)
indemnity otstupnoe (n.n.)
independence nezavisimost' (n.f.)
    samostoyatel'nost' (n.f.)
independent nezavisyashchii (adj.)
independent, not nesamostoyatel'nyi (adj.)
indescribable neopisuemyi (adj.)
indestructible nesokrushimyi (adj.)
index indeks (n.m.)
    pokazatel' (n.m.)
india ink tush' (n.f.)
Indian (American) indeets (n.m.)
Indian (Asian) indiets (n.m.)
indicate ukazat' (v.pf.)
    ukazyvat' (v.impf.)
indicated, not neoboznachennyi (adj.)
indicative mood iz"yavitel'nyi (adj.)
indifference ravnodushie (n.n.)
indifferent bezrazlichnyi (adj.)
indigestion nesvarenie (n.n.)
    rasstroistvo (n.n.)
indignation negodovanie (n.n.)
indirect kosvennyi (adj.)
indiscernible nerazlichimyi (adj.)
indiscriminate ogul'nyi (adj.)
indisposition nedomoganie (n.n.)
indisputable besspornyi (adj.)
    neosporimyi (adj.)
indissoluble nerazryvnyi (adj.)
indistinct nevnyatnyi (adj.)
individual edinolichnyi (adj.)
    individual'nyi (adj.)
    odinochnyi (adj.)
indivisible nedelimyi (adj.)
    nerazdel'nyi (adj.)
indomitable neukrotimyi (adj.)
Indonesian indoneziets (n.m.)
induction induktsiya (n.f.)

indulge potakat' (v.impf.)
indulgence poblazhka (n.f.)
industrial proizvodstvennyi (adj.)
industrialization industrializatsiya (n.f.)
industrious rabotyashchii (adj.)
    trudolyubivyi (adj.)
industry industriya (n.f.)
    promyshlennost' (n.f.)
industry, gold zolotopromyshlennost' (n.f.)
inedible nes''edobnyi (adj.)
inequality neravenstvo (n.n.)
inertia inertsiya (n.f.)
inertness inertnost' (n.f.)
inevitable neizbezhnyi (adj.)
    neminuemyi (adj.)
    neotvratimyi (adj.)
inexhaustible neischerpaemyi (adj.)
    neissyakaemyi (adj.)
    neistoshchimyi (adj.)
inexorable neumolimyi (adj.)
inexpensive nedorogoi (adj.)
inexperience neopytnost' (n.f.)
inexplicable neob''yasnimyi (adj.)
inexpressible neperedavaemyi (adj.)
    nevyrazimyi (adj.)
inexpressive nevyrazitel'nyi (adj.)
infallible nepogreshimyi (adj.)
infamous gnusnyi (adj.)
infant prodigy vunderkind (n.m.)
infantry pekhota (n.f.)
infect zarazhat' (v.impf.)
infection infektsiya (n.f.)
    zaraza (n.f.)
infectious infektsionnyi (adj.)
infertile neplodorodnyi (adj.)
infinitive infinitiv (n.m.)
infinity beskonechnost' (n.f.)
inflame vosplamenit' (v.pf.)
inflammable ogneopasnyi (adj.)
inflammation vospalenie (n.n.)
inflate nadut' (v.pf.)
    vzdut' (v.pf.)
    vzduvat' (v.impf.)
inflation inflyatsiya (n.f.)
inflection fleksiya (n.f.)
inflexible negibkii (adj.)
    nesgibaemyi (adj.)
inflict nanesti (v.pf.)

influence povliyat' (v.pf.)
    protektsiya (n.f.)
    vliyanie (n.n.)
    vozdeistvie (n.n.)
influenza gripp (n.m.)
influx naplyv (n.m.)
inform donesti (v.pf.)
    informirovat' (v.impf.)
    izveshchat' (v.impf.)
    izvestit' (v.pf.)
    osvedomit' (v.pf.)
    soobshchat' (v.impf.)
    soobshchit' (v.pf.)
    uvedomit' (v.pf)
information informatsiya (n.f.)
    spravka (n.f.)
    spravka (n.f.)
    svedenie (n.n.)
information bureau informbyuro (n.n.)
information, to extract vypytat' (v.pf.)
    vypytyvat' (v.impf.)
    vyvedat' (v.pf.)
informer donoschik (n.m.)
    osvedomitel' (n.m.)
infrared infrakrasnyi (adj.)
infrequently, not neredko (adv.)
infringe ushchemit' (v.pf.)
infuriate razozlit' (v.pf.)
    vzbesit' (v.pf.)
infuse nastoyat' (v.pf.)
infusion nastoi (n.m.)
    vlivanie (n.n.)
ingenious zateilivyi (adj.)
ingot slitok (n.m.)
ingratiating vkradchivyi (adj.)
inhabit naselyat' (v.impf.)
inhabitant obitatel' (n.m.)
    zhitel' (n.m.)
inhabited obitaemyi (adj.)
inhale vdokhnut' (v.pf.)
    vdykhat' (v.impf.)
inherit unasledovat' (v.pf.)
inhibitor ingibitor (n.m.)
inhospitable negostepriimnyi (adj.)
inhuman beschelovechnyi (adj.)
inimitable nepodrazhaemyi (adj.)
initial iskhodnyi (adj.)
initials initsialy (n.pl.)

initiative initsiativa (n.f.)
  pochin (n.m.)
injection in"ektsiya (n.f.)
  vpryskivanie (n.n.)
injury ushib (n.m.)
injustice nespravedlivost' (n.f.)
ink chernila (n.pl.)
inn traktir (n.m.)
innate prirozhdennyi (adj.)
  vrozhdennyi (adj.)
inner porch seni (n.pl.)
innermost sokrovennyi (adj.)
innersole stel'ka (n.f.)
innervation innervatsiya (n.f.)
innocent nevinnyi (adj.)
innovation novovvedenie (n.n.)
  novshestvo (n.n.)
innovator novator (n.m.)
innumerable neschetnyi (adj.)
  nesmetnyi (adj.)
inoculate privit' (v.pf.)
inoculation privivka (n.f.)
inopportune nesvoevremennyi (adj.)
inopportunely nekstati (adv.)
inorganic neorganicheskii (adj.)
inquire spravit'sya (v.pf.)
  spravlyat'sya (v.impf.)
inquiries, to make rassprashivat' (v.impf.)
  razuznavat' (v.impf.)
  zaprashivat' (v.impf.)
inquiry sledstvie (n.n.)
  zapros (n.m.)
inquisition inkvizitsiya (n.f.)
inquisitive pytlivyi (adj.)
insane bezumnyi (adj.)
  nevmenyaemyi (adj.)
insanitary antisanitarnyi (adj.)
insatiable nenasytnyi (adj.)
inscription nadpis' (n.f.)
insect bukashka (n.f.)
  nasekomoe (n.n.)
insecticide intektitsid (n.m.)
insecure nenadezhnyi (adj.)
insensible beschuvstvennyi (adj.)
insensitive nechuvstvitel'nyi (adj.)
inseparable nerazluchnyi (adj.)
inset vkladka (n.f.)
inside nutro (n.n.)

vnutr' (adv.)
vnutrennii (adj.)
vnutri (adv.)
inside out naiznanku (adv.)
insignificance nichtozhnost' (n.f.)
insignificant neznachitel'nyi (adj.)
insincere neiskrennii (adj.)
insinuate oneself vtirat'sya (v.impf.)
insipid vodyanistyi (adj.)
insist nastaivat' (v.impf.)
  nastoyat' (v.pf.)
insistence nastoyanie (n.n.)
insofar as postol'ku (conj.)
insolence naglost' (n.f.)
insolent naglyi (adj.)
insolent fellow naglets (n.m.)
insoluble nerazreshimyi (adj.)
inspect oglyadyvat' (v.impf.)
inspection inspektsiya (n.f.)
  obsledovanie (n.n.)
  reviziya (n.f.)
  smotr (n.m.)
inspector inspektor (n.m.)
inspire inspirirovat' (v.impf.)
  odukhotvoryat' (v.impf.)
  okrylit' (v.pf.)
  vdokhnovit' (v.pf.)
  vnushat' (v.impf.)
  voodushevit' (v.impf.)
install ustanavlivat' (v.impf.)
  vodvorit' (v.pf.)
installation vselenie (n.n.)
installation of radio radiofikatsiya (n.f.)
installments, to pay by rassrochit' (v.pf.)
instance instantsiya (n.f.)
  mig (n.m.)
instant mgnovenie (n.n.)
instead of vmesto (prep.)
instigate podstrekat' (v.impf.)
instigator zachinshchik (n.m.)
instinct instinkt (n.m.)
instinctive bezotchetnyi (adj.)
institute institut (n.m.)
institution zavedenie (n.n.)
instruct instruktirovat' (v.impf.)
instructions direktiva (n.f.)
  predpisanie (n.n.)
  ukazanie (n.n.)

instructive pouchitel'nyi (adj.)
    prosvetitel'nyi (adj.)
instructor instruktor (n.m.)
instrument instrument (n.m.)
instrumental tvoritel'nyi (adj.)
insubordination nepodchinenie (n.n.)
insufficiency nedostatochnost' (n.f.)
insulation teploizolyatsiya (n.f.)
insulator izolyator (n.m.)
insult oskorblenie (n.n.)
insulting oskorbitel'nyi (adj.)
insurance strakhovanie (n.n.)
insurance office strakhkassa (n.f.)
insurance, state gosstrakh (n.m.)
insure zastrakhovat' (v.pf.)
intact, to remain utselet' (v.pf.)
intangible neosyazaemyi (adj.)
integration integrirovanie (n.n.)
intellect intellekt (n.m.)
intelligence razvedka (n.f.)
intelligent myslyashchii (adj.)
intelligible tolkovyi (adj.)
    vrazumitel'nyi (adj.)
intend nameren (adj.)
    namerevat'sya (v.impf.)
    prednaznachat' (v.impf.)
    predpolagat' (v.impf.)
intensification usilenie (n.n.)
intensified usilennyi (adj.)
intensify usilivat'(sya) (v.impf.)
intensive intensivnyi (adj.)
intent pristal'nyi (adj.)
intention namerenie (n.n.)
    zamysel (n.m.)
interaction vzaimodeistvie (n.n.)
intercede zastupat'sya (v.impf.)
interest interes (n.m.)
    zainteresovat' (v.pf.)
interest free besprotsentnyi (adj.)
interested zainteresovannyi (adj.)
interjection mezhdometie (n.n.)
interlace spletat'(sya) (v.impf.)
interlocutor sobesednik (n.m.)
intermediate promezhutochnyi (adj.)
interminable neskonchaemyi (adj.)
intermission antrakt (n.m.)
intermit peremezhat'sya (v.impf.)
intern internirovat' (v.impf&pf.)

internal vnutrenii (adj.)
international internatsional'nyi (adj.)
    mezhdunarodnyi (adj.)
Internationale, the Internatsional (n.m.)
internationalism internatsionalizm (n.m.)
interplanetary mezhplanetnyi (adj.)
interpret istolkovat' (v.pf.)
    traktovat' (v.impf.)
interpretation interpretatsiya (n.f.)
    tolkovanie (n.n.)
interrogate doprashivat' (v.impf.)
interrogation dopros (n.m.)
    opros (n.m.)
interrupt ostanovit' (v.pf.)
    perebit' (v.pf.)
    perebivat' (v.impf.)
    prervat' (v.pf.)
    preryvat' (v.impf.)
interruption pereryv (n.m.)
intersect peresech'(sya) (v.pf.)
    peresekat'(sya) (v.impf.)
intersection peresechenie (n.n.)
interval interval (n.m.)
    promezhutok (n.m.)
intervene vmeshat'sya (v.pf.)
interview interv'yu (n.n.)
interweave perepletat'(sya) (v.impf.)
intestinal worm glist (n.m.)
intestine kishka (n.f.)
intestines kishechnik (n.m.)
intimate intimnyi (adj.)
intimidate pripugnut' (v.pf.)
    zapugat' (v.pf.)
into v (prep.)
    vo (prep.)
intolerable nevynosimyi (adj.)
intolerant neterpimyi (adj.)
intonation intonatsiya (n.f.)
intoxicated netrezvyi (adj.)
intractable nesgovorchivyi (adj.)
intransitive neperekhodnyi (adj.)
intranuclear vnutriyadernyi (adj.)
intraspecific vnutrividovoi (adj.)
intravenous vnutrivennyi (adj.)
intricate zamyslovatyi (adj.)
intrigue intriga (n.f.)
introduce otrekomendovat' (v.pf.)
    vvesti (v.pf.)
    (cont'd)

vvodit' (v.impf.)
introduction vvedenie (n.n.)
introductory vstupitel'nyi (adj.)
vvodnyi (adj.)
intuition intuitsiya (n.f.)
invade vtorgat'sya (v.impf.)
invader zakhvatchik (n.m.)
invalid invalid (n.m.)
nedeistvitel'nyi (adj.)
invaluable neotsenimyi (adj.)
invariable neizmennyi (adj.)
invasion nashestvie (n.n.)
invent izobresti (v.pf.)
vydumat' (v.pf.)
vydumyvat' (v.impf.)
invented vymyshlennyi (adj.)
inventor izobretatel' (n.m.)
inventory inventar' (n.m.)
invertebrates bespozvonochnye (n.pl.)
invest oblech' (v.pf.)
investigate rassledovat' (v.pf.)
investigate thoroughly vnikat' (v.impf.)
investigation issledovanie (n.n.)
rassledovanie (n.n.)
investigator sledovatel' (n.m.)
investment kapitalovlozhenie (n.n.)
inveterate zakorenelyi (adj.)
zavzyatyi (adj.)
zayadlyi (adj.)
invigorate bodrit' (v.impf.)
invigorating zhivitel'nyi (adj.)
invincible nepobedimyi (adj.)
inviolable neprikosnovennyi (adj.)
nerushimyi (adj.)
inviscid nevyazkii (adj.)
invisible nevidimyi (adj.)
nezrimyi (adj.)
invitation priglasitel'nyi (adj.)
invoice nakladnaya (n.f.)
involuntary neproizvol'nyi (adj.)
nevol'nyi (adj.)
involve vovlekat' (v.impf.)
vputat' (v.pf.)
involved mudrenyi (adj.)
zaputannyi (adj.)
involved in, to get vvyazat'sya (v.pf.)
invulnerable neuyazvimyi (adj.)
inward, to grow vrastat' (v.impf.)

iodine iod (n.m.)
iodoform iodoform (n.m.)
ion ion (n.m.)
ionosphere ionosfera (n.f.)
iota iota (n.f.)
Iranian iranets (n.m.)
Irishman irlandets (n.m.)
iron otgladit' (v.pf.)
otutyuzhit' (v.pf.)
utyug (n.m.)
vygladit' (v.pf.)
zagladit' (v.pf.)
zheleznyi (adj.)
zhelezo (n.n.)
iron, cast chugun (n.m.)
iron, soldering payal'nik (n.m.)
ironical ironicheskii (adj.)
ironing glazhen'e (n.n.)
irons, to put in zakovat' (v.pf.)
irony ironiya (n.f.)
irradiation obluchenie (n.n.)
irreconcilable neprimirimyi (adj.)
irregular nepravil'nyi (adj.)
neregulyarnyi (adj.)
irregularity neravnomernost' (n.f.)
irreparable nepopravimyi (adj.)
irreplaceable nezamenimyi (adj.)
irrepressible neuderzhimyi (adj.)
irreproachable bezukoriznennyi (adj.)
bezuprechnyi (adj.)
irresistible neotrazimyi (adj.)
irresponsible bezotvetstvennyi (adj.)
nesoznatel'nyi (adj.)
irretrievable bezvozvratnyi (adj.)
irreversibility neobratimost' (n.f.)
irrevocable bespovorotnyi (adj.)
nevozvratimyi (adj.)
irrigate oroshat' (v.impf.)
irrigation irrigatsiya (n.f.)
obvodnenie (n.n.)
irrigation ditch aryk (n.m.)
irritant razdrazhitel' (n.m.)
irritate razdrazhat' (v.impf.)
zlit' (v.impf.)
Islam islam (n.m.)
island ostrov (n.m.)
isolate izolirovat' (v.imp.&pf.)
isolation otryv (n.m.)

isometric ravnovelikii (adj.)
isomorphism izomorfizm (n.m.)
isosceles ravnobedrennyi (adj.)
isotherm izoterma (n.f.)
isothermal izotermicheskii (adj.)
isotope izotop (n.m.)
issue vydat' (v.pf.)
    vydavat' (v.impf.)
issuing vydacha (n.f.)
isthmus peresheek (n.m.)

it ono (p.)
it seems kazhetsya (pred.)
    mereshchit'sya (v.impf.)
Italian ital'yanets (n.m.)
italics kursiv (n.m.)
itch chesat'sya (v.impf.)
    chesotka (n.f.)
    zud (n.m.)
ivy plyushch (n.m.)

J

jack domkrat (n.m.)
jackal shakal (n.m.)
jackdaw galka (n.f.)
jacket kurtka (n.f.)
    tuzhurka (n.f.)
    zhaket (n.m.)
jacket, quilted vatnik (n.m.)
jacket, service french (n.m.)
jade klyacha (n.f.)
jag zazubrit' (v.pf.)
jam povidlo (n.n.)
    varen'e (n.n.)
    zator (n.m.)
jamb kosyak (n.m.)
janitor dvornik (n.m.)
January yanvar' (n.m.)
Japanese yaponets (n.m.)
jargon zhargon (n.m.)
jasmine zhasmin (n.m.)
jaundice zheltukha (n.f.)
jaw chelyust' (n.f.)
jealous revnivyi (adj.)
jealousy revnost' (n.f.)
jelly zhele (n.n.)
jelly, fruit marmelad (n.m.)
jellyfish meduza (n.f.)
jerk up vzdergivat' (v.impf.)
    vzdernut' (v.pf.)
jersey fufaika (n.f.)
jest, in shutya (adv.)
jest, to parry with a otshutit'sya (v.pf.)

Jesuit iezuit (n.m.)
jet reaktivnyi (adj.)
    struya (n.f.)
Jew evrei (n.m.)
jeweler yuvelir (n.m.)
jingle zvyakat' (v.impf.)
job, to leave one's uvol'nyat(sya) (v.impf.)
join primknut' (v.pf.)
    priobshchat' (v.impf.)
    prisoedinit' (v.pf.)
    skolachivat' (v.impf.)
    stekat'sya (v.impf.)
    vklyuchat'sya (v.impf.)
    vstupat' (v.impf.)
    vstupit' (v.pf.)
joiner stolyar (n.m.)
joiner's bench verstak (n.m.)
joining prisoedinenie (n.n.)
joint skreplenie (n.n.)
    sochlenenie (n.n.)
    styk (n.m.)
    sustav (n.m.)
joint, soldered spaika (n.f.)
jointly soobshcha (adv.)
    sovmestno (adv.)
joke anekdot (n.m.)
    shutit' (v.impf.)
    shutka (n.f.)
jolt, to give a tryakhnut' (v.pf.)
jolting tryaska (n.f.)
journal zhurnal (n.m.)

journey poezdka (n.f.)
    puteshestvie (n.n.)
joyless neveselyi (adj.)
jubilee yubilei (n.m.)
judge sud'ya (n.m.)
judgment suzhdenie (n.n.)
juice sok (n.m.)
juicy nalitoi (adj.)
    sochnyi (adj.)
July iyul' (n.m.)
jumble meshanina (n.f.)
jump prygat' (v.impf.)
    pryzhok (n.m.)
    skachok (n.m.)
    skakat' (v.impf.)
    vprygivat' (v.impf.)
jump away otskakivat' (v.impf.)
jump back otprygivat' (v.impf.)
jump off soskakivat' (v.impf.)
    soskochit' (v.pf.)
    sprygivat' (v.impf.)
jump out vyprygivat' (v.impf.)
    vyskakivat' (v.impf.)
    vyskochit' (v.pf.)
jump over pereprygnut' (v.pf.)
    pereskakivat' (v.impf.)

jump up podprygivat' (v.impf.)
    podskakivat' (v.impf.)
    vskakivat' (v.impf.)
    vskochit' (v.pf.)
    vsprygivat' (v.impf.)
jumper dzhemper (n.m.)
junction podsoedinenie (n.n.)
    soedinenie (n.n.)
June iyun' (n.m.)
jungle dzhungli (n.pl.)
juniper mozhzhevel'nik (n.m.)
junk rukhlyad' (n.f.)
junk, old star'e (n.n.)
junkyard svalka (n.f.)
jurisdiction of, under the podsudnyi (adj.)
jury zhyuri (n.n.)
just spravedlivyi (adj.)
just a little chut'-chut' (adv.)
justice pravosudie (n.n.)
    spravedlivost' (n.f.)
    yustitsiya (n.f.)
justification opravdanie (n.n.)
justify opravdat' (v.pf.)
justify oneself opravdyvat'(sya) (v.impf.)
jut out vdavat'sya (v.impf.)
juvenile maloletnii (adj.)

K (К, Х)

kangaroo kenguru (n.m.)
kapron (synthetic fiber) kapron (n.m.)
Karelian karel (n.m.)
Kazakh kazakh (n.m.)
keel kil' (n.m.)
keep khranit' (v.impf.)
    soderzhat' (v.impf.)
keep an eye on usledit' (v.pf.)
keep balance ustoyat' (v.pf.)
keep pace with ugnat'sya (v.pf.)
keep silent molchat' (v.impf.)
    otmalchivat'sya (v.impf.)
    promolchat' (v.pf.)
keep up podderzhivat' (v.impf.)
keeper, record uchetchik (n.m.)

keg bochonok (n.m.)
kennel konura (n.f.)
kernel yadro (n.n.)
key klavish(a) (n.m.(f))
    klyuch (n.m.)
key, major (music) mazhor (n.m.)
key, master otmychka (n.f.)
key, minor (music) minor (n.m.)
keyboard klaviatura (n.f.)
khaki khaki (adj.&n.)
khan khan (n.m.)
kick brykat'sya (v. impf.)
    lyagat'(sya) (v.impf.)
    lyagnut' (v.pf.)
kid laika (n.f.)

shevro (n.n.)
kidney pochka (n.f.)
kill ubivat' (v.impf.)
umertvit' (v.pf.)
kill with an axe zarubat' (v.impf.)
zarubit' (v.pf.)
killed pogibshii (adj.)
ubityi (adj.)
killing umershchvlenie (n.n.)
kilning obzhig (n.m.)
kilo kilo (n.n.)
kilogram kilogramm (n.m.)
kilograms, one hundred tsentner (n.m.)
kilometer kilometr (n.m.)
kilowatt kilovatt (n.m.)
kind dobryi (adj.)
vid (n.m.)
kind, of every vsevozmozhnyi (adj.)
kindle rastopit' (v.pf.)
razzhech' (v.pf.)
kindness dobrota (n.f.)
kindness, human chelovekolyubie (n.n.)
kinematics kinematika (n.f.)
king damka (n.f.)
korol' (n.m.)
kingdom tsarstvo (n.n.)
kiosk kiosk (n.m.)
Kirghiz kirgiz (n.m.)
kiss potselovat'(sya) (v.pf.)
potselui (n.m.)
tselovat' (v.impf.)
kissel (jellied food) kisel' (n.m.)
kitchen kukhnya (n.f.)
kitchen garden ogorod (n.m.)
kitchen help sudomoika (n.f.)
kite zmei (n.m.)
kitten kotenok (n.m.)
knapsack kotomka (n.f.)

ranets (n.m.)
knave valet (n.m.)
knead zameshivat' (v.impf.)
zamesit' (v.pf.)
knee koleno (n.n.)
knife nozh (n.m.)
nozhik (n.m.)
knight rytsar' (n.m.)
knit vyazat' (v.impf.)
knitting vyazanie (n.n.)
knitting needle spitsa (n.f.)
knob nabaldashnik (n.m.)
knock postuchat'(sya) (v.pf.)
stuchat' (v.impf.)
stuk (n.m.)
stuknut' (v.pf.)
knock down sshibat' (v.impf.)
knock out vykolachivat' (v.impf.)
knot uzel (n.m.)
knotty suchkovatyi (adj.)
uzlovatyi (adj.)
know znat' (v.impf.)
know, to get to poznavat' (v.impf.)
knowledge znanie (n.n.)
known, it is izvestno (pred.)
kolkhoz kolkhoz (n.m.)
Komsomol komsomol (n.m.)
Komsomol (Communist youth group)
komsomol'skii (adj.)
kopeck kopeika (n.f.)
Korean koreets (n.m.)
koumiss (a type of beverage) kumys (n.m.)
Kremlin kreml' (n.m.)
kremlevskii (adj.)
kulak kulak (n.m.)
Kurd kurd (n.m.)
kvass kvas (n.m.)

L (Л)

label étiketka (n.f.)
   nakleika (n.f.)
   yarlyk (n.m.)
labial gubnoi (adj.)
labor potugi (n.pl.)
   trud (n.m.)
   trud (n.m.)
labor, hard katorga (n.f.)
labor, woman in rozhenitsa (n.f.)
laboratory laboratoriya (n.f.)
laboratory assistant laborant (n.m.)
laborious kropotlivyi (adj.)
Laborite leiborist (n.m.)
labyrinth labirint (n.m.)
lace kruzhevnoi (adj.)
   kruzhevo (n.n.)
lace insertion proshivka (n.f.)
lace up zashnurovat' (v.pf.)
lack nedostat' (v.pf.)
   nedostatok (n.m.)
   nedostavat' (v.impf.)
laconic lakonichnyi (adj.)
ladder trap (n.m.)
lady barynya (n.f.)
   dama (n.f.)
   gospozha (n.f.)
lady, young baryshnya (n.f.)
lady's damskii (adj.)
lag otstavanie (n.n.)
   zapazdyvanie (n.n.)
laid up, to be slech' (v.pf.)
lair logovishche (n.n.)
lake ozero (n.n.)
lamb barashek (n.m.)
   yagnenok (n.m.)
lame khromoi (adj.)
lamentation prichitanie (n.n.)
lamp lampa (n.f.)
lamp shade abazhur (n.m.)
lance pika (n.f.)
lance corporal efreitor (n.m.)
land krai (n.m.)
   pozemel'nyi (adj.)
   pristat' (v.pf.)
   pristavat' (v.impf.)

   sukhoputnyi (adj.)
   susha (n.f.)
   zemel'nyi (adj.)
   zemlya (n.f.)
land, alien chuzhbina (n.f.)
land improvement melioratsiya (n.f.)
land, native rodina (n.f.)
land, pasture vygon (n.m.)
land, plot of arable nadel (n.m.)
land, plowed pakhota (n.f.)
land surveying geodeziya (n.f.)
land surveyor zemlemer (n.m.)
landing desant (n.m.)
   posadochnyi (adj.)
   prizemlenie (n.n.)
landing net sachok (n.m.)
landless bezzemel'nyi (adj.)
landlord domovladelets (n.m.)
   pomeshchik (n.m.)
landmark vekha (n.f.)
landowner zemlevladelets (n.m.)
landscape landshaft (n.m.)
   peizazh (n.m.)
landslide opolzen' (n.m.)
land-use regulations zemleustroistvo (n.n.)
language yazyk (n.m.)
language, to use foul skvernoslovit' (v.impf.)
languid tomnyi (adj.)
languor istoma (n.f.)
lantern fonar' (n.m.)
lap lakat' (v.impf.)
lapel otvorot (n.m.)
large bol'shoi (adj.)
   krupnyi (adj.)
larva lichinka (n.f.)
laryngitis laringit (n.m.)
laryngology laringologiya (n.f.)
larynx gortan' (n.f.)
laser lazer (n.m.)
lash bich (n.m.)
   khlestat' (v.impf.)
   plet' (n.f.)
last kolodka (n.f.)
   poslednii (adj.)
   prodlit'sya (v.pf.)

last, at nakonets (adv.)
    naposledok (adv.)
last, before pozaproshlyi (adj.)
last, next to predposlednii (adj.)
last year's proshlogodnii (adj.)
lasting dolgovechnyi (adj.)
latch shchekolda (n.f.)
late pozdnii (adj.)
late, to be opazdyvat' (v.impf.)
    opozdat' (v.pf.)
    zapazdyvat' (v.impf.)
lately nedavno (adj.)
later potom (adv.)
lateral bokovoi (adj.)
lathe tokarnyi stanok (adj.-n.m.)
Latin latinskii (adj.)
    latyn' (n.f.)
lattice reshetka (n.f.)
Latvian latviiskii (adj.)
laugh posmeyat'sya (v.pf.)
    smeyat'sya (v.impf.)
laugh, to make nasmeshit' (v.pf.)
    smeshit' (v.impf.)
laugh, to make somebody rassmeshit' (v.pf.)
laughable smekhotvornyi (adj.)
laughing, to burst out raskhokhotat'sya
      (v.pf.)
    rassmeyat'sya (v.pf.)
    zakhokhotat' (v.pf.)
laughingstock posmeshishche (n.n.)
laughter smekh (n.m.)
laughter, roar of khokhot (n.m.)
laughter, to roar with gogotat' (v.impf.)
launch zapuskat' (v.impf.)
    zapustit' (v.pf.)
laundry prachechnaya (n.f.)
laureate laureat (n.m.)
laurel lavr (n.m.)
    lavrovyi (adj.)
lava lava (n.f.)
law yuridicheskii (adj.)
    zakon (n.m.)
lawless bezzakonnyi (adj.)
lawn gazon (n.m.)
    luzhaika (n.f.)
lawnmower kosilka (n.f.)
laws of nature, conformity with
      zakonomernost' (n.f.)

lawyer advokat (n.m.)
    yurist (n.m.)
lax raskhlyabannyi (adj.)
laxative slabitel'noe (n.n.)
lay nastilat' (v.impf.)
    prolozhit' (v.pf.)
    snesti (v.pf.)
    ulozhit' (v.pf.)
lay a foundation zalozhit' (v.pf.)
lay aside otkladyvat' (v.impf.)
    otlozhit' (v.pf.)
lay eggs nestis' (v.impf.)
lay out raskladyvat' (v.impf)
    razlagat' (v.impf.)
    razlozhit' (v.pf.)
    vykladyvat' (v.impf.)
    vylozhit' (v.pf.)
lay upon vozlagat' (v.impf.)
    vozlozhit' (v.pf.)
layer obolochka (n.f.)
    plast (n.m.)
    prosloika (n.f.)
    sloi (n.m.)
layer, thin nalet (n.m.)
laying kladka (n.f.)
    navodka (n.f.)
    prokladka (n.f.)
    ukladka (n.f.)
    zakladka (n.f.)
laying out razbivka (n.f.)
layout komponovka (n.f.)
laziness len' (n.f.)
lazy lenivyi (adj.)
lazy fellow lentyai (n.m.)
lazy, to be lenit'sya (v.impf.)
lazy, to grow oblenit'sya (v.pf.)
    razlenit'sya (v.pf.)
lead dovozit' (v.impf.)
    operezhenie (n.n.)
    otvesti (v.pf.)
    privesti (v.pf.)
    privodit' (v.impf.)
    rukovodit' (v.impf.)
    svinets (n.m.)
    svintsovyi (adj.)
    vesti (v.impf.)
    vodit' (v.impf.)
lead round obvodit' (v.impf.)

lead, sounding lot (n.m.)
leader lider (n.m.)
   predvoditel' (n.m.)
   rukovoditel' (n.m.)
   starosta (n.m.&f.)
   vozhatyi (n.m.)
   vozhd' (n.m.)
leader, military polkovodets (n.m.)
   voenachal'nik (n.m.)
leader, team zven'evoi (n.m.)
leadership voditel'stvo (n.n.)
leading navodyashchii (adj.)
   vedushchii (adj.)
leaf list (n.m.)
leaflet listovka (n.f.)
   proklamatsiya (n.f.)
league liga (n.f.)
leak prosachivat'sya (v.impf.)
   prosochit'sya (v.pf.)
   protech' (v.pf.)
   tech' (n.f.)
leakage utechka (n.f.)
lean prislonit'sya (v.pf.)
   sukhoshchavyi (adj.)
   toshchii (adj.)
lean against pristavit' (v.pf.)
   pristavlyat' (v.impf.)
lean back otkidyvat'sya (v.impf.)
lean on operet'sya (v.pf.)
   opirat'sya (v.impf.)
lean on one's elbows oblokachivat'sya
   (v.impf.)
leapfrog chekharda (n.f.)
learn poduchit' (v.pf.)
   uchit' (v.impf.)
   uznavat' (v.impf.)
   vyuchit' (v.pf.)
learn by heart vyzubrit' (v.pf.)
   zatverdit' (v.pf.)
learned znayushchii (adj.)
learning uchenost' (n.f.)
lease arenda (n.f.)
   sdacha (n.f.)
leash privyaz' (n.f.)
least naimenee (adv.)
least, not in the nichut' (adv.)
   niskol'ko (adv.)
   otnyud' (adv.)

leather processing kozhevennyi (adj.)
leave ostavlyat' (v.impf.)
   otbyt' (v.pf.)
   otbyvat' (v.impf.)
   otpusk (n.m.)
   pobyvka (n.f.)
   uvol'nitel'naya (n.f.)
   vybyvat' (v.impf.)
   vyekhat' (v.pf.)
   vyezzhat' (v.impf.)
   zavozit' (v.impf.)
leave, to ask for otprashivat'sya (v.impf.)
leave behind obgonyat' (v.impf.)
   obognat' (v.pf.)
   peregnat' (v.pf.)
   peregonyat' (v.impf.)
leave of, to take prostit'sya (v.pf.)
   rasprostit'sya (v.pf.)
leave one's job uvol'nyat'(sya) (v.impf.)
leave, to take proshchat'sya (v.impf.)
   rasproshchat'sya (v.pf.)
leave, to take one's otklanyat'sya (v.pf.)
leave traces sledit' (v.impf.)
leaves, fall of the listopad (n.m.)
leavings ob"edki (n.pl.)
lechery razvrat (n.m.)
lecture lektsiya (n.f.)
   nravouchenie (n.n.)
lecture hall auditoriya (n.f.)
lecturer lektor (n.m.)
lecturer, senior dotsent (n.m.)
leech piyavka (n.f.)
left levyi (adj.)
left, on the sleva (adv.)
left, to the nalevo (adv.)
   vlevo (adv.)
left-handed person levsha (n.m.)
left-wing levyi (adj.)
leg noga (n.f.)
   nozhka (n.f.)
legacy nasledie (n.n.)
legal legal'nyi (adj.)
   pravovoi (adj.)
   sudebnyi (adj.)
legal adviser yuriskonsul't (n.m.)
legal procedure sudoproizvodstvo (n.n.)
legalize uzakonit' (v.pf.)
legend legenda (n.f.)

predanie (n.n.)

skazanie (n.n.)

legible chetkii (adj.)

legion legion (n.m.)

legislation zakonodatel'stvo (n.n.)

legless beznogii (adj.)

leisure dosug (n.m.)

lemon limon (n.m.)

limonnyi (adj.)

lemonade limonad (n.m.)

length dlina (n.f.)

otrez (n.m.)

lengthen nadstavit' (v.pf.)

lengthening udlinenie (n.n.)

Leninist leninets (n.m.)

**Leninist Young Communist League of the
Soviet Union** V.L.K.S.M. (abbr.)

lens linza (n.f.)

lens, crystalline khrustalik (n.m.)

Lenten postnyi (adj.)

lentil chechevitsa (n.f.)

leopard leopard (n.m.)

leprosy prokaza (n.f.)

less menee (adv.)

menshe (adj.)

lesser men'shii (adj.)

lesson urok (n.m.)

lesson, to teach a prouchit' (v.pf.)

let predostavit' (v.pf.)

puskai (part.)

pust' (part.)

let go puskat' (v.impf.)

pustit' (v.pf.)

let out vybaltyvat' (v.impf.)

vyboltat' (v.pf.)

vypustit' (v.pf.)

lethal letal'nyi (adj.)

Lett latysh (n.m.)

letter bukva (n.f.)

pis'mo (n.n.)

letter of credit akkreditiv (n.m.)

letter, small strochnaya bukva (adj.-n.f.)

letters, man of literator (n.m.)

lettuce salat (n.m.)

leukemia leikimiya (n.f.)

leukocyte leikotsit (n.m.)

leukocytosis leikotsitoz (n.m.)

level sravnivat' (v.impf)

srovnyat' (v.pf.)

uroven' (n.m.)

level of proficiency kvalifikatsiya (n.f.)

level, on a naravne (adv.)

level to the ground sryt' (v.pf.)

sryvat' (v.impf.)

level with vroven' (adv.)

leveling uravnitel'nyi (adj.)

lever rychag (n.m.)

levy dan' (n.f.)

vzimat' (v.impf.)

lexical slovarnyi (adj.)

liar lgun (n.m.)

vrun (n.m.)

liberalism liberalizm (n.m.)

liberate raskrepostit' (v.pf.)

liberator osvoboditel' (n.m.)

liberty vol'nost' (n.f.)

library biblioteka (n.f.)

knigokhranilishche (n.n.)

library, village izba-chital'nya (n.f.)

lice infested vshivyi (adj.)

license litsenziya (n.f.)

svidetel'stvo (n.n.)

lichen lishai (n.m.)

lick lizat' (v.impf.)

oblizat' (v.pf.)

lick one's lips oblizyvat'sya (v.impf.)

lid zaslonka (n.f.)

lie lezhat' (v.impf.)

lgat' (v.impf.)

lozh' (n.f.)

pokoit'sya (v.impf.)

prolegat' (v.impf.)

solgat' (v.pf.)

vrat' (v.impf.)

lie ahead predstoyat' (v.impf.)

lie down lech' (v.pf.)

lozhit'sya (v.impf.)

prilech' (v.pf.)

ulech'sya (v.pf.)

lie in wait podkaraulivat' (v.impf.)

podsteregat' (v.impf.)

lie, to tell a navrat' (v.pf.)

sovrat' (v.pf.)

lie too long zalezhat'sya (v.pf.)

lies vran'e (n.n.)

lies, to tell izolgat'sya (v.pf.)

lieutenant leitenant (n.m.)
lieutenant colonel podpolkovnik (n.m.)
lieutenant general general-leitenant (n.m.)
life pozhiznennyi (adj.)
    zhizn' (n.f.)
life, mode of byt (n.m.)
    obikhod (n.m.)
lifeless bezdykhannyi (adj.)
lifesaving spasatel'nyi (adj.)
lift podnimat' (v.impf.)
    podnyat' (v.pf.)
lift up zanosit' (v.impf.)
ligament svyazka (n.f.)
light blik (n.m.)
    legkii (adj.)
    legkovesnyi (adj.)
    nalegke (adv.)
    svet (n.m.)
    svetlyi (adj.)
    svetovoi (adj.)
light filter svetofil'tr (n.m.)
light guide svetovod (n.m.)
light, little ogonek (n.m.)
light sensitive svetochuvstvitel'nyi (adj.)
light signals semafor (n.m.)
light, to come to raskryvat'(sya) (v.impf.)
light up osveshchat' (v.impf.)
    osvetit' (v.pf.)
    ozarit' (v.pf.)
    zasvetit'sya (v.pf.)
light up a cigarette zakurivat' (v.impf.)
lighter zazhigalka (n.f.)
lighthouse mayak (n.m.)
lightly legko (adv.)
light-minded legkomyslennyi (adj.)
lightness legkost' (n.f.)
lightning molniya (n.f.)
lightning conductor gromootvod (n.m.)
lightning, summer zarnitsa (n.f.)
lights, traffic torgovat' (v.impf.)
like napodobie (prep.)
    ponravit'sya (v.pf.)
    vrode (prep.)
like, and the i.t.p.(i tomu podobnoe) (abbr.)
like one dead zamertvo (adv.)
like, to become upodobit'sya (v.pf.)
likely pravdopodobnyi (adj.)
liking pristrastie (n.n.)

    simpatiya (n.f.)
lilac siren' (n.f.)
    sirenevyi (adj.)
lily liliya (n.f.)
lily of the valley landysh (n.m.)
limb, artificial protez (n.m.)
lime izvest' (n.f.)
    izvestka (n.f.)
    izvestkovyi (adj.)
    lipovyi (adj.)
lime tree lipa (n.f.)
limestone izvestnyak (n.m.)
limit limit (n.m.)
    predel (n.m.)
limitation ogranichenie (n.n.)
limp khromat' (v.impf.)
    prikhramyvat' (v.impf.)
line amplua (n.n.)
    cherta (n.f.)
    liniya (n.f.)
    ochered' (n.f.)
    podbit' (v.pf.)
    podbivat' (v.impf.)
    strochka (n.f.)
    stroka (n.f.)
line, dotted punktir (n.m.)
line, fishing lesa (n.f.)
line, to drop a cherknut' (v.pf.)
linear lineinyi (adj.)
lined linovannyi (adj.)
linen bel'e (n.n.)
    polotno (n.n.)
linger medlit' (v.impf.)
    meshkat' (v.impf.)
linguist lingvist (n.m.)
linguistics yazykoznanie (n.n.)
lining podkladka (n.f.)
link zveno (n.n.)
linking verb glagol-svyazka (n.f.)
linseed oil olifa (n.f.)
lion lev (n.m.)
lion's l'vinyi (adj.)
lip guba (n.f.)
lips, to lick one's oblizyvat'sya (v.impf.)
liquefying ozhizhenie (n.n.)
liqueur, fruit nalivka (n.f.)
liquid zhidkii (adj.)
liquid ammonia nashatyrnyi spirt (adj.-n.m.)

liquidation likvidatsiya (n.f.)
lisp shepelyavit' (v.impf.)
    syusyukat' (v.impf.)
list kren (n.m.)
    opis' (n.f.)
    perechen' (n.m.)
    spisok (n.m.)
    vedomost' (n.f.)
list, to be on the chislit'sya (v.impf.)
list, to take a nakrenit'sya (v.pf.)
listen prislushat'sya (v.pf.)
    proslushat' (v.pf.)
    vyslushat' (v.pf.)
listen attentively vslushat'sya (v.pf.)
listener slushatel' (n.m.)
listless bezuchastnyi (adj.)
liter litr (n.m.)
literally bukval'no (adv.)
    doslovno (adv.)
literate gramotnyi (adj.)
literature slovesnost' (n.f.)
literature, specialist in literaturoved (n.m.)
lithography litografiya (n.f.)
Lithuanian litovets (n.m.)
litigation tyazhba (n.f.)
litmus paper lakmusovaya bumaga (adj.-n.f.)
litter pomet (n.m.)
    priplod (n.m.)
    sorit' (v.impf.)
little malen'kii (adj.)
    malo (adv.)
little by little malo-pomalu (adv.)
    pomalen'ku (adv.)
    ponemnogu (adv.)
little, just a chut'-chut' (adv.)
little one malysh (n.m.)
little-known maloizvestnyi (adj.)
live dozhit' (v.pf.)
    dozhivat' (v.impf.)
    prozhit' (v.pf.)
    prozhivat' (v.impf.)
    zhit' (v.impf.)
live in poverty bedstvovat' (v.impf.)
live on, sufficient to prozhitochnyi (adj.)
live, to begin to zazhit' (v.pf.)
live together uzhit'sya (v.pf.)
    uzhivat'sya (v.impf.)
liver pechen' (n.f.)

    pechenka (n.f.)
livestock skot (n.m.)
livestock, number of pogolov'e (n.n.)
living zhivoi (adj.)
living room gostinaya (n.f.)
lizard yashcheritsa (n.f.)
load gruz (n.m.)
    gruzit' (v.impf.)
    nagruzhat' (v.impf.)
    nagruzit' (v.pf.)
    nav'yuchivat' (v.impf.)
    pogruzhat' (v.impf.)
    pogruzit' (v.pf.)
    poklazha (n.f.)
    vzvalivat' (v.impf.)
    zagruzhat' (v.impf.)
    zagruzka (n.f.)
    zaryazhat' (v.impf.)
loading nagruzka (n.f.)
    pogruzka (n.f.)
loaf, long baton (n.m.)
loaf, round karavai (n.m.)
loamy soil suglinok (n.m.)
loan ssuda (n.f.)
    zaem (n.m.)
loathing omerzenie (n.n.)
lobby kuluary (n.pl.)
lobule dol'ka (n.f.)
local nizovoi (adj.)
local trade-union committee mestkom (n.m.)
locality mestnost' (n.f.)
location mestonakhozhdenie (n.n.)
locator, sound zvukoulavlivatel' (n.m.)
lock pryad' (n.f.)
    shlyuz (n.m.)
    zamok (n.m.)
    zamykat' (v.impf.)
    zaperet' (v.pf.)
    zatvor (n.m.)
lock, safety predokhranitel' (n.m.)
lock up zapirat' (v.impf.)
locked up vzaperti (adv.)
lockout lokaut (n.m.)
locomotive lokomotiv (n.m.)
    parovoz (n.m.)
locomotive, electric elektrovoz (n.m.)
locust sarancha (n.f.)
log brevno (n.n.)

koloda (n.f.)
poleno (n.n.)
logarithm logarifm (n.m.)
logic logika (n.f.)
logopedics logopediya (n.f.)
loiter okolachivat'sya (v.impf.)
slonyat'sya (v.impf.)
lonely bezlyudnyi (adj.)
odinokii (adj.)
long dlinnyi (adj.)
dlitel'nyi (adj.)
dolgii (adj.)
long ago davno (adv.)
long before zadolgo (adv.)
long, not nedolgo (adv.)
long, not for nenadolgo (adv.)
long since izdavna (adv.)
long standing, of mnogoletnii (adj.)
long-awaited dolgozhdannyi (adj.)
longer dol'she (adv.)
dolee (adv.)
longitude dolgota (n.f.)
longitudinal prodol'nyi (adj.)
long-playing dolgoigrayushchii (adj.)
long-range dal'noboinyi (adj.)
long-term dolgosrochnyi (adj.)
look poglyadyvat' (v.impf.)
posmotret' (v.pf.)
smotret' (v.impf.)
vyglyadet' (v.impf.)
vzirat' (v.impf.)
vzor (n.m.)
look after prismotret' (v.pf.)
look around osmatrivat'sya (v.impf.)
look askance kosit'sya (v.impf.)
pokosit'sya (v.impf.)
look attentively prismatrivat'sya (v.impf.)
look back oglyanut'sya (v.pf.)
look for otyskivat' (v.impf.)
podyskivat' (v.impf.)
look in zaglyadyvat' (v.impf.)
zaglyanut' (v.pf.)
look out beregis' (v.impf.)
vyglyadyvat' (v.impf.)
look round ozirat'sya (v.impf.)
look, to take a oglyadet' (v.pf.)
loop petlya (n.f.)
loophole boinitsa (n.f.)

lazeika (n.f.)
loosen razrykhlit' (v.pf.)
loot nagrabit' (v.pf.)
lord lord (n.m.)
lord, feudal feodal (n.m.)
lordly barskii (adj.)
lose lishat'sya (v.impf.)
proigrat' (v.pf.)
rasteryat' (v.pf.)
teryat' (v.impf.)
uteryat' (v.pf.)
utratit' (v.pf.)
lose a bet prosporit' (v.pf.)
lose courage strusit' (v.pf.)
lose one's way sbivat'sya (v.impf.)
lose the habit otuchat'sya (v.impf.)
otvykat' (v.impf.)
lose weight pokhudet' (v.pf.)
loss poterya (n.f.)
proigrysh (n.m.)
propazha (n.f.)
ubytok (n.m.)
utrata (n.f.)
losses uron (n.m.)
lost in thought, to be zadumat'sya (v.pf.)
lost, to get zabludit'sya (v.pf.)
lot uchastok (n.m.)
zhrebii (n.m.)
lotion primochka (n.f.)
lots uima (n.f.)
lottery lotereya (n.f.)
lotto loto (n.n.)
loud gromkii (adj.)
gromoglasnyi (adj.)
kriklivyi (adj.)
zychnyi (adj.)
loudspeaker gromkogovoritel' (n.m.)
reproduktor (n.m.)
louse vosh' (n.f.)
love lyubit' (v.impf.)
lyubov' (n.f.)
love, cease to razlyubit' (v.pf.)
love, to fall in polyubit' (v.pf.)
vlyubit'sya (v.pf.)
lover lyubovnik (n.m.)
loving lyubyashchii (adj.)
low nevysokii (adj.)
nizkii (adj.)

nizko (adj.)

low tide otliv (n.m.)

lower nizhe (adj.)

nizhnii (adj.)

nizshii (adj.)

opustit' (v.pf.)

ponizhat'(sya) (v.impf.)

ponizit' (v.pf)

snizit' (v.pf.)

spustit' (v.pf.)

lowered, to be opuskat'(sya) (v.impf.)

lowland nizmennost' (n.f.)

low-level breyushchii (adj.)

loyal loyal'nyi (adj.)

loyalty predannost' (n.f.)

lubrication smazka (n.f.)

luck, bad nezadacha (n.f.)

luck, to be in povezti (v.pf.)

luck, to have vezti (v.impf.)

lucky, to be poschastlivit'sya (v.pf.)

lug in pritashchit' (v.pf.)

luggage bagazh (n.m.)

lull ubayukat' (v.pf.)

lumbar poyasnichnyi (adj.)

luminary svetoch (n.m.)

luminescence lyuminestsentsiya (n.f.)

svechenie (n.n.)

luminous svetyashchiisya (adj.)

lump kom (n.m.)

komok (n.m.)

kuskovoi (adj.)

lump sugar kolotyi sakhar (adj.-n.m.)

lunar lunnyi (adj.)

lunatic dushevnobol'noi (adj.)

lung legkoe (n.n.)

lure zamanivat' (v.impf.)

lure out vymanivat' (v.impf.)

lust pokhot' (n.f.)

luster blesk (n.m.)

glyanets (n.m.)

losk (n.m.)

lusterless matovyi (adj.)

lute lyutnya (n.f.)

luxurious roskoshnyi (adj.)

luxury roskosh' (n.f.)

lying lzhivyi (adj.)

lymph limfa (n.f.)

lynching samosud (n.m.)

lynx rys' (n.f.)

lyre lira (n.f.)

lyric poetry lirika (n.f.)

M (M)

macaroni makarony (n.pl.)

machination makhinatsiya (n.f.)

machinations kozni (n.pl.)

machine mashina (n.f.)

mashinnyi (adj.)

obtachivat' (v.imp.)

obtochit' (v.pf.)

machine, adding summator (n.m.)

machine, automatic avtomat (n.m.)

machine building mashinostroenie (n.n.)

machine gun pulemet (n.m.)

machine tool stanok (n.m.)

machine tool construction stankostroenie (n.n.)

machine, washing stiral'naya mashina (adj.-n.f.)

machine, winnowing veyalka (n.f.)

machinist mashinist (n.m.)

macrocosm makrokosmos (n.m.)

mad sumasshedshii (adj.)

umalishennyi (adj.)

mad, to go obezumet' (v.pf.)

pomeshat'sya (v.pf.)

madcap sorvanets (n.m.)

sumasbrod (n.m.)

madden besit' (v.impf.)

madness bezumstvo (n.n.)

umopomeshatel'stvo (n.n.)

magazine zhurnal (n.m.)

magic feericheskii (adj.)

(cont'd)

magicheskii (adj.)
magician volshebnik (n.m.)
magnate magnat (n.m.)
magnesia magneziya (n.f.)
magnesium magnii (n.m.)
magnet magnit (n.m.)
magnetism magnitizm (n.m.)
magnetization namagnichivanie (n.n.)
magneto magneto (n.n.)
magnificent velikolepnyi (adj.)
magnifying glass lupa (n.f.)
magnolia magnoliya (n.f.)
magpie soroka (n.f.)
mail pochta (n.f.)
pochtovyi (adj.)
mailman pis'monosets (n.m.)
main uzlovoi (adj.)
main, gas gazoprovod (n.m.)
main road magistral' (n.f.)
mainland materik (n.m.)
maintenance remontno-tekhnicheskii (adj.)
soderzhanie (n.n.)
maize kukuruza (n.f.)
majestic velichestvennyi (adj.)
major maior (n.m.)
major key (music) mazhor (n.m.)
major, sergeant starshina (n.m.)
majority bol'shinstvo (n.n.)
sovershennoletie (n.n.)
make delat' (v.impf.)
izgotavlivat' (v.impf.)
nadelat' (v.pf.)
proizvesti (v.pf.)
sdelat' (v.pf.)
smasterit' (v.pf.)
uchinit' (v.pf.)
vydelyvat' (v.impf.)
zastavit' (v.pf.)
zavarivat' (v.impf.)
make a call sozvonit'sya (v.pf.)
make a fool of odurachit' (v.pf.)
make a fortune nazhivat'(sya) (v.impf.)
make a slip obmolvit'sya (v.pf.)
make clear vyyasnit' (v.pf.)
make friends podruzhit'sya (v.pf.)
sdruzhit'sya (v.pf.)
make fun of podsmeivat'sya (v.impf.)
make lighter oblegchat' (v.impf.)

make mistakes oshibat'sya (v.impf.)
make much noise nashumet' (v.pf.)
make noise shumet' (v.impf.)
zashumet' (v.pf.)
make one's way through probirat'sya
(v.impf.)
probrat'sya (v.pf.)
make out razglyadet' (v.pf.)
make room potesnit'sya (v.pf.)
make short work of raspravit'sya (v.pf.)
raspravlyat'sya (v.impf.)
make somebody laugh rassmeshit' (v.pf.)
make the fire zataplivat' (v.impf.)
zatopit' (v.pf.)
make up grimirovat' (v.impf.)
zagrimirovat' (v.pf.)
make up for naverstat' (v.pf.)
make up to podlazhivat'sya (v.impf.)
zaiskivat' (v.impf.)
make use vospol'zovat'sya (v.pf.)
make use of pol'zovat'sya (v.impf.)
make worse ukhudshit' (v.pf.)
makeup grim (n.m.)
makeup, to put on podkrashivat'(sya)
(v.impf.)
making izgotovlenie (n.n.)
malaria malyariya (n.f.)
Malay malaiskii (adj.)
Malayan malaets (n.m.)
male samets (n.m.)
malefactor zloumyshlennik (n.m.)
malevolent neblagozhelatel'nyi (adj.)
nedobrozhelatel'nyi (adj.)
malice zlost' (n.f.)
malicious ekhidnyi (adj.)
zlonamerennyi (adj.)
zlostnyi (adj.)
maliciously zlo (adv.)
malignant zlokachestvennyi (adj.)
malnutrition nedoedanie (n.n)
mamma mama (n.f.)
mamen'ka (n.f.)
mammals mlekopitayushchie (n.pl.)
man muzhchina (n.m.)
man, brave khrabrets (n.m.)
man, brown-haired shaten (n.m.)
man, dark-haired bryunet (n.m.)
man, drowned utoplenik (n.m.)

man, fair-haired blondin (n.m.)
man, handsome krasavets (n.m.)
man of letters literator (n.m.)
man, old starik (n.m.)
manage sladit' (v.pf.)
    upravit'sya (v.pf.)
    zavedovat' (v.impf.)
management upravlenie (n.n.)
management, apartment domoupravlenie
    (n.n.)
management, factory zavodoupravlenie
    (n.n.)
management, one-man edinonachalie (n.n.)
manager antreprener (n.m.)
    rasporyaditel' (n.m.)
    zaveduyushchii (n.m.)
mandate mandat (n.m.)
mane griva (n.f.)
manege manezh (n.m.)
maneuver lavirovat' (v.impf.)
    manevr (n.m.)
    manevrirovat' (v.impf.)
maneuvers manevry (n.pl.)
manganese marganets (n.m.)
mania maniya (n.f.)
maniac man'yak (n.m.)
manicure manikyur (n.m.)
manifesto manifest (n.m.)
manipulate manipulirovat' (v.impf.)
mannequin maneken (n.m.)
manner manera (n.f.)
    sposob (n.m.)
manner, in a businesslike po-delovomu
    (adv.)
manners manery (n.pl.)
    zamashki (n.pl.)
mansion osobnyak (n.m.)
manual ruchnoi (adj.)
    rukovodstvo (n.n.)
manual worker chernorabochii (adj.)
manufacture vydelka (n.f.)
    vyrabatyvat' (v.impf.)
manufactured promtovarnyi (adj.)
manure navoz (n.m.)
    unavozhivat' (v.impf.)
manuscript rukopis' (n.f.)
    rukopisnyi (adj.)
many mnogie (adj.)

many times mnogokratno (adv.)
many-colored mnogotsvetnyi (adj.)
many-sided mnogostoronnii (adj.)
many-storied mnogoétazhnyi (adj.)
map karta (n.f.)
maple klen (n.m.)
marathon marafonskii (adj.)
marauder maroder (n.m.)
marble mramor (n.m.)
march marsh (n.m.)
    marshirovat' (v.impf.)
March mart (n.m.)
    martovskii (adj.)
march vystuplenie (n.n.)
mare kobyla (n.f.)
margarine margarin (n.m.)
mark metit' (v.impf.)
    metka (n.f.)
    namechat' (v.impf.)
    oboznachit' (v.pf.)
    otmechat' (v.impf.)
    otmetit' (v.pf.)
    oznamenovat' (v.pf.)
    pomechat' (v.impf.)
    pometit' (v.pf.)
    razmetit' (v.pf.)
    znamenovat' (v.impf.)
marked mechenyi (adj.)
market bazar (n.m.)
    rynok (n.m.)
marksman strelok (n.m.)
marmoset martyshka (n.f.)
marriage brak (n.m.)
    zamuzhestvo (n.n.)
marry zhenit' (v.impf.)
marshal marshal (n.m.)
marshal, field fel'dmarshal (n.m.)
marshes, salt solonchaki (n.pl.)
marten kunitsa (n.f.)
martyr muchenik (n.m.)
marvelous divnyi (adj.)
Marxism marksizm (n.m.)
Marxism-Leninism marksizm-leninizm
    (n.m.)
Marxist marksist (n.m.)
Marxist-Leninist marksistsko-leninskii (adj.)
masculine muzhskoi (adj.)
maser mazer (n.m.)

mash mesivo (n.n.)
mashed potatoes pyure (n.n.)
mask maska (n.f.)
mask, gas protivogaz (n.n.)
mason kamenshchik (n.m.)
masquerade maskarad (n.m.)
mass gromada (n.f.)
   massa (n.f.)
   massovyi (adj.)
   poval'nyi (adj.)
mass meeting massovka (n.f.)
massage massazh (n.m.)
masses, the massy (n.pl.)
massive massiv (n.m.)
mast machta (n.f.)
master khozyain (n.m.)
   osvoit' (v.pf.)
   usvaivat' (v.impf.)
   usvoit' (v.pf.)
master, grand chess grossmeister (n.m.)
master key otmychka (n.f.)
mastering usvoenie (n.n.)
masterly masterskii (adj.)
masterpiece shedevr (n.m.)
mastiff dog (n.m.)
mat polovik (n.m.)
   tsinovka (n.f.)
match match (n.m.)
   spichechnyi (adj.)
   spichka (n.f.)
matching podgonka (n.f.)
material material (n.m.)
   material'nyi (adj.)
   veshchestvennyi (adj.)
material, raw syr'e (n.n.)
materialism materializm (n.m.)
maternal materinskii (adj.)
maternity rodil'nyi (adj.)
mathematician matematik (n.m.)
matrix matritsa (n.f.)
matter materiya (n.f.)
matter, printed banderol' (n.f.)
matting rogozha (n.f.)
mattress matras (n.m.)
   tyufyak (n.m.)
maturity vozmuzhalost' (n.f.)
   zrelost' (n.f.)
mausoleum mavzolei (n.m.)

maximum maksimal'nyi (adj.)
   maksimum (n.m.)
May mai (n.m.)
   maiskii (adj.)
May Day pervomaiskii (adj.)
me menya (p.)
   mne (p.)
   mnoi (p.)
meadow lug (n.m.)
meal muka (n.f.)
   trapeza (n.f.)
mealy muchnoi (adj.)
mean oboznachat' (v.impf.)
   srednee (n.n.)
   znachit' (v.impf.)
meaning znachenie (n.n.)
meaningful mnogoznachitel'nyi (adj.)
meanness podlost' (n.f.)
means sredstvo (n.n.)
means, by no nikak (adv.)
means, peasant of average serednyak (n.m.)
means, without neobespechennyi (adj.)
means of, by posredstvom (adv.)
   putem (adv.)
measles kor' (n.f.)
measure izmerit' (v.pf.)
   mera (n.f.)
   merit' (v.impf.)
   meropriyatie (n.n.)
   obmerit' (v.pf.)
   pomerit' (v.pf.)
   pomerit'sya (v.pf.)
   smerit' (v.pf.)
   zamerit' (v.pf.)
   zameryat' (v.impf.)
measure, half polumera (n.f.)
measure off otmerit' (v.pf.)
measure one's strength tyagat'sya (v.impf.)
measured mernyi (adj.)
   razmerennyi (adj.)
measurement obmer (n.m.)
measuring izmerenie (n.n.)
measuring glass menzurka (n.f.)
meat myasnoi (adj.)
   myaso (n.n.)
meat, canned tushenka (n.f.)
meat grinder myasorubka (n.f.)
meat, roast zharkoe (n.n.)

mechanic mekhanik (n.m.)
mechanical mashinal'nyi (adj.)
mechanization mekhanizatsiya (n.f.)
mechanized bakery khlebozavod (n.m.)
medal medal' (n.f.)
meddle meshat'sya (v.impf.)
vputyvat'sya (v.impf.)
mediator posrednik (n.m.)
medical vrachebnyi (adj.)
medical assistant fel'dsher (n.m.)
medication medikament (n.m.)
medicinal lekarstvennyi (adj.)
medicine meditsina (n.f.)
medieval srednevekovyi (adj.)
mediocre posredstvennyi (adj.)
zauryadnyi (adj.)
medium sreda (n.f.)
meet skhodit'sya (v.impf.)
uvidat'(sya) (v.impf.)
vstretit' (v.pf.)
meeting miting (n.m.)
skhodka (n.f.)
sobranie (n.n.)
vstrecha (n.f.)
zasedanie (n.n.)
meeting, mass massovka (n.f.)
melancholy melankholiya (n.f.)
toska (n.f.)
melancholy, to be grustit' (v.impf.)
melodious melodichnyi (adj.)
melody melodiya (n.f.)
melon dynya (n.f.)
melt rasplavit'(sya) (v.pf.)
rasplavlyat'(sya) (v.impf.)
rastayat' (v.pf.)
stayat' (v.pf.)
tayat' (v.impf.)
topit' (v.impf.)
topit'sya (v.impf.)
melt down peretopit' (v.pf.)
melted talyi (adj.)
toplenyi (adj.)
melting tayanie (n.n.)
member chlen (n.m.)
member, corresponding chlen
korrespondent (n.m.)
member, party partiets (n.m.)
members, most active aktiv (n.m.)

membership chlenskii (adj.)
membership, party partiinost' (n.f.)
membrane obolochka (n.f.)
pereponka (n.f.)
memoirs memuary (n.pl.)
zapiski (n.pl.)
memorable pamyatnyi (adj.)
memorial memorial'nyi (adj.)
memory pamyat' (n.f.)
zapominanie (n.n.)
menagerie zverinets (n.m.)
mend shtopat' (v.impf.)
zashtopat' (v.pf.)
menopause klimaks (n.m.)
menshevik men'shevik (n.m.)
mental myslennyi (adj.)
umstvennyi (adj.)
mention pominat' (v.impf.)
pomyanut' (v.pf.)
upominanie (n.n.)
upomyanut' (v.pf.)
mentor nastavnik (n.m.)
menu menyu (n.n.)
mercenary korystnyi (adj.)
merchant kupets (n.m.)
torgovets (n.m.)
mercury rtut' (n.f.)
mercy miloserdie (n.n.)
poshchada (n.f.)
merge slivat'(sya) (v.impf.)
meridian meridian (n.m.)
merit zasluga (n.f.)
mermaid rusalka (n.f.)
merry-go-round karusel' (n.f.)
message poslanie (n.n.)
message, telephone telefonogramma (n.f.)
messenger gonets (n.m.)
kur'er (n.m.)
poslanets (n.m.)
posyl'nyi (n.m.)
metabolism obmen veshchestv (n.m.)
metal metall (n.m.)
metal, rolled prokat (n.m.)
metal, to strap with okovat' (v.pf.)
metalloid metalloid (n.m.)
metallurgical metallurgicheskii (adj.)
metalworker's slesarnyi (adj.)
metalworking metalloobrabatyvayushchii
(adj.)

metaphor metafora (n.f.)
metaphysics metafizika (n.f.)
meteor meteor (n.m.)
meteorite meteorit (n.m.)
meteorological meteorologicheskii (adj.)
meter metr (n.m.)
   schetchik (n.m.)
meter, cubic kubometr (n.m.)
method metod (n.m.)
   priem (n.m.)
methyl metil (n.m.)
metric metricheskii (adj.)
metrology metrologiya (n.f.)
mew myaukat' (v.impf.)
mica slyuda (n.f.)
microbe mikrob (n.m.)
microbiology mikrobiologiya (n.f.)
micro-district of a city mikroraion (n.m.)
microphone mikrofon (n.m.)
microscope mikroskop (n.m.)
microwave mikrovolnovoi (adj.)
midday poludennyi (adj.)
middle seredina (n.f.)
   srednii (adj.)
middle, in the posredine (adv.)
midge moshka (n.f.)
midnight polnoch' (n.f.)
midnight, after popolunochi (adv.)
midst, in the posredi (adv.)
midwife akusherka (n.f.)
might moch' (n.f.)
mighty mogushchestvennyi (adj.)
migraine migren' (n.f.)
migration migratsiya (n.f.)
mild krotkii (adj.)
   nezlobivyi (adj.)
mile milya (n.f.)
militarism militarizm (n.m.)
militarization voenizatsiya (n.f.)
military voennyi (adj.)
military commissar voenkom (n.m.)
military equipment amunitsiya (n.f.)
military leader polkovodets (n.m.)
   voenachal'nik (n.m.)
militia militsiya (n.f.)
militiaman militsioner (n.m.)
milk doit' (v.impf.)

molochnyi (adj.)
moloko (n.n.)
milk pail podoinik (n.m.)
milk, sour prostokvasha (n.f.)
milk, yield of udoi (n.m.)
milking doinyi (adj.)
milkmaid doyarka (n.f.)
milky mlechnyi (adj.)
mill stan (n.m.)
millenium tysyacheletie (n.n.)
miller mel'nik (n.m.)
millet proso (n.n.)
   pshennyi (adj.)
   psheno (n.n.)
millimeter millimetr (n.m.)
milling cutter freza (n.f.)
million million (n.m.)
millstone zhernov (n.m.)
mimic peredraznivat' (v.impf.)
mimosa mimoza (n.f.)
mince semenit' (v.impf.)
mind um (n.m.)
mind, to change one's peredumat' (v.pf.)
   perereshat' (v.impf.)
   razdumat' (v.pf.)
   razubezhdat'sya
    (v.impf.)
mine dobyvat' (v.impf.)
   mina (n.f.)
   minirovat' (v.impf.)
   minnyi (adj.)
   priisk (n.m.)
   rudnik (n.m.)
   shakhta (n.f.)
miner gornorabochii (n.m.)
   rudokop (n.m.)
   uglekop (n.m.)
mineral mineral (n.m.)
   mineral'nyi (adj.)
mineral oil, black mazut (n.m.)
mineralogy mineralogiya (n.f.)
mines, clear of razminirovat' (v.pf.)
miniature miniatyurnyi (adj.)
minimum minimal'nyi (adj.)
   minimum (n.n.)
mining dobycha (n.f.)
mining and metallurgical gornozavodskii
   (adj.)

minister ministr (n.m.)
minister, prime prem'er (n.m.)
ministerial ministerskii (adj.)
mink norka (n.f.)
minor key minor (n.m.)
minority men'shinstvo (n.n.)
mint chekanit' (v.impf.)
    myata (n.f.)
minuend umen'shaemoe (n.n.)
minus minus (n.m.)
minute minuta (n.f.)
minute, every ezheminutno (adv.)
    pominutno (adv.)
minutes protokol (n.m.)
miracle chudo (n.n.)
miraculous chudodeistvennyi (adj.)
mirror zerkalo (n.n.)
miscalculate obshchityvat'sya (v.impf.)
    progadat' (v.pf.)
    proschitat'sya (v.pf.)
miscarriage vykidysh (n.m.)
miscellaneous raznoe (n.n.)
mischief prokaza (n.f.)
mischievous child ozornik (n.m.)
    shalun (n.m.)
miser skryaga (n.m.&f.)
miserable nishchenskii (adj.)
misfire osechka (n.f.)
misfortune beda (n.f.)
    napast' (n.f.)
misinterpret perevirat' (v.impf.)
    perevrat' (v.pf.)
mismanagement beskhozyaistvennost' (n.f.)
misplace zateryat' (v.pf.)
misprint opechatka (n.f.)
miss khvatit'sya (v.pf.)
    opozdat' (v.pf.)
    promakh (n.m.)
    promakhnut'sya (v.pf.)
    proslushat' (v.pf.)
    razminut'sya (v.pf.)
    soskuchit'sya (v.pf.)
    upuskat' (v.impf.)
missile raketa (n.f.)
missing, to be propadat' (v.impf.)
    propast' (v.pf.)
mission missiya (n.f.)
mist tuman (n.m.)

mistake oshibka (n.f.)
mistaken, to be zabluzhdat'sya (v.impf.)
mistakes, to make oshibat'sya (v.impf.)
misted zapotelyi (adj.)
mistress khozyaika (n.f.)
misunderstand oslyshat'sya (v.pf.)
misunderstanding nedorazumenie (n.n.)
mitten rukavitsa (n.f.)
mittens varezhki (n.pl.)
mix peremeshat' (v.pf.)
    smeshivat' (v.impf.)
mix in podmeshat' (v.pf.)
mix up naputat' (v.pf.)
    zameshat' (v.pf.)
    zameshivat' (v.impf.)
mixed raznosherstnyi (adj.)
    smeshannyi (adj.)
mixed, to get peremeshivat'sya (v.impf.)
mixer smesitel' (n.m.)
mixer, concrete betonomeshalka (n.f.)
mixture mikstura (n.f.)
    smes' (n.f.)
moan ston (n.m.)
moaning nyt'e (n.n.)
mobile podvizhnoi (adj.)
    pokhodnyi (adj.)
mobilize mobilizovat' (v.impf.&pf.)
mock izdevat'sya (v.impf.)
    nasmekhat'sya (v.impf.)
mockery nasmeshka (n.f.)
mode of life byt (n.m.)
    obikhod (n.m.)
model lepit' (v.impf.)
    maket (n.m.)
    model' (n.f.)
    naturshchik (n.m.)
    obraztsovyi (adj.)
    vylepit' (v.pf.)
modelling lepka (n.f.)
moderate umerit' (v.pf.)
    umeryat' (v.impf.)
moderation umerennost' (n.f.)
modesty skromnost' (n.f.)
modification vidoizmenenie (n.n.)
modulation modulyatsiya (n.f.)
Mohammedanism magometanstvo (n.n.)
moisten namachivat' (v.impf.)
    namochit' (v.pf.)
    (cont'd)

smachivat' (v.impf.)
smochit' (v.pf.)
uvlazhnyat' (v.impf.)
moisture vlaga (n.f.)
mold formovat' (v.impf.)
plesen' (n.f.)
slepit' (v.pf.)
slepok (n.m.)
Moldavian moldavanin (n.m.)
molder formovshchik (n.m.)
molding pressovanie (n.n.)
moldy zaplesnevelyi (adj.)
moldy, to grow plesnevet' (v.impf.)
mole krot (n.m.)
molecular molekulyarnyi (adj.)
molecule molekula (n.f.)
molibdenum molibden (n.m.)
mollycoddle nezhenka (n.m.&f.)
moment moment (n.m.)
moment, in a vmig (adv.)
monarchist monarkhist (n.m.)
monarchy monarkhiya (n.f.)
Monday ponedel'nik (n.m)
monetary denezhnyi (adj.)
money den'gi (n.pl.)
denezhnyi (adj.)
money box kopilka (n.f.)
money, lack of bezdenezh'e (n.n.)
moneylender rostovshchik (n.m.)
Mongol mongol (n.m.)
Mongolian mongol'skii (adj.)
mongrel dvornyazhka (n.f.)
monk monakh (n.m.)
monkey obez'yana (n.f.)
monoatomic odnoatomnyi (adj.)
monograph monografiya (n.f.)
monolithic monolitnyi (adj.)
monologue monolog (n.m.)
monopolist monopolist (n.m.)
monopoly monopoliya (n.f.)
monosyllabic odnoslozhnyi (adj.)
monotonous monotonnyi (adj.)
odnoobraznyi (adj.)
odnozvuchnyi (adj.)
monster chudovishche (n.n.)
izverg (n.m.)
urod (n.m.)
month mesyats (n.m.)

monthly ezhemesyachnyi (adj.)
mesyachnyi (adj.)
pomesyachnyi (adj.)
monument monument (n.m.)
pamyatnik (n.m.)
moo mychat' (v.impf.)
mood naklonenie (n.n.)
nastroenie (n.n.)
mood, thoughtful razdum'e (n.n.)
moon luna (n.f.)
moon, full polnolunie (n.n.)
moon, new novolunie (n.n.)
moon rover lunokhod (n.m.)
moonlighting khaltura (n.f.)
moor prichalivat' (v.impf.)
moorage prichal (n.m.)
mop shvabra (n.f.)
morals moral' (n.f.)
nravstvennost' (n.f.)
more bol'she (adj.)
bolee (adv.)
eshche (adv.)
more often chashche (adj.)
morgue morg (n.m.)
morning utrennii (adj.)
utro (n.n.)
morning, in the utrom (adv.)
morning, the following nautro (adv.)
morocco leather saf'yan (n.m.)
morphology morfologiya (n.f.)
mortal smertel'nyi (adj.)
zaklyatyi (adj.)
mortality smertnost' (n.f.)
mortally nasmert' (adv.)
mortar minomet (n.m.)
mortgage zakladnaya (n.f.)
zakladyvat' (v.impf.)
zalozhit' (v.pf.)
Moscow moskovskii (adj.)
mosque mechet' (n.f.)
mosquito komar (n.m.)
moss mokh (n.m.)
most naibolee (adv.)
moth mol' (n.f.)
motylek (n.m.)
mother mat' (n.f.)
mother country otechestvo (n.n.)
mother-in-law svekrov' (n.f.)

teshcha (n.f.)

mother-of-pearl perlamutr (n.m.)

motion khod (n.m.)

motive motiv (n.m.)

motive, hidden podopleka (n.f.)

motor dvigatel' (n.m.)

motor (n.m.)

motor and tractor avtotraktornyi (adj.)

motor, electric elektrodvigatel' (n.m.)

motor transport avtotransport (n.m.)

motor vessel teplokhod (n.m.)

motorcar legkovoi avtomobil' (adj.-n.m.)

motorcycle mototsikl (n.m.)

motto deviz (n.m.)

mound sopka (n.f.)

val (n.m.)

mountain gora (n.f.)

mountain pass pereval (n.m.)

mountain ridge kryazh (n.m.)

mountaineering al'pinizm (n.m.)

mountainous goristyi (adj.)

gornyi (adj.)

mountebank figlyar (n.m.)

mounting ustanovka (n.f.)

mourn oplakivat' (v.impf.)

skorbet' (v.impf.)

mournful skorbnyi (adj.)

zaunyvnyi (adj.)

mourning traur (n.m.)

mouse mysh' (n.f.)

mousetrap myshelovka (n.f.)

mouth past' (n.f.)

rot (n.m.)

ust'e (n.n.)

zherlo (n.n.)

mouthpiece rupor (n.m.)

move dvinut' (v.impf.)

perebirat'sya (v.impf.)

perebrat'sya (v.pf.)

peredvigat'(sya) (v.impf.)

peredvinut' (v.pf.)

perekochevat' (v.pf.)

perelagat' (v.impf.)

perelozhit' (v.pf.)

peremeshchat' (v.impf.)

peremestit' (v.pf.)

podat'sya (v.pf.)

podvigat'(sya) (v.impf.)

podvinut' (v.pf.)

rastrogat' (v.impf.)

sdvigat'(sya) (v.impf.)

sdvinut' (v.pf.)

shevel'nut'(sya) (v.pf.)

shevelit' (v.impf.)

move apart razdvigat' (v.impf.)

move aside otodrat' (v.pf.)

otodvigat'(sya) (v.impf.)

otodvinut' (v.pf.)

rasstupat'sya (v.impf.)

move away otkhodit' (v.impf.)

otoiti (v.pf.)

move backwards pyatit'sya (v.impf.)

move by entreaties umolit' (v.pf.)

move in vselit' (n.pf.)

move on prodvigat' (v.impf.)

prodvinut' (v.pf.)

move out vydvigat'(sya) (v.impf.)

vydvinut' (v.pf.)

move to pity razzhalobit' (v.pf.)

move up pridvinut' (v.pf.)

movement dvizhenie (n.n.)

mover, prime tyagach (n.m.)

moving pereezd (n.m.)

proniknovennyi (adj.)

mow kosit' (v.impf.)

skosit' (v.pf.)

mowing pokos (n.m.)

much gorazdo (adv.)

mnogo (adv.)

mnogoe (n.n.)

mucous slizistyi (adj.)

mucus sliz' (n.f.)

mud gryazi (n.pl.)

muff mufta (n.f.)

muffler glushitel' (n.m.)

kashne (n.n.)

mug kruzhka (n.f.)

mulatto mulat (n.m.)

mule mul (n.m.)

multinational mnogonatsional'nyi (adj.)

multiple kratnoe (n.n.)

multiplicand mnozhimoe (n.n.)

multiplication umnozhenie (n.n.)

multiply pomnozhit' (v.pf.)

razmnozhat'(sya) (v.impf.)

razvestis' (v.pf.)

multistage mnogokaskadnyi (adj.)
multitude mnozhestvo (n.n.)
mumble myamlit' (v.impf.)
  shamkat' (v.impf.)
mummy mumiya (n.f.)
mumps svinka (n.f.)
municipal munitsipal'nyi (adj.)
murder ubiistvo (n.n.)
murmur govor (n.m.)
  ropot (n.m.)
muscle muskul (n.m.)
  myshtsa (n.f.)
Muscovite moskvich (n.m.)
muscular myshechnyi (adj.)
muse muza (n.f.)
  zadumat'sya (v.pf.)
museum muzei (n.m.)
mushroom grib (n.m.)
music muzyka (n.f.)
  noty (n.pl.)
music stand pyupitr (n.m.)
must dolzhen (adj.)
  nado (pred.)
mustache, with a usatyi (adj.)

mustaches usy (n.pl.)
mustard gorchitsa (n.f.)
mustard gas iprit (n.m.)
mustard plaster gorchichnik (n.m.)
musty zatkhlyi (adj.)
mutagen mutagen (n.m.)
mutation mutatsiya (n.f.)
mute nemoi (adj.)
mutilate uvechit' (v.impf.)
mutter bormotat' (v.impf.)
mutual oboyudnyi (adj.)
mutual aid vzaimopomoshch' (n.f.)
muzzle dulo (n.n.)
  morda (n.f.)
  namordnik (n.m.)
my, mine moe (p.)
  moi (p.)
  moya (p.)
myopic blizorukii (adj.)
mysterious tainstvennyi (adj.)
mystery taina (n.f.)
mystical misticheskii (adj.)
mysticism mistika (n.f.)
myth mif (n.m.)

N (H)

nagging popreki (n.pl.)
nail gvozd' (n.m.)
  nogot' (n.m.)
  prikolachivat' (v.impf.)
naivete naivnost' (n.f.)
naked golyi (adj.)
naked, half polugolyi (adj.)
naked, stark nagishom (adv.)
name imya (n.n.)
  naimenovanie (n.n.)
  nazvanie (n.n.)
name, by poimenno (adv.)
name, of the same odnoimennyi (adj.)
name-day imeniny (n.pl.)
namesake odnofamilets (n.m.)
  tezka (n.m.&f.)
nap, to take a vzdremnut' (v.pf.)

nape zagrivok (n.m.)
naphthalene naftalin (n.m.)
napkin salfetka (n.f.)
narcissus nartsiss (n.m.)
narcotic durman (n.m.)
narration povestvovanie (n.n.)
narrow suzhivat'(sya) (v.impf.)
  uzkii (adj.)
narrow one's eyes zazhmurit' (v.pf.)
narrow-gauge uzkokoleinyi (adj.)
narrowing suzhenie (n.n.)
narrowness tesnota (n.f.)
  uzost' (n.f.)
nasal nosovoi (adj.)
nasal twang, to speak with a gnusavit'
  (v.impf.)
nasturtium nasturtsiya (n.f.)

nasty   gadkii (adj.)

nasty thing   merzost' (n.f.)

nation   natsiya (n.f.)

national   narodnyi (adj.)

    natsional'nyi (adj.)

national economic   narodnokhozyaistvennyi

    (adj.)

nationalism   natsionalizm (n.m.)

nationality, a   narodnost' (n.f.)

nationalization   natsionalizatsiya (n.f.)

nationalize   obobshchestvit' (v.pf.)

nationwide   vsenarodnyi (adj.)

native   otechestvennyi (adj.)

    rodnoi (adj.)

    tuzemnyi (adj.)

    urozhenets (n.m.)

native country   otchizna (n.f.)

native land   rodina (n.f.)

natural   estestvennyi (adj.)

    neprinuzhdennyi (adj.)

natural history   estestvoznanie (n.n.)

nature   natura (n.f.)

    priroda (n.f.)

nature, conformity with laws of

    zakonomernost' (n.f.)

nature preserve   zapovednik (n.m.)

naughty, to be   shalit' (v.impf.)

nausea   toshnota (n.f.)

navaga (fish)   navaga (n.f.)

navel   pupok (n.m.)

navigable   sudokhodnyi (adj.)

navigation   moreplavanie (n.n.)

    navigatsiya (n.f.)

navigator   shturman (n.m.)

near   bliz (prep.)

    blizhnii (adj.)

    blizkii (adj.)

    nedalekii (adj.)

    okolo (adv.)

    podle (adv.)

    pri (prep.)

nearby   vblizi (adv.)

nearest   blizhaishii (adj.)

nearly   pochti (adv.)

neat   akkuratnyi (adj.)

nebula   tumannost' (n.f.)

necessary   nuzhnyi (adj.)

necessary, to become   ponadobit'sya (v.pf.)

necessity   neobkhodimost' (n.f.)

neck   gorlyshko (n.n.)

    sheya (n.f.)

necklace   ozherel'e (n.n.)

necrosis   omertvenie (n.n.)

need   nadobnost' (n.f.)

    nuzhda (n.f.)

need, no   nezachem (adv.)

need, there is no   nechego (p.)

need, to be in   nuzhdat'sya (v.impf.)

needle   igla (n.f.)

    igolka (n.f.)

needle, knitting   spitsa (n.f.)

needles   khvoya (n.f.)

needlework   rukodelie (n.n.)

negation   otritsanie (n.n.)

negative   negativ (n.m.)

neglect   mankirovat' (v.impf.)

    prenebrech' (v.pf.)

    prenebregat' (v.impf.)

    zabrosit' (v.pf.)

    zapuskat' (v.impf.)

    zapustit' (v.pf.)

neglected   zapushchennyi (adj.)

negligence   khalatnost' (n.f.)

negligent   neradivyi (adj.)

negotiations   peregovory (n.pl.)

Negro   negr (n.m.)

    negrityanskii (adj.)

neigh   rzhat' (v.impf.)

neighbor   sosed (n.m.)

neighboring   blizhnii (adj.)

neither...nor   ni...ni (conj.)

nephew   plemyannik (n.m.)

nephric   pochechnyi (adv.)

nepotism   kumovstvo (n.n.)

nerve   nerv (n.m.)

nest   gnezdit'sya (v.impf.)

    gnezdo (n.n.)

nestling   ptenets (n.m.)

net   set' (n.f.)

netting   setka (n.f.)

nettle   krapiva (n.f.)

neuralgia   nevralgiya (n.f.)

neurasthenia   nevrasteniya (n.f.)

neurology   neirologiya (n.f.)

neuropathology   nevropatologiya (n.f.)

neutral   neitral'nyi (adj.)

neutrality neitralitet (n.m.)
neutralization neitralizatsiya (n.f.)
neutron neitron (n.m.)
never nikogda (adv.)
nevertheless vse-taki (part.)
new novyi (adj.)
New Year's novogodnii (adj.)
newborn novorozhdennyi (adj.)
newest noveishii (adj.)
new-fangled novomodnyi (adj.)
newly arrived novopribyvshii (adj.)
newly married couple novobrachnye (n.pl.)
news izvestie (n.n.)
   novost' (n.f.)
   vest' (n.f.)
newspaper gazeta (n.f.)
newspaper, factory mnogotirazhka (n.f.)
next ocherednoi (adj.)
next to last predposlednii (adj.)
nibble nadkusit' (v.pf)
nice milo (adj.)
   milyi (adj.)
niche nisha (n.f.)
nickel nikel' (n.m.)
nickel-plated nikelirovannyi (adj.)
nickname klichka (n.f.)
   prozvat' (v.pf.)
   prozvishche (n.n.)
nicotine nikotin (n.m.)
night noch' (n.f.)
   nochnoi (adj.)
nightfall, before zasvetlo (adv.)
night, first prem'era (n.f.)
night, to spend the nochevat' (v.impf.)
   perenochevat' (v.pf.)
nightcap chepchik (n.m.)
nightingale solovei (n.m.)
night-light nochnik (n.m.)
nightmare koshmar (n.m.)
nine devyat' (num.)
   devyatka (n.f.)
nine hundred devyat'sot (num.)
nineteen devyatnadtsat' (num.)
ninety devyanosto (num.)
ninth devyatyi (adj.)
niobium niobii (n.m.)
nipple sosok (n.m.)
nitrate nitrat (n.m.)

nitrate, silver lyapis (n.m.)
nitrite nitrit (n.m.)
nitrogen azot (n.m.)
no net (part.)
   nikakoi (p.)
no wonder nemudreno (adj.)
noble blagorodnyi (adj.)
nobleman dvoryanin (n.m.)
nobody nikem (p.)
   nikogo (p.)
   nikomu (p.)
   nikto (p.)
nobody to, there is nekogo (p.)
   nekomu (p.)
nobody's nichei (p.)
nod kivat' (v.impf.)
noise shum (n.m.)
   shumok (n.m.)
noise, grinding skrezhet (n.m.)
noise, to make shumet' (v.impf.)
   zashumet' (v.pf.)
noise, to make much nashumet' (v.pf.)
noiseless besshumnyi (adj.)
noisy shumnyi (adj.)
nomad kochevnik (n.m.)
nominal naritsatel'nyi (adj.)
   nominal'nyi (adj.)
nominative imenitel'nyi (adj.)
nonadjustable nereguliruemyi (adj.)
nonaggression nenapadenie (n.n.)
nonaqueous nevodnyi (adj.)
noncombatant nestroevoi (adj.)
nonconductor neprovodnik (n.m.)
noncontagious nezaraznyi (adj.)
noncorrosive nerzhaveyushchii (adj.)
non-execution neispolnenie (n.n.)
nonfissionable nerasshcheplyaemyi (adj.)
nonfulfillment nevypolnenie (n.n.)
noninterference nevmeshatel'stvo (n.n.)
nonlimiting nepredel'nyi (adj.)
nonmetal nemetall (n.m.)
non-nomadic osedlyi (adj.)
nonobservance nesoblyudenie (n.n.)
nonparty bespartiinyi (adj.)
   nepartiinyi (adj.)
nonpayment neplatezh (n.m.)
   neuplata (n.f.)
nonpolarized nepolyarizovannyi (adj.)

nonresident prikhodyashchii (adj.)

nonsense chepukha (n.f.)
    chush' (n.f.)
    dich' (n.f.)
    erunda (n.f.)
    vzdor (n.m.)

nonsmoking nekuryashchii (adj.)

nonstop besposadochnyi (adj.)
    nepreryvnyi (adj.)

nonworking nerabochii (adj.)

noodles lapsha (n.f.)

noon polden' (n.m.)

normal normal'nyi (adj.)

north nord (n.m.)
    sever (n.m.)

northeast severo-vostok (n.m.)

northwest severo-zapad (n.m.)

Norwegian norvezhets (n.m.)

nose nos (n.m.)

nose, bridge of the perenositsa (n.f.)

nose out pronyukhat' (v.pf.)

nose, to blow one's smorkat'sya (v.impf.)
    vysmorkat'sya (v.pf.)

nostril nozdrya (n.f.)

not ne (part.)
    net (part.)

not at all nimalo (adv.)

not bad nedurno (adv.)

not for long nenadolgo (adv.)

not guilty nevinovnyi (adj.)

not in the least nichut' (adv.)
    niskol'ko (adv.)
    otnyud' (adv.)

not infrequently neredko (adv.)

not long nedolgo (adv.)

notarial notarial'nyi (adj.)

notary notarius (n.m.)

notch paz (n.m.)
    zarubka (n.f.)
    zazubrit (v.pf.)

note nota (n.f.)
    primechanie (n.n.)
    zapiska (n.f.)

note, promissory veksel' (n.m.)

notebook tetrad' (n.f.)

notes zapiski (n.pl.)

nothing nichego (p.)
    nichem (p.)
    nichto (p.)

nothing, there is nechego (p.)
    nechem (p.)

notice podmechat' (v.impf.)
    podmetit' (v.pf.)
    zametit' (v.pf.)

notify opovestit' (v.pf.)
    predupredit' (v.pf.)

notion ponyatie (n.n.)

notorious preslovutyi (adj.)

nought nul' (n.m.)

noun sushchestvitel'noe (n.n.)

nourishing sytnyi (adj.)

novel roman (n.m.)

novelty novizna (n.f.)

November noyabr' (n.m.)

now nu (part.)
    seichas (adv.)
    teper' (adv.)

now and again podchas (adv.)

now and then izredka (adv.)
    poroi (adv.)

now and then, to come naezzhat' (v.impf.)

now on, from otnyne (adv.)

nowhere negde (adv.)
    nekuda (adv.)
    nigde (adv.)
    nikuda (adv.)

nowhere, from neotkuda (adv.)
    niotkuda (adv.)

nozzle soplo (n.n.)

nuance nyuans (n.m.)

nuclear yadernyi (adj.)

nucleation nukleatsiya (n.f.)

nucleus yadro (n.n.)

nude nagoi (adj.)

nudity nagota (n.f.)

nugget samorodok (n.m.)

numb, to become zakochenet' (v.pf.)
    zatech' (v.pf.)
    zatekat' (v.impf.)

numb, to grow nemet' (v.impf.)
    otsepenet' (v.pf.)

number chislo (n.n.)
    naschityvat' (v.impf.)
    nomer (n.m.)
    perenumerovat' (v.pf.)

number among prichislit' (v.pf.)

numeral chislitel'noe (n.n.)
numeration numeratsiya (n.f.)
numerator chislitel' (n.m.)
numerical chislovoi (adj.)
numerous mnogochislennyi (adj.)
numerous, not nemnogochislennyi (adj.)
numismatist numizmat (n.m.)
nurse nyan'ka (n.f.)
    nyanchit' (v.impf.)
    nyanya (n.f.)
    sidelka (n.f.)
    ukhazhivat' (v.impf.)

    vskarmlivat' (v.impf.)
    vskormit' (v.pf.)
    vykhodit' (v.pf.)
nursery pitomnik (n.m.)
    rassadnik (n.m.)
nursery school yasli (n.pl.)
nut gaika (n.f.)
    orekh (n.m.)
nut grove oreshnik (n.m.)
nutrition pitanie (n.n.)
nylon neilon (n.m.)

O (O)

oak dub (n.m.)
oaken dubovyi (adj.)
oar veslo (n.n.)
oarsman grebets (n.m.)
oasis oazis (n.m.)
oath klyatva (n.f.)
    prisyaga (n.f.)
oatmeal ovsyanka (n.f.)
    tolokno (n.n.)
oats oves (n.m.)
obdurate zakosnelyi (adj.)
obedience poslushanie (n.n.)
obedient poslushnyi (adj.)
obese tuchnyi (adj.)
obesity ozhirenie (n.n.)
obey poslushat'(sya) (v.pf.)
    povinovat'sya (v.impf.)
obituary nekrolog (n.m.)
object ob"ekt (n.m.)
    predmet (n.m.)
    vozrazhat' (v.impf.)
    vozrazit' (v.pf.)
objection otvod (n.m.)
objective ob"ektivnyi (adj.)
object-lens ob"ektiv (n.m.)
oblige obyazat' (v.pf.)
obliging usluzhlivyi (adj.)
oblivion zabvenie (n.n.)
oblong prodolgovatyi (adj.)

obscene nepristoinyi (adj.)
obscurantist mrakobes (n.m.)
obscure nevyyasnennyi (adj.)
observatory observatoriya (n.f.)
observe soblyudat' (v.impf.)
    soblyusti (v.pf.)
observer nablyudatel' (n.m.)
obsolete otzhivshii (adj.)
    ustarelyi (adj.)
obsolete, to become otzhit' (v.pf.)
    otzhivat (v.impf.)
obstacle pomekha (n.f.)
    pregrada (n.f.)
    prepyatstvie (n.n.)
obstacles, to put chinit' (v.impf.)
obstinacy stroptivost' (n.f.)
obstinate upryamyi (adj.)
obstruction obstruktsiya (n.f.)
    zagrazhdenie (n.n.)
    zasorenie (n.n.)
obtain dobit'sya (v.pf.)
    dobyt' (v.pf.)
    vykhlopotat' (v.pf.)
obtain by entreaties vymolit' (v.pf.)
obtrusive navyazchivyi (adj.)
obturator obturator (n.m.)
obtuse tupoi (adj.)
obvious ochevidnyi (adj.)
    yavnyi (adj.)

obviously po-vidimomu (adv.)

occupation okkupatsiya (n.f.)
    zanyatie (n.n.)

occupation, to pursue an podvizat'sya
    (v.impf.)

occupied, long nasizhennyi (adj.)

occupy zanimat' (v.impf.)
    zanyat' (v.pf.)

occur osenit' (v.pf.)
    osenyat' (v.impf.)
    proiskhodit' (v.impf.)
    proizoiti (v.pf.)

ocean okean (n.m.)

ochre okhra (n.f.)

octagonal vos'miugol'nyi (adj.)

octane oktan (n.m.)

octave oktava (n.f.)

October oktyabr' (n.m.)

ocular okulyar (n.m.)

odd chudnoi (adj.)
    nechetnyi (adj.)
    razroznennyi (adj.)
    strannyi (adj.)

ode oda (n.f.)

odious odioznyi (adj.)

of o (prep.)
    ob (prep.)
    obo (prep.)
    pro (prep.)

of age sovershennoletnii (adj.)

of another town inogorodnii (adj.)

of different calibers raznokalibernyi (adj.)

of equal strength, be tantamount to
    ravnosil'nyi (adj.)

of every kind vsevozmozhnyi (adj.)

of full value polnotsennyi (adj.)

of good quality dobrokachestvennyi (adj.)

of little value malotsennyi (adj.)

of long duration dolgovremennyi (adj.)

of long standing mnogoletnii (adj.)

of low standard nizkoprobnyi (adj.)

of many years dolgoletnii (adj.)

of passage prokhodnoi (adj.)

of planks doshchatyi (adj.)

of poor quality nedobrokachestvennyi (adj.)

of short duration neprodolzhitel'nyi (adj.)

of the best quality pervosortnyi (adj.)

of the same age odnoletki (n.pl.)

of the same name odnoimennyi (adj.)

offend obidet' (v.pf.)

offend (be offended) obizhat'(sya) (v.impf.)

offended obizhennyi (adj.)

offense obida (n.f.)

offensive nastupatel'nyi (adj.)
    nastuplenie (n.n.)
    obidnyi (adj.)

offer predlagat' (v.impf.)
    predlozhenie (n.n.)
    predlozhit' (v.pf.)

offering prinoshenie (n.n.)

office filial (n.m.)
    kantselyariya (n.f.)
    kontora (n.f.)

office, booking kassa (n.f.)

office, editorial redaktsiya (n.f.)

office, insurance strakhkassa (n.f.)

office, prosecutor's prokuratura (n.f.)

office, registry zags (n.m.)

officer ofitser (n.m.)

official chinovnik (n.m.)
    ofitsial'nyi (adj.)

officious ugodlivyi (adj.)

offspring otprysk (n.m.)

often chasto (adv.)
    zachastuyu (adv.)

oh o (interj.)
    okh (interj.)

ohm om (n.m.)

oil mazat' (v.impf.)
    neft' (n.f.)

oil, black mineral mazut (n.m.)

oil cake zhmykhi (n.pl.)

oil, castor kastorovoe maslo (adj.-n.n.)

oil, linseed olifa (n.f.)

oilcloth kleenka (n.f.)

oily maslyanistyi (adj.)

ointment maz' (n.f.)

old davnii (adj.)
    staryi (adj.)
    vetkhii (adj.)

old age starost' (n.f.)

old junk star'e (n.n.)

old man starik (n.m.)

old resident starozhil (n.m.)

old, to grow postaret' (v.pf.)
    sostarit'sya (v.pf.)
    (cont'd)

staret' (v.impf.)
old wives' tales rosskazni (n.pl.)
old woman starukha (n.f.)
olden times starina (n.f.)
oldest starshii (adj.)
old-fashioned staromodnyi (adj.)
oligarchy oligarkhiya (n.f.)
olive maslina (n.f.)
oliva (n.f.)
Olympiad olimpiada (n.f.)
Olympic olimpiiskii (adj.)
omelette omlet (n.m.)
omen predznamenovanie (n.n.)
ominous zloveshchii (adj.)
omission upushchenie (n.n.)
omnipotent vsemogushchii (adj.)
vsesil'nyi (adj.)
on na (prep.)
once nekogda (adv.)
odnazhdy (adv.)
once, at razom (adv.)
srazy (adv.)
oncology onkologiya (n.f.)
one odin (num.)
odna (num.)
one after another podryad (adv.)
one and a half poltora (num.)
one at a time poodinochke (adv.)
one day kak-to (adv.)
one side, from sboku (adv.)
one time grant edinovremennyi (adj.)
one year old godovalyi (adj.)
one-color odnotsvetnyi (adj.)
one-day odnodnevnyi (adj.)
one-man management edinonachalie (n.n.)
oneself, to find ochutit'sya (v.pf.)
one-sided odnostoronnii (adj.)
one-storied building odnoétazhnyi (adj.)
onion luk (n.m.)
only lish' (adv.)
tol'ko (adv.)
only, the edinstvennyi (adj.)
ooze sochit'sya (v.impf.)
opaque neprozrachnyi (adj.)
open otkryt' (v.pf.)
otkryvat'(sya) (v.impf.)
otpirat' (v.impf.)
otvorit' (v.pf.)

otvoryat'(sya) (v.impf.)
raskryvat'(sya) (v.impf.)
raspechatat' (v.pf.)
raspuskat'(sya) (v.impf.)
rastvorit' (v.pf.)
rastvorit'sya (v.pf.)
razinut' (v.pf.)
razvernut' (v.pf.)
vskryt' (v.pf.)
open, half poluotkrytyi (adj.)
open slightly priotvorit' (v.pf.)
open-hearth martenovskii (adj.)
opening otverstie (n.n.)
rastvor (n.m.)
vskrytie (n.n.)
opera opera (n.f.)
opernyi (adj.)
operable operabil'nyi (adj.)
operate operirovat' (v.impf.)
operator operator (n.m.)
operator, radio radist (n.m.)
operetta operetta (n.f.)
opinion mnenie (n.n.)
vozzrenie (n.n.)
vyskazyvanie (n.n.)
opinion, in my po-moemu (adv.)
opinion, in our po-nashemu (adv.)
opinion, in your po-tvoemu (adv.)
po-vashemu (adv.)
opinion, to express an vyskazat' (v.pf.)
opium opium (n.m.)
opponent opponent (n.m.)
protivnik (n.m)
opportune svoevremennyi (adj.)
opportunism opportunizm (n.m.)
opportunity okaziya (n.f.)
oppose protivit'sya (v.impf.)
vosprotivit'sya (v.pf.)
opposite obratnyi (adj.)
protivnyi (adj.)
opposite direction, proceeding from the
vstrechnyi (adj.)
opposition oppozitsiya (n.f.)
protivopostavlenie (n.n.)
protivostoyanie (n.n.)
oppression gnet (n.m.)
pritesnenie (n.n.)
oppressor ugnetatel' (n.m.)

optical opticheskii (adj.)
optics optika (n.f.)
optimism optimizm (n.m.)
optional fakul'tativnyi (adj.)
    neobyazatel'nyi (adj.)
or ili (conj.)
    libo (conj.)
oral slovesnyi (adj.)
    ustnyi (adj.)
orange apel'sin (n.m.)
    oranzhevyi (adj.)
orator orator (n.m.)
orbit orbita (n.f.)
orchestra orkestr (n.m.)
orchestra seats, front parter (n.m.)
order nakaz (n.m.)
    orden (n.m.)
    poryadok (n.m.)
    prikaz (n.m.)
    rasporyadok (n.m.)
    ukazka (n.f.)
    velet' (v.impf.)
    zakaz (n.m.)
order about pomykat' (v.impf.)
order, holder of an ordenonosets (n.m.)
Order of the Red Banner, holding the
    krasnoznamennyi (adj.)
order, to put in pribirat' (v.pf.)
    pribrat' (v.pf.)
orderly ordinarets (n.m.)
    vestovoi (adj.)
orders, to give rasporyadit'sya (v.pf.)
    rasporyazhat'sya (v.impf.)
ordinal poryadkovyi (adj.)
ordinary obydennyi (adj.)
ordinate ordinata (n.f.)
ore ruda (n.f.)
organ organ (n.m.)
organ, semiofficial ofitsioz (n.m.)
organ, street ulichnyi (n.f.)
organic organicheskii (adj.)
organism organizm (n.m.)
organization organizatsiya (n.f.)
    postanovka (n.f.)
organized organizovannyi (adj.)
organizer, party partorg (n.m.)
organs, internal vnutrennosti (n.pl.)
orgy orgiya (n.f.)

orient vostok (n.m.)
orientation orientatsiya (n.f.)
origin proiskhozhdenie (n.n.)
    vozniknovenie (n.n.)
    zarozhdenie (n.n.)
original original (n.m.)
    podlinnik (n.m.)
    samobytnyi (adj.)
    svoeobraznyi (adj.)
oriole ivolga (n.f.)
ornament ornament (n.m.)
orphan sirota (n.m.&f.)
orphan, to become an osirotet' (v.pf.)
orthographical orfograficheskii (adj.)
oscillation kolebanie (n.n.)
oscillator vibrator (n.pl.)
Osset osetin (n.m.)
ossified okostenelyi (adj.)
ostrich straus (n.m.)
other drugoi (adj.)
    prochii (adj.)
others drugie (n.pl.)
otherwise inache (adv.)
otitis otit (n.m.)
otter vydra (n.f.)
ottoman takhta (n.f.)
our nash (p.)
ours nash (p.)
oust izgonyat' (v.impf.)
out von (adv.)
out of vne (prep.)
out of place nevpopad (adv.)
out-argue peresporit' (v.pf.)
outcast otverzhennyi (adj.)
outcome iskhod (n.m.)
    razvyazka (n.f.)
outdo pereshchegolyat' (v.impf.)
outline nametit' (v.pf.)
    obvesti (v.pf.)
    ocherchivat' (v.impf.)
    ochertanie (n.n.)
    ochertit' (v.pf.)
outlook krugozor (n.m.)
outlook, world mirovozzrenie (n.n.)
out-of-the-way zakholustnyi (adj.)
outpost forpost (n.m.)
outpouring izliyanie (n.n.)
output vypusk (n.m.)
    (cont'd)

vyrabotka (n.f.)
outright napoval (adv.)
outside naruzhu (adv.)
   snaruzhi (adv.)
   vne (prep.)
outside, from izvne (adv.)
outstanding nedyuzhinnyi (adj.)
   vydayushchiisya (adj.)
outstretched rasprostertyi (adj.)
outstrip operedit' (v.pf.)
outward vneshnii (adj.)
outwardly vneshne (adv.)
outweigh pereveshivat' (v.impf.)
   perevesit' (v.pf.)
outwit perekhitrit' (v.pf.)
oval oval'nyi (adj.)
ovary zavyaz' (n.f.)
ovation ovatsiya (n.f.)
oven dukhovka (n.f.)
over cherez (prep.)
   nad (prep.)
   poverkh (adv.)
   sverkh (prep.)
   svyshe (prep.)
over, from sverkhu (adv.)
over, to be minovat' (v.impf.&pf.)
   minut' (v.pf.)
overalls kombinezon (n.m.)
   spetsovka (n.f.)
overbridge puteprovod (n.m.)
overcast obmetat' (v.impf.)
overcoat pal'to (n.n.)
overcome izzhivat' (v.impf.)
   odolevat' (v.impf.)
   pereborot' (v.pf.)
   poborot' (v.pf.)
   prevozmoch' (v.pf.)
overcome, to try to peremogat' (v.impf.)
overcrowded perepolnennyi (adj.)
overdo pereborshchit' (v.pf.)
   perestarat'sya (v.pf.)
   perevarivat' (v.impf.)
   perezharit' (v.pf.)
overdraft pereraskhod (n.m.)
overdue prosrochennyi (adj.)
overdue, to be prosrochit' (v.pf.)
overeat ob"edat'sya (v.impf.)
   ob"est'sya (v.pf.)

overestimate pereotsenit' (v.pf.)
   pereotsenivat' (v.impf.)
overestimation pereotsenka (n.f.)
overfeed perekarmlivat' (v.impf.)
   perekormit' (v.pf.)
overfulfill perevypolnit' (v.pf.)
overfulfillment perevypolnenie (n.n.)
overgrowing pererastanie (n.n.)
overgrown obrosshii (adj.)
overgrown, to be zarastat' (v.impf.)
overgrown, to become obrastat' (v.impf.)
overgrowth zarosli (n.pl.)
overhaul pereborka (n.f.)
overhear podslushat' (v.pf.)
overheat peregrevat' (v.impf.)
overheating peregrev (n.m.)
overlap perekrytie (n.n.)
overload peregruzhat' (v.impf.)
   peregruzka (n.f.)
overlook nedoglyadet' (v.pf.)
   nedosmotret' (v.pf.)
   proglyadet' (v.pf.)
   proglyadyvat' (v.impf.)
   prosmatrivat' (v.impf.)
   prosmotret' (v.pf.)
overpopulation perenaselenie (n.n.)
overpower osilit' (v.pf.)
   peresilivat' (v.impf.)
overpowering oduryayushchii (adj.)
overripe perespelyi (adj.)
   perezrelyi (adj.)
oversalt peresalivat' (v.impf.)
   peresolit' (v.pf.)
oversaturation peresyshchenie (n.n.)
overseas zaokeanskii (adj.)
overseer nadziratel' (n.m.)
overshoes, high botiki (n.pl.)
oversight nedosmotr (n.m.)
oversleep prospat' (v.pf.)
   prosypat' (v.impf.)
   zaspat'sya (v.pf.)
overstock zatovarivanie (n.n.)
overstrain pereutomlenie (n.n.)
overstrain oneself perenapryagat'sya (v.pf.)
overtake nagnat' (v.pf.)
   nagonyat' (v.impf.)
   nastigat' (v.impf.)
overthrow nisprovergat' (v.impf.)

nizvergat' (v.impf.)

svergat' (v.impf.)

overtime sverkhurochnyi (adj.)

overture uvertyura (n.f.)

overturn oprokidyvat'(sya) (v.impf.)

oprokinut' (v.pf.)

overwhelm nakhlynut' (v.pf.)

oburevat' (v.impf.)

overwork zaezdit' (v.pf.)

owe money zadolzhat' (v.pf.)

owl sova (n.f.)

own rodnoi (adj.)

vladet' (v.impf.)

owner sobstvennik (n.m.)

vladelets (n.m.)

ox vol (n.m.)

ox-eye daisy romashka (n.f.)

oxidant okislitel' (n.m.)

oxidation okislenie (n.n.)

oxide okis' (n.f.)

oxidizer okislitel' (n.m.)

oxidizing agent okislitel' (n.m.)

oxygen kislorod (n.m.)

oyster ustritsa (n.f.)

ozone ozon (n.m.)

ozonization ozonirovanie (n.n.)

P (П)

pace, at a walking shagom (adv.)

pace with, to keep ugnat'sya (v.pf.)

Pacific tikhookeanskii (adj.)

pacification usmirenie (n.n.)

pacifist patsifist (n.m.)

pack koloda (n.f.)

pakovat' (v.impf.)

svora (n.f.)

upakovat' (v.pf.)

zapakovat' (v.pf.)

package posylka (n.f.)

svertok (n.m.)

tara (n.f.)

tyuk (n.m.)

packed bitkom (adv.)

nabityi (adj.)

packet paket (n.m.)

packing prokladka (n.f.)

ukladka (n.f.)

uplotnenie (n.n.)

pact pakt (n.m.)

pad obit' (v.pf.)

obivat' (v.impf.)

pad, writing bloknot (n.m.)

padding nabivka (n.f.)

pagan yazychnik (n.m.)

page stranitsa (n.f.)

page, title titul'nyi list (adj.-n.m.)

pages, to make up into verstat' (v.impf.)

paid platnyi (adj.)

pail, milk podoinik (n.m.)

pain bol' (n.f.)

pain, rheumatic lomota (n.f.)

painless bezboleznennyi (adj.)

paint okrashivat' (v.impf.)

okrasit' (v.pf.)

pokrasit' (v.pf.)

vykrasit' (v.pf.)

paint over zakrashivat' (v.impf.)

zakrasit' (v.pf.)

zamazat' (v.pf.)

zamazyvat' (v.impf.)

painted krashenyi (adj.)

painter zhivopisets (n.m.)

painter, house malyar (n.m.)

painting zhivopis' (n.f.)

painting, decorated with raspisnoi (adj.)

paintings rospis' (n.f.)

pair para (n.f.)

pairs, in poparno (adv.)

pajamas pizhama (n.f.)

palace dvorets (n.m.)

palate nebo (n.n.)

pale, to grow poblednet' (v.pf.)

pale, to turn blednet' (v.impf.)

pobelet' (v.pf.)

palette   palitra (n.f.)
paling   tyn (n.m.)
pallor   blednost' (n.f.)
palm   ladon' (n.f.)
palm tree   pal'ma (n.f.)
palpitation   serdtsebienie (n.n.)
pan, frying   skovoroda (n.f.)
pan, roasting   protiven' (n.m.)
pancake   blin (n.m.)
pancake, cheese   syrnik (n.m.)
pancreatic   podzheludochnyi (adj.)
panel   obshit' (v.pf.)
      panel' (n.f.)
panic   panika (n.f.)
panicky   panicheskii (adj.)
panorama   panorama (n.f.)
pant   pykhtet' (v.impf.)
panther   pantera (n.f.)
pants   shtany (n.pl.)
paper   bumaga (n.f.)
      bumazhnyi (adj.)
paper bag   kulek (n.m.)
paper, litmus   lakmusovaya bumaga
      (adj.-n.f.)
paper, tracing   kal'ka (n.f.)
paper, writing   pischaya bumaga (adj.-n.f.)
parabola   parabola (n.f.)
parachute   parashyut (n.m.)
parade   parad (n.m.)
paradise   rai (n.m.)
paradox   paradoks (n.m.)
paraffin   kerosin (n.m.)
      parafin (n.m.)
paragraph   abzats (n.m.)
      paragraf (n.m.)
parallax   parallaks (n.m.)
parallel   parallel' (n.f.)
paralysis   paralich (n.m.)
paralyze   paralizovat' (v.pf.)
paralyzed, to be   otnimat'sya (v.impf.)
paramount   pervostepennyi (adj.)
parapet   parapet (n.m.)
parasite   parazit (n.m.)
      tuneyadets (n.m.)
parchment   pergament (n.m.)
pardon   izvinenie (n.n.)
      pomilovanie (n.n.)
      proshchat' (v.impf.)

parent   roditel' (n.m.)
parent state   metropoliya (n.f.)
parental   roditel'skii (adj.)
parity   chetnost' (n.f.)
      paritet (n.m.)
park   park (n.m.)
parliament   parlament (n.m.)
parody   parodiya (n.f.)
parotiditis   parotit (n.m.)
paroxysm   paroksizm (n.m.)
parquet   parket (n.m.)
parrot   popugai (n.m.)
parry   parirovat' (v.impf.&pf.)
parry with a jest   otshutit'sya (v.pf.)
parsley   petrushka (n.f.)
part   chast' (n.f.)
      detal' (n.f.)
      dolya (n.f.)
      partiya (n.f.)
      rasstat'sya (v.pf.)
      rasstavat'sya (v.impf.)
participant   uchastnik (n.m.)
participate   uchastvovat' (v.impf.)
participle   prichastie (n.n.)
particle   chastitsa (n.f.)
particular   chastnost' (n.f.)
particularly   osobo (adv.)
partidge   kuropatka (n.f.)
parting   probor (n.m.)
      proshchal'nyi (adj.)
parting words   naputstvie (n.n.)
partisan   partizan (n.m.)
partition   pereborka (n.f.)
      peregorodka (n.f.)
      razgorazhivat' (v.impf.)
      razgorodit' (v.pf.)
partition off   otgorazhivat' (v.impf.)
      peregorazhivat' (v.impf.)
      peregorodit' (v.pf.)
partly   otchasti (adv.)
partner   partner (n.m.)
partnership   souchastie (n.n.)
party   partiinyi (adj.)
      partiya (n.f.)
      vecherinka (n.f.)
party activists   partaktiv (n.m.)
party member   partiets (n.m.)
party membership   partiinost' (n.f.)

party organizer partorg (n.m.)
pass dopusk (n.m.)
    pasovat' (v.impf.)
    peredat' (v.pf.)
    peredavat' (v.impf.)
    proekhat' (v.pf.)
    proezzhat' (v.impf.)
    proiti (v.pf.)
    prokhodit' (v.impf.)
    provesti (v.pf.)
    provodit' (v.impf.)
pass, mountain pereval (n.m.)
pass time korotat' (v.impf.)
pass, to let propustit' (v.pf.)
passage pereezd (n.m.)
    perekhod (n.m.)
    proezd (n.m.)
    prokhod (n.m.)
passage, of prokhodnoi (adj.)
passage, underground podkop (n.m.)
passbook sberknizhka (n.f.)
passenger passazhir (n.m.)
passerby prokhozhii (adj.)
passing prekhodyashchii (adj.)
passing by, in mimokhodom (adv.)
passing, in mel'kom (adv.)
    poputno (adv.)
passion strast' (n.f.)
    uvlechenie (n.n.)
passionate strastnyi (adj.)
passive passivnyi (adj.)
    stradatel'nyi (adj.)
passport pasport (n.m.)
password parol' (n.m.)
past byloe (n.n.)
    istekshii (adj.)
    mimo (adv.)
    minuvshii (adj.)
    proshedshii (adj.)
past, the proshedshee (n.n.)
    proshloe (n.n.)
paste kleit' (v.impf.)
    okleivat' (v.impf.)
    pasta (n.f.)
    podkleivat' (v.impf.)
    raskleivat' (v.impf.)
paste in vkleivat' (v.impf.)
paste together skleit' (v.pf.)

    slepit' (v.pf.)
paste, tomato tomat (n.m.)
paste up zalepit' (v.pf.)
pasteurization pasterizatsiya (n.f.)
pastime vremyapreprovozhdenie (n.n.)
pastry, puff sloenyi pirog (adj.-n.m.)
pasture pastbishche (n.n.)
    podnozhnyi korm (adj.-n.m.)
pasture land vygon (n.m.)
pat pokhlopat' (v.pf.)
patch zaplata (n.f.)
pâté pashtet (n.m.)
patent patent (n.m.)
paternal ottsovskii (adj.)
path dorozhka (n.f.)
    tropa (n.f.)
    tropinka (n.f.)
pathos pafos (n.m.)
patience terpenie (n.n.)
patient patsient (n.m.)
    terpelivyi (adj.)
patriarch patriarkh (n.m.)
patriot patriot (n.m.)
patrol dozor (n.m.)
    patrul' (n.m.)
patron pokrovitel' (n.m.)
patronage, under the podshefnyi (adj.)
patronymic otchestvo (n.n.)
patter skorogovorka (n.f.)
pattern obtekanie (n.n.)
    shablon (n.m.)
    uzor (n.m.)
pause pauza (n.f.)
pave mostit' (v.impf.)
    vymostit' (v.pf.)
paved moshchenyi (adj.)
paved roadway mostovaya (n.f.)
pavement panel' (n.f.)
pavilion pavil'on (n.m.)
paw lapa (n.f.)
pawn peshka (n.f.)
    zalozhit' (v.pf.)
pawning zaklad (n.m.)
pawnshop lombard (n.m.)
pay platit' (v.impf.)
    poluchka (n.f.)
    poplatit'sya (v.pf.)
    vyplachivat' (v.impf.)
    (cont'd)

zaplatit' (v.pf.)
pay a visit provedat' (v.pf.)
pay attention obrashchat' (v.impf.)
pay, be worth while okupit'sya (v.pf.)
pay by installments rassrochit' (v.pf.)
pay extra priplachivat' (v.impf.)
pay, extra priplata (n.f.)
pay in addition doplachivat' (v.impf.)
pay off rasplachivat'sya (v.impf.)
payer platel'shchik (n.m.)
payment oplata (n.f.)
plata (n.f.)
platezh (n.m)
rasplata (n.f.)
uplata (n.f.)
vyplata (n.f.)
vznos (n.m.)
payment, additional doplata (n.f.)
peace mir (n.m.)
uspokoenie (n.n.)
peaceful mirnyi (adj.)
peace-loving mirolyubivyi (adj.)
peach persik (n.m.)
peacock pavlin (n.m.)
peak kozyrek (n.m.)
peaked cap furazhka (n.f.)
kartuz (n.m.)
peal raskat (n.m.)
pear grusha (n.f.)
pearl zhemchug (n.m.)
pearl barley perlovyi (adj.)
peas gorokh (n.m.)
goroshek (n.m.)
peasant krest'yanin (n.m.)
peasant of average means serednyak (n.m.)
peasant's house izba (n.f.)
peat torf (n.m.)
pebbles gal'ka (n.f.)
peck klevat' (v.impf.)
klyunut' (v.pf.)
peculiarity osobennost' (n.f.)
pecuniary denezhnyi (adj.)
pedal pedal' (n.f.)
pedant pedant (n.m.)
peddler lotochnik (n.m.)
raznoschik (n.m.)
pedestal p'edestal (n.m.)
pedestrian peshekhod (n.m.)

pedigree plemennoi (adj.)
porodistyi (adj.)
peel kozhura (n.f.)
lupit'sya (v.impf.)
peel off oblezt' (v.pf.)
peelings ochistki (n.pl.)
shelukha (n.f.)
peep podglyadet' (v.pf.)
peephole glazok (n.m.)
peer vglyadet'sya (v.pf.)
vsmatrivat'sya (v.impf.)
peg kolyshek (n.m.)
pelican pelikan (n.m.)
pelvis taz (n.m.)
pen, fountain avtoruchka (n.f.)
penalty vzyskanie (n.n.)
pencil karandash (n.m.)
pencil case penal (n.m.)
pendulum mayatnik (n.m.)
penetrate prolezat' (v.impf.)
pronikat' (v.impf.)
proniknut' (v.pf.)
penetrating pronitsatel'nyi (adj.)
penguin pingvin (n.m.)
peninsula poluostrov (n.m.)
penknife perochinnyi nozh (adj.-n.m.)
pennant vympel (n.m.)
pension pensiya (n.f.)
pensioner pensioner (n.m.)
pentagon pyatiugol'nik (n.m.)
peony pion (n.m.)
people lyudi (n.pl.)
narod (n.m.)
people, to fill with naselit' (v.pf.)
people, young molodezh' (n.f.)
pepper perets (n.m.)
pepperbox perechnitsa (n.f.)
perceive usmatrivat' (v.impf.)
percentage protsent (n.m.)
perceptible ulovimyi (adj.)
perch okun' (n.m.)
percussion cap piston (n.m.)
peremptory bezapellyatsionnyi (adj.)
perfect sovershennyi (adj.)
perfection sovershenstvo (n.n.)
perfidious kovarnyi (adj.)
perform prodelat' (v.pf.)
prodelyvat' (v.impf.)

vystupat' (v.impf.)
performance otpravlenie (n.n.)
 spektakl' (n.m.)
 vystuplenie (n.n.)
performance, amateur samodeyatel'nost'
 (n.f.)
perfume dukhi (n.pl.)
perfume, to dushit'sya (v.impf.)
perfumery parfyumeriya (n.f.)
perhaps avos' (adv.)
 mozhet byt' (adv.)
 pozhalui (adv.)
pericarditis perikardit (n.m.)
perigastritis perigastrit (n.m.)
perimeter perimetr (n.m.)
period period (n.m.)
 tochka (n.f.)
period of service vysluga (n.f.)
period, point tochka (n.f.)
periodic periodicheskii (adj.)
periodicals periodika (n.f.)
periodicity periodichnost' (n.f.)
periosteum nadkostnitsa (n.f.)
periphery periferiya (n.f.)
periscope periskop (n.m.)
perish gibnut' (v.impf.)
 pogibat' (v.impf.)
perishable skoroportyashchiisya (adj.)
perlon (synthetic fiber) perlon (n.m.)
permanent bessmennyi (adj.)
permanent staff, not on vneshtatnyi (adj.)
permeability pronitsaemost' (n.f.)
permissible dopustimyi (adj.)
permission pozvolenie (n.n.)
permit dozvolyat' (v.impf.)
 pozvolit' (v.pf.)
 propusk (n.m.)
 putevka (n.f.)
 razreshit' (v.pf.)
pernicious pagubnyi (adj.)
peroxide perekis' (n.f.)
perpendicular perpendikulyar (n.m.)
perplex ozadachit' (v.pf.)
perplexity nedoumenie (n.n.)
persecution gonenie (n.n.)
 presledovanie (n.n.)
perseverance usidchivost' (n.f.)
Persian pers (n.m.)

persimmon khurma (n.f.)
persist uporstvovat' (v.impf.)
persistent nastoichivyi (adj.)
 neotstupnyi (adj.)
 neotvyaznyi (adj.)
 upornyi (adj.)
person osoba (n.f.)
 persona (n.f.)
person, a half-educated nedouchka (n.m.&f.)
person, affected krivlyaka (n.f.)
person, left-handed levsha (n.m.)
person, self-taught samouchka (n.m.&f.)
person, touchy nedotroga (n.m.&f.)
personal personal'nyi (adj.)
personality lichnost' (n.f.)
personally lichno (adv.)
personify olitsetvoryat' (v.impf.)
personnel personal (n.m.)
perspective perspektiva (n.f.)
perspiration isparina (n.f.)
pertinent umestnyi (adj.)
pessimist pessimist (n.m.)
pestilence mor (n.m.)
pet lyubimets (n.m.)
petal lepestok (n.m.)
petition proshenie (n.n.)
petitioning khodataistvo (n.n.)
petrel, storm burevestnik (n.m.)
petrography petrografiya (n.f.)
petroleum chemistry neftekhimiya (n.f.)
petroleum cracking process kreking (n.m.)
petty melochnyi (adj.)
petty tyrant samodur (n.m.)
petty-bourgeois melkoburzhuaznyi (adj.)
phagocyte fagotsit (n.m.)
pharmacist farmatsevt (n.m.)
pharmacology farmakologiya (n.f.)
pharmacopoeia farmakopeya (n.f.)
pharyngitis faringit (n.m.)
pharynx zev (n.m.)
phase faza (n.f.)
pheasant fazan (n.m.)
phenomenon fenomen (n.m.)
 yavlenie (n.n.)
phenyl fenil (n.m.)
phial puzyrek (n.m.)
philanthropist filantrop (n.m.)
philharmonic society filarmoniya (n.f.)

philistine meshchanskii (adj.)
   obyvatel' (n.m.)
philologist filolog (n.m.)
philosopher filosof (n.m.)
phlegm mokrota (n.f.)
phlegmatic flegmatichnyi (adj.)
phone, public telefon-avtomat (n.m.)
phonetics fonetika (n.f.)
phonograph patefon (n.m.)
phosphate fosfat (n.m.)
phosphorus fosfor (n.m.)
photochemistry fotokhimiya (n.f.)
photoelectric cell fotoélement (n.m.)
photograph fotografiya (n.f.)
   sfotografirovat' (v.pf.)
   snimat'sya (v.impf.)
photographer fotograf (n.m.)
photosynthesis fotosintez (n.m.)
phrase fraza (n.f.)
phrasemonger frazer (n.m.)
phraseology frazeologiya (n.f.)
physical fizicheskii (adj.)
physical culture fizkul'tura (n.f.)
physician terapevt (n.m.)
   vrach (n.m.)
physicist fizik (n.m.)
physics fizika (n.f.)
physiognomy fizionomiya (n.f.)
physiologist fiziolog (n.m.)
physiology fiziologiya (n.f.)
physiotherapy fizioterapiya (n.f.)
phytopathology fitopatologiya (n.f.)
piano fortepiano (n.n.)
   pianino (n.n.)
piano, grand royal' (n.m.)
pick kovyryat' (v.impf.)
   narvat' (v.pf.)
   obirat' (v.impf.)
   obobrat' (v.pf.)
pick up podbirat' (v.impf.)
   podobrat' (v.pf.)
pickax kirka (n.f.)
picket piket (n.m.)
   zastava (n.f.)
pickle marinovat' (v.impf.)
pickled marinovannyi (adj.)
picnic piknik (n.m.)
picture kartina (n.f.)

picture tube kineskop (n.m.)
picturesque kartinnyi (adj.)
   zhivopisnyi (adj.)
pie pirog (n.m.)
piebald pegii (adj.)
piece kusok (n.m.)
   otrezok (n.m.)
   shtuchnyi (adj.)
   shtuka (n.f.)
piece, by the poshtuchnyi (adj.)
pieces, to vdrebezgi (adv.)
pieces, to crush into razmel'chat' (v.impf.)
pieces, to cut to izrezat' (v.pf.)
pieces, to fall to razvalivat'sya (v.impf.)
pieces, to hack to izrubit' (v.pf.)
pieces, to tear to izorvat' (v.pf.)
   rasterzat' (v.pf.)
   razdirat' (v.impf.)
   razodrat' (v.pf.)
   zadrat' (v.pf.)
piecework sdel'nyi (adj.)
pier byk (n.m.)
   mol (n.m.)
   prostenok (n.m.)
pierce prokalyvat' (v.impf.)
   prokolot' (v.pf.)
   pronizat' (v.pf.)
   pronzit' (v.pf.)
   protknut' (v.pf.)
   protykat' (v.impf.)
piercing pronzitel'nyi (adj.)
pig svin'ya (n.f.)
   svinoi (adj.)
pig breeding svinovodstvo (n.n.)
pig, suckling porosenok (n.m.)
pig tender svinar' (n.m.)
   svinarka (n.f.)
pigeon golub' (n.m.)
pigsty svinarnik (n.m.)
pike shchuchii (adj.)
   shchuka (n.f.)
pile kipa (n.f.)
   stopka (n.f.)
   svaya (n.f.)
   vors (n.m.)
pile up nagorodit' (v.pf.)
   nagromozhdat' (v.impf.)
pilfer rastaskat' (v.pf.)

pilgrim palomnik (n.m.)
pill pilyulya (n.f.)
  tabletka (n.f.)
pill, sleeping snotvornoe (n.m.)
pillar stolb (n.m.)
  stolp (n.m.)
pillow podushka (n.f.)
pillowcase navoloka (n.f.)
pilot letchik (n.m.)
  lotsman (n.m.)
  pilot (n.m.)
pin bulavka (n.f.)
  nakalyvat' (v.impf.)
  nakolot' (v.pf.)
  prikalyvat' (v.impf.)
  prikolot' (v.pf.)
  shtift (n.m.)
pin, rolling skalka (n.f.)
pin together skalyvat' (v.impf.)
  skolot' (v.pf.)
pince-nez pensne (n.n.)
pincers kleshchi (n.pl.)
  pintset (n.m.)
  shchiptsy (n.pl.)
pinch prishchemit' (v.pf.)
  shchepotka (n.f.)
  shchipat' (v.impf.)
  shchipok (n.m.)
  ushchemit' (v.pf.)
  ushchipnut' (v.pf.)
pine sosna (n.f.)
pine for iznyvat' (v.impf.)
pine forest bor (n.m.)
pineapple ananas (n.m.)
pink rozovyi (adj.)
pioneer pioner (n.m.)
  zastrel'shchik (n.m.)
pipe dudka (n.f.)
  svirel' (n.f.)
  truba (n.f.)
pipe, water vodoprovod (n.m.)
pipeline nefteprovod (n.m.)
  truboprovod (n.m.)
piping kant (n.m.)
piquant pikantnyi (adj.)
pirate pirat (n.m.)
pistil pestik (n.m.)
pistol pistolet (n.m.)

piston porshen' (n.m.)
pit yama (n.f.)
pit, ash podduvalo (n.n.)
pitch var (n.m.)
  zasmolit' (v.pf.)
pitch-dark besprosvetnyi (adj.)
  neproglyadnyi (adj.)
pitchfork vily (n.pl.)
pitiful zhalkii (adj.)
pity zhal' (pred.)
  zhalost' (n.f.)
pity on, to take szhalit'sya (v.pf.)
pity, to have smilostivit'sya (v.pf.)
pivot shtift (n.m.)
place mesto (n.n.)
  polozhit' (v.pf.)
  pomeshchat' (v.impf.)
  pomestit' (v.pf.)
  razmestit' (v.pf.)
place of residence mestozhitel'stvo (n.n.)
place one's arms akimbo podbochenivat'sya
    (v.impf.)
place, out of nevpopad (adv.)
place, reserved bronya (n.f.)
place, to find a pristraivat'(sya) (v.impf.)
place under podstavit' (v.pf.)
placenta platsenta (n.f.)
placer rossyp' (n.f.)
placidity blagodushie (n.n.)
plagiarism plagiat (n.m.)
plague chuma (n.f.)
plain nekrasivyi (adj.)
  nezateilivyi (adj.)
  ravnina (n.f.)
plainly tolkom (adv.)
plaintiff istets (n.m.)
plait kosa (n.f.)
  plesti (v.impf.)
plait into vplesti (v.pf.)
plan plan (n.m.) ·
  planirovat' (v.impf.)
  zadumat' (v.pf.)
  zamyshlyat' (v.impf.)
  zamyslit' (v.pf.)
plan, five-year pyatiletka (n.f.)
plane obstrogat' (v.pf.)
  obtesat' (v.pf.)
  ploskost' (n.f.)
  (cont'd)

rubanok (n.m.)
strogat' (v.impf.)
planet planeta (n.f.)
plank planka (n.f.)
plank bed nary (n.pl.)
planked footway mostki (n.pl.)
planks, of doshchatyi (adj.)
planned planovyi (adj.)
planning planirovanie (n.n.)
planning commission, state gosplan (n.m.)
plant nasadit' (v.pf.)
posadit' (v.pf.)
rassadit' (v.pf.)
rassazhivat' (v.impf.)
rastenie (n.n.)
sazhat' (v.impf.)
usadit' (v.pf.)
usazhivat' (v.impf.)
zasadit' (v.pf.)
plant, factory manufaktura (n.f.)
plant, heating teplotsentral' (n.f.)
plantain podorozhnik (n.m.)
plantation plantatsiya (n.f.)
planting posadka (n.f.)
plants, citrus tsitrusovye (n.pl.)
plasma plazma (n.f.)
plaster oshtukaturit' (v.pf.)
plastyr' (n.m.)
shtukaturit' (v.impf.)
plaster, mustard gorchichnik (n.m.)
plastic plasticheskii (adj.)
plastmassa (n.f.)
plate plastinka (n.f.)
plita (n.f.)
plitka (n.f.)
tarelka (n.f.)
plateau plato (n.n.)
ploskogor'e (n.n.)
platform perron (n.m.)
platforma (n.f.)
pomost (n.m.)
platinum platina (n.f.)
platitude poshlost' (n.f.)
platoon vzvod (n.m.)
platoon commander vzvodnyi (n.m.)
play igra (n.f.)
igrat' (v.impf.)
p'esa (n.f.)

razygrat' (v.pf.)
sygrat' (v.pf.)
play one's trump card kozyrnut' (v.pf.)
kozyryat' (v.impf.)
play softly naigryvat' (v.impf.)
play the buffoon payasnichat' (v.impf.)
player igrok (n.m.)
player, accordian garmonist (n.m.)
player, chess shakhmatist (n.m.)
playful igrivyi (adj.)
shalovlivyi (adj.)
playing, to finish doigrat' (v.pf.)
doigryvat' (v.impf.)
pleasant priyatnyi (adj.)
please nravit'sya (v.impf.)
pozhaluista (part.)
ugodit' (v.pf.)
ugozhdat' (v.impf.)
pleased, to be poradovat'sya (v.pf.)
pleasure otrada (n.f.)
udovol'stvie (n.n.)
plebiscite plebistsit (n.m.)
pledge zalog (n.m.)
zarok (n.m.)
plenary plenarnyi (adj.)
plenty polno (adv.)
plenum plenum (n.m.)
pleurisy plevrit (n.m.)
pliant podatlivyi (adj.)
pliers ploskogubtsy (n.pl.)
plinth tsokol' (n.m.)
plot fabula (n.f.)
plot of arable land nadel (n.m.)
plow pakhat' (v.impf.)
plug (n.m.)
vspakhat' (v.pf.)
plow up raspakhat' (v.pf.)
plow, wooden sokha (n.f.)
plowed land pakhota (n.f.)
plowing vspashka (n.f.)
zapashka (n.f.)
plowland zyab' (n.f.)
plowman pakhar' (n.m.)
plowshare lemekh (n.m.)
pluck oshchipat' (v.pf.)
potrokha (n.pl.)
plug shtepsel' (n.m.)
shtift (n.m.)

vilka (n.f.)
zatknut' (v.pf.)
plum sliva (n.f.)
plumage operenie (n.n.)
plumb otvesnyi (adj.)
plummet gruzilo (n.n.)
otves (n.m.)
plump pukhlyi (adj.)
plunder khishchenie (n.n.)
raskhitit' (v.pf.)
razgrabit' (v.pf.)
plunderer raskhititel' (n.m.)
plunge okunat' (v.impf.)
plural mnozhestvennyi (adj.)
plus plyus (n.m.)
plush plyush (n.m.)
ply kursirovat' (v.impf.)
pneumatic pnevmaticheskii (adj.)
pneumatic drill otboinyi molotok (adj.-n.m.)
pneumonia pnevmoniya (n.f.)
pocket karman (n.m.)
luza (n.f.)
pockmarked ryaboi (adj.)
pod struchok (n.m.)
poem poéma (n.f.)
stikhotvorenie (n.n.)
poet poét (n.m.)
poetry poéziya (n.f.)
poetry, lyric lirika (n.f.)
point ball (n.m.)
ochko (n.n.)
ostrie (n.n.)
punkt (n.m.)
tochka (n.f.)
pointed ostrokonechnyi (adj.)
zaostrennyi (adj.)
pointer legavyi (adj.)
strelka (n.f.)
ukazka (n.f.)
pointsman strelochnik (n.m.)
poison otrava (n.f.)
yad (n.m.)
poisonous yadovityi (adj.)
poke sovat' (v.impf.)
tknut' (v.pf.)
tykat' (v.impf.)
poke about shnyryat' (v.impf.)
poker kocherga (n.f.)

polar fox pesets (n.m.)
polarity polyarnost' (n.f.)
polarization polyarizatsiya (n.f.)
Pole pol'ka (n.f.)
polyak (n.m.)
pole polyus (n.m.)
shest (n.m.)
zherd' (n.f.)
polecat khorek (n.m.)
police politsiya (n.f.)
policeman politseiskii (n.m.)
Polish pol'skii (adj.)
polish polirovat' (v.impf.)
shlifovat' (v.impf.)
Polish Catholic priest ksendz (n.m.)
polish, floor mastika (n.f.)
Polish Roman Catholic church kostel (n.m.)
polish, shoe gutalin (n.m.)
vaksa (n.f.)
polished loshchenyi (adj.)
polisher, electric floor elektropoloter (n.m.)
polisher, floor poloter (n.m.)
polishing shlifovka (n.f.)
polite vezhlivyi (adj.)
political politicheskii (adj.)
political study group politkruzhok (n.m.)
political worker politrabotnik (n.m.)
politics politika (n.f.)
polka pol'ka (n.f.)
pollen pyl'tsa (n.f.)
pollination opylenie (n.n.)
pollution zagryaznenie (n.n.)
polyarthritis poliartrit (n.m.)
polyclinic poliklinika (n.f.)
polygamy mnogozhenstvo (n.n.)
polyglot mnogoyazychnyi (adj.)
polygon mnogougol'nik (n.m.)
polygraphy poligrafiya (n.f.)
polymer polimer (n.m.)
polynominal mnogochlen (n.m.)
polysemantic mnogoznachnyi (adj.)
polysyllabic mnogoslozhnyi (adj.)
polytechnic politekhnicheskii (adj.)
pomade pomada (n.f.)
pomegranate granat (n.m.)
pomp pompa (n.f.)
pompous napyshchennyi (adj.)
vysokoparnyi (adj.)

pond   prud (n.m.)
pond, fish   sadok (n.m.)
ponderous   tyazhelovesnyi (adj.)
    uvesistyi (adj.)
pontoon   pontonnyi (adj.)
pool   bassein (n.m.)
    omut (n.m.)
poor   maloimushchii (adj.)
    nebogatyi (adj.)
    neimushchii (adj.)
    plokhoi (adj.)
    ubogii (adj.)
poor harvest   nedorod (n.m.)
poor progress   neuspevaemost' (n.f.)
poor quality, of   nedobrokachestvennyi (adj.)
poor, to grow   bednet' (v.impf.)
poplar   topol' (n.m.)
poppy   mak (n.m.)
popsickle   ledenets (n.m.)
popular   populyarnyi (adj.)
popular belief   pover'e (n.n.)
populated   zaselennyi (adj.)
populated, thinly   malolyudnyi (adj.)
population   narodonaselenie (n.n.)
    naselenie (n.n.)
porch   kryl'tso (n.n.)
    pod"ezd (n.m.)
pore   pora (n.f.)
pork   svinina (n.f.)
    svinoi (adj.)
porous   nozdrevatyi (adj.)
    poristyi (adj.)
    rykhlyi (adj.)
port   port (n.m.)
    portovyi (adj.)
    portvein (n.m.)
portable   perenosnyi (adj.)
    portativnyi (adj.)
porter   nosil'shchik (n.m.)
porterage   perenoska (n.f.)
porthole   illyuminator (n.m.)
portion   portsiya (n.f.)
portrait   portret (n.m.)
Portuguese   portugalets (n.m.)
pose   krasovat'sya (v.impf.)
    poza (n.f.)
    risovat'sya (v.impf.)
position   dolzhnost' (n.f.)

polozhenie (n.n.)
    post (n.m.)
    pozitsiya (n.f.)
positive   polozhitel'nyi (adj.)
positron   pozitron (n.m.)
possessed   oderzhimyi (adj.)
possession   obladanie (n.n.)
possession of, to take   zavladevat' (v.impf.)
possession, to take   ovladevat' (v.impf.)
possessive   prityazhatel'nyi (adj.)
possibility   vozmozhnost' (n.f.)
possible, it is   mozhno (pred.)
possible way, in every   vsemerno (adv.)
post   stolb (n.m.)
    zastava (n.f.)
postal   pochtovyi (adj.)
postcard   otkrytka (n.f.)
poster   plakat (n.m)
postgraduate   aspirant (n.m.)
posthumous   posmertnyi (adj.)
postpone   otsrochit' (v.pf.)
    perenesti (v.pf.)
postscript   pripiska (n.f.)
postulate   postulat (n.m.)
postwar   poslevoennyi (adj.)
pot   gorshok (n.m.)
    kotelok (n.m.)
potassium   kalii (n.m.)
potatoes   kartofel' (n.m.)
    kartoshka (n.f.)
potatoes, mashed   pyure (n.n.)
potential   potentsial (n.m.)
potentialities   zadatki (n.pl.)
potentiometer   potentsiometr (n.m.)
potter   gonchar (n.m.)
pouch, tobacco   kiset (n.m.)
poultry   ptichii (adj.)
pound   funt (n.m.)
    istoloch' (v.pf.)
    toloch' (v.impf.)
pour   lit' (v.impf.)
    lit'sya (v.impf.)
    nakapat' (v.pf.)
    perelit' (v.pf.)
    podlit' (v.pf.)
    podlivat' (v.impf.)
    polit' (v.pf.)
    slit' (v.pf.)

ssypat' (v.pf.)
sypat' (v.impf.)
zalit'(sya) (v.pf.)
zalivat' (v.impf.)
pour in vlivat' (v.impf.)
pour into vsypat' (v.impf.)
pour off otlit' (v.pf.)
otlivat' (v.impf.)
pour out izlivat' (v.impf.)
nalit' (v.pf.)
nalivat' (v.impf.)
otsypat' (v.pf.)
vylit' (v.pf.)
vysypat' (v.pf.)
pour over obdavat' (v.impf.)
pour, water polivat' (v.impf.)
pouring prolivnoi (adj.)
poverty bednost' (n.f.)
nishcheta (n.f.)
poverty, to live in bedstvovat' (v.impf.)
poverty-stricken nishchii (adj.)
powder napudrit' (v.pf.)
poroshok (n.m.)
posypat' (v.impf.)
pudra (n.f.)
powder puff pukhovka (n.f.)
powder with snow zaporoshit' (v.pf.)
power mogushchestvo (n.n.)
moshch' (n.f.)
moshchnost' (n.f.)
polnomochie (n.n.)
sila (n.f.)
silovoi (adj.)
vlast' (n.f.)
power engineering énergetika (n.f.)
power of attorney doverennost' (n.f.)
power station, electric elektrostantsiya (n.f.)
power station, hydroelectric gidrostantsiya (n.f.)
powerful moguchii (adj.)
powers, within one's posil'nyi (adj.)
practical praktichnyi (adj.)
practice praktika (n.f.)
prairie preriya (n.f.)
praise khvala (n.f.)
khvalit' (v.impf.)
pokhvala (n.f.)
prevoznesti (v.impf.)

raskhvalivat' (v.impf.)
voskhvalyat' (v.impf.)
praiseworthy pokhval'nyi (adj.)
prance gartsevat' (v.impf.)
prank shalost' (n.f.)
prayer molitva (n.f.)
preach propovedovat' (v.impf.)
precancerous predrakovyi (adj.)
precaution predostorozhnost' (n.f.)
precept zavet (n.m.)
precious dragotsennyi (adj.)
precipice krucha (n.f.)
obryv (n.m.)
propast' (v.pf.)
precipitate osazhdat'sya (v.impf.)
precipitation osadki (n.pl.)
predecessor predshestvennik (n.m.)
predetermine predreshat' (v.impf.)
predicate skazuemoe (n.n.)
predicative predikativnyi (adj.)
predisposition predraspolozhenie (n.n.)
preelection predvybornyi (adj.)
preface predislovie (n.n.)
prefer predpochest' (v.pf.)
prefix prefiks (n.m.)
pristavka (n.f.)
pregnant beremennaya (adj.)
chrevatyi (adj.)
prehistoric doistoricheskii (adj.)
prejudice predrassudok (n.m.)
predubezhdenie (n.n.)
preliminary predvaritel'nyi (adj.)
premalignant predrakovyi (adj.)
premature prezhdevremennyi (adj.)
premature baby nedonosok (n.m.)
premeditated prednamerennyi (adj.)
premise predposylka (n.f.)
preoccupation ozabochennost' (n.f.)
preparation preparat (n.m.)
preparations sbory (n.pl.)
preparatory podgotovitel'nyi (adj.)
prigotovitel'nyi (adj.)
prepare gotovit' (v.impf.)
nagotavlivat' (v.impf.)
nagotovit' (v.pf.)
prigotovit' (v.pf.)
zagotavlivat' (v.impf.)
prepayment avans (n.m.)

preponderance pereves (n.m.)
   zasil'e (n.n.)
preposition predlog (n.m.)
prepositional predlozhnyi (adj.)
prerevolutionary dorevolyutsionnyi (adj.)
preschool doshkol'nyi (adj.)
prescribe propisat' (v.pf.)
prescription retsept (n.m.)
presence prisutstvie (n.n.)
present nalitso (adv.)
   nastoyashchii (adj.)
   podarok (n.m.)
   predstavit' (v.pf.)
   predstavlyat' (v.impf.)
   prepodnesti (v.pf.)
present, at nyne (adv.)
present, the nastoyashchee (n.n.)
present, to give as a podarit' (v.pf.)
present, to make a darit' (v.impf.)
presentation podnoshenie (n.n.)
present-day aktual'nyi (adj.)
   tepereshnii (adj.)
presenting podacha (n.f.)
presents, to load with zadarivat' (v.impf.)
preservation sokhranenie (n.n.)
preserve, nature zapovednik (n.m.)
president prezident (n.m.)
presidium prezidium (n.m.)
press davit' (v.impf.)
   nadavit' (v.pf.)
   napirat' (v.impf.)
   nazhat' (v.pf.)
   pozhat' (v.pf.)
   pozhimat' (v.impf.)
   press (n.m.)
   pressa (n.f.)
   prizhat' (v.pf.)
   tesnit' (v.impf.)
press conference press-konferentsiya (n.f.)
press in vdavit' (v.pf.)
press, iron zagladit' (v.pf.)
press oneself prizhimat'(sya) (v.impf.)
press out vydavit' (v.pf.)
press, the pechat' (n.f.)
press, underground samizdat (n.m.)
pressed caviar payusnaya ikra (adj.-n.f.)
pressing pressovanie (n.n.)
pressure davlenie (n.n.)

   napor (n.m.)
   nazhim (n.m.)
pressure chamber barokamera (n.f.)
pressure gauge manometr (n.m.)
pressurize germetizirovat' (v.impf.)
prestige prestizh (n.m.)
presumptuous samonadeyannyi (adj.)
pretend prikidyvat'sya (v.impf.)
   pritvorit'sya (v.pf.)
pretentious vychurnyi (adj.)
pretext otgovorka (n.f.)
   predlog (n.m.)
prettier, to grow khoroshet' (v.impf.)
pretty khoroshen'kii (adj.)
   milen'kii (adj.)
   milovidnyi (adj.)
prevail preobladat' (v.impf.)
   ulamyvat' (v.impf.)
   ulomat' (v.pf.)
   uprosit' (v.pf.)
prevent pomeshat' (v.pf.)
   predotvratit' (v.pf.)
preventive preventivnyi (adj.)
previous predydushchii (adj.)
previous conviction sudimost' (n.f.)
prewar dovoennyi (adj.)
price tsena (n.f.)
price, ask the pritsenivat'sya (v.impf.)
price, half poltseny (col)
price, to fall in deshevet' (v.impf.)
price, to reduce the udeshevit' (v.pf.)
price, to rise in dorozhat' (v.impf.)
   vzdorozhat' (v.pf.)
priceless bestsennyi (adj.)
prick kol'nut' (v.pf.)
   kolot' (v.impf.)
   ukol (n.m.)
prick up one's ears nastorazhivat'sya
   (v.impf.)
   nastorozhit'sya (v.pf.)
prickly kolkii (adj.)
   kolyuchii (adj.)
pride gordost' (n.f.)
priest zhrets (n.m.)
priest, Polish Catholic ksendz (n.m.)
primary pervichnyi (adj.)
   pervonachal'nyi (adj.)
   preimushchestvennyi (adj.)

primary source pervoistochnik (n.m.)
prime tsvet (n.m.)
prime cost sebestoimost' (n.f.)
prime minister prem'er (n.m.)
prime mover tyagach (n.m.)
primitive pervobytnyi (adj.)
  primitivnyi (adj.)
primus stove primus (n.m.)
prince knyaz' (n.m.)
principal osnovnoi (adj.)
principle printsip (n.m.)
print napechatat' (v.impf.)
  pechatat' (v.impf.)
printed pechatnyi (adj.)
printed cotton sitets (n.m.)
  sittsevyi (adj.)
printed matter banderol' (n.f.)
printing knigopechatanie (n.n.)
printing house tipografiya (n.f.)
prism prizma (n.f.)
prismatic prizmaticheskii (adj.)
prison tyur'ma (n.f.)
  tyuremnyi (adj.)
prisoner plennik (n.m.)
  uznik (n.m.)
prisoner of war voennoplennyi (n.m.)
private boets (n.m.)
  neglasnyi (adj.)
  ryadovoi (adj.)
privilege l'gota (n.f.)
  privilegiya (n.f.)
privileged privilegirovannyi (adj.)
prize premiya (n.f.)
  priz (n.m.)
  vyigrysh (n.m.)
prize, to award a premirovat' (v.impf.&pf.)
probability veroyatnost' (n.f.)
probably verno (adv.)
probe zond (n.m.)
problem problema (n.f.)
  zadacha (n.f.)
procedure protsedura (n.f.)
procedure, legal sudoproizvodsto (n.n.)
proceed iskhodit' (v.pf.)
proceeding from the opposite direction
  vstrechnyi (adj.)
process pererabatyvat' (v.impf.)
  pererabotat' (v.pf.)

protsess (n.m.)
processing obrabotka (n.f.)
procession protsessiya (n.f.)
  shestvie (n.n.)
proclaim provozglasit' (v.pf.)
procrastination volokita (n.f.)
proctology proktologiya (n.f.)
procurement, grain khlebozagotovka (n.f.)
prodigy, infant vunderkind (n.m.)
produce proizvodit' (v.impf.)
  stavit' (v.impf.)
producer rezhisser (n.m.)
producers' promyslovyi (adj.)
product produkt (n.m.)
  proizvedenie (n.n.)
production produktsiya (n.f.)
  proizvodstvo (n.n.)
productivity produktivnost' (n.f.)
  proizvoditel'nost' (n.f.)
profanation oskvernenie (n.n.)
  profanatsiya (n.f.)
profane oskvernit' (v.pf.)
profession professiya (n.f.)
professional professional'nyi (adj.)
professor professor (n.m.)
proficiency, level of kvalifikatsiya (n.f.)
profile profil' (n.m.)
profit barysh (n.m.)
  nazhiva (n.f.)
  pozhivit'sya (v.pf.)
  pribyl' (n.f.)
  vygoda (n.f.)
profitable dokhodnyi (adj.)
  rentabel'nyi (adj.)
program programma (n.f.)
progress progress (n.m.)
  uspevaemost' (n.f.)
progress, poor neuspevaemost' (n.f.)
progression progressiya (n.f.)
progressive postupatel'nyi (adj.)
project proekt (n.m.)
projectile snaryad (n.m.)
projection proektsiya (n.f.)
  ustup (n.m.)
  vystup (n.m.)
proletarian proletarii (n.m.)
proletariat proletariat (n.m.)
proliferation proliferatsiya (n.f.)

prolific plodovityi (adj.)
prologue prolog (n.m.)
prolongation prodlenie (n.n.)
prominence protuberanets (n.m.)
    vypuklost' (n.f.)
promisary note veksel' (n.m.)
promise obeshchanie (n.n.)
    poobeshchat' (v.pf.)
    sulit' (v.impf.)
promising mnogoobeshchayushchii (adj.)
promotion, to gain vysluzhivat'sya (v.impf.)
prompt podskazat' (v.pf.)
    pospeshnyi (adj.)
prompter sufler (n.m.)
promptly zhivo (adv.)
promulgate obnarodovat' (v.impf.&pf.)
prone nichkom (adv.)
    plashmya (adv.)
pronoun mestoimenie (n.n.)
pronounce proiznesti (v.pf.)
pronunciation proiznoshenie (n.n.)
proof dokazatel'stvo (n.n.)
proof, without goloslovno (adv.)
proofreader korrektor (n.m.)
prop podporka (n.f.)
prop up podperet' (v.pf.)
    podpirat' (v.impf.)
propaganda propaganda (n.f.)
propaganda station agitpunkt (n.m.)
propaganda team agitbrigada (n.f.)
propagandist agitator (n.m.)
propagate plodit'sya (v.impf.)
propeller propeller (n.m.)
proper dolzhnyi (adj.)
properly po-nastoyashchemu (adv.)
propertied imushchii (adj.)
properties butaforiya (n.f.)
property dostoyanie (n.n.)
    imushchestvo (n.n.)
    sobstvennost' (n.f.)
    svoistvo (n.n.)
prophecy prorochestvo (n.n.)
prophet prorok (n.m.)
prophylaxis profilaktika (n.f.)
proportion proportsiya (n.f.)
proportional proportsional'nyi (adj.)
propose as husband (wife) svatat' (v.impf.)
props rekvizit (n.m.)

proscenium avanstsena (n.f.)
prose proza (n.f.)
prosecutor, public prokuror (n.m.)
prosecutor's office prokuratura (n.f.)
prosperity protsvetanie (n.n.)
    rastsvet (n.m.)
prosperous zazhitochnyi (adj.)
prostitute prostitutka (n.f.)
protect obezopasit' (v.pf.)
    predokhranit' (v.pf.)
protect (oneself) uberegat'(sya) (v.impf.)
protection predokhranenie (n.n.)
protective cover protektor (n.m.)
protector protektor (n.m.)
protege stavlennik (n.m.)
protein protein (n.m.)
protein-free bezbelkovyi (adj.)
protest oprotestovat' (v.pf.)
    protest (n.m.)
proton proton (n.m.)
prototype prototip (n.m.)
protoxide zakis' (n.f.)
protrude vydavat'sya (v.impf.)
protruding navykat(e) (adv.)
protuberance protuberanets (n.m.)
proud gordelivyi (adj.)
    samolyubivyi (adj.)
proud, to be gordit'sya (v.impf.)
prove dokazat' (v.pf.)
prove oneself zarekomendovat' (v.pf.)
prove someone guilty ulichat' (v.impf.)
prove to be okazat'sya (v.pf.)
    okazyvat'sya (v.impf.)
proverb poslovitsa (n.f.)
provide obespechit' (v.pf.)
    prokormit' (v.pf.)
provide oneself with obzavestis' (v.pf.)
providing general education
    obshcheobrazovatel'nyi (adj.)
province guberniya (n.f.)
    provintsiya (n.f.)
provinces periferiya (n.f.)
provincial provintsial'nyi (adj.)
provisions pripasy (n.pl.)
    proviziya (n.f.)
provocation provokatsiya (n.f.)
provoke provotsirovat' (v.impf.)
    sprovotsirovat' (v.impf.)

proximity blizost' (n.f.)
prunes chernosliv (n.m.)
pseudonym psevdonim (n.m.)
psyche psikhika (n.f.)
psychiatrist psikhiatr (n.m.)
psychiatry psikhiatriya (n.f.)
psychoanalysis psikhoanaliz (n.m.)
psychologist psikholog (n.m.)
psychology psikhologiya (n.f.)
psychosis psikhoz (n.m.)
public glasnyi (adj.)
     obshchenarodnyi (adj.)
     publichnyi (adj.)
     publika (n.f.)
public garden skver (n.m.)
public health zdravookhranenie (n.n.)
public phone telefon-avtomat (n.m.)
public prosecutor prokuror (n.m.)
public, the obshchestvennost' (n.f.)
publication izdanie (n.n.)
     opublikovanie (n.n.)
publicity glasnost' (n.f.)
     oglaska (n.f.)
publish izdat' (v.pf.)
     izdavat' (v.impf.)
puck shaiba (n.f.)
pudding, baked zapekanka (n.f.)
puddle luzha (n.f.)
puff klub (n.m.)
puff pastry sloenyi pirog (adj.-n.m.)
puff, powder pukhovka (n.f.)
puffy odutlovatyi (adj.)
pull dergat' (v.impf.)
     potyanut' (v.pf.)
     terebit' (v.impf.)
     tyanut' (v.impf.)
pull down odergivat' (v.impf.)
     odernut' (v.pf.)
     snosit' (v.impf.)
pull off sdergivat' (v.impf.)
     sdernut' (v.pf.)
     stashchit' (v.pf.)
     staskivat' (v.impf.)
pull out vydergivat' (v.impf.)
     vydernut' (v.pf.)
     vyrvat' (v.pf.)
     vyryvat' (v.impf.)
pull over nadvigat' (v.impf.)

     nadvinut' (v.pf.)
pull through protaskivat' (v.impf.)
pull through (an illness) vykhazhivat'
     (v.impf.)
pull up podtyanut' (v.pf.)
pulley blok (n.m.)
     shkiv (n.m.)
pulling down slom (n.m.)
pulmonary legochnyi (adj.)
pulpit kafedra (n.f.)
pulse pul's (n.m.)
     pul'sirovat' (v.impf.)
pulverization raspylenie (n.n.)
pulverize raspylyat'(sya) (v.impf.)
pumice pemza (n.f.)
pump nagnetat' (v.impf.)
     nakachat' (v.pf.)
     nasos (n.m.)
     pompa (n.f.)
pump house vodokachka (n.f.)
pump out otkachat' (v.pf.)
     vykachat' (v.pf.)
pumpkin tykva (n.f.)
pun kalambur (n.m.)
punch kompostirovat' (v.impf.)
Punch petrushka (n.m.)
punch probivat' (v.impf.)
punctual punktual'nyi (adj.)
punctuation punktuatsiya (n.f.)
puncture proboi (n.m.)
punish karat' (v.impf.)
     nakazyvat' (v.impf.)
punishment nakazanie (n.n.)
punishment room kartser (n.m.)
punitive karatel'nyi (adj.)
puny shchuplyi (adj.)
     tshchedushnyi (adj.)
pupil pitomets (n.m.)
     zenitsa (n.f.)
     zrachok (n.m.)
puppet marionetka (n.f.)
puppy shchenok (n.m.)
purchase pokupka (n.f.)
     zakupat' (v.impf.)
     zakupka (n.f.)
pure gold chervonnyi (adj.)
purifier ochistitel' (n.m.)
purple bagrovyi (adj.)

purpur (n.m.)
purpurovyi (adj.)
purpose tsel' (n.f.)
purpose, not without nesprosta (adv.)
purpose, on narochno (adv.)
purpose, to no vpustuyu (adv.)
zrya (adv.)
purpose, to send for a podoslat' (v.pf.)
podsylat' (v.impf.)
purposeful tseleustremlennyi (adj.)
purposeless netselesoobraznyi (adj.)
purr murlykat' (v.impf.)
purse koshelek (n.m.)
pursue an occupation podvizat'sya (v.impf.)
pursuit pogonya (n.f.)
pursuit of, in vdogonku (adv.)
pus gnoi (n.m.)
push tolchok (n.m.)
tolkat' (v.impf.)
tolknut' (v.pf.)
push apart rastalkivat' (v.impf.)
rastolkat' (v.pf.)
push aside spikhivat' (v.impf.)
push away otpikhivat' (v.impf.)
ottalkivat' (v.impf.)
ottolknut' (v.pf.)
push in vdvigat' (v.impf.)
vpikhivat' (v.impf.)
vtalkivat' (v.impf.)
vtolknut' (v.pf.)
zapikhat' (v.pf.)
push into zadvigat' (v.impf.)
zatolkat' (v.pf.)
push out vytalkivat' (v.impf.)
vytolknut' (v.pf.)
push through prosovyvat' (v.impf.)
prosunut' (v.pf.)
protalkivat' (v.impf.)
push up pododvigat' (v.impf.)
pushing aside otstranenie (n.n.)
pussy willow verba (n.f.)
put det' (v.pf.)
klast' (v.impf.)
postavit' (v.pf.)
pristavit' (v.pf.)

pristavlyat' (v.impf.)
stavit' (v.impf.)
ustanovit' (v.pf.)
put an end presekat' (v.impf.)
put in vlozhit' (v.pf.)
vsovyvat' (v.impf.)
vstavit' (v.impf.)
vsunut' (v.pf.)
vvernut' (v.pf.)
put in a word for zamlovit' (v.pf.)
put in irons zakovat' (v.pf.)
put in order pribirat' (v.pf.)
pribrat' (v.pf.)
put into vdet' (v.pf.)
vdevat' (v.impf.)
put obstacles chinit' (v.impf.)
put on nadet' (v.pf.)
nadevat' (v.impf.)
nakladyvat' (v.impf.)
nalagat' (v.impf.)
nalozhit' (v.pf.)
put on airs vazhnichat' (v.impf.)
put on makeup podkrashivat'(sya) (v.impf.)
put on shoes obut' (v.pf.)
obuvat'(sya) (v.impf.)
put on weight polnet' (v.impf.)
rastolstet' (v.pf.)
put out vykalyvat' (v.impf.)
vykolot' (v.pf.)
vysunut' (v.pf.)
put scent on nadushit' (v.pf.)
put to sleep usypit' (v.pf.)
put together sostavit' (v.pf.)
put under podkladyvat' (v.impf.)
podlozhit' (v.pf.)
podsovyvat' (v.impf.)
podsunut' (v.pf.)
puttees obmotki (n.pl.)
putty shpaklevat' (v.impf.)
puzzle golovolomka (n.f.)
puzzled nedoumennyi (adj.)
puzzled, to be nedoumevat' (v.impf.)
pyramid piramida (n.f.)
python piton (n.m.)

Q

quack kryakat' (v.impf.)

quadrangular chetyrekhugol'nyi (adj.)

quagmire tryasina (n.f.)

quail perepelka (n.f.)

qualification tsenz (n.m.)

qualified, highly vysokokvalifitsirovannyi
    (adj.)

qualitative kachestvennyi (adj.)

quality kachestvo (n.n.)

quality, of good dobrokachestvennyi (adj.)

quality, of poor nedobrokachestvennyi (adj.)

quality, of the best pervosortnyi (adj.)

quantitative kolichestvennyi (adj.)

quantity chislennost' (n.f.)
    kolichestvo (n.n.)
    velichina (n.f.)

quarantine karantin (n.m.)

quarrel peressorit'sya (v.pf.)
    porugat'sya (v.pf.)
    possorit'(sya) (v.pf.)
    povzdorit' (v.pf.)
    rassorit'sya (v.pf.)
    ssora (n.f.)

quarrelsome neuzheli (part.)
    svarlivyi (adj.)

quarry kamenolomnya (n.f.)
    kar'er (n.m.)

quarter chetvert' (n.f.)

quartermaster intendant (n.m.)

quarters, sick lazaret (n.m.)

quartet kvartet (n.m.)

quartz kvarts (n.m.)

quay pristan' (n.f.)

queen ferz' (n.m.)
    koroleva (n.f.)

quench utolit' (v.pf.)

utolyat' (v.impf.)

question oprashivat' (v.impf.)
    vopros (n.m.)

quick bystryi (adj.)
    provornyi (adj.)
    prytkii (adj.)
    rastoropnyi (adj.)

quickly bystro (adv.)

quick-tempered zapal'chivyi (adj.)

quick-wit soobrazitel'nost' (n.f.)

quiet spokoinyi (adj.)
    tikhii (adj.)
    tishina (n.f.)

quiet, to grow pritikhat' (v.impf.)

quietly smirno (adv.)
    tikho (adv.)

quilt pododeyal'nik (n.m.)
    stegat' (v.impf.)

quilt cover pododeyal'nik (n.m.)

quilted steganyi (adj.)

quilted jacket vatnik (n.m.)

quinine khina (n.f.)

quinsy angina (n.f.)
    zhaba (n.f.)

quit vybyvat' (v.impf.)

quite sovsem (adv.)
    vpolne (adv.)

quite unexpectedly nevznachai (adv.)

quits kvity (adj.)

quorum kvorum (n.m.)

quota kontingent (n.m.)
    norma (n.f.)

quotation tsitata (n.f.)

quotation marks kavychki (n.pl.)

quotient chastnoe (n.n.)

R (P)

rabbit krolik (n.m.)
rabbit breeding krolikovodstvo (n.n.)
raccoon enot (n.m.)
race begovoi (adj.)
  gonka (n.f.)
  naperegonki (adv.)
  rasa (n.f.)
race, relay estafeta (n.f.)
racecourse ippodrom (n.m.)
races gonki (n.pl.)
racial rasovyi (adj.)
racing gonochnyi (adj.)
racket raketka (n.f.)
radial luchevoi (adj.)
radiance siyanie (n.n.)
radiant luchezarnyi (adj.)
  luchistyi (adj.)
radiate izluchat' (v.impf.)
radiation lucheispuskanie (n.n.)
  radiatsiya (n.f.)
radiation, gamma gamma-izluchenie (n.n.)
radiator radiator (n.m.)
radical radikal (n.m.)
  radikal'nyi (adj.)
radio radio (n.n.)
radio engineering radiotekhnika (n.f.)
radio, installation of radiofikatsiya (n.f.)
radio operator radist (n.m.)
radioactivity radioaktivnost' (n.f.)
radioelectronics radioélektronika (n.f.)
radiology radiologiya (n.f.)
radioscopy prosvechivanie (n.n.)
radiotherapy radioterapiya (n.f.)
radish rediska (n.f.)
radish, black red'ka (n.f.)
radium radii (n.m.)
radius radius (n.m.)
raft plot (n.m.)
rafter stropilo (n.n.)
rag loskut (n.m.)
  tryapka (n.f.)
ragamuffin oborvanets (n.m.)
rage beshenstvo (n.n.)
  bushevat' (v.impf.)
  razbushevat'sya (v.pf.)

ragged oborvannyi (adj.)
rags lokhmot'ya (n.pl.)
  otrep'ya (n.pl.)
  rubishche (n.n.)
raid nabeg (n.m.)
  nalet (n.m.)
  oblava (n.f.)
  reid (n.m.)
raider naletchik (n.m.)
rail rel's (n.m.)
railroad zheleznodorozhnyi (adj.)
railroad station vokzal (n.m.)
railway car vagon (n.m.)
rain dozhd' (n.m.)
  dozhdevoi (adj.)
rainbow raduga (n.f.)
raincoat plashch (n.m.)
rainy dozhdlivyi (adj.)
raise povyshat' (v.impf.)
  povysit' (v.pf.)
  rastit' (v.impf.)
  vodruzhat' (v.impf.)
  vozvysit' (v.pf.)
  vyrastit' (v.pf.)
  vzvesti (v.pf.)
  vzvodit' (v.impf.)
  zanosit' (v.impf.)
raise a little pripodnyat' (v.pf.)
raising snyatie (n.n.)
raisins izyum (n.m.)
rake grabli (n.pl.)
  gresti (v.impf.)
  razgrebat' (v.impf.)
rake up sgrebat' (v.impf.)
  zagrebat' (v.impf.)
rally slet (n.m.)
  splachivat'(sya) (v.impf.)
  splotit'(sya) (v.pf.)
rallying splochenie (n.n.)
ram baran (n.m.)
  taranit' (v.impf.)
  trambovat' (v.impf.)
  utrambovat' (v.pf.)
rancid progorklyi (adj.)
rancor, full of zlopamyatnyi (adj.)

random, at   naobum (adv.)
    naugad (adv.)
range   diapazon (n.m.)
range, firing   poligon (n.m.)
rank   chin (n.m.)
    sherenga (n.f.)
    zvanie (n.n.)
ransom   vykup (n.m.)
rape   iznasilovat' (v.pf.)
rapid gallop   kar'er (n.m.)
rapid-fire   skorostrel'nyi (adj.)
rapprochement   sblizhenie (n.n.)
rare   maloupotrebitel'nyi (adj.)
    redkii (adj.)
rascal   merzavets (n.m.)
    prokhodimets (n.m.)
rash   syp' (n.f.)
rashness   oprometchivost' (n.f.)
raspberry   malina (n.f.)
rat   krysa (n.f.)
rate   otnoshenie (n.n.)
    stavka (n.f.)
    temp (n.m.)
rather   dovol'no (adv.)
ratification   ratifikatsiya (n.f.)
ratio   otnoshenie (n.n.)
ration   paek (n.m.)
rational   ratsional'nyi (adj.)
rationalization   ratsionalizatsiya (n.f.)
rationing   normirovanie (n.n.)
rattle   drebezzhat' (v.impf.)
    gromykhat' (v.impf.)
    pogremushka (n.f.)
    treskotnya (n.f.)
rave   besnovat'sya (v.impf.)
raven   voron (n.m.)
ravine   ovrag (n.m.)
raw   neobrabotannyi (adj.)
    syroi (adj.)
raw material   syr'e (n.n.)
rawboned   kostlyavyi (adj.)
ray   luch (n.m.)
rayon   viskoza (n.f.)
rays, beta   beta luchi (n.pl)
razor   britva (n.f.)
reach   dobirat'sya (v.impf.)
    dobrat'sya (v.pf.)
    doekhat' (v.pf.)

    doezzhat' (v.pf.)
    doiti (v.pf.)
    dokhodit' (v.impf.)
    donosit'sya (v.impf.)
    dostat' (v.pf.)
    dostich' (v.pf.)
reach agreement   dogovarivat'sya (v.impf.)
    dogovorit'sya (v.pf.)
reach one's ears   donestis' (v.pf.)
reaches, the lower   nizov'e (n.n.)
reaches, upper   verkhov'e (n.n.)
react   reagirovat' (v.impf.)
reactance   reaktivnost' (n.f.)
reaction   reaktsiya (n.f.)
reactionary   reaktsioner (n.m.)
reactivation   reaktivatsiya (n.f.)
reactivity   reaktivnost' (n.f.)
reactor   reaktor (n.m.)
read   chitat' (v.impf.)
    perechest' (v.pf.)
    perechitat' (v.pf.)
    perechityvat' (v.impf.)
    pochitat' (v.pf.)
    prochest' (v.pf.)
    prochitat' (v.pf.)
read attentively   vchitat'sya (v.pf.)
reader   chitatel' (n.m.)
    khrestomatiya (n.f.)
readiness   gotovnost' (n.f.)
reading   chitka (n.f.)
    chtenie (n.n.)
reading and writing   gramota (n.f.)
reading room   chital'nya (n.f.)
read-out   schityvanie (n.n.)
ready   gotovyi (adj.)
    nagotove (adv.)
real   sushchii (adj.)
real estate   nedvizhimost' (n.f.)
realism   realizm (n.m.)
realistic   realisticheskii (adj.)
reality   real'nost' (n.f.)
realization   realizatsiya (n.f.)
realize   osoznat' (v.pf.)
    realizovat' (v.pf.)
really   pravo (adv.)
    razve (part.)
    uzh (adv.)
ream   stopa (n.f.)

reap pozhat' (v.pf.)
    pozhinat' (v.impf.)
    szhat' (v.pf.)
    zhat' (v.impf.)
reaper zhneika (n.f.)
    zhnets (n.m.)
rear tyl (n.m.)
    vykormit' (v.pf.)
rear-guard ar'ergard (n.m.)
rearm perevooruzhat' (v.impf.)
rearrange perestavit' (v.pf.)
reason rassudok (n.m.)
    rassuzhdat' (v.impf.)
    razum (n.m.)
reason, bring to obrazumit' (v.pf.)
reason, not without nedarom (adv.)
reasonable blagorazumnyi (adj.)
    razumnyi (adj.)
    rezonnyi (adj.)
reassure obnadezhit' (v.pf.)
rebel povstanets (n.m.)
rebellion myatezh (n.m.)
rebuff otpor (n.m.)
rebuild perestroit' (v.pf.)
rebuilding perestroika (n.f.)
recalculation pereraschet (n.m.)
recede skhlynut' (v.pf.)
receipt chek (n.m.)
    kvitantsiya (n.f.)
    raspiska (n.f.)
receipts prikhod (n.m.)
receive poluchat' (v.impf.)
    poluchit' (v.pf.)
    prinimat' (v.impf.)
receiver priemnik (n.m.)
    trubka (n.f.)
recent nedavnii (adj.)
receptacle rozetka (n.f.)
reception priem (n.m.)
    priemnyi (adj.)
reception room priemnaya (n.f.)
receptive vospriimchivyi (adj.)
receptor retseptor (n.m.)
reciprocity vzaimnost' (n.f.)
recite deklamirovat' (v.impf.)
reciter chtets (n.m.)
reckless bezrassudnyi (adj.)
recoil otpryanut' (v.pf.)

    otshatnut'sya (v.pf.)
recollect vspominat'(sya) (v.impf.)
    vspomnit' (v.pf.)
recollection vospominanie (n.n.)
recombination rekombinatsiya (n.f.)
recommend rekomendovat' (v.impf.&pf.)
reconcile mirit' (v.impf.)
    pomirit' (v.pf.)
reconciliation primirenie (n.n.)
reconnaissance rekognostsirovka (n.f.)
reconsider peresmatrivat' (v.impf.)
    peresmotret' (v.pf.)
reconstruct rekonstruirovat' (v.impf.&pf.)
reconstruction rekonstruktsiya (n.f.)
record plastinka (n.f.)
    rekord (n.m.)
record keeper uchetchik (n.m.)
record of service stazh (n.m.)
record, to enter in the zaprotokolirovat'
    (v.pf.)
recorder, automatic samopisets (n.m.)
recording gramzapis' (n.f.)
    zapis' (n.f.)
recording, sound zvukozapis' (n.f.)
recover opravlyat'sya (v.impf.)
    vyzdoravlivat' (v.impf.)
recover one's breath otdyshat'sya (v.pf.)
recovery izlechenie (n.n.)
    vyzdorovlenie (n.n.)
recruit novobranets (n.m.)
    verbovat' (v.impf.)
    zaverbovat' (v.pf.)
rectal pryamokishechnyi (adj.)
rectangular pryamougol'nyi (adj.)
rectifier vypryamitel' (n.m.)
red krasnyi (adj.)
    ryzhii (adj.)
Red Army man krasnoarmeets (n.m.)
red bilberry brusnika (n.f.)
red bunting kumach (n.m.)
Red Guard krasnogvardeets (n.m.)
Red Navy man krasnoflotets (n.m.)
red-cheeked krasnoshchekii (adj.)
redden alet' (v.impf.)
redeem iskupat' (v.impf.)
    vykupat' (v.impf.)
redemption iskuplenie (n.n.)
red-hot dokrasna (adv.)

redistribution pereraspredelenie (n.n.)
reduce sbavit' (v.pf.)
   sokrashchat'(sya) (v.impf.)
   sokratit' (v.pf.)
   svesti (v.pf.)
reduce, take svodit' (v.impf.)
reduce the price udeshevit' (v.pf.)
reduction oslablenie (n.n.)
reduction gear reduktor (n.m.)
reed kamysh (n.m.)
   trostnik (n.m.)
reeducation perevospitanie (n.n.)
reef rif (n.m.)
reel smatyvat' (v.impf.)
   smotat' (v.pf.)
reelect pereizbirat' (v.pf.)
reequipment pereoborudovanie (n.n.)
reexamination pereékzamenovka (n.f.)
   pereosvidetel'stvovanie (n.n.)
refer soslat'sya (v.pf.)
reference otzyv (n.m.)
   ssylka (n.f.)
reference book spravochnik (n.m.)
referred, to be ssylat'sya (v.impf.)
refine ochishchat'(sya) (v.impf.)
refined izoshchrennyi (adj.)
   izyskannyi (adj.)
refinement utonchennost' (n.f.)
refining ochistka (n.f.)
reflect otrazhat' (v.impf.)
   otrazit' (v.pf.)
reflection otblesk (n.m.)
   otobrazhenie (n.n.)
   razmyshlenie (n.n.)
reflector otrazhatel' (n.m.)
   reflektor (n.m.)
reflex refleks (n.m.)
   reflektornyi (adj.)
re-form pereformirovat' (v.pf.)
reform perestraivat'(sya) (v.impf.)
   reforma (n.f.)
refraction prelomlenie (n.n.)
refractor refractor (n.m.)
refractory ogneupor (n.m.)
   tugoplavkii (adj.)
refrain pripev (n.m.)
   uderzhivat'(sya) (v.impf.)
refresh osvezhat' (v.impf.)

refreshments ugoshchenie (n.n.)
refrigerator kholodil'nik (n.m.)
refuge pribezhishche (n.n.)
   ubezhishche (n.n.)
refugee bezhenets (n.m.)
refusal otkaz (n.m.)
refuse otbrosy (n.pl.)
refuse, repeatedly otnekivat'sya (v.impf.)
refute oprovergat' (v.impf.)
regain consciousness ochnut'sya (v.pf.)
regale lakomit'sya (v.impf.)
regard vmenyat' (v.impf.)
regardless nevziraya (adv.)
regards privet (n.m.)
regeneration regeneratsiya (n.f.)
regime rezhim (n.m.)
regiment polk (n.m.)
regimental polkovoi (adj.)
region oblast' (n.f.)
regional oblastnoi (adj.)
regional committee obkom (n.m.)
register oformit' (v.pf.)
   registr (n.m.)
   vedomost' (n.f.)
   zaregistrirovat' (v.pf.)
registration propiska (n.f.)
   registratsiya (n.f.)
   uchetnyi (adj.)
registry office zags (n.m.)
regret sozhalet' (v.impf.)
regroup peregruppirovat' (v.pf.)
regular kadrovyi (adj.)
   regulyarnyi (adj.)
   shtatnyi (adj.)
regulate regulirovat' (v.impf.)
   sorazmerit' (v.pf.)
   sorazmeryat' (v.impf.)
   uregulirovat' (v.pf.)
regulations reglament (n.m.)
regulations, land-use zemleustroistvo (n.n.)
rehabilitate reabilitirovat' (v.impf.&pf.)
rehearsal repetitsiya (n.f.)
rehearse repetirovat' (v.impf.)
reign tsarit' (v.impf.)
   votsarit'sya (v.impf.)
rein povod (n.m.)
reincarnated, to be perevoplotit'sya (v.pf.)
reinforced concrete zhelezobeton (n.m.)

reinforcement popolnenie (n.n.)
reins vozhzhi (n.pl.)
reject otvergat' (v.impf.)
    zabrakovat' (v.pf.)
rejection ottorzhenie (n.n.)
rejuvenation omolozhenie (n.n.)
relapse retsidiv (n.m.)
related rodstvennyi (adj.)
related, to become porodnit'sya (v.pf.)
relation rodstvennik (n.m.)
    vzaimootnoshenie (n.n.)
relations snosheniya (n.pl.)
relationship rodstvo (n.n.)
relative otnositel'nyi (adj.)
relax oslabit' (v.pf.)
relaxation razryadka (n.f.)
relay rele (n.n.)
relay race éstafeta (n.f.)
release osvobozhdat' (v.impf.)
    otpustit' (v.pf.)
reliability nadezhnost' (n.f.)
    solidnost' (n.f.)
reliable blagonadezhnyi (adj.)
    dostovernyi (adj.)
    obstoyatel'nyi (adj.)
relief rel'ef (n.m.)
relieve oblegchat' (v.impf.)
religion religiya (n.f.)
    veroispovedanie (n.n.)
religious religioznyi (adj.)
    veruyushchii (adj.)
reload perezaryadit' (v.pf.)
reluctance neokhota (n.f.)
remain ostat'sya (v.pf.)
    ostavat'sya (v.impf.)
    vysidet' (v.pf.)
remain intact utselet' (v.pf.)
remain seated usidet' (v.pf.)
remainder ostatok (n.m.)
remains ostanki (n.pl.)
remark replika (n.f.)
    zamechanie (n.n.)
    zametit' (v.pf.)
remarkable dostoprimechatel'nyi (adj.)
    zamechatel'nyi (adj.)
remarks, to make witty ostrit' (v.impf.)
remedy sredstvo (n.n.)
remember pomnit' (v.impf.)

pripominat' (v.impf.)
zapominat'(sya) (v.impf.)
zapomnit' (v.pf.)
remember suddenly spokhvatit'sya (v.pf.)
remind napomnit' (v.pf.)
reminder napominanie (n.n.)
remold perekovat' (v.pf.)
remorse raskayanie (n.n.)
    ugryzenie (n.n.)
remoteness davnost' (n.f.)
removal otdalenie (n.n.)
    snyatie (n.n.)
    udalenie (n.n.)
remove otdalit' (v.pf.)
    smeshchat' (v.impf.)
    smestit' (v.pf.)
    svezti (v.pf.)
    svozit' (v.impf.)
    ubirat' (v.impf.)
    ubrat' (v.pf.)
    udalyat'(sya) (v.impf.)
    ustranit' (v.pf)
renal pochechnyi (adv.)
rename pereimenovat' (v.pf.)
render okazat' (v.pf.)
    vozdavat' (v.impf.)
render habitable obzhit' (v.pf.)
render harmless obezvredit' (v.pf.)
renegade otshchepenets (n.m.)
    renegat (n.m.)
renew obnovit' (v.pf.)
    vozobnovit' (v.pf.)
renewed obnovlennyi (adj.)
renounce otrekat'sya (v.impf.)
    otreshat'sya (v.impf.)
renovate podnovit' (v.pf.)
rent nanyat' (v.pf.)
    prokat (n.m.)
    prorekha (n.f.)
    renta (n.f.)
renunciation otrechenie (n.n.)
reorganization pereustroistvo (n.n.)
    reorganizatsiya (n.f.)
repair chinit' (v.impf.)
    naladit' (v.pf.)
    pochinit' (v.pf.)
    pochinka (n.f.)
    popravit' (v.pf.)

remont (n.m.)

remontnyi (adj.)

reparation reparatsiya (n.f.)

repartition peredel (n.m.)

repatriation repatriatsiya (n.f.)

repayment otplata (n.f.)

repeal otmena (n.f.)

repeat tverdit' (v.impf.)

repeated povtornyi (adj.)

repeatedly neodnokratno (adv.)

repeatedly refuse otnekivat'sya (v.impf.)

repeller otrazhatel' (n.m.)

repent kayat'sya (v.impf.)

raskaivat'sya (v.impf.)

repertoire repertuar (n.m.)

repetition povtorenie (n.n.)

replaceable zamenimyi (adj.)

replenish popolnit' (v.pf.)

report doklad (n.m.)

donesenie (n.n.)

otchitat'sya (v.pf.)

otchityvat'sya (v.impf.)

raport (n.m.)

report, shorthand stenogramma (n.f.)

report, to make a dolozhit' (v.pf.)

reporter reporter (n.m.)

reprehensible predosuditel'nyi (adj.)

represent izobrazhat' (v.impf.)

representation predstavitel'stvo (n.n.)

representative predstavitel' (n.m.)

predstavitel'nyi (adj.)

upolnomochennyi (n.m.)

representative, trade torgpred (n.m.)

repressed zataennyi (adj.)

repression repressiya (n.f.)

reprimand notatsiya (n.f.)

otchitat' (v.pf.)

otchityvat' (v.impf.)

vygovarivat' (v.impf.)

vygovor (n.m.)

reprint perepechatat' (v.pf.)

reproach penyat' (v.impf.)

poprekat' (v.impf.)

popreknut' (v.pf.)

poritsanie (n.n.)

ukor (n.m.)

ukoryat' (v.impf.)

uprek (n.m.)

uprekat' (v.impf.)

reproachful ukoriznennyi (adj.)

reproduction razmnozhenie (n.n.)

reproduktsiya (n.f.)

vosproizvedenie (n.n.)

reproof otpoved' (n.f.)

reprove zhurit' (v.impf.)

reptile gad (n.m.)

reptiles presmykayushchiesya (n.pl.)

republic respublika (n.f.)

republish pereizdavat' (v.impf.)

repulse otbit' (v.pf.)

otbivat' (v.impf.)

otrazhat' (v.impf.)

otrazit' (v.pf.)

repulsion ottalkivanie (n.n.)

repulsive, to become oprotivet' (v.pf.)

reputation reputatsiya (n.f.)

reputed, to be proslyt' (v.pf.)

request pros'ba (n.f.)

zatrebovat' (v.pf.)

required, to be nadlezhat' (v.impf.)

requirements potrebnost' (n.f.)

requisition rekvizirovat' (v.impf.&pf.)

rekvizitsiya (n.f.)

reregistration pereregistratsiya (n.f.)

rescue spasti (v.pf.)

rescuer spasitel' (n.m.)

rescuing spasenie (n.n.)

research izyskanie (n.n.)

nauchno-issledovatel'skii (adj.)

resection rezektsiya (n.f.)

resell pereprodat' (v.pf.)

resemble pokhodit' (v.impf.)

reservation nedomolvka (n.f.)

reserve bronirovat' (v.impf.)

rezerv (n.m.)

vygovorit' (v.impf.)

zabronirovat' (v.pf.)

reserved place bronya (n.f.)

reserved seat ticket platskarta (n.f.)

reserved, to become zamknut'sya (v.pf.)

reservist voennoobyazannyi (n.m.)

reservoir rezervuar (n.m.)

vodoem (n.m.)

vodokhranilishche (n.n.)

reshape perekraivat' (v.impf.)

perekroit' (v.pf.)

reshuffle peretasovat' (v.pf.)
residence rezidentsiya (n.f.)
residence, place of mestozhitel'stvo (n.n.)
resident, old starozhil (n.m.)
residual ostatochnyi (adj.)
resin smola (n.f.)
resist protivostoyat' (v.impf.)
 uperet'sya (v.pf.)
resistance soprotivlenie (n.n.)
resistance, heat zharostoikost' (n.f.)
resistant, frost morozoustoichivyi (adj.)
resistor soprotivlenie (n.n.)
resolution postanovlenie (n.n.)
 reshimost' (n.f.)
 rezolyutsiya (n.f.)
resonance rezonans (n.m.)
resonant zvuchnyi (adj.)
resort, health zdravnitsa (n.f.)
resort to pribegat' (v.impf.)
resourcefulness smetlivost' (n.f.)
resources resursy (n.pl.)
respect pochitanie (n.n.)
 pochtenie (n.n.)
respected uvazhaemyi (adj.)
respected, greatly mnogouvazhaemyi (adj.)
respectful pochtitel'nyi (adj.)
respite peredyshka (n.f.)
respond otkliknut'sya (v.pf.)
response otklik (n.m.)
 priemistost' (n.f.)
responsibility otvetstvennost' (n.f.)
rest otdokhnut' (v.pf.)
 otdykh (n.m.)
 pochit' (v.pf.)
 pokoi (n.m.)
 support (n.m.)
rest, the ostal'noe (n.n.)
rest, to take a peredokhnut' (v.pf.)
restaurant restoran (n.m.)
restless bespokoinyi (adj.)
 nespokoinyi (adj.)
 neugomonnyi (adj.)
restoration restavratsiya (n.f.)
restore vosstanavlivat' (v.impf.)
 vosstanovit' (v.pf.)
restrain sderzhat' (v.pf.)
restrain oneself uterpet' (v.pf.)
restraint sderzhannost' (n.f.)

uderzh (n.m.)
restriction ogranichenie (n.n.)
result privesti (v.pf.)
 privodit' (v.impf.)
 rezul'tat (n.m.)
result from proistekat' (v.impf.)
resultant force ravnodeistvuyushchaya (n.f.)
resurrected, to be voskresat' (v.impf.)
resuscitate ozhivit' (v.pf.)
 voskresit' (v.pf.)
retail roznitsa (n.f.)
retaliate vymeshchat' (v.impf.)
 vymestit' (v.pf.)
retardation zaderzhka (n.f.)
retelling pereskaz (n.m.)
reticence skrytnost' (n.f.)
 zamknutost' (n.f.)
retina setchatka (n.f.)
retire udalyat'(sya) (v.impf.)
retort kolba (n.f.)
retouch retushirovat' (v.impf.&pf.)
retrain perepodgotovit' (v.pf.)
retraining perekvalifikatsiya (n.f.)
 pereobuchenie (n.n.)
retreat otboi (n.m.)
 otstuplenie (n.n.)
retribution kara (n.f.)
 vozmezdie (n.n.)
return otdacha (n.f.)
 vernut' (v.pf.)
 vozvrashchat'(sya) (v.impf.)
 vozvrat (n.m.)
return fire otstrelivat'sya (v.impf.)
reunion vossoedinenie (n.n.)
reveal vskryvat' (v.impf.)
 vyyavit' (v.pf.)
revelry razgul (n.m.)
revenge mest' (n.f.)
 otmestka (n.f.)
 revansh (n.m.)
revenge oneself on otomstit' (v.pf.)
 otygrat'sya (v.pf.)
revenge, to take mstit' (v.impf.)
reverberation reverberatsiya (n.f.)
reverently svyato (adv.)
reverse oborotnyi (adj.)
 obratnyi (adj.)
reversibility obratimost' (n.f.)

reversing gear revers (n.m.)
review retsenziya (n.f.)
reviewer obozrevatel' (n.m.)
revile izrugat' (v.pf.)
revision peresmotr (n.m.)
   revizionnyi (adj.)
revisionism revizionizm (n.m.)
revive ozhit' (v.pf.)
   ozhivat' (v.impf.)
   vozrodit' (v.pf.)
revolt vzbuntovat'sya (v.pf.)
revolution oborot (n.m.)
   perevorot (n.m.)
   revolyutsiya (n.f.)
revolutionary revolyutsioner (n.m.)
revolve vrashchat' (v.impf.)
revolver revol'ver (n.m.)
reward nagrada (n.f.)
   voznagradit' (v.pf.)
rheostat reostat (n.m.)
Rhesus rezus (n.m.)
rheumatic pain lomota (n.f.)
rheumatism revmatizm (n.m.)
rhinoceros nosorog (n.m.)
rhizome kornevishche (n.n.)
rhombus romb (n.m.)
rhyme rifma (n.f.)
rhythm ritm (n.m.)
rib rebro (n.n.)
ribbon lenta (n.f.)
rice ris (n.m.)
   risovyi (adj.)
rich bogatyi (adj.)
rich in content soderzhatel'nyi (adj.)
rich, to get razbogatet' (v.pf.)
rich, to grow bogatet' (v.impf.)
riches bogatstvo (n.n.)
rickshaw riksha (n.m.)
ricochet rikoshet (n.m.)
rid of, to get otdelat'sya (v.pf.)
   otdelyvat'sya (v.impf.)
rid, to get sbyt' (v.pf.)
   sbyvat' (v.impf.)
riddle zagadka (n.f.)
ride, to give a podvezti (v.pf.)
ride, to go for a prokatit'sya (v.pf.)
ride, to take for a katat' (v.impf.)
rider sedok (n.m.)

   vsadnik (n.m.)
rider, horse naezdnik (n.m.)
ridge gryada (n.f.)
ridge, mountain kryazh (n.m.)
ridicule osmeivat' (v.impf.)
   osmeyat' (v.pf.)
   vysmeivat' (v.impf.)
riding katanie (n.n.)
riffraff sbrod (n.m.)
rifle strelkovyi (adj.)
   vintovka (n.f.)
rift rasselina (n.f.)
rig osnastit' (v.pf.)
rigging osnastka (n.f.)
   snast' (n.f.)
   takelazh (n.m.)
right pravo (n.n.)
   pravyi (adj.)
right, to have a vprave (pred.)
right, to the napravo (adv.)
   sprava (adv.)
   vpravo (adv.)
right up to vplot' do (adv.)
right wing pravyi (adj.)
rightness pravota (n.f.)
rights, deprived of bespravnyi (adj.)
rights, enjoying full polnopravnyi (adj.)
rights, equality of ravnopravie (n.n.)
rigidity prochnost' (n.f.)
rim obod (n.m.)
   oprava (n.f.)
ring kol'tso (n.n.)
   persten' (n.m.)
   pozvonit' (v.pf.)
   ring (n.m.)
   zazvonit' (v.pf.)
   zvenet' (v.impf.)
ringing zvon (n.m.)
   zvonkii (adj.)
ringleader glavar' (n.m.)
ringlet kolechko (n.n.)
rink, skating katok (n.m.)
rinse propoloskat' (v.pf.)
   spolaskivat' (v.impf.)
   spolosnut' (v.pf.)
rinse out vypoloskat' (v.pf.)
rinsing poloskanie (n.n.)
riot bunt (n.m.)

rip off otparyvat'(sya) (v.impf.)
    otporot' (v.pf.)
    sporot' (v.pf.)
rip up rasparyvat' (v.impf.)
    rasporot' (v.pf.)
ripe spelyi (adj.)
ripen dozrevat' (v.impf.)
    pospet' (v.pf.)
    pospevat' (v.impf.)
    sozrevat' (v.impf.)
    spet' (v.impf.)
    urodit'sya (v.pf.)
    zret' (v.impf.)
ripening sozrevanie (n.n.)
ripple ryab' (n.f.)
    ryabit' (v.impf.)
    zhurchat' (v.impf.)
    zyb' (n.f.)
rise podymat'sya (v.impf.)
    voskhod (n.m.)
    vosstat' (v.pf.)
    vosstavat' (v.impf.)
    vskhodit' (v.impf.)
    vysit'sya (v.impf.)
rise, half pripodnimat'sya (v.impf.)
    privstat' (v.pf.)
rise in price dorozhat' (v.impf.)
    vzdorozhat' (v.pf.)
rising vosstanie (n.n.)
    vstavanie (n.n.)
risk risk (n.m.)
rival sopernik (n.m.)
river rechka (n.f.)
    reka (n.f.)
riverbed ruslo (n.n.)
rivet klepat' (v.impf.)
    zaklepka (n.f.)
road doroga (n.f.)
    dorozhnyi (adj.)
    reid (n.m.)
roads, icy condition of gololeditsa (n.f.)
roads, lack of bezdorozh'e (n.n.)
roads, season of bad rasputitsa (n.f.)
roadway, paved mostovaya (n.f.)
roam bluzhdat' (v.impf.)
    iskolesit' (v.pf.)
roar rev (n.m.)
    revet' (v.impf.)

    zarychat' (v.pf.)
roar of laughter khokhot (n.m.)
roar with laughter gogotat' (v.impf.)
roast podzharivat'(sya) (v.impf.)
roast meat zharkoe (n.n.)
roasting obzhig (n.m.)
roasting pan protiven' (n.m.)
rob grabit' (v.impf.)
    obkradyvat' (v.impf.)
    obokrast' (v.pf.)
    ograbit' (v.pf.)
robbery grabezh (n.m.)
    razboi (n.m.)
robe mantiya (n.f.)
rock kachat' (v.impf.)
    kachnut' (v.pf.)
    pokachat' (v.pf.)
    pokachivat' (v.impf.)
    poroda (n.f.)
    skala (n.f.)
    utes (n.m.)
rock to sleep ukachat' (v.pf.)
rocket raketa (n.f.)
rocking chair kachalka (n.f.)
rod, fishing udilishche (n.n.)
    udochka (n.f.)
rodent gryzun (n.m.)
roentgen rentgen (n.m.)
roentgenology rentgenologiya (n.f.)
role rol' (n.f.)
roll bulka (n.f.)
    katit'sya (v.impf.)
    obvalyat' (v.pf.)
    podkatit' (v.pf.)
    raskatat' (v.pf.)
    saika (n.f.)
    ukatat' (v.pf.)
    valyat' (v.impf.)
roll away otkatit' (v.pf.)
roll call pereklichka (n.f.)
    poverka (n.f.)
roll down skatit' (v.pf.)
    skatyvat' (v.impf.)
roll in vkatit' (v.pf.)
roll under zakatit' (v.pf.)
    zakatyvat' (v.impf.)
roll up skatat' (v.pf.)
    skatyvat' (v.impf.)

svernut' (v.pf.)
svorachivat' (v.impf.)
zakatat' (v.pf.)
zakatyvat' (v.impf.)
zasuchivat' (v.impf.)
rolled metal prokat (n.m.)
roller rolik (n.m.)
val (n.m.)
rolling pin skalka (n.f.)
Roman rimskii (adj.)
romance romantika (n.f.)
romanticism romantizm (n.m.)
romp vozit'sya (v.impf.)
roof krovlya (n.f.)
krysha (n.f.)
roofing (iron) krovel'nyi (adj.)
rook grach (n.m.)
lad'ya (n.f.)
room komnata (n.f.)
pokoi (n.m.)
room, boiler kotel'naya (n.f.)
room, punishment kartser (n.m.)
room, reception priemnaya (n.f.)
room, to find umestit'sya (v.pf.)
roommate sozhitel' (n.m.)
roost nasest (n.m.)
root koren' (n.m.)
kornevoi (adj.)
root out korchevat' (v.impf.)
vykorchevat' (v.pf.)
root plant korneplod (n.m.)
root, to take ukorenit'sya (v.pf.)
rooted vkorenivshiisya (adj.)
rooted in, to be korenit'sya (v.impf.)
rootlet koreshok (n.m.)
rope kanat (n.m.)
tros (n.m.)
verevka (n.f.)
rose roza (n.f.)
rostrum tribuna (n.f.)
rot gnit' (v.impf.)
sgnit' (v.pf.)
tukhnut' (v.impf.)
rot, to let sgnoit' (v.pf.)
rotation, crop sevooborot (n.m.)
rotor rotor (n.m.)
rotten gniloi (adj.)
prelyi (adj.)

tukhlyi (adj.)
rotten through, to be prognivat' (v.impf.)
rotting gnienie (n.n.)
zagnivanie (n.n.)
rouge rumyana (n.pl.)
rough koryavyi (adj.)
sherokhovatyi (adj.)
shershavyi (adj.)
rough copy chernovik (n.m.)
roughly nacherno (adv.)
round kruglyi (adj.)
krugom (adv.)
obkhod (n.m.)
tur (n.m.)
vokrug (adv.)
round dance khorovod (n.m.)
round loaf karavai (n.m.)
round off okruglit' (v.pf.)
roundabout okol'nyi (adj.)
round-faced kruglolitsyi (adj.)
round-the-world krugosvetnyi (adj.)
rout razgrom (n.m.)
route marshrut (n.m.)
trassa (n.f.)
routine rutina (n.f.)
rover, moon lunokhod (n.m.)
row gresti (v.impf.)
ryad (n.m.)
verenitsa (n.f.)
row, scandal skandal (n.m.)
rowdy buyan (n.m.)
rowing greblya (n.f.)
rowlock uklyuchina (n.f.)
rub nateret' (v.pf.)
natirat' (v. impf.)
potirat' (v.impf.)
rastirat'(sya) (v.impf.)
teret' (v.impf.)
rub in vteret' (v.pf.)
rub oneself nateret'sya (v.pf.)
rub out zateret' (v.pf.)
zatirat' (v.impf.)
rubber kauchuk (n.m.)
rezina (n.f.)
rubbish khlam (n.m.)
ruble rubl' (n.m.)
ruby rubin (n.m.)
rudder rul' (n.m.)

rude nevezhlivyi (adj.)
rude, to be grubit' (v.impf.)
rudely, to speak nagrubit' (v.pf.)
rudeness grubost' (n.f.)
rudiments nachatki (n.pl.)
ruffian khuligan (n.m.)
ruffle up nakhokhlit'sya (v.pf.)
rug pled (n.m.)
ruin dokonat' (v.pf.)
    gibel' (n.f.)
    pogubit' (v.pf.)
    razorenie (n.n.)
    razoryat' (v.impf.)
    razrukha (n.f.)
    zagubit' (v.pf.)
ruin, to go to razrushat'sya (v.impf.)
ruins razvaliny (n.pl.)
rule pravilo (n.n.)
    razgrafit' (v.pf.)
    vlast' (n.f.)
ruler lineika (n.f.)
ruling pravyashchii (adj.)
rum rom (n.m.)
Rumanian rumyn (n.m.)
rumble gul (n.m.)
rummage obsharivat' (v.impf.)
rumor molva (n.f.)
rumors, false krivotolki (n.pl.)
run begat' (v.impf.)
    bezhat' (v.impf.)
    pobezhat' (n.pf.)
    probeg (n.m.)
    rastech'sya (v.pf.)
    rastekat'sya (v.impf.)
    razbegat'sya (v.impf.)
    razbezhat'sya (v.pf.)
    sbegat' (v.pf.)
run across perebegat' (v.impf.)
run after pognat'sya (v.pf.)
run against nabegat' (v.impf.)
    nabezhat' (v.pf.)
run away ubegat' (v.impf.)
    ubezhat' (v.pf.)
    udirat' (v.pf.)
    udrat' (v.pf.)
run down sbezhat' (v.pf.)
run fast primchat'sya (v.pf.)
run high razygryvat'sya (v.impf.)

run in vbegat' (v.impf.)
run into narvat'sya (v.pf.)
    naryvat'sya (v.impf.)
    naskakivat' (v.impf.)
    naskochit' (v.pf.)
    natknut'sya (v.pf.)
    natykat'sya (v.impf.)
run off otbegat' (v.impf.)
run out vybegat' (v.impf.)
    vylivat'sya (v.impf.)
run through prodergivat' (v.impf.)
    prodernut' (v.pf.)
run up podbegat' (v.impf.)
    vzbegat' (v.impf.)
run up to dobegat' (v.impf.)
runner begun (n.m.)
runners poloz'ya (n.pl.)
running beg (n.m.)
    begom (adv.)
running about, to be tired out with
    nabegat'sya (v.pf.)
running start razbeg (n.m.)
running, to come pribegat' (v.impf.)
    pribezhat' (v.pf.)
    sbegat'sya (v.impf.)
rupture proboi (n.m.)
rural derevenskii (adj.)
    sel'skii (adj.)
rush nestis' (v.impf.)
    prilit' (v.pf.)
    rinut'sya (v.pf.)
    rvanut'sya (v.pf.)
rush along mchat' (v.impf.)
rush back otkhlynut' (v.pf.)
rush by proskochit' (v.pf.)
rush forward vylazka (n.f.)
rush past promchat'sya (v.pf.)
    pronestis' (v.pf.)
    pronosit'sya (v.impf.)
rusk sukhar' (n.m.)
Russian rossiiskii (adj.)
    russkii (adj.)
Russian, in po-russki (adv.)
Russian salad vinegret (n.m.)
Russian woman russkaya (adj.)
rust rzhavchina (n.f.)
    rzhavet' (v.impf.)
rustle shelest (n.m.)

shelestet' (v.impf.)
shorokh (n.m.)
shurshat' (v.impf.)
rusty zarzhavlennyi (adj.)
rusty, to become zarzhavet' (v.pf.)

rut koleya (n.f.)
ruthless besposhchadnyi (adj.)
bezzhalostnyi (adj.)
rye rozh' (n.f.)
rzhanoi (adj.)

S (С, Ш, Щ)

saber sablya (n.f.)
sable sobol' (n.m.)
sabotage diversiya (n.f.)
sabotazh (n.m.)
saboteur diversant (n.m.)
sack meshok (n.m.)
sacred nenarushimyi (adj.)
svyashchennyi (adj.)
sacrifice pozhertvovat' (v.pf.)
zhertva (n.f.)
sad gorestnyi (adj.)
grustnyi (adj.)
sad, to become zagrustit' (v.pf.)
saddle osedlat' (v.pf.)
sedlat' (v.impf.)
sedlo (n.n.)
support (n.m.)
sadness grust' (n.f.)
safe besproigryshnyi (adj.)
bezopasnyi (adj.)
nadezhnyi (adj.)
seif (n.m.)
safety sokhrannost' (n.f.)
tselost' (n.f.)
safety lock predokhranitel' (n.m.)
saffron shafran (n.m.)
sag obvisat' (v.impf.)
sage mudrets (n.m.)
sail otplyvat' (v.impf.)
parus (n.m.)
sail away uplyvat' (v.impf.)
sail up to priplyvat' (v.impf.)
sailing parusnyi (adj.)
sailor matros (n.m.)
moryak (n.m.)
sake of, for the radi (prep.)

salable khodkii (adj.)
salad salat (n.m.)
salad, Russian vinegret (n.m.)
salary zhalovan'e (n.n.)
salary scale oklad (n.m.)
sale prodazha (n.f.)
sbyt (n.m.)
sale, clearance rasprodazha (n.f.)
sale, to have a rasprodavat' (v.impf.)
saline solenyi (adj.)
saliva slyuna (n.f.)
sally, rush forward vylazka (n.f.)
salmon lososina (n.f.)
semga (n.f.)
salmon, Siberian keta (n.f.)
salt posolit' (v.pf.)
sol' (n.f.)
solenyi (adj.)
solit' (v.impf.)
solyanoi (adj.)
zasalivat' (v.impf.)
zasolit' (v.pf.)
salt marshes solonchaki (n.pl.)
saltcellar solonka (n.f.)
salted, lightly malosol'nyi (adj.)
salting solenie (n.n.)
zasol (n.m.)
saltpeter selitra (n.f.)
salute salyut (n.m.)
salvo zalp (n.m.)
same, the samyi (adj.)
samovar samovar (n.m.)
sample obrazchik (n.m.)
sanatorium sanatorii (n.m)
sanction sanktsionirovat' (v.impf. &pf.)
sanktsiya (n.f.)

sand pesochnyi (adj.)
  pesok (n.m.)
sand, grain of peschinka (n.f.)
sandal sandaliya (n.f.)
sandpiper kulik (n.m.)
sandstone peschanik (n.m.)
sandwich buterbrod (n.m.)
sanity vmenyaemost' (n.f.)
sapper saper (n.m.)
sapphire sapfir (n.m.)
sapping podryvnoi (adj.)
sarafan sarafan (n.m.)
sarcasm sarkazm (n.m.)
sarcoma sarkoma (n.f.)
sardine sardina (n.f.)
sash kushak (n.m.)
sateen satin (n.m.)
satellite satellit (n.m.)
satiate nasytit' (v.pf.)
satiety sytost' (n.f.)
satin atlas (n.m.)
satin stitch glad' (n.f.)
satire satira (n.f.)
satirical article fel'eton (n.m.)
satisfaction dovol'stvo (n.n.)
  udovletvorenie (n.n.)
satisfied sytyi (adj.)
satisfied, to be udovol'stvovat'sya (v.impf.)
satisfy udovletvorit' (v.pf.)
  utolit' (v.pf.)
  utolyat' (v.impf.)
saturate nasyshchat' (v.impf.)
  propitat' (v.pf.)
saturated nasyshchennyi (adj.)
saturated, to be propityvat'sya (v.impf.)
Saturday subbota (n.f.)
sauce podlivka (n.f.)
  sous (n.m.)
saucepan kastryulya (n.f.)
saucer blyudechko (n.n.)
  blyudtse (n.n.)
sausage kolbasa (n.f.)
  sardel'ka (n.f.)
savage dikar' (n.m.)
savagery dikost' (n.f.)
save izbavit' (v.pf.)
  kopit' (v.impf.)
  sberech' (v.pf.)

skopit' (v.pf.)
  spasti (v.pf.)
save up priberegat' (v.impf.)
saving sberegatel'nyi (adj.)
  sberezhenie (n.n.)
savings bank sberkassa (n.f.)
saw perepilivat' (v.impf.)
  pila (n.f.)
  podpilivat' (v.impf.)
saw down spilivat' (v.impf.)
saw off otpilivat' (v.impf.)
saw out vypilivat' (v.impf.)
saw up raspilivat' (v.impf.)
sawdust opilki (n.pl.)
sawmill lesopil'nya (n.f.)
saxophone saksofon (n.m.)
say molvit' (v.pf.)
  progovorit' (v.pf.)
  skazat' (v.pf.)
saying pogovorka (n.f.)
scaffold éshafot (n.m.)
  lesa (n.pl.)
scaffolding podmostki (n.pl.)
scald obvarit' (v.pf.)
  oshparit' (v.pf.)
scald oneself obvarivat'(sya) (v.impf.)
scale chasha (n.f.)
  gamma (n.f.)
  masshtab (n.m.)
  shkala (n.f.)
scale, salary oklad (n.m.)
scales cheshuya (n.f.)
  vesy (n.pl.)
scales, to tip the peretyagivat' (v.impf.)
scalpel skal'pel' (n.m.)
scandal skandal (n.m.)
scandalous vozmutitel'nyi (adj.)
scanning razvertka (n.f.)
scanty malochislennyi (adj.)
  mizernyi (adj.)
  skudnyi (adj.)
scar rubets (n.m.)
  shram (n.m.)
scare kosynka (n.f.)
scarecrow chuchelo (n.n.)
  pugalo (n.n.)
scarf sharf (n.m.)
scarlet alyi (adj.)

scarlet fever skarlatina (n.f.)
scatter raskidyvat' (v.impf.)
    razbegat'sya (v.impf.)
    razbezhat'sya (v.pf.)
    razbrasyvat' (v.impf.)
    razbrosat' (v.pf.)
    zakidat' (v.pf.)
    zakidyvat' (v.impf.)
scatterbrain razinya (n.m.&f.)
    rotozei (n.m.)
scattered razbrosannyi (adj.)
scattering rossyp' (n.f.)
scene stsena (n.f.)
scenery dekoratsiya (n.f.)
scenic stsenicheskii (adj.)
scent chut'e (n.n.)
    chuyat' (v.impf.)
    nyukh (n.m.)
scent, to put on nadushit' (v.pf.)
scepter skipetr (n.m.)
schedule raspisanie (n.n.)
schedule, ahead of dosrochno (adv.)
scheme skhema (n.f.)
    zateya (n.f.)
schemes proiski (n.pl.)
schist slanets (n.m.)
schnitzel shnitsel' (n.m.)
scholarship stipendiya (n.f.)
scholasticism skholastika (n.f.)
school shkola (n.f.)
school, boarding internat (n.m.)
    pansion (n.m.)
    shkola-internat (n.m.)
school, nursery yasli (n.pl.)
school, secondary uchilishche (n.n.)
school, technical tekhnikum (n.m.)
schoolboy shkol'nik (n.m.)
schoolmate souchenik (n.m.)
schooner shkhuna (n.f.)
sciatica ishias (n.m.)
science nauka (n.f.)
scientific nauchnyi (adj.)
scissors nozhnitsy (n.pl.)
sclerosis skleroz (n.m.)
scoff zasmeyat' (v.pf.)
scold branit' (v.impf.)
    vyrugat' (v.pf.)
scolding nagonyai (n.m.)

scolding, severe golovomoika (n.f.)
scoop cherpat' (v.impf.)
    kovsh (n.m.)
    sovok (n.m.)
scoop dry vycherpat' (v.pf.)
scoop up zacherpnut' (v.pf.)
scooter motoroller (n.m.)
scope okhvat (n.m.)
    razmakh (n.m.)
scorching palyashchii (adj.)
    raskalennyi (adj.)
scorching heat peklo (n.n.)
score partitura (n.f.)
scoring a hit popadanie (n.n.)
scorpion skorpion (n.m.)
Scot shotlandets (n.m.)
Scots, the shotlandtsy (n.pl.)
scrap klochok (n.m.)
    obryvok (n.m.)
scrape peredryaga (n.f.)
    skoblit' (v.impf.)
    skresti (v.impf.)
scrape out vyskablivat' (v.impf.)
    vyskoblit' (v.pf.)
scraper skrebok (n.m.)
scratch chesat' (v.impf.)
    chesat'sya (v.impf.)
    otsarapat' (v.pf.)
    pochesat'(sya) (v.pf.)
    rastsarapat' (v.pf.)
    tsarapat' (v.impf.)
scratch out vytsarapat' (v.pf.)
scrawl karakuli (n.pl.)
screen ékran (n.m.)
    shirma (n.f.)
    zavesa (n.f.)
screen play stsenarii (n.m.)
screw vint (n.m.)
screw in vvintit' (v.pf.)
screw out vyvintit' (v.pf.)
    vyvorachivat' (v.impf.)
screw up privintit' (v.pf.)
    zavintit' (v.pf.)
screwdriver otvertka (n.f.)
scribbler pisaka (n.f.)
scrofula zolotukha (n.f.)
scrupulous razborchivyi (adj.)
    shchepetil'nyi (adj.)

sculptor skul'ptor (n.m.)
sculpture vayanie (n.n.)
scum nakip' (n.f.)
scurvy tsinga (n.f.)
scythe kosa (n.f.)
sea more (n.n.)
   morskoi (adj.)
seacoast poberezh'e (n.n.)
seagull chaika (n.f.)
seal opechatat' (v.pf.)
   opechatyvat' (v.impf.)
   pechat' (n.f.)
   tyulen' (n.m.)
   zaplombirovat' (v.pf.)
seal, fur kotik (n.m.)
seal up zapechatat' (v.pf.)
   zapechatyvat' (v.impf.)
sealed, hermetically germeticheskii (adj.)
sealing uplotnenie (n.n.)
sealing wax surguch (n.m.)
seam shov (n.m.)
   zaleganie (n.n.)
seamstress beloshveika (n.f.)
   shveya (n.f.)
search iskat' (v.impf.)
   obysk (n.m.)
   obyskivat' (v.impf.)
   poisk (n.m.)
   razyskivat' (v.impf.)
   rozysk (n.m.)
   sharit' (v.impf.)
search for doiskivat'sya (v.impf.)
searchlight prozhektor (n.m.)
seashore vzmor'e (n.n.)
seaside primorskii (adj.)
season sezon (n.m.)
season, fishing putina (n.f.)
season of bad roads rasputitsa (n.f.)
seasoning priprava (n.f.)
seat posadit' (v.pf.)
   rassadit' (v.pf.)
   rassazhivat' (v.impf.)
   siden'e (n.n.)
   usadit' (v.pf.)
   usazhivat' (v.impf.)
seat, to take a usazhivat'sya (v.impf.)
   usest'sya (v.pf.)
seat, to take another peresest' (v.pf.)

seated, to remain usidet' (v.pf.)
seats, front orchestra parter (n.m.)
seats, to take rassest'sya (v.pf.)
seaweed vodorosl' (n.f.)
secluded ukromnyi (adj.)
second sekunda (n.f.)
   vtorichnyi (adj.)
   vtoroi (adj.)
secondary pobochnyi (adj.)
   vtorichnyi (adj.)
   vtorostepennyi (adj.)
secondary school uchilishche (n.n.)
secondhand poderzhannyi (adj.)
secondhand bookseller bukinist (n.m.)
secondly vo-vtorykh (adv.)
secret konspirativnyi (adj.)
   potainoi (adj.)
   sekret (n.m.)
   sekretnyi (adj.)
   zataennyi (adj.)
secretary sekretar' (n.m.)
secretion sekretsiya (n.f.)
   vydelenie (n.n.)
secretly taikom (adv.)
   vtaine (adv.)
secretory sekretornyi (adj.)
sect sekta (n.f.)
section podotdel (n.m.)
   sechenie (n.n.)
   sektsiya (n.f.)
sector sektor (n.m.)
secular svetskii (adj.)
security obespechenie (n.n.)
sedative boleutolyayushchee (n.n.)
sedentary sidyachii (adj.)
sedge osoka (n.f.)
sediment gushcha (n.f.)
   osadok (n.m.)
sedimentation osazhdenie (n.n.)
   sedimentatsiya (n.f.)
seduce obol'shchat' (v.impf.)
   sovrashchat' (v.impf.)
   sovratit' (v.pf.)
seducer obol'stitel' (n.m.)
see nasmotret'sya (v.pf.)
   povidat' (v.pf.)
   uvidet' (v.pf.)
   videt' (v.impf.)

see enough of, to   naglyadet'sya (v.pf.)

seed   kostochka (n.f.)
    semya (n.n.)

seed drill   seyalka (n.f.)

seedling   sazhenets (n.m.)

seedlings   rassada (n.f.)

seeing off   provody (n.pl.)

seem   chudit'sya (v.impf.)
    kazat'sya (v.impf.)
    pochudit'sya (v.pf.)

seeming   mnimyi (adj.)

seems, it   kazhetsya (pred.)
    mereshchit'sya (v.impf.)

seethe   burlit' (v.impf.)

segment   segment (n.m.)

seine   nevod (n.m.)

seismology   seismologiya (n.f.)

seize   nakhvatat' (v.pf.)

seize hold of   vtsepit'sya (v.pf.)

seize upon   dorvat'sya (v.pf.)

seizure   vzyatie (n.n.)
    zakhvat (n.m.)
    zanyatie (n.n.)

selected   izbrannyi (adj.)

selection   otbor (n.m.)
    otborochnyi (adj.)
    podbor (n.m.)
    selektsiya (n.f.)

selenium   selen (n.m.)

self-acting   samodeistvuyushchii (adj.)

self-awareness   samosoznanie (n.n.)

self-confidence   samouverennost' (n.f.)

self-control   samoobladanie (n.n.)
    vyderzhka (n.f.)

self-criticism   samokritika (n.f.)

self-deception   samoobman (n.m.)

self-defense   samooborona (n.f.)
    samozashchita (n.f.)

self-determination   samoopredelenie (n.n.)

self-education   samoobrazovanie (n.n.)

self-government   samoupravlenie (n.n.)

self-humiliation   samounizhenie (n.n.)

self-interest   koryst' (n.f.)

self-interested   korystolyubivyi (adj.)

selfishness   égoizm (n.m.)

selfless   samozabvennyi (adj.)

selflessness   samootverzhennost' (n.f.)

self-portrait   avtoportret (n.m.)

self-preservation   samosokhranenie (n.n.)

self-propelled   samokhodnyi (adj.)

self-recording   samopishushchii (adj.)

self-restrained   vyderzhannyi (adj.)

self-sacrifice   samopozhertvovanie (n.n.)

self-satisfied   samodovol'nyi (adj.)

self-service   samoobsluzhivanie (n.n.)

self-taught person   samouchka (n.m.&f.)

self-willed   samovol'nyi (adj.)
    svoevol'nyi (adj.)

sell   prodat' (v.pf.)
    prodavat' (v.impf.)

sell cheap   prodeshevit' (v.pf.)

semantics   semantika (n.f.)

semen   semya (n.n.)

semicircle   polukrug (n.m.)

semiconductor   poluprovodnik (n.m.)

semidarkness   polumrak (n.m.)
    polut'ma (n.f.)

semiliterate   malogramotnyi (adj.)
    polugramotnyi (adj.)

seminal   semennoi (adj.)

seminar   seminar (n.m.)

seminary   seminariya (n.f.)

semiofficial organ   ofitsioz (n.m.)

semiprecious stone   samotsvet (n.m.)

senate   senat (n.m.)

send   otpravit' (v.pf)
    otpravlyat' (v.impf.)
    pereslat' (v.pf.)
    peresylat' (v.impf.)
    poslat' (v.pf.)
    posylat' (v.impf.)
    prislat' (v.pf.)
    prisylat' (v.impf.)
    razoslat' (v.pf.)
    zasylat' (v.impf.)

send about   rassylat' (v.impf.)

send for a purpose   podoslat' (v.pf.)
    podsylat' (v.impf.)

send off   otoslat' (v.pf.)
    otsylat' (v.impf.)

sender   otpravitel' (n.m.)

sending   peresylka (n.f.)

senile   starcheskii (adj.)

senior lecturer   dotsent (n.m.)

seniority   starshinstvo (n.n.)

sensation   oshchushchenie (n.n.)
         (cont'd)

sensatsiya (n.f.)
sense chuvstvo (n.n.)
rassuditel'nost' (n.f.)
smysl (n.m.)
tolk (n.m.)
sense of smell obonyanie (n.n.)
senseless bessmyslennyi (adj.)
sensible neglupyi (adj.)
zdravyi (adj.)
sensitive chutkii (adj.)
sensitive to cold zyabkii (adj.)
sensitiveness chuvstvitel'nost' (n.f.)
sensor datchik (n.m.)
sensuality chuvstvennost' (n.f.)
sentence predlozhenie (n.n.)
prigovor (n.m.)
prisudit' (v.pf.)
sentimental sentimental'nyi (adj.)
sentry chasovoi (n.m.)
separate obosobit' (v.pf.)
otdel'nyi (adj.)
otdelyat'(sya) (v.impf.)
raz"ekhat'sya (v.pf.)
razdel'nyi (adj.)
razobshchat' (v.impf.)
razvesti (v.pf.)
separatnyi (adj.)
separately porozn' (adv.)
separation obogashchenie (n.n.)
otdelenie (n.n.)
razluka (n.f.)
separator otdelitel' (n.m.)
September sentyabr' (n.m.)
Serbian serb (n.m.)
serenade serenada (n.f.)
serene bezmyatezhnyi (adj.)
serf krepostnoi (adj.)
serfdom krepostnichestvo (n.n.)
sergeant serzhant (n.m.)
sergeant major starshina (n.m.)
serial seriinyi (adj.)
series seriya (n.f.)
series, in posledovatel'no (adv.)
serious neshutochnyi (adj.)
ser'eznyi (adj.)
serious, not neser'eznyi (adj.)
sermon propoved' (n.f.)
serum syvorotka (n.f.)

servant sluga (n.m.)
servants prisluga (n.f.)
serve otsluzhit' (v.pf.)
podavat' (v.impf.)
posluzhit' (v.pf.)
servirovat' (v.impf.)
service obsluzhivanie (n.n.)
posluzhnoi (adj.)
serviz (n.m.)
sluzhba (n.f.)
sluzhebnyi (adj.)
sluzhenie (n.n.)
usluga (n.f.)
service for the dead panikhida (n.f.)
service jacket french (n.m.)
service, record of stazh (n.m.)
service, to do someone a udruzhit' (v.pf.)
usluzhit' (v.pf.)
serviceman voennosluzhashchii (n.m.)
servile rabskii (adj.)
servility nizkopoklonstvo (n.n.)
podobostrastie (n.n.)
rabolepie (n.n.)
servitude kabala (n.f.)
session sessiya (n.f.)
set garnitur (n.m.)
stoika (n.f.)
vpravit' (v.pf.)
zadat' (v.pf.)
set aside otstavit' (v.pf.)
set, complete komplekt (n.m.)
set fire zazhech' (v.pf.)
set free osvobodit' (v.pf.)
set off otpravit'sya (v.pf.)
set on natravit' (v.pf.)
set on fire podzhech' (v.pf.)
podzhigat' (v.impf.)
set square ugol'nik (n.m.)
setting oprava (n.f.)
ukladka (n.f.)
settle obosnovat'sya (v.pf.)
osest' (v.pf.)
otstaivat'sya (v.impf.)
otstoyat'sya (v.pf.)
poselit' (v.pf.)
poselyat'(sya) (v.impf.)
rasselit' (v.pf.)
selit'sya (v.impf.)

uladit' (v.pf.)
ulazhivat' (v.impf.)
ustraivat'(sya) (v.impf.)
zasest' (v.pf.)
settle accounts raskvitat'sya (v.pf.)
settle down ostepenit'sya (v.pf.)
settlement poselok (n.m.)
settler, new novosel (n.m.)
settling osazhdenie (n.n.)
osedanie (n.n.)
rasselenie (n.n.)
settlor pereselenets (n.m.)
poselenets (n.m.)
seven sem' (num.)
semerka (n.f.)
semero (num.)
seven-hundredth semisotyi (adj.)
seventeen semnadtsat' (num.)
seventh sed'moi (adj.)
seventieth semidesyatyi (adj.)
seventy-year-old semidesyatiletnii (adj.)
seven-year semiletnii (adj.)
several neskol'ko (adv.)
severance otsechenie (n.n.)
severe surovyi (adj.)
sew obshivat' (v.impf.)
shit' (v.impf.)
sew in vshit' (v.pf.)
vshivat' (v.impf.)
sew on nashivat' (v.impf.)
prishivat' (v.impf.)
sew together sshivat' (v.impf.)
sew up zashivat' (v.impf.)
sewage nechistoty (n.pl.)
sewer stok (n.m.)
sewing poshivka (n.f.)
shveinyi (adj.)
sex pol (n.m.)
sexual polovoi (adj.)
seksual'nyi (adj.)
shabby iznoshennyi (adj.)
oblezlyi (adj.)
obtrepannyi (adj.)
ponoshennyi (adj.)
zakhudalyi (adj.)
shackles kandaly (n.pl.)
shade ottenit' (v.pf.)
ottenok (n.m.)

ottenyat' (v.impf.)
ten' (n.f.)
tushevat' (v.impf.)
shade in zatushevat' (v.pf.)
shade, lamp abazhur (n.m.)
shadow ten' (n.f.)
shadowing slezhka (n.f.)
shady tenevoi (adj.)
shaft ogloblya (n.f.)
val (n.m.)
shaggy kosmatyi (adj.)
lokhmatyi (adj.)
shah shakh (n.m.)
shake drognut' (v.pf.)
pokachnut' (v.pf.)
pokolebat' (v.pf.)
poshatnut' (v.pf.)
potryasat' (v.impf.)
pozhat' (v.pf.)
pozhimat' (v.impf.)
sotryasat' (v.impf.)
tryasti (v.impf.)
shake loose rasshatat' (v.pf.)
rasshatyvat' (v.impf.)
shake off otryakhivat'(sya) (v.impf.)
otryakhnut' (v.pf.)
stryakhivat' (v.impf.)
shake out vytryasti (v.pf.)
shake up vstryakhivat' (v.impf.)
vzbaltyvat' (v.impf.)
vzboltat' (v.pf.)
shaking vstryaska (n.f.)
shallow malovodnyi (adj.)
mel' (n.f.)
melkovodnyi (adj.)
neglubokii (adj.)
otmel' (n.f.)
shallow, to grow melet' (v.impf.)
sham simulirovat' (v.impf.)
shame pristydit' (v.pf.)
sram (n.m.)
styd (n.m.)
stydno (pred.)
shameful postydnyi (adj.)
shameless besstydnyi (adj.)
bezzastenchivyi (adj.)
shaped timber pilomaterial (n.m.)
shapshot snimok (n.m.)

share aktsiya (n.f.)
    pai (n.m.)
    podelit' (v.pf.)
shareholder aktsioner (n.m.)
sharing delezh (n.m.)
shark akula (n.f.)
sharp boikii (adj.)
    diez (n.m.)
    ostryi (adj.)
    rezkii (adj.)
sharpen chinit' (v.impf.)
    natochit' (v.pf.)
    navostrit' (v.pf.)
    ochinit' (v.pf.)
    ottachivat' (v.impf.)
    ottochit' (v.pf.)
    podtachivat' (v.impf.)
    podtochit' (v.pf.)
    tochit' (v.impf.)
sharpening obostrenie (n.n.)
sharpness ostrota (n.f.)
sharpshooter snaiper (n.m.)
sharp-sighted zorkii (adj.)
shave brit' (v.impf.)
    vybrit' (v.pf.)
shave off sbrivat' (v.impf.)
shave oneself pobrit'(sya) (v.pf.)
shaving struzhka (n.f.)
shawl platok (n.m.)
    shal' (n.f.)
she ona (p.)
sheaf snop (n.m.)
    svyazka (n.f.)
sheath nozhny (n.pl.)
she-bear medveditsa (n.f.)
shed sarai (n.m.)
shed a tear proslezit'sya (v.pf.)
shed, cattle khlev (n.m.)
shed tears poplakat' (v.pf.)
sheep ovechii (adj.)
    ovtsa (n.f.)
sheepbreeding ovtsevodstvo (n.n.)
sheepskin ovchina (n.f.)
sheepskin coat tulup (n.m.)
sheet list (n.m.)
    listovoi (adj.)
    prostynka (n.f.)
shelf polka (n.f.)

shell lushchit' (v.impf.)
    oblupit' (v.pf.)
    rakovina (n.f.)
    shelushit' (v.impf.)
    skorlupa (n.f.)
shell-shocked kontuzhennyi (adj.)
shelter krov (n.m.)
    ukrytie (n.n.)
shelter, bomb bomboubezhishche (n.n.)
shelter, gas gazoubezhishche (n.n.)
shepherd chaban (n.m.)
    pastukh (n.m.)
shield shchit (n.m.)
    vygorazhivat' (v.impf.)
    vygorodit' (v.pf.)
    zaslonyat' (v.impf.)
shift smeshchenie (n.n.)
shine blestet' (v.impf.)
    blistat' (v.impf.)
    losnit'sya (v.impf.)
    otsvechivat' (v.impf.)
    svetit' (v.impf.)
    zablestet' (v.pf.)
shining blestyashchii (adj.)
ship korabl' (n.m.)
    sudno (n.n.)
shipbuilder korabel (n.m.)
shipbuilding korablestroenie (n.n.)
    sudostroenie (n.n.)
shipwreck korablekrushenie (n.n.)
shipyard sudoverf' (n.f.)
    verf' (n.f.)
shirk otlynivat' (v.impf.)
shirt rubashka (n.f.)
    sorochka (n.f.)
shirtfront, false manishka (n.f.)
shiver drognut' (v.pf.)
    oznob (n.m.)
shock potryasat' (v.impf.)
    shok (n.m.)
    shokirovat' (v.impf.)
shoe bashmak (n.m.)
    botinok (n.m.)
    obuvnoi (adj.)
    tuflya (n.f.)
shoe, bast lapot' (n.m.)
shoe polish gutalin (n.m.)
    vaksa (n.f.)

shoemaker sapozhnik (n.m.)
shoes, football butsy (n.pl.)
shoes, to put on obut' (v.pf.)
  obuvat'(sya) (v.impf.)
shoes, to take off one's razut'sya (v.pf.)
  razuvat'sya (v.impf.)
shoes, walking polubotinki (n.pl.)
shoot otrostok (n.m.)
  strelyat' (v.impf.)
  zastrelit' (v.pf.)
shoot through prostrelit' (v.pf.)
shooting rasstrel (n.m.)
  s"emka (n.f.)
  strel'ba (n.f.)
shooting gallery tir (n.m.)
shop lavka (n.f.)
  tsekh (n.m.)
shop assistant prodavets (n.m.)
shop, baker's bulochnaya (n.f.)
  konditerskaya (n.f.)
shopkeeper lavochnik (n.m.)
shopwindow vitrina (n.f.)
shore bereg (n.m.)
short korotkii (adj.)
  kratkii (adj.)
  rassypchatyi (adj.)
  strizhennyi (adj.)
short breath odyshka (n.f.)
short circuit zamykanie (n.n.)
short duration, of neprodolzhitel'nyi (adj.)
short, in slovom (adv.)
short of, to be nedoschitat'sya (v.pf.)
short story novella (n.f.)
short weight nedoves (n.m.)
shortage nekhvatka (n.f.)
shortchange obschitat' (v.pf.)
shorten sokrashchat'(sya) (v.impf.)
  ukorachivat' (v.impf.)
  ukorotit' (v.pf.)
shorthand report stenogramma (n.f.)
shorthand, to take down in stenografirovat'
    (v.impf.)
short-lived nedolgovechnyi (adj.)
shortly nezadolgo (adv.)
shorts shorty (n.pl.)
  trusiki (n.pl.)
  trusy (n.pl.)
shortsighted nedal'novidnyi (adj.)

shortwave korotkovolnovyi (adj.)
shot drob' (n.f.)
  vystrel (n.m.)
shoulder plecho (n.n.)
shoulder belt perevyaz' (n.f.)
shoulder blade lopatka (n.f.)
shoulder strap pogon (n.m.)
shout krichat' (v.impf.)
  krik (n.m.)
  kriknut' (v.pf.)
  nakrichat' (v.pf.)
  okrik (n.m.)
  pokrikivat' (v.impf.)
  vopit' (v.impf.)
shout down perekrichat' (v.pf.)
shout to one another pereklikat'sya (v.impf.)
shove about rassovat' (v.pf.)
shove in zasovyvat' (v.impf.)
  zasunut' (v.pf.)
shove, to give a podtalkivat' (v.impf.)
  podtolknut' (v.pf.)
show okazat' (v.pf.)
  pokaz (n.m.)
  pokazat' (v.pf.)
  pokazyvat' (v.impf.)
  predstavlenie (n.n.)
  proyavit' (v.pf.)
  seans (n.m.)
  vykazat' (v.pf.)
show booth balagan (n.m.)
show, for napokaz (adv.)
  pokaznoi (adj.)
show off shchegol'nut' (v.pf.)
show oneself pokazat'sya (v.pf.)
show the door to vyprovazhivat' (v.impf.)
  vyprovodit' (v.pf.)
show through skvozit' (v.impf.)
shower dush (n.m.)
shrapnel shrapnel' (n.f.)
shred klok (n.m.)
  kromsat' (v.impf.)
shredder terka (n.f.)
shreds, torn to izodrannyi (adj.)
shriek raskrichat'sya (v.pf.)
shrink s"ezhivat'sya (v.impf.)
shroud savan (n.m.)
Shrovetide maslenitsa (n.f.)
shrubbery kustarnik (n.m.)

shudder sodrogat'sya (v.impf.)
shuffle sharkat' (v.impf.)
   tasovat' (v.impf.)
shuffle along bresti (v.impf.)
shun gnushat'sya (v.impf.)
   izbegat' (v.impf.)
shutter stavnya (n.f.)
shuttle chelnok (n.m.)
shy sharakhat'sya (v.impf.)
   zastenchivyi (adj.)
shy, to feel stesnyat'sya (v.impf.)
shyness stydlivost' (n.f.)
Siberian sibirskii (adj.)
Siberian salmon keta (n.f.)
sibilant shipyashchii (adj.)
sick bol'noi (adj.)
   bolen (adj.)
sick quarters lazaret (n.m.)
sick rate zabolevaemost' (n.f.)
sick, to feel toshnit' (v.impf.)
sickle serp (n.m*)*
sickly boleznennyi (adj.)
side bok (n.m.)
   bort (n.m.)
   gran' (n.f.)
   pobochnyi (adj.)
   storona (n.f.)
side by side naryadu (adv.)
side, from one sboku (adv.)
side, on one nabok (adv.)
side street pereulok (n.m.)
sideboard bufet (n.m.)
sidelong koso (adv.)
sidewalk trotuar (n.m.)
sideways bokom (adv.)
siding raz''ezd (n.m.)
siege osada (n.f.)
   osadnyi (adj.)
sieve resheto (n.n.)
   sito (n.n.)
sift otseivat'(sya) (v.impf.)
   otseyat' (v.pf.)
   proseivat' (v.impf.)
   proseyat' (v.pf.)
sifting out otsev (n.m.)
sigh okhat' (v.impf.)
   okhnut' (v.pf.)
   vzdokh (n.m.)

   vzdykhat' (v.impf.)
sight pritsel (n.m.)
   zrenie (n.n.)
sight, lovely zaglyaden'e (n.n.)
sighted zryachii (adj.)
sign podpisat' (v.pf.)
   primeta (n.f.)
   priznak (n.m.)
   raspisat'sya (v.pf.)
   raspisyvat'sya (v.impf.)
   znak (n.m.)
signal signal (n.m.)
signaller svyazist (n.m.)
signalling, block blokirovka (n.f.)
signals, light semafor (n.m.)
signature podpis' (n.f.)
signboard vyveska (n.f.)
significant znamenatel'nyi (adj.)
signify oznachat' (v.impf.)
   znachit' (v.impf.)
   znamenovat' (v.impf.)
silage silos (n.m.)
silent bezmolvnyi (adj.)
silent, to become umolkat' (v.impf.)
silent, to grow smolkat' (v.impf.)
   zamolchat' (v.pf.)
   zamolkat' (v.impf.)
silent, to keep molchat' (v.impf.)
   otmalchivat'sya (v.impf.)
   promolchat' (v.pf.)
silently molcha (adv.)
   potikhon'ku (adv.)
silhouette siluét (n.m.)
silica kremnezem (n.m.)
silicate silikat (n.m.)
silicon kremnii (n.m.)
silk shelk (n.m.)
   shelkovyi (adj.)
silkworm shelkovichnyi cherv' (adj.-n.m.)
silky shelkovistyi (adj.)
silt il (n.m.)
silver serebristyi (adj.)
   serebro (n.n.)
   serebryanyi (adj.)
silver fir pikhta (n.f.)
silver fox cherno-buryi (adj.)
silver nitrate lyapis (n.m.)
similar pokhozhii (adj.)

skhodnyi (adj.)

skhozhii (adj.)

similarity podobie (n.n.)

simple neslozhnyi (adj.)

nezamyslovatyi (adj.)

prostoi (adj.)

simple-hearted prostodushnyi (adj.)

prostoserdechnyi (adj.)

simpleton prostak (n.m.)

simplicity prostota (n.f.)

simplify uproshchat' (v.impf.)

uprostit' (v.pf.)

simply poprostu (adv.)

prosto (adv.)

simulate simulirovat' (v.impf.)

simulation modelirovanie (n.n.)

simulator trenazher (n.m.)

simultaneous odnovremennyi (adj.)

sin grekh (n.m.)

greshit' (v.impf.)

sin, to commit a sogreshit' (v.pf.)

since poskol'ku (conj.)

raz (conj.)

sincere chistoserdechnyi (adj.)

dushevnyi (adj.)

iskrennii (adj.)

sine sinus (n.m.)

sinew zhila (n.f.)

sinewy zhilistyi (adj.)

sinful greshnyi (adj.)

sing pet' (v.impf.)

raspevat' (v.impf.)

spet' (v.pf.)

sing, to begin to zatyanut' (v.pf.)

singe opalit' (v.pf.)

singer pevets (n.m.)

singer, leading zapevala (n.m.)

singing penie (n.n.)

pevchii (adj.)

singing, to start zapet' (v.pf.)

singing voice, in a naraspev (adv.)

single file gus'kom (adv.)

single-breasted odnobortnyi (adj.)

single-seater odnomestnyi (adj.)

single-track odnokoleinyi (adj.)

sink opuskat'(sya) (v.impf.)

potopit' (v.pf.)

tonut' (v.impf.)

utopit' (v.pf.)

zatonut' (v.pf.)

sinusoid sinusoida (n.f.)

sip glotok (n.m.)

sip, to take a khlebnut' (v.pf.)

siren sirena (n.f.)

siskin chizh (n.m.)

sister sestra (n.f.)

sister-in-law zolovka (n.f.)

sit prosidet' (v.pf.)

sidet' (v.impf.)

sit down podsazhivat'sya (v.impf.)

podsest' (v.pf.)

prisazhivat'sya (v.impf.)

prisest' (v.pf.)

sadit'sya (v.impf.)

sest' (v.pf.)

sit up late zasidet'sya (v.pf.)

sitting sidyachii (adj.)

situation kon''yunktura (n.f.)

situatsiya (n.f.)

six shest' (num.)

shesterka (n.f.)

shestero (num.)

six-month shestimesyachnyi (adj.)

six-month-old polugodovalyi (adj.)

sixteen shestnadtsat' (num.)

sixteenth shestnadtsatyi (adj.)

sixth shestoi (adj.)

sixtieth shestidesyatyi (adj.)

six-year-old shestiletnii (adj.)

size format (n.m.)

razmer (n.m.)

skater kon'kobezhets (n.m.)

skater, figure figurist (n.m.)

skates kon'ki (n.pl.)

skating rink katok (n.m.)

skeleton kostyak (n.m.)

skelet (n.m.)

skeptic skeptik (n.m.)

sketch éskiz (n.m.)

nabrasyvat' (v.impf.)

nabrosat' (v.pf.)

nabrosok (n.m.)

zarisovka (n.f.)

ski lyzha (n.f.)

ski binding kreplenie (n.n.)

ski jump tramplin (n.m.)

skill navyk (n.m.)
   snorovka (n.f.)
   umenie (n.n.)
skillful iskusnyi (adj.)
   umelyi (adj.)
skimmer shumovka (n.f.)
skin kozha (n.f.)
   nakozhnyi (adj.)
   obdirat' (v.impf.)
   obodrat' (v.pf.)
   penka (n.f.)
   sdirat' (v.impf.)
   shkura (n.f.)
   sodrat' (v.pf.)
skin, thin kozhitsa (n.f.)
skipper shkiper (n.m.)
skirmish perestrelka (n.f.)
   skhvatka (n.f.)
   stychka (n.f.)
skirt yubka (n.f.)
skull cherep (n.m.)
sky nebo (n.n.)
skylark zhavoronok (n.m.)
skyscraper neboskreb (n.m.)
slabbing slyabing (n.m.)
slack vyalyi (adj.)
slag shlak (n.m.)
slander kleveta (n.f.)
   nagovarivat' (v.impf.)
   ochernit' (v.pf.)
   ogovarivat' (v.impf.)
   ogovorit' (v.pf.)
   oklevetat' (v.pf.)
   poklep (n.m.)
slanting kosoi (adj.)
slap nashlepat' (v.pf.)
   shlepnut' (v.pf.)
slap in the face opleukha (n.f.)
   poshchechina (n.f.)
slash iskromsat' (v.pf.)
slate-pencil grifel' (n.m.)
slaughter uboi (n.m.)
   zakolot' (v.pf.)
   zarezat' (v.pf.)
   zakalyvat' (v.impf.)
slaughterhouse boinya (n.f.)
Slav slavyanin (n.m.)
slave rab (n.m.)

   rabskii (adj.)
slave-owning rabovladel'cheskii (adj.)
sledge salazki (n.pl.)
sleep son (n.m.)
   spat' (v.impf.)
sleep, to get some pospat' (v.pf.)
sleep, to have a good vyspat'sya (v.pf.)
   vysypat'sya (v.impf.)
sleep, to put to usypit' (v.pf.)
sleep, to rock to ukachat' (v.pf.)
sleeper shpala (n.f.)
sleeping sonnyi (adj.)
sleeping pill snotvornoe (n.n.)
sleepless bessonnyi (adj.)
sleepwalker lunatik (n.m.)
sleepy sonnyi (adj.)
   zaspannyi (adj.)
sleeve rukav (n.m.)
sleigh narty (n.pl.)
   sani (n.pl.)
slice lomtik (n.m.)
slide zolotnik (n.m.)
slide down skatyvat'sya (v.impf.)
sliding skol'zhenie (n.n.)
slight tretirovat' (v.impf.)
slightest maleishii (adj.)
slightly chut' (adv.)
   slegka (adv.)
slime shlam (n.m.)
   sliz' (n.f.)
   tina (n.f.)
slimy slizistyi (adj.)
sling strop (n.m.)
slip poskol'znut'sya (v.pf.)
   skol'znut' (v.pf.)
slip away uliznut' (v.pf.)
   uskol'zat' (v.impf.)
slip down spolzat' (v.impf.)
slip in proskal'zyvat' (v.impf.)
slip off soskal'zyvat' (v.impf.)
slip out vyskal'zyvat' (v.impf.)
   vyskol'znut' (v.pf.)
slip past proskakivat' (v.impf.)
slip, to let prozevat' (v.pf.)
slip, to make a obmolvit'sya (v.pf.)
slippers tapochki (n.pl.)
slippery skol'zkii (adj.)
slobbery slyunyavyi (adj.)

slogan lozung (n.m.)

slope kosogor (n.m.)

    otkos (n.m.)

    skat (n.m.)

    sklon (n.m.)

sloping otlogii (adj.)

    pokatyi (adj.)

    pologii (adj.)

slops pomoi (n.pl.)

slot paz (n.m.)

    prorez (n.m.)

Slovak slovak (n.m.)

Slovakian slovatskii (adj.)

sloven neryakha (n.m.&f.)

slow medlitel'nyi (adj.)

slow down zamedlit' (v.pf.)

slowing down zamedlenie (n.n.)

slowly medlenno (adv.)

slow-witted nedogadlivyi (adj.)

    neponyatlivyi (adj.)

sludge shlam (n.m.)

slum trushchoba (n.f.)

slurry shlam (n.m.)

slush slyakot' (n.f.)

sly lukavyi (adj.)

    pronyrlivyi (adj.)

small mal (adj.)

    malyi (adj.)

    melkii (adj.)

    nebol'shoi (adj.)

small, a little too malovat (adj.)

small of the back poyasnitsa (n.f.)

small town mestechko (n.n.)

smaller men'she (adj.)

smallpox ospa (n.f.)

smart boikii (adj.)

    shikarnyi (adj.)

smash gromit' (v.impf.)

    razmozzhit' (v.pf.)

    sokrushat' (v.impf.)

smear izmazat' (v.pf.)

    vymazat' (v.pf.)

smell chuyat' (v.impf.)

    pakhnut' (v.impf.)

    ponyukhat' (v.pf.)

    zapakh (n.m.)

smell, sense of obonyanie (n.n.)

smelt pereplavit' (v.pf.)

    plavit' (v.impf.)

    vyplavit' (v.pf.)

smelting plavil'nyi (adj.)

smelting, steel staleplavil'nyi (adj.)

smile ulybat'sya (v.impf.)

    ulybka (n.f.)

    usmekhat'sya (v.impf.)

    usmeshka (n.f.)

smoke dym (n.m.)

    koptet' (v.impf.)

    koptit' (v.impf.)

    kurit' (v.impf.)

smoke out vykurivat' (v.impf.)

smoke, to fill with nakurit' (v.pf.)

smoker kuryashchii (adj.)

smoking kurenie (n.n.)

smoky zakopchennyi (adj.)

    zakoptelyi (adj.)

smooth gladkii (adj.)

    plavnyi (adj.)

    sgladit' (v.pf.)

smooth out razgladit' (v.pf.)

    vyravnivat' (v.impf.)

    vyrovnyat' (v.pf.)

smooth surface glad' (n.f.)

smoulder tlet' (v.impf.)

smouldering tlenie (n.n.)

snack zakuska (n.f.)

snack, to have a zakusit' (v.pf.)

snag zagvozdka (n.f.)

snail ulitka (n.f.)

snake zmeya (n.f.)

snake, grass uzh (n.m.)

snake's zmeinyi (adj.)

snap ogryzat'sya (v.impf.)

    shchelchok (n.m.)

snarl oskalit' (v.pf.)

snatch khvatat' (v.impf.)

    khvatat'sya (v.impf.)

    khvatit' (v.pf.)

    raskhvatat' (v.pf.)

    urvat' (v.pf.)

    uryvat' (v.impf.)

    vykhvatit' (v.pf.)

sneak krast'sya (v.impf.)

sneer glumit'sya (v.impf.)

    izdevka (n.f.)

sneeze chikhat' (v.impf.)

sniff sopet' (v.impf.)
sniff round obnyukhat' (v.pf.)
snore khrapet' (v.impf.)
snort fyrkat' (v.impf.)
snout rylo (n.n.)
snow sneg (n.m.)
   snezhnyi (adj.)
snow crust nast (n.m.)
snow, to powder with zaporoshit' (v.pf.)
snowball snezhok (n.m.)
snowdrift sugrob (n.m.)
snowdrifts zanosy (n.pl.)
snowdrop podsnezhnik (n.m.)
snowfall snegopad (n.m.)
snowflake snezhinka (n.f.)
Snow-Maiden snegurochka (n.f.)
snowplow snegoochistitel' (n.m.)
snowstorm buran (n.m.)
   metel' (n.f.)
   purga (n.f.)
   v'yuga (n.f.)
snow-white belosnezhnyi (adj.)
snub-nosed kurnosyi (adj.)
so nastol'ko (adv.)
   stol' (adv.)
   tak (adv.)
so many stol'ko (adv.)
so much stol'ko (adv.)
so much the tem (conj.)
so much the more podavno (adv.)
soak promochit' (v.pf.)
   razmochit' (v.pf.)
   zamochit' (v.pf.)
soak in vpityvat'(sya) (v.impf.)
soap mylit' (v.impf.)
   mylo (n.n.)
   namylivat' (v.impf.)
soap dish myl'nitsa (n.f.)
soar parit' (v.impf.)
   vitat' (v.impf.)
soaring parenie (n.n.)
sob rydat' (v.impf.)
   vskhlipyvat' (v.impf.)
   zarydat' (v.pf.)
sobbing, to burst out razrydat'sya (v.pf.)
sober otrezvit' (v.pf.)
sobriety trezvost' (n.f.)
sociable obshchitel'nyi (adj.)

social bytovoi (adj.)
   sotsial'nyi (adj.)
Social Democrat sotsial-demokrat (n.m.)
social security sotsstrakh (n.m.)
socialism sotsializm (n.m.)
socialist sotsialist (n.m.)
   sotsialisticheskii (adj.)
socialist emulation sotssorevnovanie (n.n.)
society obshchestvo (n.n.)
society, philharmonic filarmoniya (n.f.)
sock nosok (n.m.)
socket rozetka (n.f.)
soda soda (n.f.)
sodium natrii (n.m.)
sofa divan (n.m.)
soft myagkii (adj.)
soft part (of loaf) myakish (n.m.)
soft, to become obmyakat' (v.impf.)
soft-boiled vsmyatku (adv.)
soften razmyagchat' (v.impf)
   smyagchat'(sya) (v.impf.)
soil grunt (n.m.)
   ispachkat' (v.pf.)
   pachkat' (v.impf.)
   pochva (n.f.)
soil, loamy suglinok (n.m.)
soil, virgin tselina (n.f.)
soiled, easily markii (adj.)
solar solnechnyi (adj.)
solar power engineering gelioénergetika (n.f.)
sold by weight razvesnoi (adj.)
solder payat' (v.impf.)
   spaivat' (v.impf.)
   spayat' (v.pf.)
   zapaivat' (v.impf.)
   zapayat' (v.pf.)
soldered joint spaika (n.f.)
soldering iron payal'nik (n.m.)
soldier soldat (n.m.)
soldier, front-line frontovik (n.m.)
sole podmetka (n.f.)
   podoshva (n.f.)
solemn torzhestvennyi (adj.)
solicit domogat'sya (v.impf.)
solid osnovatel'nyi (adj.)
solidarity solidarnost' (n.f.)
solidification otverdevanie (n.n.)
   zatverdenie (n.n.)

solidity solidnost' (n.f.)
solitude odinochestvo (n.n.)
  uedinenie (n.n.)
solo solo (n.n.)
soloist solist (n.m)
solution rastvor (n.m.)
solution, alkaline shchelok (n.m.)
solve razgadat' (v.pf.)
  razgadyvat' (v.pf.)
solvent kreditosposobnyi (adj.)
  platezhesposobnyi (adj.)
  rastvoritel' (n.m.)
some koe-kakoi (p.)
  nekotoryi (p.)
some, a kind of kakoi-to (p.)
some, a little nemnogo (adv.)
  nemnozhko (adv.)
some, any kakoi-nibud' (p.)
somebody koe-kto (p.)
somehow chto-to (p.)
  kak-nibud' (p.)
  kak-to (adv.)
someone nekto (p.)
something chto-libo (p.)
  chto-to (p.)
  koe-chto (p.)
  nechto (p.)
sometimes inogda (adv.)
somewhat neskol'ko (adv.)
somewhere gde-libo (adv.)
  koe-gde (adv.)
  koe-kuda (adv.)
son syn (n.m.)
song pesn' (n.f.)
  romans (n.m.)
son-in-law zyat' (n.m.)
soon skoro (adj.)
soon after vskore (adv.)
soot kopot' (n.f.)
  sazha (n.f.)
soothe unimat'(sya) (v.impf.)
  unyat' (v.pf.)
  uspokoit' (v.pf.)
sop podachka (n.f.)
sophomore vtorokursnik (n.m.)
sore bolyachka (n.f.)
  nabolevshii (adj.)
sorrel shchavel' (n.m.)

sorrow pechal' (n.f.)
sorrowful priskorbnyi (adj.)
sorry for, to feel pozhalet' (v.pf.)
  zhalet' (v.impf.)
sort sort (n.m.)
sort out perebirat' (v.impf.)
  perebrat' (v.pf.)
  rassortirovat' (v.pf.)
sorting razbrakovka (n.f.)
soul dusha (n.f.)
sound vyslushat' (v.pf.)
  zazvuchat' (v.pf.)
  zvuchat' (v.impf.)
  zvuk (n.m.)
  zvukovoi (adj.)
sound locator zvukoulavlivatel' (n.m.)
sound recording zvukozapis' (n.f.)
sounding lead lot (n.m.)
soundless bezzvuchnyi (adj.)
soundly zdravo (adv.)
soundproof zvukonepronitsaemyi (adj.)
soundproofing zvukoizolyatsiya (n.f.)
soup pokhlebka (n.f.)
  sup (n.m.)
  supovoi (adj.)
soup, cabbage shchi (n.pl.)
soup, fish ukha (n.f.)
  kislyi (adj.)
sour kvashenyi (adj.)
sour cream smetana (n.f.)
sour milk prostokvasha (n.f.)
sour, to turn perekisat' (v.impf.)
  prokisat' (v.impf.)
  skisat' (v.pf.)
  zakisat' (v.impf.)
source istochnik (n.m.)
  istok (n.m.)
source, primary pervoistochnik (n.m.)
south yug (n.m.)
  yuzhnyi (adj.)
southeast yugo-vostochnyi (adj.)
  yugo-vostok (n.m.)
southerner yuzhanin (n.m.)
southwest yugo-zapad (n.m.)
  yugo-zapadnyi (adj.)
sovereign polnovlastnyi (adj.)
  suverennyi (adj.)
Soviet sovet (n.m.)
  (cont'd)

sovetskii (adj.)
Soviet, village sel'sovet (n.m.)
sow poseyat' (v.pf.)
   zasevat' (v.impf.)
   zaseyat' (v.pf.)
sowing posev (n.m.)
   sev (n.m.)
soybean soevyi (adj.)
spa kurort (n.m.)
space prostranstvo (n.n.)
space, dwelling zhilploshchad' (n.f.)
space suit skafandr (n.m.)
spacer rasporka (n.f.)
spacious pomestitel'nyi (adj.)
spaciousness prostor (n.m.)
spade lopata (n.f.)
   zastup (n.m.)
spades piki (n.pl.)
span perekrytie (n.n.)
   prolet (n.m.)
   pyad' (n.f.)
   razmakh (n.m.)
Spaniard ispanets (n.m.)
spare shchadit' (v.impf.)
   udelit' (v.pf.)
   udelyat' (v.impf.)
   zapasnoi (adj.)
spark iskra (n.f.)
spark plug svecha (n.f.)
sparkle iskrit'sya (v.impf.)
   sverkat' (v.impf.)
sparrow vorobei (n.m.)
spasm spazm(a) (n.m.&f.)
spatial prostranstvennyi (adj.)
spawn ikra (n.f.)
   otrod'e (n.n.)
speak govorit' (v.impf.)
   razgovarivat' (v.impf.)
speak rudely nagrubit' (v.pf.)
speak with a nasal twang gnusavit' (v.impf.)
spear kop'e (n.n.)
special ékstrennyi (adj.)
specialist in literature literaturoved (n.m.)
specialization spetsializatsiya (n.f.)
specialty spetsial'nost' (n.f.)
species vid (n.m.)
specific spetsificheskii (adj.)
   vidovoi (adj.)

specific gravity udel'nyi ves (adj.-n.m.)
specification spetsifikatsiya (n.f.)
specimen ékzemplyar (n.m.)
specious blagovidnyi (adj.)
spectacle zrelishche (n.n.)
spectacular éffektnyi (adj.)
spectator zritel' (n.m.)
specter prizrak (n.m.)
spectrogram spektrogramma (n.f.)
spectrometry spektrometriya (n.f.)
spectrum spektr (n.m.)
speculate spekulirovat' (v.impf.)
speech rech' (n.f.)
speed bystrota (n.f.)
   pryt' (n.f.)
   skorost' (adv.)
speedboat glisser (n.m.)
spelling pravopisanie (n.n.)
spend istratit' (v.pf.)
   izderzhat' (v.pf.)
   izraskhodovat' (v.pf.)
   raskhodovat' (v.impf.)
   zatratit' (v.pf.)
spend the night nochevat' (v.impf.)
   perenochevat' (v.pf.)
sphere sfera (n.f.)
spherical sfericheskii (adj.)
   sharovidnyi (adj.)
sphinx sfinks (n.m.)
spice pryanost' (n.f.)
spider pauk (n.m.)
spill luchina (n.f.)
   prolit' (v.pf.)
   prolivat' (v.impf.)
   prosypat' (v.pf.)
   rassypat' (v.pf.)
   razlit' (v.pf.)
spill out vysypat'sya (v.pf.)
spin pryast' (v.impf.)
spin round zavertet'sya (v.pf.)
spinach shpinat (n.m.)
spinal spinnoi (adj.)
spine khrebet (n.m.)
spinning pryadil'nyi (adj.)
spinning wheel pryalka (n.f.)
spiral spiral' (n.f.)
   vintovoi (adj.)
spirit dukh (n.m.)

spirits, low unynie (n.n.)
spiritual dukhovnyi (adj.)
spit kosa (n.f.)
    naplevat' (v.pf.)
    oplevat' (v.pf.)
    plyunut' (v.pf.)
    splevyvat' (v.impf.)
    splyunut' (v.pf.)
    vertel (n.m.)
spit out vyplevyvat' (v.impf.)
    vyplyunut' (v.pf.)
spite nazlo (adv.)
    zloba (n.f.)
spite of, in nesmotrya (prep.)
    vopreki (prep.)
spittle plevok (n.m.)
spittoon plevatel'nitsa (n.f.)
splash bryzgat' (v.impf.)
    bryznut' (v.pf.)
    obryzgat' (v.pf.)
    plesk (n.m.)
    raspleskat' (v.pf.)
    vsplesk (n.m.)
    vsplesnut' (v.pf.)
splash out vypleskivat' (v.impf.)
spleen khandra (n.f.)
    selezenka (n.f.)
splendor pyshnost' (n.f.)
splint lubok (n.m.)
splinter oskolok (n.m.)
    zanoza (n.f.)
split raskalyvat'(sya) (v.impf.)
    raskol (n.m.)
    rasshchepit' (v.pf.)
    razbit' (v.pf.)
    sech'sya (v.impf.)
spoil balovat' (v.impf.)
    isportit' (v.pf.)
    izbalovat' (v.pf.)
    portit' (v.impf.)
sponge gubka (n.f.)
    obteret'(sya) (v.pf.)
sponge cake biskvit (n.m.)
sponger nakhlebnik (n.m.)
sponging obtiranie (n.n.)
spontaneous combustion samovozgoranie
      (n.n.)
spool katushka (n.f.)

shpul'ka (n.f.)
spoon lozhka (n.f.)
spore spora (n.f.)
sport sport (n.m.)
sporting sportivnyi (adj.)
sports festival spartakiada (n.f.)
sportsman sportsmen (n.m.)
spot krapinka (n.f.)
    pyatno (n.n.)
spotted pyatnistyi (adj.)
spout nosik (n.m.)
sprain rastyanut' (v.pf.)
    rastyazhenie (n.n.)
sprat kil'ka (n.f.)
sprats shproty (n.pl.)
sprawl razlech'sya (v.pf.)
sprayer raspylitel' (n.m.)
spread namazat' (v.pf.)
    nasypat' (v.impf.&pf.)
    postilat' (v.impf.)
    postlat' (v.pf.)
    rasplastat' (v.pf.)
    rasplyt'sya (v.pf.)
    rasplyvat'sya (v.impf.)
    rasstilat' (v.impf.)
    razmazat' (v.pf.)
    razostlat' (v.pf.)
    stlat' (v.impf.)
spread under podostlat' (v.pf.)
    podstilat' (v.impf.)
spreader rasporka (n.f.)
spree, to go on a zagulyat' (v.pf.)
spring klyuch (n.m.)
    pruzhina (n.f.)
    ressora (n.f.)
    rodnik (n.m.)
    vesennii (adj.)
    vesna (n.f.)
spring crop yarovoi (adj.)
spring flood polovod'e (n.n.)
spring floods pavodok (n.m.)
springboard tramplin (n.m.)
sprinkle opryskivat' (v.impf.)
    spryskivat' (v.impf.)
    vspryskivat' (v.impf.)
sprint, one hundred meter stometrovka (n.f.)
sprout pobeg (n.m.)
    rostok (n.m.)
    (cont'd)

vskhodit' (v.impf.)

spur prishporivat' (v.impf.)

shpora (n.f.)

spurs otrogi (n.pl.)

sputnik sputnik (n.m.)

spy lazutchik (n.m.)

podsmatrivat' (v.impf.)

podsmotret' (v.pf.)

shpion (n.m.)

spyglass podzornaya truba (adj.-n.f.)

squabble skloka (n.f.)

squabbler sklochnik (n.m.)

squadron éskadra (n.f.)

éskadril'ya (n.f.)

squall shkval (n.m.)

squander motat' (v.impf.)

promatyvat' (v.impf.)

promotat' (v.pf.)

razbazarivat' (v.impf.)

squandering motovstvo (n.n.)

square kvadrat (n.m.)

square, to set ugol'nik (n.m.)

squash kabachok (n.m.)

squeak pishchat' (v.impf.)

pisk (n.m.)

vzvizgivat' (v.impf.)

squeal vizg (n.m.)

squeamish brezglivyi (adj.)

squeamish, to be brezgat' (v.impf.)

squeeze sdavit' (v.pf.)

stiskivat' (v.impf.)

tiskat' (v.impf.)

zazhat' (v.pf.)

zhat' (v.impf.)

squeeze in vtiskivat' (v.impf.)

squeeze out vyzhat' (v.pf.)

vyzhimat' (v.impf.)

squeezed sdavlennyi (adj.)

squint kosit' (v.impf.)

kosoglazie (n.n.)

prishchurivat'sya (v.impf.)

shchurit' (v.impf.)

skosit' (v.pf.)

zhmurit'sya (v.impf.)

squirrel belichii (adj.)

belka (n.f.)

squirrel, ground suslik (n.m.)

stab zakalyvat' (v.impf.)

stability ostoichivost' (n.f.)

ustoichivost' (n.f.)

stabilization stabilizatsiya (n.f.)

stable konyushnya (n.f.)

stabil'nyi (adj.)

stack kopna (n.f.)

shtabel' (n.m.)

skird(a) (n.m.&f.)

stog (n.m.)

stadium stadion (n.m.)

staff kadry (n.pl.)

shtab (n.m.)

shtat (n.m.)

staff, not on permanent vneshtatnyi (adj.)

stage éstrada (n.f.)

kaskad (n.m.)

peregon (n.m.)

stadiya (n.f.)

stsena (n.f.)

stupen' (n.f.)

stagger zashatat'sya (v.pf.)

stagnant kosnyi (adj.)

stoyachii (adj.)

stagnation kosnost' (n.f.)

zastoi (n.m.)

stain zapyatnat' (v.pf.)

stain with grease zasalivat' (v.impf.)

stainless nezapyatnannyi (adj.)

staircase lestnitsa (n.f.)

stake kol (n.m.)

prikol (n.m.)

stavka (n.f.)

stale cherstvyi (adj.)

stale, to become zacherstvet' (v.pf.)

stale, to grow cherstvet' (v.impf.)

stall larek (n.m.)

stoilo (n.n.)

stamen tychinka (n.f.)

stammerer zaika (n.m.&f.)

stamp marka (n.f.)

shtamp (n.m.)

shtempel' (n.m.)

shtempelevat' (v.impf.)

topat' (v.impf.)

topnut' (v.pf.)

stamping tisnenie (n.n.)

stand stanovit'sya (v.impf.)

stend (n.m.)

stoyanka (n.f.)
stoyat' (v.impf.)
vyderzhivat' (v.impf.)
stand empty pustovat' (v.impf.)
stand, music pyupitr (n.m.)
stand out mayachit' (v.impf.)
vyrisovyvat'sya (v.impf.)
stand still zameret' (v.pf.)
zamirat' (v.impf.)
stand up postoyat' (v.pf.)
stand up for vstupat'sya (v.impf.)
vstupit'sya (v.pf.)
standard merilo (n.n.)
standart (n.m.)
standartnyi (adj.)
standard, of low nizkoprobnyi (adj.)
standard-bearer znamenosets (n.m.)
standby system dublirovanie (n.n.)
standing stoyachii (adj.)
standing, of long mnogoletnii (adj.)
stanza strofa (n.f.)
staple shtapel'nyi (adj.)
star zvezda (n.f.)
starch krakhmal (n.m.)
nakrakhmalit' (v.pf.)
starched krakhmal'nyi (adj.)
stare glazet' (v.impf.)
glyadet' (v.impf.)
tarashchit' (v.impf.)
ustavit'sya (v.pf.)
vytarashchit' (v.pf.)
starling skvorets (n.m.)
starry zvezdnyi (adj.)
start razgon (n.m.)
start (n.m.)
trogat'sya (v.impf.)
vstrepenut'sya (v.pf.)
vzdragivat' (v.impf.)
vzdrognut' (v.pf.)
zavesti (v.pf.)
zavodit' (v.impf.)
start up sharakhat'sya (v.impf.)
starting otpravnoi (adj.)
pusk (n.m.)
startle vspoloshit' (v.pf.)
starve izgolodat'sya (v.pf.)
starving vprogolod' (adv.)
state derzhava (n.f.)

gosudarstvennyi (adj.)
gosudarstvo (n.n.)
kazennyi (adj.)
konstatirovat' (v.impf.&pf.)
shtat (n.m.)
state bank gosbank (n.m.)
state farm sovkhoz (n.m.)
state, general samochuvstvie (n.n.)
state insurance gosstrakh (n.m.)
state, parent metropoliya (n.f.)
state planning commission gosplan (n.m.)
statement vyskazyvanie (n.n.)
vystuplenie (n.n.)
statesman deyatel' (n.m.)
station stantsiya (n.f.)
station, electric power elektrostantsiya (n.f.)
station, filling benzokolonka (n.f.)
station, first aid medpunkt (n.m.)
station, hydroelectric power gidrostantsiya (n.f.)
station, propaganda agitpunkt (n.m.)
station, railroad vokzal (n.m.)
stationary statsionarnyi (adj.)
stationery pischebumazhnyi (adj.)
statistics statistika (n.f.)
statue izvayanie (n.n.)
statuya (n.f.)
stay prebyvanie (n.n.)
probyt' (v.pf.)
rasporka (n.f.)
stay with gostit' (v.impf.)
steadfast nepokolebimyi (adj.)
steady neuklonnyi (adj.)
steal krast' (v.impf.)
pokhitit' (v.pf.)
raskradyvat' (v.impf.)
raskrast' (v.pf.)
stashchit' (v.pf.)
ukrast' (v.pf.)
vorovat' (v.impf.)
steal in vkradyvat'sya (v.impf.)
zakradyvat'sya (v.impf.)
zakrast'sya (v.pf.)
steal into prokradyvat'sya (v.impf.)
steal up to podbirat'sya (v.impf.)
podkradyvat'sya (v.impf.)
podkrast'sya (v.pf.)
podobrat'sya (v.pf.)

stealthily ispodtishka (adv.)
   ukradkoi (adv.)
steam par (n.m.)
   parit' (v.impf.)
   parovoi (adj.)
steamer parokhod (n.m.)
steel stal' (n.f.)
steel founder stalevar (n.m.)
steel foundry staleliteinyi zavod (adj.-n.m.)
steel rolling staleprokatnyi (adj.)
steel smelting staleplavil'nyi (adj.)
steep krutoi (adj.)
   obryvistyi (adj.)
steepness krutizna (n.f.)
steering rulevoi (adj.)
steering wheel shturval (n.m.)
stem stebel' (n.m.)
stench smrad (n.m.)
   von' (n.f.)
   zlovonie (n.n.)
stencil trafaret (n.m.)
step pa (n.n.)
   podnozhka (n.f.)
   postup' (n.f.)
   shag (n.m.)
   shagat' (v.impf.)
   stupat' (v.impf.)
   stupen (n.f.)
   stupit' (v.pf.)
step aside postoronit'sya (v.pf.)
step back otstupat' (v.impf.)
   otstupit' (v.pf.)
step over pereshagnut' (v.pf.)
stepdaughter padcheritsa (n.f.)
stepfather otchim (n.m.)
stepladder stremyanka (n.f.)
stepmother machekha (n.f.)
steppe stepnoi (adj.)
stepson pasynok (n.m.)
step-up povysitel'nyi (adj.)
stereometry stereometriya (n.f.)
stereophonic stereofonicheskii (adj.)
stereoscope stereoskop (n.m.)
stereotype stereotip (n.m.)
sterile besplodnyi (adj.)
   steril'nyi (adj.)
sterilization sterilizatsiya (n.f.)
sterlet (fish) sterlyad' (n.f.)

stern korma (n.pl.)
stethoscope stetoskop (n.m.)
stew tushit' (v.impf.)
stewardess styuardessa (n.f.)
stewed tushenyi (adj.)
stick khvorostina (n.f.)
   kleit'sya (v.impf.)
   palka (n.f.)
   prilepit' (v.pf.)
stick, bacillus palochka (n.f.)
stick, hockey klyushka (n.f.)
stick in uvyazat' (v.pf.)
   uvyaznut' (v.pf.)
   vtykat' (v.impf.)
stick into vsadit' (v.pf.)
stick out ottopyrivat'sya (v.impf.)
   torchat' (v.impf.)
stick together skleivat'(sya) (v.impf.)
   slipat'sya (v.impf.)
stick, walking trostochka (n.f.)
sticky kleikii (adj.)
   lipkii (adj.)
stiff chopornyi (adj.)
stiff, to become okochenet' (v.pf.)
stiffen kochenet' (v.impf.)
still eshche (adv.)
   kadr (n.m.)
   vse eshche (adv.)
stilts khoduli (n.pl.)
stimulant razdrazhitel' (n.m.)
stimulus pobuditel' (n.m.)
   razdrazhitel' (n.m.)
   stimul (n.m.)
   vozbuditel' (n.m.)
sting uzhalit' (v.pf.)
   zhalit' (v.impf.)
   zhalo (n.n.)
stinginess skupost' (n.f.)
stingy skarednyi (adj.)
   skupoi (adj.)
stingy, to be skupit'sya (v. impf.)
stipulate obuslovit' (v.pf.)
   ogovarivat' (v.impf.)
   ogovorit' (v.pf.)
stipulation ogovorka (n.f.)
stir boltat' (v.impf.)
   meshat' (v.impf.)
   pomeshat' (v.pf.)

pomeshivat' (v.impf.)
razmeshat' (v.pf.)
shelokhnut'sya (v.pf.)
vskolykhnut' (v.pf.)
stir up mutit' (v.impf.)
rasshevelit' (v.pf.)
stirrup stremya (n.n.)
stitch stezhok (n.m.)
strochit' (v.impf.)
strochka (n.f.)
stock levkoi (n.m.)
stock, empty porozhnyak (n.m.)
stockbreeding zhivotnovodstvo (n.n.)
stocking chulok (n.m.)
stocky korenastyi (adj.)
stoicism stoitsizm (n.m.)
stoker istopnik (n.m.)
kochegar (n.m.)
stolen kradenyi (adj.)
stomach zheludok (n.m.)
zhivot (n.m.)
stomach, on an empty natoshchak (adv.)
stomatology stomatologiya (n.f.)
stone kamen' (n.m.)
kamennyi (adj.)
tumba (n.f.)
stone, crushed shcheben' (n.m.)
stone, semiprecious samotsvet (n.m.)
stony kamenistyi (adj.)
stool taburet(ka) (n.m.(f.))
stoop gorbit'sya (v.impf.)
nagibat'sya (v.impf.)
sgorbit'sya (v.pf.)
sutulit'sya (v.impf.)
stop ostanavlivat'(sya) (v.impf.)
ostanovit' (v.pf.)
ostanovka (n.f.)
perestat' (v.pf.)
perestavat' (v.impf.)
prekratit' (v.pf.)
stat' (v.pf.)
stop! stoi (imp.)
stop stop (n.m.)
stoyanka (n.f.)
stoyat' (v.impf.)
unimat'(sya) (v.impf.)
stop short osekat'sya (v.impf.)
stop up zakuporivat' (v.impf.)

zatknut' (v.pf.)
zatykat' (v.pf.)
stoppage pereboi (n.m.)
storage khranenie (n.n.)
zapominanie (n.n.)
store magazin (n.m.)
pripasat' (v.impf.)
zapasti (v.pf.)
storehouse baza (n.f.)
sklad (n.m.)
storeroom chulan (n.m.)
kladovaya (n.f.)
stork aist (n.m.)
storm burya (n.f.)
bushevat' (v.impf.)
grozovoi (adj.)
shtorm (n.m.)
shturm (n.m.)
shturmovat' (v.impf.)
storm petrel burevestnik (n.m.)
stormy burnyi (adj.)
story povest' (n.f.)
rasskaz (n.m.)
story, imaginary nebylitsa (n.f.)
story, short novella (n.f.)
story, true byl' (n.f.)
storyteller skazitel' (n.m.)
stout, to grow tolstet' (v.impf.)
stove pech' (n.f.)
pechka (n.f.)
plita (n.f.)
plitka (n.f.)
stove, primus primus (n.m.)
straight napryamik (adv.)
pryamo (adv.)
pryamoi (adj.)
straighten raspravit' (v.pf.)
raspravlyat' (v.impf.)
vypryamit' (v.pf.)
vypryamlyat' (v.impf.)
straighten out razgibat'(sya) (v.impf.)
razognut' (v.pf.)
straightforward pryamolineinyi (adj.)
strain napryach' (v.pf.)
napryagat' (v.impf.)
strain off stsedit' (v.pf.)
strait(s) proliv (n.m.)
strange postoronnii (adj.)
(cont'd)

strannyi (adj.)

strangle dushit' (v.impf.)

    udavit' (v.pf.)

    zadushit' (v.pf.)

strap lyamka (n.f.)

strap, shoulder pogon (n.m.)

strap with metal okovat' (v.pf.)

strategist strateg (n.m.)

stratification nasloenie (n.n.)

    rassloenie (n.n.)

    stratifikatsiya (n.f.)

stratified sloistyi (adj.)

stratified, to become rasslaivat'sya (v.impf.)

stratospheric balloon stratostat (n.m.)

stratum plast (n.m.)

straw soloma (n.f.)

strawberries, wild kaban (n.m.)

strawberry klubnika (n.f.)

stray plutat' (v.impf.)

stream struit'sya (v.impf.)

streamlined obtekaemyi (adj.)

street ulichnyi (adj.)

    ulitsa (n.f.)

street, back zakoulok (n.m.)

street organ sharmanka (n.f.)

street, side pereulok (n.m.)

streetcar tramvai (n.m.)

strength krepost' (n.f.)

    prochnost' (n.f.)

    sila (n.f.)

strength, beyond one's neposil'nyi (adj.)

strength, of equal ravnosil'nyi (adj.)

strength, to measure one's tyagat'sya (v.impf.)

strengthen krepit' (v.impf.)

    podkrepit' (v.pf.)

    ukrepit' (v.pf.)

    uprochit' (v.pf.)

stress upor (n.m.)

    usilie (n.n.)

stretch natyagivat' (v.impf.)

    natyanut' (v.pf.)

    natyazhka (n.f.)

    prostirat'sya (v.impf.)

    protyagivat' (v.impf.)

    protyanut' (v.pf.)

    rastyagivat'(sya) (v.impf.)

    rastyanut' (v.pf.)

    tyanut'sya (v.impf.)

    vytyagivat'(sya) (v.impf.)

    vytyanyt' (v.pf.)

stretch oneself potyagivat'sya (v.impf.)

    potyanut'sya (v.pf.)

stretcher nosilki (n.pl.)

stretching rastyazhenie (n.n.)

strew obsypat' (v.pf.)

    useivat' (v.impf.)

    usypat' (v.pf.)

strewn useyannyi (adj.)

strict strogii (adj.)

strictly nastrogo (adv.)

    sobstvenno (adv.)

strike chirkat' (v.impf.)

    porazit' (v.pf.)

    probit' (v.pf.)

    stachka (n.f.)

    udarit' (v.pf.)

    zabastovka (n.f.)

strike a bargain storgovat'sya (v.pf.)

strike, hunger golodovka (n.f.)

strike out vycherkivat' (v.impf.)

    zacherkivat' (v.impf.)

strike, to be on bastovat' (v.impf.)

strike, to go on zabastovat' (v.pf.)

strikebreaker shtreikbrekher (n.m.)

striker stachechnik (n.m.)

striking razitel'nyi (adj.)

string bechevka (n.f.)

    nanizat' (v.pf.)

    shnur (n.m.)

    shpagat (n.m.)

    struna (n.f.)

    strunnyi (adj.)

    zavyazka (n.f.)

strip ogolyat'(sya) (v.impf.)

    polosa (n.f.)

    polosatyi (adj.)

stripe nashivka (n.f.)

strive dobivat'sya (v.impf.)

stroke gladit' (v.impf.)

    makh (n.m.)

    vzmakh (n.m.)

stroll gulyan'e (n.n.)

    razgulivat' (v.impf.)

strong krepkii (adj.)

    sil'nyi (adj.)

strong, to grow okrepnut' (v.pf.)
stronger, to get krepnut' (v.impf.)
stronger, to grow krepchat' (v.impf.)
stronghold oplot (n.m.)
   tverdynya (n.f.)
strong-willed volevoi (adj.)
strontium strontsii (adj.)
struck dumb, to be otoropet' (v.pf.)
structure stroenie (n.n.)
   struktura (n.f.)
   uklad (n.m.)
struggle bor'ba (n.f.)
   borot'sya (v.impf.)
stubborn nepodatlivyi (adj.)
stuck in, to be pogryazat' (v.impf.)
stuck, to get zastrevat' (v.impf.)
   zastryat' (v.pf.)
   zavyaznut' (v.pf.)
student kursant (n.m.)
   student (n.m.)
   uchashchiisya (n.m.)
   uchenik (n.m.)
student, excellent otlichnik (n.m.)
student, external vol'noslushatel' (n.m.)
   zaochnik (n.m.)
studies ucheba (n.f.)
   uchenie (n.n.)
studio atel'e (n.n.)
   studiya (n.f.)
study étyud (n.m.)
   izuchat' (v.impf.)
   kabinet (n.m.)
   prorabatyvat' (v.impf.)
   razuchivat' (v.impf.)
study group, political politkruzhok (n.m.)
stuff nachinit' (v.pf.)
   pichkat' (v.impf.)
stuffed animal chuchelo (n.n.)
stuffing farsh (n.m.)
stuffy dushno (adj.)
stumble ostupat'sya (v.impf.)
   spotknut'sya (v.pf.)
stump obrubok (n.m.)
   pen' (n.m.)
   ogryzok (n.m.)
stun oglushit' (v.pf.)
   oshelomit' (v.pf.)
stupefied, to be obaldevat' (v.impf.)

   obomlet' (v.pf.)
stupefy odurmanivat' (v.impf.)
stupid bestolkovyi (adj.)
   odurelyi (adj.)
stupid, to do something sglupit' (v.pf.)
stupid, to grow glupet' (v.impf.)
stupidity tupoumie (n.n.)
stupidly glupo (adv.)
stupor odur' (n.f.)
stupor, dull otupenie (n.n.)
stupor, to be in a otupet' (v.pf.)
sturgeon osetrina (n.f.)
sturgeon, beluga beluga (n.f.)
sty yachmen' (n.m.)
style slog (n.m.)
   stil' (n.m.)
stylistic stilisticheskii (adj.)
subbotnik subbotnik (n.m.)
subconscious podsoznatel'nyi (adj.)
subcortex podkorka (n.f.)
subdivision podrazdelenie (n.n.)
subdue smirit' (v.pf.)
subject poddannyi (adj.)
   podlezhashchee (n.n.)
   podvergnut' (v.pf.)
   sub"ekt (n.m.)
subject to, to be podlezhat' (v.impf.)
subjunctive soslagatel'nyi (adj.)
sublimate, corrosive sulema (n.f.)
submachine gunner avtomatchik (n.m.)
submarine podvodnyi (adj.)
submariner podvodnik (n.m.)
submission pokornost' (n.f.)
submit pokorit'sya (v.impf.)
   smiryat'sya (v.impf)
subordination podchinenie (n.n.)
subscribe podpisyvat'sya (v.impf.)
subscription abonement (n.m.)
   podpiska (n.f.)
subside skhlynut' (v.pf.)
   spadat' (v.impf.)
subsidiary podsobnyi (adj.)
subsidize subsidirovat' (v.impf.)
subsidy subsidiya (n.f.)
subsistence propitanie (n.n.)
subsonic dozvukovoi (adj.)
substance substantsiya (n.f.)
   veshchestvo (n.n.)

substation podstantsiya (n.f.)
substitute surrogat (n.m.)
   zamenitel' (n.m.)
substitution podmena (n.f.)
   zamena (n.f.)
substrate substrat (n.m.)
subtitle podzagolovok (n.m.)
subtraction vychitanie (n.n.)
subtrahend vychitaemoe (n.n.)
subtropical subtropicheskii (adj.)
suburb okraina (n.f.)
   predmest'e (n.n.)
   prigorod (n.m.)
subway metro (n.n.)
succeed preuspet' (v.pf.)
   preuspevat' (v.impf.)
   sumet' (v.pf.)
success udacha (n.f.)
   uspekh (n.m.)
success, to be a udat'sya (v.pf.)
   udavat'sya (v.impf.)
successful uspeshnyi (adj.)
succession preemstvennost' (n.f.)
successor preemnik (n.m.)
such takoi (adj.)
   takov (p.)
suck sosat' (v.impf.)
suck in vsasyvat' (v.impf.)
   vsosat' (v.pf.)
   zasasyvat' (v.impf.)
   zasosat' (v.pf.)
suck out vysasyvat' (v.impf.)
   vysosat' (v.pf.)
suckling pig porosenok (n.m.)
sudden skoropostizhnyi (adj.)
   vnezapnyi (adj.)
suddenly vdrug (adv.)
suede zamsha (n.f.)
suffer naterpet'sya (v.pf.)
   postradat' (v.pf.)
   poterpet' (v.pf.)
   preterpevat' (v.impf.)
   stradat' (v.impf.)
   terpet' (v.impf.)
   vystradat' (v.pf.)
suffered, to have perestradat' (v.pf.)
sufferer stradalets (n.m.)
sufficient dostatochnyi (adj.)

sufficient, to be khvatat' (v.impf.)
   khvatit' (v.pf.)
suffix suffiks (n.m.)
suffocate udushat' (v.impf.)
   zadokhnut'sya (v.pf.)
   zadykhat'sya (v.impf.)
suffocating udushlivyi (adj.)
suffocation udush'e (n.n.)
sugar sakhar (n.m.)
sugar, lump kolotyi sakhar (adj.-n.m.)
sugary slashchavyi (adj.)
suggest predlozhit' (v.pf.)
   vnushat' (v.impf.)
suggest (an idea) natolknut' (v.pf.)
suggestion predlozhenie (n.n.)
suicide samoubiistvo (n.n.)
suit kostyum (n.m.)
suit, diving skafandr (n.m.)
suit, space skafandr (n.m.)
suitable podkhodyashchii (adj.)
suitable, to be godit'sya (v.impf.)
suitcase chemodan (n.m.)
suite svita (n.f.)
suited, not neprisposoblennyi (adj.)
sulfate sul'fat (n.m.)
sulfide, hydrogen serovodorod (n.m.)
sulfureous sernistyi (adj.)
sulfuric sernyi (adj.)
sulky nadutyi (adj.)
sulky, to be dut'sya (v.impf.)
sullen ugryumyi (adj.)
sullenly ispodlob'ya (adv.)
sulphur sera (n.f.)
sultan sultan (n.m.)
sum itog (n.m.)
   summa (n.f.)
sum up podytozhivat' (v.impf.)
summarize rezyumirovat' (v.impf.)
summary konspekt (n.m.)
   svodka (n.f.)
   svodnyi (adj.)
summer letnii (adj.)
   leto (n.n.)
summer cottage dacha (n.f.)
summer lightning zarnitsa (n.f.)
summit vershina (n.f.)
summon sozvat' (v.pf.)
   vyzvat' (v.pf.)

summons povestka (n.f.)
  vyzov (n.m.)
sun solnechnyi (adj.)
  solntse (n.n.)
Sunday voskresen'e (n.n.)
sunflower podsolnechnik (n.m.)
sung couplets chastushki (n.pl.)
sunset zakat (n.m.)
  zakhod (n.m.)
suntan zagar (n.m.)
suntanned zagorelyi (adj.)
suntanned, to get zagorat' (v.impf.)
super statist (n.m.)
superconductivity sverkhprovodimost' (n.f.)
superficial poverkhnostnyi (adj.)
superfluous lishnii (adj.)
superhuman nechelovecheskii (adj.)
supernatural sverkh''estestvennyi (adj.)
supernumerary sverkhshtatnyi (adj.)
superprofit sverkhpribyl' (n.f.)
supersonic ul'trazvukovoi (adj.)
superstition sueverie (n.n.)
superstructure nadstroika (n.f.)
supervision nadsmotr (n.m.)
  nadzor (n.m.)
supper uzhin (n.m.)
supplement dopolnit' (v.pf.)
  prilozhenie (n.n.)
supplementary earnings prirabotok (n.m.)
supply snabdit' (v.pf.)
  zapas (n.m.)
support opora (n.f.)
  podderzhat' (v.pf)
supporter storonnik (n.m.)
supposition predpolozhenie (n.n.)
suppress podavit' (v.pf.)
  podavlyat' (v.impf.)
  umalchivat' (v.impf.)
  umolchat' (v.pf.)
suppression podavlenie (n.n.)
suppuration nagnoenie (n.n.)
supremacy glavenstvo (n.n.)
supreme verkhovnyi (adj.)
surf priboi (n.m.)
surface poverkhnost' (n.f.)
surface, smooth glad' (n.f.)
surface, to come to the vsplyvat' (v.pf.)
surfeit presytit'sya (v.pf.)

surgeon khirurg (n.m.)
surgical operativnyi (adj.)
surname familiya (n.f.)
surpass prevoskhodit' (v.impf.)
  prevzoiti (v.pf.)
surplus izlishek (n.m.)
surprise syurpriz (n.m.)
surprised, to be porazhat'sya (v.impf.)
surrender sdacha (n.f.)
  sdavat'(sya) (v.impf.)
surreptitiously vtikhomolku (adv.)
surround obstupat' (v.impf.)
  okruzhat' (v.impf.)
  otsepit' (v.pf.)
survey obzor (n.m.)
survey, geological geologorazvedka (n.f.)
surveying, land geodeziya (n.f.)
surveyor, land zemlemer (n.m.)
survival perezhitok (n.m.)
survive vyzhit' (v.pf.)
  vyzhivat' (v.impf.)
susceptible vospriimchivyi (adj.)
suspect podozrevat' (v.impf.)
  zapodozrit' (v.pf.)
suspend priostanavlivat' (v.impf.)
  priveshivat' (v.impf.)
  privesit' (v.pf.)
suspender podvyazka (n.f.)
suspenders podtyazhki (n.pl.)
suspension suspenziya (n.f.)
  vzves' (n.f.)
sustained nezatukhayushchii (adj.)
swaddle pelenat' (v.impf.)
  zapelenat' (v.pf.)
swaddling clothes pelenki (n.pl.)
swaggering chvanstvo (n.n.)
swallow glotat' (v.impf.)
  lastochka (n.f.)
  proglatyvat' (v.impf.)
swamp boloto (n.n.)
swampy bolotistyi (adj.)
  bolotnyi (adj.)
  topkii (adj.)
swan lebed' (n.m.)
  lebedinyi (adj.)
swarm koposhit'sya (v.impf.)
  roi (n.m.)
  roit'sya (v.impf.)

sway kolykhat'(sya) (v.impf.)
   raskachivat'(sya) (v.impf.)
   shatat' (v.impf.)
swear obrugat' (v.pf.)
   poklyast'sya (v.pf.)
swearing bran' (n.f.)
   rugan' (n.f.)
swearword rugatel'stvo (n.n.)
sweat pot (n.m.)
   potet' (v.impf.)
   vspotet' (v.pf.)
sweater sviter (n.m.)
sweaty potnyi (adj.)
Swede shved (n.m.)
sweep mesti (v.impf.)
   podmetat' (v.impf.)
   vymesti (v.pf.)
   vymetat' (v.impf.)
sweep away otmesti (v.pf.)
   otmetat' (v.impf.)
   razmetat' (v.pf.)
   smesti (v.pf.)
   smetat' (v.impf.)
sweep up zamesti (v.pf.)
   zametat' (v.impf.)
sweepings sor (n.m.)
sweet pritornyi (adj.)
   sladkii (adj.)
sweet tooth slastena (n.f.)
sweetness sladost' (n.f.)
swell nabukhat' (v.impf.)
   nabukhnut' (v.pf.)
   opukhat' (v.impf.)
   otech' (v.pf.)
   otekat' (v.impf.)
   pukhnut' (v.impf.)
   raspukhat' (v.impf.)
   razbukhat' (v.impf.)
   razduvat'sya (v.impf.)
swelling opukhol' (n.f.)
   vzdutie (n.n.)
swift molnienosnyi (adj.)
swill poilo (n.n.)
swim doplyvat' (v.impf.)
   plavat' (v.impf.)
   plyt' (v.impf.)
   proplyvat' (v.impf.)
   zaplyvat' (v.impf.)

swim away uplyvat' (v.impf.)
swim out vyplyvat' (v.impf.)
swimmer plovets (n.m.)
swimming plavanie (n.n.)
swimming across vplav' (adv.)
swindler moshennik (n.m.)
   zhulik (n.m.)
swing kacheli (n.pl.)
   pomakhivat' (v.impf.)
   raskachat' (v.pf.)
   raskachivat'(sya) (v.impf.)
Swiss shveitsarets (n.m.)
switch pereklyuchat' (v.impf.)
   pereklyuchatel' (n.m.)
   vyklyuchatel' (n.m.)
switchboard kommutator (n.m.)
switchman strelochnik (n.m.)
swollen raspukhshii (adj.)
sword mech (n.m.)
   shashka (n.f.)
   shpaga (n.f.)
sword-hilt éfes (n.m.)
syllable slog (n.m.)
symbiosis simbioz (n.m.)
symbol podpisat' (n.m.)
   simvol (n.m.)
symbolize simvolizirovat' (v.impf.)
symmetry simmetriya (n.f.)
sympathetic otzyvchivyi (adj.)
   uchastlivyi (adj.)
sympathize simpatizirovat' (v.impf.)
   sochuvstvovat' (v.impf.)
symphony simfonicheskii (adj.)
   simfoniya (n.f.)
symptom simptom (n.m.)
synagogue sinagoga (n.f.)
synchophasotron sinkhofazotron (n.m.)
synchronization sinkhronizatsiya (n.f.)
syndicate sindikat (n.m.)
syndrome sindrom (n.m.)
synod sinod (n.m.)
synonym sinonim (n.m.)
synonymous odnoznachnyi (adj.)
syntax sintaksis (n.m.)
synthesis sintez (n.m.)
syphilis sifilis (n.m.)
syringe shprits (n.m.)
   sprintsevat' (v.impf.)

syrup sirop (n.m.)
system sistema (n.f.)
  stroi (n.m.)

system, standby dublirovanie (n.n.)
systematic planomernyi (adj.)
systematization sistematika (n.f.)

T (T, Ц)

table nastol'nyi (adj.)
  stol (n.m.)
  tablitsa (n.f.)
tablecloth skatert' (n.f.)
tachometer takhometr (n.m.)
taciturn nerazgovorchivyi (adj.)
tack smetat' (v.impf.)
tact delikatnost' (n.f.)
  takt (n.m.)
tactful taktichnyi (adj.)
tactics taktika (n.f.)
tactile osyazatel'nyi (adj.)
tactless bestaktnyi (adj.)
  netaktichnyi (adj.)
tadpole golovastik (n.m.)
Tadzhik tadzhik (n.m.)
taffeta tafta (n.f.)
tail khvost (n.m.)
tailor portnoi (n.m.)
take brat' (v.impf.)
  podkhvatit' (v.pf.)
  privivat'sya (v.impf.)
  razobrat' (v.pf.)
  snesti (v.pf.)
  svozit' (v.impf.)
  vzyat' (v.pf.)
  zavesti (v.pf.)
take a hair of the dog that bit you
  opokhmelit'sya (v.pf.)
take apart razobrat' (v.pf.)
take as far as dovezti (v.pf.)
take aside otozvat' (v.pf.)
takc away otbavit' (v.pf.)
  otbirat' (v.impf.)
  otnyat' (v.pf.)
  otobrat' (v.pf.)
  otvezti (v.pf.)
  otvozit' (v.impf.)

  unesti (v.pf.)
  unosit' (v.impf.)
  uvesti (v.pf.)
  uvezti (v.pf.)
  uvodit' (v.impf.)
  uvozit' (v.impf.)
  zabirat' (v.impf.)
  zabrat' (v.pf.)
take care berech' (v.impf.)
  pozabotit'sya (v.pf.)
take heart muzhat'sya (v.impf.)
  vospryanut' (v.pf.)
take into consideration uchest' (v.pf.)
  uchityvat' (n.impf.)
take leave proshchat'sya (v.impf.)
  rasproshchat'sya (v.pf.)
take leave of prostit'sya (v.pf.)
  rasprostit'sya (v.pf.)
take off snyat' (v.pf.)
  vzletat' (v.impf.)
take out vynimat' (v.impf.)
  vynut' (v.pf.)
  vyvesti (v.impf.)
  vyvezti (v.pf.)
take over perenimat' (v.impf.)
  perenyat' (v.pf.)
take pity on szhalit'sya (v.pf.)
take possession ovladevat' (v.impf.)
take possession of zavladevat' (v.impf.)
take root ukorenit'sya (v.pf.)
take to otnesti (v.pf.)
  otnosit' (v.impf.)
  zaladit' (v.pf.)
taken back, to be opeshit' (v.pf.)
takeoff otlet (n.m.)
  vzlet (n.m.)
talc tal'k (n.m.)
tale skazka (n.f.)

talent darovanie (n.n.)
    talant (n.m.)
talisman talisman (n.m.)
talk besedovat' (v.impf.)
    nagovorit' (v.pf.)
talk back perechit' (v.impf.)
talkative boltlivyi (adj.)
    govorlivyi (adj.)
    slovookhotlivyi (adj.)
talking, to finish dogovarivat' (v.impf.)
    dogovorit' (v.pf.)
talking, to start zagovarivat' (v.impf.)
    zagovorit' (v.pf.)
tall roslyi (adj.)
    vysokii (adj.)
tallow stearin (n.m.)
tally with vyazat'sya (v.impf.)
tame priruchat' (v.impf.)
tamer ukrotitel' (n.m.)
tangent kasatel'naya (n.f.)
    tangens (n.m.)
tangerine mandarin (n.m.)
tangible oshchutimyi (adj.)
tangilbe osyazaemyi (adj.)
tank tank (n.m.)
    tsisterna (n.f.)
tantalum tantal (n.m.)
tantamount to, to be ravnosil'nyi (adj.)
tape tes'ma (n.f.)
    tesemka (n.f.)
tar gudron (n.m.)
target mishen' (n.f.)
    tsel' (n.f.)
tariff taksa (n.f.)
    tarif (n.m.)
tarpaulin brezent (n.m.)
tarry zameshkat'sya (v.pf.)
tart terpkii (adj.)
Tartar tatarin (n.m.)
TASS (Telegraph Agency of the Soviet Union)
    TASS (abbr.)
taste vkus (n.m.)
taste bitter gorchit' (v.impf.)
taste, bitter gorech' (n.f.)
tasteless bezvkusnyi (adj.)
tavern pivnaya (n.f.)
tax nalog (n.m.)
    obrok (n.m.)

    podat' (n.f.)
taxation oblozhenie (n.n.)
taxi taksi (n.n.)
taxpayer nalogoplatel'shchik (n.m.)
tea chai (n.m.)
teach nauchit' (v.pf.)
    uchit' (v.impf.)
    vyuchit' (v.pf.)
teach a lesson prouchit' (v.pf.)
teacher pedagog (n.m.)
    uchitel' (n.m.)
teaching prepodavanie (n.n.)
teach-yourself book samouchitel' (n.m.)
team upryazhka (n.f.)
    zapryazhka (n.f.)
team leader zven'evoi (n.m.)
team, propaganda agitbrigada (n.f.)
teapot chainik (n.m.)
tear drat' (v.impf.)
    nadorvat' (v.pf.)
    porvat' (v.pf.)
    poryvat' (v.impf.)
    razorvat' (v.pf.)
    razryvat' (v.impf.)
    rvat' (v.impf.)
    rvat'sya (v.impf.)
    sleza (n.f.)
tear gas slezotochivyi gaz (adj.-n.m.)
tear off otdirat' (v.impf.)
    otorvat' (v.pf.)
    sorvat' (v.pf.)
    sryvat' (v.impf.)
tear to pieces izorvat' (v.pf.)
    rasterzat' (v.pf.)
    razdirat' (v.impf.)
    razodrat' (v.pf.)
    zadrat' (v.pf.)
tear, to shed a proslezit'sya (v.pf.)
tears, to burst into rasplakat'sya (v.pf.)
tears, shed poplakat' (v.pf.)
tear-stained zaplakannyi (adj.)
tease draznit' (v.impf.)
    poddraznivat' (v.impf.)
    podtrunivat' (v.impf.)
    razdraznit' (v.pf.)
technical tekhnicheskii (adj.)
technical school tekhnikum (n.m.)
technician tekhnik (n.m.)

technological tekhnologicheskii (adj.)
technologist tekhnolog (n.m.)
technology tekhnika (n.f.)
tectonics tektonika (n.f.)
tedious nudnyi (adj.)
teem with kishmya kishet' (v.impf.)
teenager podrostok (n.m.)
telegram telegramma (n.f.)
telegraph telegraf (n.m.)
telephone telefon (n.m.)
   telefonirovat' (v.impf.)
   telefonnyi (adj.)
telephone message telefonogramma (n.f.)
telescope teleskop (n.m.)
television televidenie (n.n.)
tell a lie navrat' (v.pf.)
   sovrat' (v.pf.)
tell lies izolgat'sya (v.pf.)
tell on skazyvat'sya (v.impf.)
teller schetchik (n.m.)
tellurium tellur (n.m.)
temper zakalyat' (v.impf.)
temper, hot vspyl'chivost' (n.f.)
temper, in a fit of sgoryacha (adv.)
temperament temperament (n.m.)
temperature temperatura (n.f.)
tempering zakal (n.m.)
temple khram (n.m.)
   visok (n.m.)
tempo temp (n.m.)
temporary vremennyi (adj.)
tempt iskushat' (v.impf.)
temptation soblazn (n.m.)
ten desyat' (num.)
   desyatok (n.m.)
ten times vdesyatero (adv.)
tenacious tsepkii (adj.)
tenant s''emshchik (n.m.)
   zhilets (n.m.)
tend vykhodit' (v.pf.)
ten-day desyatidnevnyi (adj.)
ten-day period dekada (n.f.)
tendency tendentsiya (n.f.)
tendentious tendentsioznyi (adj.)
tender laskovyi (adj.)
tenderness nezhnost' (n.f.)
   umilenie (n.n.)
tendon sukhozhilie (n.n.)

tenfold desyatikratnyi (adj.)
ten-kopeck coin grivennik (n.m.)
tennis tennis (n.m.)
tenor tenor (n.m.)
ten-ruble bill desyatka (n.f.)
tent palatka (n.f.)
   shater (n.m.)
tentacle shchupal'tse (n.n.)
ten-year desyatiletnii (adj.)
term semestr (n.m.)
   srok (n.m.)
   termin (n.m.)
terrace terrasa (n.f.)
terrible uzhasnyi (adj.)
   zhutkii (adj.)
territorial territorial'nyi (adj.)
territory territoriya (n.f.)
terror terror (n.m.)
terse nemnogoslovnyi (adj.)
tertiary tretichnyi (adj.)
test proba (n.f.)
   zachet (n.m.)
test tube probirka (n.f.)
testify zasvidetel'stvovat' (v.pf.)
tetanus stolbnyak (n.m.)
tete-a-tete naedine (adv.)
text tekst (n.m.)
textile tekstil'nyi (adj.)
thallium tallii (n.m.)
than chem (conj.)
thank blagodarit' (v.impf.)
   poblagodarit' (v.pf.)
thanks spasibo (part.)
thanks to blagodarya (prep.)
that chto (conj.)
   ta (p.)
   to (p.)
   togo (p.)
   tomu (p.)
   tot (p.)
that is why ottogo (adv.)
   potomu (adv.)
that'll do budet (pred.)
thaw ottepel' (n.f.)
   rastayat' (v.pf.)
thaw out ottaivat' (v.impf.)
   ottayat' (v.pf.)
theater teatr (n.m.)

theft   krazha (n.f.)
    pokrazha (n.f.)
their   ikh (p.)
them   ikh (p.)
    im (p.)
then   nu (part.)
    to (adv.)
    togda (adv.)
    zatem (adv.)
theorem   teorema (n.f.)
theoretical   teoreticheskii (adj.)
theoretician   teoretik (n.m.)
theory   teoriya (n.f.)
therapeutic   lechebnyi (adj.)
there   tam (adv.)
    tuda (adv.)
    von (part.)
    vot (part.)
there, from   ottuda (adv.)
there is nobody to   nekogo (p.)
    nekomu (p.)
therefore   poétomu (adv.)
thermal   teplovoi (adj.)
    termicheskii (adj.)
thermodynamics   termodinamika (n.f.)
thermometer   termometr (n.m.)
thermonuclear   termoyadernyi (adj.)
thermos   termos (n.m.)
thermostat   termostat (n.m.)
these   éti (p.)
thesis   dissertatsiya (n.f.)
    tezis (n.m.)
they   oni (p.)
thick   gustoi (adj.)
    tolstyi (adj.)
thick and fast   gradom (adv.)
thick pancake   olad'ya (n.f.)
thick, to get   zagustet' (v.pf.)
thicken   gustet' (v.impf.)
    sgushchat'(sya) (v.impf.)
    sgustit' (v.pf.)
thickening   utolshchenie (n.n.)
thicket   chashcha (n.f.)
thickets   debri (n.pl.)
thickness   tolshchina (n.f.)
thick-skinned   tolstokozhii (adj.)
thief   vor (n.m.)
thigh   bedro (n.n.)

    lyazhka (n.f.)
thimble   naperstok (n.m.)
thin   khudoi (adj.)
    khudoshchavyi (adj.)
    tonkii (adj.)
thin, to become   osunut'sya (v.pf.)
thin, to grow   khudet' (v.impf.)
    redet' (v.impf.)
thing   veshch' (n.f.)
think   dumat' (v.impf.)
    mnit' (v.impf.)
    myslit' (v.impf.)
    podumat' (v.pf.)
    polagat' (v.impf.)
think better of   odumat'sya (v.pf.)
think fit   zablagorassudit'sya (v.pf.)
think of   pridumat' (v.pf.)
    zagadat' (v.pf.)
think out   soobrazhat' (v.impf.)
think over   obmozgovat' (v.pf.)
    produmat' (v.pf.)
    vdumat'sya (v.pf.)
thinker   myslitel' (n.m.)
thinking   myshlenie (n.n.)
thinness   tonkost' (n.f.)
third   tretii (adj.)
thirst   zhazhda (n.f.)
thirteen   trinadtsat' (num.)
thirteenth   trinadtsatyi (adj.)
thirtieth   tridtsatyi (adj.)
thirty   tridtsat' (num.)
this   éta (p.)
    éto (p.)
    étot (p.)
    sei (p.)
thorium   torii (n.m.)
thorn   ship (n.m.)
thorny   ternistyi (adj.)
thorough   ot"yavlennyi (adj.)
thoroughbred   chistokrovnyi (adj.)
thoroughly   khoroshen'ko (adv.)
those   te (p.)
    tekh (p.)
    tem (p.)
    temi (p.)
thought   duma (n.f.)
    mysl' (n.f.)
    pomysel (n.m.)

thought, to be lost in   zadumat'sya (v.pf.)
thoughtful   glubokomyslennyi (adj.)
thoughtful mood   razdum'e (n.n.)
thoughtful, to become   prizadumat'sya
     (v.impf.)
thoughtlessness   nedomyslie (n.n.)
thousand   tysyacha (num.)
thousandth   tysyachnyi (adj.)
thrashing, to give a   pokolotit' (v.pf.)
thread   nit' (n.f.)
     nitka (n.f.)
     rez'ba (n.f.)
threat   ugroza (n.f.)
threaten   grozit' (v.impf.)
     prigrozit' (v.pf.)
     ugrozhat' (v.impf.)
     zamakhivat'sya (v.impf.)
threatening   groznyi (adj.)
three   tri (num.)
     troe (num.)
     troika (n.f.)
three, all   vtroem (adv.)
three hundred   trista (num.)
three times   trizhdy (adv.)
     vtroe (adv.)
three-colored   trekhtsvetnyi (adj.)
three-day   trekhdnevnyi (adj.)
threefold   troekratnyi (adj.)
three-month   trekhmesyachnyi (adj.)
three-seater   trekhmestnyi (adj.)
three-shift   trekhsmennyi (adj.)
three-story   trekhétazhnyi (adj.)
three-year   trekhgodichnyi (adj.)
     trekhletnii (adj.)
thresh   molotit' (v.impf.)
     obmolachivat' (v.impf.)
thresher   molotilka (n.f.)
threshhold   porog (n.m.)
threshing   molot'ba (n.f.)
     obmolot (n.m.)
threshing barn   riga (n.f.)
threshing floor   gumno (n.n.)
thrifty   berezhlivyi (adj.)
throat   glotka (n.f.)
     gorlo (n.n.)
throat, to clear one's   otkashlivat'sya
     (v.impf.)
throbbing   bienie (n.n.)

throne   prestol (n.m.)
     tron (n.m.)
throng   kishet' (v.impf.)
     povalit' (v.pf.)
through   cherez (prep.)
     naskvoz' (adv.)
     navylet (adv.)
     skvoz' (prep.)
through with, to be   razdelat'sya (v.pf.)
throw   brosat' (v.impf.)
     brosit' (v.pf.)
     kidat'(sya) (v.impf.)
     kinut' (v.pf.)
     metat' (v.impf.)
     zabrasyvat' (v.impf.)
     zabrosat' (v.pf.)
     zabrosit' (v.pf.)
     zakidyvat' (v.impf.)
     zakinut' (v.pf.)
throw away   otbrasyvat' (v.impf.)
     otkinut' (v.pf)
throw back   zaprokidyvat' (v.impf.)
throw down   povalit' (v.pf.)
     povergat' (v.impf.)
     sbit' (v.pf.)
     sbrasyvat' (v.impf.)
     sbrosit' (v. pf.)
     svalivat' (v.impf.)
     valit' (v.impf.)
throw off   skinut' (v.pf.)
throw on   nabrasyvat' (v.impf.)
     nabrosit' (v.pf.)
     nakidyvat' (v.impf.)
     nakinut' (v.pf.)
throw open   raspakhivat' (v.impf.)
throw out   vybrosit' (v.pf.)
     vykidyvat' (v.impf.)
     vykinut' (v.pf)
throw over   perebrasyvat' (v.impf.)
     perebrosit' (v.pf.)
     perekidyvat' (v.impf.)
throw up   izvergat' (v.impf.)
     podbrasyvat' (v.impf.)
     podkidyvat' (v.impf.)
throwing   metanie (n.n.)
thrush   drozd (n.m.)
thrust   vonzat' (v.impf.)
thrust in   votknut' (v.pf.)

thrust out vykalyvat' (v.impf.)
    vykolot' (v.pf.)
thud, to fall with a shlepat'sya (v.impf.)
thunder gremet' (v.impf.)
    grom (n.m.)
thunderous gromovoi (adj.)
thunderstorm groza (n.f.)
thus itak (conj.)
thyroid shchitovidnyi (adj.)
tic tik (n.m.)
tick tikan'e (n.n.)
ticket bilet (n.m.)
ticket, reserved seat platskarta (n.f.)
ticking tik (n.m.)
tickle shchekotat' (v.impf.)
tickling shchekotka (n.f.)
tide, high priliv (n.m.)
tide, low otliv (n.m.)
tidy opravit' (v.pf.)
    opryatnyi (adj.)
tie galstuk (n.m.)
    obvyazat' (v.pf.)
    povyazat' (v.pf.)
    povyazyvat' (v.impf.)
    privyazat' (v.pf.)
tie, bind svyazat' (v.pf.)
tie, connection, communication svyaz' (n.f.)
tie up perevyazat' (v.pf.)
    podvyazat' (v.pf.)
    podvyazyvat' (v.impf.)
    uvyazat' (v.pf.)
    uvyazyvat' (v.impf.)
    vyazat' (v.impf.)
    zavyazat' (v.pf.)
    zavyazyvat' (v.impf.)
tiger tigr (n.m.)
tight natyanutyi (adj.)
    tugoi (adj.)
    uzkii (adj.)
tight, to become okhmelet' (v.pf.)
tight, to make obuzit' (v.pf.)
tighten styagivat' (v.impf.)
    styanut' (v.pf.)
    zatyagivat' (v.impf.)
    zatyanut' (v.pf.)
tightfisted prizhimistyi (adj.)
tightly naglukho (adv.)
tights kolgotki (n.pl.)

triko (n.n.)
tilde til'da (n.f.)
tile cherepitsa (n.f.)
    izrazets (n.m.)
    plitka (n.f.)
tilted nabekren' (adv.)
timber tembr (n.m.)
timber, shaped pilomaterial (n.m.)
timbered brevenchatyi (adj.)
time pora (n.f.)
    priurochit' (v.pf.)
    raz (n.m.)
    vremya (n.n.)
time, for a long nadolgo (adv.)
time for, to find udosuzhit'sya (v.pf.)
time for, to have uspet' (v.pf.)
time, in vo-vremya (adv.)
time, in good zablagovremenno (adv.)
time, one at a poodinochke (adv.)
time, there is no nekogda (adv.)
time, to be in pospet' (v.pf.)
    pospevat' (v.impf.)
time, to come in podospet' (v.pf.)
time, to have no nedosug (n.m.)
time, to pass korotat' (v.impf.)
times, many mnogokratno (adv.)
times, olden starina (n.f.)
timesheet tabel' (n.m.)
timetable grafik (n.m.)
timid boyazlivyi (adj.)
    robkii (adj.)
timid, to be robet' (v.impf.)
tin ludit' (v.impf.)
    olovo (n.n.)
    zhest' (n.f.)
tinfoil staniol' (n.f.)
tinsel mishura (n.f.)
tiny krokhotnyi (adj.)
tip konchik (n.m.)
    nakonechnik (n.m.)
tipsy navesele (adv.)
    podvypivshii (adj.)
tiptoe tsypochki (n.pl.)
tire shina (n.f.)
    utomit' (v.pf.)
tire out zagnat' (v.pf.)
    zagonyat' (v.impf.)
tired out with running about, to be
    nabegat'sya (v.pf.)

tired, to get   ustat' (v.pf.)
    ustavat' (v.impf.)
titanic   titanicheskii (adj.)
titanium   titan (n.m.)
title   titul (n.m.)
    zaglavie (n.n.)
    zagolovok (n.m.)
title page   titul'nyi list (adj.-n.m.)
title, to give a   ozaglavit' (v.pf.)
titmouse, blue   sinitsa (n.f.)
to   k (prep.)
    ko (prep.)
toad   zhaba (n.f.)
toadstool   mukhomor (n.m.)
toady   podliza (n.f.)
toast   tost (n.m.)
    zdravitsa (n.f.)
toastmaster   tamada (n.m.)
tobacco   tabachnyi (adj.)
    tabak (n.m.)
tobacco, coarse   makhorka (n.f.)
tobacco pouch   kiset (n.m.)
today   segodnya (adv.)
together   slitno (adv.)
    vdvoem (adv.)
    vmeste (adv.)
    voedino (adv.)
toil   trudit'sya (v.impf.)
toiler   truzhenik (n.m.)
toilet   tualet (n.m.)
    ubornaya (n.f.)
toilet bowl   unitaz (n.m.)
token   zheton (n.m.)
tolerance   dopusk (n.m.)
    terpimost' (n.f.)
toleration   veroterpimost' (n.f.)
tomato   pomidor (n.m.)
tomato paste   tomat (n.m.)
tomcat   kot (n.m.)
tomorrow   zavtra (adv.)
    zavtrashnii (adj.)
tomorrow, day after   poslezavtra (adv.)
ton   tonna (n.f.)
tone   ton (n.m.)
tongs   shchiptsy (n.pl.)
tongue   yazyk (n.m.)
tongue, to hold one's   pomalkivat' (v.impf.)

    smolchat' (v.pf.)
tongue-tied   kosnoyazychnyi (adj.)
tonsil   glanda (n.f.)
too   chereschur (adv.)
    slishkom (adv.)
tool   orudie (n.n.)
tooth   zub (n.m.)
    zubets (n.m.)
    zubnoi (adj.)
tooth, sweet   slastena (n.f.)
toothless   bezzubyi (adj.)
toothpick   zubochistka (n.f.)
top   krona (n.f.)
    predel'nyi (adj.)
    verkh (adv.)
    verkhushka (n.f.)
    volchok (n.m.)
top of a boot   golenishche (n.n.)
topic   syuzhet (n.m.)
topography   topografiya (n.f.)
topology   topologiya (n.f.)
torch   fakel (n.m.)
torment   muchenie (n.n.)
    muchit' (v.impf.)
    muka (n.f.)
    terzanie (n.n.)
tormentor   muchitel' (n.m.)
torn   khudoi (adj.)
torn to shreds   izodrannyi (adj.)
torpedo   torpeda (n.f.)
torpedo boat   minonosets (n.m.)
torpid, to grow   tsepenet' (v.impf.)
tortoise   cherepakha (n.f.)
torture   istyazanie (n.n.)
    pytat' (v.impf.)
    pytka (n.f.)
torture chamber   zastenok (n.m.)
torture to death   zamuchit' (v.pf.)
toss up   vskidyvat' (v.impf.)
tossing   kachka (n.f.)
tot   karapuz (n.m.)
totality   sovokupnost' (n.f.)
touch   dotragivat'sya (v.impf.)
    kosnut'sya (v.pf.)
    mazok (n.m.)
    oshchupat' (v.pf.)
    prikasat'sya (v.impf.)
    prikosnovenie (n.n.)
    (cont'd)

pritragivat'sya (v.impf.)
privkus (n.m.)
shtrikh (n.m.)
tronut' (v.pf.)
zadet' (v.pf.)
zadevat' (v.impf.)
touch, to the na oshchup' (adv.)
touching trogatel'nyi (adj.)
touchy obidchivyi (adj.)
touchy person nedotroga (n.m.&f.)
tour gastrolirovat' (v.impf.)
tourism turizm (n.m.)
tournament turnir (n.m.)
tourniquet zhgut (n.m.)
tousle rastrepat' (v.pf.)
trepat' (v.impf.)
vz"eroshit' (v.pf.)
tow paklya (n.f.)
toward k (prep.)
ko (prep.)
navstrechu (adv.)
towel polotentse (n.n.)
tower bashnya (n.f.)
vyshka (n.f.)
town gorod (n.m.)
town, of another inogorodnii (adj.)
townsman gorozhanin (n.m.)
toxic toksicheskii (adj.)
toxic agent otravlyayushchee veshchestvo
(adj.-n.n.)
toxicology toksikologiya (n.f.)
toy igrushka (n.f.)
trace ochertit' (v.pf.)
postromka (n.f.)
prosledit' (v.pf.)
sled (n.m.)
traceless besslednyi (adj.)
traces, to leave sledit' (v.impf.)
tracing nachertanie (n.n.)
tracing paper kal'ka (n.f.)
track sled (n.m.)
track down vysledit' (v.pf.)
tracking slezhenie (n.n.)
traction tyaga (n.f.)
tractor traktor (n.m.)
tractor building traktorostroenie (n.n.)
trade promysel (n.m.)
remeslo (n.n.)

torgovat' (v.impf.)
torgovlya (n.f.)
trade representative torgpred (n.m.)
trade union profsoyuz (n.m.)
trade-union committee, local mestkom
(n.m.)
tradition traditsiya (n.f.)
traditional traditsionnyi (adj.)
traffic lights svetofor (n.m.)
tragedian tragik (n.m.)
tragedy tragediya (n.f.)
tragic tragicheskii (adj.)
trailer pritsep (n.m.)
train dressirovat' (v.impf.)
poezd (n.m.)
priuchat' (v.impf.)
train, armored bronepoezd (n.m.)
training, to give obuchat' (v.impf.)
traitor izmennik (n.m.)
predatel' (n.m.)
trajectory traektoriya (n.f.)
tramp topot (n.m.)
trample popirat' (v.impf.)
poprat' (v.pf.)
rastoptat' (v.pf.)
trample down toptat' (v.impf)
utaptyvat' (v.impf.)
utoptat' (v.pf.)
vtaptyvat' (v.impf.)
vtoptat' (v.pf.)
zatoptat' (v.pf.)
transaction, shady afera (n.f.)
transatlantic transatlanticheskii (adj.)
transcription transkriptsiya (n.f.)
transducer datchik (n.m.)
transfer perelozhit' (v.pf.)
perenesti (v.pf.)
perenos (n.m.)
perenosit' (v.impf.)
perevesti (v.pf.)
perevodnoi (adj.)
transference perebroska (n.f.)
transferred, to be perevestis' (v.pf.)
perevodit'sya (v.impf.)
transform preobrazit' (v.pf.)
transformirovat' (v.impf.)
transformation preobrazovanie (n.n.)
transformed, to be preobrazhat'sya (v.impf.)

transformer preobrazovatel' (n.m.)
transfusion perelivanie (n.n.)
transgression transgressiya (n.f.)
transient skorotechnyi (adj.)
transit tranzit (n.m.)
transitory kratkovremennyi (adj.)
   perekhodyashchii (adj.)
translation perevod (n.m.)
translation, in perevodnyi (adj.)
translator perevodchik (n.m.)
transmission peredatochnyi (adj.)
   transmissiya (n.f.)
transmitter peredatchik (n.m.)
transparent prozrachnyi (adj.)
transplant peresadit' (v.pf.)
   peresazhivat' (v.impf.)
   vysadit' (v.pf.)
transplantation peresadka (n.f.)
transport oboz (n.m.)
   perevezti (v.pf.)
   perevoz (n.m.)
   perevozka (n.f.)
   podvoz (n.m.)
   provezti (v.pf.)
   provoz (n.m.)
   provozit' (v.impf.)
   transport (n.m.)
transport, motor avtotransport (n.m.)
trap kapkan (n.m.)
   lovushka (n.f.)
   silok (n.m.)
trapezium trapetsiya (n.f.)
trash dryan' (n.f.)
trauma travma (n.f.)
travel ob"ezzhat' (v.impf.)
travel all over iz"ezdit' (v.pf.)
traveler proezzhii (adj.)
traveling companion sputnik (n.m.)
trawler trauler (n.m.)
tray lotok (n.m.)
   podnos (n.m.)
treacherous verolomnyi (adj.)
treacle patoka (n.f.)
tread protektor (n.m.)
tread on nastupat' (v.impf.)
   nastupit' (v.pf.)
treason izmena (n.f.)
treasure klad (n.m.)

   sokrovishche (n.n.)
treasury kazna (n.f.)
treat otnosit'sya (v.impf.)
   ugostit' (v.pf.)
treat outrageously nadrugat'sya (v.pf.)
treatise traktat (n.m.)
treatment lechenie (n.n.)
   otnoshenie (n.n.)
   protsedura (n.f.)
treble utroit' (v.pf.)
tree derevo (n.n.)
tree, apple yablonya (n.f.)
tree, ash yasen' (n.m.)
tree, bird cherry cheremukha (n.f.)
tree, fir elka (n.f.)
tree, lime lipa (n.f.)
tree, palm pal'ma (n.f.)
tremble drozhat' (v.impf.)
tremble, to begin to zadrozhat (v.pf.)
trembling drozh' (n.f.)
   trepet (n.m.)
trench okop (n.m.)
   transheya (n.f.)
trench warfare pozitsionnyi (adj.)
trend veyanie (n.n.)
trestle kozly (n.pl.)
trial ispytanie (n.n.)
   probnyi (adj.)
   protsess (n.m.)
   sud (n.m.)
triangle treugol'nik (n.m.)
tribal rodovoi (adj.)
tribe plemya (n.n.)
tribunal tribunal (n.m.)
tributary pritok (n.m.)
tribute dan' (n.f.)
trick fokus (n.m.)
   podvokh (n.m.)
   prodelka (n.f.)
   tryuk (n.m.)
   ulovka (n.f.)
   vykhodka (n.f.)
trickle nakrapyvat' (v.impf.)
tricky kavernyi (adj.)
tried ispytannyi (adj.)
trifle bezdelitsa (n.f.)
   pustyak (n.m.)
trifling pustyakovyi (adj.)

trigonometry trigonometriya (n.f.)
trihedral trekhgrannyi (adj.)
trill trel' (n.f.)
trilogy trilogiya (n.f.)
trim otdelat' (v.pf.)
   otdelyvat' (v.impf.)
   podrovnyat' (v.pf.)
trinket bezdelushka (n.f.)
trio trio (n.n.)
trip reis (n.m.)
tripartite troistvennyi (adj.)
triple troinoi (adj.)
tripod shtativ (n.m.)
   trenoga (n.f.)
triumph triumf (n.m.)
   vostorzhestvovat' (v.pf.)
trivalent trekhvalentnyi (adj.)
trolley drezina (n.f.)
   telezhka (n.f.)
   trolleibus (n.m.)
   vagonetka (n.f.)
troops voiska (n.pl.)
trophy trofei (n.m.)
tropic tropik (n.m.)
tropical tropicheskii (adj.)
troposphere troposfera (n.f.)
trot rys' (n.f.)
trotter rysak (n.m.)
trouble khlopoty (n.pl.)
   utruzhdat' (v.impf.)
trough kormushka (n.f.)
   koryto (n.n.)
trousers bryuki (n.pl.)
trout forel' (n.f.)
truancy progul (n.m.)
truant progul'shchik (n.m.)
truce envoy parlamenter (n.m.)
truck gruzovik (n.m.)
truck farmer ogorodnik (n.m.)
true istyi (adj.)
true, to come sbyt'sya (v.pf.)
   sbyvat'sya (v.impf.)
trump kozyr' (n.m.)
trump card, to play one's kozyrnut' (v.pf.)
   kozyryat' (v.impf.)
trumpet truba (n.f.)
trumpeter trubach (n.m.)
trunk khobot (n.m.)

stvol (n.m.)
sunduk (n.m.)
tulovishche (n.n.)
trunk line mezhdugorodnyi (adj.)
trunks plavki (n.pl.)
truss bandazh (n.m.)
trust doverie (n.n.)
   doveryat' (v.impf.)
   trest (n.m.)
truth istina (n.f.)
   pravda (n.f.)
try isprobovat' (v.pf.)
   otvedat' (v.pf.)
   poprobovat' (v.pf.)
   popytat' (v.pf.)
   poryvat'sya (v.impf.)
   postarat'sya (v.pf.)
   silit'sya (v.impf.)
try on primerit' (v.pf.)
   primeryat' (v.impf.)
try to find izyskivat' (v.impf.)
tsar tsar' (n.m.)
tsarism tsarizm (n.m.)
t-shirt maika (n.f.)
tub kadka (n.f.)
   lokhanka (n.f.)
tube trubka (n.f.)
   tyubik (n.m.)
tube, picture kineskop (n.m.)
tuber kluben' (n.m.)
tuberculosis tuberkulez (n.m.)
tuck in zapravit' (v.pf.)
Tuesday vtornik (n.m.)
tugboat buksir (n.m.)
tulip tyul'pan (n.m.)
tulle tyul' (n.m.)
tumble kuvyrkat'sya (v.impf.)
tumble in vvalit'sya (v.pf.)
   vvalivat'sya (v.impf.)
tumult buistvo (n.n.)
tundra tundra (n.f.)
tune napev (n.m.)
   nastraivat' (v.impf.)
   nastroit' (v.impf.)
tune, out of rasstroenyi (adj.)
tungsten vol'fram (n.m.)
tuning nastroika (n.f.)
tuning fork kamerton (n.m.)

tunnel tonnel' (n.m.)
   tunnel' (n.m.)
turban chalma (n.f.)
turbid mutnyi (adj.)
turbine turbina (n.f.)
turbulence turbulentnost' (n.f.)
turf dern (n.m.)
Turk turok (n.m.)
turkey indyuk (n.m.)
Turkic tyurkskii (adj.)
Turkish turetskii (adj.)
Turkmen turkmen (n.m.)
turn chered (n.m.)
   krutit' (v.impf.)
   obrashchat' (v.impf.)
   obratit' (v.pf.)
   obtachivat' (v.impf.)
   obtochit' (v.pf.)
   ochered' (n.f.)
   perelitsevat' (v.pf.)
   povernut' (v.pf.)
   povorachivat'(sya) (v.impf.)
   povorot (n.m.)
   sklad (n.m.)
   svorachivat' (v.impf.)
   vorochat' (v.impf.)
   zavernut' (v.pf.)
   zavorachivat' (v.impf.)
turn around vertet' (v.impf.)
turn away otvorachivat'(sya) (v.impf.)
turn, half poluoborot (n.m.)
turn, in poocheredno (adv.)
   poperemenno (adv.)
turn into pretvorit' (v.pf.)
   prevrashchat'(sya) (v.impf.)
   prevratit' (v.pf.)
turn off potushit' (v.pf.)
   vyklyuchit' (v.pf.)
turn on vklyuchit' (v.pf.)
turn over perevernut' (v.pf.)
   perevertyvat' (v.impf.)
   perevorachivat'(sya) (v.impf.)
   voroshit' (v.impf.)
turn round obernut'sya (v.pf.)
   oborachivat'(sya) (v.impf.)
turn-down otlozhnoi (adj.)
turner tokar' (n.m.)
turnip bryukva (n.f.)

   repa (n.f.)
turnover oborot (n.m.)
turnover, goods gruzooborot (n.m.)
turpentine skipidar (n.m.)
turret bashenka (n.f.)
TV set televizor (n.m.)
twang, to speak with a nasal gnusavit'
   (v.impf.)
tweezers shchipchiki (n.pl.)
twelve dvenadtsat' (num.)
twentieth dvadtsatyi (adj.)
twenty dvadtsat' (num.)
twice dvazhdy (adv.)
   vdvoe (adv.)
twig prut (n.m.)
   vetochka (n.f.)
twilight sumerki (n.pl.)
twin bliznets (n.m.)
   parnyi (adj.)
twins dvoinya (n.f.)
twirl zakrutit' (v.pf.)
twist skrutit' (v.pf.)
   suchit' (v.impf.)
   svit' (v.pf.)
   svivat' (v.impf.)
twitch dernut'(sya) (v.pf.)
   podergivat'sya (v.impf.)
two dva (num.)
   dvoe (num.)
   dvoika (n.f.)
two hundred dvesti (num.)
two, in nadvoe (adv.)
two years, of dvukhletnii (adj.)
twofold dvukratnyi (adj.)
two-month dvukhmesyachnyi (adj.)
two-seater dvukhmestnyi (adj.)
two-storied dvukhétazhnyi (adj.)
two-year dvukhgodichnyi (adj.)
type shrift (n.m.)
   tip (n.m.)
typewriter mashinka (n.f.)
   pishushchaya mashinka (adj.-n.f.)
typhus sypnoi tif (adj.-n.m.)
   tif (n.m.)
typing perepiska (n.f.)
typist mashinistka (n.f.)
tyranny proizvol (n.m.)
tyrant tiran (n.m.)
tyrant, petty samodur (n.m.)

U (у)

udder vymya (n.n.)
ugly bezobraznyi (adj.)
   urodlivyi (adj.)
ugly, to grow durnet' (v.impf.)
Ukrainian ukrainets (n.m.)
ulcer yazva (n.f.)
ultimatum ul'timatum (n.m.)
ultraviolet ul'trafioletovyi (adj.)
umbilical cord pupovina (n.f.)
umbrella zont (n.m.)
unacceptable nepriemlemyi (adj.)
unaccustomed to neprivychnyi (adj.)
unanimity edinodushie (n.n.)
unanimous edinoglasnyi (adj.)
unarmed bezoruzhnyi (adj.)
   nevooruzhennyi (adj.)
unasked neproshennyi (adj.)
unattainable nedostizhimyi (adj.)
   nedosyagaemyi (adj.)
unattractive nepriglyadnyi (adj.)
   neprivlekatel'nyi (adj.)
   nevzrachnyi (adj.)
unawares vrasplokh (adv.)
unbalanced neuravnoveshennyi (adj.)
   vzbalmoshnyi (adj.)
unbearable nesnosnyi (adj.)
   nesterpimyi (adj.)
   nevmogotu (adv.)
unbeliever neveruyushchii (adj.)
unbidden neproshennyi (adj.)
unbridled neobuzdannyi (adj.)
   raznuzdannyi (adj.)
unbroken sploshnoi (adj.)
unbutton rasstegivat'(sya) (v.impf.)
unbuttoned naraspashku (adv.)
uncared for besprizornyi (adj.)
unceasing bezostanovochnyi (adj.)
unceremonious bestseremonnyi (adj.)
   famil'yarnyi (adj.)
uncertainty neizvestnost' (n.f.)

neuverennost' (n.f.)
unclasp razzhat' (v.pf.)
   razzhimat' (v.pf.)
uncle dyadya (n.m.)
unclean nechistyi (adj.)
uncomfortable neudobnyi (adj.)
   neuzhivchivyi (adj.)
uncommon nezauryadnyi (adj.)
uncomplaining bezropotnyi (adj.)
uncompromising nepreklonnyi (adj.)
unconditional bezogovorochnyi (adj.)
unconscientious nedobrosovestnyi (adj.)
unconscious bessoznatel'nyi (adj.)
unconsciousness bespamyatstvo (n.n.)
   zabyt'e (n.n.)
uncontrolled beskontrol'nyi (adj.)
   neupravlyaemyi (adj.)
unconvincing neubeditel'nyi (adj.)
uncoordinated nesoglasovannyi (adj.)
uncork otkuporivat' (v.impf.)
   raskuporivat' (v.impf.)
uncoupling rastseplenie (n.n.)
uncouth neotesannyi (adj.)
uncover raskryt' (v.pf.)
uncovered nepokrytyi (adj.)
undelivered nedostavlennyi (adj.)
undemanding neprikhotlivyi (adj.)
   netrebovatel'nyi (adj.)
   nevzyskatel'nyi (adj.)
under pod (prep.)
under, from iz-pod (prep.)
under the jurisdiction of podsudnyi (adj.)
under the patronage podshefnyi (adj.)
underage nesovershennoletnii (adj.)
underestimate nedootsenivat' (v.impf.)
   preumen'shat' (v.impf.)
undergo podvergat'sya (v.impf.)
underground podzemnyi (adj.)
underground passage podkop (n.m.)
underground press samizdat (n.m.)

underground, the podpol'e (n.n.)
undermentioned nizheprivedennyi (adj.)
undermining podryv (n.m.)
undersigned, the nizhepodpisavshiisya (adj.)
undersized maloroslyi (adj.)
    nizkoroslyi (adj.)
understand ponyat' (v.pf.)
    razbirat'sya (v.impf.)
    soobrazit' (v.pf.)
    uyasnit' (v.pf.)
understand, to make one vtolkovat' (v.pf.)
understanding ponimanie (n.n.)
understanding, to come to an poladit' (v.pf.)
understood, to be razumeetsya (v.impf.)
undertake predprinimat' (v.impf.)
undertaking nachinanie (n.n.)
undertones, in vpolgolosa (adv.)
undeveloped nerazvityi (adj.)
undisciplined nedistsiplinirovannyi (adj.)
undo porot' (v.impf.)
    rasstegnut' (v.pf.)
undoubtedly bezuslovno (adv.)
    nesomnenno (adv.)
undress razdet' (v.pf.)
undulating volnoobraznyi (adj.)
unearned netrudovoi (adj.)
unearthly nezemnoi (adj.)
uneducated nekul'turnyi (adj.)
    neobrazovannyi (adj.)
unemployed bezrabotnyi (adj.)
unenviable nezavidnyi (adj.)
unequal neravnyi (adj.)
    nerovnyi (adj.)
unequivocal nedvusmyslennyi (adj.)
unessential nesushchestvennyi (adj.)
unethical neétichnyi (adj.)
uneven skachkoobraznyi (adj.)
unexpected nezhdannyi (adj.)
unexpectedly neozhidanno (adv.)
unexplored neizvedannyi (adj.)
unfading neuvyadaemyi (adj.)
unfaithful, to be izmenit' (v.pf.)
unfashionable nemodnyi (adj.)
unfasten otkrepit' (v.pf.)
    otstegivat'(sya) (v.impf.)
    otstegnut' (v.pf.)
unfavorable neblagopriyatnyi (adj.)
unfeigned nepritvornyi (adj.)

unfinished nedokonchennyi (adj.)
    neokonchennyi (adj.)
    nezakonchennyi (adj.)
unfit neprigodnyi (adj.)
unfitness negodnost' (n.f.)
unfold razvernut' (v.pf.)
    razvertyvat'(sya) (v.impf.)
    razvorachivat' (v.impf.)
unforeseen nepredvidennyi (adj.)
unforgettable nezabvennyi (adj.)
    nezabyvaemyi (adj.)
unfortunate neblagopoluchnyi (adj.)
    neschastlivyi (adj.)
unfounded neosnovatel'nyi (adj.)
unfriendly nedruzhelyubnyi (adj.)
    neprivetlivyi (adj.)
ungrateful neblagodarnyi (adj.)
unhappy neschastnyi (adj.)
unharmed nevredimyi (adj.)
unharness otpryagat' (v.impf.)
    raspryagat' (v.impf.)
    vypryagat' (v.impf.)
unhealthy nezdorovyi (adj.)
unheard of neslykhannyi (adj.)
unhook ottsepit' (v.pf.)
    rastsepit' (v.pf.)
unicellular odnokletochnyi (adj.)
unification ob"edinenie (n.n.)
uniform formennyi (adj.)
    mundir (n.m.)
    obmundirovanie (n.n.)
uniformity edinoobrazie (n.n.)
unify unifitsirovat' (v.impf.&pf.)
unimaginable nevoobrazimyi (adj.)
unimpeded besprepyatstvennyi (adj.)
unimportant malovazhnyi (adj.)
    nevazhnyi (adj.)
uninhabited neobitaemyi (adj.)
    nezhiloi (adj.)
uninitiated neposvyashchennyi (adj.)
unintelligible nevrazumitel'nyi (adj.)
unintentional neumyshlennyi (adj.)
unintentionally nechayanno (adv.)
uninterrupted bespereboinyi (adj.)
uninvited nezvanyi (adj.)
union smychka (n.f.)
    soyuz (n.m.)
union, trade profsoyuz (n.m.)

unique nepovtorimyi (adj.)
unit agregat (n.m.)
 edinitsa (n.f.)
unite soedinit' (v.impf.)
 soedinyat'(sya) (v.impf.)
united edinyi (adj.)
 soedinennyi (adj.)
units, breaking up into smaller
 razukrupnenie (n.n.)
unity edinenie (n.n.)
 edinstvo (n.n.)
 spayannost' (n.f.)
universal universal'nyi (adj.)
 vsemirnyi (adj.)
universe vselennaya (n.f.)
university universitet (n.m.)
unjust nepravyi (adj.)
unjustified neopravdannyi (adj.)
unkind nedobryi (adj.)
 nelyubeznyi (adj.)
unknown bezvestnyi (adj.)
 nevedomyi (adj.)
 neznakomyi (adj.)
unlace rasshnurovat' (v.pf.)
unlawful nedozvolennyi (adj.)
unlike nepokhozhii (adj.)
unlikely vryad li (adv.)
 navryad li (adv.)
unlimited bespredel'nyi (adj.)
 neogranichennyi (adj.)
unload razgruzhat' (v.impf.)
 razgruzit' (v.pf.)
 sgruzhat' (v.impf.)
 vygruzhat' (v.impf.)
unloading razgruzka (n.f.)
 vygruzka (n.f.)
unlock otperet' (v.pf.)
unlocked, to be otperet'sya (v.pf.)
unlocking otpiranie (n.n.)
unloved nelyubimyi (adj.)
unmarried kholostoi (adj.)
 nezhenatyi (adj.)
unmerciful nemiloserdnyi (adj.)
 neshchadnyi (adj.)
unmerited nezasluzhennyi (adj.)
unmounted peshii (adj.)
unnatural neestestvennyi (adj.)
 protivoestestvennyi (adj.)

unnavigable nesudokhodnyi (adj.)
unnecessary nenuzhnyi (adj.)
unofficial neofitsial'nyi (adj.)
unpack raspakovat' (v.pf.)
unpaid neoplachennyi (adj.)
unpaired neparnyi (adj.)
unpalatable nevkusnyi (adj.)
unpardonable neprostitel'nyi (adj.)
unplanned besplanovyi (adj.)
unpleasant nepriyatnyi (adj.)
unpractical nepraktichnyi (adj.)
unprecedented bespretsedentnyi (adj.)
 besprimernyi (adj.)
 nebyvalyi (adj.)
 nevidannyi (adj.)
unprejudiced nepredubezhdennyi (adj.)
unpretentious neprityazatel'nyi (adj.)
unprincipled bezydeinyi (adj.)
unprintable netsenzurnyi (adj.)
unproductive maloproduktivnyi (adj.)
 neproduktivnyi (adj.)
 neproizvoditel'nyi (adj.)
unprotected nezashchishchennyi (adj.)
unpublished neizdannyi (adj.)
 neopublikovannyi (adj.)
unpunished beznakazannyi (adj.)
unquenchable neutolimyi (adj.)
unquestioning besprekoslovnyi (adj.)
unreal nereal'nyi (adj.)
unrealizable nesbytochnyi (adj.)
unrecognizable neuznavaemyi (adj.)
unreliable neblagonadezhnyi (adj.)
unrest volnenie (n.n.)
unrestrained bezuderzhnyi (adj.)
 nesderzhannyi (adj.)
 nevozderzhannyi (adj.)
 nevyderzhannyi (adj.)
unripe nespelyi (adj.)
 nezrelyi (adj.)
unruly nepokornyi (adj.)
unsaddle rassedlat' (v.pf.)
unsatisfactory neudovletvoritel'nyi (adj.)
unscrew otvernut' (v.pf.)
 otvintit' (v.pf.)
 razvintit' (v.pf)
 vykrutit' (v.pf.)
 vyvernut' (v.pf.)
 vyvertyvat' (v.impf.)

unscrupulous besprintsipnyi (adj.)
   bessovestnyi (adj.)
   nerazborchivyi (adj.)
unseal raspechatat' (v.pf.)
   vskryt' (v.pf.)
unseemly neblagovidnyi (adj.)
   nepodobayushchii (adj.)
unskilled nekvalifitsirovannyi (adj.)
unskilled worker zemlekop (n.m.)
unskillful neiskusnyi (adj.)
   neumelyi (adj.)
unsociable nelyudimyi (adj.)
   neobshchitel'nyi (adj.)
unsociable, to be dichit'sya (v.impf.)
unsolder raspayat' (v.pf.)
unsolved nerazreshennyi (adj.)
unsound nesostoyatel'nyi (adj.)
unstable nestoikii (adj.)
unsteady netverdyi (adj.)
   neustoichivyi (adj.)
   shatkii (adj.)
   zybkii (adj.)
unsteady, to be zapletat'sya (v.impf.)
unstick otlepit' (v.pf.)
unstressed bezudarnyi (adj.)
unsuccessful bezuspeshnyi (adj.)
unsuitable nepodkhodyashchii (adj.)
unsurmountable nepreodolimyi (adj.)
unsurpassed neprevzoidennyi (adj.)
unsystematic bessistemnyi (adj.)
untalented bezdarnyi (adj.)
untamed neukroshchennyi (adj.)
untidy neopryatnyi (adj.)
untie otvyazat' (v.pf.)
   razvyazat' (v.pf.)
   razvyazyvat' (v.impf.)
untilled nevozdelannyi (adj.)
untouched nepochatyi (adj.)
   netronutyi (adj,)
untrained neobuchennyi (adj.)
untranslatable neperevodimyi (adj.)
untruth nepravda (n.f.)
untwine raspletat'(sya) (v.impf.)
untwist raskrutit' (v.pf.)
   rasplesti (v.pf.)
unusual neobychnyi (adj.)
   neurochnyi (adj.)
unvarnished neprikrashennyi (adj.)

unverified neproverennyi (adj.)
unwell, to be prikhvaryvat' (v.impf.)
unwillingly nekhotya (adv.)
   neokhotno (adv.)
unwillingness nezhelanie (n.n.)
unwind razmatyvat' (v.impf.)
   razmotat' (v.pf.)
unwise nerazumnyi (adj.)
unworthy nedostoinyi (adj.)
unyielding neustupchivyi (adj.)
up naverkh (adv.)
up in arms, to be opolchit'sya (v.pf.)
up to zatevat' (v.impf.)
upholsterer oboishchik (n.m.)
upholstering obivka (n.f.)
upon na (prep.)
upper reaches verkhov'e (n.n.)
upright stoimya (adv.)
uproar gam (n.m.)
upset rasstroennyi (adj.)
upward kverkhu (adv.)
   vverkh (adv.)
   vvys' (adv.)
uranium uran (n.m.)
urbane obkhoditel'nyi (adj.)
urge pozyv (n.m.)
urge on podgonyat' (v.impf.)
   podognat' (v.pf.)
   ponukat' (v.impf.)
urgent nasushchnyi (adj.)
   neotlozhnyi (adj.)
   srochnyi (adj.)
   zlobodnevnyi (adj.)
urine mocha (n.f.)
urn urna (n.f.)
urology urologiya (n.f.)
us nam (p.)
   nami (p.)
   nas (p.)
use ispol'zovat' (v.pf.)
   pol'za (n.f.)
   pol'zovanie (n.n.)
   upotrebit' (v.pf)
use, for external naruzhnoe (n.n.)
use, for future vprok (adv.)
use, in general obshcheupotrebitel'nyi (adj.)
use, not in neupotrebitel'nyi (adj.)
use of, to make pol'zovat'sya (v.impf.)

use, to make vospol'zovat'sya (v.pf.)
used poderzhannyi (adj.)
used to, to get privykat' (v.impf.)
   svykat'sya (v.impf.)
   szhit'sya (v.pf.)
   vtyagivat'sya (v.impf.)
   vtyanut'sya (v.pf.)
useful poleznyi (adj.)
useful, to be prigodit'sya (v.pf.)
useless bespoleznyi (adj.)
uselessness nenadobnost' (n.f.)
usher kapel'diner (n.m.)
USSR SSSR (abbr.)
usurp uzurpirovat' (v.impf.&pf.)

utensils utvar' (n.f.)
uterus matka (n.f.)
utilitarian utilitarnyi (adj.)
utilization utilizatsiya (n.f.)
utopia utopiya (n.f.)
utter izrech' (v.pf.)
   izrekat' (v.impf.)
   promolvit' (v.pf.)
   proronit' (v.pf.)
   vymolvit' (v.pf.)
utterly dotla (adv.)
   nagolovu (adv.)
   vkonets (adv.)
Uzbek uzbek (n.m.)

V (B)

vacancy vakansiya (n.f.)
vacation kanikuly (n.pl.)
   otpusk (n.m.)
vaccine vaktsina (n.f.)
vacuum pustota (n.f.)
   vakuum (n.m.)
vacuum cleaner pylesos (n.m.)
vagina vlagalishche (n.n.)
vague neyasnyi (adj.)
   smutnyi (adj.)
vain tshchetnyi (adj.)
vain, in naprasno (adv.)
   ponaprasnu (adv.)
   popustu (adv.)
valence valentnost' (n.f.)
valiant doblestnyi (adj.)
valid uvazhitel'nyi (adj.)
valley dolina (n.f.)
valley, lily of the landysh (n.m.)
valor doblest' (n.f.)
valuation rastsenka (n.f.)
value dorozhit' (v.impf.)
   otsenivat' (v.impf.)
   stoimost' (n.f.)
   tsenit' (v.impf.)
   tsennost' (n.f.)
value, of full polnotsennyi (adj.)

value, of little malotsennyi (adj.)
valve klapan (n.m.)
   ventil' (n.m.)
   zolotnik (n.m.)
van furgon (n.m.)
vanadium vanadii (n.m.)
vandal vandal (n.m.)
vanguard avangard (n.m.)
vanilla vanil' (n.f.)
vanity tshcheslavie (n.n.)
vaporization paroobrazovanie (n.m.)
variable peremennaya (n.f.)
variance dispersiya (n.f.)
variegated pestryi (adj.)
   raznokharakternyi (adj.)
   raznotsvetnyi (adj.)
variety raznoobrazie (n.n.)
   raznovidnost' (n.f.)
varnish lak (n.m.)
varnished lakirovannyi (adj.)
   lakovyi (adj.)
vase vaza (n.f.)
vaseline vazelin (n.m.)
vassal vassal (n.m.)
vast obshirnyi (adj.)
vat chan (n.m.)
vaudeville vodevil' (n.m.)

vault   sklep (n.m.)
veal   telyatina (n.f.)
vector   vektor (n.m.)
vegetable   rastitel'nyi (adj.)
vegetables   ovoshchi (n.pl.)
vegetarian   vegetarianets (n.m.)
vegetate   prozyabat' (v.impf.)
vegetation   rastitel'nost' (n.f.)
vehicle, horse-drawn   povozka (n.f.)
veil   vual' (n.f.)
vein   vena (n.f.)
      zhila (n.f.)
      zhilka (n.f.)
velvet   barkhat (n.m.)
veneer   fanera (n.f.)
venerable   mastityi (adj.)
      preklonnyi (adj.)
venereal   venericheskii (adj.)
vengeance   mshchenie (n.n.)
venous   venoznyi (adj.)
vent   vymeshchat' (v.impf.)
      vymestit' (v.pf.)
ventilation   ventilyatsiya (n.f.)
ventilation window   fortochka (n.f.)
verandah   veranda (n.f.)
verb   glagol (n.m.)
verbal   otglagol'nyi (adj.)
verbose   mnogoslovnyi (adj.)
      prostrannyi (adj.)
verdure   zelen' (n.f.)
verify   proverit' (v.pf.)
      vyverit' (v.pf.)
      vyveryat' (v.impf.)
vermicelli   vermishel' (n.f.)
vermin   vreditel' (n.m.)
versatile   mnogogrannyi (adj.)
      raznostoronnii (adj.)
verse   stikh (n.m.)
versed in, not   neiskushennyi (adj.)
versification   stikhoslozhenie (n.n.)
version   variant (n.m.)
      versiya (n.f.)
vertebra   pozvonok (n.m.)
vertebrates   pozvonochnye (n.pl.)
vertical   vertikal'nyi (adj.)
very   ochen' (adv.)
very, the   samyi (adj.)
vessel   sosud (n.m.)

vessel, motor   teplokhod (n.m.)
vetch   vika (n.f.)
veteran   veteran (n.m.)
veterinary   veterinar (n.m.)
veto   veto (n.n.)
vex   razdosadovat' (v.pf.)
viable   zhiznesposobnyi (adj.)
vial   sklyanka (n.f.)
viands   yastva (n.pl.)
vibration   vibratsiya (n.f.)
vibrator   vibrator (n.pl.)
vice   porok (n.m.)
      tiski (n.pl.)
vice admiral   vitse-admiral (n.m.)
vicious   porochnyi (adj.)
      zlovrednyi (adj.)
victim   postradavshii (adj.)
      zhertva (n.f.)
victorious   pobedonosnyi (adj.)
victory   pobeda (n.f.)
Vietnamese   v'etnamets (n.m.)
view of, in   vvidu (prep.)
vigilance   bditel'nost' (n.f.)
vile   merzkii (adj.)
village   derevnya (n.f.)
      selenie (n.n.)
      selo (n.n.)
village library   izba-chital'nya (n.f.)
village Soviet   sel'sovet (n.m.)
villain   negodyai (n.m.)
      podlets (n.m.)
      zlodei (n.m.)
vindictive   mstitel'nyi (adj.)
vine   loza (n.f.)
vinegar   uksus (n.m.)
vinyl   vinil (n.m.)
violate   narushat' (v.impf.)
      narushit' (v.pf.)
violence   nasilie (n.n.)
      rasprava (n.f.)
violent   buinyi (adj.)
violet   fialka (n.f.)
      fioletovyi (adj.)
      lilovyi (adj.)
violin   skripka (n.f.)
violinist   skripach (n.m.)
virgin   devstvennyi (adj.)
virgin soil   tselina (n.f.)

virology virusologiya (n.f.)
virtue dobrodetel' (n.f.)
virtuoso virtuoz (n.m.)
virulence virulentnost' (n.f.)
virus virus (n.m.)
visa viza (n.f.)
 vizirovat' (v.impf.)
viscosoty vyazkost' (n.f.)
viscous tyaguchii (adj.)
 vyazkii (adj.)
visibility vidimost' (n.f.)
visible vidnyi (adj.)
 zametnyi (adj.)
visible, to be vidnet'sya (v.impf.)
 vyrisovyvat'sya (v.impf.)
vision videnie (n.n.)
visit naveshchat' (v.impf.)
 navestit' (v.pf.)
 pobyvat' (v.pf.)
 s''ezdit' (v.pf.)
 vizit (n.m.)
visit, to pay a provedat' (v.pf.)
visitor posetitel' (n.m.)
vista proseka (n.f.)
visual vizual'nyi (adj.)
vital zhivotrepeshchushchii (adj.)
 zhiznennyi (adj.)
vitamin vitamin (n.m.)
vitriol kuporos (n.m.)
vivid koloritnyi (adj.)
vividly zhivo (adv.)
vivisection vivisektsiya (n.f.)
vocabulary leksika (n.f.)
 leksikon (n.m.)
 slovar' (n.m.)

vocal golosovoi (adj.)
 vokal'nyi (adj.)
vocation prizvanie (n.n.)
vodka vodka (n.f.)
voice golos (n.m.)
 zalog (n.m.)
voice, in a singing naraspev (adv.)
voiceless bezgolosyi (adj.)
volatility letuchest' (n.f.)
volcano vulkan (n.m.)
volleyball voleibol (n.m.)
volt vol't (n.m.)
volume kubatura (n.f.)
 ob''em (n.m.)
 tom (n.m.)
volumes, in many mnogotomnyi (adj.)
voluntary dobrovol'nyi (adj.)
volunteer okhotnik (n.m.)
 vyzyvat'sya (v.impf.)
voluptuous sladostrastnyi (adj.)
vomit rvat' (v.impf.)
vomiting rvota (n.f.)
voracity prozhorlivost' (n.f.)
vote votum (n.m.)
voting golosovanie (n.n.)
vouch poruchit'sya (v.pf.)
vow obet (n.m.)
vow not to, to make a zarech'sya (v.pf.)
 zarekat'sya (v.impf.)
vowel glasnyi (adj.)
vulcanization vulkanizatsiya (n.f.)
vulgar vul'garnyi (adj.)
vulnerable uyazvimyi (adj.)
vulture korshun (n.m.)
vying with one another napereboi (adv.)

W

wadded vatnyi (adj.)
wadding vatin (n.m.)
waddle perevalivat'sya (v.pf.)
wafer vaflya (n.f.)
wag vilyat' (v.impf.)
wages zarabotnaya plata (adj.-n.f.)

 zarplata (n.f.)
wail vopl' (n.m.)
waist taliya (n.f.)
waistcoat zhilet (n.m.)
wait dozhdat'sya (v.pf.)
 dozhidat'sya (v.impf.)

perezhidat' (v.impf.)
podozhdat' (v.pf.)
podzhidat' (v.impf.)
povremenit' (v.pf.)
wait for vyzhdat' (v.pf.)
vyzhidat' (v.impf.)
wait, to lie in podkaraulivat' (v.impf.)
podsteregat' (v.impf.)
wait until something is over perezhdat'
(v.pf.)
waiter ofitsiant (n.m.)
waitress podaval'shchitsa (n.f.)
waive postupit'sya (v.pf.)
wake budit' (v.impf.)
razbudit' (v.pf.)
wake up probudit'sya (v.pf.)
prosnut'sya (v.pf.)
walk round obognut' (v.pf.)
ogibat' (v.impf.)
walk, to go for a progulyat'sya (v.pf.)
walk, to take a pogulyat' (v.pf.)
walk up and down raskhazhivat' (v.impf.)
walking khod'ba (n.f.)
walking pace, at a shagom (adv.)
walking shoes polubotinki (n.pl.)
walking stick trostochka (n.f.)
wall stena (n.f.)
stennoi (adj.)
wall newspaper stengazeta (n.f.)
wallet bumazhnik (n.m.)
walleye bel'mo (n.n.)
wallow in utopat' (v.impf.)
wallpaper oboi (n.pl.)
walnut gretskii orekh (adj.-n.m.)
walrus morzh (n.m.)
waltz val's (n.m.)
wander brodit' (v.impf.)
kochevat' (v.impf.)
skitat'sya (v.impf.)
stranstvovat' (v.impf.)
zabresti (v.pf.)
wanderer strannik (n.m.)
want khotet' (v.impf.)
khotet'sya (v.impf.)
want, cease to raskhotet' (v.pf.)
war voina (n.f.)
war, prisoner of voennoplennyi (n.m.)
war, to be at voevat' (v.impf.)

wardrobe shkaf (n.m.)
wares tovar (n.m.)
warlike voinstvennyi (adj.)
warm gret' (v.impf.)
otogret' (v.pf.)
sogret' (v.pf.)
teplyi (adj.)
warm oneself otogrevat'(sya) (v.impf.)
warm, to grow teplet' (v.impf.)
warm up obogret' (v.pf.)
obogrevat'(sya) (v.impf.)
podogrevat' (v.impf.)
pogret'(sya) (v.pf.)
razogrevat' (v.impf.)
warmer, to grow poteplet' (v.pf.)
warming sogrevanie (n.n.)
warmly teplo (adv.)
warmth teplo (n.n.)
teplota (n.f.)
warn predosteregat' (v.impf.)
warp korobit' (v.impf.)
pokorobit'(sya) (v.pf.)
warrant naryad (n.m.)
order (n.m.)
ruchat'sya (v.impf.)
warrior voin (n.m.)
wart borodavka (n.f.)
wash myt' (v.impf.)
obmyvat' (v.impf.)
omyvat' (v.impf.)
podmyvat' (v.impf.)
stirat' (v.impf.)
umyt' (v.pf.)
vymyt'(sya) (v.pf.)
vystirat' (v.pf.)
wash off otmyvat' (v.impf.)
smyt' (v.pf.)
smyvat'(sya) (v.impf.)
washbasin shaika (n.f.)
washing promyvanie (n.n.)
stirka (n.f.)
umyvanie (n.n.)
washing machine stiral'naya mashina (adj.-n.f.)
wasp osa (n.f.)
waste otkhody (n.pl.)
rastochat' (v.impf.)
util'syr'e (n.n.)

waste ground pustyr' (n.m.)
wasteful neraschetlivyi (adj.)
watch chasy (n.pl.)
    sledit' (v.impf.)
    sterech' (v.impf.)
    vakhta (n.f.)
watchmaker chasovshchik (n.m.)
watchtower kalancha (n.f.)
water slezit'sya (v.impf.)
    voda (n.f.)
    vodnyi (adj.)
    vodyanoi (adj.)
water, boiling kipyatok (n.m.)
water pipe vodoprovod (n.m.)
water, to pour polivat' (v.impf.)
watercolor akvarel' (n.f.)
waterfall vodopad (n.m.)
watering polivka (n.f.)
watering can leika (n.f.)
watering place vodopoi (n.m.)
waterline vaterliniya (n.f.)
watermelon arbuz (n.m.)
waterproof nepromokaemyi (adj.)
water-resistant vodostoikii (adj.)
watershed vodorazdel (n.m.)
watertight vodonepronitsaemyi (adj.)
watery vodyanistyi (adj.)
watt vatt (n.m.)
wave makhat' (v.impf.)
    makhnut' (v.pf.)
    pomakhat' (v.pf.)
    volna (n.f.)
    vzmakhivat' (v.impf.)
    zavit' (v.pf.)
    zavivka (n.f.)
waveguide volnovod (n.m.)
wavy volnistyi (adj.)
wax vosk (n.m.)
wax, sealing surguch (n.m.)
waxen voskovoi (adj.)
way put' (n.m.)
    sposob (n.m.)
way, by the kstati (adv.)
way around, the other naoborot (adv.)
way, in a friendly po-druzheski (adv.)
way, in every vsyacheski (adv.)
way, in every possible vsemerno (adv.)
way, in one's own po-svoemu (adv.)

way of life uklad (n.m.)
way through, to force one's probit'sya (v.pf.)
    protolkat'sya (v.pf.)
way through, to make one's probirat'sya
    (v.impf.)
    probrat'sya
    (v.pf.)
way, to force one's lomit'sya (v.impf.)
way, to lose one's sbivat'sya (v.impf.)
we my (p.)
    nam (p.)
    nami (p.)
    nas (p.)
weak bessil'nyi (adj.)
    slabosil'nyi (adj.)
    slabyi (adj.)
weak sighted podslepovatyi (adj.)
weak, to grow oslabevat' (v.impf.)
weak will bezvolie (n.n.)
weak willed beskharakternyi (adj.)
weaken rasslabit' (v.pf.)
    slabet' (v.impf.)
weakening oslablenie (n.n.)
weakling zamorysh (n.m.)
weakness slabost' (n.f.)
weak-willed slabokharakternyi (adj.)
    slabovol'nyi (adj.)
weapon oruzhie (n.n.)
wear iznos (n.m.)
    ponosit' (v.pf.)
wear out istrepat' (v.pf.)
    iznashivat'sya (v.impf.)
    staptyvat' (v.impf.)
    stoptat' (v.pf.)
wearisome tomitel'nyi (adj.)
weather pogoda (n.f.)
weather, foul nepogoda (n.f.)
weather-beaten obvetrennyi (adj.)
weathercock flyuger (n.m.)
weathering vyvetrivanie (n.n.)
weave splesti (v.pf.)
    tkat' (v.impf.)
    vit' (v.impf.)
    vytkat' (v.pf.)
weaver tkach (n.m.)
weaving tkatskii (adj.)
wedding svad'ba (n.f.)

wedge klin (n.m.)
wedged in, to be vklinit'sya (v.pf.)
Wednesday sreda (n.f.)
weed polot' (v.impf.)
    sornyak (n.m.)
weed out vypalyvat' (v.impf.)
    vypolot' (v.pf.)
weeding polka (n.f.)
    propolka (n.f.)
week nedelya (n.f.)
weekdays budni (n.pl.)
weekly ezhenedel'nyi (adj.)
    nedel'nyi (adj.)
weeks, for two dvukhnedel'nyi (adj.)
weep plakat' (v.impf.)
weeping plach (n.m.)
weigh otveshivat' (v.impf.)
    otvesit' (v.pf.)
    razveshivat' (v.pf.)
    razvesit' (v.pf.)
    sveshat' (v.pf.)
    veshat' (v.impf.)
    vesit' (v.impf.)
    vzveshivat' (v.impf.)
    vzvesit' (v.pf.)
weight girya (n.f.)
    shtanga (n.f.)
    tyazhest' (n.f.)
    ves (n.m.)
weight, short nedoves (n.m.)
weight, to give short obveshivat (v.impf.)
    obvesit' (v.pf.)
weight, to lose pokhudet' (v.pf.)
weight, to put on polnet' (v.impf.)
    rastolstet' (v.pf.)
weightlessness nevesomost' (n.f.)
weights, set of raznoves (n.m.)
welcome dobro pozhalovat' (col.)
weld svarit' (v.pf.)
    svarivat' (v.impf.)
welding svarka (n.f.)
welfare blago (n.n.)
well khorosho (adv.)
    kolodets (n.m.)
    ladno (adv.)
    skvazhina (n.f.)
well done zdorovo (adv.)
well, to get promokat' (v.impf.)

well-aimed metkii (adj.)
well-being blagosostoyanie (n.n.)
well-bred blagovospitannyi (adj.)
well-built statnyi (adj.)
well-disposed blagozhelatel'nyi (adj.)
well-dressed naryadnyi (adj.)
well-fed upitannyi (adj.)
well-founded obosnovannyi (adj.)
well-groomed vykholennyi (adj.)
well-known obshcheizvestnyi (adj.)
well-off sostoyatel'nyi (adj.)
well-read nachitannyi (adj.)
well-regulated uporyadochennyi (adj.)
west zapad (n.m.)
western zapadnyi (adj.)
wet mochit' (v.impf.)
    mokryi (adj.)
    podmochennyi (adj.)
wet, to get moknut' (v.impf.)
    namokat' (v.impf.)
    podmokat' (v.impf.)
wet-nurse kormilitsa (n.f.)
whale kit (n.m.)
what chego (p.)
    chto (p.)
    kakoi (p.)
    kakov (p.)
wheat pshenitsa (n.f.)
wheel koleso (n.n.)
wheel, spinning pryalka (n.f.)
wheel, steering shturval (n.m.)
wheelbarrow tachka (n.f.)
wheeze khripet' (v.impf.)
when kogda (adv.&conj.)
where gde (adv.)
    kuda (adv.)
where from otkuda (adv.)
whether li (part.)
whetstone oselok (n.m.)
    tochil'nyi kamen' (adj.-n.m.)
which kakoi (p.)
    kotoryi (p.)
while poka (adv.)
whim kapriz (n.m.)
    prichuda (n.f.)
    prikhot' (n.f.)
whimper khnykat' (v.impf.)
    skulit' (v.impf.)

whimsical prikhotlivyi (adj.)
whiner nytik (n.m.)
whip khlyst (n.m.)
   knut (n.m.)
   nagaika (n.f.)
   porot' (v.impf.)
   sech' (v.impf.)
   stegat' (v.impf.)
   stegnut' (v.pf.)
   vysech' (v.pf.)
whirl kruzhit' (v.impf.)
   zakruzhit'sya (v.pf.)
whirl away umchat'sya (v.pf.)
whirlpool vodovorot (n.m.)
whirlwind smerch (n.m.)
   vikhr' (n.m.)
whisk metelka (n.f.)
whisper peresheptyvat'sya (v.impf.)
   prosheptat' (v.pf.)
   shepnut' (v.pf.)
   shepot (n.m.)
   sheptat' (v.impf.)
whisper in someone's ear nasheptyvat'
   (v.impf.)
whistle nasvistyvat' (v.impf.)
   posvistyvat' (v.impf.)
   svist (n.m.)
   svistet' (v.impf.)
   svistnut' (v.pf.)
   svistok (n.m.)
white belok (n.m.)
   belyi (adj.)
White Guard belogvardeets (n.m.)
white hot dobela (adv.)
white, to become belet' (v.impf.)
whiteness belizna (n.f.)
whitewash obelit' (v.pf.)
   pobelit' (v.pf.)
who kem (p.)
   kogo (p.)
   komu (p.)
   kto (p.)
whole tselyi (adj.)
   vse (p.)
whole, the tseloe (n.n.)
wholehearted bezzavetnyi (adj.)
wholesale optom (adv.)
   optovyi (adj.)

wholesaler skupshchik (n.m.)
whooping cough koklyush (n.m.)
whose ch'e (p.)
   chei (p.)
why chto (p.)
   otchego (adv.)
   pochemu (adv.)
   zachem (adv.)
wick fitil' (n.m.)
wicked zloi (adj.)
wicker pletenyi (adj.)
wicket kalitka (n.f.)
wide shirokii (adj.)
wide open nastezh' (adv.)
widely shiroko (adv.)
widen rasshirit' (v.pf.)
   rasshiryat'(sya) (v.impf.)
   shirit'sya (v.impf.)
wide-screen shirokoékrannyi (adj.)
widespread rasprostranennyi (adj.)
widow vdova (n.f.)
widow, to become a ovdovet' (v.pf.)
width polotnishche (n.n.)
   shirota (n.f.)
wife zhena (n.f.)
wig parik (n.m.)
wild dikii (adj.)
   ogoltelyi (adj.)
   shal'noi (adj.)
wild, gone odichavshii (adj.)
will volya (n.f.)
   zaveshchanie (n.n.)
will, against one's ponevole (adv.)
willingly okhotno (adv.)
willow iva (n.f.)
willy-nilly volei-nevolei (adv.)
wilted chakhlyi (adj.)
win obygrat' (v.pf.)
   pobezhdat' (v.impf.)
   sklonit' (v.pf.)
   sklonyat' (v.impf.)
   sniskat' (v.pf.)
   vyigrat' (v.pf.)
win back otvoevat' (v.pf.)
win over peremanivat' (v.impf.)
winch lebedka (n.f.)
wind dukhovoi (adj.)
   izvivat'sya (v.impf.)

motat' (v.impf.)
namatyvat' (v.impf.)
namotat' (v.pf.)
veter (n.m.)
wind (powered) vetryanoi (adj.)
wind round obmatyvat' (v.impf.)
obmotat' (v.pf.)
obvivat'(sya) (v.impf.)
winding obmotka (n.f.)
winding mechanism zavod (n.m.)
windlass vorot (n.m.)
window okno (n.n.)
okonnyi (adj.)
okoshko (n.n.)
window curtain gardina (n.f.)
window, ventilation fortochka (n.f.)
windowsill podokonnik (n.m.)
windward navetrennyi (adj.)
windy vetrenyi (adj.)
wine vinnyi (adj.)
vino (n.n.)
wine making vinodelie (n.n.)
wineglass ryumka (n.f.)
wineskin mekh (n.m.)
wing fligel' (n.m.)
krylo (n.n.)
wing, right pravyi (adj.)
wing, to take vsporkhnut' (v.pf.)
winged krylatyi (adj.)
wings kulisy (n.pl.)
wink migat' (v.impf.)
peremigivat'sya (v.impf.)
podmigivat' (v.impf.)
winnow veyat' (v.impf.)
winnowing veyanie (n.n.)
winnowing machine veyalka (n.f.)
winter zima (n.f.)
zimnii (adj.)
winter crops ozimye (n.pl.)
winter, in zimoi (adv.)
winter, to spend the perezimovat' (v.pf.)
wipe obteret'(sya) (v.pf.)
proteret' (v.pf.)
protirat' (v.impf.)
uteret' (v.pf.)
utirat' (v.impf.)
vyteret' (v.pf.)
wipe off steret' (v.pf.)

stirat' (v.impf.)
wire provod (n.m.)
provoloka (n.f.)
wireless besprovolochnyi (adj.)
wiring provodka (n.f.)
wisdom mudrost' (n.f.)
wise umudrennyi (adj.)
wiser, to grow poumnet' (v.pf.)
umnet' (v.impf.)
wish okhota (n.f.)
pozhelanie (n.n.)
zakhotet' (v.pf.)
zhelanie (n.n.)
zhelat' (v.impf.)
wisp mochalka (n.f.)
wit ostroumie (n.n.)
witch ved'ma (n.f.)
witchcraft koldovstvo (n.n.)
with s (prep.)
so (prep.)
u (prep.)
with might and main vovsyu (adv.)
withdraw retirovat'sya (v.impf.&pf.)
vyvesti (v.impf.)
vyvezti (v.pf.)
withdrawal vyvod (n.m.)
wither pobleknut' (v.pf.)
vyanut' (v.impf.)
zasokhnut' (v.pf.)
zasykhat' (v.impf.)
withered uvyadshii (adj.)
within vnutri (adv.)
within, from iznutri (adv.)
without exception, all naperechet (adv.)
pogolovno (adv.)
witness svidetel' (n.m.)
witticism ostrota (n.f.)
wittingly zavedomo (adv.)
witty remarks, to make ostrit' (v.impf.)
wizard koldun (n.m.)
wolf volk (n.m.)
wolf cub volchonok (n.m.)
wolfish volchii (adj.)
woman baba (n.f.)
zhenshchina (n.f.)
woman in labor rozhenitsa (n.f.)
woman, old starukha (n.f.)
woman, Russian russkaya (adj.)

womanly zhenstvennyi (adj.)
womb utroba (n.f.)
wonder, no nemudreno (adj.)
wonderful chudesnyi (adj.)
  chudnyi (adj.)
wonderfully chudno (adv.)
wood drevesina (n.f.)
  drevesnyi (adj.)
woodcutter drovosek (n.m.)
wooded lesistyi (adj.)
wooden derevyannyi (adj.)
wooden plow sokha (n.f.)
woodlands poles'e (n.n.)
woodpecker dyatel (n.m.)
wool sherst' (n.f.)
word slovo (n.n.)
word-building slovoobrazovanie (n.n.)
word-for-word podstrochnyi (adj.)
words, combination of slovosochetanie (n.n.)
words, parting naputstvie (n.n.)
work otrabatyvat' (v.impf.)
  otrabotat' (v.pf.)
  potrudit'sya (v.pf.)
  prorabatyvat' (v.impf.)
  rabota (n.f.)
  trud (n.m.)
  trudit'sya (v.impf.)
work, capacity for rabotosposobnost' (n.f.)
  trudosposobnost' (n.f.)
work clothes spetsodezhda (n.f.)
work, cultural and educational kul'trabota
  (n.f.)
work day trudoden' (n.m.)
work hard korpet' (v.impf.)
work out razrabatyvat' (v.pf.)
  razrabotat' (v.pf.)
work, to shirk progulivat' (v.impf.)
  progulyat' (v.pf.)
work up vzvintit' (v.pf.)
worker rabochii (n.m.)
  rabotnik (n.m.)
worker, an unskilled zemlekop (n.m.)
worker, exemplary peredovik (n.m.)
worker, manual chernorabochii (adj.)
worker, political politrabotnik (n.m.)
workers' and peasants' raboche krest'yanskii
  (adj.)
working rabochii (adj.)

trudovoi (adj.)
trudyashchiisya (adj.)
works kombinat (n.m.)
works, dye krasil'nya (n.f.)
workshop masterskaya (n.f.)
world mir (n.m.)
  mirovoi (adj.)
  svet (n.m.)
world outlook mirovozzrenie (n.n.)
worldly svetskii (adj.)
  zhiteiskii (adj.)
worldly-wise byvalyi (adj.)
worm cherv' (n.m.)
worm, intestinal glist (n.m.)
wormeaten chervivyi (adj.)
wormwood polyn' (n.f.)
worn potrepannyi (adj.)
worn out izmuchennyi (adj.)
worn out, to be istomit'sya (v.pf.)
  namuchit'sya (v.pf.)
worry tormoshit' (v.impf.)
  volnovat' (v.impf.)
worse khudshii (adj.)
  khuzhe (adj.)
worse, to make ukhudshit' (v.pf.)
worship poklonenie (n.n.)
  poklonyat'sya (v.impf.)
  preklonyat'sya (v.impf.)
worst, the naikhudshii (adj.)
worthwhile, to be okupit'sya (v.pf.)
worthy dostoinyi (adj.)
wound podstrelit' (v.pf.)
  poranit' (v.pf.)
  rana (n.f.)
  ranit' (v.impf.&pf.)
wounded, severely tyazheloranenyi (adj.)
woven tkanyi (adj.)
wrangle perebranka (n.f.)
  prerekat'sya (v.impf.)
wrap pelenat' (v.impf.)
wrap oneself up kutat' (v.impf.)
wrap oneself up in zapakhivat'sya (v.pf.)
wrap up obernut' (v.pf.)
  okutat' (v.pf.)
  ukutat' (v.pf.)
  zavernut' (v.pf.)
  zavertyvat' (v.impf.)
  zavorachivat' (v.impf.)

wrapper   obertka (n.f.)
wreath   venok (n.m.)
wreathe   klubit'sya (v.impf.)
wriggle out   vyvernut'sya (v.pf.)
wring out   otzhimat' (v.impf.)
wrinkle   morshchina (n.f.)
   morshchit' (v.impf.)
   namorshchit' (v.pf.)
wrinkled   smorshchennyi (adj.)
wrist   zapyast'e (n.n.)
write   nadpisat' (v.pf.)
   napisat' (v.pf.)
   pisat' (v.impf.)

write down   zapisat' (v.pf.)
write out   vypisyvat' (v.impf.)
writer   pisatel' (n.m.)
writhe   korchit'sya (v.impf.)
writing   pis'mennyi (adj.)
writing pad   bloknot (n.m.)
writing paper   pischaya bumaga (adj.-n.f.)
writing, to cover with   ispisat' (v.pf.)
writing, to finish   dopisat' (v.pf.)
written   pis'mennyi (adj.)
wrong   neladno (adv.)
wrongly   prevratno (adv.)

X

xenon   ksenon (n.m.)
X-ray   prosvetit' (v.pf.)
   rentgenovskii (adj.)

Y   (Ы, Ю, Я)

yacht   yakhta (n.f.)
Yakut   yakut (n.m.)
yarn   pryazha (n.f.)
yawl   yalik (n.m.)
year   god (n.m.)
year, half   polgoda (n.m.)
years   leta (n.pl.)
year's, last   proshlogodnii (adj.)
years, of many   dolgoletnii (adj.)
yeast   drozhzhi (n.pl.)
yell   orat' (v.impf.)
yellow   zheltyi (adj.)
yellow, to grow   zheltet' (v.impf.)
yes   da (part.)
yes-man   podpevala (n.m.&f.)
yesterday   vchera (adv.)
yesterday, day before   pozavchera (adv.)
yet   eshche (adv.)
yield   ustupat' (v.impf.)
yogi   iog (n.m.)
yoke   igo (n.n.)
   koromyslo (n.n.)
   yarmo (n.n.)

yolk   zheltok (n.m.)
you   ty (p.)
   vy (p.)
young   molodoi (adj.)
young animals   molodnyak (n.m.)
young growth   porosl' (n.f.)
   vskhody (n.pl.)
young lady   baryshnya (n.f.)
young looking   molozhavyi (adj.)
young people   molodezh' (n.f.)
younger   mladshii (adj.)
younger, to grow   molodet' (v.impf.)
younger, to look   pomolodet' (v.pf.)
your   tvoi (p.)
yours   vash (p.)
youth   molodost' (n.f.)
   yunosha (n.m.)
   yunost' (n.f.)
youth of premilitary age   doprizyvnik (n.m.)
youthful   yunyi (adj.)
yttrium   ittrii (n.m.)
yurta, animal skin hut   yurta (n.f.)

Z   (З, Ж)

zeal   userdie (n.n.)
zealous   r'yanyi (adj.)
   retivyi (adj.)
   revnostnyi (adj.)
zebra   zebra (n.f.)
zenith   zenit (n.m.)
zero   nol' (n.m.)

zigzag   zigzag (n.m.)
   zigzagoobraznyi (adj.)
zinc   tsink (n.m.)
zinc white   belila (n.pl.)
zone   zona (n.f.)
zoo   zoopark (n.m.)
zoologist   zoolog (n.m.)